HADRIAN

HADRIAN

The restless emperor

Anthony R. Birley

London and New York

First published 1997
by Routledge
11 New Fetter Lane, London EC4P 4EE

Simultaneously published in the USA and Canada
by Routledge
29 West 35th Street, New York, NY 10001

Typeset in Garamond by Keystroke, Jacaranda Lodge, Wolverhampton
Printed and bound in Great Britain by Biddles Ltd, Guildford and King's Lynn

British Library Cataloguing in Publication Data
A catalogue record for this book is available from the British Library

Library of Congress Cataloging in Publication Data
Hadrian : the restless emperor. Anthony R. Birley.
p.   cm.
Includes bibliographical references and index.
1. Hadrian, Emperor of Rome, 76–138. 2. Roman emperors–
Biography. 3. Rome–History–Hadrian, 117–138. 4. Hadrian's Wall
(England) 5. Roman Forum (Rome, Italy)
DG295.B57 1997
937'.07'092–dc21   96–49232
CIP

ISBN 0–415–16544–X

M.I.B.

matri carissimae

CONTENTS

CONTENTS

PLATES

MAPS

PREFACE

Hadrian has long needed a new biography. The last serious attempt was in 1923, by B.W. Henderson. It now has an old-fashioned air, with the comparison of Hadrian to Lord Kitchener, headmasterly pronouncements ('for all we know, it was a pure enough friendship between Hadrian, who had no son, and Antinous') and open hostility to 'Teutonic' scholarship (the work of his predecessor Gregorovius, for example, is unjustly labelled 'an intolerable compilation . . . a veritable nightmare of a book'). In fact, Henderson was out of date even when the book first appeared – he had unaccountably ignored W. Weber's study of 1907, which was, perhaps still is, fundamental if largely unreadable. At all events, the great increase in information – mainly inscriptions and papyri – since Weber and Henderson wrote has made a new synthesis overdue. Monographs on a whole range of Hadrianic affairs, his coinage, his Wall, his building programmes at Rome and Athens, his favourite Antinous, the Jewish war or revolt of Bar Kokhba, and the 'Greek renaissance', besides intensive work on the *Historia Augusta*, have laid the foundation. Yet Hadrian has become best known through a novel, by Marguérite Yourcenar (1951). For all her intuition and literary genius, the Hadrian whose *Mémoires* Yourcenar composed is a different person from the historical emperor. All the same, despite the need for a fresh non-fictional study, I might have refrained had it not been for the persuasion of Peter Kemmis Betty.

At least I ought to have been well placed to make the attempt. As chance would have it, I was born and brought up close to that 'celebrated work of antiquity' (as Walter Scott called it), Hadrian's Wall. It is impossible to avoid noticing the name in those parts. Long ago one of the biggest local employers was 'Hadrian Paints' at Haltwhistle; 'Hadrian' has subsequently become a trade name in the Tyne valley for everything from motor panels to mineral water. More to the point, our house, Chesterholm, was largely built with stones from the Roman fort of Vindolanda across the burn and my father was an archaeologist, much occupied with the Wall. When I went to university I discovered to my surprise (or dismay) that 'ancient history' at Oxford ended with the death of Trajan, 8 August AD 117 – and 'modern history' there began with Diocletian's accession on 20 November 284. The years between, from Hadrian to the sons of Carus, were a kind of black hole. This was not by chance: ancient history in Literae Humaniores was geared to classical literature; apart from some of Juvenal's *Satires* and, so I believe (not many agree), Tacitus' *Annals*, no 'classical' Latin was written after Trajan's reign. A further reason may be that for the years 117–284 the principal source is the *Historia Augusta*, deemed unsuitable for undergraduates. Nonetheless, on graduation I began research on the Antonines and Severans and 'descended into the ocean of the Augustan History' although not 'insensibly', as Gibbon had. By good fortune I was supervised by Ronald Syme. This postgraduate work duly led to a doctoral thesis (unpublished) – and to biographies of Marcus Aurelius (1966) and Septimius Severus (1971), given a new existence in revised form by Batsford (1987 and 1988).

Hadrian is a real challenge. He was already a strange and baffling figure to his contemporaries. Can we hope to get beneath his skin? The nineteen words of his *animula* poem, his 'farewell to life', have spawned a copious literature. There is not much else to tell us what really went on behind the elegant exterior, what the real Hadrian was like – the fragments of his autobiography only reveal a version for public consumption, likewise the portraits, the coins, the inscriptions bearing his name from Northumberland to the Black Sea, from Transylvania to the edge of the Sahara. There were several competing personalities inside Hadrian. He played a series of roles. For us, at least, Hadrian has to be what Hadrian did. Even the 'facts', the chronology, and the course of events, are not always easy to establish, let alone to know *why* (for example) he built the Wall in Britain, founded the Panhellenion in Athens, or adopted Ceionius Commodus as his son and successor. In particular, his prolonged provincial tours, the most obvious special feature of his reign, are hard to date with precision. Hence there have to be (all too often, perhaps) turns of phrase such as 'probably', 'plausibly enough', 'it may be conjectured', in these pages. I have tried to provide a coherent narrative and to indicate in the Notes the sources and the modern works I have consulted. (The Bibliography could have been much bulkier. I have cited here, for example, only a selection of items discussed in my paper on his 'farewell' poem. Most of the Notes are confined to citation of sources and selected modern studies. Here and there I have added some discussion of difficult questions.) I had planned to include a further section, with chapters on 'Hadrianic policy' – financial, military, religious, legal, 'administrative'. But, if I had been able to finish it at all, the end product would have become much too long. This book remains essentially a *Life*, not a *Life and Times*. The early chapters, relying on the literature of the Flavio-Trajanic period, principally Pliny's *Letters*, are intended to flesh out the *Historia Augusta*'s sketch of Hadrian before his accession. The picture of the man that emerges from the main part is dominated by his philhellenism. In a real sense Hadrian – very much a product of his time – was reliving the past. He saw himself first as a new Augustus, then as a new Pericles or even a second Antiochus Epiphanes. His obsessive wish to turn himself into a Hellene and to revive Hellenic culture was to have tragic consequences, for Hadrian himself in the death of his beloved Antinous, and for the Jewish people, whom he tried forcibly to hellenise.

In the four years and more since I began work, I have incurred many debts. Special thanks are owed to Géza Alföldy, Antonio Caballos Rufino, Werner Eck, Dietmar Kienast, Margaret Roxan, Antony Spawforth, Michael P. Speidel, Susan Walker, Peter Weiss and Ruprecht Ziegler, not least for providing copies of their own work. Werner Eck was good enough to comment on a final draft, which helped to eliminate some errors. Those that remain are my own responsibility. Thomas Pekáry's invitation to contribute to an 'Oberseminar' at Münster led to a more intensive examination of Hadrian's 'farewell to life'. I benefited greatly from the privilege of spending the fall term 1994 at the Institute for Advanced Study, Princeton, especially from conversations with Glen Bowersock, Ted Champlin, David Frankfurter, Christian Habicht and Gabriel Herman, and from being able to use, as well as the Institute's library, those of the Speer Theological Seminary and Princeton University. It was at Princeton that I wrote my paper on the *animula* poem and drafted chapters 18–20. Dr Roger Bland (British Museum) and Dr Helmut Jung (German Archaeological Institute, Rome) readily provided photographs. The maps were drafted by my pupil Peter Nadig. Mrs Rita Kröll, secretary of the Abteilung Alte Geschichte at Düsseldorf, retyped a good deal of my first draft and has given other practical help over the past two years, as did her predecessor, Mrs Herta vom Bovert, from 1990 to 1994. The change of publisher (not affecting this book only), from Batsford to Routledge, meant some months delay in going to press; but made it possible to revise a few passages. A welcome invitation to deliver the Ronald Syme Lecture at Wolfson College, Oxford in November 1996 involved further thought on 'Hadrian and Greek senators', referred to in the Notes here. Now is a suitable moment to express again my gratitude to Peter Kemmis Betty, formerly of Batsford, for his support over the past thirty-four years.

The two teachers to whom I owe most are no longer here – neither, I know well, would have agreed with everything in this book. Ronald Syme (1903–1989) published several dozen papers on Hadrianic topics and a great deal on the *Historia Augusta*. From these, from his great *Tacitus*, and from decades of friendship, I have learned more than can be expressed in a few words. Syme disapproved, to be sure, of the genre of imperial biography. But he found Hadrian a fascinating figure. So did my father, Eric Birley (1906–1995) (a close friend of Syme for sixty years), who read and offered comment on everything I wrote since I first tried to follow in his footsteps. He was at least able to cast an eye over a large part of the typescript. I hope he would have enjoyed the finished product. I am also grateful to other members of my family. My wife Heide encouraged me to undertake the task. Without her continuing support I could never have brought it to completion. My brother Robin's excavations at Vindolanda – which, among many other startling finds, have brought to light evidence for Hadrian having stayed there – have been a constant source of inspiration. I dedicate this biography to my mother, my first teacher, who taught me to read and to love books.

Anthony Birley

High Birkshaw House, Bardon Mill,

Friedberg, Hesse

March/November 1996

NOTE

A good˙ many Greek and Roman 'technical' terms from the ancient world (archon, censor, *civitas*, consul, etc.) crop up in these pages; likewise, particularly in the Notes, numerous ancient sources, from *Anth. Pal.* to Xenophon, *Anab.* Rather than inflate the text and the Notes with explanations and citations of standard editions (that many would find superfluous), it seems simpler to refer readers for those that have been left unexplained to the *Oxford Classical Dictionary*, of which the 3rd edition, by Simon Hornblower and Antony J.S. Spawforth, has just appeared (1996) (*OCD³*). Both their list of 'Abbreviations Used in the Present Work. B. Authors and Books' (pp. xxix–liv) and in many cases the articles in this 1,640-page long work should resolve all such questions. (For one source which I cite very frequently, the *Historia Augusta*, I have preferred a different abbreviation: *HA*, rather than *SHA* as in *OCD³*.)

ACKNOWLEDGEMENTS

Frontispiece: National Museum, Jerusalem
Plates 1, 5–7, 9–15, 19–25, 27, 33, 35, 37: British Museum
Plates 2–4, 8, 26, 30–32, 34, 36: German Archaeological Institute, Rome
Plate 16: Dr D.J. Wooliscroft
Plate 17: Vindolanda Trust (photograph by Alison Rutherford)
Plate 18: Professor G.D.B. Jones
Plate 28: Dr. Susan Walker
Plate 29: Merseyside Museums

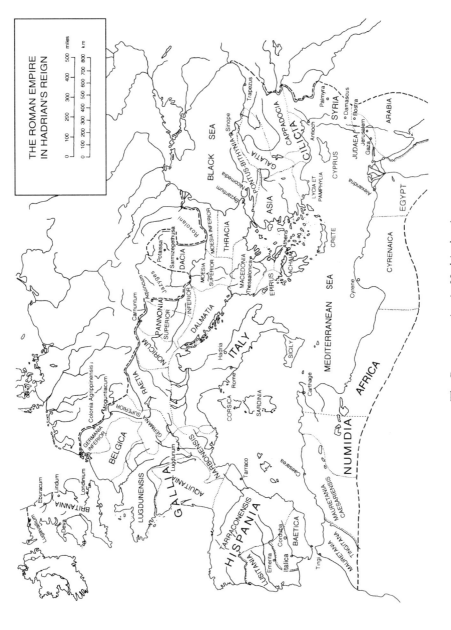

The Roman empire: in Hadrian's reign

INTRODUCTION
The Emperor Hadrian

'The most remarkable of all the Roman emperors': so a historian of imperial Rome described Hadrian nearly a century ago. What has mainly impressed ancient writers as well as modern students is the man's restless energy, 'tramping at the head of his legions through his world-wide domains', and 'his insatiable curiosity'. He spent a good half of his reign of twenty-one years away from Rome and Italy, on the move, in virtually every province of the far-flung empire. His presence in well over thirty of them can be documented. It would be simpler to list those where he cannot be proved to have set foot: Aquitania, Lusitania, Crete, Cyprus, Cyrenaica, Sardinia-Corsica – and in all but the last his presence is quite likely. Indeed, on his accession at the age of forty-one he had already spent more than half his adult life away from Rome.[1]

This concentration on the provinces, to which the series of commemorative coins from his last years gave vivid expression, was focused partly on the armies and frontiers. He made a clear and unambiguous break with the policy of his predecessor Trajan, abandoning the newly acquired territories beyond the Euphrates immediately after his accession, then evacuating some lands beyond the lower Danube. This was followed up by the construction of a series of artificial frontier lines, of which his Wall in Britain was the most elaborate. Whether these so called *limites* marked a real change at the military level may be debated. Their symbolic significance cannot be overrated – a clear signal to Roman traditionalists who still yearned for continuous extension of the frontiers, for an *imperium sine fine*. Expansion had come to an end – but the Emperor was determined to maintain the army at a peak of preparedness.

The abandonment of Trajan's conquests aroused hostile reaction; and, further, it was suspected that the deathbed adoption of Hadrian was a fake, stage-managed by Trajan's widow Plotina in the interests of her favourite. These resentments and suspicions presumably lay behind the 'conspiracy' – as it was termed – of four senior senators who were summarily put to death during the first few months of the reign. Although Hadrian claimed he had not ordered these executions, he was blamed for them and distrusted by the élite as a result. The 'affair of the four consulars' cast a shadow over the early part of his reign. He reacted with lavish generosity, with bounty for the plebs and tax remissions and a massive building

1

programme for the capital. This included an enormous new temple, of Rome and Venus, of which the foundation ceremony took place on 21 April 121, the birthday of Rome, on the eve of his first major tour – as if to demonstrate that in spite of favours to the provinces, Rome still had a central role. A few years later he began ostentatiously to portray himself as a second Augustus.

After his extended first tour – the western part, abruptly broken off in 123 when an emergency summoned him to the east, was completed with his visit to Africa in 128 – Hadrian's attention was devoted exclusively to the east. In the Greek-speaking half of the empire, after tentative experiments with the shrine of Apollo at Delphi as a new centre, he inaugurated an elaborate programme to make Athens a kind of second imperial capital, as the home of a new League of all the Hellenes, the Panhellenion. He seems to have seen himself as a new Pericles, bringing to fulfilment the vision which Pericles' Congress Decree had supposedly striven to achieve. As the seat of the Panhellenion he chose the great Temple of Olympian Zeus, inaugurated in the sixth century BC by the Athenian *tyrannos* Pisistratus. It had never been completed, even though the Seleucid king, Antiochus Epiphanes, had lavishly financed its building in the second century BC. The Greeks responded to Hadrian's Panhellenic programme with rapture. As the literature of the age demonstrates, they were only too eager to relive their glorious past. They conferred on him the name *Olympios*, once given, half in jest, to Pericles, and also the epithet of the chief god of the Hellenes.[2]

It was not merely by completing the Olympieion that Hadrian emulated and outdid the Syrian king. Like Antiochus three hundred years before him, he sought to hellenise the Jews. This is the only plausible explanation for his prohibition of circumcision and for his conversion of the ruined Jerusalem into a *colonia* under the name of Aelia Capitolina, with a temple of Jupiter or Zeus to be erected over the Holy of Holies. It was an appalling misjudgement. The uprising thus provoked grew into a major war. A charismatic leader, Shim'on ben Kosiba, or Bar-Kokhba, liberated a substantial part of Judaea and occupied Roman forces in a bloody struggle for three years.

In the meantime Hadrian had experienced a personal trauma. He had been married at the age of twenty-four to a distant kinswoman, Sabina, a grand-niece of Trajan. The marriage was childless and – at least after two decades – loveless. Hadrian was in any case more interested in males. Some time during his travels in the east he met a beautiful Bithynian boy named Antinous. He took him into his train and became besotted with him. How long the two were together is a matter of guesswork. It is legitimate to infer that Hadrian saw himself, in this as in other respects, as behaving in the tradition of classical Greece, the older man, the *erastes*, and the beautiful youth, the *eromenos*. Such relationships had always been accepted, indeed, favoured, among the Greeks. At Rome attitudes were different, although the increasing hellenisation of the upper echelons had had its effect here too, and Hadrian had been devoted to things Hellenic since his boyhood, earning the nickname *Graeculus*. Antinous – it must be supposed – was Hadrian's constant companion, especially when Hadrian was indulging his passion for hunting, at least on his last great journey, beginning in late summer 128. But in October 130 Antinous was drowned in the Nile. Whether it was suicide or even some kind of sacrifice, prompted by the advice of an Egyptian priest or 'magician', or just an accidental death, Hadrian's grief knew no bounds. The dead youth was declared a god and the Greeks, at least, responded with enthusiasm to the new cult.

Although Hadrian was able to preside at the culmination of the Panhellenic programme, the opening of the Olympieion at Athens in the spring of 132 just before the Jewish war broke out, in his last years he was something of a broken man. When he returned to Rome, at the latest in 134, his health was failing. In 136 he at last decided on a successor and adopted a young senator named Ceionius Commodus as his son and heir, giving him the new name Lucius Aelius Caesar. The choice seemed baffling and was not welcomed among the élite. Conjecture about Hadrian's motives was rife at the time and modern scholars have gone even further. There was an angry reaction from Hadrian's closest male relative, his grand-nephew Pedanius Fuscus. He made some move, evidently late in 137, and was put to death; his grandfather, Hadrian's brother-in-law, Julius Servianus, by then in his ninetieth year, was forced into suicide. Shortly after the Fuscus affair, the new Caesar expired, and Hadrian had to find another successor. This time his selection was surer, a steady man of mature years, Aurelius Antoninus. Antoninus, in turn, was instructed to adopt the young son of Aelius Caesar, Lucius, and his own nephew by marriage, Marcus, thus ensuring the succession far ahead. It seems plausible that Marcus, now sixteen years old, had been Hadrian's real choice all along, and that first Aelius Caesar, then Antoninus, were intended to keep the throne warm until Marcus was old enough to succeed. Marcus had been betrothed 'at Hadrian's wish' to the daughter of Aelius Caesar before the latter's adoption; his family was related in some way to that of Hadrian; Marcus' grandfather Annius Verus had been given signal honours by Hadrian; and Marcus had been a favourite of the Emperor, who was struck by his sterling qualities of character since his early childhood. The succession crisis thus reached a happy conclusion. But because of the deaths of Fuscus and Servianus, and evidently of others who had fallen out with Hadrian, including close friends, and whose deaths were laid at his door, Hadrian was deeply unpopular at the time of his death. Indeed, his remains were initially laid to rest hurriedly at Puteoli, close to where he died, for he was 'hated by all'. Antoninus had to struggle with the Senate to carry through his deification. There would not be many who mourned him.

Hadrian composed an autobiography during his last months. Only a fragment survives, apart from some brief quotations in two writers of the early third century, both senators, whose works, directly or indirectly, are the main source of information for Hadrian. In the early third century one of these, a biographer of the emperors, Marius Maximus, produced a second series in continuation of Suetonius' *Twelve Caesars*. He treated Hadrian in some detail: his overall picture was mixed, with stress on the dark side. But Maximus' *Vitae*

Caesarum are lost, and are known almost solely from the use made of them in the enigmatic *Historia Augusta* (*HA*), composed at the end of the fourth century. The Life of Hadrian with which the *HA* opens is a hasty compilation, not only drastically condensed, but sometimes with curious repetitions. Appended to the *HA Hadrian* is a mainly fictional life of Aelius Caesar; and the *vitae* of Antoninus, M. Aurelius and L. Verus add a little more information. Maximus' contemporary Cassius Dio wrote a *History of Rome* from its foundation to his own day. He may have used Maximus' biography of Hadrian – many items match the *HA* closely. But Book 69 of Dio's work, which covered this reign, is extant only in the form of excerpts and in a Byzantine epitome.[3]

The truncated state of the two main sources creates obvious difficulties for the historian. There are, however, other works which fill out the picture. The literature of the Flavian and Trajanic periods, even if it does not mention Hadrian, can be exploited to reconstruct the society in which he spent the first four decades of his life. The poets Martial and Statius and the professor of oratory, Quintilian, for example, are informative on the time of Domitian. Pliny's *Letters* and *Panegyric* shed a great deal of light on senatorial society and attitudes under Trajan – a good many friends and relatives of Hadrian were among Pliny's correspondents or are mentioned in his work. On the Greek side, there is plenty of useful material in Plutarch's essays (the *Moralia*), in the speeches of Dio of Prusa (Chrysostom) and in Arrian's account of the teaching of Epictetus, whom Hadrian admired and whom he probably visited at about the same time as Arrian. Arrian became a friend of Hadrian, and some of his works were addressed to him: the 'Circumnavigation (*Periplus*) of the Black Sea' and the *Tactica*, as well as the fragment of a third piece from the same period, when Arrian was governing Cappadocia, the 'Order of Battle (*Ektaxis*) against the Alani'.

Arrian is not the only contemporary writer whose works have survived. There are fragments of the voluminous production by Hadrian's freedman, Phlegon of Tralles, some of them helpful for reconstructing Hadrian's movements. A manual on siege-craft (*Poliorcetica*), attributed to the architect Apollodorus of Damascus, may shed light on the Jewish war. The Alexandrian poet, Dionysius 'the Periegete', produced a long poem describing the known world, which has indirect value for Hadrian. A curious piece is the work on physiognomy by the flamboyant sophist Antonius Polemo of Smyrna. It survives only in Arabic translation, but one passage is instructive on Hadrian's travels in the 120s. Works by another contemporary sophist, Favorinus of Arles, are also extant (one discovered, on papyrus, only in the 1930s). This all contributes to building up a picture of intellectual life in the age, backing up what may be found in a work compiled a few decades later, Aulus Gellius' *Attic Nights* – where Hadrian himself is several times quoted – and, above all, in Philostratus' *Lives of the Sophists*, written a century after Hadrian's death. Some of the leading intellectual figures of Hadrian's time, notably Favorinus, Polemo and Herodes Atticus, figure prominently in Gellius and Philostratus.[4]

There were, indeed, other writers at work under Hadrian. The poet Florus, for example, whose exchange of verses with Hadrian is quoted in the *HA*, also wrote a short history, based on Livy, of Rome's wars up to Augustus' time, which gives a little insight into attitudes at the time of writing. Another poet, Juvenal, also wrote under Hadrian. There is one clear dating indication – a suffect consul of 127 – and other *Satires* can be pressed for information on the reign. The biographer Suetonius held a major post under Hadrian, Chief Secretary, or *ab epistulis*. He was unceremoniously dismissed in 122, along with his patron, the Guard Prefect Septicius Clarus, to whom he had already dedicated at least the first two of his *Caesars*, *Julius* and *Augustus*. The remaining ten biographies, from Tiberius to Domitian, were probably composed after Suetonius had been sacked. It is a legitimate procedure to sieve through the *Caesars* for hints of Suetonius' attitudes to Hadrian. The same applies, of course, to Tacitus' *Annals*. Tacitus' earliest monographs, the *Agricola* and *Germany*, are unquestionably of indirect relevance for Hadrian's early years, when they were composed. But for the *Annals* the date of writing is disputed. Tacitus was born in the late 50s and was thus about sixty years old when Hadrian came to the throne. There is much to be said for the view that he had, at that moment, only just commenced the *Annals*. At all events, whether by coincidence or by design, a number of passages in the *Annals* afford instructive comment on Hadrian.[5]

If Hadrian's autobiography is lost, there does at any rate survive a variety of his other writings, both prose and poetry. The exchange of verses with Florus has already been referred to. There are two other Latin pieces, an epitaph for his favourite horse and – much more intriguing – his dying address to his soul, his 'farewell to life'. Some of his speeches and official letters, mostly fragmentary, preserved on stone or on papyrus, and some of his legal responses, cited in particular in the *Digest*, make up a considerable body of material in total. There is also the curious collection of *Sententiae Hadriani*, evidently his impromptu responses to petitioners for the most part, preserved as a school exercise for translation into Greek.[6]

Comment on Hadrian, implicit and explicit, from the period immediately after his death, is provided by the orators Fronto and Aelius Aristides. The former's letters, resembling in many ways those of Pliny a generation earlier, likewise shed some light on Hadrian's circle. A contemporary of these two, Pausanias, registers a series of benefactions by Hadrian in Greece, particularly at Athens, in his *Guidebook* composed in the early 170s. Later in the century a few anecdotes are included in the voluminous corpus of the doctor Galen and in the *Deipnosophistae* of Athenaeus.

The above summary account by no means exhausts the 'literary' sources for Hadrian and his reign: there are also Jewish and Christian writings, in which, of course, the main focus is on religion and on the Jewish war – together with some unfriendly comments on Antinous. Further, horoscopes of Hadrian and of his grand-nephew Fuscus compiled in the late second century were quoted by the fourth-century writer Hephaestio of Thebes. Finally, a little may be gleaned from the fourth-century chroniclers Aurelius Victor, Eutropius, Festus and the unknown author of the *Epitome de Caesaribus* – owing something, the latter especially, to the lost work of Marius Maximus.[7]

Over and above this the historian can turn to a great mass of primary material: coins, inscriptions, papyri and archaeological remains. The numismatic evidence includes not only the issues from the imperial mint but the local coinage of the Greek east, of which that of Alexandria in Egypt in the most informative. It is at least dated, whereas after 119, when Hadrian held his third consulship, precise dating disappears from the other issues – the annually renewed *tribunicia potestas* is omitted. The only sure guide is the title *pater patriae*, assumed in 128, and, in the east, the title *Olympios* from 129 onwards. But at least the broad chronological framework has been established – and some of the issues, in particular the 'province' and 'army' series, recalling, near the end of the reign, Hadrian's provincial tours, are extremely instructive. Further, the coinage issued by the rebels in Judaea provides precious indications about the nature of Bar Kokhba's regime.

Inscriptions are also available in profusion. Of especial value is the statue base from Athens giving the career up to his first consulship (108) of Hadrian himself. Comparable stones, with career details of dozens of senatorial and equestrian office-holders, allow the identification of Hadrian's principal coadjutors. One may mention also the diplomas issued to veterans, invaluable for reconstructing military history. The poems composed by Julia Balbilla, friend of the Empress, carved on the Colossus of Memnon at Thebes on the occasion of the imperial visit to Egypt, are just one striking example of the epigraphic evidence from the period, too copious and variegated to summarise further. The papyri, mainly deriving from Egypt, naturally shed light mostly on that province. Apart from small items which help to document Hadrian's stay there, fragments of two literary works celebrating Antinous have been found, also the beginning of a letter from Hadrian to his designated successor Antoninus, which may be identified as coming from his autobiography. A wholly new source of papyri, in the Judaean desert, comprises documents and letters in Greek and Aramaic, deriving from Jewish refugees hiding at the end of the revolt. Only the Greek papyri have so far been published in full, but they, and, even more, the still incompletely available Aramaic texts, give unique insight into the workings of the rebel state.

Inscriptions and coins combine to date many of the surviving remains from the reign – not least Hadrian's Wall. But all over the empire, and in particular in Rome and in Athens, major buildings for which Hadrian was responsible or with which he was associated still survive in ruined state, or, in the case of the Pantheon and his Mausoleum at Rome or Hadrian's Gate at Athens, complete. The great Villa at Tibur continues to be the subject of research. Historical reliefs, for example the so-called *tondi* from a Hadrianic hunting monument at Rome, and the obelisk with hieroglyphic inscriptions, now at Rome but originally at Antinoopolis, engage scholars in debate. Scores of sculpted portraits of Hadrian, many of Sabina, and a good hundred of Antinous, have been intensively studied.

There is thus, all told, evidence on Hadrian in abundance. But it is far from easy to put it together. The first serious study was by a French cleric, J.-G.-H. Greppo, in 1842. He focused on the imperial journeys, with special attention to the coinage. But, after introductory discussion, he confessed that because of the difficulty of the evidence, he did not feel able to attempt a 'classement chronologique de ces voyages'.[8] A few years later, in 1851, there appeared a *History of the Roman Emperor Hadrian and of his Times* by a young German academic, F. Gregorovius. It was clearly widely read, and over thirty years later the author, who had in the meantime devoted himself to the history of medieval Rome, produced a second edition, under the title *The Emperor Hadrian. Scenes from the Roman-Hellenic World in his Times* (1884). Gregorovius was immensely learned and wrote attractively. It is no surprise that an English translation appeared in 1898. But meanwhile German scientific scholarship had begun to take inscriptions (not of course neglected by Gregorovius) more seriously into account. A doctoral dissertation on Hadrian's journeys was published in 1881 by J. Dürr. In 1890 came another monograph, devoting particular attention to the sources for the reign, by J. Plew, who had already written a dissertation on Marius Maximus. The year before H. Dessau had published his epoch-making study of the *Historia Augusta*, showing that it was by a single author, not six, writing in the late fourth century, not under Diocletian and Constantine.[9] A rash of scholarly work on the *HA* and the period it covered began to pour out. O.T. Schulz tackled Hadrian in the light of new ideas on the *HA* in 1904, followed a year later by E. Kornemann. Neither work is without merit, but both propounded wholly fanciful ideas on the sources of the *HA*, obsessed with the idea that there were two main sources, a 'factual' author (labelled by Kornemann 'the last great historian of Rome') and an unserious, biographical author, a purveyor of court gossip.

Schulz and Kornemann were rapidly rendered obsolete by a work of very different quality, by Wilhelm Weber, which appeared in 1907. Weber for the first time assembled a really substantial mass of epigraphic, numismatic and papyrological evidence to date the main events in Hadrian's reign down to the Jewish war, concentrating in effect on the journeys. This monograph is unlikely to be superseded as a collection of evidence, even though it needs correcting in many places. It has to be said, though, that in spite of a few purple passages, it is a work to consult, not to read. The year after Weber's dissertation, A. v. Premerstein published a short monograph on the 'conspiracy of the four consulars', attempting to use a passage in Polemo's *De physiognomia* to date and explain this episode.

Sixteen years after Weber's book there appeared *The Life and Principate of the Emperor Hadrian* by the Oxford don B.W. Henderson. Curiously, although the author mentions in his Preface that he had been urged to write the book fifteen years before by H.F. Pelham, then Camden Professor of Ancient History at

Oxford – surely because of the appearance of Weber's book – Henderson nowhere refers to Weber. This was not because he ignored German – or 'Teutonic' – scholarship, which he frequently finds occasion to pour scorn on in a disagreeably aggressive manner. Henderson certainly managed to produce a more readable account than his predecessor, and he is still often cited – for this was to remain, as it turned out, the latest at all scholarly biography of Hadrian for over sixty years. The book by B. d'Orgeval (1950), in spite of its title, is really just an attempt to discuss Hadrian's contribution to the development of Roman law. There are, it is true, some more recent biographies, but none that can be called works of scholarship. One should also note two studies of Hadrian's life before his accession, by W.D. Gray (1919) and L. Perret (1935) – the latter also produced a short monograph on Hadrian's titulature as emperor.[10]

In spite of the lack of a new biography, since Henderson wrote there has been a remarkable series of monographs dealing with aspects of Hadrian and his reign. The coinage early received intensive treatment. P.L. Strack's substantial volume appeared in 1933, followed a year later by J.M.C. Toynbee on the Hadrianic province coins, and in 1936 by the third instalment of H. Mattingly's *Coins of the Roman Empire* in the British Museum (referred to as *BMC* III in the Notes to this volume), covering Nerva to Hadrian, in which Introduction and catalogue together devote some 300 pages to Hadrian. There have more recently been monographs on the *cistophori* minted under Hadrian in the province Asia, by W.E. Metcalf, and on the rebel Jewish coins, by L. Mildenberg. Hadrian's Wall in Britain has been repeatedly treated. One may single out here the attempt to interpret the stages of its building, by C.E. Stevens, the book by E. Birley on the history of research and the now standard work by D.J. Breeze and B. Dobson. Hadrian's building programmes in Rome and in Athens have recently been given detailed analysis in monographs by M.T. Boatwright and D. Willers respectively. Athens under Hadrian had already been the theme of a still useful book by P. Graindor (1934). The Villa at Tivoli has received repeated attention.[11]

The Jewish war has been handled in several monographs, for example by S. Applebaum and P. Schäfer. The portraiture of Hadrian – together with the imperial women associated with him – was the subject of a volume by M. Wegner, published in 1956. That on Sabina by A. Carandini (1969) is focused principally on the iconography. Antinous has also attracted much attention. R. Lambert's *Beloved and God* (1984) is a remarkable attempt at a biography of the imperial favourite, which must not be underrated. The two recent volumes by H. Meyer deal respectively with the iconography and with the obelisk.

Apart from these 'Hadrianic' monographs, various other works have shed valuable light on the period. One must note, above all, H. Halfmann's study of imperial journeys (1986), where the detailed section on Hadrian's own travels must be consulted constantly by anyone dealing with the reign. Hadrian and his age occupy a good hundred and fifty pages of J. Beaujeu's book on Roman religion in the Antonine period (1955). Further, ten contributions, by A. García y Bellido and others, in the volume *Les empereurs romains d'Espagne* (1965) are devoted in whole or in part to Hadrian. One of these, by R. Syme, on 'Hadrian the intellectual', was among the earliest of what were to amount to more than a score of papers by Syme on Hadrian. Syme's massive monograph on Tacitus (1958) , in which he again and again points to echoes of Hadrian in the *Annals*, was of course an earlier harbinger of his numerous Hadrianic studies.[12] Preserved among his papers is an outline of 'The Reign of Hadrian as Tacitus might have conceived it'. He noted that several Roman historical writers lived to an advanced age – and at the time of Hadrian's death Tacitus would have just passed eighty, had he survived. (Syme himself was about eighty-three when he made these notes.) The 'Tacitean' monograph on Hadrian was conceived in five books: Book I would have covered the years 117–121, II 121–123 or 125, III 123 or 125 to 128 – with 128 noted as a turning point in the reign, IV 128 to 134 and V 134 to 138. Suitable subjects for digressions were noted, for example Dacia and the Sarmatians, Prefects of Rome, Britain, the Parthian question, military discipline, philhellenism, Egypt and its monuments, Hadrian's travelling companions, the Jews and the Alani.

The *vita Hadriani* in the *HA* has received two commentaries, in English by H.W. Benario (1980), in French by J.P. Callu and others (1992). A collection of sources, mainly epigraphic, for the reigns of Nerva, Trajan and Hadrian by E.M. Smallwood (1966) had in the meantime made much of the primary evidence easily accessible; and J.H. Oliver's postumously published collection of Greek constitutions of Roman emperors (1989) has made a good many important Hadrianic texts more intelligible. Finally, a work of a very different nature must be mentioned: the novel by Marguérite Yourcenar, *Les mémoires d'Hadrien*, published in 1951. This book has received enormous acclaim and its literary merits are unquestioned. Yet the personality there portrayed seems to have been accepted by not a few scholars as an authentic representation of the 'real Hadrian'. Whether Yourcenar's Hadrian is in fact so close to the real man is another matter.[13]

The ancient sources at least give us an idea of Hadrian's person: a tall and imposing figure – and extremely fit, for he rode and walked a good deal, practised with weapons and at throwing the javelin, and hunted frequently. He was also elegant, 'his hair curled on a comb' and with a full beard, which was kept well trimmed. His eyes were, supposedly, bright and piercing. He could be 'pleasant to meet and had a certain charm', and he mingled readily with his humblest subjects, more of whom must have seen him than any other emperor. But his 'insatiable ambition', his burning wish to excel and to score points at the expense of the experts in every field, clearly made him a uncomfortable person to know.[14]

1

A CHILDHOOD IN FLAVIAN ROME

On the ninth day before the Kalends of February, when the consuls were the Emperor Vespasian, for the seventh time, and Titus Caesar, for the fifth time, a son was born at Rome to Domitia Paulina, wife of the young senator Aelius Hadrianus Afer. Thus the *Historia Augusta* (*HA*) records the birth of the future emperor Hadrian, on 24 January of the year 76 – at Rome, rather than at Italica in southern Spain, the home of his father. For senators their official domicile was Rome and most of them, particularly those holding or seeking one of the traditional magistracies, did indeed reside there. Cassius Dio registers the father's name as Hadrianus Afer, describing him as a senator and ex-praetor. That might simply mean that Afer reached the praetorship in the course of his career. But it is likely enough that he had been praetor a year or two before Hadrian was born. Chance has preserved on papyrus part of a letter Hadrian wrote to Antoninus just before his death: he mentions that his father lived only to his fortieth year. Afer died when Hadrian was in his tenth year, the *HA* reports, and was thus twenty-nine or thirty when his son was born, precisely the standard age for the praetorship. He could have held the office earlier. Augustus' legislation allowed senators a year off the minimum age for magistracies for each child, and Afer also had a daughter, named after her mother, probably older than Hadrian.[1]

Neither the *HA* nor other sources offer further details on Hadrian's first nine years – except for a single inscription, which records the name of the future emperor's wet-nurse, Germana, no doubt a slave. Like other women of high rank, Paulina did not breast-feed her son. Germana, to judge from her name, may have been of northern barbarian origin. She was later given her freedom and would outlive Hadrian. The *vita* does supply a single telling detail about Hadrian's mother and considerable information on his father's family. Domitia Paulina 'came from Gades [Cádiz]'. This was the oldest city in Spain and, according to tradition, the earliest of all the Phoenician settlements in the west, going back to the late second millennium BC. After centuries of independence and indeed dominance in southern Spain, Gades had fallen under Carthaginian control at the latest in the time of Hannibal's father Hamilcar Barca. After a few decades Gades switched allegiance during the Hannibalic War and was received by Rome into alliance in 206 BC. Several of its sons became Roman citizens.

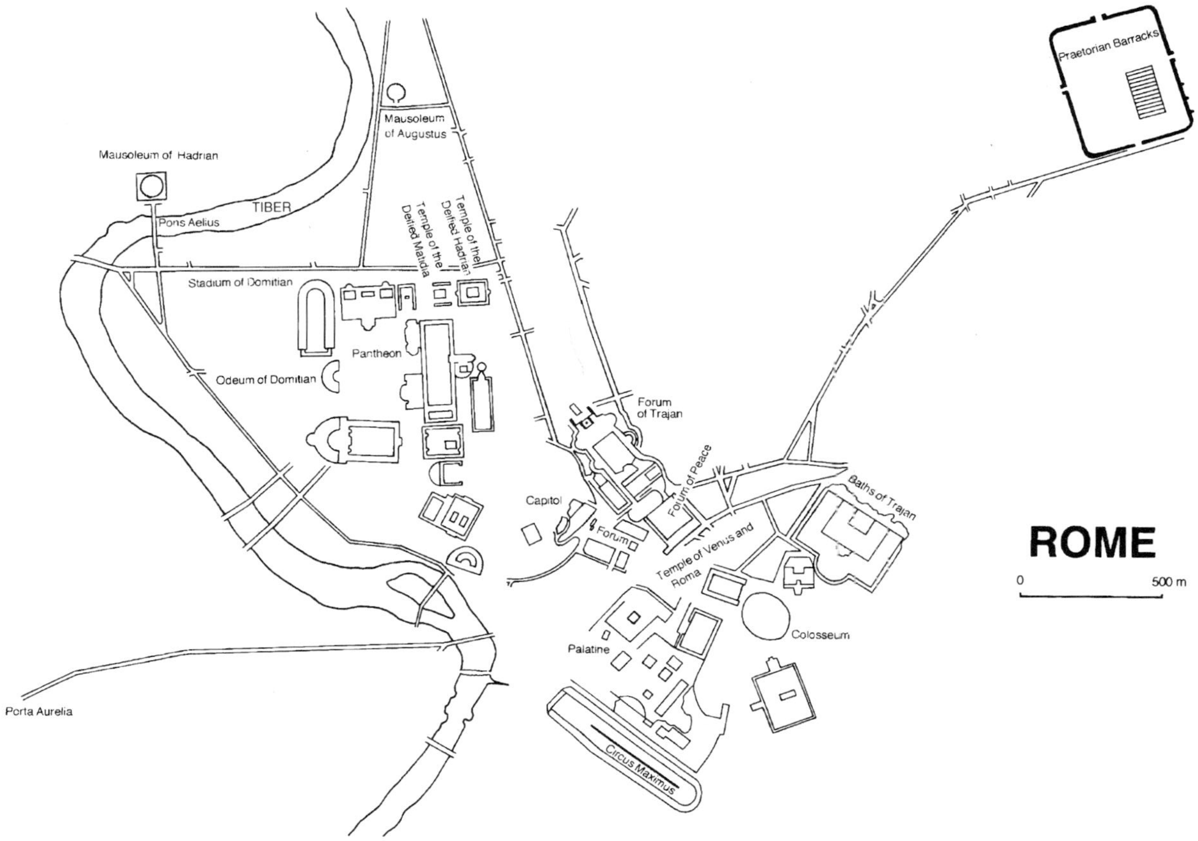

ROME

0   500 m

Praetorian Barracks

Baths of Trajan

Colosseum

Forum of Trajan

Forum of Peace

Temple of Venus and Rome

Capitol

Forum

Palatine

Circus Maximus

Mausoleum of Augustus

Temple of the Deified Hadrian

Temple of the Deified Matidia

Pantheon

Stadium of Domitian

Odeum of Domitian

TIBER

Mausoleum of Hadrian

Pons Aelius

Porta Aurelia

Map 1   Rome: the city centre

The most prominent was L. Cornelius Balbus, who achieved immense influence as Caesar's agent and after the dictator's death was actually made a member of the Roman Senate and consul in 40 BC, the first consul not to have been Italian born. In the meantime Caesar had conferred citizenship on the entire community. Gades' wealth was proverbial. Balbus himself had been extremely rich. In the Augustan age there were five hundred Gaditani with the equestrian property-qualification. Several men from these families must have followed Balbus into the Senate. One may readily postulate that Domitia Paulina's father, if not indeed earlier generations of the family, had achieved this rank. The ultimate descent was, of course, Punic: the family name Domitia points to descent from a person enfranchised through the good offices of one of the noble Republican Domitii.[2]

The paternal line was very different. The Aelii had been settled at Italica, some 5 miles (8 km) upstream from Hispalis (Seville), since 'the time of the Scipios'. In other words, an ancestor had been one of the 'sick or wounded soldiers' of P. Cornelius Scipio's army in Spain, left behind in a new settlement when he was about to return to Rome in 206 BC – the same year in which Gades had received its treaty-status – 'in a town which he named Italica after Italy'. The place was not a *colonia*, although it would later become a *municipium*, and the soldiers were doubtless allied Italians, not Roman citizens. The first Aelius of Italica came from Hadria on the east coast of Italy, as Hadrian was careful to note in his autobiography. Some two hundred years later, a member of the family, Hadrian's *atavus* Marullinus, his great-grandfather's grandfather, had entered the Roman Senate. Hence, even if the intervening generations did not serve as Roman senators, the Aelii were certainly one of the leading families of Italica, indeed of the whole province of Baetica. Two other Italica families with whom they shared this position may be identified, the Ulpii and the Trahii or Traii, the ancestors of Trajan. One or both derived from Tuder (Todi) in Umbria, and, like the Aelii, their settlement at Italica probably went back to the foundation in 206 BC.[3]

Hadrian's link with Trajan is stressed in the *HA*, his father Hadrianus Afer being described as 'a cousin (*consobrinus*) of the Emperor Trajan'. It is generally assumed that Hadrian's grandfather had married an aunt of Trajan, or, to put it another way, a sister of the elder Trajan, M. Ulpius Traianus. This man, who was thus Hadrian's great-uncle, was one of the most powerful and influential persons of the day. He was in the east at the time of Hadrian's birth, as governor of Syria, and his son, Hadrian's father's cousin, was with him, as a military tribune. Traianus owed his distinction in part, no doubt, to his military capacity, but also to a fortunate chance: he had been commanding X Fretensis, as one of the three legionary legates in the expeditionary force in Judaea led by Vespasian from late 66 onwards. Hence he was one of the men on the spot when his commander-in-chief was proclaimed emperor in July 69. Two other legionary legates in Judaea in this expedition had been a man from Vespasian's home town, Reate (Rieti), Sex. Vettulenus Cerialis – and Vespasian's own son Titus. It looks as if Vespasian had been allowed to choose these two legates himself – a most exceptional circumstance. Perhaps Traianus was also Vespasian's choice. There are hints that his wife Marcia owned property at the confluence of the Tiber and the Nar, equidistant between Tuder and Reate; and Marcia may have been a sister of Titus' first wife Marcia Furnilla. Be this as it may, as an old comrade-in-arms of the Emperor and of his elder son Titus Caesar, Traianus had a status in the 70s that was clearly exceptional. Besides, as governor of Syria he demonstrated his prowess, deterring a threatened Parthian invasion.[4]

The Aelii and Ulpii were no doubt wealthy. Membership of the Senate after all demanded a substantial property qualification. The Aelii – it is no surprise – owned productive olive plantations upstream from Italica. During the Civil Wars of 49–45 BC men from Italica had played a prominent role in the Spanish campaigns – but mostly on the side of the Pompeians. It may be conjectured that Hadrian's ancestor Marullinus had supported Caesar and that he acquired senatorial rank as a reward. The rise of the colonial élite – in particular from Gallia Narbonensis and from Baetica – continued under the Julio-Claudian dynasty, accelerated by the influence of the Guard Prefect Afranius Burrus of Vasio (Vaison-la-Romaine) and Annaeus Seneca of Corduba (Córdoba), Nero's principal advisers for the first part of his reign. That Nero's immediate successor Galba had been for many years governor of Hispania Tarraconensis at the time of his proclamation in 68 gave a further boost to the fortunes of the Spanish Romans; and Vespasian had signalled a new step forward in 73–4 when he conferred Latin status on all Spanish communities that were not yet Roman or Latin.[5]

Thus 'colonial' magnates had held the highest offices at Rome in some numbers by the time of Hadrian's birth. Valerius Asiaticus of Vienna (Vienne) had been consul *ordinarius* (holding office for the second time) in 46. Pedanius Secundus of Barcino (Barcelona) had even been Prefect of Rome under Nero. In the mid-70s there were several dozen families from the western provinces in the ranks of the Senate – joined by a handful from the Greek-speaking east who had jumped on the Flavian bandwagon in 69. As censors in 73 and 74 Vespasian and Titus had even granted patrician status, membership of the primeval aristocracy of Rome, to some provincials. Among those favoured were the Ulpii Traiani, the Annii Veri from the Baetican *colonia* of Ucubi (Espejo), Cn. Julius Agricola from Forum Iulii (Fréjus) in Narbonensis, who would shortly be consul (perhaps in 76, a few months after Hadrian's birth) and then governor of Britain, and, from Gallic Nemausus (Nîmes), the brothers Domitii, Lucanus and Tullus.[6]

Hadrian's family presumably spent the winters at Rome and the hot summer months at a cooler suburban retreat. The odds are that they already had, or would soon acquire, a villa at Tibur (Tivoli), where there was a cluster of Spanish notables with country houses in the Flavian period. Whether Hadrian's parents took him back to the old family home in his early childhood is rather doubtful. Contact with Italica and supervision of the family estates in Baetica could have been largely dealt with through bailiffs. Senators were expected to live at Rome, their official place of residence, except when on government service elsewhere. Besides, Hadrianus Afer, as a recent praetor, must be assumed to have held several posts in public service in the years immediately following his son's birth. Command of a legion is a strong possibility – up to half of the praetors each year would be called upon, particularly since Vespasian evidently made the praetorship a preliminary qualification for this post (previously younger men had become legionary legates, as in the case of Titus, legate of XV Apollinaris at the age of twenty-seven, having gone no further than the quaestorship). This could have been followed by the governorship of one of the 'imperial' provinces, as pro-praetorian *legatus Augusti* – thus Julius Agricola, praetor in 68, legate of a legion in Britain and then, for a little less than three years, governor of Aquitania.[7]

Less demanding posts were also available, for example, for twelve months only, as legate to one of the ten proconsuls, and then another twelve months – according to the rules, no earlier than five years after the praetorship – as pro-consul of one of the eight proconsular provinces reserved for ex-praetors. The majority of the proconsulships were of provinces in the Greek-speaking half of the empire. One of the few proconsular provinces in the west was Baetica – which Traianus had governed under Nero. The legate or proconsul would certainly take his wife and children with him, furthermore. Hence there is a distinct possibility that Hadrian, as a child, spent a year or two in the Greek east. This remains no more than a guess. It may, nonetheless, be noted that Traianus was proconsul of Asia in 79–80. The proconsuls of Asia and Africa were drawn from the ex-consuls and the former could nominate three *legati*. One of Traianus' legates is known, T. Pomponius Bassus, who might have been a fellow-Spaniard. Another was probably one of the new Greek senators, A. Julius Quadratus of Pergamum. The third – it is no more than a guess – could well have been the proconsul's nephew, Hadrianus Afer.[8]

That the child Hadrian could have accompanied his parents to Ephesus, Smyrna and other ancient and opulent cities of the province Asia is at least worth a thought. Childhood impressions are important and most people's earliest memories go back to about the age of three or four. Even more enticing is the thought that Afer could easily have been proconsul of Achaia in the early 80s, when Hadrian would have been a boy of four or five. Still, there is no need to invoke such speculation to explain how someone who grew up in Flavian Rome would be so attracted to all things Hellenic. Rome was by then – and had been indeed for over a century – in a real sense the largest Greek city in the world. That is to say, in the same way that at one time Glasgow was the largest Irish city or New York had the largest Jewish population, the Greek-speaking inhabitants of Rome had probably long outnumbered those of any Greek *polis* in the east. Greek culture in the capital had been further boosted by Nero's enthusiastic philhellenism and had not declined with his downfall. Some of it was no doubt very superficial, such as the fashion of having trained slaves

14

to recite Platonic dialogues as entertainment at dinner-parties. But there was genuine enthusiasm for Greek literature, philosophy and art. Greek intellectuals such as Plutarch found a ready welcome in Flavian Rome. As for Latin literature of the age, the titles of Statius' *Thebaid* and *Achilleid*, or Valerius Flaccus' *Argonautica*, speak for themselves. It is worth recalling that Quintilian, the foremost teacher of his day, recommended that small boys – he was thinking, of course, of the élite – should be taught Greek before Latin (which they would pick up anyway), although not to the extent of 'speaking and learning *only* Greek for a long time – as happens in very many cases'. This would have a bad effect on the child's command of Latin. The common practice which Quintilian thought excessive may well have applied to the boy Hadrian.[9]

If the three-year-old Hadrian was at Rome, rather than at Ephesus or elsewhere with his father in the summer of 79, the death of old Vespasian and the accession of his elder son Titus might have been the earliest public event to be imprinted in his memory. Vespasian was at Aquae Cutiliae, a Sabine spa, when he succumbed – to a fever rather than to gout, Cassius Dio reports. In spite of which, according to Dio 'there have been some who spread the story that Titus had poisoned his father at a banquet.' One of these rumour-mongers, he adds, was none other than the Emperor Hadrian. When Hadrian made the charge is not stated and where Dio found out about it is not clear. One might assume that Hadrian was quoted to this effect by Marius Maximus. Hadrian might even have found occasion to refer to the story in his autobiography. But such a claim by Hadrian might have gone the rounds in senatorial circles for years and years. The boy Hadrian can hardly have heard the allegation in 79, but the odds are that it surfaced under Domitian, who is credited with other smears against his brother. The fact that Hadrian believed it and later repeated it is perhaps an indirect sign of his attitude to Domitian.[10]

A succession of striking events in Rome and Italy from 79 onwards must have made some impact on a child at Rome. It is enough merely to list them. The eruption of Vesuvius and the disappearance of Pompeii and Herculaneum in August 79 is an obvious enough sensation. More immediate would be the fire at Rome itself the following year, less disastrous and dramatic than the great fire under Nero in 64, but serious enough to consume the rebuilt temple of Jupiter on the Capitol destroyed in another blaze at the end of 69. Also very striking – even for a child too young to attend – would be the opening of the vast new Flavian amphitheatre (the 'Colosseum') by Titus in the summer of 80, with a hundred days of spectacles. Titus' death the following September and the accession of his much younger brother Domitian was another landmark. Not much more than two years later Domitian would return from his brief participation in a northern war with the title 'Germanicus'. The eight-year-old Hadrian probably watched the triumph early in 84. Whether he also registered discussion of a famous Roman victory in the far north, won by Julius Agricola against the Caledonians at the battle of the Graupian Mountain in September 83, can be guessed with rather less confidence. The great general returned to

Rome quietly the next year and withdrew to private life. All the same, Agricola was granted the triumphal insignia, the only man so honoured under Domitian.[11]

In the course of the year 85 or at the latest in January 86 came the death of Hadrian's father. Guardians were appointed for the boy, as he had not yet assumed the toga of manhood: his first cousin once removed, Trajan, by now in his early thirties, and another man from Italica, P. Acilius Attianus, a Roman knight, aged forty-five. Their principal task was to look after the inherited property, but Trajan may perhaps have played the part of a substitute parent. He was presumably by now married, his wife being Pompeia Plotina: she was also of 'colonial' origin, from Nemausus (Nîmes) in Narbonensis. Plotina was probably only a few years older than Hadrian, and her relationship with him was very warm in later years. He would also become very fond of his second cousin Matidia, she too being not many years older than himself. She was the daughter of Trajan's sister Marciana, and was probably married in the early 80s, at the age of about fourteen or fifteen, to a man called Mindius. She bore a daughter, named after herself, and – after the loss of this husband by divorce or death – was married again, to a senator called Vibius Sabinus, and had a second daughter, Sabina, in about 86.[12]

By this time Hadrian will have had elementary teachers for several years. In 87 or 88 he was old enough to move on to secondary education with a *grammaticus*, either at a school (which Quintilian thought preferable) or with a private teacher. The *HA* happens to mention in a subsequent *vita* that the celebrated Q. Terentius Scaurus was 'Hadrian's *grammaticus*'. This is often taken to be a careless abbreviation of an original expression such as '*grammaticus* in the time of Hadrian', for Scaurus was indeed at the height of his fame when Hadrian was emperor. Still, there is something to be said for the notion that he had taught Hadrian himself. Scaurus' names suggest that he may have derived from Nemausus, from the same family as D. Terentius Scaurianus, a contemporary of Hadrian who would rise high under Trajan. One might even take this further. Pompeia Plotina, herself from Nemausus, could have been instrumental in securing Scaurus as a teacher for her husband's young ward. Scaurus was to become known as the author of a lengthy work entitled *Ars grammatica* and for other writings, including one on correct spelling, *De orthographia*, and a commentary on Horace. The latter was not one of Hadrian's favourite authors. On the contrary, he preferred writers from the second century BC, Ennius among Latin poets, the Elder Cato and the historian Coelius Antipater among prose authors. Quintilian urged that boys should not be let loose on the 'ancient authors' like Cato too soon – their harsh and powerful style would have a bad influence. Cicero was the ideal – but the mature Hadrian would prefer old Cato.[13]

Whatever he was reading in these early years, he preferred Greek to Latin literature. The *HA* and the *Epitome de Caesaribus*, both plainly deriving from Marius Maximus, state that he was already 'rather strongly' (*impensius* – which might even mean '*too* strongly') steeping himself in *Graecis litteris* or *Graecis studiis*. 'Such was his inclination in this direction', both sources add, 'that quite a few people used to call him "'little Greek".' The nickname *Graeculus* was certainly a form of mild mockery, if not necesssarily conveying the venom with which Juvenal would use the term a few decades later. Be this as it may, the ten-year-old Hadrian might be supposed to have been impressed and inspired by imperial patronage of Greek culture. Domitian instituted regular festivals at his Alban villa, held almost every year, Suetonius says, at which literary competitions for orators and poets were prominent. In 86 the Emperor inaugurated something much more lavish, a triple contest in honour of Jupiter Capitolinus, to be held every four years at Rome. A new stadium that could hold 15,000 spectators was built for the purpose. Poets and musicians, athletes both male and female, and horsemen, competed, with the Emperor presiding in Greek dress. It was in fact a Greek *agon*, with Domitian as the *agonothetes*. Another sign of imperial philhellenism was that Domitian even consented to hold office – *in absentia* – as archon at Athens.[14]

Domitian's new stadium was only a small part of the massive building programme in which he was engaged throughout his reign – continuing, in effect, what had been going on since reconstruction after the fire of 64 had been launched by Nero. Vespasian and Titus had taken this much further, with the vast new Forum of Peace, new Baths and temples, and, of course, the Colosseum. There was much to restore after the fire of 80. Apart from other projects, Domitian greatly enlarged and elaborated the imperial residence on the Palatine. The building boom, that had lasted for over thirty years by the time of Domitian's death, received a new impetus under Trajan, and Hadrian would continue building on a massive scale as Emperor, in Rome and elsewhere. Fortunes were made by some of the families with estates near Rome on which bricks and tiles were manufactured, among them by the brothers Domitii. The passion for architecture that Hadrian was to display as a young man no doubt goes back to his boyhood – likewise his skills as a player of the *cithara* (*psallendi*) and as a singer. Quintilian approved of old-fashioned singing – the praises of famous men – and a knowledge of the principles of music. The psaltery, in his view, was 'unsuitable even for a young girl of good character', never mind for a boy.[15]

Warfare continued during the 80s. After the early victory over the Chatti and the triumph, there had been a serious débâcle. The governor of Moesia, Oppius Sabinus, was defeated and killed by the Dacians. Domitian took the field again, repelled the invaders and celebrated another triumph, probably in 86. Two Spanish senators won distinction in high command, Funisulanus Vettonianus, from Caesaraugusta (Saragossa) and Cornelius Nigrinus from Liria. The Guard Prefect Cornelius Fuscus was then entrusted with a Roman offensive across the Danube. It ended in disaster, with Fuscus' death, and Domitian had to return to the front. Reinforcements were needed there, including II Adiutrix, one of the four legions in Britain – where most of Agricola's conquests were, as a result, abandoned. Things went better in 88, when the general Tettius Julianus inflicted a defeat on the Dacians. In the meantime there had been further festivities at Rome, Saecular Games. The choice of the year 88 seems at first sight surprising. The traditional Games were held at intervals of 110 years – Claudius' Games in 48 were different, celebrating the 800th anniversary of Rome's foundation. Augustus' Games had been held in 17 BC, so that, at first sight, Domitian should have waited until 94. Perhaps the *quindecimviri*, the priests responsible for these matters (one of whom was Cornelius Tacitus, also praetor in the year 88), reported that Augustus' celebration ought to have been held in 23 BC, which gave the proper interval of 110 years before 88.[16]

At the start of the year 89 came a dramatic development. News reached Rome that Antonius Saturninus, the commander of the Upper German army, at Moguntiacum (Mainz), had staged a *coup d'état*, supported by some, but perhaps not all, of his four or five legions. It may be that Domitian had had wind of Saturninus' plans in advance, and, for this reason, for the first time since he had become Emperor, refrained from holding office as consul at the start of 89. At any rate, he presumably left for Germany within a very short time of hearing the news, no doubt with the Praetorian Guard. There was the prospect of civil war, almost an exact replay, twenty years on, of Vitellius' proclamation on the Rhine. But, unlike Vitellius, Saturninus found no support from the other army commanders. His counterpart in the northern Rhineland, Lappius Maximus, moved against him with the Lower German army, likewise Norbanus, the equestrian governor of Raetia, the province to the east, with his force of auxiliaries. Other armies were also summoned. Trajan, at this time command-ing the legion VII Gemina in north-west Spain, brought his men by forced marches from Asturia to the Rhine, a good 700 miles (835 km). Lappius and Norbanus had suppressed the revolt before even Domitian arrived, let alone Trajan. A senatorial college of priests, the Arval Brethren, prayed on the Capitol for Domitian's safety, victory and return on 12 January. They were already celebrating the partial fulfilment of their *vota* ten days later; on the 25th they sacrificed to mark 'public rejoicing' and on the 29th for Domitian's safety and return – the victory had already been won.[17]

Saturninus had hoped for support from the Chatti, who evidently destroyed some of the recently constructed forts east of the Rhine. A brief campaign against them followed, and Domitian then moved down the Danube for a further expedition, against the Suebi and the Dacians. It was not the first time that there had been a conspiracy against Domitian – at least, in September 87 sacrifices had been performed by the Arval Brethren 'on account of the detec-tion of criminal acts by the sacrilegious'. Reprisals certainly followed the failed coup of 89; and there will have been uneasiness in parts of the Senate at the least. A pretender appeared in the east, with Parthian backing, claiming to be Nero. He was soon suppressed, but it was a disturbing episode. A proconsul of Asia in office at about this time, Vettulenus Civica Cerialis, specifically included by Suetonius among senior senators put to death by Domitian, was probably implicated in some way in the conspiracy of 87, or somehow compromised by the false Nero affair, rather than linked to the failed coup of Saturninus.[18]

By November 89 Domitian was back at Rome, and again celebrated a triumph – this time a double one, over Chatti and Dacians. As a further sign of the glorification of the ruler, the months September and October were renamed, respectively Germanicus – the name by which he preferred to be known since his first northern victory – and Domitianus, the former to commemorate the month of his accession, the latter the month when he was born. He began the year 90 as consul. It was the fifteenth occasion he had held the office – he had been consul six times under Vespasian, although only once as *ordinarius*, and had shared the *fasces* with Titus in 80. From 82 onwards the only year in which the Emperor had not been consul was 89. His colleague in 90 was M. Cocceius Nerva, who had already been consul with Vespasian nearly twenty years earlier: the distinction was striking, for Vespasian and Titus almost monopolised the ordinary consulship throughout the 70s. Nerva must have been valuable to Vespasian, as he had been to Nero – he had evidently given Nero useful advice in the aftermath of the conspiracy of 65, and had been suitably decorated. His role as an *éminence grise* under the Flavians can only be deduced from these distinctions. Presumably his advice was particularly useful again in 89. There was an unusually large number of suffect consuls in 90. Some of these might be men who had just displayed conspicuous loyalty. One suffect was Ser. Julius Servianus, his colleague being a man from Corduba, L. Antistius Rusticus. Another Baetican senator, L. Cornelius Pusio, was one of the other suffects. All must be supposed to have been loyal servants of Domitian. The odds are that Servianus had already become Hadrian's brother-in-law by marrying his sister Paulina. The daughter of this marriage, Julia Paulina, Hadrian's niece, would herself marry in 106 and cannot have been born much later than 91 or 92. Servianus' origin is nowhere directly attested, but he was surely from the colonial élite, rather than from Italy. Various considerations make southern Gaul more likely as his home than Spain.[19]

Some time after his next birthday, 24 January 90, Hadrian 'went back to Italica.' The language of the *HA* has given rise to the idea that he had, after all, been born there and not at Rome. Or, it is suggested, he had been taken to Italica before, as a child, which is, to be sure, perfectly possible, whether on a private visit with his parents, or, perhaps, if his father had been proconsul, or legate to a proconsul, of the province Baetica. But *rediit* probably simply conveys the sense that he 'went back to the old plantation.' Cassius Dio happens to register a curious business at Rome in this year, an alleged bout of poisoning, 'some persons smearing needles with poison and pricking people with them', resulting in many deaths – and punishment of the alleged perpetrators. It was going on not only at Rome but 'in most of the world'. In fact, an epidemic was probably raging. There were several deaths in high places, for example the younger Aurelius Fulvus, consul *ordinarius* in 89, and probably aged only about thirty-three, the wife and young sons of the Professor of Rhetoric Quintilian, and the husband of the young and beautiful Violentilla. Martial congratulated his friend Licinius Sura soon afterwards on his recovery from an almost fatal illness. One might in fact suggest that Servianus married Domitia Paulina precisely because he had been widowed – he was, after all, over forty and had surely not been a bachelor up till then.[20]

Hadrian might have been sent to Italica to escape the epidemic. A likelier reason is that he had assumed the toga of manhood and was thus under some obligation to inspect the family property at Italica and elsewhere in Baetica. The ceremony was often held when the youth was a year or two older than fourteen. But Nero had assumed the *toga virilis* at this age and the young Marcus Aurelius would do likewise. The occasion was normally the festival of the Liberalia on 17 March. It may be supposed that in March of the year 90 Hadrian went through this *rite de passage*. He was now no longer a *puer* but a *iuvenis*.[21]

2

THE OLD DOMINION

Tarraconensis and Baetica were not quite Rome's oldest overseas possessions. Sicily and Sardinia–Corsica, annexed after the First Punic War, had priority. But Rome had first established a foothold in the peninsula at Tarraco (Tarragona) in 218 BC, at the very start of the Hannibalic War. Within twelve years, building on the work of his father and uncle, P. Scipio, the later Africanus, had conquered Carthage's Spanish empire and a good deal more. It would be a hard struggle to take Roman rule as far as the Atlantic. The Cantabrians and Asturians of the north-west did not succumb until 19 BC, and for several decades Augustus retained a force of three legions in Tarraconensis, the largest of the three provinces into which the land was now divided. By the time of Nero the garrison was reduced to a single legion and that remained the case thereafter. VII Gemina, based on the new legion raised by Galba in Spain in 68, had now taken over the fortress in Asturia which was to be called Legio (León). The other two provinces, Lusitania and Baetica, had no legions and scarcely any garrison; and their governors were of lower rank than the consular legate who ruled Hither Spain from Tarraco. Lusitania, the western part of the old Further Spain, was, like Tarraconensis, an imperial province, governed by the emperor's legate, but only by an ex-praetor, being thus on a par with with the three Gallic provinces, Aquitania, Belgica and Lugdunensis. Baetica, which took its name from the Baetis (the modern name, Guadalquivir, means precisely 'the great river', as the Arab conquerors called it in the eighth century), was a 'senatorial' or proconsular province.[1]

The proconsular provinces were fundamentally, as the geographer Strabo had expressed it in Augustus' day, those that were 'peaceable and easy to rule without arms'. Furthermore, it might be added that the proconsular provinces were those that were highly urbanised. This certainly applied to Baetica, where the old Punic and Carthaginian cities such as Gades (Cádiz) and Malaca (Málaga) had been joined by a host of Roman foundations. Italica was the first in a long line. Carteia, another veteran settlement, had received a charter from the Senate in 171 BC. Meanwhile the riches of the country had attracted settlers and contractors in substantial numbers. Other and more famous city foundations followed, above all Corduba (Córdoba) and Hispalis (Sevilla). Caesar and

Augustus conferred charters on existing towns – including Italica – and established further *coloniae* in Baetica. Vespasian's grant of Latin status to the whole peninsula meant that every community that had hitherto lacked a charter could now convert itself into a *municipium*.[2]

The wealth of Spain, and especially the valley of the Baetis, is underlined by the description in Strabo's *Geography*, under Augustus. 'Turdetania', as he calls the region, was 'wonderfully blessed by nature: not only does it produce everything, but these blessings are doubled by the ease with which its products can be exported by ship.' He lists 'corn and wine and olive oil – not only in large quantities but of the best quality – wax, honey and pitch' among these products, as well as dye-stuffs, wool, cattle of all kinds, game, and seafood in abundance. Over and above this Strabo stresses Turdetania's richness in metals: gold, silver, copper and iron were all there, in a quantity and quality unsurpassed anywhere in the world. His story that the Carthaginians had found the people of that country using silver feeding-troughs and wine-jars may be only a slight exaggeration.[3]

The favoured land had not surprisingly attracted substantial numbers of immigrants over the last century and a half of the Republic, civilian traders and contractors, even political exiles, to add to the Italian element represented by veterans. The nomenclature of Roman Spain indicates that many of the immigrants came from the back country in Italy, from Etruria, Umbria, Picenum and Samnium. What the total number of settlers was can only be guessed at, but in the Civil War some ten thousand men from immigrant or veteran families served in the Pompeian forces. Relations with the native Iberians were mostly friendly and intermarriage was common. It is true that the author of the *Bellum Hispaniense*, describing Caesar's campaign against the younger Pompey in 45 BC, while noting that 'the whole of Further Spain is fertile and well-watered', adds that 'because of frequent native raids, all places remote from towns are protected by towers and fortifications, with lookout points'. The implantation of colonists by Caesar and Augustus and the establishment of peace throughout the empire ended this residual insecurity. And the new settlement took place, at least in Baetica and eastern Tarraconensis, in a country already to a large extent Latin in language and culture. 'The Turdetanians', Strabo wrote, 'have completely changed over to the Roman way of life, and do not even remember their own language any more.' Large-scale grants of Latin status and the admission of natives to colonial foundations under Caesar and Augustus helped to consolidate the process.[4]

Southern Spain early on began to make its own contribution to Latin literature. Cicero in 62 BC made a sarcastic comment about Corduban poets, unnamed, with their 'heavy and slightly foreign sound'. In spite of this, under Augustus Corduba produced another one, Sextilius Ena, whose verses praised Cicero. Better known is the celebrated *rhetor* and prose author Annaeus Seneca. His son of the same name would become even more famous, as a poet and philosopher and as tutor and *minister* to Nero; and the *rhetor*'s grandson was the epic poet Lucan. Other Baetican *litterati* include the elder Seneca's friend Porcius Latro and, probably, Junius Gallio, who was to adopt Seneca's eldest son. Both acquired a reputation as declaimers at Rome. Some of the Spanish orators of the time, for example Gavius Silo and Clodius Turrinus, remained in the province. Several other Augustan writers may also have derived from Spain, such as the historian Fenestella, the collector of moral *exempla* Valerius Maximus, and Grattius, who produced a poem on hunting, the *Cynegetica*. The attraction of Rome for provincial talents was too strong for most to resist. These three, like the Senecas, Gallio and Latro, had clearly all moved to Rome. Flavian Rome had two outstanding Spaniards – both, from their names, of Romanised Iberian origin and both from Tarraconensis: Quintilian the teacher of rhetoric (M. Fabius Quintilianus) from Calagurris (Calahorra) and the poet Martial (M. Valerius Martialis) from Bilbilis (near Calatayud).[5]

The *HA* has only a single sentence about Hadrian's brief stay at Italica. 'He at once entered military service', it begins. *Militia* for a fourteen-year-old cannot possibly mean joining the army. Hadrian must have been enrolled in the local organisation, *collegium*, for the young men of good family, the *iuvenes*. Inscriptions attest the existence of such *collegia* in the towns of Italy and the western provinces. Not much is known of what they actually did. At the still native town of Mactaris (Maktar) in Africa the *iuvenes*, sixty-five strong, dedicated a basilica and storehouses in the year 88. The basilica was no doubt a training-hall. The young men probably had a role in the imperial cult and undertook physical, perhaps military training. In case of extreme emergency they could be called up as a militia. But the few mentions in literary sources suggest that in some cases the gilded municipal youth got out of hand. In Apuleius' novel, *The Golden Ass*, the beautiful Photis warns her lover Lucius to return to his lodgings in good time: 'There is a wild band of *iuvenes* of good family that disturbs the peace – you will see the bodies of people they have killed lying in the street.' That this unruly conduct by the *iuvenes* was not entirely fictional is clear from the third-century jurist Callistratus: 'Some of those commonly called *iuvenes* have the habit of joining in popular acclamations in some disorderly communities. If they have not caused any further trouble and have not been warned by the governor, they can be punished by a beating and banned from attending shows.' Further offences were to receive more serious treatment, exile or even death.[6]

What else Hadrian did in his short stay in the old country is largely a matter of guesswork. He may have had relatives there, for example a great-uncle, also called Aelius Hadrianus. According to the *HA*, the old man, an expert astrologer, once told the young Hadrian that he would become emperor. Although Hadrian was later noted for his addiction to the science of the stars, the story may be an invention of the *HA*. If, as seems likely, his mother was with him, they may have visited her home town, Gades. A visit to the proconsul may also have been deemed appropriate for a young man of senatorial family. It is not known who the incumbent governor was in the year 90 – it could have been one Baebius

Massa, whose conduct was to result in his prosecution three years later. But Massa probably held office in 91–2 or 92–3. However this may be, the young master should at least have inspected the family estates, a few miles upstream from Italica, on the way to Ilipa, to make himself known to the estate-workers. Amphorae made to contain olive-oil from this locality, produced by the 'Virginensian Pottery' (*figlina Virginensia*), were stamped *port. P.A.H.*, plausibly interpreted as 'the warehouse, *port(us)*, of Publius Aelius Hadrianus'. One estate then was presumably the *fundus Virginiensis* recorded by a painted inscription from the great mound of amphorae at Rome, the Monte Testaccio. The names of five slave-workers appear on some of these amphorae: Augustalis, Callistus, Hermes, Milo and Romulus. Whether any of these men were already working on the estate when the young Hadrian was there is another matter. The amphorae are generally dated a little later.[7]

What impression Italica made on Hadrian can only be surmised – the fact that he studiously avoided returning there when he was in Spain as emperor may imply that his verdict was somewhat negative. This implication is not necessarily in conflict with his lavish generosity to the place, which was totally transformed during his reign. Small-town life and society may have seemed boring and petty. When Martial returned to his Spanish home a decade later, he admitted to his friend Priscus that he was living 'in a provincial desert': it was difficult to keep one's spirits up every day in a small place, without theatres, libraries and dinner parties, and subjected to the envy or malice of his fellow-*muncipales*. One 'cultural' item may have caught Hadrian's attention at Italica, a Greek work of art which must have been one of the town's treasures. A small marble plaque registered the fact that it had been donated 'to the *vicus Italicensis* by Lucius Mummius, son of Lucius, *imp(erator)*', following the 'capture of Corinth'. The consul who destroyed Corinth in 146 BC and took the name 'Achaicus' had previously served as governor of Further Spain. Little Italica had thus been singled out for a small share in the spoils – Mummius' vast plunder of statues and paintings was notorious. He had given them away with astonishing lavishness, lacking any personal interest in the arts. Hadrian may have made friends at Italica. A possible fellow-townsman and probably his exact coeval, later registered as one of his closest friends, was A. Platorius Nepos. But Hadrian and Nepos could have got to know each other at Rome or at Tibur – Aemilius Papus, also known as Messius Rusticus, another of Hadrian's close friends, whose family came from Siarum in the Baetis valley, certainly had property at Tibur.[8]

The rest of the *HA*'s report on Hadrian's stay at Italica, following immediately on his entry into the '*militia*', is much more readily intelligible: he was 'devoted to hunting, to such an extent as to incur reprimand'. This was no doubt a favourite activity of the *iuvenes* of Italica. Spain was an ideal country for such pursuits: stags, wild boar and wild goats abounded – as did the 'digging hares' (rabbits) then found only there in Europe. It is no coincidence that the book of epigrams composed by Martial at Bilbilis begins by saying that 'after the hunting-nets have been put aside and the wood is silent', he could compose – there was nothing else to do there. It may be inferred that Hadrian was still at Italica in the autumn, when the hunting season began. He may have formed another habit here. Marius Maximus reported that Hadrian's favourite dish was a game pie, the ingredients being sow's udder, pheasant and ham, baked in pastry. Hadrian – who always had a healthy appetite – called it his *tetrafarmacum*, 'four-fold medicine'. The name was probably meant as a joke, a reference to the use of the originally medical term by the Epicurean philosophers, to describe the essence of the master's doctrines. It is plausible enough that Hadrian acquired the taste for this dish in his youth and first ate it after hunting at Italica. The sport was not yet, however, an acceptable or highly thought-of occupation for upper-class Romans, as it had always been for the Greeks. Polybius specifically mentions how exceptional was the younger Scipio in his devotion to hunting – which he acquired in Macedonia after his father Paullus' conquest of that king-dom – and to other Hellenic arts and sciences. Scipio Aemilianus remained an exception: the Roman élite left hunting to slaves and freedmen – or, in the shape of staged *venationes* in the arena, hunting was a spectacle to entertain the people.[9]

This would soon change, with the advent of Trajan. A decade later Pliny was to wax rapturous at the new ruler's healthy and honourable forms of recreation, hunting and sailing. Whenever he could find time, his 'only relaxation is to range through the forests and drive the wild beasts from their lairs'. Senators such as Pliny and Tacitus followed suit, half-heartedly in Pliny's case: he took his notebooks with him, as he 'sat by the hunting-nets, with writing materials instead of hunting spears', a practice he recommended to Tacitus. In Spain it had no doubt been different. The rebel general Sertorius, who controlled much of the peninsula for a decade or so in the late Republic, 'hunted whenever he had leisure', according to Plutarch. The Spanish *rhetor* Porcius Latro, for all that he was notoriously pale from his hours of studying indoors, had at one time been devoted to hunting in forest and mountain with the peasants with such a passion that he could hardly tear himself away from the chase. The younger Seneca, who seldom even hints at his Spanish origin, seems also to have hunted, for he writes of the 'effort and danger' involved 'when we hunt'. Poems of Martial also show a few of his Spanish friends enjoying the chase. But Trajan, even if he shared the Spanish taste, was not yet emperor in the year 90. His reaction when he heard of Hadrian's excessive enthusiasm was 'to remove him' from Italica.[10]

Trajan himself was due to return to Rome by the autumn of 90 at the latest, to be consul *ordinarius* for the next year. One might suppose that he travelled from Legio to Italica and personally yanked his young ward away – the word used, *abductus*, is certainly rather strong. He might even have summoned him up to the legionary base. Be this as it may, and whether or not Hadrian had the chance to see other parts of Spain on the return journey, it may be supposed that before the end of the year 90 he was back at Rome, where he was treated by Trajan 'as a son' (*pro filio*). Trajan was now at the pinnacle of distinction. As consul *ordinarius*, with, as his colleague, M'. Acilius Glabrio, a member of whose family had first held the office nearly three hundred years before (in 191 BC), his social rank was now second to none except the Emperor, not least because so few non-members of the imperial family had been allowed to hold the ordinary consulship under the Flavians.[11]

Hadrian had probably had at least one private tutor in his household at Italica. Back at Rome he was ready to attend classes in rhetoric. It was probably too late for him to become a pupil of the foremost teacher of the day, Quintilian. He retired at about this time, after twenty years as 'Imperial Professor' at Rome – he was the first holder of the Chair in Rhetoric created by Vespasian – and was devoting himself to writing a lengthy monograph, *On the Education of an Orator*.[12]

3

MILITARY TRIBUNE

If Hadrian could not attend classes with Quintilian, he was no doubt found another teacher. He would in any case have been expected, as a senator's son himself and hence a future senator, to attach himself to leading orators. One rising star was not available: Cornelius Tacitus was away in the years 90–3, presumably holding posts in the provinces. It is probable enough that Trajan encouraged Hadrian to sit at the feet of Licinius Sura, another Spaniard, from one of the *coloniae* in Tarraconensis. Sura had already been winning applause as an advocate in the early 80s, when Martial wrote his first book of epigrams. In 92 Martial would call him 'most celebrated of learned men, whose old-fashioned speech recalls that of our grave forefathers'. He had a house on the Aventine, close to the Temple of Diana and overlooking the Circus Maximus, as Martial reveals in another poem. Sura is named third in a short list of eloquent admirers of Martial's writings, after Silius Italicus, the consular poet, and Aquillius Regulus, an aggressive orator.[1]

Early in May 92 Domitian left Rome for yet another northern campaign, against the Suebian Germans and the Sarmatians, and would be away for eight months. It may be that Trajan went with him and remained on the Danube, perhaps even to become governor of Pannonia. A few years later, at any rate, Pliny claimed that after winning approval for his rapid march from Spain to the Rhine in 89, Trajan was 'deemed worthy' by Domitian 'to conduct a series of expeditions': it is hard to see where else he could have served. The Emperor's campaign was far from a complete success, not least since a legion, XXI Rapax, was wiped out by the enemy. When Domitian returned in January 93, he marked the end of the war merely with a minor triumph, an *ovatio*. Statius attributed the Emperor's self-restraint to his 'clemency', and to his not wishing to 'dignify' the Marcomanni and the Sarmatian 'nomads' by holding a full-scale triumph over them. In December 92, anticipating Domitian's imminent return, Martial had addressed his eighth book of *Epigrams* to the Emperor, calling him by the title 'Dacicus' (which Domitian never assumed). A dozen of the eighty-two poems are devoted to praise, direct or indirect, of Domitian: 'In the month of Janus, the city sees a god returning'; 'Rome never loved a leader (*ducem*) so much'; 'It is not because of your gifts that the people loves you, Caesar, the people loves your gifts because of you.'[2]

27

Martial's ninth book, a year or two later, likewise continued to hail Domitian's victories. A new theme was added: the Emperor had banned castration, for which Martial congratulates him effusively in two poems. The poet managed, nonetheless, to include in the same book six effusive pieces on Domitian's own eunuch favourite Earinus, who had just dedicated some locks of his hair in a golden box to be deposited in the shrine of Asclepius at his native Pergamum. Statius, meanwhile, produced over a hundred lines on the beautiful Earinus and the tresses that the god was receive from the *Caesareus puer*, artfully praising the imperial ban on castration at the same time. The Emperor's 'Ganymede' was no exception in Flavian Rome. Beautiful boys – albeit mostly not eunuchs – were a feature of several households known from the literature of the age. Two poems of Statius were written to console friends on the deaths of *delicati*. 'Greek love' had once been frowned upon at Rome, and the traditionally minded professor, Quintilian, still disapproved. Martial's and Statius' writings show that it was now commonplace.[3]

In the course of 93 there was news from Baetica to create a stir, of special interest to senators from the province, no doubt. The proconsul, Baebius Massa, was accused by 'the provincials' – presumably through the provincial council – of extortion or corruption. Massa was tried before his peers, in the Senate, the prosecutors being Herennius Senecio, a senator from Baetica itself, and Pliny. Massa was convicted and his assets frozen while restitution was assessed. In the meantime the former proconsul struck back. He had experience as a *delator* (an informer or denouncer specialising in accusations of *maiestas*, treason) from the time of Nero. Together with Mettius Carus, another *delator*, he accused Senecio of treason. This would open the floodgates. Senecio was an adherent of the Stoic philosophy and closely linked with a senatorial group commonly labelled the 'Stoic Opposition'. A series of treason trials in the Senate followed, resulting in the execution not merely of Senecio but of two ex-consuls, Helvidius Priscus and Arulenus Rusticus, and the banishment of four other persons of senatorial rank, Rusticus' brother Mauricus, together with Mauricus' wife, and two women from the family of Helvidius. The charges were various, but clearly involved, in essence, criticism of the Emperor, direct or indirect, by a group that had displayed opposition to autocracy for half a century – Helvidius' father, had been condemned to death by Vespasian, his father's father-in-law Thrasea by Nero, Thrasea's father-in-law Caecina Paetus by Claudius.[4]

The trials took place after the death of Julius Agricola, who died on 23 August 93, while the prosecution of Baebius Massa was still in progress. Tacitus wrote, a few years later, that Agricola was fortunate in dying when he did, not having to witness 'the Senate House under siege, the Senate shut in by armed men.' The young Hadrian must have watched these trials – and, of course, that of Baebius Massa – with considerable interest. The consuls would have been required to preside; one of the men holding office in 93 was evidently a Spanish kinsman of Hadrian's family, L. Dasumius Hadrianus of Corduba. As for Tacitus, he was back at Rome soon after Agricola's death – he had been away for four years

28

– and, with his fellow-senators, was obliged to vote for the death sentence against Helvidius, Rusticus and Senecio. Tacitus had mixed feelings. Part of the charge against Senecio was that he had declined to stand for office after entering the Senate with the most junior magistracy, the quaestorship. What good did this passive opposition do? Agricola acted differently: he had continued to serve his country, even under Domitian – and would have been only too ready to make himself available for further service, in Syria, on the Danube, as proconsul of Asia, had Domitian permitted. Tacitus concluded, a few years later, that 'those who admire what is unlawful ought to know that there can be great men even under bad emperors, that obedience and restraint, if combined with diligence and vigour, are more laudable than seeking fame by the precipitous path that leads to an ostentatious martyrdom, which brings no benefit to the commonwealth.'[5]

Agricola's path, obedience and moderation, was, after all, the path that Trajan was following. As Trajan was later said to have remarked: 'Domitian was a bad emperor, but he had good *amici*.' There can be little doubt that Hadrian would have been content to subscribe to this view and, indeed, may even have felt that Domitian's measures against the Stoic group were justified. It is quite possible that he was present as an observer in the Senate House when the trials were in progress: Augustus had permitted sons of senators to attend Senate meetings as soon as they had taken the *toga virilis*, 'to accustom themselves to public life'. At all events, the treason trials could still have been in progress when Hadrian took his first steps in his official career. It was presumably in 94 that he held one of the offices in the vigintivirate, which Augustus had made obligatory for future senators. There were four separate boards, of varying prestige. Patricians, or plebeians with exceptionally strong patronage behind them, could become one of the three mint-masters, *tresviri monetales*. Then there were the four men assigned to supervise the streets of the capital, the *quattuorviri viarum curandarum*. Least favoured were the members of the board of three whose duties included some forms of policing, the *tresviri capitales* – at this very time they had been called upon to supervise the public burning of books by the condemned senators. Hadrian's friend Platorius Nepos, who had to be content with being a *capitalis* and must have served at about this time, could have been given this disagreeable task.[6]

Hadrian's post was as one of the remaining ten *vigintiviri*, the *decemviri stlitibus iudicandis* (the board of ten to adjudicate lawsuits), assigned by the responsible praetor to preside over one of the four panels of jurors in the Centumviral Court. This dealt with civil cases and met in the Basilica Julia. The public could and did attend. It was, however, the speeches of the advocates which attracted their attention, not the performance of the presiding *decemvir*, who is scarcely ever mentioned: his duties were clearly minimal. Pliny, who had himself appeared before the Centumviri as an advocate at the age of eighteen, and had been a *decemvir* shortly afterwards, continued to be regularly involved with cases in this court. He happens to record one which fell about the time when the young Hadrian might have been presiding. One Asudius Curianus had been disinherited by his mother, who made Pliny and another senator, Sertorius Severus, as well as several knights, her new heirs. Some of them were nervous that their friendship with the recently executed Arulenus Rusticus might jeopardise their position. Pliny made Curianus an offer just before the case was due to open, and it was settled out of court.[7]

Being a *decemvir* was not very demanding, it may be supposed, but it was an initiation into public life, a magistracy of the Roman People, if only a minor one. Hadrian would have had attendants (*viatores*) and scribes assigned to him. The same year would also bring two further opportunities to play a public role. By fortunate chance, the base survives for a statue set up to him at Athens in the year 112. It lists his *cursus honorum*, confirming and supplementing the account given in the *HA*. Two posts not mentioned in the *vita* are registered after the decemvirate: *praefectus feriarum Latinarum* and *sevir turmae equitum Romanorum*. The *feriae Latinae* were an ancient festival of the old Latin League, still held every year in the spring or early summer on the Alban mountain (modern Monte Cavi in the Alban Hills) twenty miles south of Rome. All the magistrates of the Roman People were obliged to attend and in their absence the consuls had to appoint a prefect to look after their duties in the city. The position seems regularly to have been given to a young senator or future senator, who had caught the eye of one of the consuls. It seems probable that Hadrian was picked out by the suffect consuls in office from 1 May to the end of August in 94, both of them men with a string of names, M. Lollius Paullinus D. Valerius Asiaticus Saturninus and C. Antius A. Julius Quadratus. The former was a descendant of the Gallic senator, Valerius Asiaticus of Vienna (Vienne), who had been consul for the second time in 46 and was soon afterwards killed by Claudius. Quadratus was from Pergamum and was one of the handful of Greeks who had been made senators by Vespasian. He had in all probability been legate to Trajan's father when the latter was proconsul of Asia fifteen years earlier, and he was certainly a friend of Trajan himself. It seems highly plausible that it was Quadratus who selected his friend's young kinsman for the honour of replacing the consuls.[8]

A month or two later came another ceremony, the annual ride-past of the Roman knights (*transvectio equitum*) on 15 July. They were distributed for the purpose in six squadrons (*turmae*), each of which was led by a young senator or future senator, with the title *sevir*, who would, at the very least, have to be a good horseman. Hadrian's sevirate at the ride-past is not dated on the Athens inscription, of course, but, like the honorary prefecture of Rome, it too probably fell in 94. The eighteen-year-old had now been very decisively launched on his career. Whether he had attracted the notice of the Emperor and had been favoured with an invitation to the Palace remains unknown. Statius celebrated his own attendance, for the first time, at a mass imperial banquet for senators and knights in this year or early in 95 – the 'Romulean chiefs' (senators) and the 'wearers of the *trabea*' (knights) reclined at a thousand tables – so it is not impossible that Hadrian was there. Statius expresses himself as awestruck by the vast marbled halls and the chance to 'gaze on Himself, calm-visaged and majestically serene'.[9]

Suetonius, writing over thirty years later, not surprisingly has a different emphasis. After the executions of senators Domitian 'became terrifying to all and hated', and was increasingly nervous, having the portico in the Palace where he took his exercise lined with reflecting walls so that he could see anyone coming up behind him. As for his banquets, Cassius Dio tells of a macabre entertainment for senators and knights, in a room entirely pitch black, with bare couches of the same colour on the bare floor. The guests were invited at night and a slab shaped like a gravestone was set beside them, black-painted boys danced around them before the food, again all coloured black, was served. No one spoke, except the host, 'and he conversed only about death and killing.' The guests were petrified.[10]

The year 95 was marked by further executions for conspiracy, prominent victims being Acilius Glabrio, Trajan's aristocratic consular colleague, and Domitian's own close kinsman, his cousin's son, Flavius Clemens. Clemens was also married to Domitian's grand-niece Domitilla, two of his sons had been adopted by Domitian and Clemens was consul this very year. Perhaps there were grounds for Domitian's action. Who can tell? He himself is reported by Suetonius to have complained at the unhappy lot of *principes*: no one believed in conspiracies against emperors – except when they were actually killed. Hadrian was probably glad to get away from Rome that year.[11]

Military service as a tribune was evidently no longer obligatory for future senators – some, at any rate, are known to have omitted it. But, of the twenty-eight legions that existed at this time, only the two in Egypt, from which persons of senatorial rank were debarred, did not need a *tribunus laticlavius*, 'with the broad stripe', denoting membership of the senatorial order. Some served for a few months or a year only, but, as there were only twenty *vigintiviri* each year, many of them must have joined a legion soon after their year as a minor magistrate was over. In Hadrian's case there can have been no doubts: his father's cousin, himself childless, who was now treating him 'like his own son', had spent several years as a military tribune, in at least two separate legions, in Syria and on the Rhine. He would surely have insisted that Hadrian follow his example and, furthermore, he was probably in a position to offer him a commission in his own army. Although there is not yet positive evidence, rational conjecture suggests that Trajan may have been governing Pannonia during these years. At all events, Hadrian now became tribune of II Adiutrix, stationed at Aquincum (Budapest) on the Danube. It was one of at least four legions in Pannonia and had a key role to play in guarding the empire against the Sarmatians across the river.[12]

II Adiutrix was a relatively new legion, only formed in the course of the Civil Wars, from marines in the Ravenna fleet. It had soon afterwards been sent to Britain and had had fifteen years of unbroken campaigning there, until it was transferred in 86 to the Danube, initially to Moesia. Three years later, after the end of Domitian's first Pannonian campaign, it moved to Aquincum and built itself the first legionary fortress there, of timber. It had certainly just participated in Domitian's second Pannonian campaign, of 92, not long before Hadrian took up his commission. As *tribunus laticlavius* Hadrian was, according to the hierarchy, second-in-command to the legion's commander, the legate (whose identity is unknown). He would have accommodation within the fortress on a substantial scale, his own house, in fact, with a good many rooms, and he would have brought with him slaves and freedmen from his own household in Rome.[13]

What his duties were is not so easy to say. Although in theory deputy commander, in practice he would have been expected to learn from the professional officers, the centurions, mostly men risen from the ranks, and from his five fellow-tribunes, all Roman knights. The centurions and men of the legion would have had plenty to tell him, about campaigning against the Sarmatians, and about their time in Britain during Agricola's long command. Some of them would have been at the great battle of the Graupian Mountain in 83, and could have offered opinions on the Caledonians. Hadrian, one likes to assume, will not have been one of those who 'devoted his service to the pursuit of pleasure, with as much leave as possible, to bring back the title of the tribunate, with nothing learned.' Rather, like the young Agricola thirty-five years earlier, he will have set out 'to get to know the province, to make himself known to the army, to learn from the experienced, to follow the best, to strive after nothing for the sake of ostentation, to refuse nothing through fear, to be at once cautious and alert.' Like Agricola, he probably spent some time with the governor, whose headquarters was at Carnuntum – not least if his kinsman Trajan was holding the post.[14]

Hadrian would later be known for his ability to mix easily with persons from all walks of life and for his fondness for talking to plebeians; for his astonishing capacity to remember names, not least of soldiers and veterans; and for his readiness to share the soldiers' simple diet. These qualities probably stood him in good stead in his first military posting. Later, as Emperor, he had the reputation of being 'most skilled with weapons and most expert in military science'. The odds are that he laid the groundwork for this proficiency at Aquincum in the years 95–6. At least one contact that he surely made in 95 was to be of great importance. An inscription from Aquincum registers a centurion of II Adiutrix called M. Turbo. The name Turbo is so uncommon that this can hardly be other than Q. Marcius Turbo (Marcius being abbreviated by analogy with the *praenomen* Marcus). This man from the Dalmatian *colonia* Epidaurum (near Dubrovnik) would serve Hadrian as Guard Prefect for over fifteen years.[15]

After not much more than a year with II Adiutrix, Hadrian's tour of duty came to an end, in the summer of 96 – perhaps because a new *tribunus laticlavius* had come to take his place, which in turn might mean that a new governor had arrived, bringing his own protégé as tribune with him. Be that as it may, Hadrian did not part company with the army, but received a new commission in one of the legions of Lower Moesia, V Macedonica, based at Oescus at the confluence of the river of the same name with the Danube. The governor to whom he owed this appointment cannot be identified with complete certainty, but was very probably L. Julius Marinus. He is surely the Julius Mar[ ], recorded as legate of Lower Moesia the following January. Marinus had an estate at the Sabine town of Cures, but may well have come from the east – the *colonia* of Berytus (Beirut) in Syria has been suggested as his home. At any rate, the young Hadrian was probably known to him, or strongly recommended: a second military tribunate was exceptional for a *laticlavius*.[16]

On 18 September 96, not long after Hadrian had arrived at Oescus, a dramatic event took place at Rome. The news probably took no more than a week to reach the Lower Danube: the Emperor had been assassinated. His successor – not the conspirators' first choice – was already installed and recognised by the Senate, indeed, had been acclaimed by that body with enthusiasm: Marcus Cocceius Nerva. Domitian's memory was condemned, his statues in silver and gold were melted down, his name was erased from public monuments. The plebs at Rome reached with indifference, but the soldiers were not at all pleased. Some tried to have Domitian deified, so Suetonius reports. Elements of the Danubian army, probably in Hadrian's province, were mutinous. They were brought to their senses – according to an admittedly somewhat implausible story in Philostratus – by the wandering philosopher Dio of Prusa (Bursa). Hadrian had probably only been with V Macedonica for a few weeks when the news came through – this appointment is dated to 'the very end of Domitian's reign' (*extremis iam Domitiani temporibus*) by the *HA*.[17]

Domitian had been the victim of a palace conspiracy, within his own household, including his chamberlain and other palace freedmen, and the Empress, not a plot by senators, let alone army-commanders, although the Guard Prefects were involved. But his relations with the Senate had been steadily deteriorating since 89, if not earlier, and the trials and executions in late 93 had made things worse. Now *libertas* was proclaimed, the exiles returned, and there was a rush to settle scores against those who had served the 'tyrant' as *delatores*. But the new Emperor's position was far from secure. Nerva was anything but a military man and the soldiers were angry. Further, the state finances were soon in a parlous condition. Nerva was obliged to sell off imperial property to raise funds; and he established an economy commission. He was to hold the consulship himself for 97, as was to be expected. The name of his colleague, however, may have come as a surprise. It was L. Verginius Rufus, who had a played a significant role in the Civil Wars of 68–9, and had then prudently withdrawn from public life. Rufus was now eighty-three years old. The reason for the choice may be divined. Nearly thirty years earlier Rufus had been offered the throne by the soldiers, more than once – first after the battle of Vesontio (Besançon) in June 68, after his Upper German army had thrashed the Gallic rebels of Julius Vindex; the offer was repeated shortly afterwards, on the news of Nero's death, then again after the death of Otho in April 69. Rufus had declined each time. Nerva may have wanted to send a signal to the army commanders: they should follow this salutary example.[18]

4

PRINCIPATUS ET LIBERTAS

The year 97 began inauspiciously. Old Verginius Rufus, rehearsing his address of thanks to Nerva for the grant of the consulship, fell and broke his hip as he bent to pick up a heavy book. A long illness followed. Meanwhile Nerva was calling on other elderly men. His friend Arrius Antoninus, who had offered Nerva his commiserations rather than congratulations on his accession, was given a second consulship. His first had been in the Year of the Four Emperors, AD 69. Julius Frontinus, who had been governor of Britain under Vespasian, emerged to be curator of Rome's aqueducts. Corellius Rufus, nearly eighty years old and crippled by painful gout for over forty years, was appointed to a land commission. Frontinus, Corellius and Verginius were all friends and patrons of Pliny. He himself had been one of the prefects of the military treasury in Domitian's last years. Now, temporarily out of office, he reflected that 'once Domitian had been killed, there was a beautiful opportunity for attacking the guilty, avenging the victims – and promoting my own prospects.' Early in 97, after consulting Corellius, he launched an attack on Publicius Certus, one of the men in charge of the other treasury, the *Aerarium Saturni*. Certus had played a major role in the downfall of Helvidius.[1]

Pliny's attack on Certus caused a general outcry. There were too many in the Senate who had compromised themselves under Domitian. Pliny was taken aside and warned that Certus had a powerful friend, 'then commanding a large army in the east, about whom serious if unconfirmed rumours were circulating.' But Pliny's main speech won the House round. When the aged Fabricius Veiento, one of Domitian's long-serving advisers, tried to reply, he could not get a hearing. Certus was not prosecuted, but was removed from his Treasury post and denied the expected consulship.

Pliny's reference to the threatening posture of the unnamed army commander in the east reflects the tense situation in which Nerva found himself. He desperately needed the support of the armies. The danger in the east must mean the army of Syria, and its commander had clearly made people wonder if he would try a *coup d'état*. He can be identified as M. Cornelius Nigrinus, from Liria in eastern Tarraconensis, highly decorated by Domitian for service on the Danube. Nerva acted quickly. Nigrinus was dismissed. A young senator

35

serving as quaestor in Asia, Larcius Priscus, was appointed, anomalously, commander of the Syrian legion IV Scythica and acting governor of the province; the legate of one of the other Syrian legions, XVI Flavia, was also replaced hurriedly. Nigrinus evidently gave no trouble, retiring to his Spanish home. The German armies also required loyal commanders. The governor of the Upper province, with headquarters at Moguntiacum (Mainz), had probably been appointed soon after Nerva's accession: M. Ulpius Traianus. Pliny would soon embroider the circumstances, recalling a propitious omen. As Trajan mounted the Capitol to sacrifice, as was usual, before leaving for his command, 'some citizens, gathered there for other reasons', suddenly cried out 'Imperator!' – so Pliny would claim, some four years later. 'It was thought at the time that they were saluting Jupiter.'[2]

In the course of the summer Verginius Rufus finally expired. The public funeral was a great occasion, 'a credit to the Emperor and our times, to the Forum and its speakers', as Pliny reported, in a letter to a provincial friend. It fell to one of the suffect consuls in office, Cornelius Tacitus, to deliver the address, 'a most eloquent orator, whose tribute put the crowning touch to Verginius' good fortune.' Rufus had prepared a brief verse epitaph for his own tomb: 'Here lies Rufus, who once defeated Vindex and set free the imperial power – not for himself but for his country'. Tacitus will certainly have expatiated at much greater length on Rufus' role in 68 and 69. That the circumstances in 97 were uncannily similar to those in 68, following the death of Nero, with an aging, childless new ruler, was no doubt apparent to all. Tacitus himself was surely inspired, at least in part, by the commission to commemorate Verginius Rufus, to compose something else – the biography of Agricola, a kind of substitute for the funeral speech that his absence had made impossible in 93. Besides which, in 93 he could not have spoken freely. For fifteen years – a substantial portion of a man's life – silence had been imposed. Now a happier era had dawned: Nerva Caesar reconciled what had once seemed an impossible combination, principate and liberty.[3]

By the time that the *Life of Agricola* had been published, there had been further dramatic developments. In October 97 the Praetorian Guard mutinied and besieged the Palace. They demanded vengeance for the murder of Domitian. Nerva was panic-stricken, vomiting with fear, but still attempted resistance, inviting the men to kill him. It was no good. He was forced to hand over Domitian's killers, who were lynched by the troops – and the Princeps was compelled by the Guard Prefect Casperius Aelianus to offer solemn thanks. His position was becoming desperate. Secret and urgent consultations must have followed. Meanwhile better news came, from the Danube. A minor victory over the eastern German tribes had been won by the governor of Pannonia. Nerva assumed the title Germanicus and proceeded to the Temple of Jupiter on the Capitol, to deposit the laurels of victory. Then – under divine inspiration – Pliny would claim, he made a proclamation: 'May Good Fortune attend the Roman Senate and people and myself: I adopt Marcus Ulpius Traianus.'[4]

Trajan, Pliny asserts, was reluctant and had to be persuaded to accept the adoption, which carried the title Caesar and the succession. He added the name of Nerva to his own, together with the newly assumed title Germanicus, and was shortly afterwards granted the *imperium* and the *tribunicia potestas;* but remained on the Rhine. A late source, the *Epitome de Caesaribus,* using Marius Maximus' lost lives of Nerva and Trajan, has a brief but striking remark about Trajan's coming to power: he seized it (*imperium arripuerat*), with the support of Licinius Sura. Even Pliny hints at something other than a totally unexpected elevation. For Nerva to have acted otherwise, he pronounced, would have been wanton and tyrannical: it was clear that Trajan would have become Emperor even if Nerva had not adopted him. Sura's role in this is obscure; it is not even certain whether he was at Rome or perhaps governing a province in the vicinity of Upper Germany. Trajan had, in any case, other support, above all from two senior senators at Rome, Julius Frontinus and Julius Ursus. Their 'care and vigilance' in Trajan's interests would be rewarded with high honours from Trajan. Most people must, nonetheless, have been surprised. Trajan, for all his distinction and the eminence of his father, was of provincial stock. Tacitus, completing the biography of his father-in-law at this time, claims, it is true, that Agricola used to prophesy Trajan's accession to the power 'in our hearing', and pray for it – this would have been at least seven years before it happened. One may have leave to doubt.[5]

The elevation of Hadrian's kinsman produced an understandable reaction in the province where he was stationed. He was chosen to take the Lower Moesian army's congratulations to the new Caesar on the Rhine – as one of a great host of such emissaries from all over the empire, there can be no doubt. Before he left, he may have sought out an astrologer. At any rate, the only other item that the *Historia Augusta* (*HA*) has to report on Hadrian's stay in Lower Moesia is that there 'a certain *mathematicus* confirmed what his great-uncle Aelius Hadrianus had already predicted, that he would become emperor.'[6]

On Hadrian's arrival in Germany, he was retained, with yet another tribunate, this time in the Moguntiacum legion, XXII Primigenia. Trajan handed over his Upper German command and moved to the residence of the Lower German governor, the Colonia Agrippinensis (Cologne), evidently taking over the role of legate himself. His replacement at Moguntiacum was Julius Servianus, Hadrian's brother-in-law, and himself close to Trajan – and to the influential Julius Ursus, probably Servianus' kinsman. Hadrian's third military tribunate is unparalleled – only one other case is attested, some twenty-five years later. But the circumstances in 97 were very special: Hadrian, was now, after all, the nearest male kinsman of the heir to the throne. His relations with his new immediate chief were not very happy. At least, the *HA* claims that Servianus reported adversely to Trajan: Hadrian was spending money lavishly and was running up debts – no doubt there were plenty of people willing to lend to such a well-placed young man. One wonders what opportunities there were for spending money on the Rhine. Over the river from Moguntiacum was a small spa, Aquae Mattiacae

(Wiesbaden), which might have offered some modest scope for the high life. All the same, fifteen years later, visiting the Rhine armies as Emperor, Hadrian himself made a determined attempt to stamp out 'luxury' in the military bases. Perhaps he was buying expensive horses and dogs, to indulge his passion for hunting: it was the right season of the year. Aside from pleasure, he will have had the chance of seeing for himself the new frontier system of forts and watch-towers which Domitian had set in place in the lands across the river, the fertile plain bounded by wooded hills to the north and east, by the River Moenus (Main) to the south. A fellow-tribune of senatorial rank, Junius Avitus, praised by Pliny (who had probably recommended him) for 'his deference to Servianus' high standards', was certainly more congenial to Servianus than his self-assertive young brother-in-law.[7]

News from Rome in early February brought Hadrian the chance of escape: Nerva had died on 27 January and Trajan was declared emperor the next day. A courier probably arrived at Moguntiacum within a week. Hadrian was determined to inform Trajan at Cologne in person. Servianus, for his part, sent his own messenger – and, another sign of his bad relations with Hadrian, had the carriage Hadrian was using put out of commission, so the *HA* reports. Undeterred, the story goes on, Hadrian proceeded on foot and completed the 110 miles or so (180 km) before Servianus' man. That his carriage broke down is not impossible, and that he was obliged to walk some of the way is also likely enough. But whether Servianus had got someone to tamper with the vehicle is another matter; and one may suspect that Hadrian was able to commandeer horses for a good part of the distance. The version in the *HA* surely derives from Hadrian's autobiography, written forty years later, when he had reason to blacken Servianus' memory, and at the same time to exaggerate his own youthful fitness.[8]

Hadrian remained with Trajan – who still chose to stay on the Rhine – and was now 'in his favour'. Trajan's first measure, no doubt, was to order the deifi-cation of Nerva and the burial of his remains in the Mausoleum of Augustus. He promised the Senate by letter that he would 'neither put to death nor exile any good man'. He was able to instal his trusted supporters in positions of influence. Frontinus and Ursus were rewarded with second consulships early in the year. Two close friends, Cornelius Palma and Sosius Senecio – the latter, the son-in-law of Frontinus, as governor of Belgica was probably close by – were designated to be *consules ordinarii* for 99.[9]

The Guard Prefect, Casperius Aelianus, duly appeared, to take up his post at the new ruler's side. But his role in the mutiny of the previous October could not be overlooked. He was put to death, and a successor appointed, Attius Suburanus. This man was already on the spot. He had been serving as procurator of Belgica, hence as paymaster of the Rhine armies. When Trajan handed him his sword of office, he bared the blade, held it up and told Suburanus: 'If I rule well, use this for me – if badly, against me.' Trajan had already created his own élite troops, as a counterweight to the Praetorians, converting the mounted guards of

Plate 1 Coin portrait of Trajan, from the period 104–114 (*BMC* III Trajan no. 853)

the legate of Lower Germany into Imperial Horse Guards, *equites singulares Augusti*. In effect this was to revive the German bodyguards of the Julio-Claudian emperors, the *corpore custodes*. The majority of these men had been Batavians (from modern Netherlands), and so too were Trajan's new Horse Guards. The *ab epistulis*, the Imperial Chief Secretary, Titinius Capito, must also have arrived, with a host of other high officials. He was the first man of equestrian rank in this post, previously held by imperial freedmen. Capito had been appointed by Domitian at the end of his reign and retained in office by Nerva. Trajan too kept him on, an important sign of continuity between the 'despotism' of Domitian and the new dawn of liberty.[10]

Capito will have had numerous letters to draft. Trajan must have been flooded with correspondence. Pliny's letter to the new Emperor happens to survive: 'Your filial loyalty, Most Sacred Emperor, made you wish to succeed your father as late as possible, but the immortal gods have hastened to put the government of the commonwealth in your hands.' No reply is preserved – perhaps it was too brief to be published. He used his friendship with Servianus for something more specific, a personal privilege, the *ius trium liberorum* (the honorary rights of a father of three children), useful for his career: fatherhood, which Pliny had failed to achieve despite two marriages, brought more rapid advancement. Trajan was duly thanked 'for granting this at the wish of Julius Servianus, an excellent man and most favoured by yourself'.[11]

39

The fact that Trajan remained on the northern frontier may have provoked speculation that he intended to launch a German campaign. One of those who may have hoped for, or expected, such a development was Cornelius Tacitus. His biography of Agricola was completed, his debt of *pietas* to his father-in-law paid. At the same time, the short work constituted a powerful political statement in justification of those who, like his father-in-law and himself, and, to be sure, like Trajan, had continued their careers under the 'despotism' of Domitian. He had also poured scorn on Domitian's 'pretended' German victory, contrasted with the true glory of Agricola's British conquests. Now Tacitus began a monograph on the Germans. He was well equipped for the task, for his own father had served as procurator of Belgica and the Germanies, and he himself had in all likelihood commanded a legion on the Rhine. All the same, he obviously used existing literature on Germany, for example a book by the elder Pliny, as the basis for his own treatise. He may simply have picked on the subject because it was topical, all eyes being focused on the new Emperor. He summarises Rome's relations with the Germans from the invasions of the Cimbri and Teutones in the late second century BC down to AD 98 as '210 years of (alleged) Roman successes' against this people, over whom (a contemptuous dismissal of Domitian's wars) in recent times 'triumphs have been celebrated rather than victories won'.[12]

If Tacitus hoped for a new German expedition, he was disappointed. Instead, Trajan moved from the Rhine across to the Danube, taking with him Julius Servianus, who was made governor of Pannonia – and brought Pliny's protégé Junius Avitus, his *tribunus laticlavius*, with him. Trajan himself wintered in Moesia, to assess the peoples – Sarmatians and Dacians – across the Danube that had caused repeated problems for Rome in the past decade and more. Pliny dutifully enlarges on the respect shown to Trajan by Rome's enemies and the admiration his own men had for his active participation in manoeuvres. It was quite late in the year 99 before he eventually set off for Italy. 'Your people's prayers were calling you home', Pliny was to say. The imperial *adventus* was suitably modest and unpretentious, Trajan dismounting to enter the city on foot, to proceed through the assembled ranks of Senate, knights and plebs, amid universal delight. After sacrifice on the Capitol, the imperial party proceeded to the Palace, Trajan 'walking with the same demeanour as if entering a private house'. Plotina added to the favourable impression by turning round on the steps to the people and saying: 'I enter this building the same woman as I hope to leave it.'[13]

Hadrian, who presumably returned to Rome in the imperial entourage, still enjoyed Trajan's approval. A problem would soon arise, duly reported by the *HA*, but in a passage where the text is defective. Hadrian had trouble with 'the *paedagogi* [attendants or tutors] of the boys that Trajan very greatly loved'. The reference is clearly to pages of the imperial household. Trajan's fondness for boys – and for wine – is attested by Cassius Dio. Like Domitian, then, Trajan had his Ganymedes – but this did no one any harm, Dio adds, and he could hold

Plate 2 Plotina, Trajan's Empress (bust from Museo Vaticano, Rome)

his drink. It is difficult to avoid the conclusion that Hadrian had encroached on the Emperor's prerogative and had got too close to the page-boys. His open passion, thirty years later, for a beautiful youth would make his own homosexuality universal knowledge. Someone called Gallus evidently intervened on Hadrian's behalf, but he was still anxious about the Emperor's attitude to him, the *HA* goes on. It is then claimed that Hadrian resorted to consulting the 'Virgilian lots', opening the *Aeneid* at random to gain a prophecy of his future – the answer was allegedly a passage in the Sixth Book, describing King Numa. This may be an invention by the author of the *HA*, like what follows: the Virgilian oracle, 'according to others', may have 'come from the Sibylline Verses'. All the same, even if the story was invented, the chances are that it was Hadrian himself who was reponsible. There are clear signs that he deliberately fostered a comparison between himself and Numa when he became Emperor. The *HA* further asserts that he also, at this time, learned that he would become Emperor from an oracular response in the Temple of Jupiter (Zeus) Nicephorius (at Antioch). The *HA* cites as its source for the latter story the work of an otherwise unknown 'Syrian Platonist' named Apollonius. If there is anything – other than the fantasy of the *HA* – in this, it too should belong later, when Hadrian was himself in Syria.[14]

More plausible is the next item in the *HA*, that Hadrian was restored to a totally friendly relationship with Trajan through the good offices of Licinius Sura. There is no doubt that Sura was one of Trajan's closest friends and advisers, closer to him, perhaps, than anyone else. Julius Frontinus, it is true, was obviously the most senior adviser, sharing the ordinary consulship with Trajan in the year 100. But Frontinus was an old man – he expired a few years later. Dio singles Sura out for the mutual 'friendship and confidence' between him and the Emperor. There was some jealousy and hostile criticism, Dio adds, which Trajan took pains to disarm by turning up for dinner uninvited at Sura's mansion, dismissing his guards, and having his friend's barber shave him. The next day he said to his other friends, who had been disparaging Sura, 'If Sura had really wanted to kill me, he would have done it yesterday.' Among his other services, Sura functioned as imperial speechwriter. Hadrian also enjoyed the backing of the Empress, and it was through her urging that Trajan's grand-niece Sabina was assigned to Hadrian as a bride. According to Marius Maximus (so the *HA* records), Trajan's enthusiasm for this match had been less than whole-hearted. It was indeed a significant further step forward for Hadrian. He was now twenty-four, his bride some ten years younger, so it is assumed. It was everything other than a love-match – although Hadrian was devoted to Matidia, his mother-in-law, now widowed, whom the childless Trajan treated like a daughter.[15]

The marriage must have taken place in AD 100, shortly before Hadrian entered the Senate as quaestor in early December of that year. As he was approaching his twenty-fifth birthday (24 January 101) when he took up this first senatorial magistracy, he was at the normal age. In other words, he had not

Plate 3 Matidia, Hadrian's mother-in-law
(bust from Museo del Palazzo dei Conservatori, Rome)

43

Plate 4 Sabina, with the attributes of the goddess Ceres
(statue from Ostia Museum)

received accelerated advancement because of his kinship with Trajan; but he was at least one of the Emperor's own quaestors. It may be, however, that he had by now been enrolled in two of the priestly colleges reserved for senators, the *VIIviri epulonum* and the *sodales Augustales*. The Athens *cursus*-inscription of Hadrian, which registers these priesthoods, puts them out of chronological order. It is reasonable to conjecture that he received this distinction when he became a senator. The *VIIviri* – by now ten in number – were the most junior of the four great colleges of priests, less prestigious than the *pontifices* or augurs or *XVviri*. But they were nonetheless counted as one of the 'four great colleges', in which only a minority of the senators could expect enrolment; and the priests of the deified Augustus stood not far behind in public esteem.[16]

Admission to the priestly colleges, like most other distinctions, was controlled by the Emperor. When a vacancy arose, the existing members could make nominations – thus Pliny, when he finally became an augur, told a friend that he had been nominated repeatedly by Frontinus. He finally got in when Frontinus died, as his replacement. As it happens, there was a vacancy in the college of *VIIviri* precisely in the year 100, not, as was usually the case, through death. One of the members, a recent proconsul of Africa, Marius Priscus, had been expelled. He had been tried in the Senate for extortion, the prosecuting counsel being Tacitus and Pliny. In any case, another *VIIvir* had died the previous year – L. Vibius Sabinus, the presumed father of Hadrian's bride. Pliny had also approached Trajan himself on his own behalf: 'No higher tribute could be paid to my reputation than some mark of favour from so excellent a *princeps*. I pray you, therefore, to add to the honours to which I have been raised by your generosity by granting me a priesthood, either an augurate or a septemvirate, as there is a vacancy in both orders.' Pliny had to wait. Someone else got the augurate and it may have been Hadrian who became a *VIIvir*.[17]

Of the surviving members of the college, it is a fair guess that Hadrian was supported by Julius Quadratus, the influential man from Pergamum, who, it was suggested earlier, may have nominated Hadrian as Prefect during the Latin festival in 94. Membership of this college would bring Hadrian into close touch with his fellow-*VIIviri*, for example at the banquets (*epulae*) which, as their title indicates, they had to hold in honour of Jupiter and the other gods (hardly anything else is known about their duties). They were an impressive group of men, including, as well as Quadratus, Atilius Agricola, from Augusta Taurinorum (Turin), one of the up-and-coming senators who had Trajan's favour, like Hadrian also a *sodalis Augustalis*, Cilnius Proculus, from Arretium (Arezzo) in Etruria, Neratius Priscus, from Saepinum in the Samnite country, consul in 97 and then for a brief term legate of Germania Inferior, and the now elderly Domitius Tullus, the immensely wealthy and influential Narbonensian.[18]

Not yet a senator in 100, Hadrian will not have had to sit through the lengthy speech of thanks delivered by one of the consuls that summer, Pliny's *Panegyric*, although, as a senator's son he would have been entitled to attend. If Trajan himself had to listen to it, his warm feelings towards the effusive orator may

45

have been slightly reduced. In its published form the speech would have taken up to six hours to deliver, and even the original may have tried the imperial patience. Whether or not he was present when the consul Pliny delivered the original version before the Senate, Hadrian might have had the chance of hearing a revised and expanded *Panegyric*, read in instalments on three successive days to an invited audience, and later published. Pliny's aim was not merely to pay tribute to the Emperor, but to show his successors what path to follow. More to Hadrian's taste may have been an address by the Bithynian Greek intellectual, Dio of Prusa, *On Kingship*, probably delivered before Trajan at this time.[19]

As quaestor of the Emperor, Hadrian had the task of reading out Trajan's speeches in his absence. It is somewhat surprising to learn from the *HA* that 'he was laughed at for his rather "rustic" accent.' His reaction was 'to give attention to the study of Latin until he had acquired complete proficiency and fluency.' It is hard to believe that he had picked up a 'Spanish' accent in his short stay at Italica a decade earlier. Perhaps, rather, his unusually long spell in the army and association with centurions and rankers affected his diction. In any case, he had no doubt been continuing to devote himself to Greek rather than Latin. He is known to have attended at some point lectures by the Syrian Greek sophist Isaeus, who was in Rome in about the year 100. Pliny enthused about the sixty-year-old sophist: he spoke perfect Attic Greek and charmed his audience with brilliant extempore efforts. 'If you are not eager to meet him', he told his correspondent, 'you must really be iron-willed and stony-hearted.'[20]

Hadrian was also given another duty, mentioned by the *HA* but not listed on the Athens inscription, 'curator of the Acts of the Senate', in other words, responsibility for the official reports of proceedings in the House. This record was a valuable source for historians; Tacitus, for one, would make good use of the *Acta Senatus*. Whether he was already combing the senatorial archives in 101, for his *Histories* of the years 69–96, cannot be known. For one thing, he might have been governing a province at this time.[21]

Hadrian's first senatorial duties at Rome were not to last more than a few months. On 25 March 101 Trajan left to wage war against the Dacian king Decebalus and took with him Hadrian, still his quaestor but now also a member of his staff, *comes Augusti*, as the Athens inscription makes clear. As *comes* he served alongside Sura, Servianus and other leading figures. Trajan had been preparing for the war for over two years; this was, no doubt, the principal reason for his visit to Moesia in 98–9. The Dacians had been recognised as a threat since the time of Julius Caesar and the growth of the kingdom under Decebalus had given Domitian considerable trouble. Rome's loss of face in his wars had not been made good. A force of ten legions now stood ready on the Danube, together with a good 60,000 men from the regiments of *auxilia* and additional detachments from the armies of Britain and the east. Trajan brought the Praetorians, with a new Guard Prefect, Claudius Livianus, and the Horse Guards. The war was to last for two campaigning seasons and would end in a Dacian surrender.[22]

The *HA* has a characteristically brief and trivial record of Hadrian's involvement: 'He followed Trajan to the Dacian War in a position of fairly close intimacy; at this time, indeed, he [Hadrian] states that he indulged in wine too, so as to fall in with Trajan's habits, and that he was very richly rewarded for this by Trajan.' Hadrian thus clearly wrote something about his service in his autobiography. But, it seems from what follows, he was only at the front for the first year. It may be inferred that he accompanied Trajan in his capacity as quaestor, in good old Republican fashion, and that when his term of office expired he returned to Rome to pursue his career.[23]

The *HA* records next that he was made tribune of the plebs, giving as the date the consuls of the year 105. But a few lines later, Hadrian's next office, the praetorship, is dated to the consulship of 'Subuninus and Servianus', both for the second time. There must be a confusion here, first between Suburanus and Sura. The latter held his second consulship, as colleague of Servianus, in 102. Suburanus, who had been Guard Prefect from 98 onwards, after giving up this office had become a senator and suffect consul in 101, and was consul for the second time, as *ordinarius*, in 104. Either the *HA*, or its source Marius Maximus, has muddled the names and dates. The most plausible solution is that Hadrian returned to Rome in the late autumn of 101, to hold office as tribune of the plebs for 102 – starting, according to the old practice for tribunes, on 10 December 101. If this is right, it means that the normal requirement of the *cursus honorum*, that there should be a year's interval between offices, was waived in his case: there will have been less than a week between the end of the quaestorship on 4 December and the start of the tribunate on 10 December. Such an exemption could, then, be a modest sign of favour from Trajan, enabling his kinsman to become tribune a little before the completion of his twenty-sixth year.[24]

Servianus and Sura, as *ordinarii* for 102, ought in the normal course of events to have been at Rome, but, because of the war, they may have held office in *absentia*. Servianus, it may be noted, had in the meantime changed his name, being styled 'L. Julius Ursus Servianus' instead of 'Ser. Julius Servianus'. He had clearly inherited the new items from Trajan's powerful ally L. Julius Ursus. Sura, at least, played a personal role in Dacia during 102, being sent with the Guard Prefect Claudius Livianus to negotiate with the Dacian king. In the event, Decebalus 'was afraid and would not meet them.' As for Servianus, he too had surely been on Trajan's staff, at least in 101. A letter to him from his friend Pliny, anxious for news, suggests that he was at the front. One major victory was already won in the first campaign. In 102 further victories were achieved. The Moorish chieftain Lusius Quietus, commanding a force of his fellow-countrymen, and Laberius Maximus, governor of Lower Moesia, are singled out for their successes in the scanty historical record. Decebalus was compelled to sue for peace. He surrendered his 'arms, engines and engineers, demolished forts, gave back deserters, withdrew from captured territory and became an ally of the Roman people. Trajan left garrisons all over Dacia and returned to Rome to hold a triumph and take the title Dacicus.' Large tracts of land north of the lower Danube were annexed, south-west Dacia being added to Upper Moesia, and a very much greater slice of territory on its eastern side to a much expanded province of Lower Moesia.[25]

In the course of his service Hadrian would have had the opportunity to form links with members of the high command. Sosius Senecio, who played a prominent role, is explicitly listed as a personal friend of his ten years later, likewise the Guard Prefect Claudius Livianus, a Lycian from Sidyma. Q. Pompeius Falco, later to become Senecio's son-in-law, commanded V Macedonica in this war, and was to hold important posts under Hadrian. It may be assumed that they became acquainted in 101, if not before. He should also have got to know another legionary legate, Julius Quadratus Bassus of Pergamum, commander of XI Claudia. Two further important figures, Atilius Agricola, governing Pannonia, and Cilnius Proculus, legate of Upper Moesia, were fellow-*VIIviri*. Another person whom Hadrian must have met was Trajan's architect, Apollodorus of Damascus, responsible for erecting the bridge across the Danube at Drobeta (Turnu Severin) at the end of the first campaign.[26]

Hadrian supposedly had something to say about his tribunate of the plebs in his autobiography. 'He claims that in this magistracy he was given an omen that he would receive perpetual tribunician power [a prerogative of the Emperor], in that he lost the *paenulae*, cloaks which the tribunes of the plebs used to wear when it rained, but which the emperors never wear.' Thus the *HA*. But, as it stands, this little story can hardly be authentic. The *paenula* was the standard Roman raincoat, worn by all Romans, including emperors. At best, the *HA* has misunderstood or distorted something in its source. Whether as tribune of the plebs Hadrian had any serious duties to perform or made any effort to be active in the Senate is doubtful. Pliny mentions an intervention by a tribune in the debate of 97, when he himself attacked Publicius Certus. He also describes at some length a sitting of the Senate in 105, when another tribune, Avidius Nigrinus, took a personal initiative, denouncing the taking of fees by advocates. Hadrian was probably content to keep a low profile, even if the times were now different from forty years earlier, when Agricola as tribune passed his year in 'quiet inactivity', knowing that *inertia* was the wise way to comport oneself. The very fact that Hadrian was tribune of the plebs at all is worth dwelling on: it means that, in spite of his kinship with Trajan, he had not been made a patrician. Indeed, the Athens inscription does not mention that he was the Emperor's candidate in this post, or for the praetorship. For the time being, it seems, Trajan wanted his former ward to be treated to some extent like a normal senator. Nonetheless, as has been argued, he was allowed to become tribune a year earlier than was laid down by the rules.[27]

Hadrian's absence from Rome for most of 101 probably meant that he had missed the prosecution for extortion, conducted by Pliny, of the proconsul of Baetica, Caecilius Classicus. He had surely been kept informed by correspondents about a case which affected his 'home' province. In 102–3 Pliny was involved in another such trial, this time for the defence, of a proconsul of Pontus-Bithynia, Julius Bassus. Business such as this may have seemed worthy of the Senate, but Hadrian will not have gained a very positive impression from some other senatorial sessions. Pliny reports with some indignation how voting-tablets at a secret ballot had been found to have jokes and obscenities scribbled on them.[28]

In spite of such lapses, in 104 Hadrian duly secured election as praetor for the next year. He was marginally younger than the prescribed age of thirty or 'in one's thirtieth year': he would be twenty-nine on 24 January 105. An attempt was made, it seems, to raise standards. One of his colleagues as praetor, Licinius Nepos, conducted himself with old-fashioned sternness, even fining a senator for non-attendance as a juror. As president of the Centumviral Court Nepos later warned both prosecution and defence that he would enforce the regulations over accepting fees strictly, the same question which was raised by the tribune Nigrinus in 105. Nepos also intervened the next year in connection with another extortion trial, again of a proconsul of Bithynia, Varenus Rufus. One of the praetors of 106, Juventius Celsus, later a noted jurist, attacked Nepos 'violently and at length, as a would-be reformer of the Senate'. No activity of this sort is recorded for Hadrian, only that he received a large sum of money from Trajan to pay for the games he had to put on as praetor – games which, as it turned out, he must have held *in absentia*. All the same, the years in which Hadrian went through the old republican magistracies must have given him some opportunity to familiarise himself with Roman law. Perhaps he presided over a court as praetor. If so, it was only for five months at the most.[29]

Hadrian was not to see out his year of office at Rome. For some time it had been clear that Decebalus had been infringing the terms imposed on him in 102 – at least, that was the official Roman version. Trajan had been preparing for a new campaign, his measures including the raising of two new legions, II Traiana and XXX Ulpia Victrix. War was declared against Dacia in May 105. Trajan set off for the Danube on 4 June and once again he took Hadrian with him, this time giving him the command of the legion I Minervia.[30]

5

THE YOUNG GENERAL

I Minervia, of which Hadrian took command in summer 105, was presumably known to him. It had been stationed at Bonna on the Rhine, close to the Colonia Agrippinensis (Cologne) where he had spent the early part of the year 98. He could also have come across the legion in the first Dacian war, for which it had been moved to the Danube. It had remained there at the end of the war, as one of the fourteen or so legions now concentrated for the new war in Pannonia and Moesia. I Minervia was a relatively new creation: it had been formed by Domitian and given a name honouring that ruler's favourite deity.[1]

The Roman offensive, carefully prepared – with the advantage of Apollodorus' massive new stone bridge across the Danube – had not even begun when Decebalus launched a pre-emptive strike. He evidently attacked Roman forces in south-western Dacia, which had been occupied since 102 and added to Moesia Superior. When the onslaught was repulsed, Decebalus attempted to have Trajan murdered by Roman deserters, but this too failed. He now offered to negotiate with the Roman commander north of the river, Pompeius Longinus, and treacherously took him prisoner. Decebalus tried bargaining with the high-ranking hostage to force the evacuation of Rome's newly won territory. Trajan gave an ambiguous response and Longinus solved his dilemma by committing suicide. That Trajan had been the object of an assassination attempt may well have prompted speculation about the succession. He had no children and had given no sign that he would adopt a son, whether his young kinsman Hadrian or some-one else. Pliny, in his *Panegyric* five years before, had prayed to Jupiter that Trajan 'may be granted a successor born to him . . . but, if fate denies him this, direct his choice to someone worthy to be adopted in your Temple on the Capitol.' The chances of a son being born were now remote. It was surely in the aftermath of Decebalus' plot to kill him that Trajan pointed elsewhere. He is reported by the *HA* to have 'once said to Neratius Priscus: "I commend the provinces to you if anything should befall me."' Neratius Priscus was at this time, it seems, gov-erning Pannonia. In other words, he was one of the men on the spot, although the main focus of the Roman war effort was further down the Danube.[2]

Neratius Priscus was to become best known as a jurist, and, jointly, with Juventius Celsus, praetor the next year, as the leader of the 'Proculian school', one of the two principal traditions in the interpretation of Roman law that grew up in the early principate. In spite of his renown as a jurist, Priscus' service as governor of two major military provinces demonstrates that he was an 'all-rounder'. Furthermore, his brother Marcellus had been governing Britain shortly before. Neratius Priscus might have made an ideal emperor. Whether or not Trajan was entirely serious, and whether his 'entrusting the provinces' to Priscus 'if anything should happen to me' was really intended as the nomination of a successor, is another matter. Another story, in an excerpt from Cassius Dio for which no date can be conjectured, has Trajan at a banquet asking his friends to name him 'ten men capable of being emperor' – *capax imperii*, as Tacitus would have put it. 'After a moment's pause, he added – "I only need nine names, one I have already, Servianus."' Hadrian's brother-in-law undoubtedly enjoyed high favour from Trajan, as his second consulate with Sura in 102 had shown. But this anecdote, too, can hardly be taken as an indication of Trajan's real intentions. He was strong and active, not quite 50 years old, and did not need or want to nominate a successor.[3]

The tortuous transactions involving a high Roman officer's fate may have occupied the remainder of the campaigning season of 105. At any rate, the decisive Roman offensive was launched in the spring of 106. In a series of battles the Dacian forces were pushed back into the interior. Their capital, Sarmizegethusa, was captured, and Decebalus committed suicide to avoid capture. A Roman cavalryman named Claudius Maximus, arriving just too late to capture the king alive, cut off his head and brought it to Trajan at a place called Ranisstorum. It was sent to Rome, to be hurled down the Gemonian Steps, the traditional fate for enemies of the Roman People. His kingdom was now annexed: Dacia was to be a new Roman province, the first such acquisition for more than half a century. To add to the sense of revived glory and expansion, in the same year (106) another new territory was added to the empire in the east: the governor of Syria, Cornelius Palma, peacefully took over the Nabataean kingdom east of the River Jordan and in the Negev, creating the province of Arabia. Mopping up operations in Dacia no doubt followed the death of Decebalus, but by the end of 106, with victory won, Roman units were busily erecting new forts around the frontiers.[4]

The new province of Dacia, with a garrison of at least two legions, was assigned to Julius Sabinus. There was plenty for him to do. If he is the Sabinus who received a letter from Pliny – in response to Sabinus' own request for long and frequent missives – his 'life under arms, the camps, bugles and trumpets, sweat and dust and heat of the sun' would hardly put him in the frame of mind to read about Pliny's trivial activities, so Pliny modestly put it. The organisation of the newly conquered province was a major undertaking. According to the fourth-century chronicler Eutropius, 'to cultivate the fields and inhabit the cities [including a newly founded *colonia Ulpia Sarmizegethusa*, replacing, at a different site, the old royal capital], countless settlers were brought in from all over the Roman world, for Dacia had been drained of its manpower during the long war.' Apart from loss of life, tens of thousands of Dacian prisoners of war had been taken, to be sold as slaves or die as gladiators in the spectacles held in 107 to celebrate the victory.[5]

Hadrian's personal role in the war is described only briefly by the *HA*: 'At this time, certainly, his many outstanding deeds became renowned.' The Athens inscription adds that he received military decorations (*dona militaria*) from Trajan for both Dacian wars. What he actually did to earn the decorations the second time round can only be conjectured. The leading part was played, as in the first war, by Sura and Senecio. Their reward was a further consulship each, Sura's third, Senecio's second, for 107. Hadrian apparently got something else, though: 'Having been presented with a diamond which Trajan had been given by Nerva, he was encouraged to hope for the imperial succession.' The 'encouragement' may have been a subjective reaction on Hadrian's part. There is no guarantee that Trajan mentioned the succession when he made the gift.[6]

Hadrian remained in the north when the war ended. The province of Pannonia was now divided into two, Superior and Inferior, and Hadrian became governor of the latter, smaller part. Pannonia Inferior retained only one legion, II Adiutrix, and the governor was thus at the same time legate of the legion. The model was Numidia, where the legate of III Augusta was – in his case only *de facto* – also the governor. Judaea had been, since 71, a second example of a one-legion province and now there was also the newly formed province of Arabia. Thus ten years after his first service at Aquincum Hadrian was back as the chief, taking office perhaps precisely on 11 June 106, which, as has been plausibly conjectured, was probably the day when Pannonia was divided. This is, at any rate, a good reason why 11 June was subsequently treated as an important anniversary in both Pannonias for several hundred years to come. Hadrian had been promoted after barely twelve months as legate of I Minervia. He thereby no longer had a front-line role in the Dacian war just when it reached its decisive phase, between June and the beginning of August. He may nonetheless have had a new and important task, to guard the Roman western flank.[7]

Lower Pannonia faced the Sarmatian Jazyges of the Hungarian plain, an unruly people which had several times fought against Rome. While they may have supported Rome against the Dacians, they apparently had to be 'restrained' by Hadrian. Perhaps what was involved was a precautionary move, to ensure that the Sarmatians behaved while the final drive against the Dacians was in full swing. The *HA* supplies no further details. Trouble with the Sarmatians no doubt continued when the Dacian war ended: Trajan declined to return to them territory which they had lost to Decebalus, so Cassius Dio reports. Perhaps they tried to grab it back in the summer of 106 and were 'restrained' from this by Hadrian.[8]

As the first governor of a 'new' province, Hadrian was justified in creating suitable accommodation, for himself and a substantial household. He may now have been joined by his wife Sabina, but will certainly have had personal servants suitable to his rank. The gubernatorial palace, on an island in the Danube, later to become the most impressive building at Aquincum, may well have been commissioned by Hadrian. Indeed, given his later reputation as a would-be architect, he probably designed it himself. Its commanding position, facing the potentially hostile Sarmatians, represented in itself a statement of Roman self-confidence.[9]

Two further laconic remarks about Hadrian's service in Lower Pannonia are offered by the *HA*: 'He preserved military discipline and checked the procurators who were overstepping the mark.' A drive to restore discipline in the army was to be one of the keynotes of his policy in the early years of his reign. As for his firm hand with the procurators, this is an instructive contrast with the conduct of Agricola in a comparable governorship thirty years before. As Tacitus had written a few years earlier, his father-in-law as legate of Aquitania had refrained from 'disputes (*contentione*) with procurators'. Who is meant by 'procurators' in Hadrian's case is not clear, perhaps freedmen as well as the senior Roman knight responsible for collection of taxes and paying the army. The wise governor refrained from involvement in fiscal matters, which were the equestrian procurator's responsibility. If the procurator of the Emperor or his freedmen assistants were behaving oppressively or infringing on the legate's prerogatives, Hadrian may have acted, confident of Trajan's backing. As Emperor, he himself would clamp down on procurators and governors alike with an iron hand.[10]

Governorships, especially of provinces with a garrison, gave the opportunity for patronage. There were commissions for six tribunes, one senatorial, in the legion, and at least as many for equestrian officers commanding auxiliary regiments. Army commanders could appoint their friends and protégés – and would receive letters from fellow-senators recommending suitable persons. Pompeius Falco, at this time governing another one-legion province, Judaea, was approached by Pliny. 'You will be less surprised how much I press this recommendation for a military tribunate, when you learn who the man is and what he is like.' Cornelius Minicianus was 'an ornament of my home district'. Pliny's request may have been turned down by Falco. He had had more success a few years earlier with Neratius Marcellus, from whom he procured a tribunate in the army of Britain for his scholarly young friend Suetonius Tranquillus (who then backed out). Pliny was a correspondent of several persons close to Hadrian, including Servianus and Sura, but Hadrian himself is absent from the nine books of private letters. All the same, a man from the 'Pliny country', P. Clodius Sura of Brixia (Brescia), who was to be made curator of Comum by Hadrian as Emperor, had earlier served as equestrian tribune of II Adiutrix. One may at least ask whether he could have been recommended to Hadrian by Pliny, but it remains, of course, pure speculation. Another man who served under Hadrian as equestrian tribune of the legion may have been M. Vettius Latro, who had been decorated for service in the first Dacian war as prefect of a Pannonian unit, went on to be tribune of II Adiutrix and then to command a cavalry regiment in Dacia. Latro was then to hold a few procuratorships, of modest rank. Over twenty years later

Hadrian would give this man, whose home was in African Thuburbo Maius, a considerable boost to his career.[11]

It was also part of the governor's duties to appoint and promote centurions. Whether Marcius Turbo, known to have become Hadrian's trusted friend, was still a centurion in II Adiutrix is, of course, uncertain. Perhaps not by coincidence it was at about the time when Hadrian returned to Pannonia Inferior that Turbo achieved a major step up the ladder, becoming *praefectus vehiculorum*, in charge of the imperial posting-service, the *cursus publicus*. He had by then, presumably, been chief centurion of a legion, not necessarily, of course, II Adiutrix. Turbo may at least have had backing from Hadrian.[12]

A praetorian imperial province carried with it the expectation of the consulship. Hadrian might have hoped for the prestige of being *ordinarius*, opening the year and giving it his name. But once again, as with the withholding of patrician rank, he had to be content with a lesser prize. The *consules ordinarii* of the year 108, Ap. Annius Gallus and M. Atilius Bradua, were men of consular parentage, which Hadrian lacked, and Bradua at least was also a patrician. Hadrian achieved only a suffect consulship, with M. Trebatius Priscus. But it came a mere two years or less after he had begun his governorship, probably in May 108, and he was only thirty-two. He had thus reached, almost a decade earlier than most plebeians, the office to which all senators still aspired. The republican minimum age, forty-two, or the forty-second year, was still enforced. But Augustus had allowed patricians and members of consular families to hold the *fasces* as young as thirty-one. The *HA* attributes Hadrian's consulship to his successful conduct as governor. In truth, unless he had made a complete hash of his duties, the office followed almost automatically.[13]

It may be that he held his consulship in *absentia* and continued to govern his province on into 109. His presumed successor, Julius Maximus Manlianus, is first attested in Pannonia in July 110 and became consul in 112. However this may be, while Hadrian was holding the consulship, 'he learned from Sura that he was to be adopted by Trajan, and was then no longer despised and ignored by Trajan's friends.' This report probably goes back to Hadrian's autobiography, and must be treated with some caution. Sura himself died shortly afterwards, to be honoured by Trajan with a public funeral and a statue. Whether Hadrian was already back in Rome for his consulship in early summer 108 or only some months later, perhaps just before Sura died (unless Sura imparted Trajan's intentions by letter), he acquired a new closeness to Trajan. Further, other protégés of Sura, such as Minicius Natalis of Barcino, may now have looked to Hadrian as their patron. Sura had composed Trajan's speeches for him, and this role now fell to Hadrian, as the *HA* reports – not mentioning that Sura had been the previous imperial speechwriter. Sura and Hadrian may also have assisted the Emperor to compose his own history of the Dacian wars.[14]

Sura was not the only person of distinction to pass away at this time. Domitius Tullus, one of the richest men in Rome, died in late 108 or early 109. His will provided opportunity for gossip: 'we talk about nothing else in the city',

Pliny wrote to a friend. The old man, 'crippled and deformed in every limb, unable to turn over in bed without assistance or to clean his own teeth', had been the object of attention from numerous legacy-hunters. In the event, he made his niece and adoptive daughter, Domitia Lucilla, his principal heiress, with legacies to his grandsons and great-granddaughter. 'In fact, the whole will is ample proof of his affection for his family, and so all the more unexpected.' His widow, who had been severely criticised for marrying the old man, inherited beautiful villas and a large sum of money.[15]

It seems that parts of the testament of Tullus have survived on stone, from a large marble funerary monument on the Via Appia. In modern times the testator was identified as a Dasumius, from the Corduban family related to Hadrian. A newly discovered fragment has ruled this name out. The inscription, of which the text had been drawn up between May and August 108, while Hadrian was consul, can be assigned instead to Domitius Tullus. The funeral, so it was laid down, was to be supervised by the testator's friend Julius Servianus, whose daughter Julia Paulina, Hadrian's niece, was a beneficiary. So too, among many others, but named in a special codicil at the end, were the Emperor and Sosius Senecio. Tullus' son-in-law, P. Calvisius Ruso, husband of Lucilla (not her first – she already had a granddaughter from a previous marriage), was to take the testator's name. He duly appears, as consul for 109, under the style 'P. Calvisius *Tullus*'. Tullus' widow turns out to have been called Dasumia Polla, from a Corduban family linked to that of Hadrian. The testator, himself of southern Gallic origin, is shown by this inscription to have been closely linked to Baetica. His family network epitomises high Roman society in the early second century, the Baetican Emperor and his Narbonensian Empress being merely the apex of the now dominant colonial élite. The infant daughter of Tullus Ruso and Lucilla would become, after her marriage to a young man from another Baetican family, the mother of Marcus Aurelius. Another link in this aristocratic colonial network had been forged two years before the death of Domitius Tullus. Hadrian's niece Julia Paulina had married Pedanius Fuscus Salinator, scion of a family from Barcino (Barcelona) that had been at the summit of Roman society for three generations. Young Fuscus was an admiring disciple of Pliny, who congratulated Servianus on his choice of son-in-law, 'who will prove better than your fondest hopes could wish – it only remains for him to give you grandchildren like himself as soon as possible.' Julia Paulina may have had children soon after her marriage. But only the son born in April 113, Hadrian's grand-nephew, would survive.[16]

How aware of provincial origins Roman society was in the case of these high-ranking persons is a question. For senators like Pliny, himself from the remotest corner of Italy, more important was the fact that the Emperor was 'one of us'. True, he had been loaded with adulation, and was constantly encouraged to take the title *Optimus*, best of emperors; and he had made not only his wife but even his sister an Augusta. But Trajan was able to maintain his image as a *civilis princeps*, a citizen prince. It was no doubt not mere coincidence that Trajan had as his seal a figure of Marsyas, which he presumably acquired from the family of his mother, the Marcii: it was a potent symbol of freedom for the Romans. Otherwise, Trajan was content to cultivate the image of a bluff military man, one of those Romans who 'looked stupid and were believed honest'. As he rode in his triumphal chariot through the streets of Rome, he had the Greek sage Dio of Prusa with him, so Philostratus records. 'I have no idea what you are talking about', the Emperor told the sage, 'but I love you as myself.' As for the provincial origin, he had taken steps to deal with any residual resentments from Italian senators by implementing what Nerva had begun, the state-supported welfare scheme (*alimenta*) for poor children, confined to Italy, and obliging senators from the provinces to invest at least a third of their capital in Italian land.[17]

Besides all this, his popularity was guaranteed by the vast riches won in Dacia. They made possible a programme of public building on a scale not seen since the time of Augustus – notwithstanding the massive building in Rome undertaken by the Flavian dynasty. Rome itself now began to acquire a real city centre for the first time, the Forum Ulpium, dwarfing the existing Fora. Trajan also constructed a new harbour for the capital, to replace that of Ostia. Hadrian took an active interest in this activity. But, Dio reports, when he interrupted a discussion between Trajan and his master-architect Apollodorus, the latter curtly advised him to stick to his still-life drawing. Hadrian never forgot this slight.[18]

After a year or two in Rome – there is no other evidence of how he occupied himself in this period – it must be supposed that Hadrian felt restless. He may have hoped for a consular appointment from Trajan, and none was forthcoming, let alone adoption and the role of Caesar. The city may have begun to seem unattractive to him. There were, it is true, various forms of entertainment available. But Hadrian may have been bored by dinner parties with mimes and clowns and dancing catamites laid on to divert the guests, even if not disgusted, as was Pliny's earnest friend the rhetoric teacher Julius Genitor. There were also intellectual occasions. Tacitus may have been holding public readings of his *Histories* of the Flavian period. Pliny had reacted with enthusiasm when he had been invited to read parts of the work, and prophesied that it would become immortal. Whether Tacitus was the unnamed author to whom Pliny refers in another letter is uncertain: he had never been 'more conscious of the powers of history, its dignity, its majesty, its divine inspiration' than at a recent public reading. The author had left part to be read on another day and afterwards was begged not to proceed. 'Such is the shame that people feel at hearing about their conduct. The author complied' – but: 'the book remains and will remain and will always be read.' This would fit well with Tacitus' account of the Flavian period. Whether Hadrian would have found anything of much interest in such work, or in other literary novelties, such as Caninius Rufus' poem on the Dacian wars or readings by Titinius Capito 'on the deaths of famous men', or Pliny's published speeches, is another matter. He probably spent time hunting, perhaps with Trajan, now that the Emperor had made this an acceptable pursuit for the

56

élite. He could have been building on his own country estate – at Tibur, one assumes. But he clearly wanted something different.[19]

Friends of his, above all Sosius Senecio, and contemporaries, such as Minicius Fundanus, now a fellow-*VIIvir* of Hadrian's, had strong links with Greece. But he had never been there (so far as is known). At about the time of Hadrian's consulship Pliny found an excuse to write to his young friend Valerius Maximus, who had been appointed to a mission in the province of Achaia, as '*corrector* of the free cities'. He told him to remember that

> you have been sent . . . to the pure and genuine Greece, where civilisation and literature, and agriculture, too, are believed to have originated; and you have been sent to set in order the constitution of free cities . . . to free men who are both men and free in the fullest sense . . . Respect the gods their founders . . . pay regard to their antiquity, their heroic deeds, and the legends of the past . . . always bear in mind that it is Athens you go to and Sparta that you rule.[20]

Hadrian would not need the encouragement of Pliny, who is not known ever to have been to Greece, whereas the recipient of his sententious advice, Quinctilius Valerius Maximus, was from the colony of Alexandria Troas and thus certainly familiar with the Greek world. Greece was a magnet for all educated Romans and for a philhellene like Hadrian his lack of office provided an ideal chance to go there at last. His presence at Athens is not firmly attested until the year 112, but it is plausible to suppose that he sought permission from Trajan to leave Rome for a visit to Greece some time before. It may be that he was invited to stay at Athens, for example by one of the suffect consuls of 109, C. Julius Antiochus Epiphanes Philopappus, 'King Philopappus'. This man was a long-time resident at Athens, but must have been at Rome to hold his consulship. In any case, from about 109 onwards Trajan himself was evidently turning his eyes eastwards. For one thing, the Parthian empire was in turmoil, with two, if not three, rival claimants to the throne. Trajan's appointment of the *corrector* Maximus is only one small sign. A further new mission was being planned, for Pliny, which he would take up in 110: imperial legate with consular power, replacing the normal annual proconsul, in the province of Pontus-Bithynia. His particular mandate was to restore the finances of the cities. Trajan's reasons for concern with the state of this province may have had wide-reaching implications. His thoughts were already turning to the eastern part of the empire, and it should have suited his purposes for his kinsman to take up residence in the cultural capital of the Hellenic east.[21]

6

ARCHON AT ATHENS

The route to Athens meant a journey south along the Via Appia, then across to Beneventum and on to Brundisium (Brindisi). From 109 or 110 onwards major road-building was under way, on a Via Nova Traiana to the great south-eastern port. The man in charge of the project was Pompeius Falco, now married to Sosia Polla, daughter of Hadrian's friend Senecio (probably not Falco's first wife). Hadrian, it may be guessed, will have called on Falco in the course of his journey. Whether he had much company for this trip is a matter of guesswork. He presumably took Sabina with him, and a considerable household. Some like-minded friends may have joined him. But of known friends, his contemporaries who were senators, Platorius Nepos and Aemilius Papus, were probably pursuing their careers, being a stage or two behind Hadrian in the *cursus honorum*. His two equestrian friends were probably also both holding office, Claudius Livianus as Guard Prefect – with Hadrian's former guardian Acilius Attianus by now his colleague, it may be conjectured – and Marcius Turbo as a tribune in the Rome garrison and then as procurator of the main gladiatorial training-school. For his stay at Athens and for stops on the way, he had no doubt made arrangements about accommodation in advance. Sosius Senecio would have been well placed to give advice and introductions, and at Athens itself Hadrian probably had a host who had invited him.[1]

A standard destination from Brundisium was Dyrrachium (Dürres) in Epirus, from which the traveller for the east could join the Via Egnatia. Anyone heading for Athens would sail for a more southerly port, such as Buthrotum, and then coast down into the Corinthian Gulf. There is good reason to suppose that Hadrian made for Nicopolis, on the peninsula opposite Actium, at the mouth of the Gulf of Ambracia – the city had been founded by Augustus to commemorate the victory of 31 BC – and stayed there for some time. Nicopolis had become famous in the time of Trajan as the home of the philosopher Epictetus. The lame Phrygian had once been a slave at Rome, belonging to an imperial freedman, Epaphroditus. He had become a pupil of the Roman Stoic Musonius Rufus, and had been banished, along with other philosophers, under an edict of Domitian – probably a sequel to the trials and executions of Stoic senators in late 93. He settled at Nicopolis and chose to remain in spite of Domitian's death.

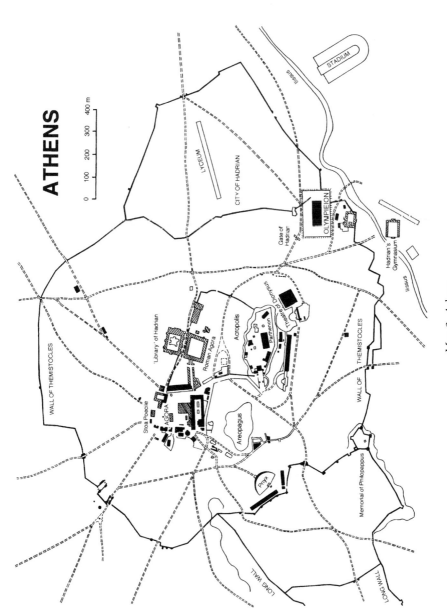

ATHENS

0 100 200 300 400 m

LYCEUM

CITY OF HADRIAN

WALL OF THEMISTOCLES

'Library' of Hadrian

Roman Agora

Stoa Poecile

AGORA

Acropolis

Theatre of Dionysus

Parthenon

Areopagus

Pnyx

WALL OF THEMISTOCLES

Memorial of Philopappus

Gate of Hadrian

OLYMPIEION

Hadrian's Gymnasium

Ilissus

Ilissus

STADIUM

LONG WALL

LONG WALL

Map 2 Athens

It had become a place of pilgrimage for seekers after truth, who came to sit at the feet of Epictetus. The *HA* registers Epictetus as one of only two named philosophers with whom Hadrian was on particularly close terms. It is difficult to avoid the conclusion that the friendship with Epictetus was formed when Hadrian was on his way to Athens for the first time, in about the year 110 or 111.[2]

Epictetus wrote nothing, but one of his admirers who was at Nicopolis in these years made copious notes of the master's discourses, or his dialogues with pupils and various visitors, some of them eminent persons; they were only published long afterwards. The author, or compiler, was then a young man, from Bithynian Nicomedia (Izmit), a Roman citizen of the rank of knight, L. Flavius Arrianus. Some of the conversations at Nicopolis which he transcribed may even include ones at which Hadrian was present. Further, a passing reference by Epictetus may give a hint of where Hadrian stayed at Nicopolis – 'at the house of Quadratus', where Epictetus evidently held forth from time to time. The name is not particularly uncommon and there might have been a local worthy called Quadratus. But it could have been Julius Quadratus the consul of 94 who, it was suggested, may have nominated Hadrian to be his Prefect during the Latin Festival, and perhaps also for membership of the *VIIviri epulonum* in about the year 100. Quadratus was in high favour with Trajan. He had been governor of Syria for a few years, consul a second time, as *ordinarius*, in 105, and at this time was probably completing a year as proconsul of Asia. He could even have been spending some time at Nicopolis on his way back from Asia to Rome. Epictetus comments that 'if some man who has been consul twice hears this [the notion that no bad man can be truly free], he will agree with you if you add – "but you are a wise man, this does not apply to you."' There were, it is true, at least seven persons still alive in the middle years of Trajan who had been consul twice – Servianus, Laberius Maximus, Suburanus, Quadratus and his colleague Julius Candidus, Senecio and Cornelius Palma.[3]

Epictetus was a Stoic, although he spoke with sympathy of the Cynics and, like them, thought nothing of birth or rank. Apart from the sarcastic remarks directed at a man twice consul (whether present or not), there were plenty of cutting comments directed at other eminent persons. A man destined to receive high equestrian office – as Prefect of the *annona* – was handled by Epictetus with justifiable scepticism when he claimed to lack ambition. The *corrector* Maximus, who was an Epicurean, received quite a grilling when 'he sailed all the way to Cassiope during the winter' to visit Epictetus. 'I sit as judge over the Hellenes', said Maximus, but this did not impress Epictetus. The procurator-governor of Epirus, the little province to which Nicopolis belonged, probably a man named Cn. Cornelius Pulcher from Epidaurus in the Peloponnese, got no sympathy when he complained about being insulted by the people for his ostentatious support of a comic actor. Epictetus is repeatedly quoted as expatiating on the worthlessness of seeking imperial preferment. These attitudes may well have been attractive to Hadrian. Two passages in Arrian's *Discourses of Epictetus* look as if they could have been directed at Hadrian himself. To be a son of God or a citizen of the universe was what counted, Epictetus said. 'Shall kinship with Caesar or with any other powerful persons at Rome be enough to enable men to live in security, immune from contempt and fearing nothing?' Who else other than Hadrian could claim kinship with the Emperor at this time? Even closer to Hadrian is another remark. No one could think ill of himself if he regarded himself as begotten of God. 'But – if Caesar adopts you, no one will be able to endure your conceit.' Irrespective of the story in the *HA* that Hadrian had learned, when consul in 108, that he would be adopted by Trajan – which could have become widely known, even if not made public – many must have looked on him as the heir apparent.[4]

Epictetus and his pupils may have become weary of Dacian war bores. Someone had evidently complained about his host 'telling every day how he fought in Moesia . . . how he climbed up to the crest of the hill, how he began to be besieged again.' Epictetus dismissed the war as having come about through ignorance, just like the Persian or Peloponnesian – or Trojan – wars. It was all very well, for 'the profound peace that Caesar now seems to provide – no wars any more, no battles, no large-scale brigandage: we can travel by land at any hour, we can sail from sunrise to sunset.' Yet Caesar could not provide 'peace from fever, from shipwreck, fire, earthquake, lightning . . . or from love, sorry, or envy'. True peace could only come from God.[5]

In a discourse on providence and the gifts of nature, Epictetus had occasion to mention facial hair. At first sight, 'can there be anything more useless than the hairs on a chin?' But the beard is nature's way of distinguishing men and women: 'we should preserve the signs that God has given; we should not throw them away and confuse the sexes.' Shaving had been the norm in Roman society for several hundred years, but traditionally minded Greeks – after a brief period when Alexander set the fashion for shaving – stuck to their beards. Dio of Prusa registers his satisfaction at having seen in Olbia, a remote Black Sea outpost of Hellenism on the River Borysthenes (Dnieper), only one man who was clean-shaven. This was to curry favour with the Romans – and he was looked down on by his fellow-citizens. As emperor Hadrian is regularly shown bearded – not with the flowing beard of the philosopher, but with the traditional well-tended beard of the Greeks. He might of course have stopped shaving some years before. But it is a plausible conjecture that his visit to Greece, when he was in his mid-thirties, was decisive, that it made him wish to look like a Greek, whether or not Epictetus' comments had a direct influence. The *HA* has another explanation for Hadrian's beard: he grew it 'to conceal facial blemishes'.[6]

While Arrian was a pupil of Epictetus at Nicopolis he certainly took the opportunity to visit the surrounding areas. In his other writings he reveals familiarity with Ambracia and Amphilochia, and gives details of how one sails between Acarnania, south of Nicopolis, and the island of Leucas. Given his passion for hunting, Arrian is likely to have spent time in this pursuit as well. It is at least plausible to imagine Hadrian joining him. Arrian was also at Delphi.

By the time he went there, he had probably ended his studies with Epictetus. An inscription shows Arrian as a member of the advisory council of a high Roman official settling boundary disputes between Delphi and her neighbours. This was Avidius Nigrinus, who probably came to Greece as imperial legate with a special mission soon after his consulship in the first half of 110. Nigrinus, it has been suggested, was appointed after the *corrector* Maximus had completed his tour of duty – the fact that Trajan found it necessary to send a second special commissioner, this time a consular, must be taken as a sign of concern for the state of Greece. Nigrinus may even have replaced the normal annual proconsul, as Pliny had just done in Pontus-Bithynia. Nigrinus was particularly well equipped for the task. His father of the same names and his uncle Avidius Quietus had strong links with Greece, and had been friends of Plutarch.[7]

Hadrian's older friend Sosius Senecio was also closely linked to Plutarch. Senecio had probably met him many years before, when serving as quaestor in Achaia. The friendship lasted and was cemented at Rome. Plutarch dedicated to Senecio one of his most substantial works, the nine books of *Table Talk*, in which he recalls their conversations in Greece, at Athens and Patras, and at Chaeronea, Plutarch's home in Boeotia, where Senecio had attended the wedding of Plutarch's son, as well as at Rome. At least several pairs of the *Parallel Lives* of great Greeks and Romans, Plutarch's other major work, on which he was still engaged at this time, were also dedicated to Senecio, as was his essay *On Making Progress in Virtue*. Another Roman friend of Plutarch who must have been well known to Hadrian was Minicius Fundanus of Ticinum (Pavia), who was on close terms with Pliny and was a fellow-*VIIvir* of Hadrian's. Much of Plutarch's life was centred on Delphi, where he held an important priesthood of Apollo. It is plausible enough to suppose that Hadrian visited Delphi on his way to Athens, but whether it was there or elsewhere, he surely made the acquaintance of Plutarch during this stay in Greece.[8]

At Athens Hadrian had, no doubt, ample opportunity for dinner parties with witty, literary, or philosophical conversation of the kind that Senecio obviously so much relished. At least one of the guests at an Athenian party immortalised in the *Table Talk* was still at Athens, 'King Philopappus', as Plutarch calls him, by his full names C. Julius Antiochus Epiphanes Philopappus. He was a grandson of the last king of Commagene, Antiochus IV, deposed by Vespasian in 72. Antiochus' sons and this grandson (whose last name mean 'lover of his grandfather') still retained the royal title. Philopappus had taken up residence at Athens, of which he had become a citizen, holding office as archon and becoming a lavish bene-factor. What is more, Philopappus had become a Roman senator and was even consul suffect in the year 109. It had been a nice gesture to confer the *fasces* on this man at precisely this moment: it was almost the three-hundredth anniversary of the battle of Thermopylae, at which his ancestor Antiochus the Great had been defeated by the consul M'. Acilius Glabrio. The consul Antiochus Epiphanes marked a symbolic coming together of the western and eastern élites. As has been suggested, Hadrian could easily have got to know Philopappus at Rome in the summer of 109, and could well have been invited to stay with him at Athens. Be this as it may, it would have been difficult for a high-ranking Roman visitor to Athens in these years not to come into contact with the king. His sister Balbilla turns up many years later as a close friend of Hadrian's wife Sabina. It is a fair bet that their friendship began, if not in 109, then at the latest about the year 111, when Hadrian – surely with his wife – first came to Athens.[9]

Other prominent persons likely to have entertained Hadrian or to have made his acquaintance include the young Spartan notable who was a cousin of Philopappus and Balbilla, C. Julius Eurycles Herculanus. Plutarch dedicated an essay to Herculanus, *On the Art of Self-Praise Without Incurring Disapproval*. Most of the piece is devoted to historical examples from Greek history, but towards the end comes some practical advice. Boasting about one's success, some 'act or word that found favour with the governor', should be avoided. After attending gubernatorial banquets, people should refrain from recounting 'gracious remarks illustrious or royal persons have addressed to them'. One can readily imagine Herculanus at dinner with the imperial legate Nigrinus – who was also active at Athens – and Hadrian among the other guests.[10]

Herculanus, 'thirty-sixth in descent from the Dioscuri' and a member of a family, the Euryclids, that had dominated Sparta since the time of Augustus, was related not only to King Philopappus but to the leading family of Athens, that of Ti. Claudius Atticus Herodes. Atticus claimed descent from Miltiades and Cimon, and indeed from the legendary hero Aeacus. The family was immensely rich, Atticus' father Hipparchus having managed to secrete a large part of his fortune when on trial under the Flavians. Atticus 'discovered' the treasure after Nerva's accession, and was permitted to take possession. This enabled him to play the role of benefactor on the grand scale, and he seems to have acquired honorary senatorial rank under Trajan. But neither Atticus nor Herculanus, even though their families had enjoyed Roman citizenship since the Julio-Claudian period, nor indeed any other Greeks from 'old Greece' (the province Achaia and the 'free cities' such as Athens that were, at least in theory, enclaves within the province) had become Roman senators. The consul 'King' Philopappus was only an honorary Athenian. Greeks from Asia Minor had entered the Senate, in some numbers, a few even rising to the consulship, under the Flavians, and Trajan had given high command to men like the Pergamenes Quadratus and Quadratus Bassus. It must be supposed that Athenians and Spartans still felt a certain reserve and declined to seek senatorial rank. For one thing, they may not have been good enough at Latin. It was doubtless to give his young son a good grounding in this respect that Atticus arranged for the boy, aged about eleven or twelve at this time, to stay at Rome in the house of Calvisius Tullus Ruso, the son-in-law of old Domitius Tullus.[11]

Hadrian liked Athens, of that there can be no doubt. His repeated visits there when Emperor make this clear. To see the Acropolis and the Parthenon and other famous monuments was in itself an aspiration shared by most cultivated persons in this age. Hadrian may have been particularly struck by the vast

Temple of Olympian Zeus, inaugurated over 600 years earlier by Pisistratus, but never completed. Antiochus Epiphanes, the Seleucid king whose names Philopappus bore, had spent large sums to take the work further, but it was still not finished. Athens, in turn, liked Hadrian. He was invited to become an Athenian citizen, and, when the offer was accepted, was made a member of the deme Besa. King Philopappus was enrolled in the same deme, and one may suppose that he played a part. Hadrian was then elected *archon eponymus* – in other words, was to hold the ancient chief magistracy, and the Athenian year would take his name. His own freedman, the learned Phlegon of Tralles, who was probably already with him, would later write a chronicle in which his patron's archonship is registered for the year 112. As the Athenian year began and ended in the summer, it is not certain whether his term of office began in 111 or 112. However this may be, it was a striking gesture. 'The *Boule* of the Areopagus, the *Boule* of the Six Hundred and the *Demos* of the Athenians' honoured 'their *archon* Hadrianos' with a statue in the Theatre of Dionysus. They took care to preface this simple three-line inscription on the base with seven lines in Latin setting out their archon's career as a Roman senator. A few other Romans of his rank had accepted this honour, but only a few. One was a man called Trebellius Rufus, from Tolosa (Toulouse), who had evidently settled at Athens and ceased to pursue the senatorial career. Under Domitian the great Vibius Crispus, three times consul, had accepted enrolment in the deme Marathon and the archonship – but in *absentia*. And Domitian himself, whose patron goddess was the Roman version of Athena, had likewise consented to be archon without coming to Athens.[12]

An eminent senior senator, on his way to become proconsul of Asia, may have passed through Athens in the spring of the year 112, or a year later, on his way back, and witnessed the Roman archon carrying out his duties – Cornelius Tacitus. His *Histories* complete, Tacitus may now have been beginning his research for a new work – not the sequel that he had promised, the reigns of Nerva and Trajan, but the *Annals* of the Julio-Claudian emperors, from Tiberius to Nero. Athens is mentioned only briefly in the surviving books. Tacitus related the visit in AD 18 of Germanicus Caesar who went from Nicopolis to the ancient allied city, where the 'Greeks received him with elaborate honours, expatiating on their own history and literature to make their flattery seem more dignified.' (The visit shortly after by the Caesar's enemy Piso, who was harshly critical of the Athenians, is also described.) Hadrian was not yet a Caesar like Germanicus, and the Athenians, however delighted with so eminent an archon, may not have displayed such elaborate flattery to him. All the same, the position of Hadrian's wife Sabina, already unusually distinguished, became even more special in the summer of 112. Her grandmother, Trajan's sister Marciana Augusta, died at the end of August and was promptly deified; on the same day her daughter Matidia, Sabina's mother, was named Augusta. Sabina was thus daughter of an Augusta and granddaughter of a Diva.[13]

The year 112 had already been marked at Rome by the formal opening on

1 January of Trajan's colossal new Forum and Basilica and adjacent market. To show the extent of the excavation that had been required, a mighty column was to be erected, completed and dedicated in May of the following year. The simple inscription proclaimed that the work had been paid for *ex manubiis*, 'from the booty'. Whether the column was already decorated with reliefs commemorating in visual form the two Dacian wars which had made all this possible, must remain uncertain.[14]

In the course of 113, developments in the east took a turn which gave Trajan the opportunity he had clearly been waiting for. Rome's only serious rival, Parthia, had been seriously split for some years between rival kings, Pacorus, Vologaeses and Chosroes. This alone provided an excellent opportunity for the settling of old scores. There was even a more recent provocation. Not long before, Pliny had informed Trajan that a man called Callidromus had turned up at Nicomedia: apparently a slave of Laberius Maximus, he had been captured by Decebalus – presumably in 101 or 102 – and sent as a gift to King Pacorus. If the story of Callidromus were true – Pliny in turn sent the man to the Emperor – it suggested an attempt had been made by Decebalus to enlist Parthian support. Pacorus had been king for a long time, over thirty years, but in comparison with his rivals Vologaeses and Chosroes was now a spent force. Chosroes, for the time being the most powerful contender, now took a step which could be construed as an infringement of the agreement reached fifty years before. It had been established that the king of Armenia had to be nominated by Rome, even if he were a member of the Parthian royal house. Chosroes simply deposed the incumbent, Axidares, son of Pacorus, and installed a successor, Parthamasiris, also a son of Pacorus, without reference to Trajan. Axidares may have resisted, and have appealed to Rome. Threatening missives were sent and Trajan began preparations for war. As a young man serving under his father in Syria, forty years earlier, he had had the chance of fighting the Parthians; but peace had then been preserved. Now he could hope to win new glory, in the footsteps of Alexander the Great with whom flatterers had been comparing him. Troop reinforcements on a massive scale were set in motion for the eastern frontier provinces, to proceed down the Danube, through Pontus-Bithynia and Galatia and on towards the Euphrates. The Emperor himself, with his court – including Plotina and Matidia, the two Augustae – set off from Rome at the end of October. The day of his *profectio*, no doubt deliberately chosen as propitious, was the sixteenth anniversary of his adoption by Nerva. He travelled by the Via Appia and his own new road, the Via Traiana, just completed the previous year, to Brundisium, then headed for Athens. The Misenum fleet under the command of its new prefect, Marcius Turbo, and no doubt a great flotilla of merchantmen, would then convey the Imperator, his staff, his household and his entourage.[15]

7

THE PARTHIAN WAR

Trajan's stay at Athens was no doubt relatively brief, just long enough to enable the sixty-year-old Emperor to refresh himself after the sea crossing, and to make further dispositions and appointments. Ambassadors from King Chosroes were awaiting him. They 'asked for peace and proffered gifts', Dio records, 'for when he heard of Trajan's departure, the king was terrified, since Trajan's practice was to make good his threats. So he humbled his pride and begged Trajan not to make war on him. Further, he requested that Armenia be awarded to Parthamisiris. He had deposed Axidares, he wrote, because he had been unsatisfactory to both Romans and Parthians.' Trajan made no formal reply, either in writing or verbally, except for an ominous comment: 'Friendly relations are determined by deeds, not by words. When I reach Syria I shall take appropriate action.'[1]

Arrangements had already been made for the major commands in the east. Quadratus Bassus, who had been governing Cappadocia-Galatia for several years, after sterling service in both Dacian wars and the governorship of Judaea in between, was now transferred to Syria. His successor in Cappadocia was M. Junius Homullus. Not much is known about Homullus, except that he had been consul in 102, hence was now quite senior, and had spoken in the Senate at the trials of the two proconsuls of Pontus-Bithynia defended by Pliny – 'with subtlety, acuteness and elegance' in the second instance. An anecdote in the *HA* suggests that the outspoken Homullus was on good terms with the Emperor: 'he told Trajan that Domitian was, indeed, a very bad man but had good friends – whereas the ruler who entrusts the commonwealth to men of evil ways is hated the more, for it is better to endure one bad man than many.' As for Pontus-Bithynia, Trajan's special commissioner Pliny had by now died – probably in the course of the previous year, 112, after less than two years in office. He had been replaced by another consular legate, Cornutus Tertullus. This province was too important for troop movements from the Danube to the eastern front for it to be given back to an annual proconsul.[2]

The new province of Arabia remained in the hands of its first governor, C. Claudius Severus, although he had been in office since Cornelius Palma had annexed the Nabataean kingdom in 106, and had in the meantime become consul. Egypt acquired a new Prefect in 112 or 113, M. Rutilius Lupus, taking over from Ser. Sulpicius Similis. Further afield too, new governors were in place. Minicius Natalis became legate of Upper Pannonia. One of his legions, I Adiutrix, left for the east, where it was commanded by Hadrian's friend and coeval Platorius Nepos. Pompeius Falco, another friend, may now have been sent to govern Moesia Inferior. Who was governing Moesia Superior and the new acquisition, Dacia, is not clear. Whether Claudius Livianus was still Guard Prefect, and if so with the Emperor, is also uncertain. He is mentioned along with Senecio, Aemilius Papus, Platorius Nepos, Acilius Attianus and Turbo as among Hadrian's particular friends at the time of the Parthian expedition. As a Greek, from Lycia, Livianus would have been an appropriate choice for service in the east, but he was no longer in office at the end of the war, when Attianus was with Trajan as Prefect. Livianus was probably soon replaced, by Sulpicius Similis, who may be supposed to have taken the place of Attianus at Rome when the latter joined Trajan in the east.[3]

An impressive galaxy of senior men no doubt accompanied the Emperor as his *comites*, perhaps including Cornelius Palma and Publilius Celsus, the two men most recently honoured with a second consulship, the former in 109, the latter this very year. These two, and Senecio, had been singled out by the public erection of statues, Dio mentions, 'so greatly did he esteem them above the rest.' Senecio's services in the Dacian wars and Palma's successful annexation of Arabia are well attested. The reasons for Celsus' distinction remain obscure. The *HA* biographer names all three in connection with Hadrian at this time, Senecio as one of his close friends, Palma and Celsus as his enemies. Of the other men given a second consulship by Trajan, one had fallen into disfavour: Laberius Maximus, who had played a major role in the first Dacian war, had been suspected of treasonable designs and sent into exile on an island. Nonetheless, his son-in-law, Bruttius Praesens, after some years out of public life – for which withdrawal Pliny had gently chided him – was given a command as legate of one of the Syrian legions, VI Ferrata. Laberius was one of only two senators known to have suffered banishment under Trajan, the other being the blue-blooded aristocrat Calpurnius Crassus: he had already been suspected of planning a coup against Nerva, and had allegedly tried it again under Trajan; he too was confined to an island.[4]

Others who were to hold important commands included two recent consuls, Julius Maximus Manlianus, Hadrian's successor as legate of Pannonia Inferior, and Catilius Severus, a friend of Pliny and a recently elected colleague of Hadrian in the *VIIviri epulonum*. Catilius, a 'colonial', but not from the west – his home was the Bithynian *colonia* Apamea – had, it seems, now married Dasumia Polla, the wealthy widow of Domitius Tullus, an advantageous connection. The Dasumii of Corduba were related to Hadrian. Of the other commanders, Lusius Quietus, the formidable North African chieftain who had done signal service against the Dacians, was back again with Trajan in command of his Moorish auxiliaries. As for Hadrian himself, the influence of Plotina, so the *HA* claims, secured him appointment on Trajan's staff, as *legatus* 'at the time of the Parthian expedition' – presumably as *legatus Augusti pro praetore* and *comes* of the Emperor.[5]

The imperial party must have left Athens well before the end of the year. Trajan's route, briefly registered by Dio, took him through the provinces of Asia and Lycia. From there he took ship to the main harbour of Syria, Seleucia in Pieria, close to the mouth of the River Orontes, which he reached in December, according to the Byzantine chronicler John Malalas. The same Malalas, whose history is focused on Antioch, notes Hadrian's presence: Trajan 'set out with a large force of soldiers and senators and sailed for the east. Among the senators was Hadrian, his relative by marriage through his sister.' From there, via the pleasant garden settlement of Daphne, Trajan reached Antioch, again according to Malalas, on 7 January 114. The information is plausible enough, except that it is preceded by a detailed account of an alleged 'Persian' capture of Antioch, liberated by the Antiochenes themselves, following Trajan's instructions. Although Malalas has some convincing enough details, the presence in his narrative of fantasies of this kind makes it dangerous to prefer him to other sources. But the alternative and superior account, written by Arrian – the last part of his *Parthian History* – survives only in fragments, and Cassius Dio, who used Arrian's work, is likewise not preserved in full. Xiphilinus' summary of Dio, supplemented by some excerpts from Dio's full text, provides only an outline. As a result, the chronology of Trajan's war remains uncertain in several important respects.[6]

During the early part of the year, while Roman forces assembled, or perhaps, indeed, shortly after landing in Syria, Trajan made a dedication from the spoils of Dacia to Zeus Casius, the god of the mountain near the mouth of the Orontes. A verse inscription accompanied the gift, composed – according to Arrian, who quotes part of it, and the *Palatine Anthology* in which the full text is preserved – by Hadrian on his behalf: 'Trajan, descendant of Aeneas, to Casian Zeus, the ruler on earth to the ruler above, makes offering from the plunder of the Getae.' Further spoils, from the Arsacid rulers of Parthia, were promised, if Zeus vouchsafed another victory. Trajan is also supposed to have consulted the oracle of Jupiter of Heliopolis (Baalbek), to enquire whether he would return to Rome when the war was over: the answer, supplied by an elaborate rigmarole, was negative.[7]

Trajan had to deal with Armenia. Antioch was not the most promising place from which to launch an expedition in that direction. He had presumably decided to avoid crossing Anatolia in the winter, but, in any case, at Antioch he was better placed to assess the situation and inform himself about the position in the Parthian empire as a whole and Mesopotamia in particular. Just across the Euphrates, the little kingdom of Osrhoene was in the hands of a native ruler again, Abgarus, who had apparently purchased it from Pacorus a few years before – the latest trace of the old king in the written sources, although coins were still struck for him as late as 115–16. 'Abgarus sent gifts and a message of friendship on Trajan's arrival at Antioch', Dio reported, 'but did not appear in person. He was afraid of Trajan and the Parthians alike and was trying to stay neutral. For that reason he would not come to confer with the Emperor.'[8]

Trajan's objective in 114 was Satala, north of the upper Euphrates, in Lesser Armenia, which had been part of the empire for over fifty years. Here the reinforcements from the Danube provinces were assembled. It was a long march by any standards, some 475 miles (760 km) through difficult country, and must have taken at least seven weeks. On the way he registered an early success: whether led by Trajan in person or by one of the senior commanders, a Roman force crossed the Euphrates beyond Melitene, entered 'enemy' territory, and captured Arsamosata on the River Arsanias (Murat su), an eastern tributary of the Euphrates. This was one of the four principal cities of the Armenian kingdom. At Satala Trajan held court, a kind of durbar: 'the satraps and princes came to meet him with gifts, one of which was a horse that had been taught to do obeisance, kneeling on its forelegs and placing its head beneath the feet of whoever stood near', Dio's account reports. Two fourth-century chroniclers, Eutropius and Festus, list some of the kings who did homage: the Iberi from the Caucasus, the Colchi, Bosporani and Sauromatae. Amazaspus, a kinsman of the Iberian king, took service in the Roman forces. As for the eastern neighbours of the Iberi, the Albani, Trajan appointed a new ruler. Anchialus of the Heniochi and Machelones and Julianus of the Apsilae are also known to have been confirmed in their little kingdoms by Trajan. The ceremony at which 'kingdoms were assigned' – *regna adsignata* – was duly celebrated on the imperial coinage. Three men in short tunic and trousers are portrayed standing before Trajan, wearing his breastplate and seated on a tribunal, with the Guard Prefect and a lictor at his side. He extends his right hand to the barbarian in the foreground who raises both arms in salute.[9]

But the new Parthian nominee to the throne of Greater Armenia, Parthamasiris, whose installation had provided Trajan with the *casus belli*, did not appear. 'He wrote to Trajan, calling himself king.' As Trajan declined to reply, he wrote again, dropping the royal title, requesting that the governor of Cappadocia, Homullus, be sent to him. Instead, Trajan sent Homullus' son, serving under his father as *tribunus laticlavius*. From Satala Trajan now moved eastwards to Elegia, where Parthamasiris arrived, to be received by Trajan before the Emperor's tribunal. The king 'saluted Trajan, removed his crown and laid it at Trajan's feet, expecting to be given it back. But the assembled troops now loudly acclaimed Trajan as *imperator*', the traditional sign of a victory. Parthamasiris, terrified, took it as an insult and a sign of his impending doom. He turned as if to flee but was surrounded; he begged for a private audience with Trajan, but was rebuffed. In rage, he left the camp, but was ordered back by Trajan. Before the army Trajan told the king to say what he wanted in the hearing of all. Parthamasiris 'declared that he came not because he had been defeated but of his own free will. He believed that he should not be treated wrongfully but should receive back his kingdom, as Tiridates had from Nero.'

Trajan replied that 'he would surrender Armenia to no one: it belonged to the Romans and would have a Roman governor.' Parthamasiris' Armenian courtiers were obliged to stay – they were now Roman subjects. He himself was allowed to leave, with his Parthian companions and an escort of Roman cavalry. The humiliation of the Parthian king of Armenia was depicted on several coin issues, with the legend *rex Parthus*: the Parthian is shown, knees bending and both hands outstretched as he approaches Trajan. However, the sequel was something of a blot on Trajan's reputation: on his journey – presumably back to Parthia – the deposed monarch was killed, in unknown circumstances.[10]

There was some fighting to be done. Bruttius Praesens, legate of VI Ferrata, was faced with snow 16 feet deep in the mountains east of Lake Van. Native guides supplied his men with snowshoes. The experience may have been too much for Praesens – at least, his *cursus*-inscription registers as his next post the curatorship of the Via Latina, perhaps a kind of paid leave. But he was back in the east before the war ended. The exploit with snowshoes is recorded by a fragment of Arrian's *Parthica*, in which Trajan's war was treated at some length. It might well be that Arrian had been able to obtain a commission as an equestrian officer and had been with the army in Armenia in 114. Otherwise, Lusius Quietus, so an admittedly late source claims, campaigned against the Mardi east of Lake Van. Several other kings were 'won over', some submitting of their own accord, which meant that they were treated as 'friends' by Trajan, others without a battle. Greater Armenia was organised as a Roman province – or, rather, perhaps, added on to Cappadocia, from which Galatia was now detached. Catilius Severus may already have been installed as legate of Cappadocia-Armenia Maior before the end of 114. A procurator of Armenia Maior is also attested, T. Haterius Nepos. The new conquest inspired the Senate to bring about what had long been proposed: Trajan was officially to be called *Optimus* – 'the best'. The Emperor had lived up to his reputation, marching on foot with the men throughout the entire campaign, fording rivers with them, sometimes even deliberately sending out false reports of impending enemy attack to keep the soldiers up to the mark.[11]

The war was far from finished, however. To annexe Armenia meant that Mesopotamia had to follow. Trajan and the armies moved south, and Nisibis and Batnae were rapidly captured, which prompted the Senate to vote him – prematurely – the title Parthicus. Trajan did not accept yet. He knew only too well that a lot more fighting lay ahead. 'Leaving garrisons at opportune points, he went to to Edessa, and there saw Abgarus for the first time.' Abgarus could no longer stay neutral:

> Partly through fear of Trajan and partly through the persuasion of his son Arbandes, a handsome youth who was in favour with Trajan, he came to meet Trajan on the road, made his apologies and obtained pardon – for he had a powerful intercessor in the boy. He therefore become Trajan's friend and entertained him at a banquet, and during the dinner brought in his son to perform a barbarian dance.

Trajan was very taken with the boy, who wore gold earrings: 'I blame you for not coming to me and joining in my expedition and sharing in the hard work – for this reason I would gladly tear off one of your earrings!', he told Arbandes. Other Parthian vassals were less compliant, particularly a certain Mannus, and the ruler of Adiabene, Mebarsapes.[12]

Trajan returned to Antioch for the winter. Early in the new year, disaster struck: Antioch was hit by a violent earthquake. Vast numbers perished, the most prominent victim being one of the *consules ordinarii* of 115, M. Pedo Vergilianus, who must have been holding office in *absentia*. Trajan himself escaped out of a window with only minor injuries, 'led out by some being of superhuman stature', according to Dio. As the aftershocks continued for several days, he remained out of doors, in the city's hippodrome. Nothing is reported about how Plotina managed, or other members of the imperial household – except that Malalas specifically mentions that 'Hadrian, before he began to reign, was with the Emperor Trajan, because he was his relative by marriage, when the great city of Antiochus suffered from the wrath of God – he was then a senator.' Malalas also reports, in connection with the earthquake, the martyr-dom of the Bishop of Antioch, Ignatius, who 'had incurred the Emperor's anger by abusing him.' The firm tradition in the church is that Ignatius was sent to Rome for execution. Now whereas Xiphilinus' abbreviation of Dio supplies a lengthy account of the disaster, Malalas, by paradox, has less detail on this dramatic event at his native city, but supplies a precise date, Sunday 13 December, two years after Trajan's arrival in the east. However, 13 December 115 was not a Sunday. Further, Pedo the *consul ordinarius* of 115, who died in the earthquake, was replaced by a suffect consul early in the year, although his colleague continued in office for some time. Elaborate attempts have been made to defend Malalas' date, but they create unnecessary difficulties. It is more plausible to accept that Pedo was still in office as consul when the earthquake struck, probably in January 115. Malalas is likely enough to have invented, or assumed, the date of 13 December on the assumption that the earthquake was about a week before the martyrdom of Ignatius, who he knew had died under Trajan – and supposed had been condemned at Antioch when the Emperor was there. The saint was commemorated at Antioch on 20 December.[13]

The war had to go on: after the long account of the earthquake, Dio–Xiphilinus proceeds with the statement that 'Trajan at the beginning of spring hastened into the enemy's country.' The year 115 apparently saw a whole series of battles. For one thing, Trajan received a further four imperatorial accla-mations. The scanty nature of the sources makes it difficult to be sure where Roman forces were engaged, and in what order. His first target was Adiabene, the kingdom across the Tigris, 'a district of Assyria opposite Ninus [Nineveh]'. In the winter trees had been felled in the forests around Nisibis and collapsible boats constructed. They were taken on wagons to form a pontoon bridge over the Tigris. After an opposed crossing, the Romans conquered the whole of Adiabene, Dio goes on, adding that 'Arbela and Gaugamela, near which places

Alexander defeated Darius, are in this country.' This historical background may well have been in the forefront of Trajan's mind. But the Parthian king, the contemporary equivalent of the Persian Darius, remained to be tackled. In a separate excerpt evidently belonging to the account of this action, Lusius Quietus is credited by Dio with capturing Singara in Mesopotamia, on the south side of the mountain ridge beyond the River Chaboras. Mebarsapes the ruler of Adiabene may have exercised control west of the Tigris as far as this point.[14]

Presumably leaving substantial forces on the Tigris, with orders to proceed southwards, Trajan himself now returned west, to lead an army down the Euphrates for the attack on the Parthian capital, Ctesiphon. At Dura Europus, an old Macedonian foundation, a triumphal arch was erected in his honour. Further down the river, at Ozogardana, the 'tribunal of Trajan' was still to be seen two hundred and fifty years later. In the course of the campaign, Trajan still had the business of the empire to deal with. One item which happens to be recorded must have come to his attention in late summer, a disturbance at Alexandria, the Egyptian metropolis. Inter-communal rioting between the Greeks and the substantial Jewish minority had broken out again. The animosity between the two communities went back a long way and both sides frequently sent delegations to Rome to seek imperial backing. Trajan had been appealed to in this way not long before he left Italy, and had favoured the Jews, according to an Alexandrian Greek version preserved on papyrus. The rioting had obliged the Prefect Rutilius Lupus to intervene against the Jews. In an an edict of 13 October 115 Lupus referred to 'a battle between Romans and Jews'. The Prefect demanded restraint from the Greeks and announced that a 'judge' had been sent by the Emperor to examine the matter.[15]

Trajan had planned to join the Euphrates to the Tigris by a canal to bring his boats across the narrow strip of land between the rivers, but was advised against it and had them hauled across instead. 'Then he crossed the Tigris and entered Ctesiphon' – apparently meeting no resistance. Chosroes had fled, but Trajan captured one of his daughters and the royal throne. It was a moment to relish. The Parthians had inflicted defeats on Crassus and the Triumvir Antonius which had been only partially avenged by the victory of Ventidius, the sole Roman who had ever held a triumph *de Parthis*. Augustus had restored Roman prestige and recovered the lost standards, but by diplomacy, not war. Parthia, and the bone of contention, Armenia, had gone on presenting problems for Rome; and till now no Roman army had ever reached the Parthian capital.[16]

'When he had taken possession of Ctesiphon, he was acclaimed *imperator* and confirmed the title Parthicus', Dio reports. The *Fasti Ostienses* of the year 116 supply a date: on 20 or 21 February 'laurelled despatches were sent to the Senate by the Emperor Trajan, on account of which he was named Parthicus.' There is much to be said for the suggestion that Trajan deliberately chose the anniversary of his accession, 28 January, to enter the enemy capital – if it could be supposed that there was time for despatches sent out on that day to reach the Senate three and a half weeks later. The Senate voted new honours to Trajan.

Meanwhile circus games were held on three days. The imperial coinage went to town, proclaiming 'the conquest of Parthia' (*Parthia capta*) and 'Armenia and Mesopotamia subjected to the power of the Roman People'. A further new province was now to be created: southern Mesopotamia, called 'Asorestan' by its Iranian rulers, was to be the Roman province of Assyria. Trajan sailed down the Tigris and the united stream of the two rivers in a vast imperial barge, adorned with gold, holding 'conferences' on board, as a fragment of Arrian's *Parthica* registers.[17]

The Emperor was able to stand at the head of the Persian Gulf, having won over Athambelus, ruler of the little kingdom of Mesene in the Tigris island (in the area of modern Basra). When he saw a ship sailing for India, he expressed regret that he was too old to follow further in Alexander's footsteps to that country. Nonetheless, he wrote to the Senate, perhaps in the despatches reported in the *Fasti Ostienses* under 6 May, that he had advanced further than Alexander had – a sophistical argument could, of course, make such a claim, given that the Spanish Emperor could be deemed to have started from the River Bactis. But Trajan probably meant his Armenian campaign – and he may have counted his conquest of Dacia in the same calculation. The Senate responded that 'he should have the honour of celebrating triumphs over as many peoples as he pleased, since on account of the large number of peoples which he named in his frequent despatches, they were not always able to understand or even pronounce the names correctly.' Trajan's interest in Alexander – an obsession, it might almost be called – was further evident when he sacrificed to the king's shade at Babylon. But, unlike Alexander, Trajan had failed to defeat the Great King in the field.[18]

While at Babylon, Trajan was informed that during his voyage to the Gulf and back rebellion had broken out in 'all the territories previously conquered'. What is more, in the late spring or early summer a massive Jewish uprising had begun in three Roman provinces, Cyrenaica, Egypt and Cyprus. In Armenia, Catilius Severus was confronted by a Parthian named Vologaeses. Before it came to a battle, Vologaeses obtained an armistice. Trajan made him an offer of part of Armenia, in return for peace. Meanwhile he sent two generals against the insurgents in Mesopotamia, Maximus and Quietus. Maximus, a man of consular rank, perhaps the governor of Mesopotamia, was defeated and killed. Quietus, with his Moorish cavalry, was more successful, recovering Nisibis and, after a siege, Edessa, which was burned to the ground. The great Greek city of Seleucia on the Tigris, close to Ctesiphon, was also sacked, by the legionary commanders Erucius Clarus and Julius Alexander. Trajan evidently realised that his dream of equalling Alexander's conquests was beyond attainment. At Ctesiphon a great ceremony was held and a Parthian prince, Parthamaspates, a renegade son of Chosroes, was crowned as king by the grace of Rome. The event was duly celebrated on the imperial coinage, with the Emperor placing a diadem on the head of the kneeling vassal and the legend *Rex Parthis datus*, 'a king given to the Parthians'.[19]

The Jewish revolt in the diaspora was now reaching alarming proportions. In Cyrenaica, which had had a large Jewish population for several centuries, the rebels, with a man called Andreas at their head, according to Dio – perhaps the same as the Lukuas said by Eusebius to have been proclaimed king by the Jewish rebels – were 'destroying both Romans and Greeks'. Dio reports horrific atrocities allegedly committed by the insurgents and gives the number of dead as 220,000. At Cyrene itself several temples and other public buildings were wrecked, and even the roads leading to the city were 'torn up and broken'. From Cyrenaica the Jewish host poured into Egypt, where their fellow-Jews rose in their support. On Cyprus, where Dio names the Jewish leader as Artemio, even more were killed by the insurgents than in Cyrenaica – Dio's figure is 240,000. Salamis, the principal city, was sacked. The timing of the revolt in the Nile valley can be gauged from the receipts for the Jewish tax – imposed by Vespasian after the destruction of the Temple in 70. None is dated later than 18 May 116. The Prefect Lupus could not cope with the crisis; a legion was defeated by the Jews, as a vivid report in a papyrus letter attests. The native Egyptian population had to be mobilised – and fought with fierce enthusiasm, tempered by fear of 'the unholy Jews', winning a victory outside Memphis. Trajan sent in new troops, commanded by Marcius Turbo, prefect of the Misenum fleet, which had come to Syria for the war. Turbo campaigned himself in Egypt and Cyrenaica, 'many tens of thousands of Jews' being killed. An inscription from Berytus (Beirut) commemorates one of the officers in Turbo's expeditionary corps, a citizen of the *colonia*, who, as tribune of the Upper Moesian legion VII Claudia, 'was sent with a detachment to Cyprus on the expedition' and was decorated by Trajan.[20]

There was still a large Jewish community in Mesopotamia dating back to the time of the Babylonian exile. According to Eusebius, 'Trajan suspected that the Jews there would also attack . . . and ordered Lusius Quietus to clean them out of the province. He mustered his forces and massacred a great multitude of them.' To what extent the Jewish uprisings in Cyrenaica, Egypt and Cyprus were coordinated with the outbreak of resistance in Mesopotamia is unclear from the sources. The Parthian king may well have been able to stir up the Cyrenaean Jews – who seem to have taken the initiative – to create a 'second front'. The earthquake at Antioch may also have had an effect, and been seen by the Jews as a sign of impending doom for the imperial power. Further, the fact that the Jews had a king surely means that they had messianic expectations. At all events, the diaspora revolt played a decisive part in forcing Trajan to abort his plan for wider conquests.[21]

On his way back northwards, Trajan took personal charge of the siege of the desert city of Hatra, which had also thrown off the Roman yoke. His forces managed to undermine part of the city wall, but the ensuing cavalry charge was repulsed. Even the Emperor himself was nearly wounded as he rode past. In spite of his having 'laid aside his imperial uniform to avoid being recognised', the enemy shot at the majestic figure and killed one of his *equites singulares*. The heat, the flies and the intense discomfort proved too much. 'Trajan therefore departed, and a little later began to fail in health.'[22]

Trajan was still determined to restore the situation and to make another expedition into Mesopotamia. But there was more bad news: war had broken out in Dacia. The man chosen to deal with the situation there was Julius Quadratus Bassus, who had been governor of Syria since the beginning of the Parthian expedition. As Bassus' successor in Syria, Trajan appointed Hadrian. At last Hadrian had a consular command and real responsibilities again – not that there is much direct evidence for what he did as legate of Syria. His literary freedman must have been with him, for in one of his books, *On Marvels*, Phlegon registers a case of a woman changing sex in the year 116. It happened at the Syrian town Laodicea on Sea – and Phlegon saw the person himself. Another story is mentioned in passing by Ammianus Marcellinus – Hadrian received a prophecy from the 'talking Castalian springs' at Daphne, outside Antioch. The *HA*'s report that Hadrian had a similar response from the shrine of Zeus Nicephorius, although placed in the context of his early career, may, if it is not invented, belong to his time in Syria. More to the point, the *HA* has two other items to report on Hadrian's position in late 116 or early 117. His 'enemies' Palma and Celsus fell under suspicion of plotting a coup: this was 'a guarantee' that Hadrian would be adopted. Further, he was designated to a second consulship – as *ordinarius* for 118 – thanks to the influence of Plotina. This probably took place in January 117, and 'it served to make his adoption a foregone conclusion.' Another nomination to the consulship was much more startling. Lusius Quietus, the Moor, was suddenly made a senator, given a suffect consulship – some time in 117 – and installed as governor of Judaea, presumably with an extra legion, given his consular rank. Trajan evidently wanted to be sure that the Jews in their homeland did not follow the example of the diaspora.[23]

There was, no doubt, widespread opposition to the idea of Hadrian becoming Trajan's successor. Hence, presumably, 'the widespread rumours' reported by the *HA*, that 'he had bribed Trajan's freedmen, had cultivated his boy favourites and had frequent sexual relations with them when he was an inner member of the court.' But Trajan still took no further step.

> Many say [the *HA* reports] that he intended to die without a successor, following the example of Alexander the Macedonian. Many also say that he intended to advise the Senate by letter that if anything should befall him, the Senate should give a *princeps* to the Roman common-wealth, adding some names, from which it should choose the best man.

The Emperor's illness was becoming worse; he was convinced he had been poisoned. In fact, as Dio – who registers the alleged poisoning – records, he had had a stroke, was partly paralysed and was suffering from dropsy. In late July or early August 117, probably persuaded by Plotina and his beloved niece

Matidia, he set off back to Rome, accompanied by the Augustae and the Guard Prefect Attianus. At Selinus in Cilicia, the imperial party had to stop. Trajan was too ill to go further. Hadrian remained in Syria, holding the fort, and waiting for news.[24]

8

THE NEW RULER

Trajan's 'letter of adoption' reached Hadrian in Syria on 9 August 117. He was now Caesar. Whether this was made public, at Antioch or otherwise, and what took place that day or on the next, is not recorded. In the night of 10–11 August, so Dio reports, Hadrian had a dream, that 'fire came down from the sky, which was clear and bright, striking his throat first on the left side and then on the right, but neither frightening him nor hurting him.' On the following day came another dispatch, announcing Trajan's decease. Hadrian would treat 11 August as his *dies imperii*. The news was at once communicated to the troops, who duly acclaimed him as Imperator. A double donative was awarded – no doubt to all the legions and to the Guard, not just to the Syrian army.[1]

It was not the first time that the eastern legions had raised a general to the throne: nearly fifty years earlier Vespasian owed the power to the armies of Syria, Judaea and Egypt. But that had been a *coup d'état*; and six months had to pass before the Danubian troops that had espoused his cause could capture Rome. In 97, before Trajan's adoption by Nerva was announced, the governor of Syria had probably been tempted to bid for the succession by force; but Trajan's men quickly stifled that threat. The position in August 117 was not as desperate as in 69, to be sure; but it was far more dangerous than in 97. Trajan was dead and Hadrian had long been the obvious heir. But the adoption was, at best, by a dying man and stage-managed by the Empress. Of course Hadrian could call not only on the eastern armies but on the large contingents from Rhine and Danube that were still in the East. But the troops were demoralised and Trajan's death acted as a signal to Rome's enemies in every quarter. The empire was in a state of disarray not seen since the Year of the Four Emperors. It could easily have turned into a catastrophe.[2]

Besides, Hadrian had rivals and enemies, at Rome and elsewhere. A letter from Attianus urged rapid and ruthless action. Three men were named. If the City Prefect, Baebius Macer, seemed likely to resist confirming Hadrian's nomination, he should be killed; likewise two prominent exiles, Laberius Maximus, the disgruntled former marshal, alleged to have aspired to the throne, and Crassus Frugi, who had plotted against Nerva as well as Trajan, both languishing on islands. What Macer could have done is far from clear. But, the *HA* claims, 'there was a widespread belief that Trajan had intended to make Neratius Priscus and not Hadrian his successor – and many of his friends approved – and had actually said to him: "I entrust the provinces to you, should anything happen to me."' There were other stories current: 'that Trajan wanted to die without naming a successor, like Alexander; or that he had planned to write to the Senate inviting it to choose a Princeps for the commonwealth, in the event of his death, supplying names from which the Senate should choose the best man.' Perhaps Attianus thought Macer had actually received such a missive and might proceed on these lines. The remark about Neratius probably went back a long way. He was to become known as a jurist, but he had governed Pannonia at the time of the Dacian wars, when such a statement by Trajan could plausibly have been made. Trajan had even once given the impression that he regarded Servianus, Hadrian's brother-in-law, as a potential successor, according to Dio. 'At a banquet he invited his friends to name ten men capable of sole rule [the Latin phrase was surely *capax imperii*], then, after a short pause, added – "I only need to know nine: one I have already, Servianus".'3

However this may be, Hadrian declined to act against the three that Attianus had named. For one thing, Laberius' son-in-law, Bruttius Praesens, was governing Cilicia – and he was Hadrian's man. But when Crassus, descendant of more than one great Republican house, chose to leave his island without authorisation (so at least it was claimed), a procurator had him killed. As for Baebius Macer, whom Pliny had once favoured with details of his polymath uncle's literary production, nothing more is heard of him. He was clearly replaced as soon as Attianus reached Rome. Macer was himself an historian, who wrote an account of Augustus. Perhaps he went back to writing history, as another senator of his generation was doing at this very time – subtly hinting at parallels with current events: Cornelius Tacitus, at work on his *Annales*.4

Within a few days, perhaps within a few hours, of his acclamation, Hadrian gave the order for the total evacuation of Mesopotamia, Assyria and Greater Armenia. In truth, much of the newly conquered territory had in effect been surrendered by Trajan himself. But as the *HA* reports the action, Hadrian 'abandoned' everything beyond the Euphrates and Tigris. That meant the immediate withdrawal from the three new provinces. Further, by early in the next year at the latest he had arranged the removal of the puppet Parthian king crowned by Trajan at Ctesiphon, Parthamaspates, and had him installed as ruler of Osrhoene. The rest could be left to Chosroes and his rival Vologaeses to fight over. Hadrian was following, so he was to claim, the example of Cato, who pronounced that 'the Macedonians must have their freedom because they cannot be protected'. Hadrian's devotion to early Latin literature was well known: 'He preferred Cato to Cicero, Ennius to Virgil, Caelius [Antipater] to Sallust', the *HA* notes later on. Hadrian must have quoted the old Censor's speech *De Macedonia liberanda*, still extant in late antiquity. It was not a convincing precedent, on any count.5

The second desperately necessary move was also decided at once. Lusius Quietus was removed from his new command in Judaea. He was 'suspected of designs on the throne', says the *HA*. Such aspirations seem preposterous for the Moorish chieftain, in spite of his startling promotion by Trajan: senatorial rank, a consulship, and the mandate to continue, as governor of Judaea, his savage suppression of dissent or revolt among the Jewish people. Quietus was still regarded as a barbarian, and besides must have been an old man now. But Hadrian and he were enemies. The fear that Quietus might lend his support to a rival might well have seemed serious enough in the summer of 117.[6]

The letter of dismissal was presumably carried by Quietus' successor, probably one of the men on the spot with Hadrian in Syria. But there may have been an acting governor. At about this time the procurator Claudius Paternus Clementianus, a man from Raetia, replaced an unnamed legate of Judaea. It might have been Quietus in 117. The disgraced governor was also deprived of his 'private army', the Moorish tribesmen he had led in Rome's wars for some twenty-five years. They were sent back home – and, within weeks this treatment and indignation at it among their fellow-countrymen led to open revolt in Mauretania. In Judaea the reaction was understandably quite the opposite: the fall of the butcher of Babylonian Jewry was to lead at least one Jew to hail Hadrian as a deliverer. Something may even have led to the mistaken belief that they would be allowed to rebuild their Temple.[7]

Who was physically with Hadrian at this moment is hard to establish. The identity of the officers in the army of Syria, for example, is not known. One may conjecture that one of the *tribuni laticlavii* was young Haterius Nepos, whose father had been procurator of Greater Armenia two years before. The younger Haterius was evidently with Hadrian when he returned to Rome the following summer. Another who was to return to Rome with Hadrian was M. Hosidius Geta, perhaps legate of one of the eastern legions in 117. Only one companion at Antioch in August 117 is recorded by name, the sharp-witted Greek intellectual, Valerius Eudaemon: the *HA* calls him *conscius imperii*, an 'accomplice in gaining the throne'. Eudaemon was evidently despatched almost at once to Egypt with the appointment of 'procurator for the administration of Alexandria' (*ad dioecesin Alexandriae*), a relatively junior post but one which would enable him to keep an eye on things there. More important, Eudaemon probably came with a letter of dismissal for the Prefect Rutilius Lupus. The new Prefect was Q. Rammius Martialis, a former commander of the *vigiles* at Rome. He must surely have been in the east with Hadrian, for he was already in office in Egypt before the end of August. Eudaemon, one might conjecture, may have encouraged Hadrian to issue an edict confirming the privileges to philosophers, rhetors, *grammatici*, and doctors granted by Vespasian and Trajan. At any rate, a letter of Antoninus Pius, preserved in the *Digest*, refers to Hadrian's edict as coming 'straight after his accession to power'.[8]

After these urgent measures Hadrian left Antioch 'to view Trajan's remains, which were being conducted by Attianus, Plotina and Matidia.' They were presumably travelling from Selinus towards him. 'When he had intercepted them', the *HA* proceeds, 'he put them on a ship to be transported to Rome.'

With Trajan's ashes, conveyed by the dowager Empress, with Matidia, and with Attianus – Sabina presumably stayed with her husband – went Hadrian's letter to the Senate, 'and it was composed with very great care'. He requested divine honours for Trajan (anything else would have been unthinkable) and asked the Senate's pardon for not submitting to it the question of his accession: his salutation by the soldiers had been over-hasty, to be sure, but the commonwealth could not be left without an emperor.[9]

A curious by-product of Trajan's death has been detected. Not only was Selinus renamed Trajanopolis, it received the status of *ius Italicum*, even though it was not made a *colonia*. Trajan was the first emperor to have died outside Italy. Was it deemed expedient to create the fiction that the place where he expired was in fact equivalent to part of Italy – or was Trajan himself, indeed, supposed to have declared Selinus to have this status? In other words, was it thought important that his last action, the adoption of a successor, should have taken place on 'Italian' soil?[10]

The remains of another person who had just died had been left at Selinus. On 12 August, a few days after his master's death, Trajan's butler, the freedman Phaedimus, expired. He was only twenty-eight years old. Given Trajan's propensities, the servant in charge of the imperial wine cabinet was bound to have been in close contact with his master. And since Trajan – according to Dio – had been convinced that he was being poisoned, people might have wanted to interrogate Phaedimus. Perhaps he committed suicide, out of panic, or just from grief. But Attianus may have eliminated him in case he said too much. Phaedimus' remains would only be interred at Rome more than twelve years later.[11]

By the time the ship was under sail for Italy, Hadrian will have known the dimensions of the crisis. A century later Marius Maximus rose to Tacitean heights (it may be argued), when summarising the simultaneous eruption of revolt and invasion which had flared up all around the frontiers. The *HA* biographer perhaps allowed himself a direct quotation of Maximus' sombre sentences, in a passage which echoes the opening of Tacitus' *Histories*: 'The nations conquered by Trajan were in revolt; the Moors were on the rampage; the Britons could not be kept under Roman sovereignty; Egypt was ravaged by uprisings; finally, Libya and Palestine displayed the spirit of rebellion.' The last three, Egypt, the Cyrenaica and Judaea, were all part of the same business: the Jewish revolt, most drastic in the diaspora, but, as signalised by the appointment of Quietus, breaking out or expected in the homeland too. Marcius Turbo had by now virtually crushed the rebels in Egypt and the Cyrenaica, even if some fighting was still going on. At any rate, Turbo, still based in or near Egypt, with his mixed force from fleet and army, could now be sent to deal with the very different outbreak of trouble further west, in Mauretania.[12]

But Hadrian could not yet return to Rome. There was another threat, more serious than any other: beyond the Danube. Quadratus Bassus, sent there by Trajan from Syria to defend the new territories, the jewel in the imperial crown, 'died on campaign in Dacia.' Whether in action against the enemy – who would

80

have been free Dacians, it may be assumed, as well as the Sarmatians to east and west of Trajan's Dacia – or simply from natural causes, his loss was a heavy blow. The garrison of Dacia and the Danubian provinces was below strength: several legions and numerous auxiliary regiments had been drawn off for the Parthian expedition. Hence 'the armies were sent ahead' from the east to 'Illyricum'. Hadrian would follow as soon as he could safely leave Syria. There were still matters to deal with, not least finding a successor for Quadratus Bassus. Hadrian's choice fell on Avidius Nigrinus – so at least it may be conjectured. Nigrinus, it seems probable, had been in Achaia as imperial legate during Hadrian's stay in Greece before the war, and was probably regarded as a friend.[13]

By late September Hadrian should have learned the Senate's response to his letter: it was effusive and conciliatory. The honours voted for Trajan went beyond his own proposal; and he himself was to hold a triumph and was to be called *Pater Patriae*. These honours for himself Hadrian rejected. Coins had now been issued at Rome, one with Trajan as emperor on the obverse, on the reverse Hadrian, with the name 'Hadrianus Traianus Caesar'; the other showing Hadrian as emperor, 'Traianus Hadrianus', with Trajan's titles 'Optimus Augustus Germanicus Dacicus', and, on the reverse, the legend *adoptio*, with Trajan and Hadrian clasping hands and Hadrian as *Pater Patriae*, along with other titles, and son of the deified Parthicus Traianus. The need to proclaim the legitimacy of the succession is manifest.[14]

Plate 5 Hadrian as Caesar, a unique gold coin from late summer 117
(*BMC* III p. 124)

For the majority of the inhabitants of the empire, who had not yet seen Hadrian, these first coin issues would in any case have conveyed a startling novelty: the new ruler wore a beard. He was the first high-ranking Roman not to be clean-shaven for many centuries. One need not suppose that Hadrian had suddenly thrown his razors away when he was acclaimed Emperor. He might have stopped shaving as a young man, one of the aspects of his behaviour which earned him the nickname *Graeculus*. Or his Greek beard of the traditional kind was a result of his conjectured visit to Epictetus a few years earlier. At all events, within a short time the adult male population of the empire followed suit: beards became the norm for almost a century.[15]

Plate 6 Hadrian's 'adoption' celebrated by the imperial coinage
(*BMC* III Hadrian no. 8)

The official ceremony of deification would have to wait until Hadrian was in
Rome. Meanwhile Trajan could already be called Divus Traianus, as the Senate
had voted. In the Greek east this was in any case a mere technicality: emperors
were regularly treated as divine in their lifetime. Panegyrists were no doubt at
work all over the empire at festivities to hail the new ruler's accession. A specimen
happens to be preserved on papyrus, an extract from a speech delivered at one of
the Egyptian *nome*-capitals, it seems. The orator imagines a divine message:

> I have mounted with Trajan to Heaven in a white-horsed chariot and
> return to you, my people, I who am not unknown to you, the god
> Phoebus, and proclaim to you the new King Hadrian. To him let all things
> be happily subject, both by reason of his virtue and on account of his
> divine father's blessed fortune. It is for us now to make sacrifice of burnt
> offerings, to drink draughts from the fountains, to make merry with oil
> from the gymnasium, all these things furnished for you by the Governor,
> from his loyalty towards the Emperor and from his love towards you.

The author might have been a certain Orion, whose *Panegyric* on Hadrian
was still extant in Byzantine times. At any rate, the Prefect Rammius Martialis
no doubt regarded some use of public funds as desirable in the ravaged
province.[16]

Martialis or his advisers may have had an even better idea. The eastern provinces would no doubt have been particularly impressed by the symbolism of the Phoenix, which featured on Hadrian's early coins. To be sure, the legendary bird was supposed to appear only once every 500 years – and a sighting had been reported in Egypt in the reign of Tiberius, less than a century earlier. Tacitus has a learned digression on the subject in his *Annals* – how the reborn phoenix dutifully transported its parent's ashes to the temple of the Sun. He expresses doubt as to the authenticity of the Tiberian manifestation, but, he solemnly adds, 'there is no dispute that the bird in question is seen in Egypt from time to time.' As it happens, Claudius had produced a phoenix to symbolise and authenticate his new *saeculum* only a few years after. Nobody believed in it. Tacitus may have been gently mocking a recent claim: that the Phoenix had been sighted soon after Hadrian's accession. Be that as it may, the royal bird that died on the fire, to be reborn from the ashes, was a powerful symbol, which Hadrian will not have scorned.[17]

When the moment came to leave Syria for the Balkans, Catilius Severus, after leading his men out of Greater Armenia, joined Hadrian at Antioch and was installed as legate of Syria. There is one other action that Hadrian took in Syria between his accession and his departure for the north: he blocked up the Castalian spring at Daphne with a great mass of stone. The prophetic waters had foretold his rule; he did not want them to do the same for anyone else. An inscription from Rome has been plausibly claimed to register a few stages in Hadrian's journey north-westwards: what survives is an itinerary for the days 13–19 October, from Mopsucrene, 12 miles beyond Tarsus, then northwards over the Taurus into Cappadocia, via Tyana. He was heading for Ancyra in Galatia, which – if he continued to travel at 15–18 miles (25–30 km) a day, as suggested by the itinerary – he probably reached by the end of October. A detachment of the Praetorian Guard and the Horse Guards – the 'Batavians' – must be assumed to have been with him. The bulk of the forces sent back to the west had gone on ahead.[18]

At Ancyra a descendant of the Galatian kings, Latinius Alexander, donated to the city the funds needed for the accommodation of 'the greatest emperor Caesar Traianus Hadrianus Augustus on his visit, and of his sacred armies' – during 'a whole year'. This should mean that some units had arrived in Ancyra well before Trajan's death, probably accompanying Quadratus Bassus on his way to counter the attack on Dacia. The generosity of Alexander was gratefully registered on the base of a statue set up to his daughter Cleopatra.[19]

Hadrian probably stayed for some days at Ancyra, capital of the province Galatia and the nodal point of important routes across Anatolia, to recuperate a little and to deal with incoming dispatches. He was at any rate there long enough to found a 'mystic contest' (*mystikos agon*) for the worship of Dionysus. As was later recorded in a decree of the association of artists who performed, Hadrian himself, as '*neos Dionysos*', was included in the ceremonies jointly with the god. On later visits to the Greek half of the empire he would receive countless honours

– or worship – of this kind, and would be able to stay long enough to relish them. This time desperately urgent business demanded that he press forward.[20]

On 11 November he was already just inside Bithynia, about five days' journey west of Ancyra on the Nicaea road, at Juliopolis, 'a frontier place, with a great deal of traffic passing through it', as the governor of Pontus-Bithynia had written to Trajan a few years before. 'The little town' found this a heavy burden and Pliny had asked Trajan to post a legionary centurion there (Trajan declined). How Juliopolis coped with Hadrian and the army is not known – and there were other visitors as well. There happens to be record of a delegation from the 'Synod of *Neoi* (young men)' of Pergamum, congratulating Hadrian on his succession. Hadrian dictated a rapid reply: '11 November, from Juliopolis. Noting from your letter and through your representative Claudius Cyrus the great joy you have expressed at our succession, I consider this a sign of your excellence.' A copy of the letter was duly engraved in a public place at Pergamum. Hadrian would be greeted by delegations of this kind everywhere he went for the rest of his reign. Pergamum may have been very much in Hadrian's thoughts. It was the home of Quadratus Bassus. At some time during his journey Hadrian decided to signify openly his respect for the great marshal: he ordered that his remains should be conveyed under military escort back to Pergamum, to be interred in a tomb paid for by the imperial fisc. It was a kind of substitute for the public funeral, *funus censorium*, reserved for Rome's greatest sons.[21]

All the while missives must have been arriving from every part of the empire: from Attianus at Rome, from Turbo in Mauretania, but especially from the Danube. The man on the spot, with whom Hadrian was hurrying to confer, was Pompeius Falco, governor of Moesia Inferior. Falco was an experienced general, who had commanded V Macedonica in the first Dacian war and governed both Lycia-Pamphylia and Judaea before becoming consul in the same year as Hadrian, 108. He had been legate of the now massive Lower Moesian province for at least two years, and must have been leading the resistance against the Roxolani and free Dacians together with Quadratus Bassus. Falco can be regarded as a personal friend of Hadrian: for one thing, he was married to Sosia Polla, Senecio's daughter. Polla had been with Falco in his province; she bore him a son in 117 or 118. Another friend (explicitly and repeatedly so described in the *HA*), Platorius Nepos, who had commanded a legion in the Parthian war, had by now become governor of Thrace. This was a province that Hadrian would be staying in for some time. It would be good to have Nepos there.[22]

Hadrian's movements and their timing in the next six months can only be reconstructed in their bare outlines. What is clear is the outcome, which was – in the eyes of many – shocking and demeaning for Rome. Large portions of Trajan's conquests north of the Lower Danube were abandoned: the great plains of Oltenia and Muntenia, the south-eastern flank of the Carpathians and southern Moldavia, which had all been added to Moesia Inferior after the first Dacian war, were restored to the Sarmatian Roxolani. No doubt on the advice of Falco, the order was even given to dismantle the superstructure of the Danube bridge below the Iron Gates, constructed by Trajan's master-architect Apollodorus. Probably it was only an emergency measure, taken because an enemy breakthrough westwards across the River Alutus (Aluta or Olt) or, in the case of the Jazyges, southwards from a point between the legionary base Berzovia and Trajan's Dacian *colonia*, was a real threat. On no account could Hadrian allow an invasion across the Danube.[23]

It is perhaps understandable that he should be accused of surrendering 'Dacia', even by someone who should have known better, the orator Cornelius Fronto, who must have been in his late teens at the time of Hadrian's accession. But so soon after the evacuation of the new eastern provinces, this further withdrawal must have provoked anger, resentment and exaggeration. Hadrian could with some plausibility be alleged to have contemplated giving up Dacia itself. His rivals and enemies now had even better grounds for seeking to overthrow him.[24]

It has been suggested that he wintered at Nicomedia or Byzantium, combining the amenities of the Marmara with the strategic advantages of the imperial highway to the west, the Via Egnatia. Whether he could permit himself the luxury of more than a few weeks in either city is perhaps doubtful, given the urgency of the crisis. Still, one may conjecture that he inaugurated the year 118, as consul for the second time, at the city which became 'the second Rome' two centuries later. His consular colleague, Pedanius Fuscus, the husband of his niece Julia, will surely have held office at Rome. Whether or not Hadrian stayed at Byzantium, at the start of 118 or later, he did at some stage accept honorary office there for two successive years. Three weeks later, on 24 January, was Hadrian's birthday. He was forty-two, exactly the age prescribed by the old *lex annalis* for the tenure of the consulship. There was not much for him to celebrate, although loyal messages no doubt poured in. Perhaps the presence of Platorius Nepos made some kind of party feasible. Whether Sabina was with him is unknown: she had to accompany him on his future travels, even though her relations with Hadrian were doubtless already cold and formal. Hadrian was still receiving – or replying to – messages of congratulation on his accession after the start of the new year: his letters of thanks to Delphi and to little Astypalaea in the Cyclades happen to be preserved. Four days after his birthday, the thirtieth anniversary of Trajan's accession on 28 January was a further occasion for festivities throughout the empire. Many admirers of the great Imperator must have gritted their teeth as they reflected on what his successor was doing.[25]

Hadrian's presence this winter in 'Scythia' can perhaps be inferred from a little ditty the poet Florus sent him a few years later: Hadrian had had to 'endure the Scythian frosts'. The trouble is that 'Scythia' and 'Scythians' were elastic terms – theoretically it could be argued that the poem means Hadrian actually went well beyond the Danube mouths into what is now Ukraine. More likely Florus meant the territory between the Danube and the Black Sea that was later called Scythia Minor. Twenty years earlier Hadrian had spent a few months as tribune of V Macedonica. His old legion was now based at Troesmis, which would not have been a bad place for him to supervise the withdrawal of Roman garrisons – including the most northerly, Piroboridava on the River Hierasus (Sereth), some 60 miles (100 km) to the north-west. At Troesmis, if not at one of the cities of the coast, Tomis or Histria or Callatis, he could have conducted negotiations with the king of the Roxolani. Quite what the status of this people had been under the Trajanic dispensation is not clear. Perhaps they had been allowed an enclave within the Transdanubian part of Moesia Inferior that Hadrian now gave up. The *HA* says that 'the king was complaining at the reduction of his subsidy.'[26]

At all events, peace was concluded. The king became a Roman citizen, taking the names P. Aelius Rasparaganus, and must be assumed to have been granted the status of 'friend of the Roman people'. In return for these concessions and favours Hadrian may have received something from Rasparaganus: a splendid horse. His favourite hunter a few years later was an animal called Borysthenes, an 'Alan', still in youthful prime. It has been suggested plausibly enough that it was bred among the Alani, neighbours and kinsmen of the Roxolani, somewhere near the River Borysthenes (Dnieper), and that Hadrian acquired it at this time. Of course, the horse could equally have been a gift from the Greeks of Tyras (on the estuary of the Dniester) or of Olbia (on the Dnieper), or from the king of the Bosporus (Crimea) – all clients of Rome, who will have confirmed their allegiance at this time.[27]

If peace could have been made with the Roxolani before the winter was over – which is far from certain – matters were not so easily settled with the other branch of the Sarmatians, the Jazyges on the western flank of the Dacian province. Perhaps Hadrian came to Dacia first before he acted, perhaps the reports of what was being done by the governor of that province and by the legate of Pannonia Inferior suggested that something more drastic was needed. At all events, probably as soon as he heard that peace had been restored in Mauretania, he sent for Marcius Turbo. This was a friend he could trust. It is at least attested that before Hadrian left the Danube for Rome, Turbo was made acting governor of both Dacia and Pannonia Inferior. He was not a senator, yet was to command an army of several legions. That there was a sense of outrage in some quarters need not be doubted. Particular resentment would be felt by the senators serving in the two provinces – the two governors who lost their posts to a hard-bitten former centurion, and the legionary legates.[28]

It has been conjectured above that the man who had taken over Dacia when Quadratus Bassus died was Avidius Nigrinus. His tenure of the office is known only from an undated dedication made at the legionary base Apulum in northern Dacia by M. Calventius Viator, centurion of IV Flavia and training officer (*exercitator*) of Nigrinus' horse guards (*equites singulares*). Nigrinus is unlikely to have governed Dacia until several years after his consulship, which was in 110, and could not have held the office later that 118 – for the good reason that he did not survive that year.

The *HA* reports that Nigrinus conspired to kill Hadrian, that Lusius Quietus and 'many others' were his accomplices, and that Hadrian escaped their attempt on his life while he was sacrificing. Cassius Dio's version, which survives only in the epitome by John Xiphilinus, is slightly different. That he places the (alleged) assassination plot during a hunt instead of 'while Hadrian was sacrificing' is not a real discrepancy: hunts would begin and end with a sacrifice. Unlike the *HA*, which states it as a fact that 'Hadrian escaped Nigrinus' ambush', Dio treats the whole affair as a frame-up. But even if Nigrinus and his 'accomplices' were framed, there must have been an occasion in the early part of 118 when he could have been in a position to strike Hadrian down. It is surely plausible that Hadrian did indeed go hunting with Nigrinus and that something happened which – perhaps only later – could be construed as an abortive assassination attempt. The allegation against him would otherwise have been too absurd to invent. Nigrinus must have been with Hadrian. As to the whereabouts of Lusius Quietus at this time, nothing is known. It is hardly likely that Hadrian had obliged him to remain with the imperial entourage. His alleged complicity need only mean that Nigrinus was claimed to have been in touch with him.[29]

If Nigrinus plotted – or could plausibly be alleged to have plotted – to kill Hadrian, his real motives, and those of his supposed fellow-conspirators, are not far to seek: deep resentment at the abandonment of Trajan's conquests. In Nigrinus' own case, the *HA*, after stating that 'he had prepared an ambush against Hadrian as he was sacrificing, Lusius being his accomplice, and many others', adds a curious comment, '*even though Hadrian had intended him as his own successor.*' That Hadrian within a few months of his accession seriously planned to make Nigrinus his heir seems hardly credible. Could the *HA* biographer have misunderstood his source? It is easy to explain why he could have taken 'successor' in the wrong sense: eighteen years later Nigrinus' step-son Ceionius Commodus would become Hadrian's adopted son and heir. With a simple change in the Latin word order – as was long ago suggested – a quite different meaning merges: Nigrinus plotted against Hadrian '*because* Hadrian had appointed a successor *for him* as *well*', in other words, as well as for Lusius. Both men, in other words, were alleged to have acted purely out of wounded pride.[30]

On this interpretation, Nigrinus' attempt on Hadrian's life was made immediately following his dismissal, after only a few months in office as legate on Dacia, and his replacement by Marcius Turbo. He and Lusius Quietus would have been confident of support from influential quarters. Be this as it may, Nigrinus was allowed to go home, to Faventia (Faenza) in northern Italy. But there he was killed; Quietus was put to death 'on a journey'; and two other leading men were also struck down, Cornelius Palma at the Campanian resort of Baiae, Publilius Celsus at Tarracina in Latium. Both had enjoyed great distinction under Trajan, with second consulships and other honours. But – so it was claimed – they were known as old enemies of Hadrian, who had been out of favour for several years, indeed under suspicion of planning to seize power. Their fall from grace in the closing stages of the Parthian war had supposedly given Hadrian the signal that his own adoption was a matter of course.[31]

The order to execute the four ex-consuls for treason was given by the Senate and carried out by Attianus. Hadrian was to assert that he had not wanted them to die, and he put the blame on Attianus. This wretched affair cast a blight over Hadrian's relations with the Senate. The account in the *HA* reflects the official version, designed to show that all four acted from unworthy personal motives. It may be more plausible to postulate that they had all opposed Hadrian's change of policy. But whether there was a 'conspiracy' in which these four men – not to mention the 'many others' of which the *HA* speaks – were participants may be doubted.[32]

Few probably mourned Lusius Quietus; and, in spite of his undoubted distinction, virtually nothing is known of Publilius Celsus. But Palma had certainly been one of Trajan's closest associates: consul for the first time, as *ordinarius* indeed, in 99, with Sosius Senecio as colleague, he must above been an especial favourite, to whom Trajan owed something. He had earned further esteem as governor of Syria, when he carried through the bloodless annexation of Arabia.

Less is recorded about Nigrinus' career, but something of the man, earnest and conscientious, is conveyed in Pliny's *Letters*. As tribune of the plebs in 105 he had read out in the Senate 'an eloquent and important statement', denouncing the – illegal – acceptance of fees by advocates, and asked that Trajan should remedy the evil. He was again active in 106, as prosecution counsel against a proconsul of Bithynia whom Pliny was defending. Pliny called a speech of his 'concise, impressive, well-phrased'. Besides this, Nigrinus' father and uncle Quietus were close friends of Plutarch. Both had governed Achaia, where Nigrinus was also to serve, and it was to them that Plutarch dedicated his treatise *On Brotherly Love*. Hadrian ought to have known 'perhaps the most admired of Plutarch's philosophical writings', addressed to Quietus, *On the Delays of Divine Vengeance*. Quietus had also been a close friend of the great Stoic senator Thrasea, Nero's victim.[33]

Some people may have reflected on these matters when Quietus' nephew and his three 'fellow-conspirators' were condemned to death by the Senate, not least those who had to vote for the motion. Cornelius Tacitus might have been there, although his age (he was now about 60) could have exempted him from attendance. It is possible to detect veiled allusions to this affair in his *Annales*. At the beginning, there are curious remarks on the four alleged rivals of Tiberius and their extinction. In the last book, when he has to recount the fate of Thrasea and others, Tacitus' tone becomes weary. Even if he were writing of men who died for the fatherland in foreign wars, he would be sickened and his readers would avert their gaze from 'deaths of fellow-citizens, honourable perhaps, but depressing in their cumulation'. As it is, 'servile passivity and so much blood shed at home weary the spirit and cramp it with sorrow. I ask no excuse from those who know about these matters – except that I do not hate those who perished so tamely.'[34]

A minor figure has been supposed to have done well out of this sad business: Calventius Viator, the training-officer of Nigrinus' guards, was later to become the acting commander of Hadrian's own Horse Guards. It has been argued that he 'was given the position because he had served the Emperor well with respect to his personal safety, obviously by betraying Nigrinus' plot.' The notion is ingenious – but Viator is first record in charge of the *equites singulares Augusti* ten years later. All that can really be said is that Hadrian clearly did not hold it against him that he had once served Avidius Nigrinus. For that matter, Nigrinus' cousin, the younger Quietus, was allowed to pursue his career and a few years later became proconsul of Asia.[35]

By the spring Hadrian was in Pannonia, and his Horse Guards, the 'Batavians', were with him. Dio reports the impact made by these men: 'so beautifully trained were his troops that the cavalry of the "Batavians", as they were called, swam across the Danube fully armed. Seeing this, the barbarians were terrified of the Romans, and, turning to their own affairs, they used Hadrian as arbitrator in their disputes.' The tombstone of one of the troopers who swam the river boasted of his feat: 'I am the man once well known on Pannonian shores, brave and foremost among a thousand Batavian men: with Hadrian as my judge I was able to swim the vast waters of the deep Danube fully armed.' He added another achievement: 'from my bow I shot an arrow, while it hung in the air and was falling I hit and split it with another – neither Roman nor barbarian, no soldier with a spear, no Parthian with a bow, could ever outdo me.'[36]

The Danube crops up again in a quite different anecdote about Hadrian's stay in Pannonia at this time. As always, delegations sought the Emperor out, wherever he might be. A young man from an ancient and powerful Athenian family had to speak before Hadrian, Herodes Atticus. Hadrian must have met young Herodes at Athens six years earlier. Herodes' father Atticus was by a long way the most powerful and influential man in that city and one of the richest men in the empire, in spite of the confiscation of some of the family fortune. Herodes was now barely seventeen years old and the occasion was too much for him: he broke down in the middle of his speech. 'In his humiliation he rushed to the River Danube as though he was going to throw himself in. So overwhelming was his ambition to become a famous orator that he treated the penalty of failure as death.' Hadrian was no doubt merely amused by the episode: both Herodes and his father Atticus would enjoy imperial favour within a few years.[37]

It may be assumed that while he was in Pannonia Hadrian conferred with the governor of the Upper province, Minicius Natalis, an experienced and senior man – he had been consul in 106 and in Pannonia since before the start of the Parthian war. Furthermore, Natalis came from Barcino and had probably been a protégé of Licinius Sura. He may be regarded as a friend and supporter of the new Emperor.[38] Hadrian remained in the Danube lands throughout the spring and into the early summer of 118. Much must have remained to be done.

The display of their prowess by the Horse Guards which so impressed 'the barbarians' and induced them to make Hadrian the arbitrator in their disputes may have been a show of strength on the eve of his departure for Rome. Whether the war against the Jazyges of the Hungarian plain was already over is not certain. Hadrian perhaps campaigned in person against this people – as he may have done twenty years earlier when governing Pannonia Inferior. It may have been at this time, the only moment in his reign when he is known for certain to have been in Pannonia, that he founded a *colonia* in the Lower province, at Mursa (Osijek). It was the last *colonia* to be established in the Danubian lands as a new city – later creations in the region were promoted *municipia*. No details are known about Mursa, even whether it was a settlement for legionary veterans of the traditional type.[39]

It may also have been the impressions gained during this stay that made Hadrian decide to confer charters on a string of other communities, making them *municipia*. Three were major centres already, the seats of the governors of Upper and Lower Pannonia and of Upper Moesia: Carnuntum, Aquincum and Viminacium. All three were separate and distinct communities from the *canabae* or civil settlements that nestled close to the legionary fortresses. If the decision was taken in principle now, it was not implemented at once – Aquincum was still just a *vicus* four years later. In addition, a number of communities in the interior of Pannonia became *municipia* under Hadrian: Bassiana and Cibalae in the south of the Lower province, between the rivers Save and Danube; in Pannonia Superior Mogentiana, Municipium Iasorum, Salla and perhaps Halicanum and Mursella. These were all, unlike the first three, essentially native *civitas* capitals. This was, of course, the territory that Hadrian, who had governed Lower Pannonia ten years earlier, knew best of all the provinces in the Latin west. Even so, the impetus thus given to 'romanisation' is very striking. A single community in the interior of Upper Moesia, Ulpianum, also received municipal status. It was clearly connected to the lead-silver mines (*metalla Ulpiana*) opened up under Trajan.[40]

The troubles elsewhere in the empire had not all been settled. In Britain the rebellion – presumably in the far north of the province – would cost many Roman lives. Hadrian decided to send Falco there as governor. An inscription at Tomis on the Black Sea coast commemorates his appointment. He presumably went straight from Moesia Inferior, along the Danube, where he could confer with Hadrian before proceeding via the Germanies to his new command.[41]

It is probable enough that Falco, in collaboration with Marcius Turbo, had begun the new settlement of the Transdanubian territories. The remaining part of Moesia Inferior north of the river now became a separate province and was labelled 'Dacia Inferior'. It had no legion and was assigned to an equestrian procurator as governor. Trajan's Dacia at first received the name Dacia Superior, but within a short time, perhaps only after a few months, it was to be sub-divided: the heart of the province, in Transylvania, was designated Dacia Superior, with its capital at the *colonia Ulpia* (Sarmizegethusa) and a single legion, XIII Gemina, at Apulum. The legate of the legion would in future be the governor, on the model of Pannonia Inferior and a few other provinces. The northernmost part, however, was detached, and, like 'Dacia Inferior', was assigned to a procurator-governor, under the name 'Dacia Porolissensis' (from the base of Porolissum). There had only been a single chartered town in Trajan's Dacia, the *colonia Ulpia*, now in the Upper province. Napoca in Porolissensis and Drobeta in the southern part of Dacia Superior certainly acquired the status of *municipium* under Hadrian. Malva, formerly in Moesia, now in Dacia Inferior, was perhaps already a *colonia*.[42]

New governors were, for the time being, not installed in the newly demarcated provinces. The *HA* preserves, in a confused form, a statement – repeated with a slight variation in the space of a few lines – about Hadrian's arrangement. In the first version, 'he put Marcius Turbo – after Mauretania – temporarily in charge of Pannonia and Dacia, adorned with the insignia of the Prefecture.' In the second version Hadrian 'came to Rome, having entrusted Dacia to Turbo, adorned with the title of the Egyptian prefecture, so that he should have more authority.' Something has been garbled in the *HA* biographer's hasty excerpting of Marius Maximus' *Vita Hadriani*. Turbo had been in Egypt shortly before, but as commander of a task-force (perhaps continuing to hold the rank of admiral of the Misenum fleet), not as Prefect of that province. But he was to become Guard Prefect: Hadrian dismissed Attianus and installed Turbo in his stead. It may well be that this appointment was made while Hadrian was still on the Danube front. He would have already been informed of the outrage that followed the killing of the four consulars. He needed to shift the blame onto Attianus, who had carried out the deed.[43] The *HA* puts Hadrian's move a little later, after he was back at Rome:

> Since he could not tolerate any longer the power of Attianus, his Prefect and former *tutor*, he tried to kill him – but was deterred, because he was already under pressure from the hostility aroused by the killing of the four consulars – of course, he was trying to shift the responsibility for the decision for their deaths onto Attianus' shoulders.

At first Attianus refused to resign. He was 'leaned on' – and Turbo replaced him.[44]

An altar set up in one of the cities in Moesia Inferior, somewhere on the Black Sea coast, by a freedman of Turbo, ought to mean that Turbo himself was there – furthermore, the dedicator, Capito, gives his patron the title 'Prefect of the Guard'. This implies that Turbo had already been named Guard Prefect before he left the Danube area – and that he was active well beyond the provinces with which, according to the *HA*, he was explicitly entrusted by Hadrian. However this may be, a military *diploma* confirms that he was the commanding general in both Pannonia Inferior and Dacia Porolissensis, under whom men from one *ala* in the former province and two *alae* and a cohort in the latter were serving when they received the privileges of discharge. Unfortunately the dating of

Turbo's mission is not clarified by the document: the men in these units were forgotten about for several years – the *constitutio* was not issued until 10 August 123, long after Turbo had gone back to Rome.[45]

Turbo might conceivably have gone to Moesia Inferior to keep an eye on the province until a successor arrived for Pompeius Falco. The man chosen for this task – a delicate one, given that a large portion of Moesia Inferior had just been abandoned to the Roxolani or assigned to the newly created Dacia Inferior – was, it seems clear, a favourite of Hadrian, Ummidius Quadratus. He was serving as suffect consul in May of 118, as one of a series of replacements for Pedanius Fuscus to have the honour of being Hadrian's colleague. If Quadratus was in Rome at all as consul, the odds are that he completed his term of office in *absentia*. This earnest young aristocrat – who had been, like Fuscus, praised and cherished by Pliny – was also, it has been conjectured, a son-in-law of Annius Verus, Hadrian's principal ally in the Senate and already City Prefect.[46]

In June, it seems, Hadrian finally left for Rome, probably overland, to Emona (Ljubljana), then across the Julian Alps, along the coast to Ariminum (Rimini) and down the Via Flaminia. He may have had a reminder of the Jazyges, against whom he had – for the second time – had to fight. Twenty years later a Jazygian huntsman was with him, a man named Mastor. 'He had been a prisoner of war and had been employed by Hadrian as a huntsman because of his strength and daring', Dio records. Mastor had doubtless seen service already. That Hadrian went hunting, for boar, in Pannonia, mounted on Borysthenes, was registered by Hadrian himself four years later, when he composed his horse's epitaph in Gaul.[47]

9

RETURN TO ROME

For many months the mint at Rome had been dutifully anticipating Hadrian's return with coins bearing the legend *Fort(una) Red(ux)*. By mid-June at the latest he must have been in Italy. A delegation from the Senate is likely enough to have gone some way north to greet him. It was 9 July when he entered the city. The Arval Brethren promptly foregathered to sacrifice, as they did on every solemn state occasion, as well as for their own peculiar worship of the Dea Dia – they had already had seven sessions this year. Hadrian himself had, as was normal, been co-opted into the brotherhood when he became Emperor. He would have had to go to the Capitol in any case himself, to give thanks to Jupiter – as Trajan had done in 99. Even so, it seems somewhat astonishing that he chose to attend in person, as one of the *fratres*, while the *magister* Trebicius Decianus sacrificed seven beasts in the name of the college, one each to Jupiter, Juno, Minerva, Salus Publica, Mars the Avenger, Victoria and Vesta, in thanksgiving for Hadrian's 'auspicious advent'.[1]

No source gives a description of his *adventus* – the coins issued shortly afterwards have only a symbolic depiction. Roma, sitting on a cuirass, holds a sceptre in her left hand and extends her other hand to the Emperor standing before her. No doubt the magistrates, senators, equestrians, suitably garlanded and festive – and Sulpicius Similis with the Guard cohorts that had stayed in Rome – were on hand to greet the Princeps as he and his party and escorting soldiers approached the city.[2]

There were newly installed consuls, in office from 1 July. Hadrian and his latest colleague Ummidius Quadratus had laid down the *fasces* at the end of June, Quadratus as well as Hadrian probably in *absentia* – he is likely to have left Rome some time earlier, to replace Pompeius Falco in Moesia Inferior. One of the new pair of consuls, Sabinius Barbarus, was probably not there either, but in Numidia (he had become legate of III Augusta the previous year). The other suffect consul, L. Pomponius Bassus, a well-connected aristocrat, presumably did the honours. The City Prefect would also be there, Annius Verus, and, surely, the imperial ladies, the Dowager, Plotina, and the junior Augusta, Matidia, the mother-in-law that Hadrian so much cherished. Hadrian's sister Paulina should have been present, and her now elderly husband Servianus was probably obliged

Plate 7 Hadrian's return to Rome in 118: ADVENTVS AVG.
(*BMC* III Hadrian no. 1120)

to put in an appearance. Servianus is unlikely to have been enthusiastic about Hadrian's accession to power. Still, his daughter Julia Paulina was Hadrian's niece, his son-in-law Fuscus, consul with Hadrian earlier in this year, was the heir apparent – and as Emperor Hadrian treated Servianus with studied deference.[3]

Nineteen years before the city had seen Trajan's first *adventus* as Emperor, 'so long awaited and longed for', as Pliny lovingly described it: the streets packed, cheers and rejoicing everywhere, delight as he embraced the senators, singled out the leading knights to greet them by name, moved among the people, letting himself be jostled by the crowd. Hadrian was to cultivate *civilitas*: 'He did every-thing in the style of a private citizen', the *HA* says of his first stay at Rome, and, in general comment on his demeanour in a later passage, reports that 'in conversation even with people of the humblest class he acted very much as an ordinary citizen, denouncing those who – as if they would preserve the Princeps' high eminence – tried to begrudge him this pleasure in human nature.' The circumstances in 118 were very different. All the same, it was in Hadrian's nature, as well as in his own interest, to comport himself as a *civilis princeps*.[4]

The plebs would be in attendance in large numbers, there is no question. To be sure, largess had already been distributed in Hadrian's absence, three gold pieces a head. But further bounty would be hoped for, and it was deemed expedient: the public mood was still very ugly after the killing of the four consulars. Tacitus, in the *Annals* that he was then composing, called the murder of Agrippa Postumus 'the *first* crime of the new principate' – of Tiberius. He was surely thinking of Hadrian when he wrote these words – and was doubtless not alone in fearing that more and worse might follow. If Hadrian did not sense it from the demeanour of Senate and People, Verus and Similis and the Augustae no doubt made clear to him what the situation was. 'To dispel the rumours about himself he gave the people a double *congiarium*, in person (*praesens*)', reports the *HA*. In other words, this time it was six *aurei* a head. A coin issue from the summer shows Hadrian on a platform, seated in his chair of state, while an official distributes money: *liberalitas Aug.*, imperial generosity – rather than *congiarium*, merely largess – was proclaimed by the coin legend.[5]

Hadrian would at any rate not emulate Tiberius' tight-fistedness. This was only the first in a series of measures to buy back the good will dissipated by the death of Nigrinus and the others. Money alone would not be enough to win round the Senate. Hence perhaps his attendance at the Arvals' rituals within hours of his arrival, although the Brethren were mostly far from being distinguished or influential. Nor were they numerous – and in any case there were two vacancies to fill. As it happens, the records of the Arval Brethren show that letters from Trajan recommending persons to fill gaps in the college were only now delivered. The co-options were dealt with during the next few weeks. Hosidius Geta and the younger Haterius Nepos, the two new Brethren, had probably been in the east and on Hadrian's staff on the long journey back to Rome.[6]

Hadrian had to face the House. It is likely enough that the consul Bassus summoned a meeting for dawn on the next day, 10 July, at any rate within a short time of the *adventus*. It had, of course, been the Senate itself that had ordered the executions. That no doubt made matters worse. Twenty-five years before, as Tacitus had bitterly recalled, 'it was *our* hands that led Helvidius to prison, *we* were shamed by the sight of Mauricus and Rusticus, Senecio's innocent blood was poured out on *us*' – us senators, who had had to vote the death penalty for Domitian's victims.[7]

Hadrian was to assert in his autobiography that the four had been killed against his will; and he put the blame on Attianus. According to Dio, Hadrian 'was so sensitive about what was being rumoured that he spoke in his own defence and declared on oath that he had not ordered their deaths.' This must be a version of Hadrian's statement to the Senate in July 118. The *HA* has a slight variation: 'before the Senate he made excuses for what had been done and swore an oath that he would never punish a senator except in accordance with a vote of the Senate.' It is perfectly plausible that he swore twice, first that he had *not* ordered the four to be killed, second that he would not punish any senator without the Senate's vote. This latter oath – first firmly attested for Nerva in 96 – had already become traditional. But it cannot have had more than token significance. Even had he already sworn it straight after becoming Emperor, the previous August, it would not have prevented the executions: the Senate had ordered them.[8]

As for Attianus, who had forced the senators to impose the death penalty, he had been dismissed, but hardly disgraced. Hadrian made him a senator, with consular rank, and told him that there was no greater honour he could bestow. The old man is unlikely to have attended the Senate after his ennoblement. He probably sulked on one of his estates, at Praeneste, or on Elba, if not back in Baetica. Attianus already had a successor. But Turbo was still with the Danube armies. The other Prefect, Similis, was old too, and weary, perhaps uneasy at the thought of serving Hadrian. He submitted his resignation, which was not at once accepted. Hadrian was obviously reluctant to lose him.[9]

Similis, like Turbo, had risen from the centurionate. His successor was of quite different mould, the cultivated Septicius Clarus, the friend of Pliny to whom the nine books of *Letters* had been dedicated. As Pliny had written, Septicius had often urged him to collect and publish these pieces. Nothing whatever is known about Septicius' previous career. He had no doubt seen military service as an equestrian officer in his youth, and must have held several appointments of high rank. It would be no surprise if he turned out to have been imperial Secretary, *ab epistulis*. However this may be, a new holder of that post would shortly take office, promoted from the directorship of the imperial libraries. It was another, younger, friend of Pliny, Suetonius Tranquillus, who was already enjoying a reputation as a scholar. His *Lives of Famous Men* had been published at least ten years earlier and he no doubt owed his first two appointments, as *a studiis* and *a bibliothecis*, to the reputation the work had brought him. Hadrian presumably thought that Suetonius and Septicius would be congenial as well as useful members of his team. Suetonius was perhaps already launched on a new literary work, *Lives of the Caesars* – competition for Tacitus' *Annales*. But the *Caesars* would begin with the Dictator and Augustus, not covered by Tacitus. Suetonius would dedicate the first *Lives* to Septicius Clarus. He also took pains to win the Emperor's favour. A scholarly aside early in the *Life* of Augustus, to demonstrate that the future Emperor had had the additional name 'Thurinus' as a boy, quotes as evidence a tiny bronze bust (*imaguncula*) of the boy Octavius, with a rusty inscription in iron letters. 'It was once in my possession', he adds, 'but I have presented it to the Princeps, who has placed it among the household gods (*Lares*) in his bedroom.'[10]

This is one of many signs of Hadrian's pronounced devotion to Augustus. When the Arval Brethren received a written communication from Hadrian in February 118, 'the tablets were opened, sealed with the *signum* impressed by a head of Augustus.' In other words, Hadrian had a portrait of the first Princeps on his signet-ring. It is not fanciful to detect here and there, in the *Divus Augustus*, a subtle attempt to justify Hadrian's renunciation of expansion. Indeed, Suetonius credits Augustus with a purely pacific policy, of a suspiciously Hadrianic character. To be sure, at the end of his reign Augustus was obliged to renounce expansion. But he had practised it for several decades first.[11] Hadrian may have been glad enough to receive this literary support. He certainly had to explain publicly what he had done. The abandonment of 'the many provinces acquired by Trajan' had not been well received. No doubt this remark refers to the territories beyond the Lower Danube as well as to Armenia and Mesopotamia. At any rate, Hadrian's attempt at justification only made matters worse. It may have been now that he quoted the Elder Cato's speech on what to do about Macedonia: that may have been irritating enough for some of his audience. But the *HA* comments here that because 'he pretended that all the measures which he had realised were unpopular had been taken in accordance with secret instructions from Trajan, the reaction was even more bitter.'[12]

Characteristically, the *HA* lumps together with this important policy change a minor action affecting Rome itself, that was also badly received: the demolition of a theatre erected by Trajan on the Campus Martius – this too was justified by appeal to Trajan's orders. In fact, Hadrian had ambitious building plans of his own, not least for the Campus Martius. The plebs, whose favour he was apparently forfeiting, would soon benefit from a construction programme that would rival even Trajan's. Besides, there were more immediate ways to win over the people of Rome. An action mentioned by no literary source may be inferred from coins of 118 and 119: a supplementary corn distribution.[13] But a whole series of measures was presently launched which was designed to conciliate all sectors of society. Hadrian had already in the previous autumn 'waived for Italy the crown gold [the traditional 'voluntary' contribution offered to a new emperor] and reduced the sums paid by the provinces – at the same time seeking to court popularity by a carefully worded exposition of the problems of the public treasury.' Now that he was face to face with public opinion in the capital, he decided that large outlays were essential, whatever the state of the imperial finances.[14]

Marius Maximus, the main source of the *HA*, must have supplied copious detail, and much of it seems to be reproduced in the *vita Hadriani*. The first measure – taken 'immediately' – was presumably a response to what Hadrian had probably noticed again and again during his eight months' journey across a dozen provinces and Italy itself. Requisitioning of transport and accommodation for those travelling on official business placed an intolerable burden on local communities. 'He organised a transport service (*cursus*) funded by the *fiscus*, so that the magistrates should not be weighed down by this charge.' It was not a new problem. The *cursus publicus* instituted by Augustus had regularly created difficulties – and Hadrian's solution was probably little more than window-dressing. For the moment it would alleviate concern.[15]

Much more important – and effective – was a sweeping amnesty for tax arrears. 'Neglecting nothing in his effort to win popularity, he remitted to private debtors in the city and in Italy an immense sum of money which was owed to the *fiscus* and did the same for huge arrears from the provinces too. To reinforce confidence, the tax documents (*syngrafi*) were publicly burned in Trajan's Forum.' Such is the *vita*'s version, confirmed and amplified by other sources. Dio too reports the measure, adding that the period covered was fifteen years, that is the years 104–18 inclusive. The response was extremely favourable.

At Rome Senate and People jointly erected a monument in the place where the ceremonial burning had taken place. On the base Hadrian was honoured as 'the first of all *principes* and the only one who, by remitting nine hundred million sesterces owed to the *fiscus*, provided security not merely for his present citizens but also for their descendants by this generosity.' The coins would in due course celebrate the act again: 'nine million HS of outstanding debts cancelled' ran the legend, and a lictor is shown setting fire to a pile of tax-records, watched by three gratified taxpayers. A fine relief has even survived, showing a group of soldiers carrying the records past a portico. It was perhaps part of the monument in Trajan's Forum from which the inscription also came. The effusive gratitude expressed in that dedication was perfectly appropriate. An analysis of economic activity in the second century has concluded that Hadrian's measure provided a needed stimulus, with beneficial consequences over many years. People were encouraged to spend, and they did.[16]

Further announcements followed – it may well be that Marius Maximus had access to a collection of speeches by Hadrian, before the Senate and indeed before the People. But several of these measures could have been made known on a single occasion. The property of condemned persons was to be assigned, not to the 'privy purse' (*fiscus privatus*), but to the public treasury (*aerarium publicum*). It may be that the *vita* or its source reproduced the name of the former department

Plate 8 The burning of the tax debt tablets
(relief from Rome now at Chatsworth House, Derbyshire)

98

anachronistically, but the sense is clear enough, and the intention. It was an answer to any who might have been muttering that the palace might still profit from the four consulars, even if Hadrian denied responsibility for their deaths. Another measure directly benefited a good many individual senators: those whose property rating had, through no fault of their own, fallen below the necessary minimum to maintain their membership, received a suitable subsidy, in accordance with the number of their children – some of them enjoyed this support for the rest of their lives, the *vita* reported. This would win gratitude from 'backbenchers'. Funds were also made available to office-holders – not merely to his friends, to help defray their expenses: the reference is to the games which magistrates of the Roman People were obliged to mount, a costly obligation. (Hadrian's own *ludi praetorii*, eleven years earlier, had been paid for by Trajan.) A number of women were also 'assisted with expenses to keep up their position', widows or daughters of distinguished senators, perhaps.[17]

A measure to reinforce the child-support scheme created by Trajan, the *alimenta*, was a subtle way to honour his adoptive father's memory and reinforce his own position in Italy (which alone benefited). He raised the age-limit for payments to 14 for girls (the age of marriage) and 18 for boys. The coins duly put the message across: Hadrian is shown seated on the *sella curulis* extending his right arm towards Italia, who stands before him, one child on her left arm, another beside her. Instead of a direct mention of the *alimenta*, the legend proclaims 'liberty restored', echoing Pliny's welcome for the original programme – 'It is a great thing indeed to have children in the hope of receiving *alimenta* and *congiaria*, a greater thing when there is hope of liberty and security.'[18]

The financial benefits of Hadrian's inaugural programme were indeed thoroughly emphasised by the coinage. *Securitas Augusti* recalls the inscription of thanks for the tax remission, which would make this and future generations *securos*. In the next two years, by then perhaps confident that the policy was already bearing fruit, Hadrian could let himself be called restorer (*restitutor*) and even 'enricher' (*locupletator*) of the world.[19]

A triumph for the Parthian victories had been offered to Hadrian in the autumn and, very properly, refused; and he himself had proposed Trajan's deification. Now that Hadrian was back the deification could be ceremonially carried through. No details are recorded, except that the ashes of the dead Imperator were deposited in the base of his great Column, an unusual distinction, and contrary to Roman practice. The Tomb of Augustus on the Campus Martius was now full anyway (room had been found there for Nerva's remains). As for the triumph, the decision was taken – it seems somewhat bizarre – to hold a posthumous one for Trajan himself (his third). Senate and army paraded along the triumphal way with a statue of the deified conqueror. Was this supposed to assuage the bitterness engendered by the surrender of Trajan's conquests? In all truth, the Parthian expedition had turned into a catastrophe well before Trajan expired. All the same, games were held – and were to be repeated annually, the *ludi Parthici*, with one of the praetors regularly assigned to preside. It may have been during the ceremonies of summer 118 that 'in honour of Trajan he ordered that balsam and saffron should flow over the steps of the theatre.' The decision was certainly now implemented to erect a temple to the deified Trajan. It may also only now have been decided – by Hadrian himself – to decorate the Column with a continuous frieze celebrating the Dacian wars.[20]

Other 'games in the circus were voted' – the Senate may, perhaps, have proposed thus to celebrate the first anniversary of his accession on 11 August. But Hadrian 'spurned' the offer, says the *HA*. He made an exception, however, for his forty-third birthday, on 24 January 119. A gladiatorial show was put on which lasted for six successive days, with a thousand wild beasts being slaughtered. Dio adds the detail that one hundred lions and one hundred lionesses were among them, an expensive business; but Hadrian was aware what the people needed. *Panem et circenses*, bread and games, that is all that the once sovereign Roman People cared about, as a contemporary satirist – Juvenal – would shortly comment. Corn had been distributed already, now came the games. Juvenal himself affected to be indifferent to the excitements of the *ludi*: 'let the young men watch', he would rather soak his wrinkled skin in the spring sunshine at home.[21]

As for Hadrian, the *HA* asserts, in a summary of his conduct as Emperor, that 'he often watched the gladiators.' Dio has an extended anecdote on this topic. When the crowd was baying loudly at a gladiatorial contest, the Emperor ordered a herald to reject their demand with the cry for 'Silence'. That had been Domitian's way, as the herald and the crowd will have known. The tactful herald simply raised his hand without uttering the word and the shouting ceased. 'His wish', responded the herald. Hadrian was grateful to the man, not angry. To have been perceived as a new Domitian would have been a serious setback.[22]

A man who had served in the east, as procurator of the short-lived province of Greater Armenia, the elder Haterius Nepos, had recently become procurator of the *ludus magnus*, in charge of training gladiators for imperial occasions. The startling rise of Haterius Nepos offers an insight into Hadrian's situation at this time: he had to rely on a few trusted men. Haterius, although mentioned in no written source, was certainly one of them – and his son of the same name, already launched on a senatorial career, enjoyed Hadrian's favour. By August of 119 the elder Haterius had become Prefect of Egypt – yet his career inscription from his home town, Umbrian Fulginiae, lists no fewer than five posts between his service in Armenia Maior, which cannot have begun before 114, and the Egyptian prefecture. He might have come back to Rome from Armenia to take charge of the gladiators before the end of the Parthian war, and at the latest in the previous autumn. But four further posts are listed between the *ludus magnus* and Egypt. Several of them must have been held simultaneously, for example 'the imperial inheritances' (*hereditates*) and the posts *a censibus* and *a libellis*. Even so, Haterius cannot have devoted more than a few months to these duties – important as they were, particularly the *libelli*, petitions to the Emperor, of which there will have been a great flood at the start of the reign. Before going to Egypt Haterius had also served as Prefect of the *vigiles*, in charge of the capital's security at night and of fire prevention. Until Marcius Turbo returned, it may be guessed, Haterius Nepos was there to use a strong hand, if it was needed.[23]

There is not much more that can be gleaned about the holders of posts at Rome in 118–19: the other new Guard Prefect, Septicius Clarus, and the *ab epistulis* Suetonius, have already been mentioned. As for the major army commands, the particularly sensitive areas were in safe hands. Catilius Severus still held Syria, Bruttius Praesens was in Cappadocia, Ummidius Quadratus had just taken over Moesia Inferior. Further, Minicius Natalis may have stayed on in Pannonia Superior for some months, although he had been there for over five years. But Turbo's special command in Dacia and Pannonia Inferior is likely to have terminated at the latest early in 119. Turbo and Natalis may have both recommended the man who took over the major part of Trajan's Dacia, now redesignated Dacia Superior. A *novus homo* from the *colonia* of Aequum in Turbo's home province Dalmatia, Sex. Julius Severus, got the job of legate, commanding the single legion left in Dacia, XIII Gemina, as well as being governor, on the model of Pannonia Inferior. That province probably went to L. Cornelius Latinianus, although his presence there is not exactly dated. Julius Severus is first attested in Dacia on 20 June 120 – and would stay there a long time; but he had probably already taken up the post in 119. He had been commanding the legion XIV Gemina in Upper Pannonia. Of course, he may not have needed to be pushed forward by Natalis, his chief, or by Turbo. When Hadrian was in Pannonia, he could himself have observed and approved Severus – and, for that matter, Severus' *cursus honorum* shows that he had been favoured from the start. A dozen years later, he would be regarded as 'the foremost among Hadrian's leading generals'.[24]

There was still fighting in Britain, so it seems: Pompeius Falco was engaged against the rebels in the north of the province. In Egypt Rammius Martialis was coping with the aftermath of the Jewish uprising. Back in November of 117, Martialis had received a request for leave from the district administrator (*strategus*) of Apollinopolis-Heptacomias. 'Because of the attack by the unholy Jews', the official told the Prefect, 'practically all my property in the villages of the Hermoupolite *nome* and in the *metropolis* needs my attention.' Other papyri refer to damage caused by the rising – and to the confiscation of Jewish property. Further documents from Egypt indicate that Hadrian issued an order within the first few months of his reign granting tax-alleviation to cultivators of royal land. As for the aftermath of the Jewish uprising, when he returned to Rome Hadrian probably had to listen to accusations and counter-accusations from Jewish and Greek delegations sent from Alexandria. At any rate, an unofficial – probably fictional – account of such a hearing was later in circulation.[25]

During the two and three-quarter years that followed his return, Hadrian must have been reflecting on the best means of ensuring stability and security for the empire; and he no doubt early on conceived the plan to see all the provinces for himself. But for the time being it was better to remain in Rome, to stamp his authority on the capital. He himself would be consul again, for the third time, in 119, and would actually carry out the traditional duties for several months. His first colleague was Dasumius Rusticus, a kinsman of a kind – albeit only by adoption into the Dasumii, the Cordoban family related to Hadrian. Of the suffect consuls, Platorius Nepos, Hadrian's friend, enjoyed the distinction of replacing Rusticus and serving alongside the Emperor. Nepos may, indeed, have remained in his province of Thrace during his consulship, and have proceeded directly from there to his next province, Lower Germany.[26]

After his third consulship Hadrian never held the office again, an interesting decision: it was a studied contrast to the hogging of the *fasces* by the Flavian dynasty – and, one might add, to a lesser extent by Trajan, who had held five consulships as Emperor. As consul for the third time, Hadrian served until the end of April and frequently administered justice in that capacity, so the *HA* reports, in a passage listing examples of his conciliatory posture towards the Senate. When he was in the city, or nearby, he always attended the regular sittings (*senatus legitimus*), and frequently went to official functions of the consuls and praetors. Sometimes he would join the consuls when they were sitting as judges, Dio adds, and he showed them honour at the horse-races. If hearing cases as Princeps (that is, rather than when consul), he would invite senators and *equites* to join him in his *consilium* and deliver his verdict only after all had offered their views. But *equites* were debarred from giving judgement on senators. He denounced those predecessors who had showed insufficient deference to the Senate. Leading senators were invited to the palace – 'admitted to the intimacy of the imperial majesty', as the *HA* rather pompously phrases it. Dio says that 'both in Rome and when abroad he always kept the noblest men about him and used to join them for banquets; often he would have three persons riding with him in his carriage.' By the same token, he frequently accepted invitations to dinner from friends – occasions for all manner of discussions, Dio notes. He would visit them several times a day if they were ill – including some who were only knights or freedmen, the *HA* stresses, reviving them with sympathetic words – and always invited them back to dinner with himself. 'He did everything in the style of a private citizen', the *HA* concludes.[27]

In a later passage, already quoted, it is emphasised that this openness was also displayed towards the common people, 'even with the humblest he acted very much as an ordinary citizen.' What survives of Dio's account, already quoted from in part, is on similar lines to that of the *HA* – Dio may well have drawn on the same source. He too stresses the partnership with the Senate and Hadrian's manifest aim to show himself a *civilis princeps*. He notes that when Hadrian was holding court, whether in the palace, the Forum or elsewhere, it was 'from a raised tribunal, so that what was transacted was in the public domain.' He took pains to avoid excessive formality, for this reason returning to the palace in a litter, 'so as not to put anyone to the trouble of accompanying him.' Also 'to spare people a burdensome duty', he accepted no callers on *dies religiosi* (when there were no official engagements). No one should have been left in any doubt: he did not want to be a despot. Hadrian made clear, the *HA* says, in frequent speeches both to the Senate and to the People (*in contione*) that he was their servant: he would administer the commonwealth in the consciousness that the state belonged to the people and was not his property.[28]

In this section on Hadrian's first years at Rome the *HA* asserts that after 'he had been consul for the third time, he appointed a great many to a third consulship and bestowed the honour of a second consulship on an immense number.' The author has either misunderstood or exaggerated something in his source. Only two men received a third consulship from Hadrian, one less than under Trajan. Still, that was remarkable enough, considering that Hadrian himself held no further consulship after 119. Furthermore, no one other than emperors or Caesars was to have such an honour again for more than three hundred years. As for second consulships, this considerable distinction, enjoyed by more than a dozen senators in the previous reign (some only as suffects), went to only five men under Hadrian. The first was Catilius Severus, in 120, and Annius Verus followed in 121. Verus got a third consulship in 126, and there were three more iterations, in 128 and 129. That is all, apart from Servianus' long-delayed third tenure, in 134 – which suggests that the chosen few had special significance. It may mean, for one thing, that Hadrian did not have many real friends and allies among the highest echelons. Besides which, he may have been reluctant to boost, by such a distinction, persons who might conceive dangerous ambitions. The last *consul iterum* from Trajan's reign had been Publilius Celsus, in 113, the one before him his alleged fellow-conspirator Palma, in 109. And Laberius Maximus, who had actually held his second consulship as Trajan's colleague, back in 103, was presumably still in his place of exile. Their second consulships had gone to their heads, it might be thought.[29]

It could be that Marius Maximus reported the designation of Catilius Severus in comment on the year 119, adding remarks which the *HA* transmitted in inflated form on Hadrian's policy regarding the consulship. At any rate, Hadrian had a special debt to Catilius, for crucial support in August 117 and the months that followed. Now he had his reward, a second consulship only ten years after his first. Catilius Severus was from a provincial *colonia*, but, unlike so many of the new élite, who came from the western provinces, he was an easterner: his home was Apamea in Bithynia. His career was at first far from distinguished, although he was not exactly a *parvenu* and he had some social graces. At least Pliny had once accepted an invitation to dinner from him – on condition that it be a brief and frugal meal, with philosophical conversation (in moderation). After a long series of posts, Catilius' career suddenly accelerated, helped by an advantageous marriage – to Dasumia, the widow of the immensely wealthy Domitius Tullus, as has been plausibly conjectured. Hadrian's friendship may have been useful too. The marriage (no doubt his second) would in due course attach Catilius to a powerful nexus of families, at the centre of which was the City Prefect Annius Verus. It was no coincidence that the other consul of 120 was a son-in-law of Verus, Aurelius Antoninus. Verus himself gained his own second consulship the next year. This had come to be a customary accolade for City Prefects, even if Verus' predecessor Baebius Macer, abruptly removed for dangerous unreliability in September 117, had been denied it. The remarkable thing about Verus is that five years after his second consulship, in 126, he, rather than Servianus, held the *fasces* a third time. Servianus was treated by Hadrian with ostentatious respect, but it was Verus and Verus' kin who enjoyed Hadrian's confidence.[30]

Hadrian may have made plans as early as 119 to leave the capital, so at least it has been inferred from coins of this year with the legend *Fort(una) red(ux)*. The intended destination was the western provinces, other coin issues seem to suggest. Hercules of Gades could indicate that Spain was on the agenda, but Britain was obviously causing concern: sestertii show the personified province sitting on a rock, with shield and lance. The precise message that this somewhat doleful Britannia was intended to convey is not entirely clear. Victory was being proclaimed on other coins, with both the goddess herself and related images: Mars the Avenger, Augustan Peace, Jupiter the Victor, Victorious Rome. The Alexandrian mint took up the theme in its issues in the Egyptian year beginning late August 119: the goddess Nike's shield bears the words 'Victory to Caesar'. This should mean personal participation by Hadrian, which also applies to a coin from the mint at Rome hailing the *virtus Augusti*, the personal manly virtue of the ruler. What really lies behind all this is another matter: the stamping out of the British revolt has been suggested. More likely perhaps is the restoration of order on the Danube: the end of Marcius Turbo's special mission would mean business as usual in that quarter. Furthermore, Hadrian had actually taken a personal part in what could be called a war against the Sarmatians. In any case, Britannia reappears on the coinage of 120. The odds are that the rebellion was not yet over – and Hadrian may have toyed with the idea of going to deal with it himself.[31]

Instead of taking off for the provinces, Hadrian made do for the time being with a trip to Campania, what Tiberius had called a *peregrinatio suburbana*, Tacitus reports – when he went there, instead of to Gaul, at the time of the great uprising. Perhaps the historian was conscious of a parallel with Hadrian: going to Campania instead of crushing the rebellious Britons in person. Apparent echoes of Hadrian crop up in the *Annals* again and again, not least in the Tiberian books. It has to be reiterated that Tacitus could perfectly well have been composing the greater part of the *Annals* after Hadrian became Emperor – he was, after all, little more than sixty in the year 119. A second imperial visit to Campania gets more detailed mention in the fourth book of the *Annals*, under the year 26. The stress there is on predictions by astrologers – which proved to be correct – that Tiberius would never return. Tiberius himself was an expert in astrology and an addict. So was Hadrian, as is repeatedly illustrated by the *HA*, reproducing Marius Maximus. It is a legitimate speculation that astrologers were busy with such forecasts in 119. If so, Hadrian, better informed than the experts in this as in other branches of learning and science, will have cheerfully ignored them.[32]

That Campania was chosen for an excursion is significant in another respect. The region, or at least Neapolis, still lovingly preserved its Hellenic identity; there at least Hadrian could indulge his passion for things Greek. The *HA* does not offer much detail: 'He gave support to all its towns by benefactions and largess, attaching all the leading men to his friendship.' Inscriptions from the year 121 presumably register the completion of public works set in motion by this visit. In a later passage there is brief mention of something more specific: he held office as *demarch* at Naples, no date being given. It might, of course, have been merely honorific, *in absentia*, at any time in the reign. But just as he had served as archon at Athens seven or eight years earlier, it is not unlikely that he honoured the Campanian Greeks, at least for a week or two, by holding the chief magistracy at Neapolis.[33]

The Greeks will have been in Hadrian's thoughts anyway, wherever he was – no emperor could stem the constant flow of embassies and petitions from cities and individuals all over the empire, but none were so assiduous and insistent as those in the eastern Mediterranean. He had already, for example, sent two separate replies to Delphi the previous year, which chance has preserved, a mere fraction of what must have been thousands of such letters. In 119 he wrote, for the second time, to the council and people of Aphrodisias in Caria, a city allied to Rome for centuries. He had already confirmed their 'freedom and autonomy'. Now he had to assure them that they were also immune from paying the tax on nails; he had written to the procurator Claudius Agrippinus, who was to instruct the nail-tax farmer to stay away from Aphrodisias.[34]

Letters like this will not have caused either Hadrian or his *ab epistulis* much effort or exertion. The business could of course have been dealt with by freed-men or slave clerks drafting the reply on standard lines once the incoming mail had been read to him and the response decided. For all that, Hadrian probably dealt with much correspondence himself. He was proverbially capable of 'writing, dictating, listening, and conversing with friends at one and the same time'. He also had a phenomenal memory, could quote extensively from books that he had just read (even ones that most people had never heard of), and never forgot a name, veterans that he had discharged from the army included.[35]

A more substantial matter, affecting sons of soldiers who had died on service, and sons of veterans, occupied his attention in the summer of 119. It is a pleasing thought that the new *ab epistulis* Suetonius may have played some modest part in composing Hadrian's letter, which was posted in the fortress of the Egyptian legions III Cyrenaica and XXII Deiotariana on 4 August 119. Presumably he had received an enquiry from the Prefect, Rammius Martialis. (Soon after the reply arrived Rammius would be replaced by Haterius Nepos.)

I am well aware, my dear Rammius, that those whom their parents have brought up as their offspring during their time of military service have been denied access to the paternal property. Now this does not seem harsh: the men themselves have acted contrary to military discipline' [soldiers were debarred from marriage]. But I very gladly take the opportunity of interpreting in a more humane way the rather strict rule laid down by the emperors before myself.

Veterans are not referred to specifically until the end of the letter; and the precise interpretation of what the change meant is not entirely straightforward. It was a modest enough measure: illegitimate sons could still not become the principal heirs – as if they were legitimate – but were nevertheless granted a claim on their fathers' property. Those who had no competition from legally born brothers or from uncles would benefit. Two years later, *disciplina militaris* – here, in the Greek version, *stratiotike didache* – was to be overhauled drastically. For the present, it was desirable to conciliate the soldiers, not least when there had been recent fighting and considerable casualties. 'You should make this benefit of mine for soldiers and veterans public', the letter concludes, 'not so that I may gain credit in their eyes, but so that they make use of it if they act amiss.' If the word translated 'gain credit' really means that (an alternative has been suggested), Hadrian was being disingenuous. The ruling would not have been confined to Egypt, in any case, but applied to all soldiers and to all legionary veterans – by a seeming paradox, sons of veterans of the non-citizen *auxilia* had a more favoured position.[36]

Also in the summer of 119, Hadrian had an enquiry from Macedonia. Terentius Gentianus, son of Trajan's marshal Scaurianus, serving there with special powers and the title *censitor*, had written to ask what punishments were appropriate for the offence of moving boundary stones. Hadrian's reply, composed on 17 August, lays down that the penalty should depend on the rank of the offender – if persons of standing have done it, it is obviously to grab other people's land and they should be banished – for a lengthy term if still young. Servants should only receive two years hard labour – and if they simply stole the stones or moved them through ignorance, a beating would suffice.[37]

The year was marked by the death of two prominent persons. An aged Stoic philosopher, Euphrates of Tyre, sought and gained Hadrian's permission to take his own life. The Emperor 'permitted him to drink hemlock in consideration of his extreme age and his malady', Dio reported. Euphrates had certainly been around for a very long time – Pliny had first met him in Syria when serving as military tribune nearly forty years before, and had 'taken pains to win his affection'. Euphrates had been at Rome for decades – soon after Trajan's accession, Pliny told a friend that 'if ever liberal studies flourished in our city, now is the time of their greatest flowering – I need only name the philosopher Euphrates.' He enlarged on the charms of the tall, white-bearded and distinguished sage and his wholly blameless life. A century later Philostratus would denounce Euphrates for having fawned on the powerful and for accumulating vast wealth as a result. That would not necessarily have damaged his standing in the eyes of Pliny, who had a proper respect for money and was himself a skilled flatterer. Hadrian had a leaning towards philosophers – Epictetus, another aged survivor and perhaps still alive in his retreat at Nicopolis, was said to have been his friend. But it is not recorded whether Hadrian had been one of the powerful persons captivated, like Pliny, by Euphrates' subtle arguments, profound reasoning and language which echoed the sublimity and richness of Plato. Other, younger philosophers were now vying for attention at Rome, including a remarkable specimen from Gallic Arelate (Arles), Favorinus, who would in due course have dealings with Hadrian.[38]

The second death affected Hadrian more directly, and he felt it keenly. His 'most-beloved mother-in-law' – so he called her – Trajan's niece, and thus his cousin by adoption, the Augusta Matidia, died in December 119. Hadrian delivered the funeral address, ascribing to her a remarkable string of qualities. He was overcome and upset, as he said, the distressing image of her in her last illness still fresh in his mind, and he could not do justice to all her virtues. But he praised her combination of gentleness and gravity, her chastity combined with great beauty, her tenderness, modesty, amiability to all, and family loyalty. His sincerity cannot be doubted in this speech, of which the text was engraved at Tibur. Matidia had perhaps expired at this fashionable watering-place. The family had probably had a country seat there for a long time, which Hadrian was to favour and extend enormously.[39]

Matidia had been widowed as a young woman and lived at court, treated by Trajan like a daughter. She had been honoured with the name or title 'Augusta' when her mother Marciana was declared a 'diva'. It seems probable, although direct evidence is lacking, that Hadrian now followed the precedent set by Trajan and granted Sabina the name Augusta. Still, although he mentioned 'my Sabina' in the funeral speech for her mother, Hadrian's empress was to remain for the most part in the background. The Dowager Plotina, now by the act of adoption Hadrian's mother, was still alive, and probably influential, although after the first few months of the reign she had disappeared from view, as far as the imperial coinage, on which Matidia had featured prominently, is concerned. Coins also proclaimed Matidia's deification. The *HA* registers in a single sentence, as the last item in this more or less chronological narrative of Hadrian's first two years, his granting of 'special honours to his mother-in-law, with gladiatorial games and other ceremonies'. In a later passage summarising his shows and building at Rome, there is the further statement that 'after other enormous delights, he presented the people with spices in honour of his mother-in-law.' There happens to be record of the date: on 23 December 119 the *magister* of the Arval Brethren in the name of the college marked the *consecratio Matidiae Aug.* with 2 pounds of perfume and 50 pounds of incense.[40]

Records of the Arvals for the year 120 are also preserved, but supply no information on out-of-the-ordinary events. As normal, and was done all over the empire, on 3 January they assembled on the Capitol – seven of the twelve Brethren were there, the five others, and Hadrian, the supernumerary thirteenth, were absent – to pronounce the vows for the health and safety (*salus*) of the Emperor. Four days later, in the portico of the Temple of Concord, only five of the *fratres* were there as the *magister* announced the customary annual sacrifice on 27 May to the Dea Dia, with prayers for Hadrian and all his house, for the Roman People and for themselves. On 7 February they had to meet to co-opt a new member. Old Bittius Proculus had expired and Hadrian nominated one Manlius Carbo. His letter was opened by the *magister*, after solemn prayers. The *Acta* describe the Emperor's seal, as was the case with Trajan's letter received the previous year. Trajan's was a mythological figure, Marsyas, a symbol of liberty and associated with the family of his mother, the Marcii. Hadrian, as already mentioned, had the head of Augustus, not a casual choice. There may have been some, such as Tacitus, who looked on Hadrian as another Tiberius, indeed a Nero or a Domitian. Whether or not Hadrian was aware of such subversive views, he would soon show unmistakable signs of wishing to model himself on the first Princeps. As already indicated, his *ab epistulis*, busy with his *vitae Caesarum*, seems to have been aware of Hadrian's thinking: Suetonius' *Divus Augustus* incorporates what can be read as a Hadrianic interpretation of Augustan policy, a rewriting of history indeed.[41]

Hadrian's decision to remain in Rome throughout 120 and into the spring of 121, contrary perhaps to his own inclinations, is hardly surprising. On one estimate, it was simply to make certain that his position was unchallengeable. Put another way, it would allow Rome to benefit from the imperial presence – after all, Trajan had left the capital for ever in early autumn 113, over the next four years no member of the imperial house had been seen there, no emperor for nearly five. But whether Hadrian was at the capital or on the move, there was work to be done. His responses to requests from the Greeks during these years happen to be preserved in three cases. The *Gerusia* of Ephesus, a college of older men entrusted with protecting the shrine of Artemis, upholding Ephesian traditions and administering funds associated with the cults, had had difficulty in recovering moneys. The proconsul of Asia for the year 119–20, Mettius Modestus, had found in favour of the *Gerusia*, but they sent an ambassador to Hadrian all the same. He simply affirmed his approval of Modestus' decision and sent a copy of the college's resolution to the new proconsul, Cornelius Priscus, 'who will appoint someone to collect funds owing in future cases.'[42]

That he could be exasperated by cases sent to him is apparent in a reply from the year 121, later quoted in a dossier about a property dispute at Tebtunis in Egypt. Hadrian had already given a reply; but was appealed to again. 'It was just the other day that I replied to you that my decision is helpful to you – and I think that Philotera, being a woman of rank and most favourably known to me, will do you no injustice, especially as she knows that unjust possession has no validity.' At this point his impatience breaks through – 'but you want to burden me with matters which are not in dispute.'[43]

The third case was one which Hadrian would in any case have found more interesting and would certainly have dealt with sympathetically had he been appealed to direct. As it was, he could hardly refuse, for the petitioners, the School of Epicurean philosophy at Athens, had enlisted the Dowager Empress as their intermediary. Her letter to Hadrian, with his reply, both in Latin, together with Plotina's letter in Greek to the School, were set up on slabs of Pentelic marble. 'What interest I have in the sect of Epicurus, you know very well, my Lord', she began. The headship of the School was transmitted by the testament of the incumbent. It turns out that the succession had been restricted to Roman citizens, at first sight a surprising state of affairs – Athens was, after all, a free city. Presumably the rule had been laid down for good reason. The current head, one Popillius Theotimus, had a non-citizen in mind as his successor or at least wanted to be free to choose such a person and to make his will in Greek. Hadrian assented to all the details: Theotimus himself and future heads of the Epicureans would be free to choose a successor, irrespective of his citizenship.

Plotina sent the correspondence with an effusive covering letter: 'Plotina to all the friends, Greeting. We have what we were so eager to obtain.' Either a Hellene or a Roman could preside over the School. 'For this fine grant of authority, we owe a debt of gratitude to him who is in truth the benefactor and overseer of all culture and therefore an emperor most worthy of reverence, and to me very dear in every way as both an outstanding guardian and a loyal son.' She went on to stress that the privilege must not be abused, the chosen successor should be the best man, not merely someone congenial to the incumbent. The philosophy of 'the Garden' probably had some appeal to Hadrian himself, difficult though it is to pin down his real beliefs. He had two friends who were philosophers, according to the *HA*, one the aged Epictetus, a Stoic (with tendencies to Cynicism), whom he had probably met a good while earlier, the other a certain Heliodorus. There are problems about the identity of this man, but it seems at least very probable that he was an Epicurean, named on another Epicurean document at Athens, after a further letter from Hadrian, four years later. But Hadrian may not have met Heliodorus the Epicurean until he went to Athens in 124. Plotina herself, it is clear, was a devotee of the Garden. Her Greek 'bristles with verbal substantives ending in -*ma*, a characteristic of the style of Epicurus himself.'[44]

Another letter supposedly from Hadrian to Plotina is preserved in the '*sententiae* of Hadrian', a collection made for schoolchildren of a dozen of his responses to petitioners, with a Greek translation. Suitably enough for a school primer, several of the interchanges show Hadrian dealing with family problems. The last one has him sternly reminding a son of his duty to honour his mother. 'If you do not recognise this woman as your mother, I will not recognise you as a Roman citizen', it ends, adding details of the terrible punishment for parricides. In one version a letter from Hadrian to Plotina is abruptly appended, as if to illustrate the Emperor's own filial piety. It is an invitation to dine on his birthday. If authentic, it could only belong to 24 January 120 or 121. (He had held the great games on that day in 119.) He greets his 'best and dearest mother':

As you make many prayers to the gods for me, so also I pray to them for you. For your piety and dignity can achieve everything. But I am glad, by Hercules, that everything I do pleases you and wins your praise. You know, mother, that today is my birthday and we ought to dine together. If you wish, then, come in good time after the bath, with my sisters, for Sabina has set off for the villa – but has sent a present of her own. Be sure to come early so that we can celebrate together.

Only the reference to Sabina – apart from the letter's inclusion in the Hadrianic *sententiae* – identifies Hadrian as the writer and by inference his adoptive mother as the recipient. How such a private letter, if genuine, was transmitted can only be guessed – perhaps by Hadrian's freedman Phlegon, a copious writer; or the *ab epistulis*, Suetonius, might perhaps have taken the opportunity of making a copy and have included it in one of his numerous essays. (He certainly made use of various purely private letters by Augustus.) The reference to 'sisters' has been treated as a sign that the letter is a piece of fiction, for only one sister, Paulina, Servianus' wife, is firmly recorded. But if Hadrian's real mother Paulina, widowed early, had remarried, he could have had a half-sister. Otherwise, 'sisters' might refer to the younger Paulina and to Hadrian's sister-in-law, the younger Matidia, very much alive at this time (she survived for another forty years). Hadrian's private devotion to most of the women of his family was no doubt genuine enough, even if it no longer extended to his wife – her withdrawal to 'the villa', perhaps at Tibur, and absence from the birthday party might be taken as a sign of the letter's authenticity. One could even speculate that if the occasion was 24 January 120, Sabina was still in mourning for her mother Matidia.[45]

Irrespective of Hadrian's private feelings, public honouring of Sabina's mother was important. The funeral and consecration of Matidia at the end of 119 were followed by the construction of a substantial temple in a prominent part of the Campus Martius, adjacent to the Saepta Julia. This was the first time that a temple had been erected exclusively for a Diva; and it was flanked on each side by a Basilica, named after Matidia herself and her mother Marciana. Besides this, work went ahead on the great temple of Trajan himself between Trajan's Forum and the Via Lata.[46]

These constructions were only a small part of what Hadrian set in motion during this first stay in Rome. Trajan's monumental building programme, which had transformed the centre of the city, had largely come to an end in 114. Many considerations spoke for renewed building activity. It was the traditional way for a ruler to win the favour and gratitude of his people. Grandiose projects could provide employment for thousands, not merely humble labourers, but craftsmen and entrepreneurs – and members of the ruling élite could profit too. The brickworks that supplied the materials needed in vast quantities were situated around Rome on land owned by these people, their names registered by the stamping of the bricks. Rutilius Lupus, lately Prefect of Egypt, is a notable example,

Hadrian's friend Platorius Nepos is another; and the family of Annius Verus' daughter-in-law Domitia Lucilla had been growing steadily richer for more than half a century through the building projects of Nero, of the Flavians and of Trajan.[47]

New buildings were needed for the newly deified. But repair and renewal was also required. The Campus Martius, in particular, adorned with great monuments under Augustus and the Flavians, could properly be given attention. Further, it was still liable to flooding, and major work was undertaken to consolidate the Tiber embankment. Hadrian adopted what might be called an ostentatiously modest approach. The *HA* biographer stresses that 'although he was responsible for an infinite number of buildings everywhere, he never had his own name inscribed on them except for the temple of his father Trajan.' This somewhat exaggerates Hadrian's restraint, but the statement certainly applies to the magnificent rebuilding of the Pantheon, close to the temple of Matidia. The 'restored' Pantheon was in effect a totally new structure, far larger than the original – and a work of unexampled architectural brilliance. Yet the inscription continued to give the credit to the man who built the original temple, M. Agrippa, thrice consul – Augustus' son-in-law. The Saepta Julia and the Baths of Agrippa close by are also listed as having been consecrated by Hadrian under the names of their initiators.[48]

Here, as elsewhere, by such restoration, Hadrian was able to revive the memory of Augustus and associate himself with that name. The Augustan character of the northern Campus Martius, marked in particular by Augustus' Mausoleum and the Ara Pacis, was respectfully maintained, but newly emphasised by Hadrian's programme of renewal. Some work was also undertaken in the Forum of Augustus. Besides all these considerations, there is no doubt that such activity was intensely congenial to Hadrian. Architecture was one of his passions, and he had a special scheme of his own. In the first months of 121, at the latest, he must have decided on an extensive tour of the western provinces. Senate and People should have no ground for resentment that he was neglecting or slighting the Eternal City by his departure. On the contrary, he would show the world that his devotion to Rome was second to none. By tradition Romulus had founded the city on 21 April, the day on which the sacred boundary, the *pomerium*, was traced. Whether by coincidence or not, an ancient festival, the Parilia, was celebrated on this, the city's birthday. Coins of 121 proclaimed something new: 'In the Eight Hundred and Seventy Fourth Year Circus Games have been founded for the Parilia on the Birthday of the City.' The *natalis urbis* was to be a major festival. Further, Roma herself was to have her own temple, shared with the divine ancestress of the Roman People. A further coincidence was that 21 April was the birthday of Rome's second king, Numa Pompilius. There are signs that Hadrian liked to have himself compared to Numa – the peaceful successor of the warlike Romulus. As for the *pomerium*, it was, by tradition, only extended when the boundaries of the republic had been increased. Trajan had not ordered an extension, although he could have done so with good grounds after

111

the annexation of Dacia and Arabia. In 121 Hadrian had the existing line of the *pomerium* emphatically renewed with a series of inscribed boundary-stones. It was a clear sign that the empire was to stay within its existing limits; and he would shortly make those limits clearer and more visible than ever before.[49]

The Temple was to stand in a vast precinct east of the Forum, dominating the Sacred Way on a great platform, stretching from just beyond the Arch of Titus with its reliefs that glorified the sack of Jerusalem, almost as far as the great Flavian amphitheatre, the Colosseum. The new temple was be raised on all four sides and, housing two goddesses, Roma and Venus, would face in two directions, with twenty columns on each of the long sides. It would take years to complete; even the commencement of the construction work would have to wait until lengthy preparations had been carried out. For one thing, the Colossus of Nero had to be moved to make room for the temple's foundations. The *HA* biographer, careless and in a hurry, forgot to mention Hadrian's most ambitious building project, but managed to supply a detail. Decrianus, the architect, moved the Colossus – which was more than one hundred feet high – with the aid of twenty-four elephants supplied by the Emperor. The Colossus had been adapted after Nero's downfall and represented the Sun God instead of its hated creator. Now, the *HA* goes on, Hadrian commissioned Apollodorus, Trajan's master-architect, to make a similar colossal statue of the moon-goddess.[50]

Whether Apollodorus responded is another question. He and Hadrian were alleged to have been on bad terms since the time when the architect was remodelling the centre of Rome for Trajan and had offended the young man by a sarcastic comment. Dio claims that Apollodorus had been banished after Hadrian's accession – and that worse followed. The alarming sequel should belong some years later, after the new temple was complete. The story is part of a pattern that is matched by a string of anecdotes in the *HA* about Hadrian's jealous and vindictive treatment of his friends in his last years. Here it need only be noted that Dio tells the story of Apollodorus as an illustration of Hadrian's burning ambition to excel in every art and science. This characteristic cannot be doubted, the *HA* having a long list of his manifold talents – and of his jealousy of the experts in each field. For the moment, it is enough to note that Dio believed Hadrian to have designed the temple himself, which is plausible enough.[51]

But the temple was still only on the drawing-board when the new Festival of the Parilia for 21 April was proclaimed. Hadrian presumably thought he had done all he could at Rome, for the time being: coins of the year 121 proclaimed a new Golden Age, *Saec(ulum) aur(eum)*. The coin legend was personified by the figure of Aion, whose name means 'eternity' – which Sol and Luna also symbolised. Now he could turn to the provinces and frontiers; and the army needed to be re-educated for its new role.[52]

10

TO THE GERMAN FRONTIER

Hadrian's departure for the provinces probably followed shortly after the new Festival of the Parilia. The exact date is a matter of guesswork. Even the coins do not announce a *Profectio Augusti*. That Hadrian was outside Italy during the year 121 is at any rate indicated by inscriptions of this year which give him the title *proconsul* – Trajan, as a show of republicanism or traditionalism of some sort, had started this practice. But there is no doubt about his destination: 'after this he set out for the Gallic provinces', the *HA* biographer states emphatically. There he continued the drive to gain popularity that he had displayed at Rome the past three years: 'He supported all of them [either all the provinces of Gaul or all the communities in Gaul] with largesses.'[1]

'After this' is not, however, very helpful for chronology: the previous sentence refers to the posthumous honours for Matidia, which were awarded at the end of 119. Hadrian's activity at Rome in 120 and 121 is passed over in silence in this section, and nothing more is said about the Gallic provinces – it is only an informed guess that he sailed from Ostia to Massilia and proceeded up the Rhone valley. At all events, the commemorative coinage issued a dozen years later signals not only Hadrian's advent in Gaul but calls him its 'restorer' (*restitutor*). The personified Gallia, kneeling before the Emperor, is dressed in the long robe, *chiton*, standard throughout the Mediterranean, rather than in the Celtic cloak, *sagum*. Most of the *restitutor* coins show her with the horn of plenty, on her head a mural crown; some show her helmeted, and on some she bears spear and sword; on one she holds up an olive-branch to the Emperor. 'From there' – from Gaul – 'he passed on to Germany', the biographer continues, and then begins a lengthy exposition of Hadrian's new programme for the army.[2]

Germany was no doubt his real goal – and Britain. He wanted to settle the north-western provinces in person, and had plans for the frontiers. He was to spend some months in Gaul on his return from Britain in the following year, hence there is no particular reason to suppose that he wintered at Lugdunum and only went on north to the Rhine in the spring of 122. He had spent a winter at Moguntiacum (Mainz) and then at the Colonia Agrippinensis (Cologne) as a young man twenty-three years earlier. The odds are that he wintered on the frontier in 121–2. A reference in Dio to him enduring 'German snows' might

Plate 9 Hadrian on the move: the imperial galley
(*BMC* III Hadrian no. 1395)

perhaps be claimed to support this. There was much to inspect: not merely the two German provinces, but Raetia and perhaps Noricum as well, the small Upper Danubian provinces, seem to have been on his agenda. It is probable enough that he already intended to conclude with a visit to Spain and to the North African provinces, an inspection of the remaining Latin part of the empire, completing what had been undertaken in 118. He could be confident that Rome was in safe hands in his absence. Of the two Guard Prefects, his old friend Turbo was to stay in the capital: that alone would guarantee order. The Prefect of the City, whose task was also to keep the peace, would be able to keep the Senate sweet. This was M. Annius Verus, consul for the second time this year, a quiet, steady man, whose network of marriage alliances undoubtedly bolstered his influence – besides, he was of Spanish origin and some sort of kinsman of Hadrian. The family was flourishing: five days after the Parilia a grandson of Verus was born, who was given his names. The child was the future Marcus Aurelius.[3]

Hadrian no doubt had a large retinue. The Guard Prefect Septicius Clarus, commanding elements of the Praetorians, was certainly with him. This literary man was perhaps expected to be a congenial travelling companion, so too the Chief Secretary, Suetonius Tranquillus, who, one may suppose, welcomed the chance to see the Rhineland. After all, although he had probably already completed his *Lives* of Caesar and Augustus, dedicated to Septicius, he would now be at work on the next instalment: several of the following Caesars had been involved with Germany and Britain. The Empress was also of the party – at least, her presence and that of the two high officials is registered by the *HA* in the following year, in Britain. No other names are securely preserved by the literary or epigraphic sources. But an inscription at Olympia evidently called M. Atilius Bradua Hadrian's *comes*. Bradua, probably an exact coeval of the emperor, had been governor of one of the German provinces and then of Britain in the later part of Trajan's reign. He would have been a suitable adviser for this tour. One can only guess at other likely members of the party. The Neratii brothers might have gone to the north-west with Hadrian: Priscus had governed Germania Inferior twenty-five years earlier, Marcellus had been governor of Britain a few years later. Hadrian might have taken one of his quaestors with him. More likely at least one stayed in Rome, to read out his letters to the Senate. But one quaestor was allowed to leave in another direction. The younger Minicius Natalis accompanied his father, the new proconsul of Africa, to Carthage, to serve there as legate.[4]

Moguntiacum (Mainz), with the fortress of the legion XXII Primigenia, and residence of the governor of Germania Superior, is a likely enough base from which Hadrian could have launched his inspection of the frontier. He might of course have preferred to stay with his friend Platorius Nepos, now governor of Germania Inferior, at the Colonia Agrippinensis. But Hadrian was due to go the Lower German province at the end of this section of the tour; from there he would cross to Britain. From Moguntiacum he could have moved easily into the lands east of the Rhine, the *Agri Decumates*, to look at the frontier installations. The *limes* first established by Domitian north of the Main nearly forty years earlier, following his war against the Chatti, had enclosed a fertile plain, the Wetterau, opposite Moguntiacum. At first the frontier had been little more than a cleared strip of land, with a series of signalling towers along it. Trajan had ordered the moving forward of some of the auxiliary regiments from the hinterland to the *limes* itself. Tacitus had not been prepared to count the cultivators of the 'Tenth-lands' among the peoples of Germany – they had been drawn from the penniless adventurers of Gaul, who settled in what had been a no man's land. By now, 'when the *limes* had been traced out and the garrisons moved forward, they have become a projection of the empire and part of the province.'

Rome's frontier indeed projected unevenly northwards at this point: the aim was surely to keep the Chatti at arm's length beyond the Taunus and Vogelsberg. The fruitful Wetterau, already dotted with farmsteads which the descendants of these mixed adventurers had established, could supply the troops. Further south, the line of forts ran along the River Main, which for some 30 miles (48 km) itself formed the frontier. Then the *limes* was driven through the forested hills of the Odenwald, across to the valley of the River Nicer (Neckar), which it followed as far as Grinario (Köngen), commanding a wide view of the Neckar and Lauter valleys. At this point the direction turned east, or rather north-east, to meet the boundary between Germania Superior and Raetia just beyond Lorch. From there it went another 100 miles (160 km), curving gradually southeast, to meet the Danube at Abusina (Eining), a few miles west of Castra Regina (Regensburg).[5]

Although the network of watchtowers and forts established under Domitian and Trajan was already recognisably an effective frontier and there was no obvious sign of a military threat from the free Germans, Hadrian effected a striking change. The limit of the empire was to be marked by a continuous palisade. It was formed by great oak posts, split through the middle, with the flat side facing outwards, strengthened by cross-beams. Here was a major undertaking for the armies of Germania Superior and Raetia. Thousands of trees would have to be felled, transported to the frontier and carefully erected. It presumably took some years before the whole line was complete. The *HA* does not mention the palisade in its account of Hadrian's visit to Germany, which is devoted solely to his reform of military discipline. Instead, there is a general statement a few pages later, that 'at that time and frequently at other times he marked off the barbarians in many places, where they are separated not by rivers but by *limites*, with great posts driven into the ground and joined together like a wall.' The inference that it was Hadrian who ordered the erection of the palisade is inescapable, even if no section of it has been proved to belong to his reign. It is also a matter of guesswork how high this imperial frontier fence was: it could have been as much as 10 feet (3 m).[6]

As a military obstacle, the palisade was doubtless of restricted value. Its symbolic significance was another matter. To the barbarians it marked off the empire more clearly than ever before. How it was perceived by the Romans is perhaps equally or even more important. It was surely Hadrian's way of making plain that the policy of expansion really was at an end. The ideology of 'boundless empire', immortalised in Virgil by the divine promise of an *imperium sine fine*, without end in time or space, was thereby unmistakably buried. It was a clear signal to any surviving admirers of Trajan's expansionist policies that the empire was indeed precisely defined: thus far and no further. Tacitus, writing his account of Tiberius at this time, complains about his subject.

> No one should compare my *Annals* with the writings of those who covered the ancient deeds of the Roman people: they could record great wars, cities besieged, kings defeated or captured . . . we must labour in a confined space, with no glory. There was undisturbed – or scarcely troubled – peace, gloom in the city – and a Princeps with no interest in extending the empire.

Tacitus' final comment, four words heavy with disdain, 'princeps proferendi imperii incuriosus', could readily have been applied to Hadrian as well as to Tiberius. When he came to the reign of Claudius, Tacitus would recall how the great Corbulo, planning to establish Roman garrisons beyond the Lower Rhine, was recalled by Claudius. 'The Roman generals of old were fortunate', was

Corbulo's laconic comment. Instead of pushing forward the bounds of empire, he set his men to dig a 23-mile (37 km) long canal between the Maas and the Rhine. It kept the troops occupied.[7]

Hadrian's palisade, apart from any practical or symbolic purpose it may have had as a frontier line, was also a means of keeping the soldiers fit and active. A programme of converting forts and signal-towers from timber to stone, already under way during Trajan's reign, was also in hand. The *HA* biographer devotes considerable space to measures Hadrian set in motion to restore military discipline. Indeed, it is the only subject mentioned in connection with his stay in Germany at this time. 'Albeit eager for peace rather than for war, he trained the soldiers as if war were imminent.' Example rather than precept was his watchword, 'instilling into them the example of his own endurance'. He lived the military life with the men, 'cheerfully eating camp fare out of doors, bacon and cheese with rough wine.'[8]

His models, the biographer relates, were 'Scipio Aemilianus, Metellus and his own father Trajan'. In all probability the biographer's source, Marius Maximus, derived these names and the whole section on the programme to restore discipline from Hadrian's autobiography. There is every reason to suppose that Hadrian would have presented such a picture of his own conduct, and it would be entirely in character for him to cite Republican models – just as he had invoked Cato to justify his abandonment of the new provinces. Scipio was famed as the man who destroyed Carthage, but it was his conduct on his last campaign, at Numantia, that was the model for Hadrian. The great general went ahead with a small escort, having heard that the army in Spain was full of idleness, discord and luxury: he knew full well that he could never overcome the enemy unless he could first bring his own men under strict discipline. On his arrival he expelled all traders, harlots and soothsayers from the camp, had all wagons and their superfluous contents sold, restricted cooking utensils to a spit, a brass kettle and one cup. Food was limited to plain boiled and roasted meats, beds were banned, and the general set the example of sleeping on straw. A rigorous training programme followed, new camps being constructed every day, with deep trenches being dug and high ramparts built – which were then demolished the next day and the ditches filled. As for Metellus, this was the consul of 109 BC, who turned the tide in the war against Jugurtha (only for Marius to seize the credit for victory). He too had had to take over an army that was weak and unwarlike, incapable of withstanding danger or hardship, subject to no discipline or restraint. Metellus would not take the field until he had forced the men to undergo old-style discipline, the *disciplina maiorum*. He banned the sale of bread or cooked food within the camp, expelled merchants, forbade the soldiers to have a slave or pack animal in camp or on the march, and 'set a strict limit on other practices of the kind.'[9]

Hadrian used carrot as well as stick, 'giving rewards to many and honours to a few, so that they could put up with the harsher conditions he was imposing. For he did indeed take army discipline in hand. After Caesar Octavianus it had

Plate 10   Hadrian in the west: DISCIPLIN. AVG.
(*BMC* III Hadrian no. 1484)

been on the decline, owing to the neglectfulness of previous emperors' – *incuria
superiorum principum* implies criticism of Trajan too, in spite of Hadrian's claim
that his adoptive father, as well as Scipio and Metellus, was his exemplar. The
appeal to 'Caesar Octavianus' is significant: before long Hadrian would make a
concentrated effort to present himself as a new Augustus. After this introduction,
the biographer presents a string of specific measures. Headquarters staff (*officia*)
and accounts were regulated. No one was to be absent from camp without
proper authorisation. Officers would win approval for just conduct rather than
for popularity. He encouraged the men by his example, marching as much as 20
miles (32 km) in armour. Then, in Scipionic fashion, came the purge: dining-
rooms, porticoes, covered galleries and ornamental gardens were demolished.
This measure probably mainly affected the officers, who were also specifically
prohibited from accepting presents from their men. Fancy uniforms were probably forbidden. This is not explicitly stated – but the biographer next reports that
Hadrian himself would wear the humblest form of dress, with an ungilded
sword-belt and a clasp without a jewel for his cloak, only with reluctance allowing
himself an ivory hilt for his sword. In general, 'he cleared out luxury from all
sides, while making improvements in arms and equipment.'[10]

It was very much part of the tradition of what constituted good generalship
that he took pains to visit sick soldiers. His pronouncement that no one should
serve in camp contrary to ancient usage at a younger age than his strength called

118

for recalls a law to this effect attributed to Gaius Gracchus. Hadrian would certainly have been aware of this. He added that there should be an upper age limit as well. Neither the lower nor the upper limits are specified. His criteria for appointment to the centurionate and the equestrian *militiae* were also spelled out, at least in general terms: 'He would not award the vine-staff [the emblem of the centurion's rank] to anyone who was not bodily robust and of good reputation, nor would he appoint anyone tribune who did not have a full beard, in other words of an age to assume the powers of a tribunate with prudence and maturity.' (The 'full beard' is an implicit reminder that Hadrian's abandonment of shaving had become the norm already.) Hadrian's 'practice was always to be acquainted with them and to know their units', the biographer adds. In later sections it is recorded that 'he regularly presented those that he appointed to commissions with horses, mules, uniform, expenses and their entire equipment', while his ability to recall the names of veterans he had discharged is given as an instance of his phenomenal memory.[11]

Further practical measures are registered in this section on the stay in Germany. 'He would choose the site for forts himself', again a traditional sign of a good general, attributed, for example, by Tacitus to Agricola as governor of Britain. It is a reminder that some new forts were founded at this time. Finally, 'he made an effort carefully to familiarise himself with the military stores, so that if there was any particular deficiency anywhere he could make it good. But more than any other emperor, he aimed never at any time to buy or to maintain anything that was unserviceable.'[12]

What survives of Cassius Dio's Book 69 has a rather less detailed but in general similar version of Hadrian's 'military reforms' – Dio may have taken it direct from the autobiography – and, as in the *HA*, it is placed at the beginning of a section covering the provincial tours, confirming the impression that it was indeed in Germany that the policy was first unveiled. Hadrian 'inspected all the garrisons and forts, some he removed to more suitable sites, others he closed down, and established some new ones.' Once again the stress is on Hadrian's 'personal inspection and investigation not merely of the usual military items, weapons, engines, ditches, ramparts and palisades, but even the private affairs of rankers and officers, their lives, their quarters and their habits. Luxuries were cut out. The men were drilled for every kind of battle, some were honoured, others reprimanded – and Hadrian showed them personally how everything should be done, and set an example by living austerely, using neither chariot nor four-wheeler, but walking or riding everywhere, bareheaded alike amid German snows or the heat of Egypt.' (The mention of Egypt shows that Dio summarised the whole series of travels: it would be nearly a decade after coming to Germany before Hadrian visited Egypt.) The result, in Dio's view, was that 'even today' – in other words a hundred years later – 'the regulations he laid down are the basis for military service.' The same opinion is expressed at the end of the fourth century by the author of the *Epitome de Caesaribus*: apart from some changes by Constantine, Hadrian's *officia militiae* were still in force. Vegetius, the late

119

Roman author of a military treatise, states at the outset that among his sources for military discipline are 'regulations (*constitutiones*) of Augustus, Trajan and Hadrian'. Vegetius specifically registers regular route marches in full armour, of 10 miles, to be carried out three times a month, by the infantry. The cavalry were to cover a similar distance, practising pursuit and retreat. Otherwise, apart from some innovations in cavalry tactics, reported by Arrian in his treatise on the subject, and a change in the ranking of equestrian officers which has been inferred from inscriptions, this is the sum total of the evidence for Hadrian's army reforms. The keynote was doubtless the stress on regular training and manoeuvres – and on discipline.[13]

Military matters were not Hadrian's only concern, even if the provinces he was now in were dominated by the army. At some stage Hadrian was in Noricum. Indeed, the commemorative coinage from the later part of the reign records not only the army of this province, as is the case with Raetia, but quite specifically his *adventus*, and furthermore the Norican mines. The *adventus* coins show the personified Noricum, bare-headed, wearing short tunic and military cloak and with a military standard (*vexillum*). He could of course have made a detour from Pannonia into Noricum in 118, but it seems plausible to suppose that he visited both Raetia and Noricum during 121 or 122. For one thing, the coins illustrating his inspection of the *exercitus Noricus* show Hadrian accompanied by a high-ranking officer, surely the Guard Prefect. Septicius Clarus was with him in 121–2. In 118 there was presumably no Prefect at his side.[14]

Noricum, 'the Kingdom of Noricum', as it was still called, was certainly given some attention by Hadrian. Two communities, Ovilava (Wels) and Cetium (St. Pölten), were granted the status of chartered town, *muncipium*, by Hadrian. This did not necessarily happen during the Emperor's visit, nor did Hadrian necessarily even visit these places personally, but it is likely enough. Whether he found time to go to the iron-mining district in the south, to which the *metalla* of the commemorative coins refer, is doubtful. A statue of Hadrian was set up in the theatre at Virunum (near Klagenfurt), the town where the governor of Noricum had his residence, and which Hadrian surely went to when in this province. The principal city in Raetia, Augusta Vindelicum (Augsburg), gained higher status under Hadrian, becoming a *muncipium*. Perhaps this elevation in status was conferred by the Emperor in person? Raetia is not included in the *adventus* series, but there is a coin of its *exercitus* – not showing a Guard Prefect with Hadrian, who is mounted for his harangue. As it happens, the governor of Noricum who was in office at about this time, Claudius Paternus Clementianus, was himself a native of Abudiacum (Epfbach) in Raetia – his Roman citizenship probably went back to the original annexation by Augustus' stepson Tiberius, at that time still a Claudius. It could be that Paternus had performed a useful service for Hadrian a few years earlier. His first administrative post had been as financial procurator of Judaea, in which capacity he had also served as temporary governor, replacing the legate – possibly when Lusius Quietus had been summarily dismissed in August 117. The man who succeeded Paternus, Censorius Niger, was himself a Norican, from Flavia Solva (Leibnitz) in the south of the province.[15]

There is just a hint that Hadrian's Greek friend Arrian might have been with him. In one of his works Arrian reveals that he had seen the confluence of the Inn and the Danube, close to the fort which was to become known as Batava Castra (Passau), on the borders of Raetia and Noricum. Arrian might, of course, have been there earlier in his career, perhaps as an equestrian officer, before he became a senator. But it is an attractive possibility to suppose that Hadrian might have had at least one Greek intellectual in his retinue during his tour of the Celtic west.[16]

Civic development in the region of a more modest kind was not neglected. South of the Main a new *civitas* was created for the Auderienses and a small town as its centre was founded (at Dieburg). The two communities on the other side of the Main, the Taunenses with their centre at Nida (Heddernheim, Frankfurt) and the Mattiaci, whose capital was at Aquae (Wiesbaden), may also have come into being at this time. In Germania Inferior, the only clear sign of Hadrian's activity in this sphere is more obvious: a settlement in the territory of the Canninefates, close to a fort of the Rhine Flotilla (*classis Germanica*) on Corbulo's canal, took the name Forum Hadriani (Voorburg). This should be a clue to his movements, and suggests that he went down the Rhine to the North Sea coast, giving him the opportunity to visit the Batavi, who occupied the Rhine island, *insula Batavorum*, and were the source of most of his Horse Guard. The Batavians, 'the most outstandingly courageous' among all the German peoples, so Tacitus had written, retained their old privilege, freedom from taxation in return for military service, in spite of their great revolt in 69–70. It may also have been Hadrian who conferred the rank of *municipium* on the *civitas* of the Tungri (Tongeren).[17]

Hadrian's tour of the Upper Danubian and Rhine provinces ended in Germania Inferior. He may have taken the opportunity of visiting Belgica as well. A faint hint that the imperial party went along the Moselle might be gleaned from Suetonius' *Life* of Caligula, where he discusses the Emperor's place of birth, and meticulously cites a statement of the Elder Pliny that it was at the *vicus* of Ambitarvium in Treveran territory, above Confluentes (Koblenz). He does not mention that he had been there himself, nor that he had inspected the altars which, he says, Pliny reported were set up there 'for Agrippina's delivery of a son'. But there are two other, slightly more positive signs later in the *Twelve Caesars* that Suetonius made use of his presence in the Rhineland. In the *Life* of Claudius he reports that there was more than one canal dug beyond the Rhine by the emperor's father Drusus and 'they are still called the Drusine canals today.' (Tacitus only knew one canal of Drusus.) Then he records that the future Emperor Titus had served as military tribune in both Germany and Britain, winning a high reputation, 'as evidenced by the statues still to be seen of him in these provinces.' A meagre harvest, to be sure; but Suetonius tended to cite books or manuscripts he had seen, rather than places or objects. For Hadrian, at any rate, there was a reunion with an old friend. The governor of Germania Inferior, Platorius Nepos, had been there since soon after his consulship in 119, it may be assumed. In the last stage of his tour, if not before, Hadrian will have stayed with Nepos in the governor's palace at the Colonia Agrippinensis (Cologne) while discussing plans for the next stage. Nepos was to accompany Hadrian to Britain and to replace Pompeius Falco as governor.[18]

More than a decade later Hadrian's tour of the German provinces was commemorated on the imperial coinage. The figure of Germania had been a common feature on the coins in Hadrian's youth, in particular the *Germania capta* issues of the 80s, with a captive figure celebrating Domitian's victories. Trajan too put Germania on his early coins, no longer dishevelled and submissive in defeat, but seated, erect and confident. The Hadrianic Germania is shown standing, a large spear in one hand, the other supporting her characteristic hexagonal shield. She wears a long, sleeveless tight-fitting tunic which leaves one shoulder and breast bare. The portrayal is just as Tacitus describes German women's dress – 'no different from that of men, except that the women often have no sleeves to their costume, their arms and shoulders are bare and part of the breast is exposed.' On some examples she also wears the Celtic cloak (*sagum*). The single coin issue of the German army is similar to that of several other *exercitus*: it shows Hadrian on horseback addressing three soldiers.[19]

Plate 11   Hadrian in Germany: EXERCITVS GERMANICVS
(*BMC* III Hadrian no. 1679)

11

HADRIAN'S WALL

Having completely transformed the soldiers, in royal fashion, he made for Britain, where he set many things right and and – he was the first to do so – erected a Wall along a length of eighty miles, which was to separate barbarians and Romans.

So the *HA* biographer recounts the journey of the year 122.[1] Britain was certainly on Hadrian's agenda many months before he set foot on the island. Only the *HA* explicitly records both the visit and its principal result, the erection of the Wall 'to separate barbarians and Romans'. It also has some anecdotes in the context of the British journey, and later quotes the poet Florus' allusion to the Emperor's 'stroll among the Britons'. But there is also documentary evidence for Hadrian being in Britain. Later coins commemorate the province herself, the *adventus Aug. Britanniae* and depict the Emperor addressing the *exercitus Britannicus*. Other coins with the legend *exped(itio) Aug(usti)* can also be referred to his British venture. Two inscriptions specifically name the 'British expedition'. One honours T. Pontius Sabinus, an officer who took reinforcements, 3,000 men, from the Spanish legion VII Gemina and from the two legions of Upper Germany, on an *expeditio Brittannica*, which can only be Hadrianic. The other records that M. Maenius Agrippa was 'selected by the deified Hadrian and sent on the British expedition' – as tribune of the First Cohort of Spaniards. Finally, a document newly discovered at one of the forts on the frontier indicates that someone stationed there hoped to present an appeal to the Emperor when he arrived to inspect or to inaugurate his new Wall.[2]

There had been trouble in the province at the outset of the reign, curtly referred to in the *HA* with the remark that 'the Britons could not be kept under Roman control.' Hadrian had sent Pompeius Falco from Lower Moesia to Britain and Falco had presumably restored the position – but only after heavy Roman losses. The figure of Britannia on coins datable to 119–20 can only allude to this fighting. A little over forty years later the orator Cornelius Fronto referred in passing to the great number of soldiers killed by the Britons when Hadrian was Emperor. It used to be thought that the entire Ninth Legion, IX Hispana, was wiped out.[3] The last dated record of the Ninth in Britain shows

Plate 12 Hadrian on the move: EXPED. AVG. (*BMC* III Hadrian no. 1313)

it building at its fortress Eburacum (York) in the year 108. But other evidence has come to light which suggests that the legion survived: the service in it of several officers can hardly be dated earlier than the 120s. It may have been operating away from Eburacum, at or near Luguvalium (Carlisle); and part of it may have been transferred to Noviomagus (Nijmegen) in Lower Germany.[4]

Whatever the truth about the whereabouts of IX Hispana in 122, Hadrian decided on an important change. Another legion, VI Victrix, was to move from Lower Germany, from its base at Vetera (Xanten) on the Rhine, to join the garrison of Britain. It was part of the army commanded by Hadrian's friend Platorius Nepos. Now Nepos was to succeed Falco in Britain. By 17 July 122 at the latest the handover had taken place. It seems probable that Hadrian crossed with Nepos and the Sixth Legion in June. The detachments commanded by Pontius Sabinus had perhaps gone ahead. The commander of the Sixth was evidently P. Tullius Varro, a native of Tarquinii in Etruria. Varro's brother, adopted into the Spanish Dasumii, had been Hadrian's colleague as consul in 119. Varro had already commanded a legion, XII Fulminata in Cappadocia. By chance we know the name of the senatorial tribune of the Sixth Legion at this time. More than fifty years later M. Pontius Laelianus was honoured with a statue in Trajan's Forum. On the base is listed his long career, beginning with the post of 'military tribune of legion VI Victrix, with which he crossed from Germany to Britain'.[5]

124

Enormous logistical efforts must have been undertaken by Falco and his officers and by the imperial procurators in advance of the imperial visit. Over 5,000 men of VI Victrix and the 3,000 legionaries from Spain and Upper Germany had to be housed. A detachment of the Praetorian Guard, together with the Horse Guards, and the whole imperial entourage also needed accommodation at a string of likely halting-places across the province. The Empress Sabina, the Guard Prefect, Septicius Clarus, the Chief Secretary, Suetonius Tranquillus, with other officials, and courtiers of various kinds were there too. There is no certain record of senators who accompanied Hadrian on this western tour as his *comites*, but two names may be suggested, Neratius Marcellus and Atilius Bradua. Marcellus had governed Britain twenty years earlier, when he had appointed Suetonius to a military tribunate, on the recommendation of Pliny. Suetonius had, however, resigned his commission before taking it up. Neratius is the most likely person to be the Marcellus described as a close friend of Hadrian. As for Bradua, he was an exact coeval of the Emperor, had also governed Britain, in the latter part of Trajan's reign, and he is known to have been a *comes* of Hadrian at some time.

Sabina's presence was deemed advisable, no doubt. For one thing, even if – or rather, because – she and Hadrian already hated each other, she could have posed a threat if she had been left at Rome, the focus of potential intrigue. An attempted coup may still have seemed a real possibility, although Marcius Turbo and the rest of the Guard remained in the capital, with the steady Annius Verus as City Prefect to keep Senate and plebs under a firm hand.[6]

The *HA* states that Hadrian 'corrected many abuses in Britain' and 'settled matters' there. His presence at any specific place in the island other than on the line of the Wall is not explicitly attested. Nor is it known where he embarked: Gesoriacum (Boulogne), the main base of the *classis Britannica*, is probable, but he could perfectly well have set out from the mouth of the Rhine, coasted up to the Humber and sailed into Eburacum – or indeed, have gone direct to the Tyne. The renaming of the settlement at Voorburg as Forum Hadriani might seem suggest his presence close to the mouth of the Rhine. But from whatever port he set out, it may be imagined that he and Nepos first went to Londinium, the seat of government, to stay in the legate's palace on the Thames, where Sabina and some other members of his party, such as Suetonius, could have been deposited. From there the Empress and her entourage may have preferred to move on elsewhere, for example to the principal spa in the province, Aquae Sulis (Bath).[7]

Suetonius was to let fall a stray indication of personal observation deriving from his visit. In Britain, as in Germany, now over forty years after Titus' death, there were still numerous statues of that emperor to be seen, he reported in the *Divus Titus*. Correspondence from all parts of the empire no doubt kept flowing in. It must have been, for example, during Hadrian's stay in Germany or Britain that a letter arrived from the proconsul of Asia, Licinius Silvanus Granianus: the provincial council had tried to persuade him to do something about the

Plate 13 Head of Hadrian found in the Thames at London (British Museum)

Christians. Granianus sought guidance from Hadrian, but by the time the reply was composed, it had to go to a new proconsul, Minicius Fundanus. As *ab epistulis*, Suetonius must have had to deal with a whole series of letters of all kinds. He was, as it happens, unusually well placed to offer Hadrian some advice in this case, for he had been with Pliny in Pontus just over ten years earlier when the latter had written his famous enquiry about the Christians to Trajan.

A text of Hadrian's letter to Minicius Fundanus was soon in Christian hands and was quoted by Justin in his *Apology*. One need not doubt either that Fundanus was proconsul of Asia in 122–3, nor that Hadrian wrote to him about the treatment of Christians following an enquiry by Granianus. It is plausible, too, that the provincial council had tried to persuade Granianus to initiate some kind of purge of the new religion. As Trajan had made clear in his reply to Pliny, that was not to be imperial policy. Fundanus, who had been a friend of Pliny, had probably read the correspondence. Whether Hadrian did more than reiterate the line taken by Trajan is another matter. Justin's version, surviving only in a Greek translation made by Eusebius for his *Ecclesiastical History*, has Hadrian going some way beyond Trajan's laconic statement. He not only insists that Christians must be prosecuted in the normal way, he lays down that they must be shown to be guilty of specific crimes before they can be sentenced – that would mean that 'the name alone' was no longer sufficient for a conviction. Besides this, he threatened severe punishment for false accusation. It looks as if Christians may have 'adapted' his rescript: other evidence indicates that there was no change in the practice followed by Pliny and confirmed by Trajan.[8]

A document issued to a veteran of the army in Britain may shed some light on what Hadrian was up to shortly after his arrival in the province. On 17 July 122 he granted the customary privileges to

> the cavalrymen and infantrymen, who have been serving in the thirteen *alae* and thirty-seven cohorts (the names of all fifty regiments follow), which are in Britain under Aulus Platorius Nepos, having been discharged with an honourable discharge by Pompeius Falco . . . to themselves, their children and descendants, the citizenship and the right of legal marriage with the wife they had at the time that citizenship was granted to them, or, if any are unmarried, with the wife they subsequently marry (provided that each takes only one wife).

To be sure, the formula was now standard and the Emperor's presence was not required. But given Hadrian's known fondness for addressing the troops, his presence in Britain in that summer, and, not least, the unparalleled number of units given their privileges at one and the same time, one may suspect that some special ceremony had been arranged. It was very unusual for two governors – the old and the new – to be named in these documents. Had Falco deferred the award because Hadrian wished to be involved?

Newly privileged veterans had to arrange for their own notarised copies of the award to be made, if they wanted a permanent record on bronze. One copy of this award of July 122 has been found. The recipient was called Gemellus, NCO of the *ala I Pannoniorum Tampiana*, commanded by Fabius Sabinus. He had gone home to his native Pannonia. Many of the veterans of the year 122 will have settled in Britain. Local recruitment, which Hadrian's policy was to foster, surely resulted in the majority of future veterans of British-based units staying in the province after discharge. Nothing more is known of the prefect of the *ala Tampiana*, Fabius Sabinus. But we do at least have the names of two other commanding officers of the auxiliary regiments in Britain at this moment. One, Maenius Agrippa, has already been mentioned, and will crop up again. A local magnate at Camerinum in Picenum, Agrippa was to serve at the newly constructed fort of Alauna (Maryport) on the Solway coast for four years, later to return to Britain as Prefect of the Fleet and then as procurator of the province. Agrippa's newly raised regiment of Spaniards, an addition to the garrison, does not feature in the diploma list. The other known officer, Q. Baienus Blassianus, from Tergeste (Trieste), was holding his first appointment, as prefect of the Second Cohort of Asturians, number 24 in the diploma list. Blassianus was to go on to a long and distinguished career, which also included the British fleet prefecture.[9]

Wherever else Hadrian went in Britain, there can be no doubt that he visited the 'frontier'. As in Germany, he had decided to mark the limits of the province by an artificial barrier. It must be assumed that extensive preparations had been undertaken before his arrival. That the British frontier-work was to be a stone wall, with regularly-spaced guard-posts every Roman mile and two towers between these posts, rather than, as in Germany, a simple timber palisade, may have been his own advance decision. Lack of suitable forests to furnish the posts for a palisade may have been the basic reason. Once it was seen to be necessary to build the new frontier in stone, there was scope for something on the grand scale.[10]

Hadrian had every reason to be well informed about North Britain. It is not fanciful to recall that his earliest memories should have included some aware-ness of Agricola's – apparently final – conquest of the northernmost part of the island. Hadrian was already a seven-year-old when the great victory over the Caledonians was won at the Graupian Mountain. When he began his own military service just over ten years later, it was on the Danube, but in a legion, II Adiutrix, that had been transferred there from Britain not long before. Numerous soldiers and centurions that he served with in the mid-90s will have had tales to tell about their fifteen years campaigning in Britain. When Hadrian returned to Rome from his three military tribunates, in 99, he could hardly have failed to read, perhaps even hear a public recital of the tribute to Agricola by the general's son-in-law, Rome's foremost orator, Cornelius Tacitus. A few years later Tacitus' first major work, recounting the history of Rome under the Flavian dynasty, began to be made public. It included an extended treatment of the wars in Britain – and a bitter indictment of Domitian for his surrender of what Agricola had won for Rome. It probably did not impress Hadrian – it had

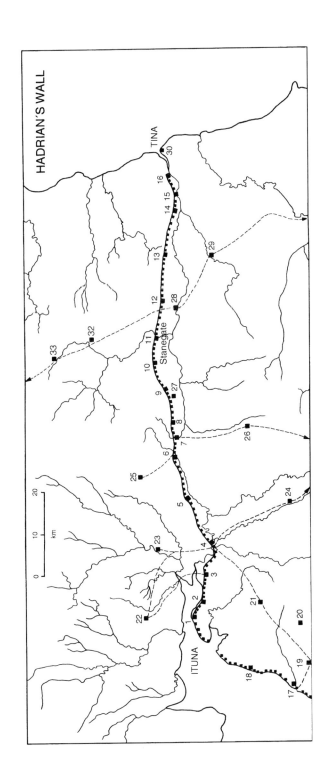

HADRIAN'S WALL

Map 3 Hadrian's Wall

Key

1 Bowness (*Maia*), 2 Drumburgh (*Congavata*), 3 Burgh-by-Sands (*Aballava*), 4 Stanwix (*Petriana? or Uxellodunum*), 5 Castlesteads (*Camboglanna*), 6 Birdoswald (*Banna*), 7 Carvoran (*Magnis*), 8 Great Chesters (*Aesica*), 9 Housesteads (*Vercovicium*), 10 Carrawburgh Chesters (*Brocolitia*), 11 Chesters (*Cilurnum*), 12 Halton Chesters (*Onnum*), 13 Rudchester (*Vindovala*), 14 Benwell (*Condercum*), 15 Newcastle (*Pons Aelius*), 16 Wallsend (*Segedunum*), 17 Maryport (*Alauna*), 18 Beckfoot, 19 Papcastle, 20 Caermote, 21 Old Carlisle, 22 Birrens (*Blatobulgium*), 23 Netherby (*Castra Exploratorum*), 24 Old Penrith (*Voreda*), 25 Bewcastle (*Fanum Cocidii*), 26 Whitley Castle, 27 Chesterholm (*Vindolanda*), 28 Corbridge (*Coria*), 29 Ebchester (*Vindomora*), 30 South Shields (*later Arbeia*), 31 Carlisle (*Luguvalium*), 32 Risingham (*Habitarcum*), 33 High Rochester (*Bremenium*)

certainly had no effect on Trajan. At about the time that the first part of the *Histories* was appearing, the great Imperator, basking in the glory of his second Dacian triumph and pondering new adventures in the east, assented to a further withdrawal of Roman forces from northern Britain south of the Forth–Clyde isthmus. Here, Tacitus had written, 'were the valour of the army and the glory of the Roman name to permit, a limit might be found within Britain', between the Firths of Clota and Bodotria. The tidal sea on either side was separated by a narrow neck of land, and 'the enemy could be pushed out, as if into a different island.' Agricola's forts between the Firths and most of what lay between them and the Tina–Ituna (Tyne–Solway) line to the south had been evacuated at the latest by 105. Neratius Marcellus, probably the man who had implemented the withdrawal, can be assumed to have had no regrets.[11]

At any rate for most of Trajan's reign the front line in Britain was back where it had been forty years before. To be sure, Rome's authority had still been exercised over the lands beyond, it seems: in the early years of Trajan Haterius Nepos, then prefect of cavalry, had conducted a census of the *Brittones Anavioneses*, the people of the Anava (Annan) valley on the north side of the Solway. This may have been followed by the enforced enrolment of young Britons to serve as frontier guards in Upper Germany. Some may have come from what is now southern Scotland, others from the Pennines, above all from the Brigantes, the 'largest people in Britain', as Tacitus calls them. The Brigantian lands straddled the backbone of the British province and stretched from sea to sea. Near Cataractonium (Catterick), the site of an important base for military supplies close to where the Great North Road forks, a western route crossing the moors and going to Luguvalium (Carlisle), the Brigantian leader Venutius had made a last stand against Rome over fifty years before. The Flavian governors had occupied and garrisoned the whole Brigantian territory and Agricola had taken the army to the far north. But the north-westernmost Brigantians were located beyond the new Trajanic frontier-line, which Hadrian now chose to make irrevocably permanent.[12]

It was surely the Brigantes, with the support of the peoples across the Solway, who had caused the trouble at the time of Hadrian's accession, suppressed by Falco, but only after heavy Roman losses. Conscription of their young men, derisively referred to by Roman officers as *Brittunculi*, 'the little Brits', looked down on and more harshly treated than soldiers who came from overseas, the *transmarini*, may be supposed to have goaded the Brigantes to rebellion.[13]

In 122, the Sixth Legion seems to have been sent straight to the north. Part of the headquarters staff may, indeed, have gone straight to Eburacum to take over the fortress built by IX Hispana. The rest sailed into the Tyne. On its arrival the legion dedicated two simple altars, one to Neptune, adorned with a relief of the sea-god's trident, a dolphin curled around it, the other to Oceanus, with a ship's anchor. Alexander the Great had once sacrificed to the same deities in the Far East, at the River Hydaspes (a branch of the Indus). Hadrian's friend Arrian was to describe the scene. In another version Alexander sacrificed after sailing

Plate 14 Oceanus: a commemoration of Hadrian's crossing to Britain
(*BMC* III Hadrian no. 129)

out into the Ocean, past the mouths of the great river. At all events, that act had marked the end of his Indian campaign. Now, nearly 450 years later, Hadrian, one may fancy, consciously imitated the great conqueror – whom Trajan had been so anxious to emulate. Was not Hadrian the first ruler of the world to reach this distant limit, a western counterpart to Alexander at the Indus? Allusion to Hadrian's presence at this place has even been detected on the imperial coinage, which shows Oceanus and a river-god identified as the Tyne (in spite of the feminine termination of Tina). By the shrine where the altars were set up, the legionaries built a bridge. It was named Pons Aelius, 'Hadrian's Bridge', and was to mark one end of the new frontier. First rafts of massive iron-shod piles were laid in the Tyne, on which stone piers were built, each with cutwaters down-stream and upstream for the tidal river. On top came the bridge itself, with a roadway some 18 feet (5.5 m) wide, presumably set on segmental timber arches.[14]

That the bridge bore his name is surely a sign that Hadrian was there during its construction, indeed that he took a personal hand in its design. Architecture was, after all, one of his great passions. Here, close by the Aelian Bridge, the work on the new frontier barrier began. It was to be a massive stone wall, 10 feet (3 m) broad and 14 feet (4.2 m) high to the rampart walk, no doubt with battlement. On the north side a great ditch was to be dug, 30 feet (9 m)

Plate 15 River-god – perhaps the River Tyne? (*BMC* III Hadrian no. 132)

wide and nine feet (2.7 m) deep. Every mile, measured westwards from the bridge, a small fort or guard-post – a 'milecastle' – was to be incorporated into the Wall, and between each pair of milecastles two towers – 'turrets' – for signalling were to be erected. These structures were to be built first, then, to connect them, three hundred paces of curtain wall.[15]

Hadrian himself may have approved the construction of a memorial at the eastern end of the frontier. Two fragments from an inscription have been preserved, reused in a church on the south side of the Tyne. Their size suggests that the original text measured a good 6 feet across and was nearly 8 feet high. It would have been on the base of a monumental piece of statuary – perhaps representing Hadrian and the newly protected province Britannia. Hadrian's names came at the beginning, preceded by the label . . . *omnium fil[ius]*, perhaps 'son of all the [deified]' – his ancestry now included Nerva and Trajan, both *divi*, not to mention his mother-in-law Matidia. Otherwise one might restore a superlative, *[principum] omnium fid[issimus]*, 'most steadfast of all emperors'. In the next lines come the words *necessitate* and then *[conser]vati divino praecepto*: necessity was invoked, it is clear, and 'divine injunction'. From the lower fragment there survives: *diffusis[. . .] provinc[ia . . .]Britannia ad[. . .]utrumque O[ceani] litus? . . .]exercitus pr[ovinciae . . .]sub cur[a . . .]*. 'The scattering' – surely of the enemy or the barbarians – is proclaimed, then perhaps the restitution of the security of Britain, and the erection of a barrier between 'the two shores of Ocean by the army of the province, under the supervision' of Platorius Nepos. This interpretation is at least plausible: the text probably represents in part a speech by Hadrian, delivered to the troops on the banks of the Tyne – it may be, of course, that the inscription was restored and amended under Severus or Caracalla.[16]

The Wall itself was faced with cut stone, with a clay and rubble core. Only for the milecastles was mortar used, it seems, perhaps so that the work could proceed even in winter (Julius Frontinus had recommended restricting aqueduct-construction to the period from April to October because of the effects of frost on mortar). The finished work was to be rendered with plaster and whitewashed, with grooves cut into the plaster to give the appearance of regular ashlar coursing: it would gleam in the sunlight and be visible for miles. Whatever calculations have been made in modern times about the way the building operations were organised, how long it took to complete the whole work, and the sequence in which the various elements in the system were initiated, it is reasonable to conjecture that at least a sample section was completed to full height for imperial inspection and approval. The army was easily capable of rapid construction-work – and not just the Roman army. Diodorus tells how the tyrant of Syracuse, Dionysius I, with a labour force of 60,000 men, backed up by 6,000 yokes of oxen, completed his great Syracusan citadel of the Euryalus and a wall 3 miles (nearly 5 km) long in less than three weeks. According to tradition the same Dionysius was the founder of Hadria, the Italian city from which Hadrian's forebears claimed to derive. Hadrian will certainly have known that Dionysius was the founder of Hadria: it was recorded by his freedman Phlegon. No doubt he also knew the story of the record-breaking building project at Syracuse.[17]

The defences erected by Dionysius should have been even more familiar to Pompeius Falco, whose family came from Sicily. This is not to say that the idea of building the Wall derived from Syracuse. Other sources of inspiration could equally well be invoked. Appeal has even been made to travellers' tales from China – hardly plausible. Ten years earlier, Hadrian had been in Greece. At Athens, he would have seen the remains of the Long Walls joining the city with its harbour of Piraeus, a double barrier some 5 miles (3 km) in length, with internal towers and fortified gateways. More likely is the appeal to earlier Greek history: at Thermopylae and at the Isthmus, the Greeks had undertaken major works to wall out the barbarians. But whatever gave Hadrian the idea for such a barrier, it is clear enough what he wished to achieve. The official policy was no doubt that announced on the monument by the banks of the Tyne – invoking necessity, the precept of heaven, the scattering of the barbarians and the protection of Britannia. The *HA* version, 'to separate Romans and barbarians', might well derive, via Marius Maximus, from the autobiography. What is nowhere stated may nonetheless be inferred: by the construction of this monumental barrier Hadrian was again, as in Germany, indicating that the age of expansion was over. Jupiter's promise to Aeneas of an 'empire without end' in time or space for his descendants, *imperium sine fine*, as Virgil had rendered it, was significantly adjusted. The empire was still to last forever, no doubt, but it had now a precise and tangible spatial limit.[18]

The restless and inquisitive traveller will not have waited by the Tyne for weeks on end while the legionaries built the Aelian Bridge and began the Wall. He would wish to see the whole line for himself. At the very least a journey to the Solway must be envisaged, with Emperor, his friend Nepos, perhaps some *comites* (such as Marcellus and Bradua), praetorian guardsmen, and Horse Guards proceeding westwards, *per lineam valli*, as it would later be called. He could, to be sure, have done the first part of the journey by water, up the Tyne as far as Coria (Corbridge), where the Great North Road from Eburacum crossed the river. But the remark of the poet Florus about Hadrian's 'walk among the Britons' may be invoked in favour of his going on foot, studying each and every part of the new frontier-line. Further, albeit the Wall was to mark the limit of the empire, the lands beyond it were given some direct protection. There were to be several northern outposts, two of them on the high road from Coria to the north, at Habitancum (Risingham) and Bremenium (High Rochester). Further up the northern highway, Trimontium (Newstead), abandoned some seventeen years before, might have been worth a visit. It is easy to envisage the energetic Emperor climbing the triple peak of the Eildon Hills to survey the Tweed valley. Another likely point for him to inspect was the place where the Wall itself had to be taken across another river, the North Tyne. Here, at Cilurnum (Chesters), the proudly named *ala Augusta ob virtutem appellata* ('named Augusta for valour'), dedicated an altar to 'the Discipline of the Emperor Hadrian'.[19]

The concern to restore discipline, already manifested in Germany, was now to be institutionalised as part of the army's religion. *Disciplina* also features on the imperial coinage (see Plate 10). Enough evidence of commercial dealings by the military, some of them perhaps slightly shady and some from just before Hadrian's visit, can be found in the Vindolanda writing tablets. This may suggest that tightening up was needed in the army of Britain as well as that of the Germanies. Other dedications to the Emperor's Discipline, not naming Hadrian, have been found along the line of the Wall. The young senatorial tribune of VI Victrix, Pontius Laelianus, never forgot this lesson. Forty years on, 'an eminent man and a disciplinarian of the old school', as *comes* of Lucius Verus in Syria, he would rip open the soldiers' cuirasses – ornamental but ineffective for defence – with his finger-tips and order their padded saddles to be slit open.[20]

Some of the older men in the Horse Guards – the Batavians – could conceivably have served on the British frontier. The Ninth Cohort of Batavians, part at least of the Third as well, had been based for some years at Vindolanda until moved to the Danube twenty years before Hadrian came to Britain. Vindolanda, first occupied in the 80s, lies on the east–west road from Coria to Luguvalium – the Stanegate – in a little sheltered valley about a mile south of the Whin Sill, the north-facing basaltic crags along which the Wall was to run. Vindolanda, as Batavians in his Horse Guards who had served there might have

Plate 16 View of Vindolanda with the line of the Wall in the background

been able to tell Hadrian, would have been an ideal base from which he could inspect the central part of the new frontier. At all events, what has been found there, dating exactly to the period at which the Wall was begun, certainly looks as if it was constructed to house persons of high rank. An unusually large and solid building, with *opus signinum* floor and walls lined with painted plaster, would have been suitable accommodation for the imperial visitor. Besides this, it seems that someone stationed there was expecting to be able to hand the Emperor a petition. One of the documents from Vindolanda, dated by its context to this period, is a three-page account registering distribution of grain. On the back of the second and third sheets an unknown man – probably the clerk who had written the account – penned an impassioned appeal. He had been flogged – till he bled – but should not have been, he protested: he was a *trasmarinus*, an 'overseas man', and innocent – the first word clearly implies that floggings for Britons were normal. He had not been able to appeal to the Prefect, who had been 'detained by ill-health'. Now, he writes, 'I implore Your Majesty not to let a man who is from overseas and innocent suffer in this way.' Hadrian was noted for his accessibility to petitioners and concern for the common soldier. But whether he read this letter is rather doubtful. At least, the draft was found in what has been identified as a centurion's quarters of a barrack-building at Vindolanda. The same centurion who had flogged the writer had probably confiscated it. Supposing that the appeal did get to Hadrian, the odds are that he was unimpressed, if the appellant was indeed the same person as the accounts-clerk: several items in the grain-distribution look highly irregular.[21]

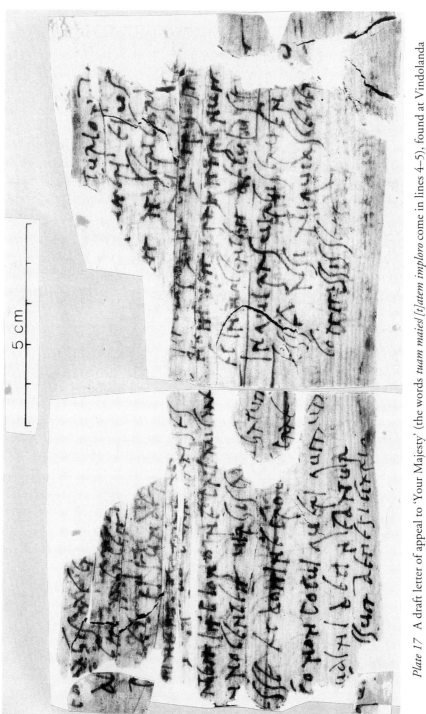

Plate 17 A draft letter of appeal to 'Your Majesty' (the words *tuam maies[t]atem imploro* come in lines 4–5), found at Vindolanda

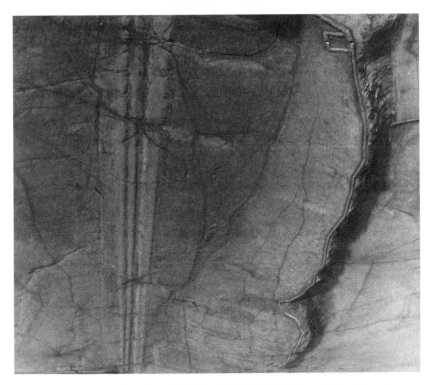

Plate 18 Aerial view of Hadrian's Wall, with Cawfields Milecastle (no. 42) at the top right. South of the Wall runs the line of the so-called Vallum

From the hillside east of Vindolanda, where the road from Coria approached the fort, the imperial visitor will have been able to see to the north on the sky-line the central, highest part of the line selected for his Wall, where it would run along the top of the crags. He would have been able to say, as another visitor did over 1,400 years later, 'verily I have seene the tract of it over the high pitches and steep descents of hills, wonderfully rising and falling.' Time will have been found for entertainment, at least for hunting. Flavius Cerialis, Prefect of the Ninth Batavians at Vindolanda twenty years earlier, had written to his friend Brocchus, 'If you love me, brother, please send me some hunting-nets.' Hunting with nets had evidently gone out of fashion in the meantime, to judge from the essay on the subject by Arrian. Celtic greyhounds, *vertragi*, were now used to catch hares. Hadrian would probably have hunted bigger game in the British frontier land, wild boar. The imperial huntsman would have had no difficulty in procuring the ingredients, which included boar's meat, for his favourite game pie, his *tetrafarmacum*. An altar in the northern Pennines records the fulfilling of a vow by an equestrian officer who 'had taken a boar of exceptional fineness, which many of his predecessors had been unable to bag.' The country north of the Wall would also have attracted: the local Celtic deity, Cocidius, was identified not only with the Roman war-god Mars but with Silvanus the god of the wild and of huntsmen. One of the outpost forts north of the western part of the Wall was, it seems, placed at Cocidius' principal sanctuary, Fanum Cocidii (Bewcastle).[22]

The frontier system stretched not merely from 'one shore of Ocean to the other', as the inscription at the eastern end put it. The fortlets and towers carried on for some 40 Roman miles along the western coast. This too will have demanded Hadrian's attention. A visit to Maryport, where Maenius Agrippa had been sent, may be regarded as probable. This man was a favourite of Hadrian, who was later to stay with him at his home, Camerinum in Picenum.[23]

What else Hadrian would wish to see in Rome's remotest province had no doubt been a matter for speculation by Pompeius Falco. In anticipation of his arrival road-building or road improvement had been undertaken. Shortly before parts of the system at least, north of Cataractonium (Catterick), were in a poor state. Octavius, probably a centurion based somewhere near Vindolanda, had written to Candidus, a colleague at that fort, demanding to know what had happened to a wagon-load from Cataractonium he should have been sent. 'I would have collected it myself', he commented, 'except that I did not want to wear out the beasts while the roads are bad.' Three British milestones survive, which may attest preparatory roadworks ordered by Falco. In 120 the old road linking the *colonia* of Lindum (Lincoln) was being renewed, as the milestone 2 miles (3.2 km) east of Ratae (Leicester) shows. In the next year a remote stretch in Snowdonia, west of Kanovium (Caerhun), was being worked on – Hadrian's propensity for climbing mountains was doubtless known to Falco, who may well have ordered improvements there in case the Emperor chose to ascend the highest peak in the province. A third milestone, not closely dated, 4 miles (6.5 km) from Lancaster, may suggest that Hadrian was expected to return south down the west side of the island.[24]

Developments in the now largely civilian southern part of the province have been plausibly enough attributed to Hadrian's initiative. Eight years after his visit the *civitas Cornoviorum* set up a monumental inscription over the main entrance to the newly completed forum at their chief centre, Viroconium (Wroxeter). The reshaping of this place may have been launched by the Emperor on a flying visit. Other British towns may likewise have been substantially developed in the years following 122. Further, it has been suggested that a large-scale programme of canal construction and land reclamation in the Fenland was inspired by Hadrian. His concern to extend the cultivation of marginal land is well attested elsewhere in the empire.[25]

Except that Hadrian did not winter in Britain, it is impossible to say how long his stay lasted. But sooner or later he had to leave his brainchild, the most elaborate and costly of all Rome's frontier-works. The *HA* biographer places a startling incident immediately after mentioning the voyage to Britain and the erection of the Wall. Hadrian 'replaced Septicius Clarus, Prefect of the Guard, and Suetonius Tranquillus, Director of the Chancery, and many others, because they had at that time, in their relations with his wife Sabina, behaved with greater familiarity than the etiquette of the court required.' Suetonius and Septicius had clearly been left with the Empress. But the exact nature of their offence must remain a mystery. What sort of impropriety can be meant? Had Sabina started an affair with one or more of these men? Or should one speculate that Suetonius had caused offence by giving a reading of his work *On Famous Whores*, or perhaps by relating the fruits of his researches about Tiberius' private life on Capri, destined for a forthcoming volume of his *Caesars*? But this is merely to make a flippant guess: the mystery must remain. There is, for one thing, a slight uncertainty in the text. 'In their relations with his wife Sabina' translates *apud Sabinam uxorem in usu eius*, but the last three words are emended. The MSS read *uniussu eius*, corrected in one to *iniussu eius*, which could mean 'without his consent', or even 'without her consent'. The *HA* biographer adds the comment: 'He would have dismissed his wife too, as he himself used to say, for being moody and difficult, if he had been a private citizen.' The *Epitome de Caesaribus*, which, like the *HA*, is evidently based on the lost *vita Hadriani* by Marius Maximus, contains what one may call Sabina's riposte. 'She used to boast openly that she had taken steps to make sure she did not become pregnant by him – offspring of his would harm the human race.'[26]

The *HA* for its part goes on to relate how Hadrian 'used to investigate not only his own household but those of his friends: through commissary-agents (*frumentarii*) he used to unearth all their secrets, and his friends were unaware that their private lives were known to the Emperor until he indicated it to them himself.' An illustration is supplied. A man applied for leave. Hadrian had intercepted a letter in which the man's wife reproached him for not wishing to come home because of his fondness for 'pleasures' and the baths. He now reproved the man for his vices. 'What!' said the startled officer, 'has my wife complained to you as well?'[27]

At all events, it looks clear enough that Hadrian had received secret reports from *frumentarii* about the conduct of his wife – and of his high officials. Hadrian was surely not responsible for creating this body of men as a kind of 'secret police' – their headquarters at Rome, the *castra peregrina*, were already in being under Trajan. But he may have used them, for political or indeed private purposes, in a way that Trajan had not. In any case, the real nature of the offence committed by Septicius, Suetonius and the unnamed 'many others' is obscure. Infringement of court protocol – at an excessively informal literary soirée on the Thames or at Aquae Sulis? – was no doubt merely the pretext. Septicius and Suetonius were perhaps simply deemed incompetent – unless they had been intriguing against Hadrian. Suetonius, who had already dedicated to Septicius the first instalment of his *Vitae Caesarum*, would have to complete the work in retirement.[28]

Septicius' successor is unknown, but if the *HA* biographer's language is taken literally he and Suetonius and the other dismissed persons were indeed replaced. Yet no new colleague for Marcius Turbo can be identified. It is of course only

Plate 19   Hadrian in Britain: BRITANNIA
(*BMC* III Hadrian no. 1723)

Plate 20   Hadrian and the army of Britain:
EXER BRITANNICVS (*BMC* III Hadrian no. 1672)

an argument from silence, but Turbo may have served a sole Prefect of the Guard until near the end of the reign. The replacement for Suetonius as *ab epistulis* may not have been appointed at once. Hadrian may have found the right man where he was to go next, in southern Gaul, on his way to Spain.[29]

Alone among the provinces, Britannia had already appeared on the imperial coinage before Hadrian went there. The personified province has been described as 'Britain subdued', a figure of dejection, sitting with her right elbow resting on her knee and supporting her head, her right foot placed on rocks. Others prefer to see her as vigilant, rather than sorrowing. She is in native dress, with short tunic and breeches, boots and an ample cloak, fringed at the bottom; against her left side is a large spiked shield. Her hair is turned back from her face in thick, waving locks. At all events, the issue commemorated the war which Pompeius Falco had waged and which Hadrian's *expeditio* formally brought to an end. A dozen years or more later, Britain reappears, with other issues recalling Hadrian's provincial tours. On the province issue, Britannia resembles the earlier personification, with spear and shield. But the *adventus* issue shows a purely civilian Britannia greeting Hadrian, in long robe, with a cloak partly veiling her head. There are two versions of the *exercitus Britannicus* issue. On one (see Plate 20), Hadrian is shown on horseback, haranguing five soldiers, one carrying a *vexillum* (flag), three with standards. On the other, the Emperor stands on a platform, addressing three soldiers, one with legionary eagle, one with *vexillum* and shield, the third with a standard.[30]

12

A NEW AUGUSTUS

'After settling matters in Britain he crossed to Gaul', the *HA* biographer reports. But the goal was Spain. A general inspection was planned and a summons had no doubt already been sent out all over the peninsula for a special assembly at Tarraco (Tarragona) in the spring. His obvious route would be to proceed to Lugdunum (Lyons), down the Rhone valley and then along the coast by the Via Domitia and Narbo Martius (Narbonne) to the Pyrenees. It is plausible enough that he may have intended a detour to the south-west, to Aquitania.[1]

A 'disturbing' dispatch that reached him after he had crossed may have curtailed his itinerary. There was rioting at Alexandria – provoked by religion. It was only five years since the bloody confrontation there between Greeks and Jews had been crushed by Marcius Turbo. The Jews were not involved this time, nor indeed the Greeks, but rather the native Egyptians. Their sacred bull, Apis, had been identified again at last, giving rise to violent rivalry. Coins of Alexandria minted in the Egyptian year 29 August 121 to 28 August 122 proclaim the happy event. But the god Ptah, in whose temple at Memphis the bull was kept, does not appear on the coinage until the next year, perhaps indicating some delay and dispute. At all events, the Prefect of Egypt, Haterius Nepos, may have urged an imperial visit, fearing the outbreak of serious fighting. Instead, Hadrian was able to restore order with a firmly worded letter. 'Thus', commented Cassius Dio, 'a word from an emperor can have more effect than the use of force.' Hadrian may have taken some time to discuss the question with his advisers. It is possible that he was able to turn to an ideally qualified person in southern Gaul, L. Julius Vestinus. At any rate, it is a plausible guess that Vestinus had become the new Chief Secretary, *ab epistulis*. His previous post had been exactly that held by Suetonius before the Secretariat: Director of Imperial Libraries, *a bibliothecis*, and Cultural Secretary, *a studiis*. Vestinus' occupation before that in Rome was highly relevant to the problem over Apis: 'High Priest', *archiereus*, of Alexandria and Egypt, in other words, the official responsible for temple administration. Although a cultivated exponent of Greek letters, Vestinus was a Gaul, from a distinguished family at Vienna (Vienne) near Lugdunum. It could well be that he had already been named *ab epistulis* straight after Suetonius' dismissal and had joined Hadrian in Gaul to take up his duties.[2]

Whether or not Vestinus replaced Suetonius as Secretary, there is simply no information about a replacement for the sacked Guard Prefect Septicius. Hadrian ought to have had a Prefect with him – Septicius' colleague, the trusty Turbo, remained in Rome, so it is supposed. Only a guess can be offered. Q. Rammius Martialis, Prefect of Egypt from 117 to 119, would have been a suitable candidate: holders of this post went on to the Guard Prefecture often enough. Besides, Rammius, like Vestinus, might have been readily available: at any rate, the rare name is found in southern Gaul, and a freedman of a Q. Rammius is attested at Narbo. Perhaps this was Martialis' home, and he could have taken up his duties almost at once.[3]

A missive, less depressing than the despatch from Egypt, that Hadrian probably also received in Gaul at this time, was a jokey little poem sent by the now elderly writer Florus. The poet made fun of Hadrian's already evident passion for travelling:

> *ego nolo Caesar esse*
> *ambulare per Britannos*
>
> ———
>
> *Scythicas pati pruinas.*

The third line of four seems to be missing, since the reply that Hadrian dashed off is a quatrain:

> *ego nolo Florus esse*
> *ambulare per tabernas*
> *latitare per popinas,*
> *culices pati rotundos.*

A free rendering might run as follows:

> I don't want to be Caesar, please
> – To tramp round the Britons, weak at the knees,
>
> ———
>
> In the Scythian frosts to freeze.

> I don't want to be Florus, please,
> To tramp round pubs, into bars to squeeze,
> To lurk about eating pies and peas,
> To get myself infested with fleas.

If, as seems logical, Florus referred to Hadrian's travels in reverse order, the latest being the visit to Britain, the first being that to the Danube delta – 'Scythia' – in 117–18, the missing line ought to have been about the tour of the Rhine and Upper Danube frontier in 121. One could restore '*latitare per Sugambros*' or '*per Batavos*', or the name of some other people in that region, perhaps just '*Germanos*'.[4]

Annaeus Florus had had mixed fortunes. Born in Africa, he had come to Rome as a youth and entered the poetry competition at Domitian's Capitoline *Ludi*. His entry was acclaimed by the audience, but he was denied the prize because, so he later maintained, the Emperor did not want Africa to gain 'Great Jupiter's Crown'. The disappointed poet took to travel, going to Sicily, Crete, the Cyclades, Rhodes and Egypt, then returning to Italy, turning northwards, crossing the Alps into Gaul, to settle finally at Tarraco, where he opened a school. The city appealed to him: the people were honest, sober, peaceful, taking their time to welcome strangers but when they did so they were judicious hosts. The climate was particularly temperate – it was like spring all through the year – and the country was fertile. Early in the reign of Trajan a group of old acquaintances returning from Rome to Baetica came across him at Tarraco and persuaded him to return to the capital, 'where your verses are recited.'[5]

Hadrian should have known Florus personally. Perhaps he knew and valued his poetry, not all of it so banal as the lines quoted above. Florus could write about wine and roses, about carving the name of his beloved on the fruit-trees that he planted. He had become disenchanted with women: 'Every woman hides dangerous poison in her breast: Sweet the talk of their lips, hurtful their heart.' He was also suspicious of foreign ways (*sperne mores transmarinos*). If he had read them, Hadrian may have preferred the former of these two poems to the latter.[6]

Florus was to turn his hand to history, producing a brief account, suitable for schoolboys, of Rome's expansion up to the time of Augustus, with comments on imperial *inertia* under later emperors – until, under Trajan, Rome was rejuvenated. At first sight, this suggests enthusiasm for conquest. But Hadrian would have relished some of Florus' comments, for example, 'It is harder to hold on to new provinces than to create them.' The new Emperor could with justice have quoted this remark when confronted with the legacy of Trajan's Parthian war. The last campaign that Florus recounts in detail is the final conquest of northwest Spain by Augustus, who learned of the subjugation of the Cantabrian strongholds by his legates while 'wintering at Tarraco on the coast'. The little work ends with a celebration of the Augustan peace; the last sentence recalls how it had been debated whether to call the new founder of the empire Romulus – but that it had seemed more fitting to give him the name Augustus.[7]

Hadrian 'wintered at Tarraco', the *HA* biographer writes. He mentions first in a single sentence an action of Hadrian's in Gaul, the erection of a basilica 'of remarkable construction' at Nemausus (Nîmes) in honour of the dowager-empress Plotina, whose family, it seems, came from that city. That Plotina had died is not stated explicitly here, but in the *Epitome* of Cassius Dio her death and Hadrian's reaction follow immediately after the story of how he mourned for his favourite horse Borysthenes – honoured by a tomb and a verse epitaph composed by himself. A stone with just such an epitaph was found at Apta (Apt), not far from Nemausus, in the sixteenth century. The *HA* biographer probably found the same story in Marius Maximus, but only alludes to it in a later section summarising Hadrian's character: 'He loved horses and dogs so much that he set up tombs for them' – no details about Hadrianic dogs have yet come to light.[8]

Apta, on the high road from the Rhone up the Durance to the Cottian Alps and Turin, was no doubt the scene of a hunting trip. The city itself is on a river but its territory included mountains, especially on the north, where it stretched into the foothills of the Alps. At this prosperous little place, a *colonia* since Caesar's time, Hadrian would have found congenial company for a hunt, witness two dedications to the hunters' god Silvanus at Apta itself and three more at the old hill-fort of St-Saturnin nearby.[9]

Somewhere in these parts in autumn or early winter 122 Borysthenes died. Hadrian probably dashed off the verses the same day, no masterpiece, to be sure (hence some argue the lines are not authentic), but deserving quotation – at least in prose: 'Borysthenes the Alan, Caesar's hunting-horse, used to fly over plains and marshes and hills and thickets, at Pannonian boars – nor did any boar, with tusks foaming white, dare to harm him as he followed, or spray the tip of his tail with spittle from its maul (as tends to happen), but in unimpaired youth, with limbs unscarred, after meeting his day of fate, he lies in this field.' When Alexander's famous horse Bucephalus died in India, the great conqueror allegedly founded a city at the spot. Hadrian was to show himself prone to gestures of this kind – a new city in the province of Asia would commemorate a successful hunt. The smaller and intensely romanised Gallia Narbonensis hardly needed a new foundation.[10]

As for the commemoration of Plotina, the erection of the basilica at Nemausus cannot, it seems, have been ordered before the start of 123. At any rate, stamped tiles from brickworks she owned near Rome dated by the consuls of this year bear her name as though she were still alive. Wherever Hadrian was when he heard of the death of his great supporter – and mother by adoption – he no doubt went in person to Nemausus. There cannot have been time for more than the choice of a site, the drawing up of plans and the guarantee of funding. The construction presumably took several years to complete. An inscription from Nemausus records an *exactor*, overseer, of the 'marble- and stonework of the basilica'. Dio records that 'when Plotina, through whose love he gained the throne, died, he honoured her in exceptional fashion, wearing black for nine days, building her a temple and composing some hymns about her.' Whether the 'temple' is in fact the basilica at Nemausus is unclear. Plotina was in due course deified, perhaps not until Hadrian returned to Rome nearly three years later. Another excerptor quotes a little more: 'when Plotina died, Hadrian praised her, saying that "she asked much of me but was never refused anything", meaning by this no more than that "her requests were such that they were neither difficult to fulfil nor gave any grounds for refusal."'[11]

Nemausus would have no doubt earned a visit from Hadrian in any case. It had produced senators for several generations, the first notable example being the caustic orator Cn. Domitius Afer, consul under Caligula and a celebrated figure in Claudio-Neronian Rome. One of his sons by adoption, the immensely wealthy Domitius Tullus, would have been well-known to Hadrian as a fellow-*VIIvir epulonum*. Besides, Tullus' granddaughter Domitia Lucilla was daughter-in-law of Hadrian's City Prefect, Annius Verus. Verus' own daughter Faustina was married to another prominent man from Nemausus, T. Aurelius Fulvus. Even if these families of the new élite had by now little personal contact with their place of origin, they may be assumed to have still possessed estates there. Hadrian would have had ample choice of accommodation. Vienna (Vienne), Arelate (Arles), Vasio (Vaison) and other cities of Narbonensis could also boast citizens with seats in the Roman Senate – and they could have had more. An inscription from the Rhone valley in honour of one Q. Valerius Macedo, a magnate of Vienna, registers that 'the deified Hadrian offered him the broad stripe [of senatorial rank] with the quaestorship and permitted the honour to be declined.'[12]

When the time came to move on to Spain, Hadrian's route will certainly have been along the old Via Domitia, and he may be assumed to have visited Narbo Martius, the original *colonia*, founded in 118 BC as 'a bulwark of the empire against barbarous peoples' (as Cicero had put it), and capital of the province. The possibility that he now had a new Guard Prefect (Rammius Martialis) from the *colonia* has already been mentioned. Unlike the once native Gallic cities such as Vienna and Nemausus, Narbo is not known to have produced senators yet. Hadrian now elevated one of its leading citizens to this status, L. Aemilius Arcanus, who had held three commissions as an equestrian legionary tribune, the third being in II Augusta of the army of Britain. Arcanus did not, like Valerius Macedo, disdain 'adlection into the *amplissimus ordo*'. Hadrian might have come across Arcanus in Britain, and he might have registered the fact, if Arcanus did not remind him of it, that the man's father had been a friend of the poet Martial.[13]

Martial ought to have been in Hadrian's thoughts anyway, as he approached Tarraco. One of his finest poems, to his fellow-townsman Licinianus, celebrates a visit by his friend to Bilbilis – but not to stay for the winter: come the December snows and the hoarse north wind, Licinianus will head for 'Tarraco's sunny shores' and spend his time hunting. These lines should have appealed to Hadrian, and he should have known them – the addressee was, like Hadrian, a protégé of Licinius Sura, who is mentioned at the end of the poem. On the road down to Tarraco Hadrian could have seen numerous inscriptions, and no doubt statues, of the great man. Sura, though probably deriving from the now decayed inland *colonia* at Celsa, had clearly possessed property and influence at Barcino (Barcelona), which lay on Hadrian's route. At Tarraco, too, an ancestor of Sura was commemorated – by an arch across the road leading to the city. Hadrian surely stayed first at Barcino: this was the home-town of Pedanius Fuscus, husband of his niece Julia. Fuscus, if anyone, must have been regarded as Hadrian's likely heir at this stage. The couple were, indeed, probably travelling with Hadrian.[14]

Hadrian had doubtless been to Tarraco before – perhaps over thirty years before, on his way to and from Italica in his youth, for he probably travelled by land like the group of Baeticans who came across Florus at Tarraco. Hadrian will have been well informed about the city's history: the oldest Roman foundation in Spain, founded by the brothers Scipio in 218 BC at the start of the Hannibalic War – massive walls they constructed survived. The son of the younger brother, the future Scipio Africanus, had founded Italica twelve years afterwards. Tarraco had been his headquarters from 211 to 206 BC. Here in 211 and 210 he had summoned representatives of Rome's Spanish allies. Hadrian may perfectly well have had this distant historical precedent in mind when he planned his own *conventus* of all the 'Hispani'. There can be no doubt that he was also thinking of Augustus, who had wintered at Tarraco almost exactly 150 years before. The first thing that the *HA* biographer reports about Hadrian's stay at Tarraco is that 'he rebuilt the Temple of Augustus at his own expense.'[15]

Tacitus, as it happens, had recently been reporting its original construction in the first book of his *Annals*, under the year 15: 'Approval was given [by Tiberius] to the request of the Hispani, who applied to erect a Temple to Augustus in the *colonia* of Tarraco – which provided an example for all the provinces.' Tarraco was laid out in two parts, divided by a great Circus. On two terraces on the north-east side of the city were the principal public buildings, including two Fora and the Temple of Augustus, and the area set aside for the meetings of the Council of the Province of Hispania Citerior, which administered the imperial cult. Here, it may be assumed was the venue for Hadrian's *conventus*.[16]

Hadrian's presence at Tarraco in the 150th year after the first emperor was given the name Augustus (16 January 27 BC) seems to coincide with an important policy development. The imperial coinage at about this time drastically abbreviates Hadrian's titulature. Instead of being styled 'Imp. Caesar Traianus Hadrianus Aug.', he would soon be presented simply as 'Hadrianus Augustus'. The message thereby conveyed is plain enough: he wished to be seen as a new Augustus. Such a notion had clearly been in his mind for some time. It cannot be mere chance that caused Suetonius to write, in his newly published *Life of the Deified Augustus*, that the first emperor had been 'far removed from the desire to increase the empire or for glory in war' – an assertion which his own account appears to contradict in a later passage. Tacitus, by contrast, out of touch – and out of sympathy – with Hadrian from the start, but aware of his aspirations to be regarded as an Augustus *redivivus*, seems subversively to insinuate, in the *Annals*, that a closer parallel could be found in Tiberius.[17]

Be this as it may, whatever symbolism may be read into Hadrian's residence at Tarraco in early 123, the great assembly was the principal event. Hadrian may have had much to pronounce upon. Only one item is recorded: he proclaimed a levy, *dilectus*. That Spain should provide soldiers was nothing new. Auxiliary regiments of Asturians, Bracaraugustani, Celtiberi, Vardulli, Vascones, as well as undifferentiated 'Hispani', testify to the continuation of the peninsula's martial traditions under the principate. Hadrian probably meant service in the legions, of which Spain itself had for more than two generations had only one on its soil, VII Gemina, at Legio (León) in the north-west. A thousand men from VII Gemina had just been sent to Britain, where they probably had to remain for good, assigned to the British legions, no doubt an unwelcome transfer. Now VII Gemina will have needed supplementation. Besides which, Hadrian may have already planned an intervention across the Straits, in Mauretania. For this too troops from Spain might be required.[18]

At all events, there was an unfavourable reaction. 'The "Italici" demurred, with a humorous speech, the others in all seriousness;' Hadrian 'deliberated the matter with circumspection and skill', reports the *HA* biographer, quoting Marius Maximus. This leaves us uncertain of the outcome, but it seems likely that a levy was held, and that it continued to be held at regular intervals for a good forty years. A further puzzle is the identity of the *Italici*. Unless the author has been careless – or the text is corrupt – *Italicis* cannot refer to the representatives of Hadrian's native city: they would properly be described as *Italicensibus*. As it stands, the sentence implies that there was a distinction between the Spaniards of Italian descent and the enfranchised natives. This is indeed perfectly plausible: there were, after all, separate words for the two categories, *Hispanienses* for the descendants of immigrants, *Hispani* for the natives. This still does not make the story entirely intelligible. Why should the Italo-Spaniards protest with 'humour', the others with passion? If anything, the former category might have been expected to protest much more strongly – for the Italians themselves were by now, in practice, spared from military service, the colonial or Romanised provincials, by contrast, supplying the bulk of the recruits to the western legions. The answer may be that all the Spaniards had been taking for granted that the legions were going to be supplied principally from the *coloniae* in the frontier provinces. The *Italici* may have jokingly commented that the levy could hardly apply to them.[19]

Perhaps while the assembly was in progress – 'at this time', writes the *HA* biographer, which may just mean 'while he was at Tarraco' –

> he came into very great danger, but not without winning great credit. While he was strolling through some gardens, a slave of his host rushed at him with a sword in a mad frenzy. Hadrian took hold of him and had him handed over to the attendants who ran up. When it was established that the slave was insane, he passed him to doctors for treatment, he himself being in no way agitated.

Hadrian's unnamed host, it may be conjectured, was perhaps C. Calpurnius Flaccus, former High Priest of the provincial emperor-cult, correspondent of Pliny, and father of a senator. As was to be expected, the provincials did their best to honour Hadrian. The precinct of the Temple of Augustus would soon be swarming with his statues. Some years later a High Priest was commissioned by the Council of the province 'to gild the statues' of Hadrian – presumably they were bronze and beginning to turn green.[20]

Hadrian's movements after the conclusion of the Spanish assembly can only be guessed. But his coinage later commemorates the *exercitus Hispanicus* and depicts him addressing the troops, with a legionary eagle clearly displayed. It is a natural inference that he visited the sole legionary base, that of VII Gemina, at Legio (León). The route from Tarraco would have taken him past Ilerda (Lérida), where Caesar had won a victory in the Civil War in 49 BC, Celsa and Caesaraugusta (Saragossa). From there he could have proceeded via Numantia (near Soria) and Clunia. But if, as here argued, he was consciously treading in Augustus' footsteps, the northerly route is more probable, on up the Ebro, through Calagurris (Quintilian's home) and then west to Segisama, where Augustus himself had established his camp in the Cantabrian war, before withdrawing to winter at Tarraco. From there Hadrian could go on to Legio. He might have been there already, a long time before, when Trajan was commanding VII Gemina. A visit to Asturica (Astorga), seat of the procurator and of the *iuridicus*, only a few miles west of Legio, may also be conjectured. The *iuridicus*, Ti. Claudius Quartinus, had been there for several years, it seems. His fragmentary *cursus*-inscription from a statue-base at Ostia, combined with another one from Lugdunum, shows that he had two special assignments at 'Hadrian's command'. The first was very probably to 'carry out a levy', the second would take him far from Spain.[21]

It is commonly denied that Hadrian visited the other two Spanish provinces, Lusitania and Baetica. The later commemorative coinage simply celebrated Hispania, Hadrian as the 'restorer' of the whole peninsula and his *adventus* there. The three separate provinces are not shown, simply an elegant female figure of Hispania, with corn-ear, olive branch and a rabbit to symbolise Iberian natural products. All that is certain is that he ostentatiously avoided his native Italica, as Cassius Dio explicitly comments: his 'compatriots' had presumably been expecting him, and may have been preparing to petition him to enhance the status of the town. They had to submit the request in writing: Hadrian would respond in a speech before the Senate. However this may be, there is no reason why he should not have gone south from Legio, on the high road across the Meseta via Salmantica (Salamanca) and Norba (Cáceres) to Emerita (Mérida), then down the Baetis valley to Corduba. It is perhaps too much to suggest that he could have gone on down the great river to Hispalis (Seville). That would have made his snub to Italica a few miles away on the opposite bank the more pointed. He had plenty of friends in other cities of Baetica. Furthermore, he may have wished to visit Gades (Cádiz), his mother's home town. As for Italica, even if he declined to appear there in person, Hadrian poured funds into his home town, which was rebuilt on a lavish scale, being equipped with public buildings quite out of proportion to the town's importance – the new amphitheatre, for example, was to be one of the largest in the entire empire.[22]

Even if Hadrian's itinerary is very uncertain, the *HA* appears to point him in a southerly direction in its tightly condensed summary. After the episode of the mad slave at Tarraco, the biography suddenly seems to revert to a previous theme, the erection of artificial frontiers, with the passage quoted in connection with the *limes* in Upper Germany – how he set the barbarians apart, where there no rivers as a dividing-line, by great stakes 'in the manner of a palisade'. The passage might be misplaced, and should belong just before the description of the British visit and the building of the Wall. But the next sentence reports not only a further item concerning Germany – 'he appointed a king for the Germans' – but adds that 'he suppressed revolts among the Moors and earned a public thanksgiving from the Senate.'

In the *HA*'s source the remarks about frontier fortifications – the German palisade – could have been explicitly linked with the appointment of a German king, perhaps of the Chatti just beyond the new Wetterau-*limes* or the Hermunduri of Thuringia. There is no reason, indeed, why Hadrian might not have implemented both these measures by letter from southern Spain. In other words, the erection of the German palisade may have been decided upon only after the Wall in Britain had been begun.[23]

The suppression of the *motus Maurorum* is another matter. It is surely plausible that Hadrian went to Mauretania himself – otherwise the 'thanksgiving' voted by the Senate would seem out of place. Whether the disturbances were a resurgence of the trouble suppressed by Marcius Turbo five years earlier – provoked, it was conjectured, by the downfall and death of the Moors' great man, Lusius Quietus – is impossible to tell. At any rate, this time Hadrian was available himself, and not far away, and there is no reason to deny his personal intervention. If he had acted through subordinates, the *HA* was perfectly capable of saying so (as with Antoninus Pius' military successes). Furthermore, the fact that artificial frontiers are mentioned just before the 'Moorish disturbances' permits the conjecture that Hadrian instructed the governors of the two Mauretanian provinces to give their attention to this matter too. He very probably intended a personal inspection of the North African provinces and in particular of the frontier.[24]

The *HA* biographer, intent on condensing his source, has telescoped Hadrian's movements drastically. Reports arrived, it is clear, that made Hadrian curtail the next stage in his tour: his presence in the East was essential: 'A war with Parthia was getting under way at this very time.' Hadrian sent for the *iuridicus* of Hither Spain, Claudius Quartinus, who was instructed to collect detachments of two eastern legions and move to the Euphrates frontier. He himself would follow. When the news from the other side of the empire reached him, he was in all probability in Mauretania – at least, this is implied by the order of events in the *HA*. The postulated crossing from southern Spain to Mauretania in 123 was to be Hadrian's last personal contact with the westernmost European provinces of the empire. The new Augustus had more to do in the east.[25]

13

RETURN TO THE EAST

Hadrian's progress from the western to the eastern end of the Mediterranean in the course of the year 123 has been called the most poorly documented stage in all his journeyings, at least as far as the major source, the *HA vita*, is concerned. The biographer, after mentioning the thanksgiving for the suppression of Moorish disturbances, abruptly proceeds: 'War with the Parthians was in prospect at this same time and it was checked by a personal intervention (*conloquium*) on Hadrian's part.' In other words, the Emperor negotiated with the Parthians, presumably on the Euphrates. Nothing is said about how he got there. Probability points to a journey by sea along the North African coast and then to the port of Antioch in Syria, Seleucia in Pieria. The ship that appears on the coinage of Alexandria from the year 123–4 is presumably an allusion to this voyage.[1]

However urgent the business, it need not follow that Hadrian sailed direct to Syria. Pauses must be postulated, and two or three stations may be suggested. Nor need one assume that they were only for rest and recreation. It is too much to suppose that Hadrian was able to get to the Numidian frontier, far inland. He may have originally planned this – extensive road-building on the trunk route from Carthage to Theveste was undertaken in 123. But he could well have summoned the commander of the legion III Augusta, Metilius Secundus, for a conference and instructed him to draw up plans for a new fortified frontier line.[2]

A fragment from a lost source may be invoked, which supports the case for Hadrian's presence on the soil of Africa at this time. His freedman Phlegon devoted the last two books, 15 and 16, of his historical work, *The Olympiads*, to Hadrian's reign. Only a few isolated extracts survive, but they suggest that Phlegon's account of these years followed the imperial itinerary. Phlegon himself was probably a member of Hadrian's entourage, along with the freedman Alcibiades from Nysa, Hadrian's chamberlain (*a cubiculo*), to whom he was to dedicate the work. Book 15 seems to have covered the years 117–25. Phlegon referred in it to 'Furnita, a city in Africa, whose inhabitants are called Furnitani'. This should mean that Hadrian had some dealings with a town of this name before his main visit to Africa in 128, which would have been dealt with in

Book 16. There were two places called Furni, or rather Furnos: Furnos Minus, a little way west of Carthage, in the Bagradas valley, on the main road to Membressa, and Furnos Maius, some 60 miles (100 km) south-west of Carthage, on the road to Theveste and the Numidian frontier. It might seem more plausible that Hadrian spent a few days at Furnos Minus, close to Carthage. Yet Furnos Minus did not get its charter as a *municipium* until the next century. Furnos Maius enjoyed this status in the 180s – and had perhaps gained it from Hadrian during this fleeting visit. A considerable number of other cities in Roman North Africa certainly did receive privileges from Hadrian: it is preferable to assign these measures to the later visit. Furnos Maius might, for example, have hosted the postulated conference between Hadrian and the legate Metilius Secundus.[3]

The identity of the proconsul, who would have received Hadrian at Carthage, is not known. It might well have been Atilius Bradua, who had been consul the same year as Hadrian, and had been governor of Britain under Trajan. Bradua seems to have accompanied Hadrian on his travels, to judge from his career inscription. It might be that he first joined the imperial party at this stage. But he could have been with Hadrian for the past two years, and have stayed at Carthage to take up his proconsulship.[4]

Another plausible station on the route eastwards is Cyrenaica. The province – or half-province, for it was administered jointly with Crete – had been badly ravaged in the great Jewish revolt a few years before. Hadrian's measures had been launched already: an inscription of the year 119 at Cyrene registers his order to restore 'baths, with porticoes and ball-courts and other adjacent buildings, destroyed and burned down in the Jewish disturbances'. Over twenty years later the Cyrenaeans had occasion to set up in a public place – probably the Caesareum – a series of imperial decisions relating to their city. One of these texts has been identified as an address by Hadrian before the assembled people (rather than as a letter from him). The fragmentary inscription refers to the donation of funds for the training of the young men of good family, the ephebes, exactly the kind of benefaction that was characteristic of Hadrian. He was later to display especial benevolence to the ancient Dorian colony, now over seven centuries old and fiercely proud of its status as mother-city of the North African Hellenes. Apart from this, imperial coins call Hadrian 'the restorer of Libya' and he is known to have founded a new city there. Called after himself, Hadrianopolis became the sixth member of the previously existing Pentapolis (now renamed Hexapolis). It was sited on the coast, between Arsinoe or Tauchira (Tocra) and Berenice (Benghazi), with its water-supply being brought from a spring in 'the eyebrow of the Gebel' (as later inhabitants would call the lower slopes of the Green Mountain that rises above the fertile plain). Hadrianopolis was probably intended to provide a new home for the many Greeks who had lost everything in the Jewish uprising. Whether or not Hadrian did set foot in Cyrenaica at this time, he will certainly have been aware of – and no doubt affected by – extreme hostility towards the Jews on the part of the Cyrenaican Greeks.[5]

From Apollonia (Marsa Sousa), the port of Cyrene, it can be postulated that the imperial party sailed across to Crete. The evidence that has been cited to support a stay by Hadrian on the island is, admittedly, inadequate. It is, at least, perfectly plausible that he touched Crete and then moved to the north, rather than hugging the shore of Libya and Egypt, on his way to Syria. Similarly, a visit to Cyprus is quite possible. The proconsul of the island in 123, it may be noted, was Calpurnius Flaccus, a Spaniard, son of the man who has been suggested as Hadrian's host at Tarraco. The 'explorer of all curiosities' ought not to have missed the chance of seeing the two great islands of the eastern Mediterranean. Against visits to Crete and Cyprus it can be argued that the Parthian threat was too important and that Hadrian would have needed to sail east with all possible speed. But stops along the way were certainly needed – and measures to deal with the emergency were in hand. Claudius Quartinus had surely gone ahead, to collect elements of the legion II Traiana from Judaea and III Cyrenaica from Egypt and then take this force to the Euphrates to await Hadrian.[6]

It is a plausible guess that Hadrian was at the Syrian capital in June 123. The early Byzantine chronicler John Malalas, muddled and incompetent though he may have been, seems to have much information about Antioch. He reports that Hadrian founded a 'festival of the springs', to be held each 23 June. It was clearly to mark the completion of a round of endowments. Extensive rebuilding after the earthquake eight years earlier must have been very much a necessity. Malalas lists public baths and an aqueduct, for Antioch, at Daphne 'a theatre of the springs' and a shrine of the nymphs. The 'Hadrianic Baths' were still in existence over a century later. Further, the Byzantine encyclopaedia, the *Suda*, notes Hadrian's construction of a 'very elegant temple of Trajan' at Antioch to mark his predecessor's deification. He would have ordered the start of this construction before leaving Syria in autumn 117. Nearly six years seem long enough for it to have been completed. Honouring the great conqueror – for all that his last campaign had ended in near disaster and that Hadrian had abandoned the new provinces – may have seemed a timely act when a meeting with the Parthian ruler was about to take place. It is surely no coincidence that the Alexandrian coinage for the Egyptian year 123–4 commemorated Trajan again.[7]

Hadrian must have proceeded to the frontier for the *colloquium*: traditionally these diplomatic encounters took place on the Euphrates, with each side coming across in turn for dinner. The Syrian army will have been there in force, along with elements of the Guard, the Horse Guards, and Quartinus with his task force. The army of Cappadocia might well have sent troops as well. Who was there on the Parthian side is not further specified. It is assumed that it was the king – but which king? There were still two rival rulers and it must be guessed that it was Chosroes that came. He it was, at any rate, who had dealings with Hadrian five years later, shortly before he disappeared from the scene for good, leaving his rival Vologaeses unchallenged (for a while). Hadrian had conciliated Chosroes in 117 by deposing Parthamaspates, his renegade son, whom Trajan had installed at Ctesiphon as a Roman puppet. But he had given Parthamaspates a consolation prize, shoving him into the temporarily vacant principality around Edessa (Urfa), Osrhoene, the fertile north-west corner of Mesopotamia. For nearly four years, according to the Edessene records, 118–22, Parthamaspates reigned jointly with one Ialud, then for another ten months alone. Now the Abgarid dynasty was restored at Edessa, in the person of Mannus (Ma'nu VII bar Izates). What happened to Parthamaspates is not known. Perhaps the continued presence of his estranged son on his borders had been the reason for Chosroes to threaten war. If so, Hadrian settled the matter by giving way. But on another cause of dissent, nothing is said, although the matter was surely raised: Chosroes' daughter remained for the time being in Roman hands, as did the Parthian throne of state. Both had been captured by Trajan, and were retained as bargaining counters.[8]

The 'summit' on the Euphrates seems to be reflected in the imperial coinage, which had for some time continued to announce that Hadrian was on campaign with the legend *expeditio Aug*. This must be assumed to cover the visits to Britain, to Mauretania and to the eastern frontier. Now the god Janus appears on the coins, a strong hint that Hadrian's warlike activities were coming to an end. When the gates of Janus' temple – the 'Gates of War' – were closed, peace reigned throughout the empire. Hadrian is unlikely to have delegated to anyone else the performance of such a ceremony and our meagre sources do not report one. The fifth-century historian Orosius, who had special reasons for being interested in this pagan ritual, complained that he could not recall anything being said about it being performed between the opening of the Gates by Vespasian and Titus (presumably in 72) and that by Gordian III (in 242).[9]

However this may be, Hadrian remained on the frontier. He had no doubt accompanied Trajan and the army right into Armenia nine years earlier, at the opening of the War. Now he could survey the northern part of the eastern *limes*, in the province of Cappadocia. If, as seems probable, the governor at this time was his friend Bruttius Praesens, Hadrian was assured of congenial company as he inspected the garrisons in the Upper Euphrates valley and the sweltering Anatolian uplands, principally the fortresses of the two legions, XII Fulminata at Melitene and Satala above the River Lycus in Lesser Armenia, now garrisoned by XV Apollinaris. At Satala in 114, Hadrian had probably witnessed Trajan receiving the king of the Heniochi, and gone on with him eastwards to Elegia, where the annexation of Greater Armenia as a Roman province had been staged. 'Hadrian allowed the Armenians to have a king', the *HA* reports laconically, but says no more.[10]

Hadrian is unlikely to have gone to Elegia this time. Perhaps an Armenian envoy paid his respects at Satala. It is, indeed, a question whether he went all along the Euphrates frontier line. He might well have left the difficult Euphrates route after Melitene and then gone northwest to Sebastia (Sivas), and north to Neocaesarea in the Lycus valley. Both Neocaesarea and Nicopolis, well to the east on the Satala road, took additional names in his honour, 'Hadrianopolis' and 'Hadriane' respectively. This does not prove his presence there. Still,

Neocaesarea probably got a mention in Book 15 of Phlegon's *Olympiads*, which is a pointer to it being on his itinerary before 125. Another town in the region also began to call itself Hadrianopolis, Amasia, in the valley of the River Iris, some 70 miles (110 km) west of Neocaesarea. Once again, a visit is not proved, either at this time or later. The fact that Amasia was the birthplace of the geographer Strabo may not have meant anything to Hadrian, even though he had a weakness for literary tourism: hardly anyone seems to have read the copious *Geography*, at least until Byzantine times.[11]

A few years later Arrian, as governor of Cappadocia, addressed several reports to Hadrian. His *Periplus* or *Circumnavigation of the Pontus Euxinus* opens, abruptly enough: 'We reached Trapezus [Trebizond], a Greek city, as Xenophon says, situated on the sea, a colony of the Sinopeans. And it was from the very same point as did Xenophon – and you – that we looked down with pleasure on the sea, the Euxine.' Hadrian will have known the famous moment in the *Anabasis* when the vanguard of the Ten Thousand reached the summit of the road over Mount Theches – the Zigana Pass, over 6500 feet (2000 m) above sea level. 'A great shout went up.' Xenophon and the rearguard assumed there was an enemy attack. He hurried forward with the cavalry – and then made out what the men were shouting: '*Thalatta! Thalatta!*', 'The sea! The sea!' Xenophon and his men had to fight their way down to the coast, where their fellow-Greeks at Trapezus 'received them kindly', supplying oxen, barley and wine; and they sacrificed 'to Zeus for deliverance, to Heracles for guidance and to the other gods as they had vowed.'[12]

That Hadrian followed this example is implied by Arrian, who goes on to report that 'the altars are already set up, but of rough stone and hence the inscriptions are not cut clearly enough; and there are mistakes in the Greek inscription (*epigramma*).' The mason had evidently been a 'barbarian', a non-Greek. Arrian had had the altars recut, with clear lettering on white stone. The Greek inscription – the other one was presumably in Latin – may well have been a verse epigram composed by Hadrian. Arrian goes on to comment on the temple, 'of squared stone and no mean piece of work' – but the statue of Hadrian himself, although beautifully positioned, with one hand pointing out to sea, was a poor likeness and in other respects inadequate. He asked for a replacement, 'for the place deserves an everlasting memorial.' The statue was probably designed to point to the new harbour that Hadrian ordered to be built, which Arrian refers to later in the *Periplus*. The statue of Hermes was also unworthy of the shrine and its situation. Arrian asked Hadrian to send a replacement for this too: 'it should be five feet high; also one of Philesius (Apollo), four feet high.'[13]

Hadrian seems, from Arrian's language, to have gone no further east from Trapezus than the next settlement, just over 20 miles (32 km) along the coast, the port of Hyssus, where there was an infantry cohort in garrison. Nothing in Arrian's description of the more distant parts suggests this. He does refer, in several places, to the native rulers, several of whom are specifically stated to have 'received the kingship from you', not necessarily all four at the time of Hadrian's stay at Trapezus, to be sure. Arrian, writing his *Periplus* a few years later, registers as recent the death of a more significant client of Rome, the king of the Cimmerian Bosporus – the Crimea. This was Cotys, whose reign may be dated to the years 123/4–131/2. He was a descendant of the ruler installed by Julius Caesar, Asander, who had married Dynamis, granddaughter of Mithridates the Great. Dynastic links had also been forged later with the kings of Thrace and Pontus: neither of these client states now existed, but the Bosporan kingdom survived into the third century AD. Its rulers, Roman citizens since the time of Tiberius, proudly advertised the titles 'friend of Rome and friend of Caesar'. It seems clear that Cotys was formally recognised by Hadrian at this time. Phlegon recorded in Book 15 of his *Olympiads* that 'Hadrian ordered a diadem to be brought to Cotys the Bosporan king and placed cities under his rule, including Cherson.' Cherson, or rather Chersonesus Taurica, was a Greek city of the Crimea, which had for some time enjoyed independent status. The transfer of this and other Greek *poleis* to the kingdom was to ensure their security. It was no doubt welcome to Cotys; and good relations with the Bosporan kingdom were important. In effect it ensured that the north shore of the Black Sea was to all intents and purposes an integral part of the empire. On the analogy of British India, it was a 'princely state' under indirect rule.[14]

Hadrian's goal after Trapezus was the neighbouring province of Pontus-Bithynia. In his summary account of the approach to Trapezus along the Black Sea coast from the west, Arrian adds, 'but I am telling you what you already know.' Clearly, when Arrian was writing in the early 130s, he was aware that Hadrian had sailed this way already. Stops at harbours such as Amisus, Sinope, Amastris and Heraclea Pontica may be inferred. If he chose, Hadrian could probably have had with him for light reading a copy of a recently published Latin work, the tenth and last book of the *Letters* of Plinius Secundus. Pliny had governed Pontus-Bithynia just over a decade earlier. He had prepared the first nine books of his letters for publication himself and dedicated them to Septicius Clarus. Septicius may have edited Book 10, the letters to – and from – Trajan, almost all from the two years while Pliny was governor. Or, if not Septicius, a likely editor is Suetonius, who may, indeed, have had a hand in their composition, for he was evidently on Pliny's staff in the province. At any rate, the likelihood that Hadrian had seen the collection is strong.[15]

Pliny had devoted rather less time to the Pontic half of the double province than to Bithynia: death cut short his mandate before the end of his second year as legate. The first Pontic letter concerns Sinope, where he recommended the construction of a new aqueduct. Trajan had agreed, if they could pay for it. The only other Pontic cities Pliny mentions were Amisus and Amastris, the latter described as 'an elegant and ornamental city, among its outstanding features a very beautiful and very long street' – but the river which flowed throughout its length was 'in truth a stinking sewer'. Pliny proposed that it should be covered. Here then were matters for Hadrian to inspect or for the local authorities to raise when, for the first time, an emperor visited the region. Hadrian presumably also read at some point the two letters that precede the one about Amastris: a request to grant Pliny's protégé Suetonius the privileges of a father of three children; and the long enquiry about the Christians. There were plenty of them around in Pontus – Sinope had a bishop – but they no doubt were studiously inconspicuous. Pliny had, after all, executed a batch of them; Trajan had approved this course of action with diehard members of the sect, even if he had specifically prohibited searching them out and ordered anonymous denunciations of the sect to be ignored.[16]

Further west, Heraclea instituted athletic contests for boys and men in Hadrian's honour: this might well have been in advance of a visit by him or a response to his presence. When he reached Bithynia proper, he would be on familiar ground: he had come there from Syria overland through Cappadocia and Galatia a few months after his accession six years earlier, and may have been based for some time at Nicomedia, if not at Byzantium. At any rate, it seems highly probable that he wintered at Nicomedia on this occasion. For one thing, Nicomedia (Izmit), which was rivalled for primacy in Bithynia only by its near neighbour Nicaea (Iznik), was the home of Arrian. It is attractive to speculate that Arrian, with whom he had so many interests in common, was Hadrian's host on this occasion, as he might have been in 117. In any case, Nicomedia is the only city in the empire other than Alexandria which is commemorated on the imperial coinage: Hadrian is hailed as its 'restorer'. The city had been damaged in an earthquake shortly before his visit, as had Nicaea. Both were rebuilt with lavish donations from Hadrian, as late chroniclers explicitly record. Inscriptions in his honour above the gates of Nicaea supply a specific example of this programme. The imperial benefactions to Bithynia were to be commemorated in coin issues registering his advent and calling him 'restorer' of the province.[17]

The earthquake may well have rendered some of the rather numerous building projects brought to Trajan's attention by Pliny of little more than academic interest, for example the unfinished aqueduct at Nicomedia or, at Nicaea, the half-built theatre and badly planned reconstruction of the gymnasium. Hadrian may have winced if he noticed one of Trajan's laconic remarks in response to Pliny: 'These little Greeks – *Graeculi* – love gymnasia.' After all, he had in his youth had to put up with the nickname *Graeculus*. No doubt he reacted more positively than Trajan did to the opening and closing comments in one letter, in which Pliny proposed a grandiose scheme to link Lake Sophon, 18 miles (29 km) north-west of Nicomedia, by a canal with the Sea of Marmara. 'As I observe your fortune and your greatness of spirit, it seems to me most fitting to bring to your notice projects which are worthy of your immortal name and your glory – and which combine beauty with public benefit', he began. After outlining the scheme, he reported that one of the kings of Bithynia (the last of whom had bequeathed his kingdom to Rome almost two hundred years earlier) had begun a canal. But he had either died or simply given up in despair: 'But by this very fact – for you will allow me to be ambitious to further your glory – I am inspired, indeed fired, with the wish that something should be brought to completion by you, which the kings had merely begun.' *Peragi a te quae tantum coeperant reges*: this might have been a motto for Hadrian in the Greek east.[18]

Visits to a few other cities in Bithynia may be conjectured, for example to Bithynium-Claudiopolis (Bolu). Pliny had reported that the people there had been 'building – or rather excavating – gigantic public baths in a hollow below the mountain'. He expressed doubts about the financing of the project; the odds are that it was still in progress. This city also was to take the name Hadriane, but so did dozens of others. Something else is more important: it was the home-town of the youth who was to become the object of Hadrian's passion, Antinous. More specifically, Antinous was a country lad, from the forested uplands of Bithynium's territory, his home being at a place called Mantinium near the old border between Bithynia and Paphlagonia. Nothing is said by the sources about when or where Hadrian first met him. Of the very numerous portraits of Antinous most are idealised, and depict a youth in his mid-teens, but one, at least, seems to be of a young man aged about 20. This might permit the inference that he was with Hadrian for up to seven years – in other words, from the autumn of 123 or spring of 124 until his death in October 130. Hadrian is not very likely to have been to Claudiopolis in late 117, on his way from Ancyra to the Danube. In any case, Antinous was surely too young then – and Hadrian too preoccupied – for any significant encounter. At all events, it is plausible that Hadrian first saw him at Claudiopolis, unless it is supposed that Antinous had been – for example – to Heraclea to compete in the boys' athletics. But whenever Antinous joined Hadrian, whether in 123–4 or later, his public presence with the Emperor is nowhere alluded to before the tour of Egypt in 130. Still, the imperial entourage on these journeys was certainly very considerable: apart from the military escort, and various officials – including the Chief Secretary – with their staff, there would be Hadrian's personal household of freedmen and slaves, and a variety of specialists. The *Epitome de Caesaribus*, perhaps deriving from Marius Maximus – and perhaps generalising from one specific episode – refers to his 'column of companions', *agmen comitantium*, on his provincial tours. It adds that he had organised on military lines a team of 'builders, stonemasons, architects and every kind of specialist for constructing walls or decorating buildings'. The contrast with Trajan, whose reluctance to second military architects or engineers to his governor Pliny is several times apparent, could hardly be plainer. Specialists of another kind with the imperial party would have been huntsmen. Antinous could initially have been taken on to the imperial staff in this capacity.[19]

A Bithynian city which should have been favoured with a visit is Apamea, not just because it was a Roman colony, but for the good reason that its most promi-nent citizen was a friend and old comrade-in-arms, Catilius Severus. He was the man to whom Hadrian had handed over the province of Syria at his accession. Catilius had evidently done his work well: he had been honoured with a second consulship in 120. He could well have thought it desirable to sail home to welcome Hadrian in person. Catilius also had links with Nicaea – and no doubt property in that city – and could have received Hadrian there too. Other Roman families at Nicaea could have entertained Hadrian, such as the Cassii, ancestors of the historian Cassius Dio, with their attractively situated estate on the north shore of Lake Ascanius, lying between Nicaea and the Sea of Marmara.[20]

One might also postulate a visit to Prusa ad Olympum (Bursa), which took its epithet from the great mountain behind the city, named after the seat of the gods in the Greek motherland. The sight of this massive peak (Ulu Dag) might have been enough to attract Hadrian, with his known propensity for scaling mountains. The famous orator, Dio of Prusa, whom he must have known, was surely now dead, but his building activities in his home town, which had led to appeals to the governor Pliny, might have attracted Hadrian's curiosity. Further, Hadrian is said to have had a close friend called Polyaenus, whose native city was probably Prusa. At any rate, a prominent Bithynian of this name had been at Rome in 106–7, appearing before the Senate in the prosecution of the proconsul Varenus Rufus. A few years later Pliny had to deal with a problem at Prusa. The house of one Claudius Polyaenus, bequeathed to the Emperor Claudius – over fifty years before – and thus imperial property, had fallen into ruin. Claudius Polyaenus had intended a shrine to Claudius to be erected there, but nothing had been done and Pliny proposed to allocate the site for new public baths, with a hall and colonnades, dedicated to Trajan. As likely as not, the site was still in a ruinous state – Trajan's reply had been somewhat less than whole-hearted. Here was something for Hadrian to inspect.[21]

It would have been natural for Hadrian to move on direct from Bithynia into the next-door province of Asia, where his presence in the summer of 124 is well documented, from Cyzicus in the north down as far south as Ephesus. But a source of an unusual nature, written by someone who accompanied Hadrian on his travels in these parts, the sophist and teacher of rhetoric Polemo, suggests that before entering Asia Hadrian crossed the Sea of Marmara to Thrace. He relates how 'I once accompanied the greatest of emperors on his travels.' The episode that he chose to describe took place on a hunt in the province of Asia, during the journey, which began when 'we set out from Thrace to Asia, with soldiers and carriages escorting the emperor.' There seems to be no other journey which this route fits except the one in 124. Polemo's story is told in his *De Physiognomia*, a work on the detection of character from facial features – which survives only in Arabic translation; and the place-names that he mentions are understandably not all at first sight recognisable. 'Thrace', for example, Arabic *Traqa*, is an emendation of the manuscript reading *Braqa*. But the route can be satisfactorily reconstructed: from Thrace into the province of Asia, then to Ionia, Sardes and parts of Lydia and Phrygia, from the mainland by sea via the islands to Rhodes and thence to Athens.[22]

Antonius Polemo was about ten years younger than Hadrian. He was one of the outstanding figures in the Greek world. The family derived from Laodicea on the River Lycus on the borders of Phrygia and Caria, where Polemo was born and with which he retained links. But he was particularly associated with the glittering coastal city of Smyrna. His ancestor Zeno, known as a gifted orator, had acquired instant fame by leading the defence of Laodicea against a Parthian invasion in 41 BC. Zeno's son Polemo had been made ruler of a rump kingdom of Pontus by the Triumvir Antonius, founding a dynasty which ruled until Nero absorbed the kingdom into the province of Cappadocia. In the meantime the family had acquired links with the kings of Thrace and the Crimean Bosporus. Thus the great sophist of Smyrna was a distant kinsman of the newly enthroned Cotys – who, indeed, was rash enough to enrol himself as a pupil of Polemo. He was stung for a fee of ten talents. It is likely enough that Polemo had joined Hadrian on this journey precisely in eastern Pontus, where his ancestors had once ruled. He probably still had estates there. Polemo may have remained with the imperial party for the journey west along the coast, although it seems unlikely that he would have spent the winter in Bithynia. At any rate, it is easy to see why Thrace, also a land where his family had once reigned, would have been an appropriate place for him to join Hadrian.[23]

The biographer of the sophists, Philostratus, has a great deal to relate about Polemo, and makes clear what a dominant figure he was, above all at Smyrna, where 'by opening his school he benefited the city.' He attracted pupils 'from continents and islands, select and genuinely Hellenic'; he played a leading role in the city's government, bringing about internal harmony in a previously faction-ridden community; and he acted as ambassador for Smyrna at court. 'Hadrian, at any rate, had hitherto favoured Ephesus, but Polemo converted him to the cause of Smyrna', leading to generous benefactions – this journey was doubtless the occasion for winning Hadrian's favour. But a switch from favouring Ephesus to favouring Smyrna need not be taken too literally – or, if there is anything in it, it will have taken a number of years to implement.[24]

The self-confident aristocratic Greek intellectual could be regarded as arrogant: 'he conversed with cities as his inferiors, with emperors as not his superiors and with the gods as his equals', Philostratus comments. Trajan, not noted for his closeness to intellectuals, had favoured the descendants of the old royal houses of the east, such as Julius Quadratus Bassus, his great marshal. Polemo, of royal descent as well as being a sophist, even if lacking Quadratus Bassus' qualifications, obtained a remarkable privilege from Trajan, 'free travel by land and sea', according to Philostratus. Hadrian extended the right to his descendants. It presumably meant that, like a Roman office-holder on public duties, he could use the facilities of the imperial posting-system, the *cursus publicus*. Use of that service may not have been quite Polemo's style – but the privilege probably allowed him to demand accommodation wherever he went. This could have been expensive. 'He aroused criticism, because when he travelled he was followed by a long train of baggage-animals, with many horses, servants and dogs of various breeds for hunting. He himself used to ride in a Phrygian or Celtic carriage, with silver-mounted bridles.' Such was the aristocratic Greek intellectual, with a shared passion for horses, dogs and hunting, who joined Hadrian's entourage.[25]

What Hadrian did on this visit to Thrace can only be conjectured. Commemorative coins issued later in the reign give no clues: the personified province, on one issue represented by a male figure, but otherwise simply a cloaked female woman with short tunic and no distinctive attribute, is shown greeting the Emperor, and the legend registers the imperial advent. Another issue commemorated the army of the province (only a few auxiliary regiments, no legion). The renaming of Oresta (a city already refounded by Trajan) as Hadrianopolis (Adrianople) could belong to this time. Further, the seat of the governor, Perinthus, could hardly have been avoided, even if the erection of a statue to Hadrian there in 126 is not in itself proof of his presence. A new legate, Tineius Rufus, arrived in 124, and was perhaps installed by the Emperor in person. Tineius would receive a peculiarly difficult assignment a few years later – the province of Judaea. Hadrian's tour of Thrace may have concluded by the road past Perinthus, through the Claudian *colonia* of Apri, into the Thracian Chersonese. This was an unusual district, for it had been imperial domain since the time of Augustus and was administered by an imperial procurator. One of the cities on the peninsula, Coela, was converted into a *municipium* by Hadrian, an anomalous and unexpected status in a Greek-speaking district. Perhaps there was a substantial Latin element in the town. Active road-building in Thrace in 124 may also be noted – and the newly installed king of the Bosporus had had to earn his throne: an inscription from May or June 124 records his victory over the Scythians of the Crimea, which involved naval operations. Hadrian could well have deemed it prudent to remain in the neighbourhood. That he went further north, to the Danube, on this tour, has been postulated, but seems unlikely. He evidently put the army of the Lower Danube in safe hands by moving his friend Bruttius Praesens from Cappadocia to govern Moesia Inferior. Then he could cross to Asia, with Antonius Polemo, with his 'soldiers, carriages' and a motley company.[26]

14

A SUMMER IN ASIA

Early in 124 it was time to leave Thrace and cross back to Asia, this time to the Roman province of that name. The first goal should have been Cyzicus. Hadrian will have seen first the island of Proconessus and behind it the peak of Cyzicus' peninsula, on which stood the great temple of Zeus. The 'noble city', as Florus called it, with its citadel and harbour, its walls and marble towers, was the 'glory of Asia'. Cyzicus had long exerted a special appeal for Romans. A senatorial friend of the poet Propertius stayed there for many years; it had been the home of a princess from Polemo's family, Antonia Tryphaena, daughter of the King of Pontus; and the pleasure-loving Licinius Mucianus seems to have gone to Cyzicus when out of favour with Claudius – he was especially fond of Cyzicene oysters. But, like Nicaea and Nicomedia, Cyzicus had been ravaged in the recent earthquake. Help was needed: the Cyzicenes had no doubt already appealed to the Emperor.[1]

Waiting to receive Hadrian and his party as he entered the province would be not merely notables of the city and of the provincial council but the proconsul, Hadrian's friend Pompeius Falco, nearing the end to his year of office. But Falco's wife Polla will not have been by his side – she had died in the province, leaving Falco a widower with a small son. To make good the destruction caused by the earthquake would have been enough to earn Hadrian fulsome expressions of gratitude. But Cyzicus offered an opportunity for something more. The vast temple of Zeus, begun 300 years earlier by the kings of Pergamum – the queen of Attalus I, Apollonis, was from Cyzicus – had never been completed. Here was a challenge for Hadrian. He did not need to have read Pliny's eager appeal to Trajan 'to bring to completion what the kings had merely begun'. What was undertaken at Cyzicus as a result of his visit was to be called one of the seven wonders of the world, 'the largest and most beautiful of all temples', Dio was to write – and, as it turned out, would not be completed in Hadrian's own lifetime.[2]

The temple in its unfinished state was already splendid enough to attract a notice from the Elder Pliny: its marble blocks were adorned with gold thread. Hadrian provided funds on a lavish scale, but the whole province also contributed, for Cyzicus was now granted the coveted role of *neocorus*, Temple

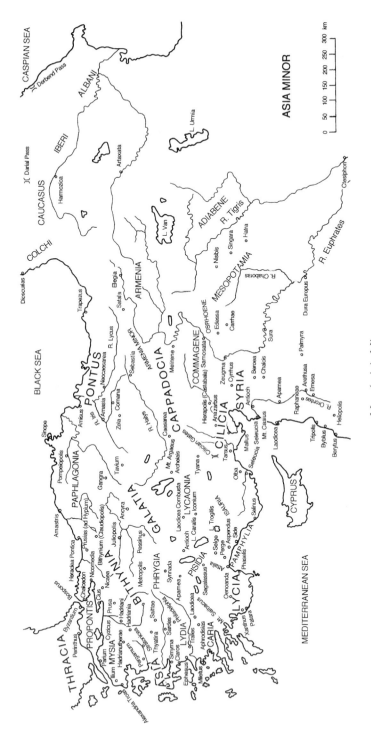

CASPIAN SEA

Derbend Pass

ALBANI

IBERI

CAUCASUS

Darial Pass

Harmozica

COLCHI

Artaxata

L. Urmia

ASIA MINOR

0 50 100 150 200 250 300 km

Dioscurias

ADIABENE

L. Van

R. Tigris

Singara

Hatra

Trapezus

ARMENIA

Satala

Begia

R. Lycus

Nisibis

Sebastia

MESOPOTAMIA

R. Chaboras

Dura Europus

Neocaesarea

ARMENIA MINOR

OSRHOENE

Edessa

Carrhae

Sura

R. Euphrates

Ctesiphon

BLACK SEA

PONTUS

Amisus

R. Iris

Amasia

Zela

Comana

R. Halys

Melitene

COMMAGENE

Samosata

Hierapolis (Castabala)

Zeugma

Cyrrhus

Beroea

Chalcis

Apamea

Raphanaea

Arethusa

R. Orontes

Emesa

Heliopolis

Sinope

Pompeiopolis

PAPHLAGONIA

Gangra

Tavium

Caesarea

Mt Argaeus

Archelais

CAPPADOCIA

Anazarbus

Tarsus

CILICIA

Mallus

Laodicea

Mt. Casus

Seleucia

SYRIA

Antioch

Tripolis

Byblus

Berytus

CYPRUS

Amastris

Heraclea Pontica

Prusias (ad Hypium)

Ancyra

GALATIA

Pessinus

Laodicea Combusta

LYCAONIA

Iconium

Tyana

Cilician Gates

Olba

MEDITERRANEAN SEA

Bosporus

Byzantium

Perinthus

THRACIA

PROPONTIS

Chalcedon

Nicomedia

Prusa

Cius

Nicaea

Hadriani

BITHYNIA

Juliopolis

Metropolis

Apamea

PHRYGIA

Synnada

PISIDIA

Antioch

Sagalassus

L. Caralis

Troglis

Selge

Aspendus

Side

ISAURIA

Perge

Attalia

PAMPHYLIA

Parium

Cyzicus

MYSIA

Hadrianutherae

Hadriania

Saittae

LYDIA

Sardes

Thyatira

Clazomenae

Smyrna

Claros

Ephesus

Miletus

ASIA

Tralles

Aphrodisias

CARIA

Laodicea

Mt. Salbacus

Cibyra

Oenoanda

LYCIA

Xanthus

Patara

Phaselis

Alexandria Troas

Warden of the imperial cult, joining Pergamum, Ephesus, Smyrna and Sardes. Hadrian himself was to share the temple with Zeus – his colossal statue was to be set on the pediment. The finished temple was built on three levels, the total effect being called labyrinthine because of the vaulted underground aisles, where, it appears, mysteries were celebrated. The sixty massive columns which surrounded the inner shrine (*cella*) were well over 6 feet (2 m) in diameter and more than 65 feet (21 m) high.[3]

As well as this great undertaking, Cyzicus evidently gained other marks of imperial favour. The city took the name 'Hadriane' and started athletic contests named 'Hadriania'; and a temple of Demeter first attested on the city's coins in his reign presumably owed at least its completion to him. The neighbouring cities of Apollonia and Miletopolis also benefited from Hadrian's presence in the area: at least, both called him 'Saviour and Founder'. But however exciting the project at Cyzicus, Hadrian can hardly have stayed more than a few weeks there. Other parts of the 'land of five hundred cities', as the province of Asia was described – with a little exaggeration – awaited him. His route seems to have taken him along the coast westwards, crossing the River Granicus, allowing the opportunity to inspect the site of Alexander's first great victory, and on to Parium, where Caesar had founded a *colonia*. At any rate, Parium took the name 'Hadriana' and Hadrian is called 'founder', *conditor coloniae*. Following in the footsteps of Alexander after the Granicus, Hadrian was aiming for Troy. Here, where the little city of Ilium proudly boasted its status as the home of Rome's Trojan ancestors, he inspected the crumbling tomb which was alleged to be that of the Achaean hero Ajax, and ordered it to be rebuilt. A little further down the coast, was the place founded by Alexander's successors, then re-established as a Roman *colonia*, Alexandria in the Troad. This city was to honour Hadrian as *restitutor*, although his major benefactions took some years to implement.[4]

The next stage of the journey was to be devoted to the mountainous wooded interior, and to hunting. 'He founded a town, Hadrianutherae, in a certain place', the *HA* biographer reports, 'because he had had successful hunting there and had on one occasion killed a she-bear.' Hadrianutherae (Balikesir), in the fertile plain of central Mysia, would commemorate its founder with bronze coins showing the mounted Emperor, with the head of his prey on the reverse. As the *HA* tells the story, the action was an autocrat's whim. But this part of Mysia was ripe for such action. He was later to found two further new cities in the fertile plains enclosed by the primeval forests: Hadriania (Balat), between the Rivers Macestus and Rhyndacus, and Hadriani (Orhaneli) at the foot of Olympus.[5]

It was perhaps somewhere in the mountains of Mysia that the curious episode described by Polemo in his *De physiognomia* took place. He wishes to demonstrate that small, deepset eyes are the mark of an evil character. He 'once met a man from *Qwrnyn*' – the name as rendered in Arabic has been variously emended, but is presumably that of a place somewhere in Mysia – with such eyes, and other dangerous facial characteristics, an insolent man, of gross shamelessness, one who stirred up trouble against authority, a man that people shunned, who hated those who are loyal, bold when it came to dishonourable acts, never ceasing to inflict harm on his own comrades – and lastly, drunken and of ungovernable rage.

After setting the scene by describing how he accompanied 'the greatest of emperors from Thrace to Asia' and briefly outlining the itinerary, he returns to his theme. 'When we had come to Asia, then, I stayed with that man' – presumably in unawareness of his true character. Perhaps Polemo had not yet studied physiognomy.

There he was with his companions, armed, surrounding the Emperor – and that was in no way to show honour to the Emperor or because he was well disposed towards him. No, he was looking for a chance of doing him harm and carrying out his evil designs, which allowed him no rest. Further, he had his companions in wickedness with him, whose chief and master he was. This was our situation then: the Emperor was preoccupied with his preparations, energetically getting ready to set off hunting, so that we had no chance of engaging him in conversation. My friends and I were sitting talking and exchanging views about the Emperor – what an uneasy position he was in, how far removed from the pleasant life people used to say he enjoyed. As our conversation continued, we also mentioned that man

and all expressed amazement at his shamelessness. In the middle of this conversation, someone startled them by coming out of the trees:

It was the evil fellow we had been talking about: he had crept up like a snake to eavesdrop. 'All that could not have been about anyone except me', he said. 'We did mention you', I said, 'and expressed amazement at your manner. Out with it, then! Tell us how you have imposed this burden on yourself and how you can bear such tensions in your soul.' This resulted in an instant outburst. He had a demon in him, the man admitted, that was responsible for the evil desire in his soul, he began to weep – 'Woe is me, I am destroyed!'[6]

This curious story can hardly be called evidence for a plot against Hadrian's life, let alone, as was once claimed, to portray an alleged attempt on Hadrian's life by Lusius Quietus in late 117. It reads rather more like an attempt by the arrogant Polemo to discredit someone who had proved an ill-tempered and discourteous – and perhaps drunken – host, when obliged to give Polemo hospitality. That he and his followers looked threatening as they stood around Hadrian, bearing arms, can hardly be taken seriously when a hunting-party, suitably equipped, was preparing to set off. All the same, Nigrinus was alleged to have plotted to kill Hadrian on a hunt or at a sacrifice before the hunt.

A deranged slave had attacked Hadrian at Tarraco the previous year – and that autumn, at Athens, it would be noticed that the knives normally carried at religious ceremonies were banned.[7]

It may be added that Polemo took the opportunity, in the same work, of portraying another person he disliked, his rival Favorinus – again unnamed – in highly unflattering terms. Hadrian, by contrast, is praised for his shining eyes, the sign of a pure and spotless character (the only such example in the entire *De physiognomia*). Hadrian's eyes, indeed, are described as possessing exactly the characteristics of a true 'Hellene and Ionian', as a later writer, Adamantius, defined them, 'languishing, bright, piercing and full of light'.[8]

From Hadrianutherae Hadrian's route seems to have taken him south up the River Macestus and across the watershed to the upper Caicus valley, where he stayed at Stratonicea. Once again, it is clear, he indulged his passion for hunting – and he was to grant the place the status of a city and the name Hadrianopolis: a few years later the people of the city honoured him as their founder under the name Zeus the Hunter (*Cynegesius*). From a letter of Hadrian's written from Rome four years later, in response to a petition from Stratonicea, it has been inferred that he stayed during this visit in the house of a certain Ti. Claudius Socrates – and that the building was subsequently consecrated, although nothing is said about these matters in the letter, which deals merely with the need to repair the building.[9]

As yet there is no explicit record of Hadrian's presence at Pergamum, but he cannot have been in this part of Asia without visiting the once royal city. He might, indeed, have been there before going to hunt in Mysia. Whichever route he followed, he must have doubled back at least for part of the journey, along the Caicus valley. Since his general plan on this occasion seems to have been to tour the northern part of the province, it seems logical that his hunting in the mountains of Mysia would have come first. There was much for him to see and to admire at Pergamum, a very considerable metropolis with well over a hundred thousand inhabitants: not least its celebrated shrines, of Zeus and Athena, of Asclepius, of Sarapis – and of Trajan. On the acropolis, beside the citadel or palace of the kings, where Hadrian presumably stayed, stood the colossal altar of Zeus and Athena, adorned with reliefs celebrating King Eumenes II's victory over the barbaric Celtic hordes three centuries earlier. The temple of Trajan was to be even larger. It was evidently conceived as a temple of Trajan and of Zeus Philius – the god of friendship. Did this perhaps reflect Trajan's close ties with the Pergamenes Julius Quadratus and Quadratus Bassus? However this may be, the plan was altered. The great sanctuary was to be turned into a shrine for Trajan and Hadrian together, their colossal statues, well over twice lifesize, seated on either side of the inner *cella*. There was no room left for Zeus Philius. As the enormous edifice was built of gleaming white marble, its appearance would outshine the other buildings on the acropolis, with their grey or pink stone.[10]

Pergamum had early on had a temple to the goddess Roma and took a prominent part in the imperial cult from its inception – not for nothing had the author of the *Revelation* told the church at Pergamum that 'thou dwellest where Satan's throne is.' It now enjoyed the superior status of 'double Temple Wardenship'. Shrines to other deities were being enlarged or constructed at Pergamum. The Asclepieum, which went back over five hundred years, was to become a vast complex, where the wealthy and cultivated élite came to take the cure. Hadrian was to be honoured there as 'a god most manifest, a New Asclepius'. The epithet 'most manifest' could be taken to confirm that Hadrian had indeed made a personal appearance in the city.[11]

Apart from inspecting the royal library in the temple of Athena, once famous for its 200,000 books – of parchment, Pergamum's own substitute for papyrus – Hadrian will have found cultivated and prominent persons to entertain him. Quadratus Bassus, whose monument he will have inspected, had been only one of a now numerous body of eminent dignitaries who resided in this city. It was probably not a coincidence that a member of a Pergamene family became consul the next year. This was L. Cuspius Camerinus, probably (to judge from his names) the descendant of an Italian trading family that had been settled at Pergamum for many generations. Camerinus' son Rufinus, thus 'ennobled' by his father's elevation, was to become consul *ordinarius* early in the next reign. Cuspius Rufinus' grandiose benefactions were to transform the great shrine of Asclepius – and testify to the considerable wealth of this family.[12]

An indirect beneficiary of Hadrian's visit, it can be inferred, was the young architect Aelius Nico, who will have prospered from the ambitious building programme. His name Aelius indicates the grant of citizenship from Hadrian. Nico's son Galenus, born five years after Hadrian's visit, will not have known the Emperor. Still, it is strange that in his voluminous writings the great doctor seldom finds occasion to mention Hadrian, and the fullest mention is an unfriendly anecdote. It is a legitimate guess that Nico or other members of Galen's family – or older friends – had passed on unfavourable recollections of Hadrian and used to tell the story because the incident took place at Pergamum.

> Hadrian the Emperor, so it is related, once struck one of his attendants in the eye with a pen. When he found out that the man had lost the sight of this eye as a result, he summoned him and invited him to request a gift. But the man stayed silent. Hadrian repeated the offer, then the man said that all he wanted was to get his eye back.

Galen supplies maddeningly few details, but at least he shows us Hadrian writing with his own hand, rather than dictating – and perhaps, if the incident did take place at Pergamum, with an iron nibbed pen rather than a stylus, to write with ink on parchment. But it is impossible to guess whether what he was writing was official or private. Further, although Galen implies that Hadrian hit his attendant – no doubt a slave – in an outburst of rage, it could well have been an accident.[13]

From the acropolis at Pergamum Hadrian could have looked far across the Caicus plain to the sea coast and the Gulf of Mytilene. Although numerous inscriptions attest the loyal gratitude of the island of Lesbos, and especially Mytilene, its principal city, they cannot in themselves prove a visit. The title 'Liberator' (*Eleutherius*) under which he was worshipped at Mytilene suggests that he may have awarded it the status of a 'free city'. It is more probable that the next stage of his journey took him inland again, to Sardes – at least, the admittedly amended Arabic text of Polemo's *De physiognomia* attests his presence there. It seems reasonable to suggest that he went by road along the Caicus valley, turning southwards by Germe, with Thyatira (Akhisar) as a halfway station. Thyatira and Nacrasa, which lies a little east of the main highway, supply testimony of public and private devotion to Hadrian for benefits received. There are indications that he may have made an extensive detour eastwards. The city of Saittae, lying between the upper reaches of the River Hermus and its tributary the Hyllus, struck coins which were surely intended to commemorate his visit. The obverse shows a bust of Hadrian, the reverse the personified city shaking hands with the Emperor. The indications in Polemo's *De physiognomia* that Hadrian travelled from Thrace to Ionia, visiting Phrygia and Lydia, including Sardes, favour a detour in this direction. Lydian Saittae was in the region known as the 'burnt land', *katakekaumene*, which was marked by the traces of extinct volcanoes. North-western Phrygia also belonged to the 'burnt land'. Hadrian perhaps went right up to the headwaters of the Hermus, to ascend the Phrygian Mount Dindymus. If he was as far inland as this, he presumably approached Sardes from the east, along the valley of the Hermus.[14]

The former Lydian capital on the River Pactolus, a far older city than Pergamum, but by now of lesser standing, did still produce notable figures, the grandest of whom, Ti. Julius Celsus Polemaeanus, had been one of the earliest of all the Greeks to become consul, back in the year 92. But Polemaeanus was now dead – and in any case he had transferred his affections to Ephesus. One of the current Sardes notables, Julius Pardalas, a Roman knight, was certainly absent in 124: he had just taken up a high position in Egypt. It had been to a man from Sardes, Menemachus, that Plutarch addressed his essay *Precepts of Statecraft*, designed to bring home to the Greeks the realities and limitations of public life under Roman rule. After some preliminary reflections, he comes to the point:

> But now – when the affairs of cities do not include leadership in wars or the overthrowing of a tyranny or concluding alliances – what positions are left for a conspicuous and brilliant public career? There are public lawsuits – and embassies to the emperor.

After more examples from both Greek and Roman history, Plutarch admits that the sort of activity now left to the Greek statesman, such as he himself undertakes in his home town – supervising public building – may seem ridiculous or trivial, but should not be despised.

At all events, Menemachus should remember not only what Pericles used to tell himself – 'Take care: you are ruling free men, you are ruling Greeks,

Athenian citizens' – he should also remind himself that 'You who rule as an office-holder are yourself under the rule of proconsuls, of imperial procurators. These are not "the spearmen of the plain", nor is this ancient Sardes nor the famed power of the Lydians . . . ' Menemachus should remember, as he carries out his duties, to 'look at the shoes of Roman magistrates just above your head . . . Many have experienced "the dread chastiser, the axe that cleaves the neck", as did your fellow-citizen Pardalas and his followers when they forgot the limits of their position.' Pardalas, it emerges later – perhaps father of the high official Julius Pardalas – had nearly brought about the destruction of Sardes 'by involving it in rebellion and war' (the circumstances are unknown).

According to Plutarch, Greeks in public life should avoid cause for blame with the 'rulers' – but should take care to have friends in high places, 'for the Romans are always eager to promote the political interests of their friends.' Favours for one's city are worth far more than procuratorships and provincial governorships which bring handsome profits. The Greek statesman should be obedient to Rome – but not servile: 'those who invite the sovereign's decision on every decree, assembly meeting, privilege, administrative measure, force him to be more of a master than he wishes.'[15]

Plutarch had written these words about twenty-five years before. The old man was almost certainly dead by now – but Hadrian had known and valued him: it had been Plutarch who had set up a statue at Delphi to celebrate Hadrian's accession, and Hadrian had awarded him some official status. So it may be imagined that he had read the essay and in any case would be only too well aware of the sentiments expressed. He could not cure the Greek inter-city competitiveness, which his travelling companion Polemo, no doubt bursting to get Hadrian to Smyrna, exemplified in extreme form. Hadrian certainly failed in the short term to make the Greeks less abject towards the ruling power. He would in due course evolve a programme to instil in them a sense of pride in Hellenism. In the meantime, it may be noted that under his rule the Greeks continued their expansion into every echelon of the Roman ruling élite. The astonishing career of the great Pergamene magnate, Quadratus Bassus, had, indeed, shown that a Greek could take high command in Rome's wars. At a more modest level, further advance was still possible. At about this time, Hadrian nominated a new legate for the legion III Augusta, in effect governor of Numidia. It was Julius Major, a man from Asian Nysa, descendant of Polemo's ancestor the King of Pontus. Another appointment, which in theory Hadrian did not control directly, had perhaps gone through the previous year: Arrian became proconsul of Hispania Baetica, the home province of Hadrian's own family. That Greeks should hold high office not merely in the east but in the far-off Latin west was a real sign that the times were changing. It would not be long before a young Pergamene, Claudius Charax, would be commanding one of the legions in Britain.[16]

Sardes could boast a poet of some quality at the time of Hadrian, a man called Strato. There is no direct evidence that Hadrian met him or knew his work, but the almost exclusive theme of Strato's verse could have appealed to the imperial visitor. Nearly one hundred of his epigrams survive: his 'heart had no place for the love of women', he was 'afire with an unquenchable flame for boys'.[17]

Sardes had special historical interest and heights to climb: the Persian fort perched on the crag above the great temple of Demeter combined both. There is an inscription in Hadrian's honour from Trocetta on Mount Tmolus, naming the proconsul Falco, but this probably predated Hadrian's arrival, for Falco's year of office may be assumed to have ended in the spring of 124. His successor, Peducaeus Priscinus, was no doubt in attendance now. A dedication to Hadrian and Sabina on the north-west slope of Mount Tmolus, facing the Smyrna road, may suggest the imperial presence – and that Sabina was there too.[18]

At any rate, is was surely in this direction, to Smyrna, that the imperial party turned next. With Polemo in Hadrian's company, expectations at Smyrna must have been high. A colossal sum of money was duly disbursed – ten million drachmae, for the construction of a grain-market and of a gymnasium grander than any other in the province, also for the temple of Zeus high up above the Gulf. Precious marble columns – from imperial quarries – were made available, not merely from nearby Phrygian Synnada, but the prized red ones from Numidia, and porphyry too, from Egypt. Polemo was entrusted with the funds in person. Smyrna was granted a second Temple Wardenship (formal approval from the Roman Senate was duly obtained): the new imperial cult was, of course, of Hadrian himself. A twenty-four strong choir was formed to hymn the God Hadrian and the grateful city duly called itself 'Hadriane'. In a fragmentary official letter written in this year, mentioning the establishment of the choir – a copy was set up on stone at Smyrna – there is also comment on the 'most happy times of the Emperor Hadrian, in which the whole world sacrifices and prays that he may live for ever and reign victoriously.' Another inscription listed benefactions from individuals and groups, 'and what we have gained from the Lord Emperor Caesar Hadrian through Antonius Polemo' (a list follows).[19]

Polemo may have claimed that he won over Hadrian to favour Smyrna rather than Ephesus. At this stage, at least, Ephesian priority was clear, apart from the second Temple Wardenship: the visit there was to be the culmination of this tour of the Asian province. Ephesus had, for one thing, been much favoured by Augustus, which was an added reason for the 'new Augustus' to be attracted to this city, which proclaimed itself 'the first and greatest Mother City of Asia'. The approach was to be by sea, as can be inferred from an inscription at Erythrae on the coast facing Chios. The city actually founded a 'Hadrianic Landing Festival' (*Hadrianeia Epibateria*) to commemorate his disembarkation there. Hadrian must have sailed out of the Gulf of Smyrna, around the Black Promontory and through the straits of Chios. No longer of any particular importance, Erythrae was nonetheless one of the original twelve members of the Ionian League and had a proud history to look back on. The Ionian League certainly appealed to Hadrian: he was to be honoured with the name 'Panionios'. Erythrae also, in common with several other places in Ionia, Smyrna and Chios to the fore, claimed to be the birthplace of Homer. That would hardly have impressed Hadrian – he rejected Homer in favour of Antimachus of Colophon, and himself wrote a work called *Catachannae*, 'medley', in imitation of that poet, 'whose very name was unknown to many', Dio claims. Still, Plato had admired Antimachus and Quintilian had praised his 'forcefulness, gravity and style that was anything but vulgar', even if Plutarch thought his strength and vigour were rather laboured. Perhaps Hadrian took to Antimachus' *Artemis*, presumably a poem in honour of the virgin huntress.[20]

Where the imperial flotilla put in to land after Erythrae is a matter of guesswork: Teos is probable enough, likewise Notium, once an Athenian naval base and the scene of a famous Athenian defeat in 407 BC. Notium was the port of Colophon, which still asserted a leading role in the Ionian League and might also have hoped for a visit – because of Antimachus (even though Colophon also claimed Homer). Be this as it may, it is hard to deny Hadrian a call at the famous oracle of Apollo at Claros, also in the territory of Colophon and not far from the coast. At any rate, a gigantic inscription at the shrine – dwarfing the majority of the very numerous dedications in tiny and elegant lettering – proclaims his benefaction. As it happens, Tacitus – who had probably visited the oracle himself ten years earlier when proconsul of Asia – was at about this time writing an account of a famous Roman's consultation of Apollo at Claros – Germanicus Caesar, on his ill-fated eastern mission. After the statutory stop at Ilium, Germanicus went to Colophon to make use of the oracle. Tacitus notes that 'it is not a woman there [that gives the responses], as at Delphi.' A priest chosen from certain families (mostly from Miletus) would listen to the questions, descend into a cave, drink the water of a secret spring and produce the response in verse from whatever came into his head – most of them were illiterate, he comments acidly.[21]

For Hadrian's presence at Ephesus itself there is firm evidence. On 29 August 124 Hadrian had occasion to write to the 'magistrates, council and people of the Termessians', that is, the little town of Oenoanda in northern Lycia, signifying his approval for the establishment of a musical competition there. The Termessians had sent three delegates to Hadrian. The letter that they took back with them ends 'from Ephesus'. How long Hadrian stayed at Ephesus, exactly what he did on this first visit, whether he made excursions to Samos across the bay or to Magnesia on the Maeander a few miles inland, all this is largely conjectural. Further, since Ephesus, exceptionally, was to be honoured with a second visit five years later, it is hard to say which of the acts of imperial generosity there belong to 124 and which to 129.[22]

A marked feature of Ephesus, distinguishing it from its rivals among the major cities of Asia, was the large number of resident Romans of Italian origin. The great trading city lay at the western end of a major route from the

Euphrates and although its harbour at the mouth of the Cayster was continually silting up, its attraction for immigrants remained. Expatriate Italian families like the Gavii were now well to the fore: Gavius Bassus had been prefect of the *classis Pontica* when Pliny was governing Pontus-Bithynia a dozen years earlier. His brother Balbus and his son Maximus were already launched on equestrian careers – Maximus would rise to the summit. The leading Ephesian families had to wait, it is true, for several generations before one of their number reached the highest rank in the senatorial career, the consulate. For the Greeks in the Senate the advantage still went to the grandees of royal descent like Quadratus Bassus of Pergamum or Celsus Polemaeanus of Sardes. Still, Celsus had elected Ephesus as his residence and Hadrian will have been able to admire the beautiful library which Celsus' son was building there in memory of his father.[23]

It may have been at this time that Hadrian selected a new member of his staff. T. Petronius Priscus, who had been serving as procurator in the province Asia, was honoured with a marble statue at Ephesus on his promotion to be Hadrian's Secretary for Petitions, *a libellis*. Petitions would certainly have flowed in regularly and an Emperor on the move was likely to be approached by provincials everywhere he went. Dio tells how 'once, when a woman approached him as he was passing by on a journey, he said to her, at first, "I don't have time" – but then, when she cried out, "Then stop being emperor!", he turned back and let her speak.' Very similar stories are told about several Greek rulers, but Dio's anecdote is likely to be genuine for all that.[24]

Ephesus, like Pergamum and Smyrna, would receive a second Temple Wardenship from Hadrian, but not at the time of this first visit. In the meantime he received honours of the usual effusive kind. An inscription recalls how 'when T. Flavius Potamo was gymnasiarch and the Lord Emperor Traianus Hadrianus Sebastus was staying in the city, the ephebes sang a hymn' for the Emperor – who 'listened to it with pleasure.' The ceremony in the theatre – where Paul had once faced the wrath of the silversmiths and the repeated cry 'Great is Diana of the Ephesians' – was suitably followed by rites in the famous temple of Artemis just outside the city.[25]

Hadrian sailed from Ephesus to Rhodes. The *HA* biographer has actually preserved a tiny trace of this journey: 'he sailed by Asia and the islands to Achaia.' Rhodes is specifically mentioned in Polemo's account and the visit is confirmed by letters of Hadrian written a few years later. He commended two men he 'sailed with from Ephesus to Rhodes', Erastus and Philocyrius. The coinage of Alexandria at this time suitably illustrated the Emperor's activity with 'an imperial galley, with square sail, small sail on bowsprit, and pennant.' Hadrian himself will have sailed on an imperial warship; Erastus, Philocyrius and other merchant captains will have transported lesser members of the entourage and necessary supplies. There was hardly time for serious stops on the way – much as Miletus, the last major city yet to see Hadrian, may have hoped for a visit. The Milesians would have to wait. But Cos would have been a convenient staging-post, even Halicarnassus, for that matter – the imperial tourist would have appreciated the famous Mausoleum – or Cnidus.[26]

As for Rhodes, there is a peculiar story in the early Byzantine chronicler John Malalas that Hadrian organised the re-erection of the Colossus, which had been toppled by an earthquake a good three hundred years earlier. Malalas even purports to know about the inscription which commemorated the massive undertaking. The team of architects, engineers and craftsmen that the *Epitome* reports Hadrian to have taken round the empire with him might very well all have been dispersed by this time on other building projects, from Cyzicus southwards. Malalas claims that the inscription registered an imperial donation of 'three *centenaria*' (3 million sesterces?) to pay for the engines, ropes and craftsmen. Colossus aside – and it has to be admitted that a project of this sort would have appealed to Hadrian – there was enough on Rhodes to attract him. The island had been Rome's ally for nearly three hundred years and still enjoyed this status; its links with Rome were for that reason closer and deeper than was the case with most of the other Greek communities. Hadrian may be imagined to have inspected the house where a famous Roman had lived for six years – Tiberius, Augustus' stepson, in resentful self-imposed exile. But, although Rhodes had a priest of the goddess Roma and festivals with the telling names of Romaea and Caesarea, a certain resistance to Roman culture has been detected there. Roman citizens were not numerous – and there were no gladiatorial shows (for which abstinence Dio of Prusa had praised the Rhodians a generation earlier). Tiberius and Hadrian were seen by Tacitus, then – surely – still writing his *Annals*, as kindred spirits, both philhellenes with intellectual interests (including astrology), both complex and tortuous characters. Hadrian, whose policies in certain respects at least (notably avoidance of imperial expansion) resembled the successor of Augustus, may have found much of interest here. Perhaps he knew the epigram of Apollonides, recalling a favourable omen – an eagle – that appeared at Rhodes 'when [Tiberius Claudius] Nero held the island of the sun' and naming Augustus' stepson 'the future Zeus'.[27]

Time must have been found for dealing with imperial business. Throughout Hadrian's long absences from Rome the centre of the empire had to move with him. Regular attention needed to be given to the filling of posts at all levels. It was about now that Bruttius Praesens was moved from Cappadocia to Moesia Inferior, replacing the excellent Ummidius Quadratus. Not much happens to be known about the governors of other provinces. Platorius Nepos was still coping with the giant Wall in Britain in 124 – it was causing problems and various modifications to the original concept were required. Hadrian was certainly kept informed by his friend. As for the high equestrians, Haterius Nepos, who had been Prefect of Egypt since 120, was probably replaced in 124. His successor is unknown (a rarity for that well-documented province). At Rome itself, Annius Verus was to lay down the City Prefecture, after a seven-year tenure, which had clearly won approval; and Marcius Turbo was there, commanding the Guard. Whether a second Prefect was with Hadrian is not recorded – but elements of the Guard would certainly have been with the Emperor, perhaps commanded by a tribune.[28]

Rhodes cannot have detained Hadrian for long, in any case. He sailed from there, via the Cyclades no doubt, to Athens, as both the *HA* and Polemo attest, and is unlikely to have set off much after mid-September. He intended to be there for the Eleusinian Mysteries, which began in the month Boedromion.[29]

15

A YEAR IN GREECE

It was some eleven years since Hadrian had left Athens, to participate in Trajan's Parthian expedition. Virtually nothing is known about how he had spent his time in Greece then. It is natural to suppose that he had taken the chance to visit at least a few of the other cities apart from Athens, where he had been archon. This time, as Emperor, he had far more scope and he was to travel widely in the Peloponnese and in central Greece. But first came the initiation into the Mysteries. He might, indeed, have undergone the preliminary initiation – as was normally prescribed – into the Lesser Mysteries at Agrae when he was archon; but if so no record of it has survived. In any case, the sources suggest that he was already Emperor when initiated into both grades. Now, presumably with a dispensation exempting him from the Agrae rituals, he could reach the first grade, becoming a *mystes*. The ceremonies lasted a whole week, beginning with the journey of the young men, the ephebes, to collect the sacred objects from Eleusis. Normally they were armed. In the year 124 they were obliged to forego their weapons, so the *HA* has it: 'During this stay in Achaia care was taken, they say, that when Hadrian was present none should enter armed, whereas generally many used to carry knives at religious ceremonies.' Recent incidents had had their impact.[1]

It may be assumed that the other rituals followed the normal pattern, with an assembly, from which murderers and barbarians were debarred, a ritual bath in the sea, with sacrifices to Demeter and to Kore, and finally the great procession of the worshippers, wearing their saffron ribbons and myrtle crowns, 14 miles (22 km) from Athens to Eleusis, ending in darkness, by torchlight. Hadrian 'undertook the Eleusinian rites following the example of Hercules and Philip', the *HA* says. A twelve-line poem composed by the priestess, *hierophantis*, who had the honour of making the Emperor a member of the cult, also alludes to Hercules. It was not the Dioscuri nor Asklepios nor Herakles that she had initiated, but 'Hadrian, the Lord of the wide earth, who poured out boundless wealth on all cities, and especially on the city of Cecrops.' Quite why the precedents of Hercules and Philip of Macedon get a mention in the *HA* is not clear. Hercules is one thing: his part in the legend of the Mysteries was well established. But Philip of Macedon, Athens' enemy, is a different matter – and there is no

Map 5 Greece and Macedonia

other evidence that he was initiated at Eleusis anyway. Still, the Macedonian royal house claimed descent from Hercules, so perhaps Philip was initiated after all. Besides this, he was regarded as a champion of panhellenism. It is probable enough that the 'example of Hercules and Philip' derived ultimately from Hadrian's autobiography. Hadrian would have been well aware that Augustus had also been initiated. Perhaps he thought that the Athenians would prefer to be reminded of authentic Greek examples of great figures from outside Athens coming to be initiated. As it happens, the name of Philip has been emended to that of Philopappus. This was the grandson of the last client king of Commagene, C. Julius Antiochus Philopappus, who, although he had been a senator, and consul the year after Hadrian, in 109, had lived many years at Athens. Philopappus' sister Balbilla turns up a few years later as a close friend of the Empress Sabina. But it seems unlikely that Hadrian, even if Philopappus had been his close friend, would have cited him in the same breath as Hercules.[2]

Nothing is said in any of the sources about where Hadrian stayed when he was in Athens. The Athenian aristocrat whom Hadrian had encountered six years before in Pannonia as a nervous young delegate of his city, Herodes Atticus, was shown special favour at this time. He had been given senatorial rank and was now to begin his senatorial career as quaestor – of the Emperor, the most honoured status possible: *inter amicos*, among the Emperor's friends, an inscription of Herodes adds. Herodes' father Atticus had in the meantime been adlected to the senate with the rank of ex-praetor. These two were no doubt in close attendance on Hadrian throughout his stay in Greece. The odds are that they acted as hosts to the Emperor and that his plans for the city were worked out in part at least in discussion with them. A few years earlier the Athenians had formally requested Hadrian 'to reform their laws'. The 'free city' was by now very much dependent on Rome. It was no doubt an Athenian who undertook suitable research into the ancient laws of Dracon and Solon, probably a man called Annius Pythodorus, who is given the title *nomothetes* on an inscription of this time. One result was that the number of members of the Council was brought down from 600 to to 500, the size it had been under Cleisthenes' dispensation. Cleisthenes had introduced the ten *phylae*, tribes, named after ancient Attic heroes, but there were by now two extra; one more, the thirteenth, was added, bearing Hadrian's name. It took the central, seventh place in the listing. Other reforms had a financial impact, notably a measure regulating the price of locally produced olive oil. This echoed a famous law of Solon. A new tax exemption for sellers of fish may have been intended to ensure ready supplies at the time of the Mysteries. At Eleusis itself Hadrian had a bridge built over the River Cephisus. Further measures would soon follow: the *HA*, like the *hierophantis*, specifically refers to Hadrian 'dispensing many favours to the Athenians.' But he was to spend a considerable time in the city, which must have been his main base during this stay. The major building programme which he initiated at Athens is best considered later.[3]

In the autumn of 124 he undertook an extensive tour of the Peloponnese. His presence at a string of famous cities at this time is well attested, even if the exact order is not quite certain in all cases. Apart from the record of inscriptions, some dated, there is the precious witness supplied by Pausanias in the *Guide to Greece* that he wrote a generation later. Again and again he refers to the results of Hadrian's visit: in particular, to temples and other monuments restored on his initiative and at his expense. Hadrian's first stop was at Athens' western neighbour and old enemy, Megara. The bad relations, which had reached a low point in the fifth century BC, still prevailed. Philostratus reports how a contemporary of Hadrian, the sophist Marcus of Byzantium (a colony of Megara), persuaded the Megarians to modify their hostility to Athens. They agreed at least to admit Athenians and their families into their houses. As at Athens, the Megarians created a new *phyle*, in their case a fourth, named Hadrianis. Megarian inscriptions from the late 130s honour Hadrian as 'their founder, lawgiver, benefactor and fosterer'. He had clearly implemented reforms as well as building work. Sabina was also honoured at Megara, as a 'New Demeter', from which one may guess that she had accompanied her husband. Pausanias specifically refers to the rebuilding of the formerly brick temple of Apollo in white stone, no doubt the 'shell stone' which he remarks on as a special feature at Megara. He also mentions the road from Megara to Corinth, formerly passable by foot only, but widened by Hadrian so that chariots could drive along it in opposite directions. An inscription dated to the following year, 125, probably belonged to the first milestone of this road. Hadrian may indeed have issued an edict ordering road improvements all over Achaia and Macedonia at this time. But at Megara, in spite of Hadrian's best efforts, according to Pausanias, he experienced 'his only failure in Greece: even he could not make them thrive.'[4]

From Megara the imperial party proceeded over the Isthmus to Epidaurus. The city erected a statue to him in 124, calling him 'its saviour and benefactor', and began a new era in the local calendar from this year. No details of his benefactions have survived. A prominent member of a local family, Cn. Cornelius Pulcher, who had been procurator of Epirus at least ten years earlier, and had evidently retired from imperial service since then, would soon take on the appointment of *iuridicus* in Egypt. One may infer that this cultivated person attracted Hadrian's attention at this time. Pulcher's forebears had already received Roman citizenship under Augustus. He himself had served as Helladarch, chairman of the Council of the Achaians – an association of Peloponnesian cities, rather than a provincial council of the normal type. There were, indeed, various competing federal organisations in Greece. Hadrian was evidently in two minds for a while as to which he should promote and foster. Pulcher had been a friend of Plutarch, who dedicated to him his essay on *How to Make Use of One's Enemies*. He had been an appreciative reader, so he had told Plutarch, of the *Precepts of Statecraft*.[5]

An inscription from Troezen, the next city to the south, honoured a local benefactor, who had, among other services to his city, made its roads passable for carriages in connection with 'the prayed-for visit of the greatest emperor'. Everything speaks for this being Hadrian, especially as the little town of Hermione, south of Troezen, erected a statue in honour of Sabina. It is plausible to suppose that the imperial party went via Troezen and Hermione to Argos. In the shrine of Hera, about 2 miles (3 km) from Mycenae, Pausanias saw 'an altar depicting, in silver, the legendary marriage of Herakles and Hebe; and the Emperor Hadrian has dedicated a peacock in gold and precious stones, because peacocks are regarded as birds sacred to Hera.' Pausanias also noted that the Heraeum still preserved a golden crown and purple dress which Nero had dedicated there on his famous visit in 67. Nero's interest in this part of Greece was largely focused on the Games in which he competed (and won all the first prizes). Hadrian did not neglect this aspect of Greek life, even if not personally inclined to participate. Pausanias happens to mention 'the boys' race on the riding-track at Nemea'. The event had died out there, he adds, 'but the Emperor Hadrian restored it to Argos for the Nemean winter Games.' These games seem to have been held at Argos in later years on 30 December; it is reasonable to infer that Hadrian watched them, indeed presided, on this day at the end of 124. It is hardly necessary to comment that Hadrian's revival of a horse-race for boys admirably suits what is known about his tastes. What else may have been on his agenda can only be guessed. He surely saw Mycenae and Tiryns. It seems likely enough that a meeting of the Council of the Achaians, which had its seat at Argos, was held to mark his visit, even if if was not the regular date for one. Other fruits of his visit included a new aqueduct and the restoration of the theatre.[6]

From Argos it was a short stretch westwards into Arcadia, to Mantinea, where three separate mentions in Pausanias' description of the city attest his presence. Not the least welcome result of his visit was that he ordered the revival of the city's original name. For ten generations, as Pausanias put it, Mantinea had been called 'Antigonia', in fact since 222 BC, in honour of Antigonus II Doson, then regent of Macedonia. Mantinea was the last resting-place of a famous Greek statesman and general of the classical epoch, Epaminondas the Theban, the man who first broke the power of Sparta and liberated the Messenians. Epaminondas, often credited with being the greatest of panhellenic patriots, was buried where he died, on the battlefield of 362 BC, four miles (6 km) along the road from Mantinea to Pallantium.

> A pillar stood over the tomb with a shield on it engraved with a serpent, to indicate that Epaminondas belonged to the people that sprang from the dragon's teeth. There are stone inscriptions on the monument, one of them ancient with a text in the Boeotian dialect, the other dedicated by the Emperor Hadrian, who composed it himself.

Honouring great figures of the past in this way was a characteristic feature of Hadrian. Pausanias does not mention that Epaminondas was buried beside a young man whose lover he had been, Caphisodorus, who had also fallen at Mantinea. Plutarch had recalled this in his essay *On Love*. At Mantinea Hadrian also ordered the building of a new temple of Poseidon the Lord of Horses, the city's chief deity, by the edge of the mountain near the stadium. He 'set inspectors to supervise the workmen to make sure that no one looked inside the ancient shrine or moved a single stone from its ruins, ordering them to build the new temple all round it.'[7]

It must be a matter of conjecture whether there was already another, very special reason for Hadrian to take an interest in Mantinea. It was supposed to be the mother-city of Bithynium, the home of Antinous – in fact, Antinous came from a small community in the territory of Bithynium that was actually called Mantinium. It is perfectly plausible that Hadrian had already met Antinous the previous year during his tour of Bithynia and had taken him into his entourage – and that he was Hadrian's constant companion from 123 until his death in Egypt seven years later. Be this as it may, the Mantineans were later to honour Antinous with particular fervour. His very name indeed recalled a Mantinean legend, which must have been known at his Bithynian home. Mantinea had originally been founded elsewhere, but, in response to the command of an oracle, so it was related, Antinoe the daughter of King Cepheus brought the people to a new site, guided by a dragon. She was revered as the city's foundress.[8]

From Mantinea the route led south to Sparta, with a stop at Tegea on the way. As had Epidaurus, Tegea revised its calendar to start a new era from the date of his arrival, and an inscription calling him 'saviour and founder' presupposes that he conferred benefits on the place. Hadrian's host at Sparta, probably in January of 125, was almost certainly the head of the Euryclid family which had dominated the place since the time of the Battle of Actium. By fighting on the winning side – unlike most of the Greeks – and making a spirited attempt to catch the fleeing Marcus Antonius, the first Eurycles, who claimed descent from the Dioscuri, had won favour for himself and the Spartans. In spite of getting into trouble with Augustus later, he was able to pass on his position of pre-eminence at Sparta and in Greece generally to his son Laco. The current Euryclid, C. Julius Eurycles Herculanus L. Vibullius Pius by his full names, 'thirty-sixth in descent from the Dioscuri', was linked by family ties to Claudius Atticus and was a cousin of Philopappus. Herculanus had become a Roman senator, first as quaestor of the province Achaia, then as tribune of the plebs, praetor – and legate to a proconsul of Baetica. He may well have only just returned from this year as assistant to the proconsul of Hadrian's home province when the Emperor came to Sparta. One may have leave to wonder which proconsul had invited this Spartan magnate to be his legate. Could it have been Arrian? Hadrian's intellectual friend from Nicomedia was to be consul a few years later, so that a proconsulship of Baetica *c.* 124–5 would fit his known career. Furthermore, a poem in Greek has been found at Corduba, dedicated to Artemis, goddess of the hunt, by a proconsul called Arrianus. Why not suppose that this was the famous Arrian, who was after all the author of a treatise on hunting? If Herculanus had already spent this year in Baetica, he had surely visited Italica, and could have amused the Emperor with gossip about his fellow-townsmen. Whether Hadrian found him congenial is another matter. Plutarch had dedicated to Herculanus his essay *How to Praise Oneself without Incurring Disapproval*, which may give some clue to his personality. Still, he evidently had some close links with Hadrian's friend Pompeius Falco – who had perhaps inherited the friendship from his father-in-law Sosius Senecio. That might have enhanced Herculanus in Hadrian's eyes.[9]

Sparta benefited directly from Hadrian's interest. The island of Caudus off the coast of Crete and the port of Corone on the Gulf of Messenia, both valuable sources of revenue, were presented to the city. A whole series of altars has been found at Sparta honouring Hadrian as 'saviour, founder and benefactor'. It has been suggested that a further practical benefaction was owed to Hadrian, a new aqueduct. Sparta was still a name to conjure with, the Spartan 'myth' was still potent. Above all, the ancient *agoge*, the training system for boys and young men ascribed to Lycurgus, was still very much in force, a subject of admiration or at least curiosity. Roman tourists were known to relish the rituals of Artemis Orthia, at which the Spartan young had to endure hours of whipping. Claudius Atticus, the great Athenian magnate, had himself spent some time at Sparta in his youth and gone through this training. Hadrian seems to have referred approvingly to 'the Laconian practices' in his speech to the Cyreneans two years earlier.[10]

Hadrian's presence at two further places in the Peloponnese, Olympia and Corinth, can be assigned tentatively to early 125. Admittedly, direct evidence for a visit to Olympia is lacking. Nor is it clear which route he would have taken from Sparta to Olympia, assuming that he did go there. He might simply have headed north-west by the most direct route, via Megalopolis. In an inscription from Lycosura, close to that city, the Megalopolitans honoured him as 'saviour and benefactor of the world and founder of their own city'. This certainly indicates some direct favour, even if not necessarily as a result of a visit. He might equally well have gone west into Messenia, across Mount Taygetus, on to Pylos, and then up the west coast. His presence at the little town of Abea, on the Gulf of Messenia, where Laconia bordered Messenia, is, however, not proved by the statue set up to him there 'in accordance with the decree of the Achaians', giving him the title 'Boulaios', '(Lord – or God) of the Council'. It does perhaps at least serve to reinforce the inference that he had attended a meeting of the Achaian Council while at Argos. The Council also had statues to him set up at Olympia itself. An inscription there records a sacrifice on his birthday, shortly after a fragmentary reference to Zeus Apobaterios, 'Zeus who brings safely to land'. Perhaps he had arrived at the nearest harbour, Pheia, on 26 January 125, his forty-ninth birthday? But Pausanias has nothing to report of buildings or benefactions by Hadrian here. Coins which were minted at Elis only during his reign portray Phidias' famous statue of Olympian Zeus. This has been taken to be a reminiscence of his visit, in particular to hint that Hadrian had paid for the restoration of the vast image of the god, made of gold and ivory, now more than five hundred years old. Olympian Zeus was at any rate very shortly to receive very particular attention from Hadrian. It is hard to believe that he did not take the chance of visiting Olympia itself.[11]

If Hadrian had approached Olympia from the south-east – or, for that matter, if he was anywhere in the vicinity – he would surely have wanted to see Scillus, where Xenophon had once lived in comfortable exile after returning with the Ten Thousand. Pausanias reports that 'Scillus is stocked with wild boar and deer for hunting', an ideal opportunity for Hadrian to indulge his passion. Here too was the sanctuary and temple Xenophon had built to Ephesian Artemis and close by a a monument with a stone portrait which local people told Pausanias was Xenophon's grave. Given Hadrian's predilection for paying homage at the tombs of famous men, this ought to have been a magnet for him.[12]

From Olympia, then, it must be assumed that Hadrian set off eastwards across the northern Peloponnese to Corinth. Philhellene Romans may sometimes have felt uncomfortable in this city, which the Republican consul Mummius had wiped off the map in 146 BC and had ceased to exist for a century until Caesar rebuilt it as a Roman colony. Hadrian himself, as a fifteen-year-old briefly back at Italica, must surely have been aware of the spoils from Corinth which Mummius had presented to the town, then Rome's most westerly settlement. Since then it had evidently been the residence of the Roman governor of Greece, the proconsul of Achaia, a Latin island, along with the other *colonia* at Patras, in the middle of Greece. But the Corinthians, even if still labelled by Pausanias as 'colonists sent by Rome', were by now thoroughly Hellenised, as the philosopher or sophist Favorinus told an audience there, not long after Hadrian's visit. Hadrian may have seen the bronze statue of this extraordinary figure in the city library. At all events, Pausanias registers Hadrian's benefactions here, an aqueduct and baths. He adds, however, that the best known baths at Corinth – there were plenty of them – had been donated by Eurycles the Spartan, made of the beautiful speckled green Laconian marble.[13]

At the latest, Hadrian was back in Athens in March of 125. At the great festival of the Dionysia he presided as *agonothetes*, president of the festival, the *HA* reports. Dio adds that 'he wore Athenian dress for the occasion and fulfilled his duties brilliantly.' The cultural life of Athens gained Hadrian's attention in other respects too. Four years before, the Epicureans had enlisted Plotina's support to obtain a privilege, the right of the head of the school to name his own successor, even a non-Roman citizen. In March 125, while at Athens, Hadrian confirmed his previous reply, in writing, and his letter was again engraved on marble. His letter is followed by a document which begins with the name (in the dative) Heliodorus, who, whether or not he was the new head of the school, was clearly an Epicurean. The *HA* happens to record Hadrian's friendship with two men – and only two – who are labelled philosophers, one being the famous Epictetus, whom he had probably met long before at Nicopolis, on his way to be archon at Athens. Heliodorus is the other name. The odds are that it was the Epicurean named on this inscription of the year 125. There is a further chance that the philosopher Heliodorus was none other than C. Avidius Heliodorus, a Syrian from Cyrrhus, whom Hadrian had very likely met ten years before in Syria. Heliodorus' Roman names point to his having been made a citizen through the good offices of Avidius Nigrinus, perhaps when Nigrinus held office as imperial commissioner in Greece. However this may be, Avidius Heliodorus turns up a few years later as the holder of an important office, in close proximity to Hadrian.[14]

Hadrian may have had contact with another philosopher of Athens at this time, Secundus, the 'silent philosopher', the teacher of Herodes. A legend developed of an encounter between Hadrian and Secundus, who defied the imperial attempt to make him break his vow of silence and provided only written answers to Hadrian's questions. There were eventually versions in Arabic, Syriac, Armenian and Ethiopic as well as Greek, all of them simply fiction, no doubt. But there may be a few authentic details preserved. In the Arabic version the 'king's cousin Salan' is named. It has been plausibly proposed that this was none other than Pedanius Fuscus Salinator, husband of Hadrian's niece Julia Paulina. Fuscus Salinator, who had been Hadrian's colleague in the consulship in his first full year as Emperor, must have been regarded as a likely heir to the throne. It is likely enough that Fuscus and Julia were in the imperial party – if they were still alive. Nothing is heard of Fuscus after the consulship he shared with Hadrian in 118. There is also a mention in the Secundus story of Hadrian losing patience and ordering a military tribune to make the philosopher speak. The officer sensibly pointed out that it would be easier to make lions or panthers talk than a philosopher. A tribune commanding a detachment of the Praetorian Guard – assuming that there was only one Prefect, Marcius Turbo, who remained at Rome – or the commander of the Horse Guards, will have been part of Hadrian's party.[15]

The church historian Eusebius claims that two Christians, Quadratus and Aristides, the latter an Athenian, addressed a defence of their faith to Hadrian – his visit to Athens in 124-5 would certainly have been a good opportunity to attempt to secure an audience or at least to deliver a written version to the Emperor. The enquiry from Asia against the Christians two years earlier, to which Hadrian had sent a reply to the proconsul Granianus, is a sign that the Christians might have felt the need to take such a step. But it is perhaps more likely that these men sent their *Apologies* to Hadrian's successor.[16]

This stay marked the opening of a colossal building programme. Nearly seven hundred years earlier the Athenian tyrant Pisistratus had begun the construction of a vast temple of Olympian Zeus in the south-east corner of the city, close to the River Ilissus. After four hundred years the Seleucid king Antiochus IV Epiphanes had taken the work a stage further, engaging a Roman architect named Cossutius. But work had ceased on Antiochus' death in 164 BC, with the marble shrine still only half built. In the time of Augustus, so Suetonius reports, 'all the client kings planned jointly to finish the temple of Olympian Jove at Athens, begun in ancient times but never finished: they were to share the costs and dedicate it to his [Augustus'] *Genius*'. Whatever may be thought of the intended rededication, the plan to exalt Athens in this way would certainly have had Augustus' approval. But again, the project was not realised; and in any case relations between the first Princeps and Athens went sour at the end of his reign. It was to be many decades before the city regained imperial favour. Now Hadrian launched the final stage of building, the erection of a vast enclosure around the temple.[17]

Another piece of public works was also begun at this time, the provision of a new aqueduct leading water from Mount Parnes. It was the first time anyone

Plate 21 Hadrian the restorer of Achaia
(*BMC* III Hadrian no. 1783)

had brought water to the city from an external source since the days of
Pisistratus. The project was ambitious, involving tunnelling, with a great reser-
voir on Mount Lycabettus, and ending with a fountain-house in the highest
point of the Agora. It would be fifteen years before this was completed. There
were to be other major building initiatives undertaken by Hadrian at Athens,
and other significant privileges which he granted to the city. Quite when each
began and how long the work lasted is difficult to establish. But one of the
first to get under way was something wholly new, called variously 'the Stoa' or
the 'Library of Hadrian'. Just north of the Roman Agora, donated to Athens by
Caesar and Augustus, in appearance the new complex was to be reminiscent of
the Forum or temple of Peace at Rome. Undoubtedly Hadrian already had it in
mind to return, to inspect progress and to dedicate the finished buildings.
Equally, he will have wished to come to the Mysteries again, to be initiated into
the higher grade. But in the spring of 125 it was time to begin the journey back
to Rome, taking the opportunity to visit other places in central and western
Greece on his way. It was four years since he had left the capital.[18]

The route taken was north-westwards, past Mount Cithaeron, into Boeotia.
At Thespiae, below Mount Helicon, the home of the Nine Muses, 'the god particularly worshipped has always been Eros', as Pausanias puts it. Here, on 'one
of the most fertile mountains in Greece', Hadrian went hunting and killed a
bear, as he had the previous year in Mysia. A few miles from Thespiae was found

184

an inscription with eight lines of Greek verse which Hadrian had composed. He had offered the bear's skin to Eros, calling him 'archer son of the sweet-tongued Cyprian (Aphrodite), dwelling at Heliconian Thespiae by Narcissus' flowering garden'. In return he asked the god to 'breathe grace soberly on him from heavenly Aphrodite'. Aphrodite Urania, so Socrates is made by Xenophon in his *Symposium* to expound it, was the patron deity of spiritual, as opposed to physical, love – in the context, to be sure, of love between man and youth: Hadrian and his Antinous, it might be thought, but this cannot be proved.[19]

Thespiae was the setting of Plutarch's essay *On Love*. It is in the form of a conversation between Plutarch's son Autobulus and his friend Flavianus, with other friends, in the shrine of the Muses on Helicon, during the festival of the Erotidia, held every fifth year. Autobulus tells his friend a story he had heard from his father Plutarch about a dispute at a previous festival, centring round a beautiful young man called Baccho. A wealthy widow called Ismenodora had fallen in love with him, to the intense exasperation of Baccho's male admirers. A friend from Tarsus, Protogenes, had been particularly vehement in his attack on Ismenodora. Marriage might be a necessity, to produce children, 'but genuine love has no connection with the women's quarters'. True love, he insisted, is the strong passion for a young and talented spirit; only the love of boys is the genuine kind. 'You will see it in the schools of philosophy or perhaps in the gymnasia . . . searching for young men, whom it encourages with a clear and noble cry to the pursuit of virtue.' Plutarch himself in due course weighs in, not least to defend married love. Other things aside, Plutarch's essay is only one of countless examples from Hellenic literature and art which treat homosexual love, in particular that between an older man and a beautiful youth, as entirely normal, indeed laudable and superior to the love between men and women. Xenophon's *Symposium*, with Socrates' praise of heavenly Aphrodite, has just been mentioned. Attitudes at Rome, even if Greek influences had had their effect, were still very much more conservative.[20]

Hadrian's philhellenism unquestionably embraced 'Greek love' too. In the Hellenic half of his empire he must have felt freer. It remains quite uncertain whether he already had Antinous with him. Even if the only possible occasion for him to have visited Bithynium seems to be the year 124, the sources make no explicit mention of Antinous being in his company until the visit to Egypt in 130. All the same, given that an emperor travelled with a massive entourage, military escort, court officials and ministers, palace slaves and freedmen, Antinous may have been found a discreet place. One may compare a tombstone from Rome, which commemorates a young man of seventeen called L. Marius Vitalis. 'Accomplished in letters', he persuaded his parents that he should learn *artefic(ium)* – what kind of art or skill is not specified – and 'left the city in the *praetorium* of Hadrianus Augustus Caesar. The envious fates snatched him from his art while he was studying.' Perhaps he had joined the great team of artists and craftsmen which the *Epitome* claims Hadrian took with him on his travels.[21]

Another place in Boeotia that Hadrian may have visited was Lebadea, famous for its oracle of Trophonius. At any rate, Trophonius seems later to have had some special significance for the Emperor. Whether he actually consulted the oracle himself may perhaps be doubted – this involved living for several days in a building consecrated 'to Good Fortune and the Good Spirit', according to Pausanias, and after a series of rituals ending up in a kiln-like structure, entered by a light, narrow ladder. 'When a man comes up from Trophonius', Pausanias recorded, 'he is still possessed with terror and hardly knows himself' – he did not write from hearsay, but from personal experience. This might have been too much for an emperor.[22]

At Boeotian Coronea Hadrian's presence left traces of a more prosaic and practical kind. A series of his letters concern the construction of dykes to control the rivers Cephisus and Hercyne at their confluence before they emptied into Lake Copais. 'Construction will begin as soon as possible', he told the archons, council and *demos* of the Coroneans in a letter from the year 125, to prevent the rivers flooding most of the arable land. He would supply the funds which the experts – perhaps members of his team of specialists – had told him were required, 65,000 denarii. A second, very fragmentary letter from the same year refers to the supply of 'wine for the soldiers [travelling] with me'. The work was to take a long time, and would include another river, the Phalarus. Further letters followed over the next ten years, also involving disputes between Coronea and its neighbours Thisbe and Orchomenus.[23]

Personal inspection of the flooding problems may have taken Hadrian to the north side of Lake Copais. At any rate, Pausanias has two items which suggest his presence north of the lake. At little Abae in Phocis, where the temples that Xerxes' soldiers had burned six hundred years before had been left in their ruined state, there was still one great shrine, and 'beside it a smaller one to Apollo, built by the Emperor Hadrian'. At nearby Hyampolis, also destroyed by Xerxes' men and later again by Philip II of Macedon, Hadrian 'built a colonnade' named after himself, a Stoa Hadriane.[24]

Perhaps the most important stage of his journey in 125 now lay before him: Delphi. If he came from Abae he would pass below Mount Parnassus. He had already written 'to the city of the Delphians' earlier in the year, announcing his decision on how many delegates each member-state in the ancient Amphictyonic Council should have. Augustus had weighted the voting-rights heavily in favour of his new city of Nicopolis near Actium, and Nero had made further changes. Now, Hadrian's letter reveals, a commission of enquiry had recommended to the Senate at Rome that the membership should be reconstituted. He refers to the proposal that the number of members should be increased and a new balance be established. In particular, excess votes hitherto held by the Thessalians 'should be transferred to the Athenians, Lacedaemonians and other cities, so that the Council (*synedrion*) should be a common Council of all the Hellenes.' On other matters, concerning both expenses for strangers (visitors) and a dispute between the Thessalians and Delphi, 'I shall decide at Delphi.'

Further, he had appointed one 'Claudius Timocrates to collect and send to me all the decrees of the Amphictyons which are in conflict with one another or with the common [i.e. Roman] laws, so that an investigation may be made.' The stress on making the Amphictyons 'a common Council of all the Hellenes' suggests that at this stage he planned to make Delphi the main Panhellenic centre, from which to revive the national self-consciousness of the Greeks.[25]

Plutarch, whom he had certainly known and admired, must have been dead by now, though he had lived to see Hadrian Emperor and had been honoured by him with an official title. Several of Plutarch's writings were devoted to Delphi and its oracle and he himself had taken a very active and prominent role in the Amphictyonic Council and as one of the two permanent priests of Apollo. He had been executive officer of the Amphictyons when they voted to honour Hadrian with a statue on his accession. In one of his essays or dialogues on Delphi, he accepted that the oracle now had more trivial questions to answer than in the great days of old, hence the answers were often in prose. 'I am perfectly happy with the settled conditions which now prevail, I welcome them', says one of the speakers in *The Oracles at Delphi*, 'and the questions put to the oracle merely reflect the circumstances: profound peace and tranquillity.' Although Plutarch had probably written the dialogue nearly twenty years earlier, Hadrian, if he read the work again before his visit, may have taken some satisfaction from these words. He no doubt felt obliged to pose a question to the priestess himself: 'Where was Homer born and who were his parents?' (Perhaps his tour of the Ionian cities of Asia the previous summer had irritated him with their competing claims to be Homer's birthplace.) The priestess made a special effort for him and produced four lines of hexameter verse: Homer was born at Ithaca, son of Telemachus and Polycaste.[26]

Pausanias has nothing to report of buildings erected by Hadrian at Delphi, but an inscription there of a *frumentarius* from the legion I Italica shows that soldiers had been left there to supervise 'the works undertaken by the Lord Caesar Traianus Hadrianus Sebastus'. Hadrian's active interest in the great religious centre continued for some time. He was to write to Delphi from Tibur later in the year and held office there too, albeit in *absentia*. He was honoured at Delphi by 'the Hellenes who meet at Plataea', who still celebrated their deliverance from the Persians in 479 BC by sacrificing regularly to Zeus the Liberator. They called him 'Emperor Hadrian the Saviour who has healed and nourished his own Hellas'. As for the Delphians, they voted to declare the days of Hadrian's visit religious holidays for the future.[27]

There is good evidence that Hadrian was at some time much further north, in the Vale of Tempe and in Macedonia, but this could have been some years later. This time his route would take him westwards, almost certainly by sea, from the Corinthian Gulf and past Cephallenia and Ithaca to Nicopolis in Epirus. He had surely been there before, on his way to be archon at Athens. It was probably then that he had first met Epictetus. If the old man was still alive, Hadrian would have wished to see him again. As likely as not, Hadrian would only have been able to pay his respects at Epictetus' tomb. Then it was time to move on, with the final Greek stage at the journey taking him up the coast to the port of Dyrrhachium. Among the party, *inter amicos*, was probably his quaestor, the Athenian Herodes Atticus.[28]

16

PATER PATRIAE

An emperor's letter to the city of Heraclea Lyncestis in Macedonia, written at Dyrrachium (Dürres in Albania) on 20 May of an unknown year, has been plausibly attributed to Hadrian and taken to indicate that he was on his way back to Italy at this time in 125. The subject of the letter was the cost of road-building and the writer, assumed to be an emperor, tells the Lyncestae that 'I have set forth in a general edict how the roads are to be paved.' They are given precise instructions on the apportionment of costs. The 'general edict' had no doubt prompted an enquiry. For the Lyncestae, through whose territory the great military trunk-road the Via Egnatia ran, the matter was serious. Hadrian could well have issued such an edict during his stay in Greece. His personal attention to the Megara–Corinth road was registered by Pausanias, and milestones from northern Greece of 124 and 125 may reflect a more general road-building programme.[1]

If Hadrian was really at Dyrrachium in late May 125, the normal thing would have been to embark from there for Brundisium (Brindisi). But, according to the *HA*, he sailed to Sicily. All that is reported of the visit is that he climbed Mount Etna, to see the sunrise, 'said to be like a rainbow'. The later coins call him the *restitutor Siciliae*, as well as registering his *adventus* on the island, but there are no clear traces of any measures he took there. The *adventus* coins show Hadrian not in a toga but in a modified military dress. Sicilia holds two corn-ears in her hand and the *triskelis*, the badge of the three-cornered island, appears behind her head. Given the direction that he came from, he presumably landed at Syracuse, which no tourist with an interest in history, private or imperial, would have missed. It may be guessed that he stayed at Centuripae, on the south-west side of Etna, with his friend Pompeius Falco, whose family came from there. In any case, it was not to be his only stay on the island. Another old friend whom Hadrian probably met now was the procurator of Sicily, M. Vettius Latro. Nearly twenty years earlier Latro had been tribune in II Adiutrix, when Hadrian, as governor of Pannonia Inferior, was the legion's commander. Since then he had had a very slow career. He was now promoted, to be procurator-governor of the Cottian Alps.[2]

Plate 22 Hadrian the restorer of Italy
(*BMC* III Hadrian no. 1825)

The best-known work in Latin literature devoted to Sicily was Cicero's denunciation of the governor Verres, never delivered in full, but written up at enormous length. Hadrian's distaste for Cicero is well-attested – he preferred the Elder Cato and the simpler style of the Middle Republic to Cicero's elaborate rhetoric. But he had probably had to read the *Orationes Verrinae* in his youth. It is a nice coincidence that at about the time of this visit to Sicily, or shortly before, a man called Verres held the consulship. Nothing else is known about him, and there is no guarantee that he was a descendant of the delinquent propraetor from the years 73–1 BC – he might, indeed, have been a Sicilian, whose ancestor had obtained the citizenship (no doubt in return for hard cash) through the mediation of the notorious governor. However this may be, one might construe the promotion of a Verres as a little joke at the expense of Cicero's memory.[3]

Hadrian's route from southern Italy back to Rome can only be guessed. He might have gone by sea from Sicily to Puteoli or Ostia. It seems unlikely that he would have crossed the Straits of Messina to go overland through Bruttium (Calabria) and all the way along the west coast. Perhaps he sailed to Tarentum, the ancient Spartan colony that had once dominated the Ionian Sea, to join the Via Appia, and so northwards into Samnium. At all events he would not have used the new Via Traiana, still under construction when Hadrian was last in these parts, in 112, with his friend Falco in charge. Whichever way he went, each city that he entered would put on a ceremony of greeting and petitions would be presented. Some traces of his activity in the region may go back to this journey, for example his appointment of a *curator* of public works at Venusia. At Aeclanum he had something more to offer. A citizen of this town, C. Eggius Ambibulus, was in high favour and was to be consul *ordinarius* the following year. It was probably as a favour to Ambibulus that Hadrian awarded the town the rank of *colonia*. Two years before Hadrian had contributed jointly with the local landowners to improve the Via Appia between Aeclanum and Beneventum.

There was something new and out of the ordinary to see at Beneventum. In 114 the Senate had voted the erection of a triumphal arch in the city in Trajan's honour. Although the inscription still bore the original date, as if Trajan had still been alive when the monument was erected, the prominence of Hadrian in at least one scene makes it clear that the design had been carefully modified. The Arch celebrates Trajan as the conqueror of Dacia and the restorer of Italy through the *alimenta* system. Hadrian is depicted close to Trajan, the only figure on the same scale, in other words as the chosen heir. This hardly represented his real position in 114, which had still been ambiguous.

From Beneventum, rather than going via the Via Appia to the Bay of Naples, which he had visited in 119, he could have proceeded through the Samnite country of the central Apennines. A stop at Saepinum, home of the influential Neratii family, is likely enough. Hadrian's freedman Phlegon referred in his *Olympiads* to an otherwise unknown place called 'Tervetia', which the Byzantine geographer Stephanus labels as 'in Sicily'. It may be that Phlegon, the last part of whose work reflected Hadrian's itinerary, really referred to Terventum in northern Samnium. If this is the case, the return journey to Rome followed a roundabout route, but it would mean he could have inspected a part of Italy he is not otherwise known to have visited. He could then have entered Rome from the east, and called on the way at Tibur.[4]

Public prayers for his safe return had been undertaken: coins were struck showing the Genius of the Roman People and the Genius of the Senate jointly sacrificing, with the legend *v(ota) s(uscepta) pro red(itu)*. It may be assumed that his entry to the city was festive. He was probably glad to be back this time, if for no other reason than because he would be able to inspect the progress of the numerous and massive building projects that had been under way. It was to be several more years before the great new temple of Roma and Venus would be finished. But the rebuilding of the Pantheon was now complete in all its magnificence. Other works of renewal in this part of Rome would soon be concluded. There was also a massive new temple, of 'the Deified Trajan and Plotina'. The *HA* singles out 'the temple of his father, Trajan' as 'the only one of the innumerable works he built on which he inscribed his own name'. From what survives of the text, it is clear that Hadrian added Plotina's name and dedicated the temple *parentibus sui[s]*. The structure was certainly magnificent, occupying a prominent place between Trajan's Column and the Via Lata, and rising to a height of some fifty Roman feet. Apart from inspection of the building work,

Hadrian may have carried out a ceremony at another temple, that of Janus, closing the Gates of War as a sign that the world was now at peace. The act is nowhere directly attested, but the god duly appears on the imperial coinage at about this time.[5]

It was not only in the city itself that Hadrian had been building. His country retreat at Tibur was being turned into a great palace. No later than the second half of August or in early September Hadrian was there, for a letter of his to the Amphictyons and Delphi was written at this time 'from his house at Tibur'. Tibur had already been favoured by the élite during the late Republic. Its situation in the Sabine Hills less than 20 miles from the city offered fresh air, especially at times of year when Rome was hot and sultry. There were groves and orchards, the cascading River Anio, the sulphurous hot springs in the plain below. Hadrian's family had probably had a country seat there for several generations. What has been aptly called a 'nest of Spanish notables' was already ensconced under the Flavians. Statius devoted over one hundred hexameters (even if the poem only took him a day to compose) to the sumptuous 'villa Tiburtina' of Manilius Vopiscus, for whom Spanish origin can be inferred. It was a cool retreat, built on both sides of the Anio, adorned with works of art, with a wooded park. The present incumbent was the son or grandson of Statius' patron. Another villa-owning family was the Minicii Natales from Barcino (Barcelona). The elder Natalis, consul in 106, had governed Pannonia Superior in Trajan's last years, the younger had been Hadrian's quaestor in 121 – but had been allowed to join his father, then proconsul, in Africa. Tibur's decurions had subscribed to erect a statue to the elder Natalis after his return from Africa: he was curator of the great temple of Hercules in the town and had consented to hold the office of *quinquennalis* (the local government equivalent of censor) there. Whether Hadrian was close to the Minicii or Manilii is unknown. But another Spaniard with a seat at Tibur, Aemilius Papus, from Siarum in Baetica, is named by the *HA* as one of Hadrian's three particular friends at the time of the Parthian war. A tombstone near Tibur was set up by Papus and his wife Cutia Prisca, to commemorate one of their sons, who died at the start of his senatorial career. Nothing is known about Papus' own career, but another son was already well launched and would soon command a legion in Britain.[6]

The imperial villa, strangely enough, was not on the heights, where the air was best, but on the flatter land below the town. Perhaps Hadrian wanted more space than the ostensibly more favoured position above would have permitted. The original villa in the north-east quarter of the site, perhaps inherited from his father, had already been extended: the new structures included a great court-yard and a throne-room, two sets of baths, a theatre and stadium. Further work was now begun, probably under the imperial architect's own direction. It is to this last phase of the palace's development that the *HA* refers:

> He completed the building of his Tiburtine villa in wonderful fashion, in
> such a way that he inscribed the most famous names of provinces and

places there, and called them, for example, the Lyceum, the Academy, Canopus, Poecile and Tempe. So that he might omit nothing, he even made a Hades.

The Canopus perhaps got its name later – Hadrian did not go to Egypt until 130 – but in any case a structure of this nature was a conventional feature for a great country-house. The long portico in the southern part of the palace, surrounding a pool, with a half-domed apsidal building at one end, corresponds in its dimensions to the Euripus of Alexandria's Canopus. As for the other names, the emphasis is on Greece, particularly Athens.[7]

It was not only wealthy senators who had a place at Tibur. The elderly satirist Juvenal had a little farm there. Whether he was able to attract Hadrian's attention – and patronage – is another matter. But he seems to have tried. His seventh *Satire* begins with a direct reference to the Emperor: 'The only hope for the arts rests with Caesar . . . he alone notices the wretched Muses in these times . . . Go to it, lads: the Emperor is surveying you and urging you on, his generosity is seeking a fitting outlet.' The days of the great patrons like Maecenas were over. 'As for you writers of history, is your labour more profitable? . . . Notching up the thousandth page and a hefty bill for papyrus: this is what the vast theme demands and the rules of your profession – but where is the profit?' It is difficult not to suspect a reference to Cornelius Tacitus, labouring at his *Annales*. Apart from Florus, whose exchange of doggerel with Hadrian was cited by the *HA*, only one other poet is attested as Hadrian's friend. Apuleius recalls how the Emperor 'honoured the tomb of his friend the poet Voconius with a line to this effect: "Wanton thou wast in thy verse, but chaste in soul."' This might be Martial's friend Voconius Victor, whose beautiful boy favourite Thestylus was the subject of one of Martial's *Epigrams*. Another poem, from the time of Nerva, expresses malicious amusement that Victor was to marry and anticipates that he will have to change his sexual practices – 'your nurse and your mother will forbid' what Victor had been used to 'and will tell you: "This is your wife, not a boy!"' Martial advised Victor to get some training with a professional in the Subura: "'She will make you a man; a virgin is not a good teacher."'[8]

The literary salons of the time were more concerned with debating pedantic niceties of linguistic usage in the classics than with current poetry or prose. It was probably during these years that Hadrian had a famous exchange, reported by the *HA*, with the sophist Favorinus of Arelate (Arles). This remarkable figure, although a Gaul by birth, was completely Hellenised, and was regarded as one of the leading Greek intellectuals among the practitioners of what was later called the 'Second Sophistic'. Described as a hermaphrodite, with no beard and a high-pitched voice, 'he was nonetheless so ardent in love that he was actually prosecuted for adultery by a man of consular rank', Philostratus, the biographer of the sophists, records. He quotes Favorinus' own remark, 'in the ambiguous style of an oracle, that there were in the story of his life these three paradoxes: though a Gaul, he lived as a Hellene; though a eunuch, he had been on trial for adultery; though he had quarrelled with an emperor, he was still alive.' Philostratus does not really report a quarrel as such. Instead, he tells how Favorinus tried to secure immunity, on the grounds that he was a philosopher, from the requirement to serve as high-priest of the imperial cult in his native Gaul. Before the claim was heard, Hadrian had indicated that he would reject it. Philosophers did indeed enjoy exemption from such expensive public duties – but Hadrian did not regard him as a philosopher. When Favorinus realised this, he informed the Emperor that his teacher Dio (of Prusa) had appeared to him in a dream and told him that it was his duty to undertake the priesthood. The people of Athens apparently reacted to the news of Favorinus' fall from favour by demolishing the bronze statue of the sophist, 'as though he were the Emperor's bitterest enemy.'[9]

Cassius Dio has a briefer version of the same story, to illustrate Hadrian's 'jealousy of all who excelled in any respect', and actually states that the Emperor 'overthrew Favorinus'. But he goes on to say that he spared him, and Philostratus too stresses that 'though Favorinus fell out with the Emperor, he suffered no harm.' Hadrian 'used to lighten the responsibilities of empire by turning his mind to philosophers and sophists', he comments, and his treatment of Favorinus was merely 'for his own diversion'. Curiously enough, Favorinus wrote *On Exile*. A papyrus copy of this work, first published in 1931, suggests that Favorinus actually was banished and was writing from exile on the island of Chios. However this may be, the affair of the immunity claim can hardly be the dispute, which neither Philostratus nor Dio properly explain. Perhaps the adultery charge was the reason – after all, Favorinus had had an affair with the wife of an ex-consul, who may have pressed Hadrian to punish the delinquent. But it may be suspected that it involved the taking of sides between Polemo, a bitter rival of Favorinus, and Herodes Atticus, his friend, and perhaps came later in the reign.[10]

As for the exchange reported in the *HA*, this too hardly seems enough to result in Favorinus' exile. There was an argument about the use of words, of the kind lovingly retailed by Aulus Gellius in his *Attic Nights* a few decades later – Favorinus featuring prominently in these literary recollections, along with the orator Fronto. The *HA* biographer introduces the story as an illustration of a general statement about Hadrian.

> Although he expressed himself with great facility in both prose and verse and was very expert in all the arts, his attitude to the professors who taught them was to mock, despise and humiliate. He often competed with these professors and philosophers by publishing books and poems turn and turn about.

Then comes the anecdote.

> In the case of Favorinus, when an expression he had used had on one occasion been criticised by Hadrian, and he had given way, his friends

reproached him: he should not have conceded to Hadrian over a word that reputable authors had used. Favorinus' reply provoked laughter: 'Your advice is misplaced, my dears. You must allow me to consider him to be more learned – he is the Lord of Thirty Legions.'[11]

The sally no doubt got back to Hadrian, who might have resented being laughed at. But it is hard to believe that his response was to send Favorinus into exile. Their relations will have to remain an enigma – the *HA*, indeed, on the following page, stresses that,

> albeit he was very ready to criticise musicians, tragic and comic actors, grammarians, rhetoricians and lawyers, yet he both honoured and enriched all the professors, even if he did always torment them by his questions. And although he was responsible for many leaving his presence in distress, he used to say that he took it badly when he saw anyone upset.

The biographer goes on to say that 'he was on close terms with the philosophers Epictetus and Heliodorus and, without mentioning names, with grammarians, rhetoricians, musicians, geometricians, painters and astrologers, but above all, as many assert, with Favorinus.'[12]

A similar anecdote is preserved in a late Roman work on grammarians, by Charisius, who cites the Emperor himself as author of *Sermones* on grammatical questions in two books. Hadrian had a dispute with Terentius Scaurus – the finest grammarian of the age, according to Gellius, and also, so the *HA* reports in a later *vita*, Hadrian's own old teacher. In one debate he rebutted Scaurus on a matter of scansion by sending for a second opinion, in another he refuted Scaurus on a question of Latin usage – of the word *obiter* – by quoting various authorities, including the mime-writer Laberius and other early authors, and finally a letter of Augustus in which the first Princeps had reproved Tiberius for avoiding the word. Of course, Hadrian added, Augustus was only a layman. As it happens, Scaurus is portrayed by Gellius precisely discussing a word coined by the poet Laberius. Lengthy and sometimes heated discussions on the right use of words take up much of the *Attic Nights*. The orator Fronto could discourse at length on the correct meaning of *praeter propter*. Favorinus, among a number of other appearances in the work, is shown sharply rebuking a young man for using obsolete words. In another vignette, he gracefully concedes to Fronto over the question of whether Greek or Latin had more words to describe colour. The exchange reported by the *HA* can readily be grasped in this context. As for Favorinus' exile – the real reason was perhaps the adultery charge, especially if the cuckolded senator had influence.[13]

The year 126 opened with the consulship of Annius Verus and Eggius Ambibulus. Verus was holding office for the third time, equalling the Emperor's score. Such an honour was rare indeed and must underline the high favour this man enjoyed. Hadrian's brother-in-law Servianus, whose first consulship had been held in 90 and who had gained a second from Trajan in 102, may have hoped for a third. He seemed to have recognised that Verus had outdone him by composing a little poem: he had thought himself the leading player in 'the glass ball game', apparently a joking reference to the game of politics – but 'I have been beaten by the thrice consul Verus, my patron, not just once but often.' Verus had now given up the prefecture of Rome, which he had probably held since 117, being succeeded by Lollius Paullinus, a scion of the Julio-Claudian aristocracy. Hadrian's closeness to the Annii Veri is also illustrated by the attention he paid to Verus' grandson. The young Marcus' father, also a M. Annius Verus, had died and the boy had been adopted by his grandfather. Hadrian, 'under whose close supervision he was brought up', the *HA* biography of Marcus reports, called him *Verissimus*, 'truest', after his father's death.[14]

A cause for celebration in 126 was the completion of a major building project, the restoration of the temple of the Deified Vespasian and Titus. The *Fasti Ostienses* register the holding of games by Hadrian in the Circus to mark the dedication: the fragmentary text concludes with the figure MDCCCXXXV, evidently referring to 1,835 pairs of gladiators. The same source is sadly limited, for Hadrian, to the years 126–8, with one further piece registering rather less lavish games in April and May of an uncertain year. But it happens to show that Hadrian was holding the office of *duumvir* at Ostia in 126, for the second time. It would not necessarily mean that he carried out the duties in person, although he might well have put in one or two appearances, for Ostia also was being restored and embellished on his initiative at this time, and land was assigned to settlers there, perhaps on an imperial estate. Other places in the vicinity of Rome also benefited from his attention. In Latium, Lavinium and Lanuvium received land-assigments and Hadrian paid for rebuilding at Gabii, long proverbial as a run-down little town. All three were part of Rome's earliest, legendary history. So too, as a deadly rival, was Veii, the Etruscan city across the Tiber, and here as well Hadrian was active. His favour to Etruria in general was shown by his accepting the office of 'praetor of the fifteen cities' of the old Etruscan league. Further to the south, Formiae was granted the status of *colonia* and he appointed a *curator* for Tarracina.[15]

Hadrian found time 126 for another activity: he agreed to be the *magister* of the Arval Brethren. On his first return to Rome, in summer 118, he had participated in their rituals on the very day he entered the city, for he had duly been co-opted to membership of this as of all the priestly colleges. Now he took his turn to preside, which would involve ceremonies at the grove of the Dea Dia on 19 May, and inviting the college to the palace, to sacrifice and to dine. In his capacity as *magister* he also paid for the erection of some building, perhaps a shrine, for the Brethren – in Rome itself, rather than at the goddess' sacred grove on the Tiber bank between Rome and Ostia, where the Arvals principally foregathered. The fragmentary inscription celebrates his action as a 'record of unusual munificence at Rome' (*[ut docume]ntum esset Romae inso[litae munificentiae]*).[16]

That he was now back in Italy and conferring benefits on communities there did not of course mean that he could not devote attention to the rest of the empire, in particular to the Greeks. He had occasion in the course of 126 to write a letter to the *Koinon* (Council) of the Achaians. Copies have been found at both Athens and Olympia. While approving the good will shown by their vote of further honours for him, Hadrian clearly wished them to show restraint. Early in 127 an ambassador arrived from Stratonicea in Lydia, which Hadrian had been to three years before. It was one of the now numerous cities that were now called Hadrianopolis, and the archons, council and people are duly so addressed. They received, indeed, no fewer than three separate missives. Writing from Rome on 11 February, Hadrian confirmed that he had read the decree thanking the ambassador, Claudius Candidus Julianus. Another letter, also from Rome, but undated, added that Hadrian had noted the city's expression of gratitude to the proconsul Avidius Quietus for benefits conferred during his year of office (125–6). Finally, on 1 March, again from Rome, Hadrian dealt with the request: he approved the city's claim to exact taxes in the rural hinterland and its wish to sell or repair a house belonging to an absentee landlord: 'you seem to be requesting what is only just and necessary for a newly established city.' Hadrian had probably already established a special secretariat for his correspondence with the Greeks. Valerius Eudaemon, the sharp-witted friend who had been at his side in August 117 and had then held high rank at Alexandria in Egypt, followed by the directorship of the imperial libraries at Rome, held as his next appointment the post of *ab epistulis Graecis*.[17]

That Hadrian wrote to the Stratoniceans from Rome suggests that he spent winters in the capital, presumably in the Domitianic palace. At any rate, from about 126 rebuilding was under way there too: the aim seems to have been to render the forbidding pile more comfortable in winter – Nerva and Trajan had evidently avoided living there. In the interior, a hypocaust system was installed in the 'Banqueting Hall of Jupiter'. Changes to the exterior on the Forum side were apparently intended to make the palace seem closer to the people. Modifications were also in hand at the other principal imperial residence, the palace in the Horti Sallustiani, towards the north-eastern edge of Rome. 'Sallust's Park', once the property of the historian's grand-nephew, had passed into imperial hands on his death and had been favoured by both Vespasian and Nerva.[18]

Within less than two years after his return from Greece, Hadrian was restless again. It was too soon to launch another tour of the provinces, but, as a precious fragment of the *Fasti Ostienses* reveals, Hadrian left Rome on 3 March 127 for *Italiam circum*[ ]. The missing part of the second word must be [*padanam*], in other words the valley of the River Padus (Po). He was to be away for five months. It may be idle to try to guess his itinerary on this journey. But stray hints can be gathered from inscriptions about places he is likely to have visited. Trebula Mutuesca, some 45 miles (72 km) north-east of Rome, on the Via Salaria, was the home of Laberia Crispina, wife of his friend Bruttius Praesens, with whom he would surely have been glad to stay. The city was assigned a *curator* by Hadrian later in the reign. Aequicoli, east of Trebula, thanked the Emperor two years later for restoring some of its public buildings, and he is also known to have made yet another effort, this time successful, at draining the Lacus Fucinus, a project begun by Claudius and revived by Trajan. That Hadrian may have travelled by the Salaria, rather than the Flaminia, is plausible enough for another reason. This would have given him the chance to make a detour to Hadria in Picenum, the city near the Adriatic coast from which the Aelii of Italica claimed to derive. The *HA* reports that this was one of the places where he held a local magistracy. It would have been in character for him to go there. Further north along this coast Hadrian's munificence is credited, precisely in the year 127, with restoring the temple of the ancient Picentine earth-goddess Cupra close to the city which bore her name, Cupra Maritima.[19]

Hadrian's restoration of an aqueduct at Cingulum in northern Picenum is not of itself proof that he was there. But it so happens that Maenius Agrippa, an equestrian officer who had been with Hadrian in Britain in 122, a prominent native of this town, proudly claims on an inscription to have been host to the Emperor. There might just have been time for Agrippa to have returned from his four-year tour of duty on the Solway Firth for some home leave, before proceeding to his third *militia* as prefect of cavalry in Moesia Inferior – he could at any rate easily have been back at Cingulum by the summer of 127. Alternatively, Hadrian could have stayed with him on his return journey. There are two other signs of Hadrianic activity in Picenum. He may have paid for the restoration of the theatre at Firmum; and he appointed a *curator* for the port of Ancona.[20]

There are a few places in the region of the Po itself, the principal object of his tour, where he would have had a reason for a visit. Faventia (Faenza) on the Via Aemilia is difficult to assess. It was the home of Avidius Nigrinus, the man put to death for alleged conspiracy nine years before. Still, Hadrian had just referred with approval, in one of his letters to the Stratoniceans, to Nigrinus' cousin Quietus. A letter of Hadrian to Quietus himself is also preserved at Aezani in Phrygia, in the gigantic temple of Zeus, with other documents regulating the temple lands. Quietus had published the 'sacred decision' with a respectful reference to 'the greatest Emperor's concern', and how 'he combined justice with philanthropy, in accordance with his care in decision-making'. A few years later Hadrian was to show favour of the most pronounced kind possible to Nigrinus' stepson and son-in-law Ceionius Commodus, by now in the early stages of his senatorial career. Perhaps he was able to bury the hatchet with the Avidii in 127. Well to the north of Faventia, north-west of Patavium (Padua), lay Vicetia (Vicenza), the home of his beloved mother-in-law Matidia. This connection might also have been grounds for a visit. At the western and eastern extremes of the vast plain between Alps and Po were two other places in which one might suggest an interest on his part. Comum (Como) was given a *curator*, a man named Clodius Sura, who had been an equestrian officer in a legion once under

Hadrian's command, II Adiutrix. Hadrian might have remembered him. A family from Aquileia, the Caesernii, certainly won high favour: two young brothers, both senators, were shortly to accompany the Emperor on the next provincial tours, and an older kinsman is found serving as an officer in the Guard, also in Hadrian's company overseas. Another man from Aquileia, Publicius Marcellus, consul in 120, had already governed Germania Superior and would soon go on to another important command, Syria. Not far from Aquileia lay Concordia, where Hadrian's niece and her husband Pedanius Fuscus seem to have had property. A visit there might also have been appropriate – whether or not the pair was still alive.[21]

Whatever the details, the tour was over by the high summer: on 1 August, the *Fasti Ostienses* register the Emperor's return to Rome. It was just in time for a further celebration: the tenth anniversary of his accession fell on 11 August. As it happens, the same inscription indicates that it was not until 19 October that 'decennial votive games' were held to mark the occasion. They lasted for ten days and included thirty *pyrrhicae*, military dances, in the Circus Maximus. The *HA* mentions that such displays were put on 'frequently' by Hadrian. It could be that he was seriously ill at this time. So, at least, it has been inferred from the especial emphasis, in the coinage of the years 127–9, on the imperial health, *salus Augusti*. The *Epitome de Caesaribus* claims that Hadrian 'had long suffered' from the condition to which he was to succumb in 138. But the suspicion arises that Hadrian retreated rapidly to Tibur, rather than spend August in the sweltering heat of Rome. On the other hand, he may simply have needed to recover from an accident: the *HA* records that once 'while hunting he fractured his collar-bone and a rib', but mentions neither the date nor the place. It could have been 127 in Italy.[22]

The most important result of the Italian tour was probably announced in the autumn or winter of 127, a major change in the government of the country. Italy was to be divided into four regions, each under an imperial legate of consular rank. Italia Transpadana was one of these districts, another included Etruria. No doubt Rome and a wide circumference around the capital were exempted. The *HA* refers briefly to the measure in three separate places, Appian mentions it once in passing. A single inscription happens to register one of the men who held the office, L. Vitrasius Flamininus, who had been consul in 122, and then, at earliest in 124, had been curator of the Tiber. Flamininus is described as *leg. pr. pr.* of Italia Transpadana and of the province of Moesia Superior. In other words, a district of Italy was being treated as a province. Hadrian presumably discussed the plan with his *consilium* (Privy Council) before implementing it, and secured agreement. But the move was not popular, and the system was abolished by his successor, Antoninus – who was himself one of the new office-holders. The *HA* reports, in the biography of Antoninus, that 'he was chosen by Hadrian as one of the four consulars to whom Italy was entrusted, to govern that part of Italy in which he owned the most property.' In the biography of Hadrian, there is only a laconic sentence: 'He established four consulars as *iudices* throughout Italy.'

Marcus Aurelius later revived the system, 'following Hadrian's example, according to which he had instructed consulars to administer justice'. But the revived version was lower-key: the Marcan officials were only ex-praetors with the title *iuridicus*, and their duties were confined to the courts. The *HA*'s use of the term *iudices* in the biography of Hadrian has given the mistaken impression that the four consular office-holders were likewise merely assize judges. But *iudices* was used here in its later sense, 'governor'.[23]

Appian's reference to the Hadrianic system is an aside in his account of the Italian revolt of 91 BC: 'It appears that there were praetors with consular power at that time governing the various parts of Italy; the Emperor Hadrian revived the custom a long time afterwards, but it did not long survive him.' This makes one wonder if Hadrian had cited ancient precedent to justify his reform. From the viewpoint of the Senate, it was an infringement of their right to supervise Italy. This had been expressed in a speech by Nero on his accession: 'The Senate should retain its ancient rights, Italy and the public provinces should come before the consuls' tribunals.' So Tacitus phrased it at any rate – did he write these words with awareness that Italy had just been removed from the *antiqua munia* of the Senate and the *consulum tribunalibus*? Be this as it may, Italy was now being treated like the provinces. Italy, it is true, also appeared in the commemorative coin series which later recalled the provincial tours, with horn of plenty – and with a sceptre, perhaps to indicate her special position.[24]

There were possibly precedents for what Hadrian had done, more recent than 91 BC, at any rate for Transpadana. A senator called Julius Proculus had been legate of the *regio Transpadana*, under Trajan, so it has been assumed. But this man may have been one of the Hadrianic legates. More interesting perhaps is the fact that Transpadana had been treated as a province under Augustus. Suetonius, in his work *On Rhetoricians*, registers the protest of the orator Albucius Silo when the eminent L. Piso sat in judgement at Mediolanum (Milan): 'It is as if we have been reduced to the status of a province again!' Suetonius had probably written this a good many years before. A more recent publication of his certainly now had relevance, his *Life* of Augustus. There he reported at some length how the first Princeps had the title *pater patriae*, Father of the Fatherland, conferred on him by a grateful People and Senate. 'There was a sudden and very great unanimity.' First the plebs sent a delegation to him at Antium, but he declined the honour. Then, when he entered the city, the attempt was repeated. Finally, in the Senate House Valerius Messalla Corvinus, the greatest orator of the day, made a speech:

> 'May all go well and fortunately for you and your house, Caesar Augustus: for we believe that with these words we pray for everlasting prosperity and happiness for this republic. The Senate, with the consent of the Roman People, salutes you as Father of the Fatherland.' With tears Augustus replied: 'Having achieved all that I have prayed for, Conscript Fathers, what else have I to ask the immortal gods, but that I am fortunate enough to retain your common good will to the end of my life?'[25]

Augustus was given the honour late, in 2 BC, twenty-five years after he had 'restored the republic.' Tiberius refused to accept it at all. But subsequent Emperors had been content to assume the title more or less at once. Hadrian had left it a long time, indeed had twice refused it when it was offered, no doubt with Augustus' late acceptance in mind. Now he judged it was the right time. Hadrian's admiration for the first Princeps and his efforts over the past few years to present himself as a second Augustus have already been stressed. A speech of Hadrian's was quoted in late antiquity in which he asked the Conscript Fathers – 'and I am particularly anxious to gain your consent', he stressed – to allow him to place a silver shield in honour of Augustus in the Senate House, close to the statue of the Emperor. It would be too much to suppose that in his imitation of Augustus he now went to the lengths of having a delegation from the Roman plebs coming to petition him at Antium, as in 12 BC – though Hadrian did have a residence there, his favourite palace, according to Philostratus, where he kept a collection of letters by the wonder-worker Apollonius of Tyana. Whether the greatest orator of the day made the speech in the Senate, as in 12 BC, is also doubtful. In any case, it is not clear who would enjoy that status in late 127 or in 128. Tacitus had been acclaimed under this appellation by his friend Pliny thirty years before; but, if he was still alive, he would have been too old and embittered to make a public appearance of this kind. Cornelius Fronto, the star of the next reign, was still too junior. Perhaps Annius Verus, the only man other than the Emperor himself to have held three consulships, did the honours. At any rate, in 128 at the latest, *pater patriae* became a regular part of the imperial titulature.[26]

Hadrian was taking a close interest in the family of Annius Verus, one of his most trusted advisers, tied to him by kinship. As already mentioned, Verus' grandson, 'Verissimus', was 'brought up under Hadrian's supervision' (literally, 'in Hadrian's lap') and had been formally enrolled among the knights at the age of only five. When the boy was seven, in 128, Hadrian made him a member of the Salii, an ancient priesthood reserved for patricians. Dio also stresses Hadrian's favourable disposition towards Marcus and actually writes that it was 'because of his kinship'. What the precise relationship was remains obscure. The Annii Veri, who came from Baetican Ucubi (Espejo), near Corduba, are likely enough to have had links with the Aelii and Ulpii of Italica. Be that as it may, the influence and respect enjoyed by Verus was bolstered by the family's enormous wealth. Verus, now in his sixties and no longer holding office, ranked higher, as a three times consul, than any of his peers. His consular sons-in-law, Aurelius Antoninus and Ummidius Quadratus, were among the most respected senators. His surviving son Libo was consul *ordinarius* in 128.[27]

Hadrian had closer kin, to be sure – his sister Domitia Paulina and her husband Julius Servianus, now in his late seventies. As already indicated, it is uncertain whether their daughter Julia Paulina and son-in-law Pedanius Fuscus Salinator were still alive – there is only a faint chance that Fuscus may have been 'the king's cousin Salan', at Athens, according to the fanciful dialogue between

Hadrian and the silent philosopher Secundus. However this may be, their son, Hadrian's grandnephew, survived. He was merely a child, not much older than Marcus if Dio's statement of his age is correct – but another source has a variant report, which would put the younger Fuscus' birth in about 113, not many years after his parents' marriage. In that case, he would be due to assume the *toga virilis* and would soon be a figure to be reckoned with, ready to enter public life some three or four years later.[28]

During these years in Italy Hadrian will have kept a close watch on the provinces. His friend Platorius Nepos was certainly now back at Rome and will have reported on the progress of the massive frontier works. The *HA* even suggests that Hadrian thought of his friend as a potential successor. Who followed Nepos in Britain is unknown, but whoever he was, he had problems. The original plan had had to be modified, with new forts built into the line of the Wall itself, and then a great flat-bottomed ditch with running mound on either side (the so-called Vallum) was dug all the way along the south side of the Wall. It would take a year or two more to complete the whole scheme. Sex. Julius Severus, the man who had spent a good seven years as governor of Upper Dacia, ensuring that the new dispensation there worked properly, was back at Rome at the end of 127, to hold the consulship. He was sent back to the same region almost at once, to be governor of Lower Moesia. Hadrian clearly valued this man more highly than any of his other army commanders. He was to go on from Lower Moesia to Britain. As for the other provinces, Hadrian was about to inspect many of them again for himself.[29]

17

AFRICA

In his recently composed biography of Augustus, Suetonius had devoted a paragraph to the first emperor's treatment of the provinces, 'and there is not one, I believe – except, to be sure, Africa and Sardinia – in which he did not set foot'. Only severe storms had prevented a planned tour in 36 BC. Reason enough for Hadrian to go to Africa, which, indeed, none of his predecessors had ever seen. He had intended a comprehensive tour of the west when he left Rome in 121, it has been argued. But thorough inspection of the North African provinces had had to be shelved when trouble threatening from the Parthians had required his presence at the other end of the empire. The immense fertility of Africa made it a 'jewel in the imperial crown'. There was much to be seen, both in the prosperous urbanised heartland and on the frontier, where a new *limes* was already under construction. The colonial élite from the proconsular province had taken a few generations longer than their peers in Narbonensis and Spain to rise to the summit – the 'first consul from Africa', a Pactumeius from Numidian Cirta (Constantine), had held office in the year 80. But now, nearly fifty years on, there were plenty of other Africans in high places, descendants both of Italian immigrants and of enfranchised natives, senators and knights. Latin literature, too, had received an injection of new blood from this direction. Suetonius came from Hippo Regius (Annaba), and a young man from Cirta, now approaching the praetorship, M. Cornelius Fronto, was later to be hailed (with no little exaggeration) as another Cicero. Hadrian would not lack cultured company in this part of the west. The ancient history of North Africa, the land of Rome's greatest rival, may also have had a special appeal.[1]

The visit to Africa must have lasted several months, and was to be followed, after a brief return to Italy, by a second tour of the east. As always when an emperor was on the move, a considerable entourage went with him. The Empress turns up in Hadrian's company in Egypt two years later. But she may have joined him only for the journey to the east. Just one name from the higher echelons happens to be registered with Hadrian in Africa. A young senator whose home was Aquileia, T. Caesernius Quinctianus, son of a high-ranking procurator from the previous reign, was *comes* of Hadrian *per Siciliam Afric(am) Mauret(aniam)*. Quinctianus' father had been governor of Mauretania

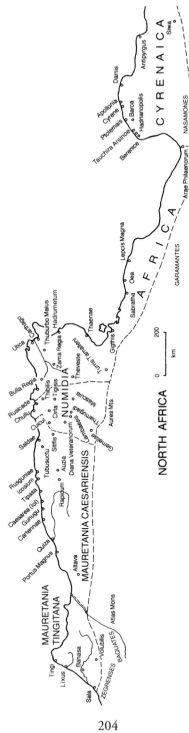

Map 6 North Africa

Caesariensis in the year 107 and Quinctianus had probably been there with him, albeit only a child at the time, and hence he hardly qualified as a Mauretanian 'expert'. Other senators were probably in the party as well, together with certain holders of high office, such as the *ab epistulis*, perhaps still L. Julius Vestinus, the conjectured replacement for Suetonius. Slaves and freedmen from the palace staff would have been in attendance too, and a detachment of the Praetorian Guard. There is a faint hint of a mention of the acting commander of the Horse Guards, the *equites singulares Augusti*, being at Hadrian's side when he addressed the troops on the frontier in July.

It has, further, been inferred that Hadrian's friend Arrian was with him. In his treatise on hunting, written at Athens fifteen or more years later, Arrian has an elaborate passage describing the skill with which Numidians ran down wild desert asses. After paraphrasing Xenophon's description of the younger Cyrus' attempts to catch these animals, he notes that 'in my day eight-year-old Numidian boys, riding bareback and without bridles, can overhaul desert asses and bring them back alive and haltered.' The vividness of this account makes it look like that of an eye-witness.[2]

The inscription of Quinctianus is the sole piece of evidence for Hadrian having visited Sicily again, only three years after his last, brief stay. Since he is known to have climbed Etna on the previous occasion, it seems likely enough that this time he visited the western end of the island, which was in any case in the right direction for Africa. But Sicily was of incidental importance. Africa was the goal, in the first instance presumably Carthage, seat of the proconsul. Who held this office in early summer 128 is not known. But the other three governors who received him in North Africa are more or less firmly attested, and all of them were newly installed. Numidia and the legion III Augusta had been for the past two or three years under the command of a Greek from Tralles in the province of Asia, Sex. Julius Major. When Hadrian arrived he had just handed over to Q. Fabius Catullinus, probably a Spaniard. Of the two equestrian governors of Mauretania, the procurator of Caesariensis was Hadrian's old friend Vettius Latro, who had just been governing the Cottian Alps. Promotion to the important province of Caesariensis for a man with his modest track record looks rather out of the ordinary. Latro's links with the Emperor from long ago, in the legion II Adiutrix, are no doubt the explanation. Latro was himself an African, from Thuburbo Maius. Tingitana was certainly governed between 129 and 132 by M. Gavius Maximus, who is likely enough to have been appointed in 128. Maximus' 'official' domicile was Rome itself, but his family had long been based at Ephesus. He was to rise to the Prefecture of the Guard at the end of the reign.[3]

The narrative section of the *HA* biography, at this point beginning to be drastically abbreviated, has little detail to offer, except that from Rome Hadrian 'crossed to Africa [the stop in Sicily is not mentioned] and conferred many benefits on the African provinces.' Two further items are added later, first, that 'he called many cities "Hadrianopolis", for example even Carthage', second, that 'when he came to Africa, it rained for the first time for five years, and for this reason he was popular with the Africans.' There is evidence in plenty for *beneficia* of various kinds bestowed by Hadrian in Africa, principally the bestowal of charters on more than a dozen towns and the granting of privileges to farmers who cultivated marginal land. The new name 'Hadrianopolis' for Carthage does not seem to have left any other record. It does at any rate imply a stay of some weeks and some benefits conferred. The construction of the great aqueduct from the mountain at Zaghouan, 35 miles (56 km) in a direct line south of the city, but taking a circuitous course totalling 82 miles (132 km), belongs to this period, and may have benefited from imperial subsidy. As for the rain after five years of drought, it may be recalled that this is precisely the lapse of time since his postulated flying visit on the way from Spain to the east.[4]

There are certainly signs, in his distribution of favours, that a sense of history did play a part in Hadrian's thinking. One recipient of privilege was the oldest city in Africa, Utica, which had been the residence of the governor during the Republic – Carthage had been wiped off the map at the end of the third Punic war in 146 BC, and not refounded until after Caesar's victory in the civil war a century later. Utica was thereafter to be remembered principally as the scene of the Younger Cato's suicide when the cause of the Republic went down. Hadrian might be supposed, further, to have recalled an episode from Rome's first civil war. Almost exactly 200 years before his visit, in 82 BC, a Roman governor had been burned to death in his own *praetorium* at Utica by hostile Roman settlers. The man was called C. Fabius *Hadrianus* – not, of course, an ancestor of Hadrian, but, as it happens, one of only two previous Romans of this name to enter the historical record. It may well be imagined that Hadrian, as a schoolboy forced to read Cicero, had registered the comment about *ille Hadrianus*, whose *avaritia* Roman citizens could not tolerate. Livy had also devoted space, in the eighty-sixth book of his great *History*, to the well-deserved end of the cruel and avaricious pro-praetor.[5]

Utica, long a *municipium* (since 36 BC), now received the title of *colonia*. Its inhabitants had requested the change, clearly regarding *colonia* as a more prestigious status. The request of the Uticenses to Hadrian was registered by Aulus Gellius in a short essay on the words *municeps* and *municipium*. He quotes Hadrian's speech before the Senate 'On the Italicenses', the people of the Emperor's home town. Hadrian held forth 'with great learning' on the subject, 'and shows himself to be surprised that his fellow-townsmen and some other ancient *municipia*, among which he names the Uticenses, whereas they could enjoy their own customs and laws, yearned for a transfer to colonial status.' Hadrian claimed, further, that Praeneste, by contrast, had actually petitioned Tiberius to be turned back from being a *colonia* into *municipium*, a request which Tiberius had acceded to – as a favour, Hadrian stressed. The point was clear enough: the old *municipia* had indeed simply acquired Roman citizenship while preserving their ancient institutions; the *coloniae* were given a standard constitutional charter. Hadrian might have mentioned a case from Africa, where the old principle had been adhered to: Lepcis Magna became a *municipium* under Vespasian, while retaining its Punic chief magistrates, *sufetes*. But Lepcis too had moved on to higher things, becoming a titular *colonia* under Trajan: *sufetes* had given way to *duoviri*. What Hadrian must have known perfectly well was that the provincial *municipia*, unlike the old Italian ones and a tiny handful in the provinces (such as Italica and Utica), enjoyed only Latin status. The *coloniae* were fully Roman, and Roman provincial towns without this title felt themselves to be at a disadvantage. Quite when Hadrian spoke in the Senate about the petition from Italica is not clear. The odds are that it was during his three years in Italy from 125 to 128, and that the petition from Utica also arrived at Rome at this time. At some stage Hadrian consented to hold office (*in absentia*) as *quinquennalis* at Italica.[6]

As for Latin status, Hadrian took an important step. The Latin right – *Latium* or *ius Latii* – meant that each year the men elected to hold office in the provincial *muncipia*, and their families, acquired full Roman citizenship. This brought with it a steady but limited spread of the citizen status among the upper stratum of the Latin west. Hadrian created an enhanced form, *Latium maius*, under the terms of which not merely the magistrates and their families, but all the town councillors – up to one hundred – became *cives Romani*. If this 'greater Latin right' was now widely granted, the effect will have been a rapid increase in Roman citizens. But further details are lacking, except for a single inscription from African Gigthis, which petitioned for the enhanced Latin status under Antoninus. This suggests that the grant was not automatic and universal for all Latin *municipia*.[7]

Four other cities in the proconsular province also gained the status of *colonia*, Bulla Regia, Zama Regia, Lares and Thaenae. Bulla had been a *municipium* for a generation, the others may have been promoted direct from the status of peregrine (that is, non-Roman) *civitas* to that of *colonia*. The favour to Bulla and Zama, whose name proudly recalled that they had once been royal residences in the old Numidian kingdom, once again points to Hadrian's feeling for the past. Lares and Thaenae also had some small place in history: Marius had captured the *oppidum* Lares, on the high road from Carthage to Theveste, during the Jugurthine war; the port of Thaenae, on the coast south of Hadrumetum, had fallen to Caesar soon after his landing in Africa. Two existing *coloniae* also received favours: Uthina, an Augustan foundation 20 miles (32 km) south-west of Carthage, and the nearby Colonia Canopitana: both registered the *indulgentia* of Hadrian. Their territory was probably augmented – at the expense of Carthage, which had been assigned a vast hinterland on its refoundation, and could easily be slimmed down in this way.[8]

Ten native communities now became *municipia* (at least ten, one should add – there may have been more). All but two were in or close to the fertile valleys of the two great rivers of the province, the Bagradas and the Miliana. Mactaris (Maktar) in the High Tell south-west of Zama Regia was the centre of an important grain-producing region. The other exception was Turris Tamalleni, an oasis 50 miles (80 km) south of Capsa, in the frontier zone. Of the eight new chartered towns further north, one may be singled out, Thuburbo Maius, which had long been under the influence of Roman Carthage. Thuburbo was also the home of Vettius Latro. One may readily suppose that Hadrian's old officer was instrumental in obtaining the promotion.

Other high-ranking Romans whose home was in Africa, whether or not they were invited to join Hadrian as his *comites*, may well have taken the opportunity of paying court to him there, and seeking advancement for themselves, if not for their fellow-townsmen. The careers of two young Africans are particularly striking. Q. Lollius Urbicus, second son of a landowner at Castellum Tidditanorum, a dependency of Cirta, had clearly already attracted Hadrian's attention. He had been tribune in the Mainz legion, XXII Primigenia – perhaps at the time of Hadrian's visit to Germany in 121–2. After his quaestorship he had spent a year as legate to a proconsul of Asia, possibly Pompeius Falco. He enjoyed the favoured status of 'Caesar's candidate' in his next two posts, tribune of the plebs and praetor, no mean achievement for a *novus homo*. Hadrian surely visited Cirta and the prosperous region around it. A tiny hint of his presence at Cirta's neighbour, Thibilis, might be invoked: a son born at about this time to the leading family there, the Antistii, received the rare *cognomen* 'Adventus'. Did the birth of Q. Antistius Adventus, who was to have a successful career under M. Aurelius, coincide with Hadrian's arrival? The other young African to benefit from Hadrian's favour was P. Salvius Julianus, whose home was apparently Hadrumetum (Sousse). He was even younger than Lollius Urbicus and his talents lay in a different direction: Roman law. Two or three years later, as Hadrian's quaestor, Julianus was to be given a special commission to codify the 'praetor's edict'.[9]

Large tracts of the province of Africa were crown land, imperial domain, supervised by procurators of the *patrimonium*. Much had fallen to the emperors by confiscation, notably under Nero: he had put to death six men who between them 'owned half the province', so the Elder Pliny claimed. Crown land throughout the empire was an important source of imperial revenue and, particularly in Africa, of food supply. The system of cultivation involved leasing substantial parcels of land to tenants-in-chief, *conductores*, who, for the peasants who actually worked the soil, were their effective landlords, to whom they paid their rent in kind. All the same, the Emperor, through his procurators, could be appealed to, particularly if the leaseholder became oppressive. Two inscriptions from imperial estates in the Bagradas valley quote a 'law of Hadrian', *lex Hadriana*, laying down new regulations for land tenure. A 'statement of the procurators' begins with reference to 'Our Caesar's tireless concern which he unceasingly exercises for the benefit of mankind'. In effect, Hadrian followed up a measure taken by Trajan at the end of his reign, which extended to imperial estates a system already operating in Africa: those who cultivated marginal waste land were exempted from rents for several years when vines, figs and olives were planted, and acquired provisional title over land unallotted in the original centuriation. This had been fostered by the *lex Manciana*, probably a measure instituted by a private landowner called Mancia, if not by a proconsul of that name. Hadrian's new dispensation – which may have applied on imperial estates across the empire, not just in Africa – instituted further and more detailed application of this policy. Those who occupied and planted centuriated land with vines and olives acquired rights of possession and inheritance.[10]

It may be conjectured that the tour of the urbanised area and of the rich agricultural hinterland took up to two months. At the latest by the end of June Hadrian was already in the military district, Numidia, where the writ of the proconsul had effectively ceased to run nearly a century before. The legate of the only legion in North Africa, III Augusta, was in practice the imperial legate of Numidia. Fabius Catullinus, not long in post, had been preparing for the visit with care, not least by training the troops so that they could impress the Emperor. He had also dedicated, on behalf of the legion, a pair of altars: to Jupiter Best and Greatest, the Lord of divine rainstorms, and to the 'Winds that have power to bring beneficent rainstorms' (*ventis bonarum tempestatum potentibus*). It was a suitable thanksgiving for the spring rains that had coincided with Hadrian's landing in Africa, after five years of drought. III Augusta had just acquired a new base, Lambaesis, over 60 miles (100 km) to the south-west of its former station Ammaedara. Work on the new fortress was still in progress. So too was the construction of the new frontier-barrier, 150 miles (240 km) further south, beyond Mons Aurasius (the Aurès Mountains). It would no doubt have been absurd to attempt to erect a continuous artificial *limes* in Africa, as was being done in Britain in stone, and in Germania Superior and Raetia with timber. Neither the materials nor the labour-force were available in Africa to demarcate the whole vast distance from the Atlantic to the borders of Egypt. Nor was a continuous barrier right across the land necessary. A desert frontier can be controlled by blocking the routes past the oases. All the same, several long stretches were constructed, which show a close resemblance in conception to the Wall in Britain.[11]

South of the outpost fort of Gemellae, which had just been established, ran a length of nearly 40 miles (60 km), screening a zone of dense palm-groves. It took the form of a wall over 6 feet (2 m) thick, of sun-dried mud bricks, with a gateway each Roman mile and a tower midway between each pair of gates. It was fronted by a continuous ditch, crossed by causeways only opposite the gates. Some 30 miles (50 km) to the north, east of the Hodna Mountains, another continuous wall, 28 miles (*c.* 45 km) long, was built, either of stone or an upcast bank, of which the width varies between 5 and 13 feet (1.5–4 m), again fronted by a ditch. The towers seem to have been placed at irregular intervals, some behind, some in front and some astride the 'Wall'. Here too there seem to have been gateways and at least in some sectors fortlets as well as towers. A third such sector has been claimed, some 44 miles (70 km) in length, far to the south-east of Lambaesis, beyond the base Ad Majores (built in the year 105 by the legate Minicius Natalis). But what has been identified as the ditch of such a *limes* may just belong to the east-west frontier road. Across the provincial border, in Mauretania Caesariensis, one further running barrier, nearly 90 miles (140 km) long, seems to have almost completely encircled a major part of the Hodna Mountains. Here too was a wall, with ditch, towers and forts.[12]

The clear evidence in the Gemellae sector for regular crossing-points shows that the system was designed to control access to the empire. Seasonal migration by the semi-nomad or transhumant peoples of the desert was to continue, but under conditions closely supervised by the army. On the Roman side of the frontier agriculture could now flourish, above all olive-cultivation. Further lengths of *limes* may await discovery, it is true. But it seems that for much of the frontier zone, particularly in Mauretania Tingitana and western Caesariensis, it was deemed sufficient to keep the peace, without building a running barrier, by means of roads, patrols and watchtowers.[13]

By good fortune substantial parts of a massive inscription at Lambaesis illuminate Hadrian's tour of some of the military bases. His visit was commemorated by the erection of an enormous column. Its base carried the text of addresses of his to three auxiliary regiments and to the senior centurions and the cavalrymen of the legion. The soldiers had performed exercises and manoeuvres before the Emperor. In the second half of June he spoke to the *cohors* II Hispanorum.

> What others would have spread over several days took you only one to finish: you have built a wall, a lengthy construction, normally made for permanent winter-quarters, in not much more time than is required for a turf rampart – and in that kind of work the turves are cut to standard size, are easy to carry and handle and can be laid without difficulty. You have built with stones, large, heavy and irregular at that, which no one can carry or lift or lay without these irregularities being noticeable. You have cut a ditch in a straight line through hard and rough gravel and have made it smooth by levelling. When the work was approved, you entered camp at speed, got your food and weapons and followed the cavalry that had gone ahead, hailing them with a great shout as they returned.

Manoeuvres followed, also evidently approved.

> I compliment my legate Catullinus for having instituted for your unit this exercise which has taken on the appearance of genuine combat and he is training you so well that I can compliment you too. Your prefect Cornelianus has also done his work to my satisfaction.

But some words of criticism were added for the cavalry section of the cohort. 'Open order tactics I do not approve of' – here he quoted an authority on military science whose name is lost in a gap. 'A trooper should ride out from cover and be more cautious in pursuit – if he doesn't watch where he's going and can check his horse at will, he is exposed to hidden pitfalls.'[14]

These words nicely illustrate Dio's statement about Hadrian and the army – his inspecting and investigating everything in person, weapons, engines, trenches, ramparts and palisades, drilling the soldiers for every kind of battle, honouring some and reproving others and teaching them what they should do. The *HA* biographer's comment, introducing the tour of the German frontier, that 'while he was eager for peace rather than war, he trained the soldiers as if war were imminent', is also amply confirmed. Fabius Catullinus, and no doubt all the army commanders, had had their instructions: the *exercitatio* of *cohors* II Hispanorum resembled real warfare, had the *verae dimicationis imago*. After Hadrian's death, Cornelius Fronto could be sarcastic about this policy: 'After the Emperor Trajan the armies had virtually no discipline. Hadrian was energetic enough in collecting his friends together and giving eloquent speeches to the armies and in general in the appliances of war' – yet he abandoned Trajan's conquests, and merely toured the empire. Fronto's further cutting comments about the armies being pandered to by being allowed to use 'wicker weapons' instead of swords and shields are specifically applied only to Asia. But Fronto was writing over twenty-five years after Hadrian's death. The decline of *militaris disciplina* in the army of Syria that he lamented in the 160s can hardly be blamed on Hadrian.[15]

'Imp. Caesar Traianus Hadrianus Augustus addressed his legion III Augusta, having inspected their exercises, in the words written below, Torquatus for the second time and Libo being the consuls, on the Kalends of July.' Parts of his remarks, directed *at pilos*, 'to the senior centurions', and to the legionary cavalry, are preserved. The legate had told him about the legion's special problems:

> that one cohort is absent, because it has been sent on the annual rota to serve in the *officium* of the proconsul; that two years ago you gave up one cohort and four men from each century to reinforce your comrades of the Third; that many outposts, and widely scattered ones, split you up; that within my own memory you have not only changed base twice but have built a new fortress.

(By 'your comrades of the Third' Hadrian meant either III Gallica in the army of Syria, or III Cyrenaica, also stationed in the east.) In view of these special circumstances, 'I would have excused you if the legion had given up training long since – but you have not given it up.' Rather, he no doubt went on to say – the text has a break here – it performed excellently. The senior centurions displayed their two customary qualities, one of which, agility, is recorded; a gap in the stone makes it necessary to guess what the other one was. The legionary cavalry, only 120 strong, were warmly praised.

> Military exercises have, in a way, their own rules: if anything is added to or removed from them, the exercise either becomes less useful or too difficult. You performed the most difficult of difficult exercises, throwing the javelin while wearing the cuirass . . . I also approve your spirit.[16]

Six days later, on the Nones (7th) of July, Hadrian was at Zarai, beyond Diana Veteranorum (Zana), on the road to Mauretania Caesariensis. Here he inspected a cohort, but neither its name nor more than two-and-a-half words from his speech have been preserved. Between 8 and 14 July he inspected two more units, the Ala I Pannoniorum and the *cohors* VI Commagenorum. He told the Pannonians that

> you have done everything according to the book: you filled the training-ground with your manoeuvres, you threw your javelins not inelegantly, even though using short and stiff ones, and you mounted both today and yesterday with agility and speed. Had anything been lacking, I would wish it to be done, if anything had particularly stood out, I would mention it – you pleased me equally throughout the whole exercise. My legate the Right Honourable (*vir clarissimus*) Catullinus devotes equal care to all the tasks he has charge of and your prefect . . . [the name is missing] appears to look after you attentively. Accept a largess!

At this point a few words follow which long defied explanation, until it was suggested that they represent, not a closing sentence from the Emperor's harangue to the Pannonians, but his order, after his speech was over, to an officer at his side: 'Viator, now to the training-grounds of the Commagenians, at the trot!' This suggests that Hadrian had spoken impromptu, not from a prepared text, and that his addresses to the troops were carefully taken down by a stenographer on the staff of the legate Catullinus. As for Viator, he was, it is argued, the centurion M. Calventius Viator. Two years later, at any rate, Viator was acting commander of the Horse Guards at Hadrian's side in Arabia. Ten years earlier he had been commanding the horse guards of the governor of Dacia, Avidius Nigrinus. It has even been inferred that his promotion to a position by the Emperor's side was a reward for services rendered, that he had revealed the treasonable plans of his chief. It has also been conjectured that Arrian was on the platform with Hadrian as he spoke to the troops. At any rate, it may not be coincidence that Arrian's own work on *Tactics*, written eight years later, seems to echo closely some of the Emperor's remarks to the Hispani and Commageni.[17]

The cavalry section of the *cohors* VI Commagenorum also performed to his satisfaction. 'It is difficult for the cavalrymen of a cohort to make a good impression, even more so after a display by troopers in an *ala*', Hadrian began. The cavalrymen in part-mounted cohorts were less well paid and of lower standard than those in the cavalry regiments proper. Hadrian made the point very specifically. 'The men in the *alae* have more space in their training-ground and more javelin-men, their right wheel is in close array, their Cantabrian attack is closely knit, their fine horses and equipment are in keeping with their pay.' The praise that followed shows that Hadrian was by now beginning to notice the burning African sun: 'You dispelled my discomfort from the heat by energetically doing what you had to do, you threw your slingstones and shot your arrows, you mounted briskly everywhere.' Once again Catullinus was singled out for praise – his merits are the more apparent 'because he has men like you under his command.' No wonder Catullinus took care to have the Emperor's words carved on stone. He received his reward eighteen months later, the consulship for the year 130, as *ordinarius*, a distinction not known to have been enjoyed by any of his predecessors in the Numidian command.[18]

In mid-July, then, it may be supposed, after the inspection of the army, Hadrian crossed from Numidia into Mauretania Caesariensis. Apart from the commemorative coinage which registers Mauretania on three separate issues, not much can be said about his visit, except that two cities on the coast received enhanced status. Tipasa, midway between Caesarea, the capital, and Icosium (Algiers), became a *colonia* and Choba, also situated between two *coloniae*, Igilgili and Saldae (Bougie), became a *municipium*. Whether the visit extended beyond Caesariensis into Tingitana is uncertain. The furthest trace of his journey in the west comes from the little town of Quiza (Pont du Chélif), on the way to Portus Magnus (Bettioua) in Caesariensis. At any rate, an arch was set up in his honour at Quiza in this year. Perhaps he chose to sail back to Italy from Portus Magnus.[19]

The tour was later to be recalled lavishly on the imperial coinage. Three issues celebrate Africa herself, Hadrian's arrival there and his work as 'restorer' of the province. The personified Africa is depicted in several different ways. In the province series she is reclining on the ground, wearing a long tunic and cloak – but on some coins her breast is bare – with an elephant-skin head-dress. Several coins allude to the fertility of Africa, showing a large basket full of fruit and corn-ears. One shows her leaning on the fruit-basket, with her right hand resting on a lion. The *restitutor* coins and some of the *adventus* ones show Africa standing to face the Emperor, holding corn-ears in her hand. There is no special issue for the army of Africa, but one of the *adventus* coins has a martial flavour: Africa wears a military style of tunic and carries a flag (*vexillum*). The visit to Mauretania was commemorated by coins showing the personified province alone and others depicting Hadrian's *adventus*, as well as by an issue for the *exercitus Mauretanicus*. Mauretania is shown in military dress, with short boots, holding one or more javelins, and she is accompanied by a horse. On some coins showing the *adventus* she is standing opposite Hadrian, with an altar between them, ready to sacrifice a bull, and has the same elephant head-dress as Africa; and one type shows her in civilian dress, long tunic and cloak, and holding corn-ears. The *exercitus* issue shows Hadrian on horseback, raising his right hand and addressing three soldiers.[20]

As soon as Hadrian's return was announced, the Senate took care to respond appropriately. An inscription found at Labici in Latium records that a senator named P. Cluvius Maximus Paullinus, an ex-praetor, had been 'a legate sent by the Senate to the Emperor Hadrian when he returned from Africa'. There were presumably other senators assigned to the task – and, indeed, it was probably standard practice for the Senate to despatch legates to receive a returning emperor. The model was the delegation that had welcomed Augustus in

Campania in 19 BC, on his return from the east. Hadrian was not going to stay in Italy very long when he arrived back in summer 128. In fact, he can hardly have remained for much more than two months: time enough to inspect the numerous building projects under way at both Rome and Tibur, and to assure himself that the capital was in safe hands. He must have made it plain to the key figures, first and foremost the Guard Prefect Marcius Turbo, that he would not be back for several years. His first goal was Greece, where his plans were now coming to fruition. From there he would go once more to Asia, this time to inspect the southern part, to Cappadocia and Syria, and then, via Arabia and Judaea, to Egypt. At least three years would be required.[21]

18

HADRIANUS OLYMPIUS

In September 128, five years after his initiation into the first grade, Hadrian took part in the Mysteries at Eleusis again. Once more he joined the *mystae* for the ritual bath in the sea, the three days fasting and the procession from Athens, with the statue of Iacchus going before. This time they could cross the stately new bridge over the Cephisus which the imperial *mystes* had had built. With the crowded throng in the *telesterion* he would wait all night for the climax of the rites, when a great fire was lit and the hierophant cried out "The Mistress has borne a sacred child!" and showed the initiates the great mystery, an ear of corn, cut in silence. So, at least, a Christian writer two generations later claimed: that was all that the secret rituals amounted to. All the same, the symbolism of death and rebirth is clear enough. Those who were ready to be moved would be affected. Hadrian, now an *epoptes*, one who had seen the mystery, may well have felt himself reborn to a new life. This is the inference to be drawn from a remarkable coin-issue, one of the *cistophori* struck in Asia Minor. Hadrian is shown standing with a corn-sheaf in his right hand, with the legend '*Hadrianus Aug[ustus] p[ater] p[atriae]*', followed by the letters *ren*. This can only mean '*renatus*', 'reborn'; the ears of corn denote the Mysteries of Demeter. On the obverse Hadrian's Roman exemplar is portrayed with the simple legend 'Imp. Caesar Augustus'. The first Princeps was the only emperor before Hadrian to have been initiated; and he had likewise advertised the fact on the Asian *cistophori* with a reverse depicting ears of corn.[1]

As always, Hadrian will have come with a great entourage: the Empress, friends and courtiers, military escort, household retainers. Hadrian's grand-nephew Pedanius Fuscus, now in his mid-teens, may have been in the party. His parents, not heard of again after the elder Fuscus' consulship in 118, were probably no longer living. The boy must have been regarded as the heir presumptive. A coeval of Fuscus, the Emperor's beloved Antinous, must surely have been there too, even though no source attests his presence. The mass of later evidence which seems to associate Antinous with Eleusis at least makes it plausible that he was initiated with Hadrian. What remains puzzling, because there are no precedents or parallels, is just how public Antinous' presence was. Hadrian was now, more than ever, revelling in his role as the reviver of

Plate 23 Hadrian 'reborn' after his initiation into the higher grade at Eleusis
(*BMC* III Hadrian no. 1094)

Hellenism. Why not suppose that he was proud and happy to display Antinous at his side, seeing himself as the traditional Hellenic lover of a beautiful youth, an *erastes*, Antinous as his *eromenos*?[2]

Of the more conventional companions of the prince, *comites Augusti*, only Caesernius Statianus is explicitly attested, the younger brother of Quinctianus, who had been with Hadrian in Sicily and North Africa. Other senators were no doubt also in attendance, for example Hadrian's former quaestor, the younger Minicius Natalis – he was, at any rate, in Greece the following summer, when he won the four-horse chariot race at the 227th Olympiad. An equestrian kinsman of the Caesernii, L. Statius Macedo, also from Aquileia, a tribune of the Guard, was probably commanding part of the military escort, a detachment of praetorians. The centurion Calventius Viator, whose presence at Hadrian's side has been detected at Lambaesis, is known to have been acting commander of the Horse Guards in Arabia the next year and was probably already in the party. Hadrian's sharp-witted friend Valerius Eudaemon may already have vacated his post as *ab epistulis Graecis*. His next appointment was as financial procurator responsible for a vast tract of southern Asia Minor, from Lycia-Pamphylia to Paphlagonia. Hadrian probably appointed a new Greek Secretary at this time, his philosopher friend Heliodorus the Epicurean. At any rate, whether or not Secretary and philosopher are identical, Avidius Heliodorus, whose home was Cyrrhus in Syria, was with Hadrian in Egypt two years later.[3]

Heliodorus' nomination provoked a sarcastic comment from a rival intellectual, Dionysius of Miletus, also called by the Roman names T. Claudius Flavianus: 'Caesar can give you money and office, but he cannot make you an orator.' Dionysius was a pupil of Isaeus, whose lectures Hadrian had also attended. Perhaps the remark was prompted by jealousy. Dionysius might have hoped for the post of Secretary himself. Philostratus reports that Dionysius was also on bad terms with another of Hadrian's secretaries, Caninius Celer

216

– 'from their earliest youth'. Celer's rhetorical talents were supposedly mediocre. Rhetorical brilliance was perhaps not what Hadrian was looking for. Heliodorus could probably offer other qualities. Not least, when there was important business to transact in Syria, a man from Cyrrhus – who may even have been linked with the old royal house of Commagene – could be particularly useful. As for Dionysius, Dio asserts that Hadrian was suspicious of him, as he was of others with great talent. Still, as Philostratus also reveals, Dionysius nonetheless received from Hadrian the rank of knight, procuratorships and membership of the Alexandrian Mouseion.[4]

Only two places in Greece are known to have seen Hadrian in 128–9, Athens (with Eleusis) and Sparta. His host at Athens was probably Atticus, now a Roman senator with prospects of a consulship not far off. It may be, though, that Atticus was away from home, on official duties. He might have been given a province to govern. It has even been suggested that he had been made legate of Dacia Superior in the previous year, which seems rather implausible for a man not known to have had any military experience. The outgoing governor, Sex. Julius Severus, the very model of a Roman *vir militaris*, had ruled the province for over seven years, from 119 or 120 until his consulship in late 127. Whether Atticus was at Athens or not, his son Herodes had probably returned from Rome again. After being Hadrian's quaestor he had held office as archon at Athens, which was probably followed by a further stay in Rome as tribune of the plebs. It seems likely that Herodes would have made sure of being at home when the Emperor took up residence again. Another house which would certainly have been able to sustain the imperial guests was that of King Philopappus, whose massive funerary monument stood on the Hill of the Muses. The grandson of the last king of Commagene was long dead, but his sister Julia Balbilla was very much alive. She was a close friend of Sabina and probably accompanied the party from Athens to the east – two years later she is found with them in Egypt.[5]

A second stay at Sparta is explicitly documented. In the interval since his visit in early 125, Hadrian had accepted, *in absentia*, the office of eponymous magistrate there, *patronomos*. He had already conferred benefits on the Spartans and may now have given authority for the city to purchase wheat from Egypt, normally strictly reserved for Rome itself. A prominent Spartan held office at about this time as 'commissioner for grain from Egypt'. The very presence of the Emperor and his entourage will have created logistical problems, here as elsewhere.[6]

It was appropriate – and surely no coincidence – that it was precisely Athens and Sparta that were to the fore among the Hellenes of Greece proper in gaining membership of the Roman Senate at this time. Some of the Greeks of Asia had taken this step a generation earlier. Athenians and Spartans may previously have been reluctant, nervous that they might feel out of place in the Roman *curia*, or simply too proud. Hadrian had perhaps been able to persuade the heads of the leading families at Athens and Sparta that they could accept senatorial status without suffering any indignity. Claudius Atticus, the leading Athenian, was given the rank of ex-praetor and within a few years would hold the consulship. His Spartan counterpart, Julius Eurycles Herculanus, was presumably considerably younger, which no doubt explains why he had a more a less normal career, beginning as quaestor, in his home province Achaia, and going on to be tribune of the plebs and praetor at Rome. This was followed by a year as legate to the proconsul of Baetica. It was suggested earlier that the proconsul under whom Herculanus had served in the far west was none other than Hadrian's friend Arrian. The Baetican legation was followed by a further post, as commander of a legion III, evidently III Gallica in Syria. Although Herculanus' ancestor Eurycles had fought at Actium, virtually no army service is known for the intervening generations. But the Spartans were traditionally the most martial of all the Greeks. It is an attractive guess that Herculanus might have been offered the command of a legion by Hadrian at the time of his second visit to Sparta. A corollary might be that Herculanus travelled to the east with the Emperor in 129, and took up his command in Syria when the imperial party arrived there.[7]

For Hadrian the visit to Sparta was surely more than sentimental. His plans for the Greeks, now crystallising, were centred, to be sure, on Athens. But it was only natural for him to treat with particular sensitivity the city which had shared the dual hegemony with the Athenians 600 years before. This would in any case be welcome in contemporary Athens. Atticus claimed descent from Miltiades and from Cimon, the great advocate of Athenian co-operation with Sparta, and he himself had spent some time at Sparta in his youth. Now the Hellenes, with Hadrian the adoptive Athenian at the forefront, were actively recreating and re-enacting their glorious past, the age of the Persian wars above all. When the Great King invaded, the Hellenes had stood together united (with a few exceptions) in 'the League against the Mede'. Their victory at Plataea, of which the 600th anniversary had recently occurred, was still commemorated in Hadrian's day. Athens had sought to continue the crusade and to liberate the Greeks of Asia. Sparta had opted out. After three decades, in the face of mounting opposition, Pericles put through the Athenian assembly a decree 'to invite all the Hellenes, wherever they lived in Europe or in Asia, whether in a small *polis* or a great one, to send delegates to Athens to deliberate on the Hellenic shrines which the barbarians had destroyed and the sacrifices owed to the gods.' Twenty Athenians of mature years had been despatched to urge their fellow-Greeks to attend 'and take part in resolutions on peace and on the common welfare of Hellas'. Nothing had come of it, because of Spartan opposition – instead, indeed, bitter decades of conflict between the Hellenes.[8]

There can be no doubt that Hadrian and his entourage, with Atticus and Eurycles Herculanus to the fore, were consciously thinking of these events. The literature of the age is focused to the point of obsession with the people and deeds of the fifth and fourth centuries BC. Perhaps it was all a charade; but for the élite, at least, it was one that gave them enormous satisfaction. Hadrian had apparently initially contemplated making the Amphictyons of Delphi the instrument for his regeneration of Hellas. In his letter to the Delphians three and a half years earlier he had recommended changes in membership, referring explicitly to a proposal to bring in the Spartans, 'so that the *synedrion* [council] should be a common *synedrion* of all the Hellenes'. But the scheme did not go through, perhaps because of Spartan resistance. The Spartans at some point sent an embassy to meet Hadrian at Nicopolis, either when he was leaving for Sicily in 125 or when he arrived in Greece in summer 128. Perhaps they had been anxious to explain their position on Panhellenic matters.[9]

Whatever the details, Hadrian was now ready to implement a new and much more ambitious plan. The '*synedrion* of all the Hellenes' at Delphi would, after all, even if reconstituted, have been only an assembly of the *poleis* of the motherland. Yet the Hellenes were spread far and wide beyond the boundaries of old Greece. It was evidently during his second stay in Greece as Emperor that Hadrian devised a new and grandiose programme. He would create a Hellenic commonwealth which would include all those *poleis* which could prove their authentic Hellenic origins. In other words, Hadrian was bringing the abortive programe of Pericles to fruition. He would create a Panhellenion, an association of all the Hellenes, with its centre at Athens. The groundwork was – literally – done: the great temple of Heavenly Zeus, the Olympieion, was being given the finishing touches. A stately enclosure was going up around it. Within this sacred *temenos* the delegates of the Hellenes would convene.[10]

The great temple of Zeus was only one item in Hadrian's Athenian building programme. He also launched the construction of two other temples, for Hera and Zeus Panhellenios, and a shrine for all the gods, a Pantheon. Further, on the north side of the Roman Agora there was to arise a magnificent structure, often referred to as Hadrian's 'Library', also known as Hadrian's Stoa, and even called, anachronistically, 'the main building of Athens University'. Although it had a section where books were kept, mentioned by Pausanias, and two auditoria can be identified in the remains, Pausanias gives no clue to its function, laying stress in particular on its hundred columns of Phrygian marble. The building's plan in fact recalls the Forum of Peace at Rome, erected by Vespasian. Other substantial public works in the vicinity might also be part of this programme. Apart from work carried out in the old city – on the north side of the Acropolis – there was considerable development in the area of the Olympieion by the Ilissus. On the opposite side of the river from the great shrine of Zeus there was to be a new gymnasium, adorned with a hundred columns of Numidian marble. This part of Athens around the Olympieion was formally reconstituted as a new deme, 'Hadrian's town'.[11]

A young senator from Cirta in Numidia, Pactumeius Clemens, who was to achieve a modest reputation as a jurist, held a special position at about this time as 'legate of Hadrian at Athens, Thespiae and Plataea, and in Thessaly'. No clue is given to the nature of his duties, but one might surmise that he played some part in the preparations for the convening of the Hellenic assembly.[12]

Plutarch, who alone records the Congress decree of Pericles, also registers the fact that the Athenian statesman was called 'Olympian'. Hadrian, the new

Pericles – who was in addition completing the temple of Olympian Zeus – now himself assumed this name. What procedure or ceremony prompted the step is not recorded – perhaps it was formally proposed in the Athenian assembly? At any rate, from the year 129 onwards he was regularly so named all over the Greek part of the empire: *Hadrianos Sebastos Olympios*, or, indeed, *Hadrianos Sebastos Zeus Olympios* – for some of the exuberant or sycophantic Greeks soon identified him with Olympian Zeus.[13]

To convene an inaugural assembly of such a body required several years of intensive planning. Lists would need to be drawn up of eligible or potentially eligible states, of which there were hundreds all over the eastern half of the empire and well beyond. Both the literature and the material remains of the age – local coinage, inscriptions and statuary – give the impression that a principal preoccupation of many a city was to demonstrate the antiquity and authenticity of its Hellenic origins. Homer and Greek mythology were deployed with remarkable ingenuity to prove foundation by Perseus or other, sometimes little known, not to say invented, figures from the heroic age. Such claims would need testing in some cases.[14]

It fitted neatly into Hadrian's Panhellenic programme that he was on his way to the eastern frontiers. The Persian empire was no more; but there was a contemporary equivalent, an Iranian power that had some pretensions to have taken its place. Invitations were being sent out at this time to client rulers and kings beyond the Euphrates to attend another 'durbar' in 129. Perhaps the Parthian Chosroes was invited to another *colloquium*. His position as Great King was no less under challenge than it had been for two and a half decades, but it evidently suited Hadrian to deal with him rather than with his rival Vologaeses. At all events, as a sweetener, Hadrian sent back the king's daughter, in Roman captivity these past twelve years or more. He also offered to return the royal throne of the Arsacids, the *sella regia*.[15]

As always, the business of the Roman state came to Hadrian, wherever he was. In early March 129 he had to give an opinion on a question of inheritance law. It resulted from the claim by the treasury on the estate of one Rusticus. Hadrian wrote to the Senate with a proposal which was laid before the House by the consuls. Juventius Celsus, holding office for the second time, was a leading jurist, one of three singled out by the *HA*, along with Neratius Priscus and Salvius Julianus, as a regular member of the imperial *consilium*. Priscus was by now probably dead. It was his brother Marcellus who held the *fasces*, also for the second time, with Celsus at the beginning of the year. Marcellus had already been replaced by a suffect when Hadrian's letter arrived. On 14 March the Senate's decree, the *SC Juventianum*, was duly implemented. Salvius Julianus, the third and youngest of the three jurists, a brilliant young man not yet a senator, may have been in Hadrian's suite at this time.[16]

Celsus, at any rate, would soon join the Emperor, for he was to take up office as proconsul of Asia in the spring. Like all proconsuls of this province, Celsus had the right to appoint three legates. But this time, it may be, one of them was chosen for him by the Emperor. A 'descendant of kings and tetrarchs', including Attalus of Pergamum, Deiotarus and Amyntas, C. Julius Severus of Ancyra, was 'legate in Asia in accordance with a letter and *codicilli* of the God Hadrian', as his inscription reveals, and the appointment can be dated to about this time. This eminent person, 'first among the Greeks' – a title which others could lay claim to – had remained outside the Senate, surprisingly enough, under Trajan, when so many of his kinsmen enjoyed this status. Hadrian had clearly persuaded him, like Claudius Atticus the Athenian and Eurycles Herculanus of Sparta, to accept Roman rank. He had entered the Senate as an ex-tribune and had held a praetorship. Now Hadrian had responsible work for him, in Asia first – other posts would soon follow. The presence of a select handful of senators with the Emperor at all times must indeed be postulated. They would form his travelling *consilium*.[17]

There was a full programme in the eastern provinces and Hadrian's departure from Greece can hardly have been later than March. The two Ephesian captains, Erastus and Philocyrius, who had brought him and his party from Ephesus to Rhodes five years before, were engaged again, as Hadrian's letters on their behalf reveal, to ship part of the imperial entourage. Hadrian wrote to the magistrates and council of the Ephesians asking that the two men be made councillors, and specifying that 'I came to you from Eleusis.' The Ephesians could congratulate themselves that Hadrian chose to come a second time to their city, rather than, for example, to one of their great rivals, Pergamum or Smyrna. In truth, the reason was simply logistical. The itinerary of this year was in effect a continuation of the journey of 124. This time Hadrian wanted to inspect the southern part of the province Asia and make a detour into Lycia. Ephesus would benefit.[18]

In an inscription of 129 'the council and people of the Ephesians' honoured Hadrian – already with the name Olympios – to express their thanks to their 'founder and saviour' for a whole series of benefactions. They list first his 'unsurpassable gifts to Artemis': the goddess now gained the right to accept legacies. A series of practical measures follow: the city was permitted to import corn from Egypt – the same concession that Sparta had received – and Hadrian had launched a scheme to make the harbours more navigable by dredging and to prevent further silting by diverting the River Cayster. The request for permission to buy Egyptian grain may have been made the previous year by a city aware from recent experience that the imperial presence for some weeks or even months would create serious supply problems. A partly preserved letter inscribed on stone at Ephesus could be Hadrian's cautious reply. It begins with a reference to 'the greatness of your . . . city and the large number of its inhabitants'. Priority has to go to 'the reigning city', but when Rome has been supplied, the other cities too can benefit – 'providing that the Nile, as we pray, floods to the usual extent and an abundance of wheat is raised among the Egyptians, then you too, among the first after my ancestral city will be considered.' Ephesus also took care to honour the Prefect of Egypt, T. Flavius Titianus, with a statue.[19]

221

There were probably frequent applications for such concessions, but the special circumstances of Hadrian's travels with a large entourage would give the cities along his route particular reason to seek such help. The organisation of his itinerary must indeed have been a matter for intense and careful planning. Some eight months before he arrived in Egypt in summer 130, preparations were in hand well up the Nile, at Oxyrhyncus, to cater for his anticipated visit. At another city in Asia, Tralles, on the route eastwards from Ephesus, the purchase of Egyptian corn was likewise permitted. The Trallians and resident Roman citizens showed their gratitude to the wealthy man, A. Fabricius Priscianus Charmosynus, who paid for the 60,000 bushels that Hadrian had authorised them to buy.[20]

Ephesus was the first city Hadrian visited after assuming the title Olympius, which from 129 would regularly appear in his titulature all over the Greek half of the empire. Another Ephesian issue of the *cistophori*, which had already celebrated Hadrian's initiation at Eleusis and 'rebirth', now proclaimed the new distinction. Hadrian is shown on the obverse with the legend '*Hadrianus Augustus cos. III p.p.*', and on the reverse, as in in continuation of these titles, appear the words '*Iovis Olympius*', the – archaic – Latin form of Zeus Olympios, who had an ancient temple at Ephesus. The god is shown sitting on his throne with sceptre in his left hand, while his outstretched right hand holds an image of the Ephesian Artemis. Identification of Emperor and Olympian Zeus is surely intended. Ephesus still did not achieve a second neocorate, temple-wardenship, of the imperial cult. The honour could not be long delayed: a new temple to the God Hadrian was being built. All in all, even if Smyrna still had the edge in some respects, Ephesus was boosted to new heights by this visit.[21]

After Ephesus another great city of western Asia had its turn to receive Hadrian: Miletus, mother-city of scores of Greek colonies. If the Emperor travelled by land, there should have been a stop on the way at Priene and the venerable shrine of the 'Panionians' nearby. Apart from Miletus itself, there was the Milesians' great temple of Apollo a few miles away at Didyma, with its oracle. The day of Hadrian's visit there was to be commemorated as holy and he was honoured as 'Olympian, saviour and founder'. One of those who may have received Hadrian was the sophist Dionysius, a native of Miletus.[22]

The imperial itinerary becomes exceptionally difficult to reconstruct at this stage. On 27 June 129 Hadrian was evidently already some distance inland, at Laodicea on the Lycus, and a few weeks later even further north, in Phrygia. One might assume that he had set off from Ephesus along the great eastern highway, following the Maeander valley. Stops at Tralles, the home of his secretary Phlegon, and nearby Nysa, from which his chamberlain Alcibiades derived, may surely be postulated. Nysa was also the residence of a rising senator, Sex. Julius Major, originally from nearby Tralles, whose Latin nomenclature masks his Greek descent – he shared an ancestor with Antonius Polemo in the shape of Pythodorus of Tralles, whose daughter had been the wife of two kings. Major's career had been much favoured: he had already governed Numidia and held the consulship and would soon be governing one of the Moesias. All the same, there are strong hints that Hadrian also went further south in 129 and visited Lycia. At Patara the governor Mettius Modestus set up a splendid arch, which may be associated with Hadrian's arrival. Several members of Modestus' family are named with the governor and may be assumed to have been with him in the province. Modestus' term of office was now ending: he evidently joined the imperial retinue and left Lycia with Hadrian – taking with him a poet, Paion of Pamphylian Side.[23]

At all events, by late June Hadrian was on the borders of Caria, at Laodicea on the Lycus, as happens to be registered by his letter 'to the council and people of the Astypalaeans. I received your embassy through which you greeted me as I was arriving just now in Caria and Petronius Heraco gave me your letter.' Hadrian's reply is dated 'five days before the Kalends' – the missing month's name may be restored as July. One would expect that Antonius Polemo, who after all came from Laodicea even if he had made Smyrna his home, would have been on hand at this stage. The presence of the Guard tribune Statius Macedo, kinsman of the Caesernii brothers, is attested at nearby Colossae, where he dedicated a statue to Hadrian. Perhaps part of the retinue or escort was quartered there – others may well have been at Hierapolis. A visit to the famous Plutonium with its sulphurous springs may be postulated – and Hierapolis was, after all, the birthplace of Epictetus.[24]

A month or so later, on 23 July, Hadrian was at Phrygian Apamea, formerly Celaenae, where the Persians had once had a royal hunting-park. Here on that day in 129 Hadrian received an embassy, according to an inscription long known but still unpublished. It refers, apparently, to the Pamphylians, and it might be that they had hoped for a visit. If so they probably had to wait. For one thing, it is likely that Hadrian was intent on hunting. At some time, it seems clear, and the journey of 129 seems more plausible than an earlier year, he and Antinous hunted wild boar together. There were also other things to attend to in the area. At some point in his reign Hadrian had the tomb of Alcibiades restored – it was a favourite occupation of his to refurbish the memory of the famous dead. It does not necessarily mean that he was there in person – but if he was, there is no better moment to fit in a visit. It would have meant a detour to the north from Apamea, for the place where Alcibiades was murdered and buried, the village of Melissa, was in northern Phrygia. Hadrian's chamberlain Alcibiades might have proposed the visit, because of his name. But there was another good reason for a northward trip: to inspect the Phrygian marble quarries around Synnada and Docimium. Other considerations aside, Hadrian had decided to donate a hundred columns of Phrygian marble for the embellishment of one of his great new buildings at Athens. Once he was in the marble area, it was not far to Melissa. Julius Severus may have been with him: he is attested in his official capacity in this part of the province, at Dorylaeum. Hadrian's visit to Phrygia is guaranteed by the two coin issues, which register his arrival (*adventui Aug. Phrygiae*) and call him the 'restorer' of the region (*restitutori Phrygiae*), which was not, indeed, a province, but had been an ancient kingdom. Phrygia herself is shown wearing the traditional cap of her people, a short tunic with cloak over it, and trousers, and holds in one hand a curved shepherd's stick.[25]

Whether or not Hadrian made this slight detour in summer 129, his route from Phrygia lay eastwards. It may be supposed that he went to Antioch 'towards Pisidia', the most successful of the veteran colonies planted by Augustus in southern Asia Minor. From there he probably moved along the Augustan road, the Via Sebaste, via Pappa-Tiberiopolis, to Iconium. But the existence of yet another city calling itself Hadrianopolis well to the north of the Sebaste might suggest that he diverged from the main road. Furthermore, there were extensive imperial estates in the area – which belonged to the province of Galatia. They might have been worth inspecting. After Iconium, the imperial party will have proceeded into Cappadocia. A stay at Archelais seems highly plausible, once the capital of a Hittite kingdom. Formerly called Garsaura, it was refounded and named after himself by the last king of Cappadocia, and had by now been for many decades a Roman *colonia*. It cannot be coincidence that precisely in 129 the governor of Cappadocia had the 'shrines reconstructed for Hadrian' at Archelais – at the expense of the priests; the *IIviri* and quaestor of the colony supervised the work. As for the governor, this was a coeval of Hadrian, Rosianus Geminus, who had been Pliny's quaestor nearly thirty years before. Rosianus' son-in-law, Pactumeius Clemens, had already attracted Hadrian's attention and was probably at this very time busy with a special mission in Greece.[26]

The narrative section of the *HA* biography, becoming ever more condensed at this point and about to break off abruptly – for some six years – after curt mention of an event of autumn 130 in Egypt, happens to report the stay in Cappadocia. A reference to Hadrian's 'tour of Asia, consecrating temples to himself', is followed by the sentence 'then he received slaves from the Cappadocians for service *castris*'. The last word has generally been rendered 'in the camp' or 'in the army'. This seems a little puzzling. It makes better sense when it is recalled that *castra* can also refer to the household of the *imperator*. In other words, the slaves in question were to join the *familia Caesaris*. Cappadocia had long been a great exporter of slaves, renowned, for example, for its temple-states such as Comana with thousands of *hieroduli*, servile retainers, of the goddess Ma. The poet Horace had once mocked the king of the Cappadocians, master of so many slaves but still short of cash. After it became a Roman province the land continued to furnish slaves for Rome. Cappadocian slaves had a high reputation as bakers. The needs of Hadrian's travelling household were perhaps now catered for better. It may be that the opportunity was also taken to improve the mobility of the court by stocking up with another celebrated Cappadocian product, horses.[27]

What else Hadrian may have done in Cappadocia this time is a matter for guesswork. His coins later celebrated both the province and its garrison. On the *exercitus Cappadocicus* issue Hadrian is shown on horseback addressing the troops, which he probably did in 129 and had certainly done already in 123. The personified province of the other issue is shown standing, wearing a short military tunic with a *chlamys* made from an animal-skin over it, and high hunting-boots. On her head is a turreted crown; in her left hand she holds a flag (*vexillum*), in the other a mountain. This should be Mount Argaeus, at the foot of which lay Caesarea, the old royal capital of Archelaus, whose own coinage had the same motif. The turreted crown alludes, it has been suggested, to the Greek or hellenised cities of the province. It may be that one of these, Arca, now became a Roman *colonia*. If so, it would be very much in line with imperial practice elsewhere: frontier provinces in the north and west of the empire gradually acquired cities of this status equal in number to the legions of their garrison. The recruiting needs of the citizen units were thus provided for locally, one *colonia* for each legion. Arca lay close to the legionary fortress Melitene.[28]

The *HA*, the sole source, does not specify where Hadrian held his second 'durbar' for the eastern princes. It has often been assumed that it was at Satala, but there is no reason to suppose that he went so far north this time. Alternatives might be Melitene, the fortress of XII Fulminata, or Samosata, the old royal capital of Commagene and now part of the province Syria. Which client rulers attended the gathering can be determined partly from the *HA* and partly from indications in Arrian. He lists four petty rulers recognised by Hadrian, who may have received regalia from him on this occasion if not in 123: Malassas of the Lazi, Rhezmegas of the Abasci, Spadagas of the Sanigae and Stachemphax of the Zilchi. Anchialus, ruler of the Heniochi and Machelones, and Julianus of the Apsilae, both long-serving clients of Rome who had been recognised by Trajan fifteen years earlier, may have paid their respects. It seems likely that the king of Armenia (whose name is not certainly known) would have turned up too, but the Parthian king certainly did not. Vologaeses III, who had finally rid himself of Chosroes, had other things to think about – and Hadrian kept the royal throne that Chosroes had been promised. There may, indeed, already have been another rival to distract and weaken Vologaeses. At any rate, Mannus, or Ma'nu, ruler of Osrhoene, just across the Euphrates from Roman Syria, should have had no difficulty in attending personally. More distant potentates probably sent envoys. Mithridates of Mesene, Rome's client on the shores of the Persian Gulf, is a case in point. Finally, a later passage in the *HA* refers to the 'kings of the Bactrians' sending envoys to Hadrian. This may refer to the great Kushan ruler Kanishka, whose reign in the distant Oxus region had just begun (according to a still disputed chronology).[29]

There were two notable absentees, whose failure to attend is stressed in the *HA*: the rulers of the kingdoms in the Caucasus, of the Iberi (Georgia) and Albani (Azerbaijan), 'scorned to come and see him'. The latter is not named, but the Iberian king is a known figure, Pharasmanes II. The *HA* three times singles out Pharasmanes' conduct towards Hadrian. 'When some kings came to Hadrian', the first passage goes, 'he acted in such a way that those who had not been willing to come regretted it, especially in the case of Pharasmanes.' Later on, it is stated that

> on many kings he conferred a great deal, but from most of them he actually purchased peace; by not a few he was despised, but to many he gave huge favours – to none more than to the king of the Iberi, to whom he presented an elephant and a fifty-man 'cohort' as well as magnificent gifts.

Pharasmanes later reciprocated, but by then relations between Rome and Iberia had seriously deteriorated, as Dio informs us. Finally, in the biography of Hadrian's successor the *HA* reports that Pharasmanes showed greater respect to Antoninus than he had to Hadrian.[30]

The hostile comment in the *HA*, that Hadrian had 'purchased peace' from the eastern rulers, is echoed in the *Epitome de Caesaribus* – surely deriving from the same source, Marius Maximus' *Life of Hadrian*: 'Having obtained peace from many kings by means of secret gifts, he used to boast openly that he had achieved more in peacetime than others by warfare.' The judgement recalls Tacitus' account of Germanicus' recall from Germany by Tiberius in AD 16. He himself, Tiberius is supposed to have told his adopted son, had been sent to Germany by Augustus nine times – and 'had achieved more by diplomacy than by force' (*plura consilio quam vi perfecisse*).[31]

Hadrian will no doubt have received, in Syria as in other provinces, delegations from the provincial councils. They would have had the opportunity to express views on the conduct of Roman officials. It seems that there was criticism. At any rate, there is a further unfriendly remark in the *HA* regarding Hadrian's tour of Asia Minor in 129: 'As he went round the provinces, he inflicted punishments on procurators and governors in accordance with their conduct. Such was his severity that he was believed to have been inciting the accusers personally.' No names or details are offered. One is left to guess that, for example, an outgoing governor of Syria or of Cilicia may have been accused of malpractice, that one or more financial procurators were convicted of corruption. The legate of Galatia at the time Hadrian passed through the province, Trebius Sergianus, can hardly have been one of them – he became consul *ordinarius* in 132 – and Rosianus Geminus continued to enjoy favour. Syria probably received a new governor at this time, Publicius Marcellus, whose home was Aquileia, a rather senior ex-consul (he had held the *fasces* in 120). It looks as if two of the three legionary commanders were also newly installed at the time of Hadrian's visit, C. Julius Severus of Ancyra for IV Scythica and Eurycles Herculanus of Sparta for III Gallica.[32]

Antioch on the Orontes, the greatest city in the region, had begun striking coins again in anticipation of Hadrian's arrival – a good deal of extra small change would be needed when the imperial retinue was in residence. The coins proclaimed Antioch's rank of *metropolis*, mother-city, of Syria. The *HA* claims that Hadrian actually intended to diminish this role and had even had plans to split the Syrian province 'so that Antioch would not be called the *metropolis* of so many cities.' It is clear that the author – or his source, Marius Maximus – has misunderstood or deliberately distorted what Hadrian actually did. Syria was indeed subdivided into two provinces nearly seventy years later, by Septimius Severus, after it had supported his rival Niger in the civil war of 193–4 (and Antioch itself was also penalised). What happened in 129–30 was quite different. The title *metropolis* of a province, in Syria as elsewhere, had been jealously reserved up till now for a single city. Under Hadrian the 'rule' was relaxed. Three other cities, each the 'capital' of a distinct region, were also granted the title: Tyre, Damascus and Samosata. Marius Maximus perhaps assumed that Hadrian's measure was motivated by the same ill-feeling towards Antioch which he knew Severus to have harboured. Yet Hadrian's benefactions to Antioch are well-attested. Even if no later coin issue commemorated Hadrian's visits to Syria, coins were struck depicting – if not naming – the guardian spirit (*Tyche*) of Antioch.[33]

The emergence of Antioch's 'rivals' as new *metropoleis* is attested by the coinage of Damascus and Samosata. For Tyre – which had already called herself *metropolis*, in a different sense, as the mother-city of Phoenician colonies all over the Mediterranean – there happens to be a notice in the Byzantine encyclopaedia, the *Suda*, about a certain Paulus of Tyre, 'a *rhetor* in the time of Philo of Byblus; under the Emperor Hadrian he went on an embassy and made Tyre a *metropolis*.' The people of Tyre and the other ancient cities of Phoenicia had been reminded of their heritage at this very time by the man associated with Paulus in this passage. Philo of Byblus was the author – or rather, as he claimed, the translator into Greek – of *The Phoenician History* of Sanchuniathon, supposedly written before the Trojan war. Philo also wrote several other works, including one on *The Selection and Acquisition of Books*, and others on *Cities and Famous Men They Produced* and *The Reign of Hadrian*.[34]

Philo had a Roman patron, the senator Herennius Severus, once a correspondent of Pliny, who called him 'very learned'. Philo introduced to Herennius his pupil Hermippus of Berytus (Beirut), author of a book on dreams. The *Suda* records that 'Herennius was consul when Philo was 78 years old', giving the date as the 220th Olympiad, equivalent to the years 101–4. That can hardly be accurate: Philo would have been practically a centenarian by the time he could have written on Hadrian's reign. If '220' could be emended to '227', equivalent to 129–32, a plausible year for Herennius' consulship would be precisely 129. A pair of suffect consuls from this time, Severus and Arrianus, might then be two persons of cultured disposition, Philo's patron and Hadrian's friend Flavius Arrianus.[35]

As for Paulus of Tyre, he is known from another source, one of the subversive propaganda tracts emanating from Alexandria in Egypt and misleadingly called the *Acts of the Pagan Martyrs*. These pieces purport to record hearings, before a succession of emperors, of disputes between Greeks and Jews. Their consistent theme is the alleged pro-Jewish policy of Rome, with victimisation of prominent

Alexandrian Greeks as a corollary. A papyrus from Oxyrhyncus which describes a hearing before Trajan lists among the Greek delegates 'Paulus the Tyrian, who offered his services as advocate for the Alexandrians'. Paulus may even have appeared for the Alexandrians a second time, before Hadrian himself, in 119. Whether, as ambassador for the Tyrians before the Emperor in 129, this man had the chance of airing his anti-semitic views cannot of course be known. But it is likely enough that Hadrian met the sage of Byblus too; he would have certainly inspected his literary productions – and the *Phoenician History* displays a certain hostility to the Jews.[36]

Paulus would no doubt have found a welcome from one prominent member of the imperial entourage. Julia Balbilla, the bosom friend of the Empress, was the granddaughter, on her mother's side, of the celebrated astrologer Claudius Balbillus. Long ago Balbillus too had represented the Alexandrian Greeks against the Jews of that city, in a hearing before Claudius Caesar. He had gone on to be Prefect of Egypt under Nero. The opinions of Balbillus' granddaughter about the Jews are of course a matter of conjecture. Still, it is relevant to notice that her father Antiochus, the prince of Commagene, had once been betrothed to a Jewish princess, Drusilla, the beautiful daughter of Herod Agrippa. The engagement had been broken off: the bridegroom balked at conversion to Drusilla's religion, which would have involved circumcision. Furthermore, Balbilla's father, like her grandfather King Antiochus of Commagene and her brother the Roman consul and honorary Athenian Philopappus, had proudly borne the names 'King Antiochus Epiphanes'.[37]

The influence on Hadrian's thinking of the first and most famous bearer of that name, Antiochus IV Epiphanes of Syria, had already been seen at Athens. It had, after all, been that king who had revived and gone a long way to completing the construction of the Olympieion. He too, like Hadrian, had promoted the cult of Zeus Olympios. There are various other aspects of the character and policies of the eccentric monarch which find an echo in Hadrian, of whom he seems to be almost a mirror image. In his long years as a hostage the Seleucid prince had acquired a fervent admiration for Roman ways. His behaviour at Antioch, mingling with the common people like a would-be *civilis princeps*, recalls Hadrian the *plebis iactantissimus amator*. Antiochus was also, at least in his latter years – and notwithstanding his promotion of Zeus Olympios – a devotee of Epicureanism.[38]

Whatever impact these various features of Antiochus may have had on Hadrian – and, considering the length of time he spent altogether at Antioch, he must have had ample opportunity for finding out about them – Antiochus Epiphanes was remembered not least for his Jewish policy, which had provoked the uprising of the Maccabees. There was considerable debate in antiquity over the circumstances and course of events which led to the emergence of an independent Jewish state. One thing is undisputed: the Temple at Jerusalem was desecrated by the 'abomination of desolation'. An altar to Olympian Zeus was set up in the Temple court and circumcision was strictly prohibited under pain of death. This assault on the Jewish religion had indeed been preceded by active Hellenising on the part of the Jewish leadership. They had 'petitioned the king to let them build a gymnasium in Jerusalem. And when he had granted this, they also concealed the circumcision of their private parts in order to be Greeks even when naked', as Josephus put it, paraphrasing the First Book of Maccabees and spelling out an important aspect of what had gone on.[39]

Whether or not Antiochus had really ordered his extreme measures in 'an attempt to wipe out their superstition and introduce Greek practices, in order to change that most repulsive people for the better', as Tacitus put it in the *Histories*, the odds are that Hadrian believed this version. There were certainly some Jews in Judaea at this time who had tried to reverse the effects of circumcision by the process known as *epispasmos*, no doubt so that they could exercise naked in the Greek gymnasia without attracting adverse comment. Hadrian was certainly making plans for Judaea on this tour. In particular, he had decided to rebuild Jerusalem, left in ruins since its destruction by Titus in 70, and to create in its place a Roman *colonia*. The *HA*, which does not register this fact, instead places immediately after its account of the policy change over *metropoleis* in Syria the statement that 'at this time, too, the Jews stirred up a war because they were forbidden to mutilate their genitals.'[40]

The harsh and hostile language probably reproduces the phrasing of an imperial edict. In Greek the word used was presumably *katatemnein* – a deliberate variant of the normal *peritemnein*. As it happens, a renegade Jew, Paul of Tarsus, had once explicitly chosen to call circumcision *katatome*, 'mutilation', instead of *peritome*, in his *Letter to the Philippians*. Writing to the Galatians, Paul had gone further: 'these agitators', who insisted on circumcision, had better 'cut themselves off' – in other words, castrate themselves. In fact, the new Hadrianic prohibition – which was universal, not confined merely to the Jews – did indeed put circumcision under the same penalty as castration: death. The practice had already been banned by Domitian and Nerva. Hadrian made castration subject to Sulla's law on murder, the *lex Cornelia de sicariis et veneficis*. He can only be supposed to have been unaware what the reaction would be, to have been led to believe that Jewish resistance to Hellenisation had now melted away. There were, indeed, signs of this. Sepphoris in Galilee, which had still been predominantly Jewish at the time of the First Revolt – although it took the Roman side – acquired a new name at about this time, Diocaesarea, the first part referring to Zeus, the second to the Emperor.[41]

Tacitus, in his brief report of Antiochus' abortive attempt to 'civilise' the Jews, adds that the king had been prevented from carrying the policy through by a war with the Parthians. Hadrian, who in all likelihood proclaimed his new policy from Antiochus' capital, could be confident that he would face no danger from that quarter. Vologaeses already had problems with a new rival. It might indeed be questioned whether he needed a precedent or an inspiration from the Seleucids. Nor need one invoke the conjectural influence of anti-semites such as Paulus of Tyre and his circle. One could also discount the small but not insignificant group of senators of Jewish descent whose families had long since abandoned their ancestral religion – men like Julius Alexander Berenicianus, soon to be proconsul of Asia, or Julius Alexander Julianus, who had been legate of Arabia a few years earlier. Although Hadrian had been perceived at least by some Jews in a favourable light at the start of the reign, the main reason was no doubt that he had disposed of the hated Lusius Quietus. His real feelings about the Jews had probably been uninterruptedly hostile at least from the time of their uprising in 116. The havoc and destruction that they had created in the Cyrenaica, in Egypt and in Cyprus, not to mention their aid to the Parthians in Mesopotamia, would surely have had a lasting impact on Hadrian's thinking.[42]

There is no need to suppose that Hadrian remained at Antioch itself throughout the winter of 129–30. He may well have gone to and fro, returning there each time, but there is no firm information about other places he might have visited in Syria – except for an ascent of Mount Casius and a trip to Palmyra. The former may have come at the end of his stay in northern Syria – it is mentioned by the *HA* just after the ban on circumcision. The mountain lay on the south side of the River Orontes near its mouth, opposite the port of Seleucia in Pieria. Hadrian climbed it in the small hours, to see the sunrise. A storm was blowing up. As he sacrificed at the summit, the heavens opened and a thunderbolt blasted both sacrificial victim and attendant. Hadrian was unscathed and no doubt took it as a good omen, perhaps as a confirmation of the dream he had had thirteen years before. The night before he became Emperor, Dio relates, he dreamed that lightning struck him from a clear sky, first on the right side of his throat and then on the left – but he was neither frightened nor injured. The story was probably told in his autobiography.[43]

There is just a hint that Hadrian may have visited Berytus (Beirut), which was after all the sole Latin community in the region, up to this moment, at any rate, the only *colonia* of the traditional kind, in other words a settlement for veteran legionaries. With plans of his own for another such foundation, Hadrian may have had a particular wish to inspect the *colonia Julia Augusta Felix*. At any rate, he had occasion to refer to Berytus in a speech, the jurist Ulpian reports, in which he called it *Augustana colonia* (quite what the term implies is not clear). Heliopolis (Baalbek) in the hinterland, with its celebrated temple, still part of the territory of Berytus, was surely likely to attract the imperial tourist. There is no direct evidence for his presence, but a local dignitary, with a splendid set of authentically 'colonial' names, M. Licinius Pompenna Potitus Urbanus, was 'granted the public horse' by Hadrian, in other words received the status of Roman knight.[44]

If Berytus was still a Latin island in a by now largely Greek-speaking world, the remaining Syrian city Hadrian visited was virtually the only place where the native language, a form of Aramaic, was still in public use. Palmyra, the great oasis trading city, may indeed have still been technically outside the empire, a client-state, even if long since under the close supervision of the governors of Syria. Hadrian's presence there is firmly attested by an inscription, in Palmyrene and Greek, in honour of a prominent citizen, Males, 'also called Agrippa'. While holding office 'during the stay in the city of the God Hadrian, he provided olive oil both for visitors and for the Palmyrenes and contributed to the reception of the soldiers.' Coin-like tokens portraying Sabina found at Palmyra point strongly to her presence with Hadrian. Tourism aside, Palmyra was a key factor in Rome's relations with the states on her eastern borders. The free city had grown wealthy by trade with Parthia and through Parthia with the far east. Some of its citizens were in the service of the king of Mesene, still a Roman client-state, at the head of the Persian Gulf. Not long after Hadrian's visit, a Palmyrene actually dedicated a temple to 'the Augusti' at the Parthian city of Vologesias.[45]

After the imperial party left Syria the next stage of the itinerary probably took Hadrian first to Arabia before Judaea. The former Nabataean kingdom, peacefully annexed just over twenty years earlier but still often called 'the new province', had a garrison of one legion, at Bostra, the commander being at the same time governor. Hadrian may have installed a new man at this time, one of his favourites, the younger Haterius Nepos. The previous incumbent, Aninius Sextius Florentinus, had died at his post and was buried in a magnificent tomb at Petra. Hadrian's presence is not directly attested at Bostra, but he was certainly at Gerasa, also in the north of the province. His Horse Guards had been quartered there for the winter. Eight members of one of the *turmae* dedicated an altar to Deania 'at Antiochia on the Chrysorhoa which is also Gerasa, the holy, inviolate and autonomous city', for the welfare of Hadrian. Their acting commander, *praepositus*, is named, M. Calventius Viator, centurion of the legion V Macedonica. Viator had probably been with Hadrian commanding the escort of *equites singulares Augusti* at least since the tour of Africa in 128. To celebrate Hadrian's arrival Gerasa erected a ceremonial arch with a triumphal statue above. Hadrian held audience here and sat in judgement. Several other statues commemorated the visit.[46]

Petra far to the south was the *metropolis* of the province and the 'rose-red city' now took the name 'Hadriane'. It is probable enough that Hadrian went on south from Gerasa, through Philadelphia (Amman) along the Via Traiana and down the east side of the Dead Sea. Two coin issues, an *adventus* and a *restitutor* type, later recalled the visit. The personified province is shown wearing a long tunic (*chiton*) and cloak. On the *restitutor* coins a dromedary stands between Arabia and Hadrian.[47]

Two sets of coins were also to commemorate Hadrian's visit to Judaea, one simply showing the personified province, the other explicitly registering Hadrian's advent. The figure of Judaea is much the same on both: a veiled woman in standard Greco-Roman dress stands opposite the Emperor. With her, exceptionally for this series of province-coins, are three small boys. Two of them are shown offering palm-branches to Hadrian, while the third clings to his mother's robe. On the province issue, Judaea is shown sacrificing – the victim, a bull, lies beside the flaming altar. There is nothing here to suggest that Judaea was any different from any of the other provinces depicted on these coins. Most

Plate 24   Hadrian comes to Judaea
(*BMC* III Hadrian no. 1655)

of the *adventus* issues show an altar with a sacrificial bull. The only unusual feature is the fact that the straightforward province issue also has the altar – and the presence of the children. They indeed may allude to the foundation of the new *colonia* at Jerusalem. Otherwise, the thoroughly Greek character of Judaea on these coins gives the impression that it had become a Hellenised province like any other in the east. The transformation of Galilean Sepphoris into Diocaesarea which evidently took place at this time would have seemed to be a harbinger of a general abandonment of Judaism.[48]

The most plausible account of the foundation at Jerusalem is supplied in the Byzantine monk Xiphilinus' abbreviation of Cassius Dio's *History*: 'At Jerusalem he founded a city in place of the one which had been razed to the ground, naming it Aelia Capitolina; and in place of the Temple of God he built another temple, for Jupiter.' The brief statement is at once continued with an account of the war which this action provoked, not at once, but when Hadrian had left the region, 'for the Jews thought it a dreadful thing that foreign peoples should be settled in their city and foreign religious rites established there.' Study of the coinage has made it certain that the foundation was undertaken in 130, in the course of Hadrian's visit. He may have been contemplating the step for some time. There are indeed some curious stories, in both rabbinical and Christian sources, that Hadrian had at some stage promised the Jews that he would allow *their* temple at Jerusalem to be rebuilt. The notion may go back to some misunderstanding at the time when Hadrian's removal of Lusius Quietus – and then his execution – won him temporary popularity with the Jews.[49]

He was, indeed, in the mood for founding cities in 130, it might be said: there seems little doubt that he had already made plans for the creation of a new Greek *polis* in Egypt. He had founded a Hadrianutherae in the northern part of the province Asia, in Mysia, where urban centres were thin on the ground. In the Cyrenaica he had created a new city, also named after himself, to resettle refugees who had been displaced in the Jewish revolt. He had, too, founded new *coloniae*, in Africa and in Pannonia. But Roman colonies were few and far between in the Greek east and none had been founded for veterans since the time of Augustus. Perhaps his visit to Pisidian Antioch and other Augustan foundations, including Berytus, had had an impact. There is, further, the point that Judaea had had a garrison of two legions, at least since the end of Trajan's reign. That might well make it seem sensible to create a second *colonia*, which, together with Caesarea, could supply citizen recruits. Hadrian's new Jerusalem was perhaps a little out of the ordinary, a colony next to a legionary base – for X Fretensis had been based at or close to the ruined Jerusalem for over sixty years. Still, at Bostra, and indeed in other eastern provinces, it was normal enough for legions to be based in or on the edge of cities.[50]

The names chosen for the new foundation hardly need emphasising: Aelia after Hadrian, Capitolina after Jupiter – and, of course, this god was the Roman equivalent of Olympian Zeus. Further, the Jews had been obliged, since the destruction of their Temple, to pay their dues to Jupiter Capitolinus as a Jewish tax. Now Jupiter was actually taking over from Jehovah. What stage the preparations for the rebuilding of Jerusalem had reached by the time of Hadrian's arrival is quite unknown – except that considerable work had been going on in the past few years on the road-network in the province. That may well have been with a view to facilitating the transport of building-materials. One may suppose that a founding ceremony took place with Hadrian's participation, the driving of a furrow around the circuit of the new city's area. The new city's coinage, already being minted within two years of Hadrian's visit, shows him personally guiding the plough. The governor of the province will also have been at hand, Q. Tineius Rufus. Whether he had just been appointed or had been there already for a year or two is not known. Rufus had previously governed Thrace, probably at the time of Hadrian's visit in 124, and had become consul in 127.[51]

Dio explicitly states that Hadrian 'passed through Judaea into Egypt', coming first to Pelusium, whereas the *HA*, in spite of mentioning the provocation of the Jews by the circumcision ban, does not directly mention a visit to Judaea at all. Instead, its version is that 'he travelled through Arabia and came to Pelusium'. Dio's version seems to be correct, since independent evidence shows Hadrian at Gaza, which was now in the province Judaea, in the summer of 130. Visits to other places in the province must also be postulated. Caesarea, the residence of the governor and a Roman *colonia* for sixty years, was probably his base. It acquired a temple in his honour – a Hadrianeum – and there was another at Tiberias, said two hundred years later to be 'a very large temple'. Visits to other parts are also plausible. The talmudic stories of his conversations with Jews, including Rabbis, are no doubt largely imaginary, but it would have been in character for Hadrian to have engaged in debate with leading local figures. Thus Hadrian – 'may his bones rot!' (as virtually every reference to him in the rabbinical literature adds) – is portrayed in the Talmud questioning Rabbi Joshua b. Hanania, about the Sabbath, about Moses and about the Jewish deity. In one anecdote Hadrian – 'may his bones rot!' – questions a centenarian peasant whom he encountered planting a fig tree.[52]

A stay at Gaza is, at all events, undeniable. Hadrian surely went on from Gaza along the coast into Egypt. Gaza began dating its coinage by a new era beginning with Hadrian's arrival, which can be narrowed down to July. A 'Hadrianic festival' was also founded there. The author of the *HA*, with an itinerary taking Hadrian from Arabia into Egypt may just have been muddled. But perhaps Hadrian made a detour to Petra on the last stage of the journey to Egypt, rather than in the course of his tour of Arabia earlier in the year. However this may be, in late July or early August 130, Hadrian entered Egypt.[53]

19

DEATH IN THE NILE

'Who does not know what monsters crazy Egypt worships' (*qualia demens Aegyptos portenta colat*)? Not long before Hadrian arrived in the country, or perhaps while he was there, Juvenal composed a ferocious satire about an incident in Upper Egypt. Something appalling had happened, near Coptus, 'recently, in the consulship of Juncus', in other words in autumn 127. During a religious festival the neighbouring communities of Ombos and Tentyra had come to blows – they worshipped rival deities – which led to a bloody riot and ended in cannibalism. Juvenal himself had been in Egypt, he is careful to stress: 'Egypt is crude, to be sure, yet the native rabble is just as prone to luxury, I have observed, as the notorious Canopus.' It is difficult not to wonder whether the old poet had not chosen to write up this gruesome traveller's tale precisely because Hadrian was in Egypt or on his way there. That Hadrian was heading for Egypt had probably been known since he left Rome in 128 – the admittedly muddled fourth-century writer Epiphanius even asserted that the whole journey was to Egypt and was undertaken for the sake of his health.[1]

Hadrian approached by land, coming from Gaza, and one must assume that as he crossed the provincial border with Judaea at Rhinocoloura he was received by his Viceroy, the Prefect Flavius Titianus. So colourless are Titianus' names that it is impossible to infer his origin – except that he was presumably provincial and only a second generation citizen, if not son of an imperial freedman. But he had a solid career behind him, which included service in Asia Minor, Rome and Gaul; and he had already been Prefect for four-and-a-half years. How the Prefect was supposed to comport himself when the Emperor was there is a question. As Viceroy the Prefect had to carry out many of the functions of the Pharaoh; now the Pharaoh was there in person. Apart from Octavian, not yet Augustus, in 30 BC, and Vespasian, who came to Egypt soon after his proclamation, no Roman predecessor of Hadrian had ever been in Egypt. At any rate, Titianus was approved of by Hadrian – he remained in office for a further three years.[2]

The first record of Hadrian in Egypt is from Pelusium, where he restored the tomb of Pompeius Magnus. This action is reported not only by Dio and the *HA*, but in some detail by Appian, himself an Alexandrian. At the end of his

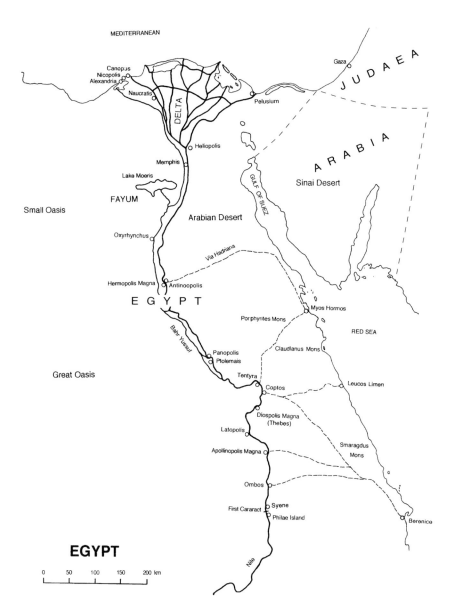

Map 7 Egypt

236

account of Pompey's murder in 48 BC, Appian adds that his head was cut off and kept for Caesar, and his body buried on the seashore in a modest tomb. In the course of time this was covered with sand and the statues of Pompey which his kinsfolk had erected had all been defaced and then removed to 'the inner recess of the temple. But in my day the Roman emperor Hadrian searched for and found them, during his visit there; and he cleared away the sand from the tomb and made it conspicuous again, and re-erected Pompey's statues.' Appian also mentions that 'someone' had composed an epigram for the tomb, which he quotes:

'How mean a tomb for one so well-endowed with shrines.'

Curiously, Appian does not seem aware that it was Hadrian who composed the verse, as duly reported by the *Palatine Anthology*, which includes the line as Hadrian's, and by Dio: 'After this he went through Judaea into Egypt and offered sacrifice to Pompeius, on whom he is said to have uttered this verse . . . and he rebuilt the tomb, which was in ruins.' Appian's apparent ignorance may be genuine: he had probably read the epigram – to which no author's name may have been attached. The *HA*, which omits mention of the poem, simply says that Hadrian 'rebuilt Pompey's *tumulus* in a more splendid way (*magnificentius*)'. The action was very much characteristic of Hadrian: restoration of tombs, with in some cases composition of verses to go on them, is attested for the Homeric hero Ajax, for Epaminondas and for Alcibiades, among others. On this occasion he honoured the memory of a great Roman who had, as Appian else-where put it, 'destroyed the Jews' greatest and to them holiest city, Jerusalem.' That Hadrian should have done this just after launching the replacement of this 'holiest city' by a thoroughly non-Jewish foundation was perhaps only coincidence, brought about by his itinerary. The Jewish inhabitants of Judaea, already seething with resentment, will have reacted with some bitterness. Hadrian would not, however, encounter such hostility in Egypt. The events of 116–17 had effectively wiped out the Jewish presence in the country.[3]

Hadrian's entry into Alexandria was already celebrated on the city coinage of his fourteenth year, which ended on 28 August 130 – the Egyptian New Year began on 1 Thoth, the equivalent of the Roman 29 August. He is portrayed standing on a *quadriga*, with the personified Alexandria standing to greet him. A later version a few years later shows him on a *quadriga* drawn by four elephants. Whether or not he actually arrived in an elephant-drawn carriage, it may at least be assumed that the date was no later than August 130. Hadrian's intention was certainly to inspect the whole province, which meant to sail up the Nile into Upper Egypt, indeed to go as far as the First Cataract and the southern frontier of the empire just beyond it, at Philae. It is safe to infer also that he came with plans to create a fourth fully-fledged Greek *polis*, alongside Naucratis, Alexandria and Ptolemais, and thus to strengthen Hellenism in Egypt. No doubt he had a general idea where this city should be established, but he would wish to select the spot himself. However, the voyage on the great river could only begin when the Nile flood had receded: there was an ancient religious taboo, of which the Romans were well aware, that the ruler of Egypt should not sail on the Nile in flood.[4]

The Alexandrian coinage of his fifteenth year – and indeed of several subsequent years – continued to depict the imperial *adventus*. Hadrian is shown being greeted by the personified city, which in one example is kissing his hand, in another offering him ears of corn; or he is shown sacrificing. Sabina too is repeatedly portrayed, standing and sacrificing, or sitting on a throne. An issue of the seventeenth year (132–3) has the great god Sarapis greeting the Emperor. Further, his temple is shown, represented by two fluted columns supporting a pediment on which an eagle perches. Inside the temple the Emperor is depicted, a sceptre in his left hand, touching with his right hand a small shrine labelled *Hadrianon*, on the other side of which Sarapis is portrayed, his right hand raised in greeting, a sceptre in his left hand. Hadrian and Sarapis thus shared a temple – which must be the mighty shrine at Alexandria, dominating the city skyline on its massive platform, approached by a hundred or more steps. The reconciliation of Rome and the Alexandrian Greeks was thus symbolically celebrated – for generations the Greeks had regarded the Roman emperors as biased protectors of the large Jewish community in their city; an image of Sarapis had gone with their envoys as a talisman to hearings at Rome. Now the Alexandrian Jewish community had disappeared. Besides the two principal deities, the Alexandrian coinage of these years shows a great variety of other gods, both Greek – Zeus, Artemis, Athena, the Dioscuri – and Egyptian – Harpocrates and the Nile – as well as personifications of Justice (Dikaiosyne) and Piety (Eusebeia).[5]

The imperial coinage struck at Rome would shortly commemorate most of the provinces and regions that Hadrian visited and Egypt was no exception, indeed was given particularly extensive treatment. Aegyptus is shown reclining on the ground, leaning on a large basket filled with corn-ears and fruit. She wears a long tunic and cloak and holds in her right hand a sistrum, the national musical instrument which was the special attribute of the goddess Isis. An ibis faces her. Exceptionally, not merely the figure of the province, but the city of Alexandria and the god Nile are also celebrated – Alexandria is the only city, apart from Nicomedia, that was honoured by this coin series. Nilus is shown as a heavily bearded old man with a garland of reeds, with hippopotamus or crocodile, and with children: these were evidently a symbolic representation of the sixteen cubits' rise of the river, on which Egypt's prodigious fertility depended. The god was normally shown on every issue at Alexandria. In Hadrian's fourteenth and fifteenth years he does not appear, which has led to the inference that the Nile floods in 130 and 131 were disappointingly low.[6]

Alexandria appears on the coins in various guises, both standing and reclining with one arm on a basket of fruit, not unlike the figure of Aegyptus. She is also depicted on coins specifically celebrating the imperial arrival, *adventui Aug. Alexandriae*. On some of these the personified city herself is

Plate 25 Egypt (*BMC* III Hadrian no. 1703)

depicted, on others she is not shown at all. Instead Hadrian is shown clasping hands with Sarapis; behind the Emperor stands Sabina, matched by Isis close to Sarapis. Rome's reconciliation with the Greeks of Alexandria is once again formally proclaimed.[7]

Before the Nile floods abated sufficiently for the great voyage up-river to begin, there was plenty for Hadrian and his party to do or simply to see at Alexandria and in the Delta. He had presumably long since authorised expenditure for rebuilding after the Jewish uprising. For what it is worth, that is stated by Jerome in his *Chronicle* under Hadrian's first year: 'Hadrian restored Alexandria which had been destroyed by the Jews.' Some of the temples shown on the Alexandrian coinage of Hadrian's eighteenth and nineteenth years (133–5), for example of Nilus and of Isis, may have been additional buildings begun during his visit – at any rate, one of the quarters of the city, which may well have been an addition, was to be named after him. A standard goal for prominent visitors was the Sema, the enclosure attached to the royal palaces, where the tombs of Alexander the Great and the Ptolemies lay. Alexander's mummified body had been placed by Ptolemy I in a gold tomb, which was later replaced by one of glass. Octavian had inspected the body closely in 30 BC, had indeed touched it, whereupon part of the nose broke off, Dio reports. The sources do not explicitly record Hadrian's inspection.[8]

Also attached to the palace-complex was another building which Hadrian certainly did visit, the 'house of the Muses', Mouseion, as it is best called, rather than the misleadingly latinised 'Museum'. This may be regarded as a Royal

Academy of Arts and Sciences. It had 'a public walk, an exedra with seats and a large house in which there is a common dining-hall for the men of learning (*philologi*) who are Fellows of the Mouseion', as Strabo had described it a century earlier. This institution of Ptolemy II, combined with the magnificent Royal Library – the stocking of which had naturally been favoured by Egypt's production of papyrus – was the pride of Alexandria. Membership of the Mouseion, which carried with it free dining-rights, was a highly regarded privilege among the intellectuals, not just of Alexandria itself. Hadrian is known to have appointed several outsiders, including his friend Antonius Polemo and Dionysius of Miletus. As Philostratus expressed it, in connection with the nomination of Dionysius, 'he was enrolled among those who had free meals in the Mouseion – by Mouseion I refer to a dining-table in Egypt, to which are invited the most distinguished men from all over the world.' Perhaps Dionysius had joined the imperial entourage, and would have the chance of enjoying his privilege in person. The institution was supervised by an imperially appointed procurator. Among known previous incumbents were the philosopher Chaeremon and his pupil Dionysius, both Alexandrians, the astrologer Claudius Balbillus, later Prefect of Egypt, and grandfather of Sabina's friend Balbilla – who was with the imperial party – and Julius Vestinus, the Gallic intellectual who had subsequently become Hadrian's *ab epistulis*.[9]

The *HA* – no longer in the narrative section of the *vita* – refers to Hadrian at the Mouseion in a single brief but revealing sentence: 'At the Museum in Alexandria he posed numerous questions to the professors and, after posing them, supplied the answers himself.' This was very much in the manner of the polymath ruler, who prided himself on being able to outdo the experts in their own fields. None of the 'professors' are named, but several of the Alexandrian and other *litterati*, including one who was probably made a member during Hadrian's stay, Pancrates, emerge in the course of the next few months in Hadrian's vicinity, further the *rhetor* Numenius, and the Alexandrian poet Dionysius 'the Periegete'. Other poets with the imperial party probably included Hadrian's freedmen Mesomedes and Phlegon of Tralles, the imperial chronicler, and, further, Paion of Side, who had links with Hadrian's other prominent freedman, who must have been there, the chamberlain Alcibiades. One should also mention again Sabina's close friend Julia Balbilla, who was shortly to reveal herself as an accomplished poetess, perhaps not the only one then in Egypt with the imperial party. Last but by no means least, the *ab epistulis* Avidius Heliodorus may properly be regarded as a man of letters; he was there, with his wife.[10]

The visit to the intellectual centre of Alexandria may have been relished by some of Hadrian's entourage. For Antinous, it may be supposed, other activities would have had more appeal, in particular hunting. It would in any case have been possible to infer from one of the reliefs – the *tondi* – which once adorned a Hadrianic monument at Rome that Antinous had accompanied Hadrian on a hunt which also left its traces in the literary record. Antinous, indeed, has been identified on all, or almost all, the eight *tondi*. On one, which should be chronologically almost the latest, he can be seen to have been with Hadrian on his lion-hunt. The lion was a 'royal beast'. That Hadrian once killed a lion is actually mentioned by the *HA*; and the event is depicted on a medallion. Besides this, there is more detail in the *Deipnosophistae* by Athenaeus of Egyptian Naucratis, an early third-century work cast in the form of a dialogue from the year 192. According to a story told here, 'a huge creature had for a long time ravaged the whole of Libya [i.e. the Cyrenaica], many parts of which this lion had rendered uninhabitable.'[11]

Athenaeus' account comes by way of explanation about an Egyptian poet named Pancrates. He had composed a poem about the hunt from which Athenaeus quotes a few lines. This episode in the Western Desert became better known when further fragments of Pancrates' poem were found on papyrus. One describes the party – including Antinous, mounted – assembling for the start of the expedition. A longer fragment begins with a description of Antinous, on horseback, awaiting the deadly lion with steel-shod spear in his hand. But it was Hadrian who struck first, throwing his bronze-tipped spear – but deliberately only wounding the beast,

> for he wished to test the aim of the handsome Antinous, son of the Argus-slayer [Hermes]. The stricken beast grew ever fiercer and tore at the ground with his paws in his rage . . . he lunged at them both, lashing his haunches and sides with his tail . . . his eyes flashing dreadful fire, his ravening jaws foaming, his teeth gnashing, the hair bristling on his mighty head and shaggy neck . . . He charged against the glorious god [Hadrian] and Antinous, like Typhoeus of old against Zeus the slayer of giants.

The remaining, very damaged lines seem to refer to the lion mauling Antinous' horse but then being struck a blow in the neck, evidently by Hadrian – who would thus have saved Antinous – and, lying in the dust, being trampled by the hooves of Antinous' mount.[12]

The Rome *tondo* shows Hadrian and a young companion side by side, each with a foot on a dead lion. If the figure at Hadrian's right hand is indeed Antinous, he is portrayed very differently from the mass of other portraits which have survived. On this hunting relief he has no luxuriant curls, indeed an almost military hair-style, and there are sideburns and down on his cheeks, the first signs of a beard. In other words, he was no longer an adolescent, an ephebe, but a young man, probably about twenty years old. It seems hardly possible that Pancrates wrote his poem about the hunt straight after it took place; rather, several months later, after further, dramatic events had intervened. It does, however, seem plausible that Hadrian met Pancrates not long after the hunt, not as a poet but in another capacity.[13]

The desert adventure – it may be guessed – occupied a week or two in September 130. Thereafter one can reconstruct Hadrian's movements in outline with some confidence over the next two months. His presence at a few places

Plate 26 Hadrian's lion hunt
(*tondo* from a Hadrianic hunting monument, reused in the Arch of Constantine).
The figure on the left, whose left foot is on the lion's head, has been identified as
Antinous (although this is often denied). If it is Antinous, it shows him as he was
shortly before his death. Next to him, with his right foot on the lion's head,
stands Hadrian (his head recut to resemble Constantine)

on specific dates is firmly established and can be postulated with confidence
elsewhere, even if the timing is less clear. It may be assumed, for example, that
he was at the pleasure-resort of Canopus, called 'notorious for its luxury' by
Juvenal, 15 miles (24 km) east of Alexandria. There was, to be sure, a great
temple of Sarapis there, known for its oracles and dream-cures. This may have
had some appeal. But Canopus was mainly renowned for

> the crowds of revellers who go down from Alexandria by the canal to the
> public festivals. Night and day there are throngs of people on the boats,
> playing the flute and dancing unrestrainedly, in fact with extreme licen-
> tiousness, men and women alike – and the people of Canopus itself have

242

establishments along the canal well-suited for this kind of relaxation and entertainment.

This is the description of the geographer Strabo. That Hadrian was at Canopus and retained favourable recollections of it is an inference from an item in the *HA*. His great Villa at Tibur had among the areas named after famous places one called 'Canopus' – the only reminder of Egypt which the biographer mentions. Canopus was a likely enough place from which the great journey up the Nile would have begun. A little over a hundred years earlier, as Tacitus reports in the *Annals*, Germanicus Caesar set off from this town, supposedly 'founded by the Spartans in memory of Menelaus' helmsman Canopus, who was buried there', for his voyage up-river to Thebes and thence to Elephantine and Syene, 'once the gateways of the Roman empire'.[14]

On the way to Canopus, if not, rather, on a special visit, it must be assumed that Hadrian was at Nicopolis, where Egypt's legionary garrison was quartered. The fortress close to Alexandria had long housed two legions and indeed there had for a time in the early principate been a third in the province. It seems that there were still two at Nicopolis, one of which, XXII Deiotariana, had been based in Egypt throughout the century and a half of its existence. Its partner, II Traiana, by contrast, first created thirty years before, had only just arrived in Egypt a year or two earlier. Lucius Macedo, tribune of the Praetorian Guard and with Hadrian as commander of his escort, after promotion to the rank of *primuspilus iterum*, 'chief centurion a second time', became commanding prefect of II Traiana: perhaps he was installed by Hadrian in person.[15]

Hadrian may have sailed on a specially constructed ship, but he would have been escorted by vessels of the *classis Alexandrina*. As it happens, a commander of the fleet under Hadrian, L. Valerius Proculus, who probably came from Malaca (Malaga) in Baetica, refers to his post as 'Prefect of the Alexandrian fleet – and of the river patrol (*potamophylacia*)', as if to emphasise an extra duty. He was probably in office at the time of Hadrian's voyage on the Nile, which should have begun on the Canopic arm. The first stop upstream would be Naucratis, the earliest Greek settlement in Egypt. Its earliest history went back nearly eight hundred years, when the Milesians had established it as a trading-post in the seventh century BC. The Pharaoh Amasis had fostered the enlargement of the town in the next century. At least twelve cities, Dorian and Aeolian as well as Ionian, had joined in the creation of the new *polis*. Such a 'Panhellenic' foundation must have been attractive to Hadrian, eagerly looking forward to the inauguration of his Panhellenion, now less than two years ahead. Furthermore, the *polis* which Hadrian himself was to found in Egypt would be given a constitution based on that of Naucratis.[16]

The next place to the south where there is evidence of a sort for Hadrian's presence is Heliopolis, as the Greeks called it, originally the city of a local sun-god, Atum, soon identified with Re, then with Horus, and worshipped there as Re-Harachte. The famous temple, the House of Re, had had a priestly school visited by Herodotus and at which Plato and the mathematician Eudoxus of Cnidus were supposed to have studied. Strabo wrote that the city was completely deserted in his day. The settlement of 'priests who studied philosophy and astronomy' had disappeared, but there were still priests 'who performed the sacrifices and explained the sacred rites to foreigners.' Further, a papyrus gives 'an extract from the spells in the holy book found in the sanctuary at Heliopolis, called the book of Hermes, written in the Egyptian language and translated into Greek'.[17]

Hadrian, with his insatiable curiosity, and perhaps with some other motive, evidently wished to learn some of the secret lore. Another papyrus, the great 'magical papyrus' now in Paris, tells of a 'spell of attraction', which 'attracts those who are uncontrollable . . . it inflicts sickness excellently and destroys powerfully, sends dreams beautifully and accomplishes marvellous dream revelations.' The text goes on to claim that Hadrian witnessed a demonstration.

> The prophet of Heliopolis, Pachrates, revealing the power of his own divine magic, demonstrated it to the Emperor Hadrian: for he attracted within one hour, made someone sick within two hours, killed within seven hours, and sent the Emperor himself dreams. Thus the prophet proved the complete truth of his magical powers. The Emperor marvelled at the prophet and ordered that he should receive a double fee.

The 'prophet Pachrates' was unquestionably a real and well-known figure. A generation later the satirist Lucian produced a caricatured portrayal in his essay *Philopseudes*, 'The Lover of Lies'. One Eucrates tells how he was sailing up the Nile and happened to meet 'a man from Memphis, one of the temple scribes (*hierogrammateis*), a remarkably wise man who knew all the teaching of the Egyptians'. He was supposed to have 'lived underground for twenty-three years, learning magic from Isis'. One of the other characters in Lucian's story at once recognises from the description his 'own teacher Pancrates, a holy man, with shaven head, clad in white in linen, speaking Greek with an accent, tall, flat-nosed, with thick lips and thin legs'. The shaven head, white linen clothes and emaciated legs were the typical features of the ascetic Egyptian priest. At this point Lucian takes off into the realm of fantasy, with Pancrates riding on crocodiles and then teaching his pupil some but not all of his spells – which resulted in Eucrates becoming the original of the Sorcerer's Apprentice.[18]

Remarkably enough, the same figure who met Hadrian in his capacity as 'prophet' seems to recur as the poet Pancrates, whose celebration of the lion-hunt has been quoted and who was to win further approval from Hadrian. There is no difficulty about the slight difference in name between the 'Pachrates' of the magical papyrus and 'Pancrates' in Lucian and Athenaeus. The former is an adaptation of a purely Egyptian name which sounded slightly similar, the latter is a 'corrected', more Hellenic version. Even if, as Lucian claimed, the man spoke Greek with an accent, there is no reason why he should not have been capable of writing passable Greek verse. As it happens, Athenaeus quotes from another work of Pancrates, the *Bocchoreis*, to illustrate the use of something called a *kondy*, a magical globe, 'from which magic wonders and profitable signs sent by the gods appear on the earth'. This directly links the poet with the practice of magic. One may speculate that his poem about the hunt had procured him an audience with the Emperor, at which he invited him to a demonstration of magical powers. Equally, of course, Hadrian might have sought out the 'prophet' first – for whatever purpose, but particularly perhaps if he was concerned about his own health – and this could subsequently have led to the poem.[19]

Hadrian may indeed have had other reasons for seeking enlightenment at Heliopolis. It was traditionally the home of the Phoenix, the legendary bird that had allegedly been sighted at the time of his accession, marking the beginning of a new era. There were very varied views on the life-span of the Phoenix. One put it at 1,460 years, the length of the so-called 'Sothic cycle'. Sothis was the Egyptian name for Sirius, the dog-star. The heliacal rising of Sirius was supposed to coincide with the Egyptian New Year's day, 1 Thoth (29 August), but in fact did so only every 1,460 years. According to the third century writer Censorinus, this coincidence occurred precisely in the year 139. Hadrian must have been well-informed about the coming event. Indeed, if one will, the proclamation of the Phoenix might be interpreted as merely an advance signal of what was soon to occur. Hadrian's construction of a massive temple of Roma and Venus and establishment of a festival for Rome's birthday on 21 April, likewise suggests that he intended, well in advance, to attune people's minds to the coming 900th anniversary of Rome's foundation, due in 148.[20]

Ahead of Hadrian and his party, only a few miles upstream from Heliopolis, lay some of Egypt's principal tourist attractions: Memphis, the 3,000-year-old original capital city of the Pharaohs, the pyramids, the Great Sphinx and the Labyrinth. No firm trace of Hadrian's presence survives at these places. That there was a temple of Hadrian at Memphis need not mean that he was there in person when it was founded – and in any case, it was probably there from soon after his accession; most places of any size would have had such a temple. Memphis had, at any rate, attracted imperial attention eight years earlier, just after Hadrian had left Britain, when he received urgent news about troubles over Apis. This was the sacred bull, variously identified as the son of Ptah or of Osiris or indeed as Osiris himself. Hadrian may be assumed to have inspected the animal about which there had been so much trouble. Each bull was ritually buried in the great Memphis Serapeum, the shrine of the original Egyptian Sarapis – Osiris-Apis or Osor-Hapi – from which Ptolemy I had derived inspiration for his new Greco-Egyptian deity. If Hadrian was concerned about his health, he might also have wanted to visit the Memphite temple of Imhotep, identified by the Greeks with Asclepius. Its priests were renowned for their skill in magic and alchemy. It must be recalled that Pachrates/Pancrates was associated by Lucian with Memphis rather than Heliopolis. There is no reason why he could not have held office as *hierogrammateus* at Memphis, and indeed his 'demonstration' to Hadrian could have taken place there, rather than at Heliopolis, which the papyrus may have named simply as his place of origin.[21]

If Hadrian left no trace of his presence at the pyramids, there is strong evidence that a high-ranking Roman woman from his party was there and climbed up the Great Pyramid of Cheops. She composed a six-line poem in Latin hexameters, which was carved on it:

> I have seen the pyramids without you, sweetest brother, and for you, as best I could, I have sadly shed my tears here and I carve my lament as a memorial of my grief. May there thus stand out from the tall pyramid the name of Decimus Gentianus, who was a priest (*pontifex*) and companion in your triumphs, Trajan, and within six *lustra* [i.e. before he was thirty] a censor and consul.

The man commemorated was D. Terentius Gentianus, son of Trajan's marshal Terentius Scaurianus. Gentianus had served in the Parthian war and early in Hadrian's reign was governor of Macedonia, where he held a census. He then held the consulship – at an unusually early age – but no further office. The *HA* reports that he was one of those that Hadrian hated – with particular violence, because 'he could see that he was esteemed by the senate'. Gentianus had apparently been one of those 'considered for the imperial position'. His sister, presumably called Terentia, was married to a senator called Lollianus Avitus, who had been proconsul of Asia in 128–9. It is plausible enough that she and perhaps her husband too had joined the imperial entourage at Ephesus in 129. It is difficult to find an an occasion otherwise when persons of senatorial rank – normally barred from entering Egypt – could have gone there, if not in the imperial entourage. Terentia would have been a suitable companion for Sabina – like Julia Balbilla, she evidently had literary leanings. It seems plausible enough that she had recently heard the news of her brother's death.[22]

South-west of Memphis, around Lake Moeris, and along the canal leading from the south shore of the lake to the Nile, were clustered a group of flourishing communities in which the Greek presence was strong. This was the region where Ptolemy II had settled the '6,475 cleruchs [colonists]', whose descendants continued to refer to themselves by this designation. Two of these communities, Berenice on Lake Moeris and Arsinoe on the canal, are known to have institutions bearing Hadrian's name, an estate (*ousia*) at the former, a temple at the latter. No evidence has yet come to light for a visit by Hadrian, but this was certainly an area where he would recruit settlers for his planned new *polis*.[23]

Some 140 miles (225 km) south of Memphis lay Oxyrhyncus, which – no doubt in common with many other places in the Nile valley – had already been making preparations for Hadrian's visit the previous December, when vast supplies of food were put in store: they included 200 *artabae* (some 7,600 litres) of barley, 3,000 bundles of hay, 372 sucking-pigs, 55 *artabae* of dates, 2,000 sheep, as well as olives and olive-oil and 'seven baskets of chaff'. Extra supplies, of barley, were evidently being collected at the end of May, as a further fragment of papyrus suggests. Oxyrhyncus later had 'Hadrianic Baths'. But whether they were so called because the Emperor used them on his visit, or donated the funds to build them, is a matter of guesswork. It is not even clear whether Hadrian stayed at Oxyrhyncus on his outward or on his return journey – or indeed on both. Oxyrhyncus, although not a Greek city, was a fairly Hellenised *nome* (district)-capital, where it seems, from the evidence of the numerous literary papyri found there, Greek literature had plenty of readers. It must in any case have been large enough to feed not merely Hadrian's immediate entourage but perhaps as many as 5,000 persons altogether, who could have been catered for at least for a few days by the supplies that had been stored there. One other point may be mentioned: Oxyrhyncus had evidently taken a prominent role in resisting the Jewish revolt in 116–17 – at any rate, a celebration for the victory over the Jews was still being celebrated there nearly a century later.[24]

By the second half of October the imperial flotilla had reached Hermopolis, some 60 miles (96 km) upstream from Oxyrhyncus. This was the city of the Egyptian Hermes, the god Thoth, who interpreted all secrets. On 22 October the festival of the Nile was due and two days later the commemoration of the death, by drowning in the river, of Osiris – at any rate, 24 October was the day which the Greeks regarded as the anniversary. It was perhaps on this very day that Antinous was drowned.[25]

The event is reported, briefly enough, by Cassius Dio, the *HA* and Aurelius Victor. Dio – himself a Bithynian – begins,

Antinous was from Bithynium, a Bithynian city which we also call Claudiopolis, and he had become Hadrian's boy favourite (*paidika*); and he died in Egypt, either by falling into the Nile, as Hadrian writes, or, as the truth is, having been offered in sacrifice. For Hadrian was in any case, as I have said, very keen on the curious arts, and made use of divinations and incantations of all kinds. Thus Hadrian honoured Antinous – either on account of his love for him, or because he had gone to his death voluntarily, for there was need for a life to be surrendered willingly, to achieve what Hadrian intended – by founding a city on the spot where he suffered this fate and naming it after him. He also set up statues of him, or rather sacred images, practically all over the world. Finally, he declared that he had seen a star, which he took to be that of Antinous, and gladly listened to the fictitious tales spun by his companions, to the effect that the star had really come into being from the soul of Antinous and had then appeared for the first time. As a result of this, indeed, he was ridiculed, especially because when his sister Paulina died he had not immediately accorded her any honours.

From this last remark it has been inferred that Paulina had died recently – and at Alexandria; in other words that she had been travelling in the imperial retinue. Her husband Servianus, now in his mid-eighties, was surely too old to have undertaken such a journey with Hadrian. He lived on, for a few years.[26]

The *HA* is much briefer still – its account forms the conclusion of the first long narrative section, which only resumes over five years later with an account of the succession crisis in the final months.

> While sailing on the Nile, he lost his Antinous, for whom he wept like a woman. There are various stories about Antinous. Some say that he offered himself as a sacrifice on behalf of Hadrian, others – what both his beauty and Hadrian's sensuality suggest. At any rate, the Greeks, at Hadrian's wish, consecrated him as a god, claiming that oracles were given through him, which Hadrian is supposed to have composed himself.

The *HA* can be seen to have condensed its source drastically.

Aurelius Victor's account presumably derived ultimately from the same lost *vita Hadriani* by Marius Maximus on which the *HA* largely depended. Victor's entire section on Hadrian's reign amounts to less than 300 words – a good quarter of them devoted to Antinous.

> As a result of Hadrian's devotion to luxury and lasciviousness, hostile rumours arose about his debauching of adult males and his burning passion for his notorious attendant Antinous; and that it was for no other reason that a city was founded named after Antinous, or that Hadrian set up statues of the ephebe. Some indeed maintain that this was done because of piety or religion: the reason being, they say, that Hadrian wanted to extend his own life-span, and when the magicians demanded a volunteer to substitute for him, everyone declined, but Antinous offered himself – hence the aforementioned honours done to him. We will leave the matter undecided although, in the case of an indulgent personality, we regard the association between persons of disparate age as suspicious.[27]

Had Hadrian not shown the deceased Antinous such remarkable honours – which will require detailed consideration – the hostile stories about his death might never have circulated. As it was, Hadrian was constrained to insist, in writing – the reference by Dio must be to his autobiography – that his death was accidental. Something else hints at an attempt to scotch the rumour that Antinous' death was voluntary. The *collegium* of worshippers of Diana and Antinous at Lanuvium, near Rome, established six years later (see Plate 32), provided among other things for the burial of its members – but suicides were explicitly debarred from this right. Other circumstantial evidence makes voluntary death seem probable. In particular, the deified Antinous, though identified with or portayed as various Greek gods, especially Hermes, Dionysus and Pan, was explicitly merged with Osiris in the city named after him. It is hard not to find the fact that his death took place, if not on the very anniversary of Osiris' drowning, at least very close to it, more than coincidental. Besides this, there was an ancient Egyptian practice that persons drowned in the Nile received divine honours. Herodotus was already aware of this in the fifth century BC. Tertullian mentions it again over 600 years later – and numerous cases are attested in the Egyptian records. Surely Antinous had heard out about this. On the other side, the concept of laying down one's life to save that of another was familiar enough to Greeks and Romans alike. The word used by the *HA* of Antinous, indeed, *devotum*, recalls precisely the Roman *devotio*, of which the most famous example was that of the Decii, father and son, each supposed to have fulfilled a vow to lay down his life to save his country.[28]

Dio states firmly – 'the truth is' – that the death of Antinous was indeed a sacrifice and alludes darkly to Hadrian's 'divinations and incantations'. Victor explicitly refers to 'magicians' (*magi*), who demanded a substitute to die for Hadrian so that they could prolong his life. Evidence for Hadrian consulting just such a 'magician', even if no details are given of the questions he posed, is supplied by the papyrus account of 'the prophet Pachrates'. It is an alarming thought that a member of the imperial suite, Julia Balbilla, may have planted the seeds of this idea that Hadrian could lengthen his life in this way. There was a story that her maternal grandfather, the astrologer Balbillus, had once advised Nero to take similar action. As Suetonius had recounted it not long before, Nero had been greatly disturbed by the appearance of a comet several nights running, apparently portending ill for himself. Balbillus had advised him to divert the wrath of heaven by putting some illustrious person to death. Tacitus has a briefer version, not naming Balbillus, but supplying a date, AD 64.[29]

There is a little more, circumstantial evidence, to be considered in due course, that may shed light on Hadrian's state of mind. It is perhaps fruitless to speculate, when the truth can never be discovered, unless by an historical novelist. A middle course might be to postulate that Antinous drowned himself as a spontaneous act, knowing that Hadrian was concerned about his health and believing – or having been told – that a 'sacrifice' was needed. It is plausible enough that Antinous had acquired a kind of death-wish anyway. He had been with Hadrian for some time, it seems clear – even if the sources are once again lacking to prove this unequivocally – and was now reaching the age when the – to the Greeks – traditionally honourable relationship with an older man was no longer sustainable. To have continued to be the Emperor's male lover after reaching adulthood could well have seemed to him shameful and degrading. Yet he may have been aware, with some dismay, that Hadrian wanted to maintain the tie – Victor, after all, accuses Hadrian of 'debauching adult males'. Not merely a great novelist but one of the leading Hellenists of modern times came to the same conclusion: that Antinous' position had become untenable and he sought a way out.[30]

At all events, it seems that it was on 30 October that Hadrian formally 'founded' the 'city of Antinous', on the right bank of the Nile, opposite Hermopolis, and close to the spot where Antinous died. Some kind of ceremony may be postulated, likewise a funeral for Antinous. But much remained to do: the recruiting of settlers, the planning and building of the city, would take several years. Even the 'paperwork' – the drafting of a constitution in particular – would take some months, and it is plausible that Hadrian deferred these matters until his return to Alexandria. It would also be necessary to shape the religious consequences, for Egypt and for the Greeks, of what had occurred. For the time being, it should be remarked that the city was founded more or less halfway between the two main centres of Hellenism outside the Delta, the Heptanomia with the descendants of the '6,475 cleruchs' and Ptolemais to the south. In other words, this is more or less where he had planned to site a new city – which he had no doubt originally intended to call Hadrianopolis. It appears that the place where Antinoopolis grew up had previously been called Bes or had at least had a shrine of this Egyptian god – a nice coincidence, for Hadrian was enrolled in the Athenian deme of Besa.[31]

The journey up the Nile continued, of that there is no doubt. Ahead lay Ptolemais, Egyptian Thebes and Philae. Hadrian was certainly close to Thebes from 18–21 November and was probably on his way north by this time. But it is quite unknown whether he had already gone as far as Philae, the island in the Nile, sacred to Isis, beyond the First Cataract and beyond the last Roman garrison post which Germanicus had visited, between Elephantine and Syene. There was a building on the island of Philae called 'Hadrian's Gate', on which the Emperor was portrayed sacrificing to Isis and Osiris; but this need not denote his presence.[32]

At all events, on 18 November Hadrian was at Thebes and before dawn on the next day was duly present to experience what no visitor to Upper Egypt could miss, the singing statue of Memnon. The colossal broken stone figure that in fact represented the Pharaoh Amenophis or Amenhotep III was called by the Greeks 'Memnon' after the Ethiopian ally of the Trojans, son of the dawn-goddess. The statue was one of two seated figures of the Pharaoh, 60 feet (over 18 m) high, set up a millennium and a half earlier to guard the Valley of the Tombs. The northern of the two statues had lost its upper half as the result of an earthquake about 150 years earlier. What remained produced a curious phenomenon: at dawn, as the stone warmed up in the sun's rays, it emitted a singing sound, 'like the twanging of a broken lyre or harp string', as Pausanias described it. To hear Memnon sing impelled many to record the experience by carving their names and the date of the visit on the statue's legs, in verse, if they were capable of this. The Prefect Titianus had been there in 126, during his first year of office, and duly 'signed'. Julia Balbilla, the friend of Sabina, immortalised the visit by Hadrian, Sabina and herself by no fewer than four poems, a total of over forty lines.[33]

The visit of 19 November was something of an embarrassment. Memnon failed to sing for Hadrian and his party. The next day Balbilla and Sabina returned and this time the Colossus duly performed. Soon afterwards Hadrian appeared and he too was favoured with the sound. On 21 November Balbilla and Sabina made a third visit and Memnon sang for them again. In her first poem Balbilla artfully claims that 'yesterday Memnon received the spouse in silence so that the fair Sabina might come back again – for the lovely form of the Queen delights you.' Then, after her return – on the 20th – he duly sang, 'lest the King be vexed at you, since for a long time you have been detaining his revered wedded wife.' According to Balbilla, 'Lord Hadrian himself loudly greeted Memnon and left for posterity an inscription declaring how much he saw and how much he heard, and it was clear to all that the gods love him.' No trace of an inscription by Hadrian himself survives.

Balbilla shows herself to be a highly educated woman, hailing Memnon as 'son of Dawn and venerable Tithonus – or Amenoth, Egyptian king, as say the priests knowledgeable in the ancients' legends'. She was not aware that the statue had been shattered in an earthquake – Strabo, who was there shortly after it occurred (in 26 BC), supplies this fact – and she repeats the widespread belief that the impious Persian king Cambyses, who had also 'killed the divine Apis', had deliberately damaged it. Nonetheless,

> I do not believe that this statue of you would therefore perish, I sense within a soul hereafter immortal. For pious were my parents and grand-parents, Balbillus the wise and King Antiochus: Balbillus the father of my mother, who was a queen, and King Antiochus, father of my father. From their stock I too have obtained noble blood, and these are my writings, Balbilla the pious.

In her last, briefest poem Balbilla reports that she 'came here with lovely Queen Sabina.' All her verses were written in the Aeolic dialect, in other words, the same form of Greek used by the great poetess of Lesbos, Sappho, over 700 years earlier. The way Balbilla refers to Sabina, combined with her imitation of the famous Lesbian poetess, raises the question whether there was in fact a lesbian relationship between the two women, whether Balbilla was Sabina's 'answer to Hadrian's Antinous'.[34]

Two further poems engraved on the Colossus probably derive from other members of Hadrian's entourage. Both are very brief: 'In vain destroyers ravaged your body. You still make a sound, as I, Mettius, have heard, o Memnon. Paion of Side wrote this.' 'That you could speak, Memnon, I, Paion of Side had previously learned but now I have experienced it in person.' It is plausible to suppose that the Mettius in question was the consular senator Mettius Modestus, member of a family from Gallic Arelate, whose father Mettius Rufus had been Prefect of Egypt forty years earlier. Modestus had been governor of Lycia-Pamphylia and his son or nephew had held the same post up to the previous year – indeed, the Mettius might be the younger Modestus. But it looks as if the poet Paion, from a town in the eastern part of the province both Mettii governed, had joined his patron as part of the imperial entourage in 129 and that they had gone on to Syria, Arabia, Judaea and Egypt. Paion later turns up as a friend of the younger Alcibiades of Nysa, son of Hadrian's chamberlain. A third possible member of the imperial party was a senator called Herennius Faustus – since senators were normally banned from entering Egypt, it is hard to see when a man evidently consul in 121 could have been there, if not with Hadrian in 130. Faustus did not attempt poetry, or even Greek. Instead he took up seven lines, in Latin, recording his names (eight in total) and *cursus honorum*, followed by the words 'I heard Memnon' (*Memnon[em audi]*) and perhaps the date – if so, it was drastically abbreviated, *C. et A. co[s]* (the consuls of 130 were Catullinus and Aper).[35]

A few days after the last visit to Memnon by Sabina and Balbilla, on 27 November, the Egyptian month Choiak which began on that day and ran until 26 December, was renamed Hadrianos. Whether any particular event was the reason for the change is not clear, although 27 November was evidently the birthday of Antinous. Some rather uncertain evidence suggests that Hadrian was at Oxyrhyncus on 29 and 30 November and at Tebtunis some 50 miles (80 km) further downstream on 1 December. It is reasonable enough to suppose that he was back at Alexandria before the end of 130. He seems to have remained there for several months.[36]

It is not difficult to infer how he occupied his time at Alexandria in this second stay. The commemoration of his dead favourite was surely elaborated here. His own freedman Mesomedes composed a hymn, the *rhetor* Numenius a prose *consolatio*. Mesomedes enjoyed a state salary – reduced by Hadrian's successor – which suggests that his effort was approved. The poem has not survived – unless the fragmentary text of a hymn to Antinous from Curium in Cyprus represents part of it. Pancrates the priest-poet produced his work on the lion-hunt, adding a personal touch which won Hadrian's favour: 'He showed Hadrian, when he was staying at Alexandria, the rosy lotus, as a great wonder, claiming that it should be called Antinoeus – for it had sprung from the earth when it received the blood of the Moorish lion which Hadrian had killed.' He duly included verses on the lotus in his poem and 'Hadrian, pleased with the originality and novelty of his thought, granted him the favour of free meals in the Mouseion.' As for Numenius' effort, it may be that he followed up Pancrates' inspiration and produced a string of parallels for the newly named rosy lotus. At any rate, part of a prose work on this theme is preserved on a papyrus from Tebtunis in the Heptanomia. It contains an anthology of various items, including a piece on the Phoenix and another on Hercules and the Eleusinian Mysteries. The longest surviving part is concerned with the Antinoan lotus, with parallels for other flowers named after beautiful youths (and one maiden) who met an early death: Narcissus, Hyacinthus, Cyparissus, Crocus, Daphne and Hylas – the last being the boy whom Hercules loved. The writer stresses that the flowers concerned were all pale in colour, unlike that of Antinous, as if the rosy red of the lotus symbolised his joy at the death for which he had wished.[37]

Another poet offered a much subtler composition at this time. Dionysius of Alexandria, who may well have been the son of the former head of the Mouseion of the same name, produced a *Guide to the Inhabited World* in nearly 1,200 hexameters. The 'Periegete', as he is known from the Greek title of the poem, artfully concealed details about himself in two acrostichs, in other words messages delivered by the first letters of successive lines. The first describes the work as the 'epic poem of Dionysius, (one) of those (who live) this side of Pharos' (*epe Dionysiou ton entos Pharou*), in other words, it identifies him as Dionysius the Alexandrian – one who lives near the famous lighthouse. In the second he refers to the 'God Hermes under Hadrian', perhaps a way of alluding to Antinous. A poem which comprises a world-tour should in any case have had an appeal to the great imperial traveller. Dionysius manages to structure the poem in a way calculated to win Hadrian's approval, for example by beginning with southern Spain. Gades, the home of Hadrian's mother, occurs right at the opening, closely followed by a mention of Canopus, and Gades crops up again several times. Adria, the Adriatic, also receives prominence, as if to echo the Emperor's name. In four places a particular name is given special emphasis by being repeated in successive lines: Carthage, the River Tiber, Ilium (Troy) – and the River Rhebas. This prominence thus given to the first three is understandable enough, but the purple passage about the obscure Rhebas is at first sight puzzling. The answer must be that the river was in Bithynia; to call this minor stream 'the fairest that sweeps the earth', with repetition of its name, was a clever way of praising Antinous' homeland.[38]

The consecration of Antinous as a god was certainly under way rapidly. At any rate, an inscription from Heraclea Pontica, on the Black Sea coast, seems to indicate the renaming before the end of the year 130 of the Association of Actors at Rome as the 'Sacred Hadrianic-Antinoan . . . *Synodos*'. The Greek cities needed little encouragement to institute a cult of the new divinity. Antinous received very particular worship, as was to be expected, at his home town of Bithynium and at Arcadian Mantinea, Bithynium's mother city. Festivals and religious insitutions of various kinds are attested above all in the Greek-speaking parts of the empire. At Naples, for example, the *phratria* (brotherhood) of the Eunostidae was renamed, the label Antinoitae being added. The Boeotian hero Eunostus was perhaps believed to have gone voluntarily to his death.[39]

As the basis for the constitution of the new city of Antinoopolis, Hadrian chose that of Naucratis, the oldest Greek *polis* in Egypt, rather than of Ptolemais or of Alexandria – the great city would have been an unsuitable model, for it had been deprived of an essential feature of the *polis*, the council (*boule*), by its Roman conquerors. It is easy to see why an emperor with such a love of antiquity should prefer the ancient Naucratis to the relative upstart Ptolemais. Such evidence as there is suggests that the settlers came from the families of the '6,475 cleruchs' in the Heptanomia and from Ptolemais; some of the men will probably have been army veterans. The settlers were encouraged to enrol by a series of very striking privileges, which would put Antinoopolis in an enviable category of its own: not least, exemption from the poll tax (*laographia*), from the tax on goods in transit (*enkyklion*) – with, initially, some extension of these exemptions to relatives of new citizens who remained in their place of origin – and exemption from compulsory public services (liturgies) outside Antinoopolis itself, were all very attractive. Further, Antinoites would enjoy the right to choose to have lawsuits in which they were involved heard at Antinoopolis, an 'alimentary' system was established – a child support scheme, and the distribution of free corn, on the model of the *frumentatio* at Rome, is also attested. At first sight the aim was to create a 'bulwark of Hellenism in Middle Egypt'. One further privilege, however, requires this view to be modified: Antinoites, both men and women, were granted the right of intermarriage with native Egyptians, *epigamia* – not enjoyed by the Naucratites. This meant that non-Greeks could become citizens of the new foundation, and thus acquire these great benefits. One must infer that Hadrian viewed this as a means of spreading Hellenism – or, put another way, that he did not regard Hellenic identity as having a racial basis.[40]

Antinoopolis seems to have become the administrative centre for the Heptanomia. To bolster its economic position a new road named after the Emperor was constructed, to link it with the Red Sea coastal route south to Myos Hormos, Claudianus Mons and Berenice, 'supplied with plentiful watering-places, rest-houses and guard-posts'. An inscription records the completion of the work in February 137. This measure seems not to have succeeded – the new route could not compete with the shorter crossings of the desert from Myos Hormos and Leucos Limen to Coptus. Another privilege, the holding of regular games, Antinoeia, would, however, unquestionably have brought lasting economic benefit to the city.[41]

Two very different sorts of evidence illustrate the Greek and the Egyptian character of Antinoopolis. A string of miscellaneous papyri referring to its citizens registers their membership of particular subdivisions of the city, tribes and demes. As at Athens under the dispensation of Cleisthenes, the tribes were ten in number; and each of those at Antinoopolis probably had five demes or parishes. The names of all ten tribes and some forty-two of the demes are known. There can be no question but that the choice of names was Hadrian's own. Most of the tribes are called after himself and members of his own family: his adoptive grandfather and father, Nerouanios and Traianios, his family name, Ailieus, his own name, Hadrianeios, his sister, Paulinios, his mother-in-law and wife, Matidios and Sabinios. Otherwise there are Sebasteios, from the first Princeps, Oseirantinoeios from Osiris-Antinous – and Athenaieus, from Athena and her city.

The demes within each tribe were clearly meant to be especially appropriate: Nerva's have names meaning 'founder of the family' and 'grandfather' and referring to Peace and Vesta, the three known for Traianios mean 'founder', 'victorious' and 'military', while the demes of Hadrianeios include Zenios, after Zeus, and Olympios and Capitolieus, again referring to Zeus and Jupiter. The remaining two in Hadrianeios, Sosikosmios, 'saviour of the universe', and Mousegetaios, 'leader of the Muses', offer an interesting reflection on Hadrian's self-perception. The demes of Matidios include Demetrieus, referring to Demeter, and Thesmophorios, both alluding to the Eleusinian Myteries, and Markianios and Plotinios, recalling Matidia's mother and sister-in-law, while Kalliteknios, 'mother of beautiful children', alludes to Sabina. As for Sabina's tribe, her demes include Heraieus, matching Hadrian's Zenios, Gamelieus, 'of marriage', and Harmonieus. The latter may just mean 'harmony' and advertise matrimonial concord, but it probably refers to Harmonia the wife of King Kadmos in the Theban legend. This couple was supposed to have lived to an advanced age under the blessing of heaven and then, in the Elysian Fields, to have been granted everlasting youth. The Theban association seems plausible in view of another deme-name of the tribe Sabinios, Trophonieus, which apparently refers to the hero whose oracle was at Boeotian Lebadea. But this, as well as the fifth deme-name of Sabinios, Phytalieus, may be argued to have associations with Eleusis, which are, indeed, implied in Gamelieus too. As for Hadrian's sister, the tribe named after her has demes that stress her relationship to the Emperor, Homognios and Philadelphios, and link her with Isis (Isideios) and Cybele (Megalesios). Perhaps this was enough to compensate for what Dio relates, Hadrian's failure to honour Paulina immediately after her death.

The four known deme-names of Oseirantinoeios tribe point to heroes from Arcadia (Kleitorios and Parrhasios), to Bithynia (Bithynieus) and to the god Hermes. As for the demes of Athenaieus: they refer to the Attic hero Erichthonios, to Marathon, Salamis and Artemision, renowned for the victories in the Persian wars – and to Eleusis. The Mysteries of Eleusis, recalled in several of the demes of the Sabinios tribe, also determined, it would seem, three of the deme-names of Sebasteios. The first two, Kaisareios and Apollonieus, simply honour the name Caesar and Augustus' patron deity Apollo. But the other three, Asklepieus, Herakleios and Dioskoureios, honour precisely the gods who had been initiated in the Mysteries before their apotheosis.[42]

As already seen from the tribe-names, Antinous was merged with Osiris at Antinoopolis. A remarkable purely Egyptian record helps to explain this in more detail. The great obelisk now standing on the Pincio at Rome must at some time have been brought to the capital from Antinous' city. The four sides of the obelisk are covered with reliefs and with hieroglyphs, making it one of the last specimens of an extended text of high quality in the ancient Egyptian writing-system. It cannot be doubted that Hadrian himself spent some considerable time, together with Egyptian priests skilled in the ancient lore, composing what was written on the obelisk.

On the east side Osirantinous addresses a prayer to Re-Harachte, 'highest of the gods, who hears the cry of gods and of men, of the enlightened ones and of the dead'. He asks Re-Harachte to reward him – Hadrian – 'who has founded a rule of worship in the temples for all men . . . he that is beloved of Hapi and of all the gods, the lord of diadems – may he live, safe and sound, may he live for ever like Re, in a fresh and rejuvenated old age!' This last phrase carries an echo of Aurelius Victor's claim that Antinous had died so that Hadrian's life could be prolonged. The Empress is also included in the new god's prayer: 'the great royal lady beloved by him [Hadrian], Sabina, who lives, is safe and in health, the Augusta, who lives forever'. The west side celebrates Antinous' deification:

> The god Osiris-Antinous, the justified, is become a youth with perfect face
> . . . his heart rejoices after he has received a command of the gods at the
> time of his death. For him is repeated every ritual of the hours of Osiris
> together with each of his ceremonies as a Mystery. . . . Lord of Hermopolis
> [Thoth], Lord of the word of god, rejuvenate his spirit!

The city of Antinoopolis is referred to on the north side, with specific reference
to the games to be held there:

> the competition place in his city in Egypt, named after him, for the strong
> [athletes] in this land, for the teams of rowers and the runners of the whole
> land and for all who belong to the place of the holy writings where Thoth
> is present, and they receive prizes and crowns on their head . . . There are
> sacrifices every day on his altars.

As well as the games, the oracles and dream-cures of the new god are praised on
this side.

Part of what is written on the fourth, southern face of the obelisk, was long
held to refer to Antinous being buried, not in his city in Egypt, but at Rome or
perhaps at Tibur. It has now been recognised that it does after all mean that his
body was laid to rest at Antinoopolis. The obelisk makes sense, not as a kind
of elaborate funerary monument, but as an integral part of the temple of
Osiris-Antinous in the new city – the only place where the god Antinous was
worshipped in this form. 'The god, who is there, he rests in this place, which
belongs to the Lord of Prosperity, [the ruler] of Rome.' Further,

> a place was named after him. The troops of Greeks of the Two Lands
> [Upper and Lower Egypt] and those who are in the temples of Egypt come
> here from their own places and are given cultivated land to make their life
> good beyond measure. A temple of this god is in that place, he is called
> there Osiris-Antinous, the justified; it is built of good white stone,
> surrounded by statues of the gods . . . and by numerous columns, made as
> they used to be made by our forefathers and also as they are made by the
> Greeks. All the gods and goddesses will give him the breath of life, so that
> he breathes, eternally rejuvenated.[43]

Such was the conception of the Greco-Egyptian cult of his new god, over
which Hadrian must have spent many days at Alexandria in the first months of
131, working with some of the most learned *hierogrammateis* in the land. The
Alexandrian coinage of Hadrian's fifteenth year continued to depict the Emperor
being greeted by the city, which offers him ears of corn and kisses his hand.
But other issues show Hadrian sitting in a ship, proclaiming his departure.
There is no indication of the time of year and it must remain a guess that he
left Egypt in the spring, after a stay of seven or eight months. But new games
were held at for the first time at Antinoopolis in March or April 131, named the
'Great Antinoan' (*Megala Antinoeia*). They were conducted 'according to the

dispositions (*taxeis*) of the divine Hadrian'. Hadrian had thus planned the arrangements for the games in detail. He may then have presided in person, involving another journey up the Nile. However this may be, he probably did attend another new festival, at Alexandria, 'the Hadrianic Philadelphian contest' – *philadelphios*, meaning 'loved by her brother', refers to his sister Paulina. This was a further gesture, comparable to the naming of an Antinoite tribe 'Paulinios', to counter the sarcasm when his initial failure to respond to her death was contrasted with the effusive honouring of his favourite.

If he did indeed return to Antinoopolis to inaugurate the first games, perhaps he took the opportunity of going south to Philae – especially if the events of the previous autumn had made this impossible then. And if he did go so far south, perhaps he performed the sacrifice traditionally performed by the ruler of Egypt in the spring, to ensure the beneficence of the river and a proper flood.[44]

Even with so much to preoccupy him, Hadrian cannot have neglected the business of empire. A new appointment to office which he probably made now was that of his friend Arrian to succeed Rosianus Geminus as legate of Cappadocia – Arrian is another person who might have been with the imperial party in 130–1. The transfer of Sextus Julius Severus from Lower Moesia to Britain may also belong to 131. At another level, one of his young companions, the brilliant young jurist Salvius Julianus, became imperial quaestor – effectively from 5 December 130, for the quaestors traditionally took office on that day. Julianus probably returned to Rome as soon as sailing conditions were suitable; and he was given a special assignment, to codify the praetorian edict. That Julianus was in Egypt is attested by one piece of evidence in his own writings: he saw there a woman of Alexandria with quintuplets, all of whom had survived. She was later to be brought to Hadrian's attention at Rome, for the fifth child was apparently born forty days after the other four. The case was important to establish the maximum possible length of a pregnancy. Another birth at Alexandria at this time was within the immediate circle of the Emperor: a son was born to the *ab epistulis* Avidius Heliodorus. Forty-four years later this son, Avidius Cassius, would briefly be recognised at Alexandria as emperor himself. There was at least one change in his retinue at about the time of Hadrian's departure from Egypt. Caesernius Quinctianus, who had been with Hadrian on the North African trip in 128, and whose younger brother Statianus had gone to the east with Hadrian in 129–30, and perhaps on to Egypt, now returned from Rome, where he had in the meantime been tribune and praetor, as the Emperor's *comes per Orientem*. Statianus in turn could now take leave of Hadrian, to pursue his *cursus honorum* in the capital.[45]

Whether Hadrian's health had been improved by his stay in Egypt is not clear. There may be a hint of this on the reverse of a coin issue from the mint at Rome, in both bronze and silver. It shows Hadrian standing, in military dress, with his left foot on a crocodile. Quite what is implied is not immediately clear. It has been argued that Hadrian is shown as the god Horus, and thus as 'King of Egypt', the vanquisher of evil forces. But it has also been pointed out that it had

Plate 27 Hadrian with foot on crocodile
(*BMC* III Hadrian no. 1617)

long been standard practice in Egypt for ill or afflicted persons to identify themselves with Horus and the demons that were causing them pain with 'scorpions,
crocodiles and serpents'. The identification, accompanied by spells, guaranteed
a cure for the patient who had taken on the god's identity. [46]

20

ATHENS AND JERUSALEM

Hadrian went from Egypt to Syria, probably sailing along the coast from Alexandria to Seleucia in Pieria, the port of Antioch, with some overnight stops on the way. At one of these, the governor of Judaea, Tineius Rufus, may have reported to him on the poor quality of the weapons which the Jews were being obliged to manufacture for the army of occupation. Hadrian would have insisted that defective items be rejected. As the *HA* noted in its section on his military measures, 'he took pains to familiarise himself with the military stores . . . and tried never to buy or to maintain anything that was unserviceable.' He will not have been aware that the Jewish craftsmen were deliberately turning out substandard weapons. The rejects were put aside, to be reworked and used when the time was ripe. These items – one may suppose that arrowheads, spearheads and swords may all have been referred to by Dio, who reports the story – were doubtless stored in the vast network of secret hideaways, caves linked by subterranean tunnels, where rebellion was being actively planned. Hostility to Rome among the Jewish population was intensifying: the ban on circumcision and the rebuilding of their holy city as a Roman *colonia* remained the prime factors. Official encouragement for the Greeks in Judaea to participate in the cult of Antinous could only have exacerbated the situation – a statue of the deified youth has been found at Caesarea.[1]

At least a short stay by Hadrian at Antioch or elsewhere in Syria must be assumed in the light of Dio's statement that he was there 'again' after being in Egypt. But the immediate goal was probably Cilicia. Hadrian had been in that province before, immediately after his accession and on his way to the Danube in the autumn of 117. But on his subsequent tours of the region, in 123 and 129, he had probably skirted round Cilicia, north of the Taurus. That he paid a formal visit some time in his reign is guaranteed by the commemorative coinage which proclaims the *adventui Aug. Ciliciae*. Hadrian, wearing short tunic and cloak, his 'travelling uniform', is shown being greeted by Cilicia. The province wears a long tunic and cloak, on her head a crested helmet like that of the goddess Athena; and she holds a military *vexillum* in her hand. Some of the Cilician cities were no doubt applying to join the Panhellenion. The allusion to Athena may suggest that their credentials passed muster in some cases.[2]

Cilicia had been one of Rome's earliest eastern provinces, but its boundaries had often been drastically adjusted. It had ceased to exist as a separate entity under the Augustan dispensation, to be revived only in AD 72, by Vespasian. Those parts that had remained under Roman rule in the interim had been attached to Syria and were also represented in the Syrian provincial council. The arrangement had continued for the next six decades. Now at last Cilicia acquired from Hadrian its own *koinon*, with its centre, the provincial temple of the imperial cult, at Tarsus, the *metropolis* of Cilicia, now also the *neocorus*, temple warden. Further, Tarsus was permitted to hold 'Hadrianic Olympics'. The new *koinon*, the *Hadriana Olympia*, and also the newly instituted worship of the 'hero Antinous', are all reflected in the city coinage of Tarsus in the 130s.[3]

Tarsus was indeed 'no mean city'. The geographer Strabo had written over a century earlier of the 'enthusiasm of its population for philosophy and the whole of Greek *paideia*', and even compares it with Alexandria as an intellectual centre – although, unlike Alexandria, 'its men of learning are all natives and foreigners are not disposed to reside there.' Tarsus had produced several noted philosophers, mainly Stoics, and had its own schools of rhetoric of all kinds. In fact, Strabo concluded, 'it is Rome that is best placed to testify to the multitude of learned men from this city, for Rome is full of Tarsians and Alexandrians.' Tarsus had been an unruly place: Augustus had been obliged to appoint one of the philosophers, Athenodorus, to rule the city with autocratic powers. More recently, on the eve of the Parthian war, Dio of Prusa had reproved the Tarsian oligarchs for their contentious rivalry with other cities, bad relations with the Roman governors and dangerously oppressive treatment of the working class, the 'linen-weavers'.[4]

The rivalries went on. Tarsus called itself 'Hadriane' – and no fewer than six other Cilician cities likewise took Hadrian's name, presumably with his permission: Mopsuestia, Adana, Zephyrium, Germanicopolis, Diocaesarea and Olba. One of the contenders with Tarsus for primacy in Cilicia, Anazarbus, and perhaps Flaviopolis as well, both inland cities in the valley of the River Pyramus, were allowed to hold Olympic-style festivals, *Hadriana Olympia*. Greek athletics were, after all, a primary means of fostering Hellenism. Several Cilician cities had long actively propagated a Greek origin: Tarsus claimed to be Argive, Olba was supposedly founded by the hero Ajax son of Teucer, Mopsuestia by the seer Mopsus, both of them just after the Trojan war. Hadrian may be supposed to have visited some of these places. Apart from this, it was probably now that the provincial boundaries were adjusted, enlarging Cilicia at the expense of Galatia, to take in the whole of Isauria and Lycaonia. In the next reign, at any rate, these 'three *eparchiae*', not previously so labelled, are regularly encountered.[5]

Hadrian may have installed a new governor in 131, T. Vibius Varus, whose term of office at any rate probably began about then. There happens to be preserved an imperial rescript to 'Vibius Varus, legate of the province Cilicia'. It is one of four similarly phrased letters quoted in the *Digest*, which nicely illustrate a characteristic feature of Hadrian. The others are to Junius Rufinus, proconsul of Macedonia, to 'Gabinius' (probably Gavius) Maximus, procurator-governor of Mauretania Tingitana, and to Valerius Verus (province unknown). All deal with the question of how to handle witnesses – Hadrian stresses that verbal evidence is much to be preferred to written depositions. The reliability of witnesses can best be established by the governor himself: 'You are better placed to tell what credit witnesses should be given, what their rank and reputation are, which ones appear to be speaking straightforwardly, whether they offer a premeditated speech or reply, convincingly, *ex tempore.*' In the letter to Rufinus Hadrian observed that 'I make a practice of interviewing witnesses in person.'[6]

Hadrian's next port of call was doubtless in Pamphylia, Cilicia's western neighbour. It seems that he had not visited that half of Lycia-Pamphylia in 129. Given that the poet Paion seems to have been in the imperial retinue in Egypt, one may conjecture that he persuaded Hadrian to make a stop at his native Side. Nearby cities were also worth a visit, Aspendus on the River Eurymedon, where Cimon and the Delian League had won a great victory over the Persians 600 years before, Perge and Attalia. The two latter could boast impressive arches in honour of Hadrian. That at Perge was erected by Plancia Magna, a senator's daughter, from an Italian settler family that was linked by marriage with Julius Severus of Ancyra. She had adorned it with statues of four empresses, Plotina, Sabina and Sabina's mother and grandmother, and of Nerva, Trajan and Hadrian. Plancia's brother, who had governed Cilicia and been consul, seems to have had a villa at Tibur not far from that of the Emperor. These people would thus have been very suitable hosts for Hadrian.[7]

Further west, at any rate, a stop is definitely attested, at Phaselis, on the once debatable boundary between Lycia and Pamphylia. The situation is impressive, on a little peninsula at the foot of the steep pine-forested slopes which lead up to Mount Solyma. Phaselis had had an evil reputation as a haunt of pirates, although Cicero spoke up for it: it had been taken over by those people because of its position – it had three separate harbours – but its inhabitants were really 'Lycians, *Graeci homines*'. Phaselis was indeed a Greek city, founded by the Rhodians, and had been a member of the Delian League. A splendid new south gateway had been erected in honour of Hadrian's visit. Statues were erected to him as 'saviour of the universe and of their country' by Phaselis itself, by a woman named Tyndaris, and by Phaselis' neighbours, Corydalla and Acalissus, 'on the occasion of his landing'. Sufenas Verus, governor of Lycia-Pamphylia, who had taken office at the time of Hadrian's visit to Lycia in 129, in succession to the younger Mettius Modestus, and was presumably in attendance, may have been designated to the consulship at this time. His colleague was to be Claudius Atticus, the Athenian millionaire, who would thus become the first consul from the Greek motherland.[8]

Hadrian's movements after the stay at Phaselis are a matter of guesswork. He probably resumed his journey by sea, but it seems that he was not finished with Asia Minor yet. A third visit to Ephesus seems likely. The city had at last, with the completion of its Temple for Hadrian, gained the second Temple wardenship it had coveted, to set it on a par with Smyrna. A possible trace of the imperial party's presence is a statue-base at Ephesus in honour of a young man of senatorial rank. He has a string of names – at least ten are preserved, and they include 'Pedanius Fuscus Salinator'. This may be Hadrian's grand-nephew. At all events, the honorand, though he had held only the pre-senatorial office of *monetalis* (*IIIvir a.a.a.f.f.*), was attended by a lictor, one Flavius Bassus, a sign of his unusual rank. The Ephesians may also have done their bit to show enthusiasm for the cult of the new god, Antinous. At any rate, some years later a sculpture was set up which seems to identify Antinous with Androclus, the legendary founder of Ephesus, son of King Codrus of Athens – and the hero is depicted in the act of slaying a wild boar. It may be that Hadrian and Antinous had hunted the boar together in the vicinity of Ephesus two years earlier.[9]

Seven years before, Hadrian had founded a new city in Mysia, in the north of the province Asia, and named it after his successful bear-hunt there, Hadrianutherae. Two further new cities in this region carrried his name, Hadriani and Hadriania. It has often been assumed that their creation was also the product of his journey in 124. But an inscription from the later second century indicates that the foundation of Hadriani was several years later than 124, in the period 128–32. The odds are that both cities were formally established in 131. If Hadrian was as far north as this, close to the boundary with Bithynia, it is natural to wonder whether he may not have gone a stage further and revisited Bithynium, Antinous' home. But this remains a guess, likewise the possibility that he went back to Cyzicus to inspect progress on the colossal temple of Zeus. That is at least plausible. He was obviously attracted to Cyzicus and twice consented to hold local office there. This may have been his last visit to the great province of Asia. What he did for the province, as its *restitutor*, his arrival there, and the personified province itself, were all commemorated on the imperial coinage shortly afterwards. The figure of Asia is shown in long tunic and cloak, with a mural crown to signify her many cities, a pruning hook in her left hand, in her right a ship's rudder, and her right foot rests on a ship's prow.[10]

On this hypothesis, his route to Athens may have been, this time, from the north – by ship across the northern Aegean to land on the coast of Macedonia, perhaps at Thessalonice. He was certainly in this province at some point, as shown by coins commemorating his *adventus* and others calling him *restitutor Macedoniae*. The province is portrayed wearing short tunic and boots, with Macedonian head-dress, carrying a whip in her left hand, a *patera* in the right. But he might, it is true, have been through Macedonia later, when he finally returned to Rome.[11]

Hadrian was now to winter at Athens for the third time as Emperor. He would surely have taken the opportunity to participate in the Mysteries again in the early autumn; a fragmentary letter to him from the Delphians of the following year may allude to this. The great festive opening of the Panhellenion was evidently timed for March or April. In the meantime there would be diversion enough: supervision of the numerous building-projects he had set in motion, and the launching of at least one more, a gymnasium. In a letter of 132 to the Athenians Hadrian formally announced a gift which may refer to this: 'Know that I take every opportunity to benefit both the city publicly and individual Athenians. To your boys I give' – here the text breaks off.[12]

Hadrian's benefits conferred on Athens and individual Athenians were indeed striking. As the priestess of the Mysteries put it, the 'city of Cecrops' was favoured by him above all others in Greece. Pausanias likewise writes that 'the Emperor Hadrian's generosity to his subjects was bestowed most of all on Athens.' Cassius Dio registers his generosity in a passage referring to this stay: 'He granted the Athenians large sums of money, an annual dole of grain, and the whole of Cephallenia'. The grain-dole was unmatched outside Rome – and, now, at Antinoopolis. As for Cephallenia, Dio may exaggerate a little, for it seems Athens did not acquire the whole of this large island. Presumably substantial tracts of land were involved, which would bring in revenues to the city coffers. A further measure mentioned here by Dio may also apply to Athens: 'Among numerous laws that he enacted was one to the effect that no senator (*bouleutes*), either personally or through the agency of another, should have any tax farmed out to him.' This may have been an attempt to enhance the dignity of the Athenian *boule*, making its members subject to the same rule as applied to the senators of Rome.[13]

The *HA*, in an undated context, mentions an individual act of lavish expenditure: 'He put on a *venatio* (wild-beast hunt) at Athens in the stadium with one thousand animals.' Hadrian had in all likelihood laid the groundwork for this display when in Africa in 128, for it must have been from there that most of the animals concerned derived. The Greeks were not accustomed to 'entertainment' on this scale – an inscription at Ephesus, for example, recalls as worthy of special note a donation of wild beasts for five days of successive display. Only twenty-five animals were involved. At this rate, Hadrian's *venatio* at Athens could have lasted for 200 days.[14]

It may have been during this winter at Athens that Hadrian received despatches from Arrian, newly installed as legate of Cappadocia, an official report in Latin and a more personal account in Greek, in the form of a letter. The Greek version survives, as the *Periplus of the Euxine Sea*. It begins with Arrian's arrival at Trapezus (Trebizond), coming from the south, 'after we had looked at the Euxine Sea from the place where Xenophon, and you, gazed at it.' He comments on the unsatisfactory statues of Hadrian and Hermes, and asks Hadrian to send replacements as well as a statue of the local god Philesius. He goes on to describe his five-day tour of the Roman military installations along the coast, up to the furthest limit of the imperial frontier at Dioscurias-Sebastopolis. One place he stopped at was called Athens – 'for there is a place of this name in the Pontus Euxinus as well, and a temple of Athena, from which it evidently takes its name.' At Apsarus east of Trapezus he refers to a particularly large garrison, no fewer than five cohorts, which may suggest that trouble was expected – perhaps a reaction to the uncooperative attitude of the Iberian king Pharasmanes in 129. At several points Arrian mentions putting the units through training manoeuvres and he notes that the fort on the River Phasis (Rioni) had been rebuilt in brick instead of earth and timber. Both items were very much in line with Hadrian's army policy. Further touches which would surely appeal to Hadrian include the description of Amisus as 'a Hellenic *polis*, a colony of the Athenians' and of the statue of the goddess Rhea in a shrine on the River Phasis, sitting on her throne 'just like the one sculpted by Phidias in the *Metroon* at Athens'. The members of the Panhellenion from outside Greece proper were to be known as the *apoikoi poleis*, 'colonial cities'. Arrian also duly notes the minor client kings in the neighbourhood, mentioning which ones had been installed by Hadrian himself.[15]

To this report of his own rapid tour Arrian appends a section describing the remainder of the Black Sea. When he comes to the Crimea, he refers to the recent death, datable to the year 131–2, of King Cotys II of the Bosporus, whose accession eight years earlier was registered by Phlegon. Towards the end of the letter Arrian dwells at length on the 'island of Achilles' off the mouth of the Danube – here he in fact confuses the '*Dromos* of Achilles' off the north-west coast of the Crimea with the island of Leuce near the Danube mouth. He writes of the numerous dedications to the hero. 'This is what I have learned of Achilles' island', he concludes, 'both from those who have been there or those who have heard about it from others'. He adds a personal comment:

> This [worship of Achilles] is readily to be believed. For I consider Achilles, if anyone, to be a hero on account of his nobility and beauty and strength of mind, and above all because he departed this life in his youth and was celebrated in Homer's poetry – and because he was a lover (*erotikos*) and devoted to his companion (*philetairos*), to the extent of being ready to die for his beloved (*paidikois*).

It is tempting to infer that Arrian intended these remarks as a delicate allusion to the death and consecration of Antinous – although the parallel between the two pairs, Achilles and Patroclus, Hadrian and Antinous, is hardly very close.[16]

No reply of Hadrian's is preserved. The only surviving letter of his to Arrian is an official rescript. It is a brief, dry piece, which deals with the withholding of evidence in cases where the imperial fisc was involved – and might of course have been written to Arrian when he was proconsul of Baetica or governing some other province.[17]

Whether in March 132 Hadrian again presided at the Dionysia, dressed in the costume of the country, as he had seven years before, is not recorded. But there was now to follow a whole series of festivities. A key moment came with the formal dedication of the vast shrine of Olympian Zeus and the gold and ivory statue of the god, which, Pausanias writes, 'exceeds all other statues in size except the Colossi of Rhodes and Rome'. As for the setting, before you go into the temple there are two statues of Hadrian in Thasian marble and two of Egyptian stone [presumably porphyry]. In front of the columns are the bronze figures which the Athenians call the 'colonies' (*apoikoi poleis*) . . . the whole enclosure is half a mile round, all full of statues. Every city dedicated a portrait of the Emperor Hadrian, but Athens outdid the rest by setting up the remarkable colossal statue of him behind the temple.

Dio and the *HA* both refer briefly to the dedication – the biographer putting it in the wrong place, in the context of the stay in 128–9. Dio at least adds a detail, that the Emperor placed in the temple 'a serpent which had been brought from India'. The association of the legendary Athenian hero Erichthonius with snakes – he was sometimes even portrayed as one – is clearly the reason for this act. Erichthonius was otherwise especially associated with Athena and, as Pausanias elsewhere notes, the snake beside the great statue of Athena in the Parthenon 'might be Erichthonius'.[18]

Pausanias mentions too the other buildings of Hadrian at Athens. In 'the common sanctuary of all the gods', in other words a Pantheon, was inscribed an account of 'all the sanctuaries of the gods he himself built and those he improved with furnishings and dedications, and all his gifts to Greek cities, and, when they asked him, to barbarian cities as well'. Then there were

a shrine for Zeus Panhellenios and one for Hera . . . but his most magnificent achievement is the Hundred Columns of Phrygian marble, with walls built just like the columns, and pavilions with gilded roofs and alabaster, decorated with statues and paintings; and books are also kept here.

This must be 'Hadrian's Library' next to the Roman Agora. Finally, Pausanias mentions the gymnasium, 'which also has a hundred columns, from the quarry in Libya' – in other words, of Numidian marble, from Simitthu.[19]

There seems nowhere to be an ancient account of the inauguration of the Panhellenion. It is difficult to avoid the conclusion that the dedication of the Olympieion and the launching of the Panhellenic organisation were one and the same occasion. Philostratus in his *Lives of the Sophists* reports how Polemo was invited to make a speech at the sacrifice for the consecration of the temple, 'completed at last after an interval of 560 years'. Polemo

fixed his gaze, as was his custom, on the thoughts that were forming in his mind, then flung himself into his speech, and delivered a long and admirable discourse from the base of the temple. As the prooemium of his speech he declared that his [the Emperor's] initiative had not been without divine inspiration.

That Polemo rather than Herodes was invited to speak on this occasion has been seen by some as some kind of rebuff. But Polemo was older; and besides, Herodes' father had just been honoured with the consulship, may indeed have been holding the office at this very time, as the first consul from Greece proper, a sufficient sign that the family was highly honoured.[20]

The *temenos* of the Olympieion could well have been served as the meeting-place of the Panhellenion. Whether the delegates, *synedroi*, from the member-cities gathered for the inauguration is not clear. At all events, the organisation will have been established. A chairman was to preside, with the title of archon, the earliest known being Cn. Cornelius Pulcher of Epidaurus, who also held the office of 'high priest of Hadrian Panhellenios'. The next five years were set aside to prepare the first festival. Members are recorded from Achaia, Macedonia, Thrace, Asia and Crete-Cyrene – none are yet attested from the Greek cities of the west, such as Massilia (Marseilles), Neapolis (Naples), Tarentum, or those of Sicily, nor from the eastern provinces of Pontus-Bithynia, Lycia-Pamphylia, Cilicia, Syria and Egypt, not to mention further afield. Amisus, for example, in Cappadocia, would surely have applied. In fact, cities in those provinces may well have been represented. Even the great Hellenic cities of Asia such as Ephesus and Smyrna are not on record as members – this surely just reflects the haphazard nature of the evidence.[21]

The Panhellenion, when complete, was to meet every four years, to celebrate the *Panhellenia*. There were also to be at Athens new Olympic games and new Panathenaic games. Finally, perhaps only after Hadrian's death, the *Hadriania* festival was instituted. Thus Athens was effectively to have a great festival every year, ensuring that there would be an annual influx of competitors, not just athletes, but poets, musicians and orators, and spectators from all over the Hellenic world. Athens, now adorned with public buildings of unequalled splendour, was indeed a new capital for the Greek part of the empire. No wonder that Hadrian alone among emperors was honoured by a portrait statue in the Parthenon – at any rate, Pausanias saw none other there.[22]

As for almost all the provinces that Hadrian visited, Achaia was commemorated on the coinage soon after this stay: in this case there is only one variety, Hadrian as restorer, *restitutor*, of Achaia. The personified province, wearing a long tunic and cloak, kneels before the emperor. Between her and Hadrian is shown a large amphora with a palm-branch emerging from its mouth. It has been identified as a 'Panathenaic' vase, of the kind made in the fifth and fourth centuries BC, clear enough symbolism – Hadrian hoped to restore Hellas to the greatness of her distant past. Close to the Olympieion was erected an arch or gate, some 60 feet (*c.* 18 m) high and over 40 feet (13 m) wide – its architecture a kind of cross between the Roman triumphal arch and the Greek city gate. It carries an inscription on each side. On that next to the old city, it reads 'This is Athens, Theseus' city once', the other proclaims 'This is Hadrian's, not Theseus' city.' No builder is named on 'Hadrian's Gate'. It was perhaps the tribute of the Panhellenion to its founder. The part of the city where the Olympieion stood had been constituted as a new deme, called 'New Hadrianic Athens', in the new tribe Hadrianis. It may be that Hadrian, before he left Athens, asked that the deme be renamed 'Antinoeis'.[23]

Plate 28   Hadrian's Gate at Athens

Some time in late spring Hadrian surely thought it was time to return to Rome. He had been away for the best part of four years. Whether he was already under way or still at Athens, news came which obliged him to remain in the east: the Roman army in Judaea had been attacked by rebels, with appalling losses. This uprising had begun gradually, it appears. 'At first the Romans took no account of the Jews', Dio reports. The trigger might have been what Dio mentions as an omen, which gave the people of Judaea 'forewarning before of the war' of the desolation to come. 'For the tomb of Solomon, whom the Jews regard with veneration, fell to pieces of its own accord and collapsed.' Perhaps this had actually been caused by the building operations in train to convert Jerusalem into Aelia Capitolina. At any rate, the legate Tineius Rufus presumably treated the first symptoms merely as an outbreak of brigandage and took measures to restore order. However, as Dio records, the insurgents

> did not dare try to risk open confrontation against the Romans, but occupied the advantageous positions in the country and strengthened them with mines and walls, so that they would have places of refuge when hard pressed and could communicate with one another unobserved undergound; and they pierced these subterranean passages from above at intervals to let in air and light.[24]

These subterranean bases were not merely to shelter the civilian population and to store weapons, including the 'rejects' originally made for Rome. Some of them were strategically situated and designed as bases for surprise attacks. As has been pointed out, their numerous entrances 'could be used not merely as escape hatches but also as sally-ports.' Clearly the initial attacks were extremely successful. It soon became too much for Tineius Rufus to handle, in spite of a garrison of two legions and a dozen or more auxiliary regiments. Publicius Marcellus, governor of Syria, brought reinforcements from the north, including the legion III Gallica, leaving Julius Severus, legate of IV Scythica, as acting governor. From Egypt, it seems, came the legion XXII Deiotariana – which appears to have been wiped out. At any rate it disappears from the Roman army list; there is in fact no trace of its existence after the year 119. There is a chance, of course, that XXII Deiotariana had in fact been Judaea's second legion for the previous few years. There had been several changes of base by the legions of Syria, Arabia, Judaea and Egypt during the previous decade and a half. If so, it must have been based in the northern part of the province, at Caparcotna in Galilee, where VI Ferrata was later in garrison.[25]

Neither Dio nor any other source mentions the destruction of an entire legion. But Fronto, writing thirty years later, did at least refer to 'the great numbers of Roman soldiers killed under Hadrian by the Jews and by the Britons'. Dio, too, at the end of his account – which, brief though it may be, is nonetheless the most detailed that survives – after listing the Jewish losses, adds that 'many on the Roman side also perished in this war.' After noting, at the start of this passage, that little attention was paid to the first signs of trouble, he goes on to stress that there was before long a real crisis.

> Soon, however, the whole of Judaea had been stirred up, and the Jews everywhere were showing signs of disturbance, were gathering together, and giving evidence of great hostility to the Romans, partly by secret and partly by overt acts; many others, too, from other peoples, were joining them from eagerness for profit, in fact one might almost say that the whole world was being stirred up by this business.[26]

Dio's statement that 'the Jews everywhere' were displaying hostility is surprising. This can only be a reference to the Jews of the Diaspora. But the Jewish population in the Cyrenaica, Egypt and Cyprus had been in effect wiped out in 116–7. He must have meant those in other provinces, perhaps Syria and Arabia in particular, possibly also in Anatolia. As for the 'many of other races' who joined the rebels, this might denote non-Jews in Judaea itself as well as malcontents from, for example, Arabia. However this may be, it was the Jews of Judaea themselves who took the lion's share.[27]

The rebels rapidly liberated part of their homeland and retained control of it for over three years. This is the startling feature of this uprising, which places it in a quite different category from that of the Britons, for example, at the beginning of Hadrian's reign. Further, what marked out this war from the great Jewish revolt that began under Nero was that this time the Jews were united under a single leader, who took the title 'Prince of Israel', *nsy' Ysr'l*. He is not named, to be sure, in the Roman sources, but they are scanty indeed. The Christian writers call him 'Bar Cocheba(s)' and attribute to him messianic claims. There is a trace of this in the Jewish – talmudic – sources: he is there called, instead, Ben or Bar Koziba, but it is clear that the later rabbis were well aware of the name b. Kokhba too, the implications of which require discussion presently. On the coins struck by the rebel regime his name appears as Shim'on, frequently with the title *Nasi* of Israel. The discovery of letters – mostly from the leader himself – and of documents issued on his authority has now clarified matters. He wrote his letters under the name Shim'on ben or bar Kos'ba (*Sm'wn bn Kwsyb'* or *br Kwsbh*) in Hebrew or Aramaic; one Greek letter has the form *Simon Chosiba*.[28]

The documents, like the coins, give Shim'on the title *nsy' Ysr'l*. Both coins and documents supply dates. The former have the legends 'Year 1 of the Redemption of Israel' and 'Year 2 of the Freedom of Israel', with later issues being less specific, 'For the Freedom of Jerusalem'. But the documents are dated by the first and second years of the 'Redemption of Israel', by the third year of the 'Freedom of Israel' and by the fourth year of the 'Redemption of Israel'. The documents also have dates within these years, the earliest being 1 *Iyyar*, April, of Year One, the latest 14 *Marhesvan*, October or November, of Year Four – with, in some cases, the year being that of Shim'on. It seems that the era began with the month *Nisan*, March/April, of 132. Thus the rebels still held some territory where the *Nasi's* writ ran in autumn 135.[29]

The name b. Kokhba is clearly a kind of nickname. *Kokhba* means 'star', alluding to Balaam's prophecy of the Messiah in the *Book of Numbers*: 'I see him, but not nigh: There shall come forth a star out of Jacob, And a sceptre shall rise out of Israel, And shall smite through the corners of Moab, and break down all the sons of tumult.' A passage from the Talmud shows that the great Rabbi Akiba, at this time in his eighties, applied the prophecy to Shim'on b. Kos'ba. This produced a sarcastic response from another Rabbi: 'Grass will sprout on your chin, Akiba, and the son of David will still not have appeared!' The passage, like others in the talmudic sources, calls the rebel leader 'b. Koziba', not b. Kos'ba. This form, from the word *Koziba*, meaning 'lie', was a rival, derogatory name, 'son of the lie' rather than 'son of the star'. Shim'on did not, to be sure, use the name b. Kokhba on the coins, nor has it, or the title 'king', been found in the letters or documents. The attempt to identify a star sign on the coins has also been dismissed. All the same, the title *Nasi* itself could have messianic connotations, as in *Ezekiel*: 'My servant David shall be king over them' is followed a few lines later by 'And David my servant shall be their prince (*Nasi*) for ever.'[30]

The support of the great R. Akiba, the most influential Jewish teacher in the period after the destruction of the Temple, was certainly important. This gesture cost Akiba his life. Jewish tradition tells of his arrest by Tineius Rufus, torture and martyrdom, along with other rabbis. Religion was unquestionably the driving force behind the uprising. The rebel coinage is entirely Jewish in its imagery and language. Its script is the old Hebrew, and the Temple, still a vital memory over sixty years after Titus had destroyed it, is repeatedly displayed, with the Ark of the Covenant within it. Other symbols, the bunch of grapes, wreaths of olive, laurel or palm, a jug, a lyre, a vine leaf or a palm tree – with seven branches – recall the Temple ritual. Foliage and a citrus fruit, the *lulav* and the *etrog*, depict the 'four species' needed for the Feast of Tabernacles. It is no surprise that a letter from Sh'imon, to Judah b. Manasseh at the base Qiryath 'Arabaya, concerns just these items, which Shim'on's 'large army' needed: palm branches and citrons are to be collected from Jonathan b. Be'ayan and Masabala – the commanders at En Geddi on the Dead Sea – and Judah himself is to supply the other two 'kinds', myrtles and willow, 'from your place and send them to the camp'. Shim'on had sent two donkeys for the purpose.[31]

The importance of religion to the rebel Jews is also shown by the appearance on the earliest coinage of the name Eleazar the Priest. This man has not been certainly identified, but he might be the same as Rabbi Eleazar of Modin, referred in the talmudic sources as an uncle of b. Kos'ba. The title 'Priest' as well as the stress on the Temple and its ritual naturally point to the Jewish aspiration to restore what Rome had destroyed two generations before and had now begun to desecrate. Negative evidence – lack of coins of the rebels at Jerusalem and no reference to Jerusalem in the letters or documents – so far indicates that this remained only an aspiration. As for the other Roman action which had provoked the revolt, the ban of circumcision, there was, not surprisingly, a firm

Jewish response. Those who had attempted to disguise their circumcision by *epispasmos* before the ban – and had perhaps thereby misled Hadrian into regarding the moment as ripe to abolish the rite – were now obliged to be recircumcised. More may perhaps be learned of the religious attitudes of the rebels when the documents are all published in full. One letter refers to a rabbi, previously unknown, Batnaya bar Meisa, evidently at En Geddi.[32]

Shim'on appears from the letters as a stern, even harsh, leader. Jonathan and Masabala, the two commanders at En Geddi, are ordered to confiscate wheat and transfer it in safe custody to Shim'on, and the 'men of Tekoa' are to be given no shelter – disobedience will result in severe punishment. In another letter they are ordered to send all the men from Tekoa and other places to Shim'on without delay. This and further letters again threaten punishment for failure to obey. Writing to the commander Joshua b. Galgula, Shim'on threatens that 'if you maltreat the Galileans with you, I will put fetters on your feet, as I did to ben Aphlul.' There is only one mention of the enemy: Shim'on, after threatening to punish his subordinates if they disobey, adds that 'I shall deal with the Romans.' Given that they were found in caves where the defeated rebels hid, the letters no doubt belong to the last stage of the war, when the situation was desperate and Shim'on was obliged to exert extreme discipline. In the earlier phases this may have been different. It should be stressed, too, that he refers to his men as 'brothers'.[33]

The talmudic sources, largely hostile to Shim'on – or 'b. Koziba' – confirm his forcefulness, not least his physical strength, but impute blasphemy rather than religious rigour to him. 'He caught [Roman] missiles on his knee, then hurled them back and killed some of the enemy', one story has it. Another tells of him cutting off a finger from each of his soldiers' hands as a test of their courage. When the rabbis protested, he substituted the requirement to uproot a cedar of Lebanon. His alleged impiety or blasphemy comes up with his supposed prayer 'as he went into battle: "Do not help us, Lord of the World, but do not put us to shame either!" That is what is written: "Hast thou not, O God, cast us off? Then go not forth with our hosts!"' There is a suggestion that he was regarded as king in the story of the 'two brothers [who] lived in Kefar Harruba, who let no Roman pass but killed them. They said "Let us take Hadrian's crown and set it on Shim'on's head, for the Romans are coming."'[34]

Christian writers are all hostile. The earliest, Justin (Flavius Justinus), a contemporary, was born of Greek parents in the province at Flavia Neapolis, the former Samaritan Shechem, and converted to Christianity at about the time of Hadrian's visit. He records debating at Ephesus with a Jew named Trypho – who had fled Judaea because of the revolt. In a later work he claims that 'in the Jewish war that happened in our day Bar Chochebas, the leader of the Jewish rebellion, ordered Christians – alone – to be punished severely if they did not deny Jesus was the Messiah and curse him.' Over a century later, Eusebius – also a native of the country, from Caesarea – put a slightly different complexion on the matter in his *Chronicle*: 'Cochebas, leader of the Jewish sect, killed the Christians with persecution of all kinds when they refused to help him against the Roman troops.' Eusebius has more in the *Ecclesiastical History*, where he calls Shim'on 'Bar Chochebas' and explains that the name 'means "star"'. He adds that 'the man was murderous and a bandit, but relied on his name, as if dealing with slaves, and claimed to be a giver of light who had come down to them from heaven and was miraculously enlightening them in their suffering.' Jerome makes Shim'on out to have been a charlatan, 'who kept fanning a lighted straw in his mouth so as to appear to be breathing out flames'.[35]

The documentary evidence provides a much more sober picture. What is striking is that land was being leased and sold, as if peace was reigning, from the beginning of the revolt all the way through to the end. What is more, land was 'leased from Shim'on b. Kos'ba'. What had been imperial domain at En Geddi had been taken over by Shim'on in the name of the people of Israel. Civil administrators with the title *prnsw* were at work as well as military commanders. Two women, Babatha, whose family came from En Geddi, and Salome, who had both been living in the province of Arabia, found refuge at En Geddi in the course of the revolt. As late as August 132, at least five months after it broke out, Babatha had still been in Arabia. Perhaps anti-Jewish reprisals there had prompted her move.[36]

The presence of Galileans at En Geddi suggests that they too were refugees or volunteers who had come to join the uprising, for there is no documentary evidence for the rebels having control of Galilee. On the other hand, in Lower Galilee, at least, caves have been found of the kind described by Cassius Dio. As for the extent of the new independent Jewish state, the finds of its coins and the places mentioned in the papyri suggest that it controlled at least a block of territory south of Jerusalem and along the Dead Sea, stretching in the west to within 18 miles (30 km) of the coast and south to beyond Hebron. There may have been isolated centres of rebel activity further north. This is suggested by finds in a cave 11 miles (18 km) north-west of Jericho. Shim'on's men may have initially reached the coast between Ascalon and Gaza – coins of these two cities were used (along with others, including some from the new Roman *colonia* of Aelia Capitolina) as the basis for their own issues. He was in a position to get supplies in by ship across the Dead Sea, so that the east side – in the province of Arabia – may have been partly under his control. There is no direct evidence yet that Jerusalem itself was won back. Whether Shim'on had a main headquarters is not clear. He was at one moment based at Herodium, due south of Jerusalem, and in the final phase at Bethar, 6 miles (10 km) south-west of the city.[37]

At some point Hadrian was back in Judaea. This must be implied by Dio, who, reporting the heavy Roman losses, adds that 'Hadrian for this reason when writing to the Senate omitted the introductory phrase normally employed by the emperors, that "If you and your children are in good health, it is well; I and the legions are in good health."' The talmudic sources have various anecdotes about Hadrian taking part in the war, and his involvement is implied by some of the Christian writers. None of these can be pressed. But a senior centurion in the

Praetorian Guard, C. Arrius Clemens of Matilica in Umbria, was decorated for war service by Hadrian, hence should have been with him in Judaea. Otherwise, all that there is to go on is the terminology in inscriptions referring to officers and men who served. The war is several times called the *expeditio Iudaica*. Given the parallels, this term must mean that the Emperor was there, at least for a token period. When this was and how long he stayed is a matter of pure conjecture.[38]

One other source has generally been taken to indicate Hadrian's presence at the front. A work on siege-engines, *Poliorcetica*, is preserved, of which the author is said to be Apollodorus of Damascus, the architect of Trajan's great Danube bridge and of many of his buildings at Rome. To be sure, Apollodorus was alleged by Dio to have been on extremely bad terms with Hadrian, and it is not clear whether he was still active at Rome at this time or in retirement. Much of the contents of the *Poliorcetica* is probably secondary, added in Byzantine times. But it begins with a letter, which is seemingly authentic, addressed to an emperor who has apparently sought his advice. 'I am honoured that you judge me worthy to share in your concern in this matter', he begins and goes on to refer to designs he is sending, with a member of his staff and a number of craftsmen. He does not know the places where the siege engines will be needed, but is aware that it is not a case of besieging cities. Rather the enemy is occupying 'heights' that are advantageous to him. Apollodorus has supplied a variety of arrangements, to produce machines quickly, even with unskilled labour. It may be, then, that Hadrian swallowed his pride and sent for advice to Apollodorus.[39]

But Hadrian was not going to finish the war in person. Dio reports that when not only 'all Judaea' had been stirred up but even 'the whole world', Hadrian 'then, indeed, sent against them his best generals, of whom the foremost was Julius Severus. He was sent from Britain, of which he was the governor, against the Jews.' Sextus Julius Severus, from a colonial family in the province of Dalmatia, had served for some seven years as the first governor of Dacia Superior, then, after his consulship at the end of 127, as legate of Moesia Inferior, before going to Britain. The moment of his transfer to Judaea, following Hadrian's summons, cannot be pinpointed exactly. His successor in Britain, a man from southern Spain, P. Mummius Sisenna, was still serving as *consul ordinarius* in April 133. But Severus could easily have left Britain before Sisenna arrived there, leaving one of the legionary legates as acting governor. The fact that a consul *ordinarius* was chosen for Britain, and straight after being consul, in itself suggests an emergency. Former *ordinarii* did not generally govern Britain, and it was also usually entrusted to men who had had previous experience in another consular province. That Hadrian sent for a general to deal with the crisis who was as far away from the theatre of war as anyone possibly could be is in itself astonishing. But Hadrian wanted the best man for the job.[40]

Severus was also able to bring reinforcements with him, both from Britain and from the provinces that he went through. What direction he took is a matter of guesswork. But if he was bringing extra troops the Rhine-Danube river route and then overland via Ancyra through Anatolia may have seemed the best. It would have taken some months. It could be that Hadrian planned his own movements so as to meet Severus on the Danube, to confer. At any rate, the Emperor's *comes* Caesernius Quinctianus was with Hadrian on a journey *per Orientem et Illyric(um)*. In other words, Hadrian's route back to Italy took him through the Balkan and Danube lands. Severus took with him from Britain at least two young officers. M. Statius Priscus, Prefect of the Fourth Cohort of Lingones, took up a commission in the Syrian legion III Gallica, and M. Censorius Cornelianus, a man from Nemausus who was commanding the First Cohort of Spaniards at Alauna (Maryport), accepted appointment as a centurion in X Fretensis. At a higher level, Severus was able to call on Q. Lollius Urbicus, then commanding the legion X Gemina at Vindobona (Vienna) as a staff officer, and an equestrian tribune of that legion took detachments to the war. Of the extra units involved, one may even have been the legion IX Hispana, which, if not still in Britain, was perhaps based in Lower Germany. Transfer of this legion to the east would explain how a man from Cilicia, who acquired citizenship from Hadrian, probably on enlistment, came to be serving in the Ninth.[41]

The losses in Judaea and the transfer there of large numbers of soldiers made various emergency measures necessary. For one thing, a batch of sailors or marines from the Misenum fleet was transferred *en bloc* to the legion X Fretensis. Two senators are found recruiting soldiers in Italy. Q. Voconius Saxa Fidus, who, after his praetorship was curator of the Via Valeria Tiburtina, was entrusted with levying of soldiers 'in these parts' as well. As he went straight on to be legate of IV Scythica, he may have brought recruits with him to Syria. Meanwhile Hadrian's young favourite Caesernius Statianus, who had just served as tribune of the plebs, was 'sent by Hadrian to recruit young men in the Transpadane region.' A third recruiting officer was the procurator-governor of the Maritime Alps – this was Valerius Proculus, who had been commander of the Alexandrian fleet, probably when Hadrian was in Egypt. The levy was not often resorted to during the principate. It was not usually popular, and will not have been now, especially if it meant serving in the war, against a dangerous enemy who had inflicted heavy losses. The missions of the three men probably represent just the tip of the iceberg. It may even be wondered if Dio's statement that more or less 'the whole world was in upheaval' refers to this recruiting drive.[42]

Before Severus arrived, Tineius Rufus had clearly been exacting a fearful revenge. 'When military aid had been sent him by the Emperor', Eusebius records, 'he moved out against the Jews, treating their madness without mercy. He destroyed in heaps thousands of men, women and children, and under the law of war, enslaved their land.' These actions presumably explain why it is Rufus, rather than his successor who finished the war, whose name is associated with the savage Roman reprisals in the talmudic tradition. No earlier than in the second half of 133, perhaps not until 134, Rufus was superseded. Severus 'did not venture to attack his opponents in the open, because of their numbers and their desperation', Dio relates. Instead, 'thanks to the number of his own soldiers and officers, by cutting off small groups, by depriving them of their food supplies and shutting them in, he was able to crush, wear out and exterminate them.' It took time, but there was less danger to his own men, Dio adds. As for the Jews,

> very few survived. Fifty of their most important outposts and 985 better known villages were rased to the ground. 585,000 were killed in the various engagements or battles. As for the numbers who perished from starvation, disease or fire, that was impossible to establish.[43]

The decisive stage, not reported by Dio but by Eusebius, and well remembered, although in a very fanciful way, in the talmudic sources, came with a siege of the fortress of Bethar. It was 'a strong citadel', as Eusebius calls it, 6 miles (10 km) south-west of Jerusalem. The siege 'lasted a long time before the rebels were driven to desperation by famine and thirst and the instigator of their madness paid the penalty he deserved.' A story in the rabbinic literature – which makes the siege last three-and-a-half years, perhaps by confusion with the duration of the whole war – has 'Bar Koziba' killing his uncle Rabbi Eleazar on suspicion of treachery. 'Forthwith the sins [of the people] caused Bethar to be captured. Bar Koziba was slain and his head taken to Hadrian . . . "Bring his body to me", he ordered.' It was found with a snake around the neck. 'Hadrian exclaimed: "If his God had not slain him, who could have overcome him?"' No doubt it was Sextus Julius Severus, rather than Hadrian, to whom the dead leader was brought. It was probably in autumn 135, or perhaps early 136.[44]

The fall of Bethar and the death of Shim'on may not have marked the end of all resistance and it was probably months before Severus' men had tracked down all the survivors hiding in their caves. A fragmentary letter surely belongs to this final phase: ' . . . till the end . . . they have no hope . . . my brothers in the south . . . of these were lost by the sword'. Hadrian marked the victory by an imperatorial acclamation, the first time in his reign that he had altered his titulature in this way. From some time in the second half of 135 he began to be *imp. II.* Severus and Publicius Marcellus received the highest military honours, an honorary triumph (*triumphalia ornamenta*), and numerous soldiers up to the rank of centurion received the usual *dona militaria*, awards for valour. Senatorial and equestrian officers, other than the two consular commanders, however, were treated on a less generous scale. Celebration of the victory on the imperial coinage was distinctly muted and indirect in comparison with previous wars.[45]

One official measure is first apparent four years later, after Hadrian's death, but may be ascribed to him. The name of the province was changed: it was no longer to be called Judaea but Syria Palaestina. This may have been intended as a punishment; but the Jewish element in the population had indeed become a minority, it must be assumed. Apart from Dio's figure of more than half a million dead, large numbers were sold into slavery. So many captive Jews were on sale at the Terebinth market at Hebron that they fetched less per head than the price of a horse, a Christian source later related. Others were taken to Gaza and disposed of there or sent to Egypt. Many perished on the way from starvation or shipwreck. There was a further punishment: the Christian writers, with more than a trace of gloating, report how 'Hadrian commanded by legal decree and ordinances that the whole nation should be absolutely debarred from entering even the district around Jerusalem, so that it could not see its ancestral home even from a distance'. Thus Eusebius. The ban on circumcision was not lifted, and the rebuilding of Jerusalem as a pagan city, Aelia Capitolina, was renewed and completed. Jerome adds the detail that 'the statue of Hadrian on horseback stands to this very day on the site of the Holy of Holies' – together with 'an idol of Jupiter', he states elsewhere. He also writes of a temple of Jupiter at the place of the resurrection and Eusebius refers to a shrine of Aphrodite at the site of Jesus' tomb or at the place of the crucifixion. Coins of the *colonia* Aelia suggest that Bacchus, Sarapis and the Dioscuri were also worshipped there. Finally, according to Jerome, outside the gate on the Bethlehem road there was a marble image of a pig: this must have been the emblem of the legion X Fretensis, a wild boar. It is hardly surprising that when Hadrian's name occurs in the rabbinical literature it is generally accompanied by the imprecation, 'May his bones rot!'[46]

If official reaction to the end of the war was muted, on the non-Jewish side at a local level there were some signs of celebration. At a Roman fort south of Scythopolis in Judaea – or, rather, in Syria Palaestina – a massive triumphal arch was erected. A bronze statue of Hadrian, slightly over life size, has been found there, the cuirass decorated with scenes of warfare, three pairs of naked hoplites. The torso may, indeed, have been reused and could once have belonged to a statue of a Hellenistic king – it would have been peculiarly appropriate if the head replaced by that of Hadrian had been that of Antiochus Epiphanes. On a more modest scale, three small pieces of sculpture, two of them from Egypt, depict a bearded warrior and defeated enemy. This may represent that province's reaction. The third piece, a marble statuette which resembles the modest ceramic reliefs from Egypt, shows the bearded *triumphator*, sword in right hand and with his left on the head of an equally bearded kneeling enemy. Was this supposed to show Hadrian and the vanquished Shim'on b. Kos'ba? It could even be that the coins portraying Hadrian as 'king of Egypt' or as Horus, with his foot on a crocodile (see Plate 27), were struck as a gesture to the Egyptians – who perceived the Jews as the evil 'people of Seth', destroyed by Horus.[47]

Before reporting Hadrian's inscription in his new Pantheon at Athens, Pausanias describes Hadrian as, 'in my own day', the one 'who has gone furthest to honour religion and among all sovereigns the one who has done the most for the happiness of his subjects. He never willingly went to war, though when the Jews who live beyond Syria rebelled, he subdued them.' It may be that on the inscription Hadrian explicitly made such a claim to be a Prince of Peace. About seventy years later, the passionate African Christian Tertullian would demand:

Plate 29 Relief perhaps commemorating Hadrian's victory
over the Jews

Quid ergo Athenis et Hierosolymis? 'What has Athens to do with Jerusalem?' Hadrian might have reversed the question, with some bitterness, when his Panhellenic triumph was overtaken by the news of the revolt, or during his stay with the army, or when, back at Rome, he heard the news of the end: 'What has Jerusalem to do with Athens?'[48]

21

THE BITTER END

On 5 May 134 Hadrian wrote a brief, not to say curt, response to a request from one Ulpius Domesticus, delegate of the Athletic Guild of the Athletes devoted to Hercules: 'Yes: I shall order a place to be given to you where you wish and a building to house your records; and if you think it necessary to change your statutes, that is your affair. Farewell. Third before the Nones of May, from Rome.' This is the first clearly dated evidence for Hadrian's whereabouts since he attended the opening of the Olympieion at Athens in the spring of 132. He had come back from the east through Illyricum, as the inscription of his young *comes* Caesernius Quinctianus shows. Which way he travelled through the Balkans and exactly when is a matter of guesswork. It is plausible, at least, that he went through Macedonia and Thrace to the Danube in the early spring of 134, taking the opportunity to inspect the Moesian and Dacian provinces and armies.[1]

Moesia and Dacia and their *exercitus* are represented on the commemorative coinage of these years, but these issues could of course refer back to Hadrian's journey in 118. Coins of Hadrian's *adventus* in Moesia show him being greeted by a sacrificing Moesia in short tunic and cloak, her hair knotted, and carrying a quiver full of arrows. On the *exercitus* coins Hadrian stands, with a lictor, facing four soldiers. In the spring of 134 Moesia Inferior had a new governor, Sextus Julius Major of Tralles, a further example of Greeks taking a full role in the running of the empire. The equivalent coins of the Dacian army are more varied: Hadrian is shown both mounted and standing, with or without a lictor. There was no *adventus* coin for Dacia, but the personified province appears, seated on a rock; she holds a standard in one hand, her curved native sword in the other. Dacia Superior would soon receive a new governor, again a Greek, the son of the great Quadratus Bassus.[2]

No coins recall Hadrian's progress through Pannonia, even though he had been there in 118. But there is an issue that must mean he was in or at least very close to Dalmatia: he is shown addressing the *exercitus Delmaticus*. This is a little surprising. That province, although still governed by a legate of consular rank, had no legions any more and only a modest auxiliary garrison. All the same, a legate of Moesia Superior under Hadrian, Vitrasius Flamininus, is specifically credited with command over the 'Dalmatian army' as well. Perhaps there had been internal disturbances which required military action. As it happens, in the silver-mining area of Dardania, in the west of Moesia Superior close to the border with Dalmatia, the miners erected a temple to 'the Hero Antinous', apparently on Hadrian's orders. It was dedicated in 136 or 137, and might well have been begun at the time when Hadrian – as here postulated – was travelling through the area in the spring of 134. Coins commemorating the mines of Dalmatia and Pannonia, and, it seems, those of Dardania – although the word *metal.* is absent from the legend – were struck at about this time, but do not name Hadrian.[3]

The year 134 had opened with Hadrian's brother-in-law Servianus as consul *ordinarius*, holding office for the third time, at the age of 84. It was a very belated gesture to the old man. Annius Verus was the only other senator to have had the exceptional honour of a third consulship from Hadrian, but he had had it eight years earlier. Servianus' colleague was Vibius Varus, who had probably been governing Cilicia when Hadrian was there in 131. Varus was apparently not the first choice. An inscription giving the consuls of this year had another name as the colleague of Servianus, which was erased. Had someone suddenly fallen out of favour? Or – if this was not simply a provincial's mistake – it might be that the originally designated consul had died at the end of 133. Servianus was now a widower: his wife Paulina, Hadrian's sister, had died, probably in Egypt, in 130. His daughter and son-in-law were, it is assumed, also dead. His grandson, young Fuscus, now about 20, had probably been in Hadrian's retinue.[4]

Coins which presumably date to 134 register Hadrian's return with Fortune the home-bringer and *adventus Augusti*. A ship on coins proclaiming 'imperial felicity' may be taken to refer to his journey. One version of the *adventus* issue shows Hadrian in military dress, mounted and holding a spear, alluding to his participation in the war. Others show him in a toga, greeted by the goddess Roma. Coins which probably also belong to this phase of the reign look like an assertion of confidence: Mars the Avenger and Jupiter Conservator, Roma Victrix and Bonus Eventus – 'successful outcome'.[5]

He had been away for six years. Servianus was probably no longer in office as consul by the time that Hadrian returned and would not have been obliged to welcome him in his official capacity. By April he had been replaced by a suffect consul, Haterius Nepos – who may have been consul in absence, however, in his province of Arabia. It is not likely that a governor in the war zone would have been replaced. Nepos' legion, III Cyrenaica, was actively engaged in the fighting. Whether Hadrian distributed largess to the people to mark his return is not directly attested. Dio merely offers an anecdote which indicates that he attended chariot-races:

> after he had returned to Rome, the crowd at a spectacle shouted out their request for the emancipation of a certain charioteer. He gave his answer by a written proclamation: 'It is not right for you either to ask me to free another's slave or to force his master to do so.'[6]

The redoutable Marcius Turbo was probably still Guard Prefect. Dio describes him as a true man of the people and a veritable workhorse.

> He would spend the entire day near the palace and would often go there even before midnight, when others were going to bed. . . . He was never seen at home in the day-time, even when he was ill; and when Hadrian advised him to stay quiet, he replied: 'A Prefect ought to die standing.'

What Dio renders as 'to stay quiet' may well mean 'to retire'; and Hadrian may not have been entirely happy with Turbo's reply – adapted from a remark of Vespasian's, applied by Vespasian to himself, as emperor.[7]

For the time being Hadrian may have retained Turbo in office. In the end he was to turn against him. The *HA* lists a string of friendships that Hadrian terminated in one way or another. Platorius Nepos, for example, was so confident of his relations with Hadrian – his long association went back at least twenty, perhaps as many as forty years – as to deny him admittance when Hadrian came to visit him on his sickbed. No action was taken against him then. Hadrian had even thought of Nepos as a possible successor, but then, he was 'led on by suspicions', and came to detest him. Elsewhere the biographer lists Nepos along with Attianus and Septicius Clarus, the ill-fated Prefects from the early part of the reign, as one of those closest of friends whom Hadrian ultimately 'regarded in the category of enemy' – having been influenced by 'whatever was whispered about his friends'. Terentius Gentianus, like Nepos supposedly thought of as a potential successor, had received similar treatment some years earlier. There would be others among the Senate. 'He compelled Polyaenus and Marcellus to suicide', the *HA* claims, with no further details. Polyaenus may have been from Bithynian Prusa but is otherwise completely unknown. Marcellus is surely the same as Neratius Marcellus, who had held a second consulship in 129. Two of Hadrian's closest equestrian advisers, Valerius Eudaemon and Avidius Heliodorus, were also the object of his disfavour. Eudaemon was 'reduced to poverty' and Heliodorus 'was provoked by a highly defamatory letter'. Heliodorus was presumably dismissed from his post of *ab epistulis*. But he survived and was evidently restored to favour by 137. Eudaemon had to wait for the next reign. The *HA* does not include in its lists of maltreated friends Favorinus, who, it asserted, was 'conspicuous above the rest' of the various intellectuals that Hadrian treated in friendly fashion. Yet it seems that he was by now languishing in exile, albeit only on the comfortable and civilised island of Chios.[8]

Whether Heliodorus was replaced as *ab epistulis* Graecis is not clear. Hadrian may not have needed a separate Greek secretariat after his return from the east. His last known secretary, in office at the end of the reign, was Caninius Celer, who may have dealt with both Greek and Latin correspondence. There were, to be sure, still plenty of letters coming from the east which required replies. The drainage works in Boeotia that had been going on for a decade were still producing problems. A letter of Hadrian's to Coronea in 135 shows that he had appointed a special commissioner for Achaia, the ex-consul Aemilius Juncus, who was to look into the matter. The newly established Panhellenion probably produced a good many enquiries about membership. Hadrian's reply to one from Cyrene from 135 is preserved. Also in 135 he accepted in a letter to the Milesians honorary office as prophet of the temple of Apollo at Didyma, which he had visited six years before.[9]

Hadrian would certainly have had other correspondence from the province of Asia in 135. The proconsul, Aurelius Fulvus Antoninus, had some exasperating experiences at the hands of the two great orators, Antonius Polemo and Herodes Atticus. When staying at Smyrna Antoninus installed himself in Polemo's mansion, 'because it was the best in Smyrna and belonged to the most notable citizen'. However, Polemo arrived home at night from a journey and raised an outcry at the door: he was being treated disgracefully, shut out of his own house – and he thereupon obliged Antoninus to move to other quarters. Hadrian 'was informed about the incident', Philostratus records, 'but held no enquiry about it, so as not to reopen the wound'. Later on, he would manage to reconcile the arrogant Greek with the mild Roman senator. Antoninus' activities in the north of his province also get mentioned. Herodes Atticus, by now an ex-praetor, had been made 'curator of the free cities' in Asia. He was devoting particular attention to Alexandria Troas. On a narrow road on Mount Ida, Herodes' carriage nearly forced that of Antoninus into the ditch – or perhaps it was the other way round, for Herodes was said to have struck the proconsul. Philostratus played down the incident: 'they did in a way shove each other aside, but this sort of thing happens in rough country on narrow roads.'

Whether Hadrian heard about this encounter is not recorded. There were certainly problems over Herodes' extravagant disbursement of public funds. He had secured Hadrian's approval for 3 million drachmae, or denarii, to improve the water-supply of Alexandria Troas, presumably by building an aqueduct, with himself to supervise the project. He overspent by more than double. When the outlay had reached 7 million, the imperial procurators in the province wrote to Hadrian: it was a scandal that the tribute from 500 cities should be spent on a single city's fountain. Hadrian expressed his disapproval to Herodes' father, who was presumably at Rome. The elder Atticus, 'in the most lordly fashion' told Hadrian he should not concern himself with trifles. He would donate the difference between the sum allocated and what had been spent to his son and Herodes would present the money to the town.[10]

Hadrian himself was still pouring out funds on building, at Rome and at Tibur. The great shrine of Venus and Rome, inaugurated in 121, was nearing completion. It may have been at this time that Hadrian finally fell out with the architect Apollodorus. At any rate, Dio associates the fate of Apollodorus with his criticism of Hadrian's design for the temple. The final straw was when the statues were ready. Apollodorus gave his opinion, in writing, that they were too tall for the *cella*: 'for now, if the goddesses want to stand up and go out, they will be unable to do so.' According to Dio, Hadrian was angry and mortified.

The mistake could not be corrected and, 'restraining neither his anger nor his grief, he killed the man.' No one seems to be able to believe this story. As far as the timing is concerned, it would make sense in about 135 or 136. That Apollodorus was actually executed may be questioned. Presumably he died shortly after writing this letter, and Hadrian was alleged to have had a hand in his death.[11]

Aurelius Victor, in his brief sketch of Hadrian, implies the construction of another important building at this time:

> More favourably disposed to eloquence and intellectual activities after settling matters in the east, Hadrian returned to Rome. Here, in the manner of the Greeks or of Pompilius Numa he began to attend to religious rites, the laws, the gymnasia, and teachers, so much so that he even established a school for the liberal arts, which they call the 'Athenaeum'. He also devoted himself at Rome in the manner of the Athenians to the mysteries of Ceres and Libera, which are called the Eleusinian Mysteries.

Victor himself clearly took the 'return from the east' to be at the start of the reign, but the source he was using probably meant the later return, of 134 – although, it is true, the east was not entirely 'settled' at that point. The location of the Athenaeum has not been established. But it looks as if Hadrian was attempting to give Rome a 'university' building of the kind which he had endowed at Athens. As for the other items stressed by Victor, privileges for teachers had been confirmed at the very outset of the reign and attention to the laws had no doubt been displayed throughout, although Salvius Julianus' revision of the praetor's edict had presumably only recently been completed. 'Religious rites' and gymnasia, likewise, were hardly a recent preoccupation, even if the deification of Antinous and the opening of the Olympieion had resulted in particularly intense activity in both these spheres since 130. It seems likely enough, too, that some kind of imitation of the Mysteries might belong to the time just after his return in 134.[12]

Hadrian was also building himself a last resting-place. The model was no doubt the massive Mausoleum of Augustus on the Campus Martius. There was no room left there, although Nerva's remains had been squeezed in; the Flavians had been buried elsewhere, and Trajan's ashes were placed in the base of his Column. The site Hadrian chose was across the Tiber from the Campus Martius, in the Ager Vaticanus. Work had begun some years earlier on a new bridge to lead to the Mausoleum. This Pons Aelius was completed and opened in 134, presumably by Hadrian in person, soon after his return. (Twelve years before he had ordered the construction of another Pons Aelius, across the distant Tyne, at the east end of his British Wall.) The great tomb was to be at least as large as that of Augustus, a good 160 feet (50 m) high, and the total effect would be more impressive: a circular drum on a square base with a central tower rising out of it. Above all, the impact must have been enhanced by the new bridge, lavishly adorned with statues, which formed a monumental approach.[13]

Plate 30 Hadrian's tomb, now the Castel Sant'Angelo

One further structure at Rome may be mentioned, the nature of which remains uncertain: The eight circular reliefs of hunting scenes known as the Hadrianic *tondi* (see Plates 26 and 31). Now on the Arch of Constantine, where they were reused (with adaptation of Hadrian's head), they have been plausibly argued to derive from a 'hunting monument', probably set up in the private grounds on the Palatine. There is a good case for the view – which has, to be sure, been denied emphatically by some – that they commemorate occasions when Hadrian and Antinous hunted together, for the bear, the wild boar and the lion. The original order of the reliefs is a matter of conjecture, but the opening scene may have been that showing a statue of Apollo, followed by the departure for the hunt. The capture of a boar would have been followed by a sacrifice to Diana, that of a bear by an offering to Silvanus, that of a lion by one to Hercules. If the monument was essentially private, that would explain why the figure identified as Antinous was portrayed not in the idealized form of the god or hero that had already proliferated across the empire, but in more realistic manner. In the lion hunt scene, on this argument, the Emperor's beloved was shown as he actually appeared shortly before his death.[14]

Not far from Rome, at Lanuvium in Latium, a new cult of Antinous and the virgin huntress Diana was being planned. When it was inaugurated, in 136, Antinous was portrayed, in a relief of some artistic merit, as Silvanus, the god of the wild and of huntsmen. The worshippers were members of a society,

Plate 31 Hadrian's boar hunt (*tondo* from a Hadrianic hunting monument, reused in the Arch of Constantine). The youthful figure in the background is clearly identifiable as Antinous. On the right, the mounted Hadrian, whose head has been recut to portray Constantine, strikes the boar

collegium, that guaranteed them proper burial. Significantly, suicides were debarred from this privilege, as if the founders of the cult were aware that talk of Antinous having taken his own life was officially denied.[15]

At Tibur, where Hadrian must have spent a large part of his time, commemoration of Antinous and of Egypt was to be extensive. Statues of Osirantinous, of Osiris-Apis, of Isis and Horus were set up in an elaborate and complex pattern. The long 'Canopus' pool, with a Serapeum at one end, probably already constructed before Hadrian was in Egypt, was now remodelled and given a new significance. While the Serapeum, dominated by two colossal statues of Osiriantinous, symbolized Egypt, so it has been argued, the Canopus now stood for the whole Mediterranean.[16]

285

Plate 32 Relief of the deified Antinous from Lanuvium

The news of the capture of Bethar and the death of Shim'on is thought to have reached Rome in autumn 135. But the end may not have come until early in 136. Hadrian responded by taking the acclamation *imp.II.* The Senate and People evidently expressed their gratitude to the Emperor for 'delivering the republic from the enemy', so a fragmentary inscription at Rome seems to indicate. Although he took the title *imp. II*, it does not appear on the imperial coinage, which nonetheless responded to the ending of the war with various portrayals of the goddess Victoria and with the legend 'virtuti Aug.', the Emperor's martial courage. Coins of Hadrian with his foot on a crocodile (see Plate 27) may, as has been suggested, have been intended to appeal particularly to traditional Egyptian perceptions of the Jews as 'Typhonians', the people of the evil Seth, with Hadrian as the beneficent Horus. Other explanations have been canvassed.[17]

Egypt had been causing concern. In two successive years the flood had been inadequate. There was hardship in the province. Hadrian was asked to take action and on 31 May 136 his edict was published at Alexandria. He had learned that once again, as in the year before, the rise of the Nile had fallen short or amounted to nothing – 'even though in the previous years the Nile achieved not only its full rise but the greater rise which was almost unprecedented and, since it reached the entire country, caused the land to bring forth very plentiful and splendid crops.' He was specifically referring here to the unusually favourable flooding in the years immediately after Antinous' drowning. Now he offered tax concessions, while expecting – 'be it said with the permission of the god' – that the Nile itself and the earth would compensate.[18]

Just after the end of the Jewish war, the empire was lucky to avoid another major outbreak in the east. Dio reported:

> A second war was begun by the Alani at the instigation of Pharasmanes. It inflicted serious damage on the territory of the Albani and Media, and then involved Armenia and Cappadocia. But when the Alani were persuaded by gifts from Vologaeses and were deterred by Flavius Arrianus, the governor of Cappadocia, it came to an end.

The Alani, a people or confederation in Transaucasia, beyond Pharasmanes' Iberian kingdom (Georgia), were closely related to the Sarmatians. Alan influence in Iberia was strong and Pharasmanes would have had no difficulty in stirring them up to create trouble and weaken the neighbours – Armenia and Albania – with whom he had bad relations. The Parthian king Vologaeses III, already in trouble from a rival, Mithridates, had to resort to Danegeld to get rid of the invaders. As Pharasmanes was supposedly a Roman client, the Parthian king sent envoys to Rome to complain. Their arrival is reported by Dio together with that of other foreign ambassadors, from the Jazyges of the Hungarian plain, who 'wished to confirm the peace'. Hadrian 'introduced them to the Senate and was empowered by it to return suitable replies, which he composed and read out to them.'[19]

Arrian's 'deterrence' is illuminated in detail by his own description of his 'Order of battle against the Alani', the *Acies contra Alanos*. The work survives only as a fragment, which is clearly from a literary reworking in Greek of an official Latin report to Hadrian. It is nonetheless a priceless record of the Roman army in action. Arrian took with him the legion XV Apollinaris from the northern base at Satala, under its legate Vettius Valens, but only a detachment from XII Fulminata further south. Six of his auxiliary regiments also sent detachments only. The emphasis was on cavalry, not least mounted archers: four cavalry regiments, *alae*, and the troopers from ten *cohortes equitatae*, grouped together, as well as the governor's horse guards and the legionary cavalry. A levy from the provincial militia of Armenia Minor and Trapezus supplemented the force. At all events, Arrian's show of force did the trick. Two-and-a-half centuries later the orator Themistius claimed that Arrian expelled the Alani from Armenia, crossed the Caspian Gates and set in order the frontier between Iberia and Albania. Arrian wrote a work on the Alani, from which the fragment doubtless derives. Themistius could well have had his information from the *Alanica*. The threat had been averted. There may have been a significant reinforcement of the Cappadocian army in the sequel. At any rate, twenty-five years later there was apparently a third legion in the province, at Elegia. Perhaps IX Hispana was moved there when the Jewish war ended.[20]

Arrian's success received no official commemoration, so far as is known. 'Wars were conducted almost without a mention' (*silentio*), as the *HA* comments. The imperial coinage had other landmarks to celebrate in 136. Coin legends such as 'To Eternal Rome' and 'To Venus the Fortunate' make it clear that the great temple, if not quite finished in every particular, was nonetheless dedicated in these years, in 136 or 137. Meanwhile an anniversary was approaching: in August 136 Hadrian would enter the twentieth year of his reign. The coins announce the taking of 'public vows' to the gods, *vota publica*, undoubtedly in connection with Hadrian's *vicennalia*. At an appropriate moment Hadrian must have distributed largess – indeed, coins from his last years refer to his 'sixth' and his 'seventh *liberalitas*', the former probably going with his anniversary. He was the first emperor since Tiberius just over a century earlier to have been able to celebrate a reign of twenty years.[21]

Arrian did his bit to mark the *vicennalia* by composing another work, his *Tactica*. It was probably dedicated to Hadrian. The opening lines where this would have been stated are missing, but, after the long section on Hellenistic tactics – heavily indebted to Aelian's work published a generation earlier – he describes this first part as 'written on behalf of the Emperor himself', before concluding with a section on Roman tactics. Further, the final remarks make clear that the author was writing for Hadrian.

> These then are the exercises of the Roman cavalry and those handed on from antiquity. The Emperor, indeed, has made the innovation of getting them to practise barbarian techniques [he refers to those of the Parthians,

288

Armenians, Sarmatians and Celts]. There are no obsolete practices that have not been revived and are now practised by the Romans, as well as those devised by the Emperor with a view to beauty, speed, the inspiring of terror and practical use. Thus, in our present empire, which Hadrian is now ruling in his twentieth year, it seems to me that these lines apply far better now than they did to the ancient Lacedaemonians:

There the spear of the young men flourishes and the sweet-voiced Muse
And Justice with her wide streets, the mainstay of fine deeds.

A poet – Terpander – whose verses had inspired the Spartans 900 years earlier would certainly have been to Hadrian's liking.[22]

Hadrian 'now began to be ill', Dio reports, in a passage that must refer to the year 136, 'for he had already been subject to nose-bleeds before this and at this time the condition became very much worse.' His behaviour in Egypt suggests that he was already concerned about his health then – even, Dio and Victor claim, to the extent of being prepared to let Antinous sacrifice himself. The text on the obelisk with Osirantinous' prayer to Re-Harachte, that Hadrian 'may live for ever like Re, with a fresh and rejuvenated age', hints that, in the immediate aftermath, Hadrian thought his health had been restored. Now, or at any rate some time after his return, coins were struck with a most peculiar portrait. They show Hadrian as a clean-shaven youth, without moustache or beard, merely with long side-whiskers. The portrayal is matched by a portrait-bust found at Tibur. He is made to look the same age that Antinous had been at his death, about twenty, three times younger than he really was – he was sixty on 24 January 136. Was he trying to convince the world – and himself – that he had been reborn or rejuvenated? A less bizarre interpretation of the portrayal might be inferred from the reverse of this coin issue, which honours Hadrian's adoptive parents. Perhaps he was merely pretending that he had already been treated as the son of Trajan and Plotina when he was only twenty. As it was, his adoption, by the dying Trajan, was thought by many to have been fraudulent.[23]

Be this as it may, he must have recognised in the course of 136 that he was not going to survive much longer. It was time to name a successor and give him the necessary powers. In the second half of 136 he suddenly announced that he was adopting as his son one of the consuls of that year, L. Ceionius Commodus. According to the *HA*, Commodus' sole recommendation was his 'beauty'. Some believed that Hadrian had bound himself to Commodus by a secret oath; when, and for what reason, is not recorded. The decision has also been seen as a belated making of amends for the killing of Avidius Nigrinus in 118. Nigrinus had been Commodus' stepfather – and his daughter, furthermore, was married to Commodus. A modern scholar has even attempted to prove that Commodus was really Hadrian's bastard son. The truth may well lie elsewhere. The chosen successor, who had now become Lucius Aelius Caesar, was tubercular. As Dio puts it, Hadrian 'appointed Lucius Commodus as Caesar for the Romans even though he frequently coughed up blood'. In fact, he was too ill to appear in the

Plate 33 Hadrian's first heir, L. Aelius Caesar
(*BMC* III Hadrian no. 1921)

Senate to thank Hadrian for the adoption. Hadrian cannot have imagined that this successor would reign for long, even though he was only in his thirties. The Caesar had a son of his own, to be sure, but he was only five years old, too young to succeed in his turn unless the next reign lasted well over ten years. But there were also daughters; and one of them, Ceionia Fabia, was already betrothed, 'at Hadrian's wish', to a favourite of Hadrian's, his 'Verissimus', the young Marcus Annius Verus, then in his fifteenth year. Marcus was 15 in April 136, at which time he had been honorary Prefect of the City during the Alban festival. No doubt he was appointed by his future father-in-law, for it was the consuls who nominated this Prefect. It is plausible to suppose that Hadrian already envisaged Marcus as the successor to his Caesar, whose role would be to keep the throne warm for a few years. The choice of this man would, at the same time, it might be thought, conciliate influential elements in the Senate.[24]

The adoption was celebrated publicly with shows in the Circus Maximus and a distribution of bounty to plebs and soldiers. Lucius was designated to be consul again, for 137, and received the tribunician power. Hadrian determined that he should go to the armies. He was sent to the Danube, to Carnuntum, with proconsular power over the two Pannonian provinces. Although the Jazyges had recently shown themselves to be submissive, by asking for their treaty to be confirmed, their northern neighbours, the Suebian German Quadi, were restive. Aelius Caesar was given a suitable staff, including, as quaestor, an adopted son of Marcius Turbo, while his own freedman Nicomedes now became his chamberlain, *a cubiculo*. A Prefect of cavalry in the Pannonian army, Domitius Rogatus, became the Caesar's own *ab epistulis*. The legate of one of the Pannonian legions, Claudius Maximus, took over much of the administrative work, with the special appointment as *iuridicus*. The province Pannonia, which had not been included on the commemorative coinage, could now be shown on issues of the Caesar, which otherwise mainly focus on abstract personifications:

concord, good fortune and hope. There may have been concord between Hadrian and his Caesar, but 'everyone [else] was against' the choice, the *HA* says. None more so than old Servianus – and his grandson Fuscus, Hadrian's grand-nephew, who undoubtedly felt cheated of his birthright.[25]

In the course of 137 young Fuscus, whose twenty-fourth birthday fell on 6 April, seems to have made a move. The evidence comes from a group of three horoscopes, compiled by one Antigonus of Nicaea, which includes that of Hadrian himself. Another, which can only refer to Fuscus, although he is not named, gives data establishing his birth on that day in 113, with further details of his origin and his end.

> He was of most eminent and illustrious birth on both his father's and his mother's side . . . he was brought up with great expectations and was already looking forward to acceding to the imperial power. Through ill counsel, he came to grief at the age of about twenty-five, and, being denounced to the Emperor he was destroyed along with an old man of his family (who was falsely accused because of him) . . . he was given to passion and fond of gladiators.

A passage in Hadrian's own horoscope can be taken to mean that he nearly met his end when aged sixty-one years and ten months, in other words, in November 137. Perhaps this was when Fuscus attempted a *coup*. The deaths of Fuscus and 'the old man of his family', who must be his grandfather Servianus, are of course reported by Dio and the *HA*. Dio evidently made a slip over Fuscus' age, which he gives as eighteen. 'Servianus and his grandson Fuscus . . . were put to death on the grounds that they were displeased [at the adoption of L. Commodus]', Dio writes. The *HA* refers four times to the death of Servianus, mentioning Fuscus only on the second occasion, without further explanation: Hadrian, 'having become anxious about a successor, at first thought of Servianus, whom he subsequently compelled to die . . . Fuscus he held in the greatest abhorrence, on the grounds that he had been aroused by prophecies and presentiments to hope for the imperial rule.'[26]

Fuscus' end is, indeed, not specifically mentioned by the *HA*, but the statement of Dio, combined with the horoscope, makes it clear that he was put to death. Servianus, the *HA* maintains, was forced to suicide, 'to prevent him surviving' Hadrian, 'although he was in his ninetieth year', the first version has it, repeated later in the last of the four mentions as 'so that he would not outlive him and become emperor'. In the third and longest passage, Servianus' death is placed not long before Hadrian's own, and the stated reasons are 'because he had provided a banquet for the imperial slaves, because he had sat on an imperial chair, placed next to his bed, because, though in his ninetieth year, he had stood up to meet the soldiers on guard-duty.' Dio, even if he is wrong in detail, reports a surely authentic story about Servianus' last moments: 'he asked for fire, and, as he offered incense, cried out: "That I am guilty of no wrong, you gods are well aware. As for Hadrian, this is my only prayer: may he long for death but be unable to die.'" It may be that Servianus was not forced to take his life in the immediate aftermath of the suppression of Fuscus. Whatever the precise timing, the whole business was deeply disturbing: Hadrian's grand-nephew had been executed for allegedly planning a coup, his brother-in-law had been ordered to take his own life. After its most detailed version of the end of Servianus, the *HA* claims that 'many others were put to death at this time, either openly or by craft.' No names are supplied. Perhaps this was when Polyaenus and Marcellus took their own lives, supposedly compelled by Hadrian to do so.[27]

The need to settle the succession, combined with Hadrian's desperate physical state, had made it impossible for him to undertake any more overseas travel. Otherwise, surely, he would have wished to go to Athens yet again, for the first Panhellenic festival of the new Commonwealth in 137. He had certainly been occupied with the Panhellenion throughout the past few years. A letter of his of 135 is preserved on stone at Cyrene. He had had an enquiry, no doubt one of many, from the president (archon) of the new body, conerning the application to join by Ptolemais-Barca in the Cyrenaica. Barca had been founded in the sixth century BC following a rift in the royal house of Cyrene. Its original population had been largely native Libyan, and relations with Cyrene long remained hostile. The Ptolemaic creation of a harbour town for Barca, Ptolemais (Tolmeita), meant that the double community became more Hellenic. Now, hundreds of years on, their application for membership was granted, but with only one delegate. Cyrene, whose people were 'of true Achaian and perfectly Dorian ancestry', Hadrian pronounced, got two.

One may conjecture that Hadrian's Greek Secretary (*ab epistulis Graecis*), Caninius Celer, dealt with this and similar letters. Celer may have been a man from the Roman *colonia* Corinth; if so, he would be particularly well equipped for Panhellenic correspondence. The Panhellenion was, after all, if in its nature Hellenic, nonetheless the creation of a Roman emperor, and the cult of the god-emperor was to play an essential part in its activities. The president to whom Hadrian sent his decision about Barca is not named in the Cyrene inscription. It has sometimes been assumed that it was Herodes Atticus, who certainly was archon of the Hellenic commonwealth at some point. But Philostratus, who reports this, does not give a date. More likely to have been the first president is a by then elderly man from Epidaurus, who was also active at Corinth where he held office in the *colonia* as Helladarch – chairman of the *koinon* of the Achaians – and as a high-ranking equestrian official, Cn. Cornelius Pulcher. Plutarch had long ago dedicated to Pulcher an essay on 'How to profit from one's enemies', and he was also known to Epictetus. Now the old man had to preside over the inaugural festival, but without Hadrian.[28]

In the winter of 137 Aelius Caesar returned to Rome. He was to deliver an important speech in the Senate on 1 January 138. But the night before he fell ill. The medicine that he was given made his condition worse and he died, from a haemorrhage, before the Senate could meet. Hadrian 'forbade public

Plate 34 Sabina deified (Museo del Palazzo dei Conservatori, Rome).
The heads of Hadrian and the attendant are restored
(also Hadrian's right arm and the masonry with flames)

293

mourning, which would have prevented the taking of the New Year vows.' His plans for the succession were now in pieces, and a new heir had to be found. The dead Caesar was not deified. There was probably need for another deification already. Just before Aelius Caesar's death, it seems, Sabina expired. She had still been alive after the adoption of the Caesar and two inscriptions from African Mactaris seem to show her still living in December 137. At all events, she predeceased Hadrian and was consecrated by him, in a ceremony which evidently took place no earlier than March 138. The event was registered on the imperial coinage and a splendid relief survives showing Sabina being carried heavenward, while a gloomy looking Hadrian sits looking up at her, his index finger pointing to the new deity. Not surprisingly, given that their relations had been known to have been bad for years, Hadrian was rumoured to have poisoned her.[29]

The observant or superstitious claimed later that they saw signs of Hadrian's own imminent end early in 138. On 23 January, the day before his birthday, someone came into the Senate wailing. The Emperor was visibly disturbed. He appeared to start talking about his own death, but his words were unintelligible. Then he made a slip of the tongue: he meant to say, 'after my son's death' but instead said 'after my death'. He had disquieting dreams – that he had asked his father, dead fifty years and more, for a sleeping draught; and that he had been overcome by a lion. The second dream suggests that his thoughts were still with Antinous and the lion-hunt in the Libyan desert.[30]

On his sixty-second birthday, 24 January, he ended the speculation. He was by now 'consumptive as a result of serious haemorrhaging, and this had led to dropsy.' He 'summoned the most eminent and respected senators to his sickbed. Lying on his couch, he made a speech' in which he made a virtue of necessity, praising the superiority of an adoptive son over a natural son – who might be mentally defective or a cripple; adoption allowed the best to be chosen. He said, according to Dio's (probably imaginary) version:

> But since heaven has taken [Lucius] from me, I have found as emperor for you in his place the man I now give you, one who is noble, mild, compassionate and prudent. He is neither young enough to do anything rash nor old enough to be neglectful. He has exercised authority in accordance with our ancestral customs, so that he is not ignorant of any matters which concern the imperial power, but can deal with them all. I am speaking of Aurelius Antoninus here. I know that he is not in the least inclined to be involved in affairs and is far from desiring such power, but still, I do not think that he will deliberately disregard either me or you, but will accept the rule, even against his will.

Antoninus did not in fact accept immediately, as the *HA* makes clear. He 'was given time to consider whether he wished to go through with it.' The ceremony of adoption took place four weeks later, on 25 February. The new heir now became Imp. T. Aelius Caesar Antoninus – *Imp(erator)* before his name shows

Plate 35 Hadrian's second heir, T. Aelius Aurelius Antoninus Caesar, AD 138
(*BMC* III Hadrian no. 1017)

that his powers were somewhat enhanced in comparison with those of L. Aelius
Caesar. He also received the tribunician power and was designated to a second
consulship, for 139. Further, he retained his name Antoninus – and his own
'Aurelius' would soon relegate to the background the 'Aelius' he had taken from
Hadrian.[31]

Antoninus was fifty-one years old, the grandson of two men who had come
to the fore in AD 69, the Year of the Four Emperors, Aurelius Fulvus and Arrius
Antoninus. Fulvus, the paternal grandfather, came from Gallic Nemausus. The
new Caesar was extremely rich and a thrifty and conscientious landlord, he was
cultured and a good speaker. His mild nature had been demonstrated in his
recent proconsulship of Asia. This year of office had been, in fact, his only
experience of the provinces – he had had no military service whatever. That was
obviously not a disadvantage in Hadrian's eyes: he wanted a man of peace.
But that other considerations were also important was demonstrated by the
condition attached to it. Antoninus in his turn was to adopt both the son of
Aelius Caesar, also called Commodus, and the young man who was betrothed
to Aelius Caesar's daughter Ceionia Fabia, Marcus Annius Verus – who was
also the nephew of Antoninus' wife Faustina. These two would now be called
L. Aurelius Commodus and M. Aurelius Verus.[32]

It is difficult to avoid the conclusion that Hadrian's real choice all along was
the young Marcus, 'Verissimus', still too young in the years 136–8 to be named
as Emperor himself. First Aelius Caesar and then Antoninus were to be place-
holders for him; both were already linked by family ties, Aelius as father-in-law
to be and Antoninus as uncle by marriage. Some support for this interpretation
may be found in what followed the choice of Antoninus. Two senior figures who
fell into disfavour at this time, Ummidius Quadratus and Catilius Severus, were
also related to Marcus, and may have seen themselves as better fitted for the role

given to Antoninus. Both men had rather more experience of government and armies than he had. What happened to them may not have been too extreme, although Hadrian is said to have 'harshly assailed' them (*insecutus*). Catilius was removed from office as City Prefect, 'for having designs on the imperial power'. There is also the mysterious case of Atilius Titianus, who had been consul *ordinarius* in 127: Hadrian is said to have 'permitted Titianus to be accused and convicted of a plot to seize power, and to be proscribed.' This case may really belong to the next reign, unless the trial began under Hadrian and the conviction and proscription was delayed, for Titianus is said to have been proscribed – by the Senate – under Antoninus.[33]

It was in 138 at the latest that the faithful Marcius Turbo was finally removed – he is linked with Quadratus and Catilius as one whom Hadrian 'assailed'. Two successors as Guard Prefects, Gavius Maximus and Petronius Mamertinus, were evidently appointed. Mamertinus was an obvious choice: he had just completed a term as Prefect of Egypt – where he had been replaced in 137 by Avidius Heliodorus, now restored to favour. Gavius seems to have been rather junior in comparison – only a few years earlier he had got no further than the procurator-ship of Mauretania Tingitana. But he was to acquire a reputation for 'very great strictness' and was highly thought of by Antoninus. Given that there would soon be a change of regime, it was clearly imperative to ensure stability in the provinces, and a firm and loyal hand in the army commands. Some names are known. Sextus Julius Severus had stayed on in the east, moving from Syria Palaestina to Syria. He may have died in office. At the end of Hadrian's reign there was something of a crisis in that province. Two or three senior consulars appear to have governed Syria in rapid succession. One was Julius Major, whose appointment was normal enough, given that he had been legate of Moesia Inferior from 134 onwards. The other known name, Bruttius Praesens, consul as much as twenty years earlier, is surprising. But he was clearly a close and trusted friend of Hadrian. Elsewhere there are some telling names. Pannonia Superior had been taken over by Haterius Nepos, a long-standing favourite of Hadrian who had not incurred his displeasure. Lollius Urbicus, who had been chief of staff to Severus in the Jewish war, governed Germania Inferior when the war was over and was appointed thereafter to Britain, perhaps by Hadrian – a standard promotion.[34]

The main consideration now, though, was stability at the centre. Hadrian's measures had guaranteed the future of the imperial position for the next two reigns. The 'two tier' adoption of 138 is, indeed, reminiscent of Augustus' plans – first, Tiberius as place-holder for Gaius and Lucius, a role Tiberius rejected, then, in AD 4, the adoption of Tiberius, who himself had to adopt Germanicus as joint second-stage heir with his own son Drusus. Hadrian, who had played the role of a 'new Augustus' for the past fifteen years, is likely enough to have been emulating the first Princeps in this sphere too. He surely knew the letter Augustus wrote on his sixty-third birthday to Gaius Caesar: he expressed great relief at passing this landmark – the 'grand climacteric' of the sixty-third year was thought to be especially perilous. Hadrian, 62 in January, was by now probably convinced that he would not reach his next birthday. After all, he was a practised astrologer and knew his own future down to the smallest detail. But the relentless progress of his illness would have made this obvious without recourse to the science of the stars.[35]

His health was now dire. He had had a particularly serious haemorrhage at Tibur shortly before forcing Servianus to die. In spite of his recourse to 'certain charms and magic rites which relieved his dropsy for a time . . . he soon filled up with water again', so Dio reports. 'As he was in fact continuously getting worse and could be said to have been dying day by day, he began to long for death. Often he asked for poison or a sword, but no one would give them to him.' The curse of Servianus was having its effect. No one dared to obey, Dio's account proceeds, 'although he promised money and immunity.' Even his Jazygian huntsman Mastor failed him. By threats and promises Hadrian got him to agree to strike the blow and drew a coloured line below his nipple, at the spot shown him by his doctor Hermogenes. But Mastor became too frightened to carry it through. Hadrian 'bitterly lamented the state to which his illness and his helplessness had reduced him – notwithstanding that it was still in his power, even when on the brink of death, to destroy anyone else.'[36]

The *HA* reports the aftermath of the bungled attempt using Mastor (whom it does not name).

Antoninus and the Prefects went in to Hadrian and begged him to endure the necessity of the disease with equanimity. Antoninus told him that he would be a parricide if, after being adopted, he allowed him to be killed. Hadrian was angry and ordered the person who had informed them to be killed – he was, however, saved by Antoninus. He at once wrote his will. But he did not lay aside the business of state . . . He did in fact try to kill himself again; when the dagger was taken from him he became more violent. He asked his doctor for poison, who killed himself rather than comply.

The tombstone of the imperial physician, Marcius Hermogenes, has been found at Rome. Two curious episodes follow in the *HA*, citing Marius Maximus as the source.

A woman appeared who said she had been warned by a dream to recommend Hadrian not to kill himself, for he would regain his health. She had gone blind for failing to do this, but the command had been repeated with the instruction to kiss Hadrian's knees, which would restore her sight.

After she had fulfilled the dream command and returned to the sanctuary – presumably she had been taking a 'dream cure' – and washed her eyes, her sight came back. Further, a blind old man from Pannonia came and touched Hadrian and likewise recovered his sight – and Hadrian's fever left him for a while.

Plate 36 Hadrian: the last portrait (Museo Vaticano, Rome), found in the imperial villa at Tivoli

Marius Maximus regarded both persons as spurious. Hadrian then made for the seaside, at Baiae, leaving Antoninus in charge at Rome.[37]

In this last phase Hadrian wrote an autobiography, from which Cassius Dio and the *HA* both quote. That it was written late on is shown by the denial, quoted by Dio, that Antinous' death was other than an accidental drowning. It also included an apologia for the death of the four consulars in 118. But it was a full account of his life, for example asserting the ultimate origin of the Spanish Aelii from Hadria in Picenum. Hadrian also claimed that he had had to drink heavily during the first Dacian war to accommodate himself to Trajan's habits. There were also omens, such as a story about losing his cloak when tribune of the plebs. It was perhaps also in the autobiography that Dio found a remarkable statement: Hadrian insisted that Vespasian had been poisoned by Titus. The *HA* has a peculiar story about the autobiography. Hadrian, it claims, was

> so eager for widespread fame that he entrusted some books that he had written about his own life to his educated freedmen, instructing them to publish them under their names – indeed, Phlegon's books are also said to have really been written by Hadrian.

If this was the case with the autobiography, the deception did not last long. As for Phlegon's works, it seems improbable that the Emperor had actually composed them. He may, to be sure, have played some part in directing Phlegon's researches.[38]

There is a more plausible suggestion about the autobiography. By some chance, part of a copy of a letter Hadrian wrote to Antoninus at this time has been preserved on a papyrus from the Fayum. It shows that he was trying to put up a front of being calm and resigned to his fate, and that he was embarrassed by his bungled suicide attempts.

> Above all I want you to know that I am being released from life neither prematurely nor unreasonably; I am not full of self-pity nor am I surprised and my faculties are unimpaired – even though I may almost appear, as I have realised, to do injury to you when you are at my side, whenever I am in need of attendance, consoling me and encouraging me to rest. This is why I am impelled to write to you, not – by Zeus – as one who subtly devises a tedious account contrary to the truth, but rather making a simple and accurate record of the facts themselves.

After this preamble, all that remains of the fragment is a remark about his real parents: 'He who was my father by birth fell ill and died as a private citizen in his fortieth year, so that I have lived half as long again as he did, and have reached nearly the same age as that of my mother.' It has been convincingly argued that the letter to Antoninus is in fact precisely the autobiography, couched in epistolary form, a practice for which there was good precedent.[39]

That he was thinking in these weeks about his real father, dead over fifty years before, as the letter to Antoninus attests, is confirmed by his dream, reported by the *HA*, that he asked his father for a sleeping potion. During his last days or weeks he composed a little poem which may show that he had at least half-way recovered his equilibrium. It is an address to his 'little soul', his companion that must now depart to the cold and gloomy underworld. The language is – surely deliberately – ambiguous and allusive, with the influence of the old Roman poet, Ennius, whom Hadrian preferred to Virgil, unmistakable. At the very end, the calm had again been shattered, if Dio can be believed: 'Finally he abandoned his careful regimen and by indulging in unsuitable food and drink met his death, shouting aloud the popular saying: "Many doctors have killed a king!"'[40]

Antoninus had been summoned to Baiae and Hadrian passed away there in his presence on 10 July 138. He was initially buried at Cicero's old villa at Puteoli, the *HA* reports, *invisus omnibus*. The phrase has two meanings – either 'unseen by all' or 'hated by all'. The interment probably was largely private, unseen. But the *HA*, or its source Marius Maximus, surely meant that Hadrian was universally loathed when he died. Dio at any rate understood it this way: 'Hadrian was hated by the people, in spite of his generally excellent rule, on account of the murders he committed at the beginning and the end of the reign, for they were unjust and impious.'[41]

EPILOGUE
ANIMULA VAGULA BLANDULA

> *animula vagula blandula,*
> *hospes comesque corporis,*
> *quo nunc abibis? in loca*
> *pallidula rigida nubila –*
> *nec ut soles dabis iocos.*

Few short poems can have generated so many verse translations and such copious academic debate as these five lines – a mere nineteen words – of the dying Hadrian, quoted in the *Historia Augusta*. Even their authenticity has been questioned. But that, at least, seems to have been settled, with the observation that the quality is evidently 'beyond the powers of the author of the *HA*'. There is also dispute over the meaning: in particular, whether the adjectives in the fourth line go with the *animula* or with the *loca*, and how the third line should be punctuated. The text here given depends on a variant reading of the third line and incorporates a conjecture, *nubila* for *nudula*, in the fourth. This produces the following sense:

> Little soul, little wanderer, little charmer,
> body's guest and companion,
> to what places will you set out for now?
> To darkling, cold and gloomy ones –
> and you won't make your usual jokes.

It seems only fitting that the great traveller, who had so often accepted hospitality and who had taken a train of *comites* with him, should at the last have thought of his soul as a wanderer, ready to take off, this time for the underworld, his soul that had been his body's *hospes* and *comes*. The key to understanding Hadrian's view of his soul's destination came when an echo was detected of Ennius' lines on the realms of the dead, the 'Acherunsia templa alta Orci', 'the lofty temples of Orcus by the river of Acheron', 'pallida leto, nubila tenebris loca', 'places deathly pale, gloomy in their darkness'. Ennius was, after all, a favourite poet of Hadrian's. The third and fourth lines, so punctuated, form question and response.[1]

301

Hadrian's character was baffling and contradictory: 'in one and the same person stern and cheerful, affable and harsh, impetuous and hesitant, mean and generous, hypocritical and straightforward, cruel and merciful, and always in all things changeable'. So the *HA* – and the *Epitome de Caesaribus* has a similar version, clearly drawn from the same source, the biographer Marius Maximus.[2] Hadrian's portraits scarcely offer a clue to his inner being: they 'show no aging or development. In what sense can one speak of his real nature? . . . Was he one of those characters that remain to some extent consistent or was his character what he did or what happened to him?' This was the verdict of a specialist on Hadrian's iconography.[3]

As for Hadrian's innermost beliefs, here too one is on uncertain ground: 'those who endeavour to reconstruct Hadrian's religion directly from his own statements, scant as they are, arrive at diametrically opposite results.'[4] His initiation at Eleusis – and the *cistophorus* coin with the legend *ren(atus)*, 'reborn', which was issued soon after he entered the higher grade – might speak for some kind of mysticism. His adventure with the Egyptian wonderworker Pachrates, the death of Antinous and its aftermath, and the strange coin-issue depicting him as a twenty-year old, point in an even more disturbing direction. In truth, his real religion had perhaps been Hellenism (beard and all), but at the last, his dying poem may suggest, he returned to a sceptical, almost Epicurean position, influenced by the old poet.[5]

The symptoms of his fatal illness – haemorrhaging, breathing difficulties, wasting and dropsy – combined with what is known of his character and behaviour, allow an easy diagnosis: coronary atherosclerotic heart disease.[6] If his portraits for the most part show no signs of change, of one at least, the latest, it has been said that it is 'not so much the depiction of an old man, rather it shows the effect of a catastrophe'[7] – by which one may understand the cumulation of blow after blow in his last years, Antinous' death, the Jewish revolt, the succession crisis.

Plate 37 Hadrian rejuvenated? (*BMC* III Hadrian no. 603)

Hadrian's favourite Marcus, when he reflected over thirty years later on those to whom he had a debt of gratitude, totally omits the man to whom he owed the throne.[8] Fronto, Marcus' teacher, in an early letter to his pupil, conceded that he had praised Hadrian often enough in speeches in the senate, *inpenso et propenso quoque*, 'earnestly – and willingly too'. Yet 'I wanted to propitiate Hadrian, like Mars Gradivus or Jupiter, rather than loved him . . . I lacked the confidence – him whom I so greatly revered I did not dare to cherish.' He was later to wax sarcastic on Hadrian's travels, 'a *princeps* energetic enough at touring the armies and haranguing them eloquently', monuments to whose journeys can be seen in many cities of Europe and Asia – but who preferred to abandon what Trajan had conquered and to train the troops with wicker weapons instead of setting them to fight with shield and sword.[9]

Six years after Hadrian's death Aelius Aristides, the young orator from Hadriani, one of the cities founded by Hadrian a decade or so earlier in Mysia, came to the capital and delivered a festive speech 'In praise of Rome'. Much of the piece can be taken as a tribute to Hadrian's work, not least the claim that the whole world was now like one single city-state and that war was a thing of the past. The empire's constitution embodied the best elements of democracy, aristocracy, oligarchy and monarchy. Its greatest 'work of perfection' was the army: in method of recruitment, conditions of service, deployment, training and discipline. In one particular respect the orator offered implied criticism of Antoninus' restless predecessor. The smooth functioning of the vast world-state could be seen in the regular succession of governors for its peoples. Their orderly conduct was ensured by their overwhelming respect for 'the great governor, for him who presided over all'. There was 'no need for him to wear himself out travelling round the whole empire, nor now in one place now in another to check on every detail in person'. This was an unmistakable contrast between the placid Antoninus – who was never to leave Italy throughout his reign – and the perpetually travelling Hadrian. The same point had already been made by Aristides in his mockery of the Persian King Cyrus, who had been obliged to wander all round his domains in perpetual motion.[10]

Nearly one hundred years after Hadrian's death, Cassius Dio, in spite of his criticisms, summed up the reign as having been 'in general excellent'. Among the positive aspects which he had earlier praised, the 'training and disciplining of the entire army throughout the whole empire' are emphasised: 'What he laid down is still the basis for military regulations today.' The author of the *Epitome de Caesaribus*, writing at the end of the fourth century, goes further: 'He established the public and palace appointments (*officia*), and those of the military, on that model, which – with a few changes made by Constantine – still exists today.' This judgement is clearly exaggerated. Hadrian's 'army reforms' were of limited scope. To be sure, he laid great stress on training and discipline, and it may be that this is what Dio and the author of the *Epitome* had in mind. There is also some evidence for him making concessions to soldiers in the legal sphere. Some tightening up of the issuing of the so-called diplomas, mainly to auxiliary

303

veterans, can be detected: the home town of the veteran's commanding officer is specified from about 129 onwards, and a few years later the order of the seven witnesses for each diploma was regularised. One small innovation seems to be that he regraded the prefecture of the *ala milliaria* as a 'fourth *militia*'.[11]

Other things aside, Hadrian's revision of imperial foreign policy and his establishment of fixed frontiers had a corollary. It became increasingly seldom for legions to be transferred from one province to another. The armies began to settle down in their bases even more than they had before, with, no doubt, effects on recruitment, which must have become more localised. Whether Hadrian's frontier policy was really an innovation has been disputed. But the symbolic effect of constructing even the palisade beyond Upper Rhine and Upper Danube and the *fossatum Africae*, let alone the elaborate and expensive set of works known as 'Hadrian's Wall' is undeniable. Only the *HA*, it is curious, specifically refers to these frontier works in connection with Hadrian. But Aelius Aristides had some lofty allusions to them six years after Hadrian's death.

> To place walls round the city itself as if you were hiding or fleeing from your subjects you considered ignoble. Nevertheless, you did not forget walls, but these you placed around the empire, not the city . . . Beyond the outermost ring of the civilised world, you drew a second line . . . An encamped army like a rampart encloses the world in a ring . . . as far as from Ethiopia to the Phasis and from the Euphrates to the great outermost island towards the West; all this one can call a ring and circuit of the walls. They have not been built with asphalt and baked brick, nor do they stand there gleaming with stucco. Oh – but these ordinary works too exist at their individual places, 'fitted close and accurately with stones and boundless in size and gleaming more brilliantly than bronze', as Homer says of the palace wall.

Ironically, just at the time Aristides delivered these sentiments, work was in full swing on a new frontier work in Britain, more modest in its construction: Hadrian's Wall had been abandoned, southern Scotland reoccupied and the Antonine Wall between Forth and Clyde erected. It is difficult not to see the decision as, among other things, a studied insult to Hadrian's memory.[12]

As to the way the empire was 'run' – its 'administration' – Hadrian made a striking innovation in Italy, creating in effect four provinces in the peninsula with four men of consular rank as their governors. The system was abolished by his successor. It may be argued that the senatorial *cursus honorum* settled down into a regular pattern under Hadrian, which lasted throughout the next reign and beyond. The tenure of only two posts, a legionary command and an imperial province or its equivalent (for example one of the treasuries), between praetorship and consulship, seems to have been a sign that a senator was on his way to govern one or more of the major military provinces after being consul. The *HA* mistakenly attributes to Hadrian a policy of extreme lavishness with third and second consulships. In fact only two men benefited from a third tenure of the *fasces* and only five second consulships are known. Despite his pronounced philhellenism, Hadrian's treatment of Greeks or easterners might seem at first sight less generous than that of Trajan; and more Greeks became consul *ordinarius* under Antoninus than under Hadrian. Still, Hadrian was evidently the first to be able to persuade Greeks of old Greece to enter the Senate; and under him Greeks are found for the first time governing provinces in the Latin west. As far as the equestrian career is concerned, the new grading of the *praefectus alae milliariae* has already been mentioned. Former holders of this post were clearly destined for important procuratorships. The *HA* attributes to Hadrian the 'innovation' of appointing *equites* rather than freedmen to be *ab epistulis* and *a libellis*, which is clearly mistaken. On the other hand, the earliest record of an *advocatus fisci* comes from Hadrian's reign and he may have instituted the post – as the *HA* claims – which, as a substitute for military service, was to afford entry into the procuratorships. In general, Hadrian's role as a reformer of the 'administration' seems to have been exaggerated.[13]

It is also questionable whether Hadrian really altered the nature of the *consilium principis*, or whether he made such an impact on Roman law as is often asserted. To be sure, he did entrust the young senator Salvius Julianus with the 'codification' of the praetorian edict. There are also a good many more of his rescripts in the *Digest* than there are of his predecessors, which may not be an arbitrary choice of the compilers: it has indeed been argued that 'rescripts intended to have permanent validity' were first issued by Hadrian. The *HA* places great stress on his innovative activity as a law-giver. One potentially far-reaching measure was the extension of *ius Latii*. The grant of *Latium maius* meant that not merely the magistrates but all members of the council of a Latin community gained full Roman citizenship. The measure must have been intended to spread Roman citizenship more widely in the western provinces, even if there is very limited evidence for its use.[14]

It is above all the provinces of the empire that were affected by Hadrian's reign. 'He aided the allied and subject cities most generously', Dio stresses. 'He had indeed seen many of them, more than any other emperor, and he assisted all of them, one might say, giving some a water supply, others harbours, food, public buildings, money and various honours.' Dio later adds that 'he also built theatres and held games as he travelled about from city to city.' The *HA* makes the same point: 'In almost all the cities he built something and gave games', and the *Epitome de Caesaribus*, with its story of the team of craftsmen organised on military lines that he took with him, talks of him 'restoring whole cities'. Even Fronto, in a basically hostile comment, notes that 'you can see monuments of his travels in a great many cities in Asia and Europe.' Dio and the *HA* stress, in particular, what he did for Athens, as does Pausanias; and the *HA* has at least a list, however incomplete, of his building at Rome.[15]

How many cities Hadrian actually founded is difficult to calculate, given that a great many eastern communities took his name. He must at least be given credit for the *colonia* of Mursa in Pannonia, evidently the last veteran colony of the traditional type in the west, for Hadrianopolis in the Cyrenaica, for Hadrianutherae, Hadriania and Hadriani in Mysia, Antinoopolis in Egypt, and Aelia Capitolina in Judaea. The last two foundations epitomise Hadrian's Hellenism, carried to extremes. His passion for the beautiful Bithynian may, to be sure, have been the reason for no more than the name of the new city on the Nile. The cult of the god Antinous which he created, for all the enthusiasm with which the Greeks took to it, seemed to Romans in the west, at least, a little bizarre. As for Hadrian's New Jerusalem, the decision to create a pagan city there and to prohibit circumcision, which together provoked the desperate last Jewish revolt, surely indicate that his Hellenism had blinded him to reality.[16]

Tertullian obviously thought Hadrian's restless travelling was prompted by his insatiable inquisitiveness – meaning a desire to know what should not be known. Julian the Apostate likewise accused Hadrian of having been 'a meddler in the mysteries'. The *HA*, too, comments that 'he was so fond of travelling that he wanted to learn further, at first hand, about everything that he had read on different parts of the world.' His 'souvenir' sections of the great Villa, recalling Athens above all, point in the same direction. A modern observer is prepared to see in Hadrian's journeys round the provinces a systematic programme: to get to know the empire at first hand and put the provinces on to a new footing. But in the last analysis the complex personality and thus the motivation eludes us, as it did Marius Maximus – for it must be his verdict that is reproduced in the *Epitome de Caesaribus*:

> changeable, manifold, fickle, born as if to be a judge of vices and virtues, controlling his passionate spirit by some kind of artifice, he expertly concealed his envious, unhappy and wanton character, immoderate in his urge for display; feigning self-restraint, affability and mildness and disguising his burning desire for glory.

Dio credits Hadrian with 'mildness' (apart from the executions at the beginning and the end of the reign), but stresses the ambition and jealousy and notes that fault was found with his 'great strictness, inquisitiveness and meddling'. Yet he was prepared to conclude that Hadrian 'balanced and made up for these defects by his careful oversight, prudence, generosity and skill' – and for his policy of peace. As for 'artifice' in Hadrian's character, one might argue that in a sense he was acting out a kind of charade during his extended presence in the east – playing the part of a reborn Pericles and trying to recreate the world of the fifth century BC.[17]

In the early fifth century AD Synesius of Cyrene wrote in a letter to a friend, that

> as for the Emperor and the Emperor's friends, and the dance of fortune – certain names shoot up like flames to a great height of glory and are then extinguished. But there is utter silence about such things here, our ears are spared from news of that sort. Maybe people know well enough that there

is an Emperor still alive – because the tax-collectors remind us of this every year. But *who* the Emperor is, that is not so clear. In fact some of us think that Agamemnon is still on the throne.

Synesius could make a joke to his friend about the remoteness of the empire's ruler. But as shown by his essay *On Kingship*, ostensibly directed to Arcadius, he strongly disapproved: an emperor should lead his armies in person, tour the provinces to see his subjects for himself and to be seen by them. Whatever else Hadrian achieved, his restless touring round the provinces made him the most visible monarch the Roman empire ever had.[18]

STEMMA

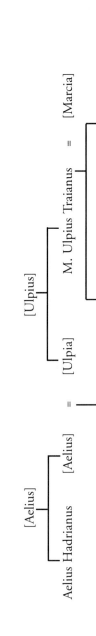

[Aelius]

[Ulpius]

[Aelius] = [Ulpia]

Aelius Hadrianus

Domitia Paulina = P. Aelius Hadrianus Afer

M. Ulpius Traianus

TRAJAN = Pompeia PLOTINA

[Marcia]

Ulpia MARCIANA = C. Salonius Matidius Patruinus

Salonia MATIDIA = (1) [L. Mindius]
= (2) L. Vibius Sabinus

SABINA   Matidia

HADRIAN = SABINA

Domitia Paulina = L. Julius Servianus

Julia Paulina = Cn. Pedanius Fuscus Salinator

Pedanius Fuscus

NOTES

Augusti and Augustae are given in capital letters. Names in square brackets are of persons whose existence is not specifically attested. (For [Marcia], [L. Mindius] and [Ulpia] cf. R.-C. nos. 521, 533, 821.) In the list below, references with a letter, A, D, etc., followed by a number are to *PIR²*. For stemmata of Antoninus Pius, the Annii Veri, Domitia Lucilla and Lucius Verus cf. A.R. Birley, *Marcus Aurelius* (1987) 235–8; for the Dasumii and Domitius Tullus, Syme, 'The Testament of Dasumius: some novelties', *Chiron* 15 (1985) 41–63 = *RP* V (1988) 521 ff., at 62 f. = 544 f. I have not taken into account the conjectures of G. di Vita-Evrard, 'Le testament dit "de Dasumius": testateur et bénéficiaires', in: *Epigrafia juridica Romana* (Pamplona 1989) 159–74, which seem to conflict with the evidence. In particular, she believes, 167 f., that the adopted daughter of Tullus, Domitia Lucilla the elder, the grandmother of M. Aurelius, had been married to Hadrian's father as her first husband; hence that Hadrian was Marcus' uncle. Yet in *HA Had.* 1.2, not discussed by di Vita-Evrard, Hadrian's mother is called Domitia *Paulina*, not Lucilla. She also supposes, 170, Tullus' wife or widow to have been a Domitia, specifically Domitia Longina, the widow of Domitian: a fascinating notion.

Aelius Hadrianus: Hadrian's great-uncle, named only in *HA Had.* 2.4.

P. Aelius Hadrianus Afer: Hadrian's father, a cousin of Trajan (*HA Had.* 1.2; *Epit. de Caes.* 14.1). Hence Hadrian was Trajan's first cousin once removed, not his 'nephew', as a good many modern writers have it. His *praenomen* P. is supplied by *ILS* 308 = Sm. 109, Hadrian's inscription from Athens. His other names are given by *HA Had.* 1.2 (Aelius Hadrianus Afer), the *Epit. de Caes.* 14.1 (Aelius Hadrianus) and Dio 69.3.1 (Hadrianus Afer). Died when Hadrian was in his tenth year (*HA Had.* 1.4), i.e. in AD 85 or at the latest January 86, aged 39 according to Hadrian's letter to Antoninus (*PFayum* 19 = Sm. 123), hence born in 45 or 46.

Domitia Paulina: Hadrian's mother, from Gades (*HA Had.* 1.2). D 185; R.-C. no. 330.

(Aelia) Domitia Paulina: Hadrian's sister (*HA Had.* 1.2, etc.). D 186; R.-C. no. 12. The letter of Hadrian in the *Corpus Glossariorum Latinorum* III 37, 44 f., refers to 'sisters' in the plural. No other full sister is attested. If the letter is not fictional (as most assume), either Hadrian had at least one other sister, nowhere attested (but di Vita-Evrard, op. cit., finds another sister in the Testamentum 'Dasumii'), or he was referring to his sister-in-law Matidia as well as to Paulina.

Julia Paulina: Hadrian's niece. Her full names are supplied in a new fragment of the Testamentum 'Dasumii', *AE* 1976. 77. Not in *PIR²*. R.-C. no. 452. The horoscope of her son, Hephaestio Thebanus 2.18.65, states that she and her husband died a violent death. This seems implausible.

L. Julius Servianus: J 569, 631. Hadrian's brother-in-law. Originally called Ser. Julius Servianus, until adopted by L. Julius Ursus (J 630).

Matidia: M 368; R.-C. no. 533. Hadrian's sister-in-law. Her father was perhaps a L. Mindius. Apparently unmarried, lived well into the reign of Antoninus Pius if not later.

Pedanius Fuscus: P 197. Hadrian's grand-nephew. Perhaps identical with the polyonymous young man honoured at Ephesus, *AE* 1977. 797 = *IKEph* 734, P. Velleius P. f. Tro. Lucullus L. Sertorius Brocchus Pedanius Fuscus Salinator Sallustius Blaesus Cn. Julius Agricola . . . Caesonius, Champlin, *ZPE* 21 (1976) 78 ff.; if so, he had perhaps been adopted after his parents' death. Born 113, died aged about 25, according to the horoscope in Hephaestio Thebanus 2.18.62–6. Dio 69.17.1 gives his age at death as only 18. Cf. also Caballos Rufino, *Senadores* (1990) 413 ff.

Cn. Pedanius Fuscus Salinator: P 200. Husband of Hadrian's niece, whom he married about 106 (Pliny, *Ep.* 6.26, a letter congratulating Servianus on his daughter's impending wedding). On his supposed violent death, see above under Julia Paulina.

Pompeia PLOTINA: R.-C. no. 631.

(Vibia) SABINA: R.-C. no. 802. Her name Vibia is not directly attested.

Salonia MATIDIA: M 367; R.-C. no. 681.

C. Salonius Matidius Patruinus: M 365.

Ulpia MARCIANA: R.-C. no. 824.

M. Ulpius Traianus: Trajan's father. The article in *RE* supp. 10 (1965) 1032 ff. (R. Hanslik) is defective. Cf. Caballos Rufino, *Senadores* (1990) 305 ff.; Franke, *Legionslegaten* (1991) 191 ff.

L. Vibius Sabinus: presumed father of Sabina, cf. R.-C. no. 802.

NOTES

ABBREVIATIONS

The following abbreviations of (mostly modern) publications are used in the Notes. For assistance in finding the full titles of ancient classical sources here given in shortened form the reader is directed to S. Hornblower and A.J.S. Spawforth, *The Oxford Classical Dictionary*, third edition (Oxford 1996).

AE	*L'Année épigraphique* (Paris 1888 ff.)
ANRW	H. Temporini and W. Haase (eds), *Aufstieg und Niedergang der römischen Welt* (Berlin–New York 1972 ff.)
BHAC	*Bonner Historia-Augusta-Colloquium* (Bonn 1964–91)
BMC III	H. Mattingly, *Coins of the Roman Empire in the British Museum* III. *Nerva to Hadrian* (London 1936)
CIG	*Corpus Inscriptionum Graecarum* (Berlin 1828–77)
CIL	*Corpus Inscriptionum Latinarum* (Berlin 1863 ff.)
CP; *Supp.*	H.-G. Pflaum, *Les carrières procuratoriennes équestres sous le Haut-Empire romain* (Paris 1961); *Supplément* (1982)
CPJ	V.A. Tcherikover and A. Fuks (eds), *Corpus Papyrorum Judaicorum* I–III (London–Cambridge, Mass. 1957–64)
DJD II	P. Benoit, J.T. Milik and R. de Vaux, *Discoveries in the Judaean Desert* II. *Les Grottes de Murabba'at* (Oxford 1961)
FGrH	F. Jacoby, *Die Fragmente der griechischen Historiker* (Berlin–Leyden 1923 ff.)
FO²	L. Vidman, *Fasti Ostienses* (2nd edn, Prague 1982)
HA	*Historia Augusta*
Historiae Aug. Coll. n.s.	*Historiae Augustae Colloquium, nova series* (Macerata–Bari 1991 ff.)
HSCP	*Harvard Studies in Classical Philology*
IG	*Inscriptiones Graecae* (Berlin 1893 ff.)
IGLS	*Inscriptions grecques et latines de la Syrie* (Paris 1929 ff.)
IGR	*Inscriptiones Graecae ad res Romanas pertinentes* (Paris 1906–27)
IKEph	*Inschriften griechischer Städte aus Kleinasien. Die Inschriften von Ephesos* I ff. (Bonn 1979 ff.)
ILAfr	R. Cagnat, A. Merlin and L. Chatelain (eds), *Inscriptions latines d'Afrique* (Paris 1923)
ILS	H. Dessau, *Inscriptiones Latinae Selectae* (Berlin 1892–1916)
ILTun	A. Merlin (ed.), *Inscriptions latines de la Tunisie* (Paris 1944)

IRT	J.R. Reynolds and J.B. Ward-Perkins (eds), *Inscriptions of Roman Tripolitania* (Rome–London 1952)
JRS	*Journal of Roman Studies*
MW	M. McCrum and A.G. Woodhead, *Select Documents of the Principates of the Flavian Emperors* (Cambridge 1966)
ODCC²	*Oxford Dictionary of the Christian Church*, 2nd edn by F.L. Cross and E.A. Livingstone (Oxford 1974)
Ol.	J.H. Oliver, *Greek Constitutions of Early Roman Emperors from Inscriptions and Papyri* (Philadelphia 1989)
PIR¹, PIR²	E. Klebs, P. v. Rohden and H. Dessau (eds), *Prosopographia Imperii Romani* (Berlin 1897–8); 2nd edn, E. Groag, A. Stein and L. Petersen (eds), (Berlin 1933 ff.)
PME	H. Devijver, *Prosopographia Militiarum Equestrium*, 5 vols (Louvain 1976–93)
POxy	B.P. Grenfel et al. (eds), *The Oxyrhyncus Papyri* (London 1899 ff.)
R.-C.	M.-T. Raepsaet-Charlier, *Prosopographie des femmes de l'ordre sénatorial (Ier–IIe siècles)* (Louvain 1987)
RE	G. Wissowa et al. (eds), Paulys *Realencyclopädie der classischen Altertumswissenschaft* (Stuttgart 1893–1978)
RIB	R.G. Collingwood and R.P. Wright, *The Roman Inscriptions of Britain* I: *Inscriptions on Stone* (Oxford 1965)
Roxan	M.M. Roxan, *Roman Military Diplomas 1954–1977* (London 1978) (I); *1978–1984* (London 1985) (II); *1985–1993* (London 1994) (III)
RP	R. Syme, *Roman Papers* I–II (Oxford 1979), III (Oxford 1984), IV–V (Oxford 1988), VI–VII (Oxford 1991)
SEG	*Supplementum Epigraphicum Graecum* (Leyden 1923 ff.)
SIG³	W. Dittenberger, *Sylloge Inscriptionum Graecarum* (3rd edn, Leipzig 1915–21)
Sm.	E.M. Smallwood, *Documents Illustrating the Principates of Nerva, Trajan and Hadrian* (Cambridge 1966)
Strack	P.L. Strack, *Untersuchungen zur römischen Reichsprägung des zweiten Jahrhunderts II. Die Reichsprägung zur Zeit des Hadrian* (Stuttgart 1933)
Toynbee	J.M.C. Toynbee, *The Hadrianic School. A Chapter in the History of Greek Art* (Cambridge 1934)
ZPE	*Zeitschrift für Papyrologie und Epigraphik*

INTRODUCTION: THE EMPEROR HADRIAN

1 'diese[r] merkwürdigste unter allen römischen Kaisern', Hirschfeld, *Kais. Verw.* (1905) 477; cf. S. Dill, *Roman Society from Nero to Marcus Aurelius* (London 1904) 503: 'the most interesting of the emperors'. Hirschfeld, like many others, no doubt attributed too many 'reforms' to Hadrian. Still, he was something of an exception to the 'passive' model of the Roman emperor in general as a ruler who *re*acted rather than acted, so convincingly laid out by Millar, *Emperor* (1977). In several respects Hadrian was *hyper*active.

2 On 'frontier policy', the symbolic intention here stressed (and reiterated below, especially in Chapters 10 and 11, with further remarks in the Notes) has been rather neglected in recent studies, e.g. Whittaker, *Frontiers* (1994) and id., in Kennedy, *Roman Army* (1996) 25 ff., in spite of the welcome new approaches there offered. – adoption, 'four consulars', 'new Augustus', etc.: Chapters 8 ff., below. – Philhellenism, etc., discussed in more detail in many places below. Panhellenion: in

an important new study (which I first saw only in November 1996), C.P. Jones, *Chiron* 26 (1996) 28 ff., takes a very different view of the role of Hadrian in the creation of this institution. Here I can only register disagreement on this question and refer to my 'Hadrian and Greek senators' (*ZPE* 116 (1997) 209ff.). – Still worth noting is the remark by M.I. Rostovtzeff, *The Social and Economic History of the Roman Empire* (Oxford 1926) 117: 'Hadrian, the intellectual, the man of refined artistic tastes, the last great citizen of Athens, the lover of antiquity.' (The title of one of Ronald Syme's choicest papers, 'Hadrian the intellectual', in *Les Empereurs romains d'Espagne* (Paris 1965, 243–53, reprinted in *RP* VI (1991) 103 ff., echoes (perhaps unconsciously) the great Russian historian.)

3   Antinous, Jewish policy, succession crisis: more detail in Chapters 19–21. – On the autobiography, see now above all Bollansée, *Ancient Society* 25 (1994) 279 ff., showing that it was probably cast in the form of a letter to Antoninus, of which *PFayum* 19 = Sm. 123 is a fragment coming from the beginning. Other items are known only from the *HA* and Dio. – I have discussed the question of sources for the *HA* in *Lives of the Later Caesars* (1976) 14 ff.; *Marcus Aurelius* (1987) 229 f.; *Septimius Severus the African Emperor* (London 1988) 205; most recently in *Historiae Aug. Coll.* n.s. 3 (1995) 57 ff.; and at length in *ANRW* II.34.3 (1997) 2678–2757. I stand by the position that the main source for the *HA Had.* and later lives up to that of Elagabalus was Marius Maximus (rejecting the 'Ignotus' postulated by Syme, supported by Barnes, in numerous contributions; for a discussion, cf. now T.D. Barnes, 'The sources of the Historia Augusta (1967–1992)', *Historiae Aug. Coll.* n.s. 3 (1995) 1–28). For the coincidence of sources of *HA Had.* and *Epit. de Caes.*, Schlumberger, *Epitome* (1974) especially 78 ff. F. Millar, *A Study of Cassius Dio* (Oxford 1964), is still valuable on that author; but the early date of writing there argued must be rejected. T.D. Barnes, 'The composition of Cassius Dio's *Roman History*', *Phoenix* 38 (1984) 240–55, makes a good case for Dio having written during the years 220–31 if not later. If so, he could have used Maximus' *Vita Hadriani* for his Book 69, as I argue in *Historiae Aug. Coll.* n.s. 3, 65 f. On the factual value of *HA Had.*, Pflaum, *BHAC 1968/69* (1970) 173 ff., is still worth consulting. There is a new discussion of the bogus letter supposedly by Hadrian in *HA Quad. tyr.* 7.6–8.10 by A. Baldini, 'L'epistola pseudoadrianea nella vita di Saturnino', *Historiae Aug. Coll.* n.s. 3 (1995) 35–56.

4   There is an extensive literature on the 'Second Sophistic'. I have benefited mainly from Bowersock, *Sophists* (1969); Bowie, 'Greeks and their past in the Second Sophistic', *Past & Present* 46 (1970) 3–41; id., in Russell (ed.), *Antonine Literature* (Oxford 1990) 53 ff.; Jones, *Plutarch* (1971); id., *Dio Chrysostom* (1978). Note also G. Anderson, *Philostratus* (London 1986); and – for an attempt at 'debunking' – P.A. Brunt, 'The bubble of the Second Sophistic', *Bull. Inst. Class. Stud. London* 39 (1994) 25–51. Swain, *Hellenism and Empire* (1996), a major new work which will make necessary a good deal of rethinking on the 'Greek renaissance', could scarcely be taken fully into account here. On Gellius, L.A. Holford-Strevens, *Aulus Gellius* (London 1988).

5   On Suetonius' implied comments on Hadrian, Carney, *PAfrCA* 11 (1968) 7 ff., is instructive. Note also id., *Turtle* 6 (1967) 291 ff., on some related matters. Cf. now A. Abramenko, 'Zeitkritik bei Sueton. Zur Datierung der *Vitae Caesarum*', *Hermes* 122 (1994) 80–94. (I am quite unconvinced by H. Lindsay, 'Suetonius as *ab epistulis* to Hadrian and the early history of the imperial correspondence', *Historia* 43 (1994) 454–68, who seeks to redate Suetonius' dismissal.) – On Tacitus and his time of writing, cf. p. 104 and note 32 to Chapter 9. Note also Potter, *ZPE* 88 (1991) 277 ff., in support of the view that Tacitus was still at work on *Ann.* under Hadrian. There are a good many more passages in the *Ann.* that I have liked to deploy (especially from the later books) than are cited in the pages that follow. But this has

largely been done, inimitably, subtly and (I believe) convincingly, by Syme, *Tacitus* (1958).

6 Some of Hadrian's own writings were collected by Cantarelli, *Studi e doc.* 19 (1898) 13 ff. and by P.J. Alexander, 'Letters and speeches of the Emperor Hadrian', *Harvard Studies in Classical Philology* 49 (1938) 141–77. On the 'Sententiae', the three papers by Schiller, *Festgabe Lübtow* (1970) 295 ff.; *Studi Grosso* IV (1971) 402 ff.; *Atti II. Congresso* (1971) 717 ff., in support of their authenticity, deserve to be retrieved from obscurity, as they have now been by Lewis, *GRBS* 32 (1991) 267 ff. I have not attempted a systematic discussion of Hadrian's 'legal policy'.

7 Fronto is cited by the traditional numbering and by page references to the new edition by M.P.J. van den Hout (Leipzig 1988). – On the horoscopes preserved by Hephaestio Thebanus, now in the edition by D. Pingree (Leipzig 1973), Cramer, *Astrology* (1954) 163 ff., was a pioneering study, developing W. Kroll, *Catalogus Codicum Astrologorum Graecorum* VI (Brussels 1903) 67 ff.; C.E. Ruelle, ibid. VIII 2 (1911) 82 ff.; cf. further O. Neugebauer and H.B. van Hoesen, *Greek Horoscopes* (Philadelphia 1959) 90 ff.; Martin, *Providentia* (1982) 291 ff.

8 Greppo, *Mémoire* (1842) 46. The other works cited in this chapter but not referred to in the Notes will be found in the Bibliography.

9 H. Dessau, 'Über Zeit und Persönlichkeit der *Scriptores Historiae Augustae*', *Hermes* 24 (1889) 337–92.

10 Note, for example, Perowne, *Hadrian* (1960) – entirely without footnotes, marred by a number of errors, and not otherwise adding anything to Henderson. Contributions on Hadrian by W. Weber subsequent to his excellent *Hadrianus* of 1907 (based on his doctoral dissertation and published when the author was still very young – he was born in 1882), e.g. in the *Cambridge Ancient History* XI (1936) and (the same in German) *Rom: Herrschertum und Reich im 2. Jhdt.* (Stuttgart 1937), were not a success. M.K. Thornton, 'Hadrian and his reign', *ANRW* 2.2 (1975) 432–76, is a rather limited bibliographical survey. Note now also M.A. Levi, *Adriano Augusto. Studi e ricerche* (1993), and *Adriano. Un ventennio di cambiamento* (1994).

11 Apart from Grenier, *MEFRA* 101 (1989) 925–1019, I have drawn mainly on Kähler, *Villa* (1950; now of course outdated in part) and the helpful survey by Boatwright, in her *City* (1987) 138 ff. I have not seen W.L. MacDonald and J.A. Pinto, *Hadrian's Villa and its Legacy* (New Haven 1995).

12 To save space, I have not listed these papers individually in the Bibliography, since all have been republished, either in his *Roman Papers* I–VI or in other volumes. Original publication details are supplied in the notes. A MSS memo in the Syme Archive at Wolfson College indicates that he had contemplated reprinting a selection in a volume of Hadrianic papers.

13 The Quebec periodical, *Cahiers d'études anciennes*, devoted a volume (21, 1988) to Yourcenar on Hadrian. I found the paper by Bernier, *CEA* 21 (1988) 7–25, on the genesis and literary fortune of the novel of considerable interest. The other contributions were of lesser value. Syme was moved to publish a lecture, 'Fictional history old and new: Hadrian', delivered in 1984 (Oxford 1986), reprinted in *RP* VI (1991) 157–81, in protest at the excessive credence given to Yourcenar's fiction. Cf. also Bruggisser, *Historiae Aug. Coll.* n.s. 5 (forthcoming), for an interesting study of Yourcenar's treatment of Hadrian (I am grateful to its author for allowing me to consult his paper in typescript). Not least instructive is the intrusion of the Yourcenarian Hadrian into scholarly works on Roman history.

14 *HA Had.* 26.1–3 has the basic description. That his beard was well-trimmed is clear from the portraits, e.g. Wegner, *Hadrian* (1956) 8. Dio 69.2.6² speaks of his charm. Polemo, *De physiognomia* 148, claims that his eyes were especially bright, Malalas 277 claims that they were blue or grey (no doubt invented, like the other descriptive items on Roman emperors). On his character, cf. esp. Dio 69.3.2 ff., and *HA*

Had. 14.9 ff., 15.10 ff., 20.1 ff., etc., discussed often enough in the pages that follow. More detail on his character and beliefs (or speculations on the question), and much more bibliography, in A.R. Birley, *Laverna* 5 (1994) 176 ff. ('Hadrian's farewell to life'). I have not thought it worth referring in this book to my narrative chapter, covering the years 117–92, delivered to the editors of *Cambridge Ancient History* XI² in 1988 ('forthcoming'). (In any case, as happens, I have changed my mind on a number of matters there treated.)

CHAPTER 1 A CHILDHOOD IN FLAVIAN ROME

1 *HA Had.* 1.2–3. There is no need to doubt that Rome was his birthplace: Syme, 'Hadrian and Italica', *JRS* 54 (1964) 142–9 = *RP* II (1979) 617 ff., at 142 = 617. Italica was his *origo* or *patria* and he was registered in the tribe, Sergia, of that place. – domicile: Talbert, *Senate* (1984) 40. – Dio: 69.3.1. – papyrus: *PFayum* 19 = Sm. 123; cf. further p. 299 and note 39, above. – father's death: *HA Had.* 11.4. – praetorship: A.R. Birley, *Fasti* (1981) 14; Talbert 17 ff. – daughter: *HA Had.* 11.2.

2 wet-nurse: *CIL* XIV 3721. – Gades: *HA Had.* 1.2; *RE* 7.1 (1910) 439–61 (Hübner). – Balbus: *RE* 4.1 (1900) 1260–8 (Münzer). – 500 Gaditari: Strabo 3.5.3, p. 169. – Domitii: cf. Syme, 'The Testament of Dasumius: some novelties', *Chiron* 15 (1985) 41–63 = *RP* V (1988) 521 ff., at 52 = 533, on a possible kinsman, Domitius Balbus (Tacitus, *Ann.* 14.40.1).

3 Italica, Hadria: *HA Had.* 1.1; Appian, *Iberica* 38. – Marullinus: *HA Had.* 1.2. – Ulpii, Trahii: Caballos Rufino, *Senadores* (1990) 309 (inscription of M. Trahius C.f.), with further bibliography; id., *Itálica* (1994) 67. – Tuder: *Epit. de Caes.* 13.1; Syme, *Tacitus* (1958) 786.

4 cousin: *HA Had.* 1.2. – career of elder Trajan: Caballos Rufino, *Senadores* (1990) 305 ff.; Franke, *Legionslegaten* (1991) 191 ff. (with slightly differing views on the career from 70–73). – Vettulenus: Syme, 'Antonine relatives: Ceionii and Vettuleni', *Athenaeum* 35 (1957) 306–15 = *RP* I (1979) 325 ff. – Marcii: Champlin, *Athenaeum* 71 (1983) 251 ff.

5 olive plantations: p. 317 and note 7 below. – civil war: [Caesar], *Bell. Alex.* 52, 57; *Bell. Hisp.* 25. – Galba: e.g. Syme, 'Partisans of Galba', *Historia* 31 (1982) 460–83 = *RP* IV (1988) 115 ff. – Vespasian: Sherwin-White, *Roman Citizenship* (2nd edn 1973) 252, 360 ff.

6 Asiaticus: Tacitus, *Ann.* 11.1.1–2. – Pedanius: Syme, 'Rival cities, notably Tarraco and Barcino', *Ktèma* 6 (1981) 271–85, at 282 = *RP* IV (1988) 89 f.; Caballos Rufino, *Senadores* (1990) 420 f. – Annii Veri: *HA M. Ant.* 1.2. – Agricola: Tacitus, *Agr.* 9.1. – Domitii: *ILS* 990–1 = MW 299–300.

7 Tibur: Syme, *Tacitus* (1958) 602; 'Spaniards at Tivoli', *Ancient Society* 13/14 (1982–3) 241–63 = *RP* IV (1988) 94 ff. – praetorian career: A.R. Birley, *Fasti* (1981) 15 ff. – Agricola: Tacitus, *Agr.* 9.1–5.

8 proconsuls, praetorian career: A.R. Birley, *Fasti* (1981) 17, 31 f., 15 ff. – Bassus: *ILS* 8797; Syme, 'Spanish Pomponii. A study in nomenclature', *Gerión* 1 (1983) 249–66 = *RP* IV (1988) 140 ff., at 253 f. = 145 f. – Quadratus: *ILS* 8819, 8819a, *AE* 1966. 463; *PIR*² J 507.

9 On the early stages of Hellenisation at Rome: MacMullen, *Historia* 40 (1991) 419 ff.; for the principate, Syme, *Tacitus* (1958) 504 ff. – dialogues: Plutarch, *Mor.* 711B (a new fashion at Rome); cf. C.P. Jones, *Plutarch and Rome* (1971), especially 20 ff. – Quintilian: *Inst. or.* 1.1.12 f.

10 Vespasian's death and Hadrian's allegation: Dio 66.17.1.

11 disasters: e.g. Dio 66.21–4. – Titus' death: Dio 66.26.1–4. – Germanicus: B.W. Jones, *Domitian* (1992) 128 ff. – Agricola: A.R. Birley, *Fasti* (1981) 73 ff.

12 father's death, guardians: *HA Had.* 1.4. Attianus' age: Caballos Rufino, *Senadores* (1990) 35 f. – Plotina, Matidia, Sabina: R.-C. nos. 631, 681, 802.

13 Scaurus: Pliny, *Ep.* 5.12; *HA Verus* 2.5; A. Gellius, *N. Att.* 11.15.3; cf. *RE* 5A.1 (1934) 672–6. The link with Scaurianus is suggested by E. Groag, ibid. 671. Sherwin-White's note on Pliny's correspondent, *Commentary* (1966) 339, is not helpful. S. Fein, *Die Beziehungen der Kaiser Trajan und Hadrian zu den Litterati* (Stuttgart–Leipzig 1994 – a useful work) 30, doubts that Scaurus taught Hadrian, but does not disprove it. – favourite authors: *HA Had.* 16.6. – Quintilian: *Inst. or.* 2.5.21 ff.

14 *HA Had.* 1.5; *Epit. de Caes.* 14.2; cf. Juvenal 3.78. – archon: *IG* II² 1996 = MW 121.

15 Building: B.W. Jones, *Domitian* (1992) 79 ff. – fortunes: *RE* supp. 15 (1978) 1514 ff. – architecture: Dio 69.4.1–5. – cithara: *HA Had.* 14.9, cf. Quintilian, *Inst. or.* 10.15.3.

16 B.W. Jones, *Domitian* (1992) 138 ff. – Funisulanus: Caballos Rufino, *Senadores* (1990) 146 ff. – Nigrinus: id. 103 ff. Saecular Games: Jones 102 f.

17 Saturninus: B.W. Jones, *Domitian* (1992) 144 f. – Arvals: MW 15. – Trajan: Pliny, *Pan.* 14.

18 further expedition: B.W. Jones, *Domitian* (1992) 150 f. – Arvals: MW 14. – false Nero: Suetonius *Nero* 57.2. – Vettulenus: Suetonius *Dom.* 10.2. On both, B.W. Jones, 'C. Vettulenus Civica Cerealis and the "false Nero" of AD 88', *Athenaeum* 61 (1983) 516–21.

19 double triumph: Suetonius, *Dom.* 6.1; B.W. Jones, *Domitian* 150 f. – months: Suetonius, *Dom.* 13.3; Talbert, *Senate* (1984) 361 f. – Nerva: Syme, *Tacitus* (1958) 1 ff., 627 ff. – Servianus: Syme, *Chiron* 15 (1985) 47 = *RP* V 528, and elsewhere. – Rusticus: Syme, 'Antistius Rusticus, a consular from Corduba', *Historia* 22 (1983) 359–74 = *RP* IV (1988) 278 ff. – Pusio: id. 367 = 287; Caballos Rufino, *Senadores* (1990) 110 ff.

20 Italica: *HA Had.* 2.1; Syme, *JRS* 54 (1964) 142 = *RP* II (1979) 647. – poisoning: Dio 67.11.6. Cf. Syme, *Some Arval Brethren* (Oxford 1980) 21 ff.; *RP* VII 564. – Fulvus: *HA Ant. Pius* 1.6. – Violentilla: Statius, *Silv.* 1.2.138, 168. – Quintilian's young wife and sons: *Inst. or.* 6 *praef.* – Martial 7.47 (Licinius Sura). – Servianus: *HA Had.* 1.2; Syme, 'More Narbonensian senators', *ZPE* 65 (1986) 1–14 = *RP* VI (1991) 209 ff., at 16 = 224 and n. 115.

21 Nero: Tacitus, *Ann.* 12.41. – M. Aurelius: *HA M. Ant.* 4.5. Cf. *RE* 6A.2 (1937) 1450 ff.

CHAPTER 2   THE OLD DOMINION

1 Caballos Rufino, *Itálica* (1994) 15 ff. – Divisions of Spain: Strabo 3.4.20, 166. There is now an extensive (and recent) literature on Roman Spain, not least Baetica. I have confined citation to what I have relied on. But I add a reference to the section 'Spain', by G. Alföldy (composed in 1987 and revised in 1988; the author was not permitted further revision), Chapter 13c of *Cambridge Ancient History*, vol. X. *The Augustan Empire, 43 BC–AD 69*, 2nd edn (Cambridge 1996) 449–63.

2 Strabo 17.3.25, 840; Dio 53.12.1 ff., especially 4 f.; cf. Alföldy, *Fasti* (1969) 149 ff.; Griffin, *JRS* 62 (1972) 1 ff.; Caballos Rufino, *Itálica* (1994) 33 ff.

3 Strabo 3.2.4, 142; 3.2.6, 144; 3.2.8, 146; 3.2.14, 151.

4 Griffin, *JRS* 62 (1972) 1 ff. – ten thousand: cf. [Caesar], *Bell. Alex.* 50, 53, 56; P.A. Brunt, *Italian Manpower* (Oxford 1980) 208, 230 f. – towers: [Caesar], *Bell. Hisp.* 8. – Caballos Rufino, *Itálica* (1994) 57 ff. – Turdetanians: Strabo 3.2.15, 151.

5 poets: Cicero, *Pro Archia* 26. – Sextilius Ena: Seneca, *Suas.* 6.27. – elder Seneca:

Griffin, *JRS* 62 (1972) 4 ff. – Latro: *PIR¹* P 638. – Gallio: *PIR²* J 756. – Silo: *PIR²* G 111. – Turrinus: Seneca, *Contr.* 10 *praef.* 14–16. – other Augustan writers: Syme, *RP* VII 466 ff. – Quintilian's origin is known only from Jerome, *Chron.* p. 190 Helm, not from his own work. Martial refers to his native Bilbilis often.

6 *HA Had.* 2.1. – *collegium iuvenum*: Gray, *Smith Coll. Stud.* 4 (1919) 155, plausibly interprets 'statim militiam iniit' this way; accepted without reference to Gray by Benario, *Commentary* (1980) 46; reported without comment by M. Jaczynowska, *Les associations de la jeunesse romaine sous le Haut-Empire* (Wroclaw 1978) 54 f., but nowhere mentioned by P. Ginestet, *Les organisations de la jeunesse dans l'Occident romain* (Brussels 1991) (the fullest study of the *iuvenes*, but playing down the military aspect). – Mactaris: *AE* 1958. 172. – Apuleius, *Met.* 2.18, cf. *Dig.* 48.19.28.3.

7 great-uncle: *HA Had.* 2.1 – Massa: Tacitus, *Agr.* 45.1; Pliny, *Ep.* 3.4.4; 6.29.8; 7.33.4–8; Eck, *Chiron* 12 (1982) 319, regards 91–2 as the probable term of office. – estates: Caballos Rufino, *Senadores* (1990) 42 and note 28, with further references.

8 Martial 12 *praef.* – Mummius: *ILS* 21d (Caballos Rufino, *Itálica* (1990) 34 f., reports an alternative, but not necessarily proven, restoration by A.M. Canto of this fragmentary text); for his conduct over the booty, e.g. Pliny, *NH* 35.24; *De vir. ill.* 60.3, cf. *RE* 16.1 (1933) 1195–1206 (Münzer). – Nepos: A.R. Birley, *Fasti* (1981) 100 ff.; Caballos Rufino, *Senadores* (1990) 249 ff. – Papus: *PIR²* M 524; Caballos Rufino, *Senadores* (1990) 217 ff.

9 *HA Had.* 2.1. – Spanish game: Strabo 3.2.6, 144–5; 3.4.15, 163; Pliny, *NH* 8.117; Martial 1.49; 10.37. – appetite: Fronto, *De feriis Alsiensibus* 5, p. 230 van den Hout, described Hadrian as a good trencherman, *prandiorum opimorum esorem optimum*; Dio, 69.7.3, also testifies to his healthy appetite. – *tetrafarmacum*: *HA Had.* 21.4, cf. *Ael.* 5.5, *Sev. Alex.* 30.6, discussed by Cazzaniga, in: *Poesia lat. in frammenti* (1974) 359 ff. (whose restoration of the text is not entirely followed here).

10 Trajan: Pliny, *Pan.* 81.1 ff. – Pliny, *Ep.* 1.6, 9.10. – Sertorius: Plutarch *Sert.* 13. – Latro: Seneca *Contr.* 1 *praef.* – Seneca, *De vita beata* 14.2. – Martial: cf. note 9 above.

11 *HA Had.* 2.2. – Glabrio: *PIR²* A 67.

12 Quintilian: *PIR²* F 59.

CHAPTER 3   MILITARY TRIBUNE

1 Tacitus away: Tacitus, *Agr.* 45.5. – Sura: Martial 1.49.40; 6.64.10 ff. Sura's origin: Syme, *Tacitus* (1958) 791; id., 'Rival cities, notably Tarraco and Barcino', *Ktèma* 6 (1981) 271–85 = *RP* IV (1988) 74 ff., at 276 = 81 f.; id., 'Hadrian's autobiography: Servianus and Sura', *BHAC 1986/89* (1991) 189–200 = *RP* VI (1991) 398 ff., at 193 = 401 – Sura a friend of Trajan: Dio 68.15.4 ff.; Victor, *Caes.* 13.8; *Epit. de Caes.* 13.6; cf. *HA Had.* 2.10, 3.10.

2 eight months: Martial 9.31.3. – Pannonia: argued by Fitz, *Verwaltung* I (1993) 162 ff., based mainly on Pliny, *Pan.* 14.5 (cf. note 12 below). – XXI Rapax: Suetonius, *Dom.* 6.1; *RE* 12.2 (1925) 1789. – Statius, *Silv.* 3.3.171. Martial 8 *praef.*; 8.8.5 f.; 8.11.7; 8.54.3 f. – Cf. on this period, Syme, 'Domitian: the last years', *Chiron* 13 (1983) 121–46 = *RP* IV (1988) 252 ff.

3 Martial 9.6 and 8, cf. Dio 67.2.3, Suetonius, *Dom.* 7.1; 9.11.13, 16–17, 36. Statius, *Silv.* 3.4, cf. 2.1, 2.6; 4.3.13 ff. – boys: Martial 9.103 praises the beautiful twins Hierus and Asylus, owner not named (it was Claudius Livianus, later Trajan's Guard Prefect: *CIL* VI 280 (= 30728); *AE* 1924. 15). – Quintilian: *Inst. or.* 1.2.2, 4; 1.3.17. MacMullen, *Historia* 31 (1982) 484ff., is instructive on the topic.

4 Massa: note 6, p. 317 above. – the opposition: Syme, *RP* VII (1991) 568 ff. – entitled to attend Senate: according to Suetonius *D. Aug.* 38.2, Augustus allowed senators' sons to be present.

5 Tacitus, *Agr.* 45.1. – Dasumius: Syme, *Chiron* 15 (1985) 41 f. = *RP* V (1988) 522 f.; *PIR²* H 5. – Tacitus: Tacitus, *Agr.* 41.2–42.4. – Senecio: Dio 67.13.2; *PIR²* H 128.

6 Trajan's remark: *HA Sev. Alex.* 65.4 f. (a bogus story according to Syme, *Ammianus and the Historia Augusta* (Oxford 1968) 170, 186; *Emperors and Biography* (Oxford 1971) 97, 108; *Historia Augusta Papers* (1983) 23, 41 f.). – vigintivirate: A.R. Birley, *Fasti* (1981) 4 ff. – Nepos: id. 100 ff.

7 The post of *Xvir*: *HA Had.* 2.2; also known from *ILS* 308 = Sm. 109, the Athens inscription. – Pliny: *ILS* 2927 = Sm. 230; *Ep.* 1.18.3; 5.8.8; 5.1.

8 *RE* 4.2 (1901) 2260 ff. – attendants etc.: e.g. *ILS* 1900, 1909, 1911, 1938. – *praef. fer.*: *ILS* 308 = Sm. 109. – *feriae*: *RE* 6.2 (1909) 2213–16. – Lollius: *PIR²* L 320. – Quadratus: *PIR²* J 507; Syme, 'Hadrian and the Senate', *Athenaeum* 62 (1984) 31–60 = *RP* IV (1988) 295 ff., at 45 = 310, suggests his involvement.

9 *transvectio*: *RE* 6A.2 (1937) 2178–87. – *seviri*: ibid. 2A.2 (1923) 2018. – Athens: *ILS* 308 = Sm. 109. – Statius: *Silv.* 4.2.22 ff., 32 f., 40 ff.

10 Suetonius, *Dom.* 14.4; Dio 67.9.1 ff.

11 Glabrio: Dio 67.14.3; Suetonius, *Dom.* 10.2. – Clemens: Suetonius, *Dom.* 15.1; Dio 67.14.1 f. – unhappy lot: Suetonius *Dom.* 21.

12 tribunate: A.R. Birley, *Fasti* (1981) 8 ff. – Trajan: Pliny, *Pan.* 14.1, 15.1–2. – Trajan's position: Syme, 'Hadrian in Moesia', *Arheolski Vestnik* 19 (1968) 101–9 = *Danubian Papers* (1971) 204–12, assuming that II Adiutrix was then in Moesia Superior, argued that Trajan was governor of that province. It is now clear that the legion was already at Aquincum in Pannonia (see next note). Fitz, *Verwaltung* I (1993) 162 ff., argues that Trajan was governor of Pannonia in 95. This remains, of course, hypothesis, neither provable nor disprovable, but at least plausible, in my view, given Pliny, *Pan.* 14.5 (*cum aliis super alias expeditionibus itinere illo dignus invenireris*).

13 II Adiutrix until 86: *RE* 12.2 (1925) 1437–43. To Aquincum in 89: Strobel, *Dakerkriege* (1984) 88; Fitz, *Verwaltung* I (1993) 163; Németh, in Hajnóczi (ed.), *Pannonia* (1994) 141.

14 Conscientious tribunes: Tacitus, *Agr.* 5.1; Pliny, *Pan.* 15.1.

15 *HA Had.* 10.2 (diet), 17.8, 20.1 (accessibility), 20.7–10 (memory), 14.10 (military skills). – Turbo: *AE* 1948.202. On Turbo: Syme, 'The wrong Marcius Turbo', *JRS* 52 (1962) 87–96 = *RP* II (1979) 541 ff.; 'More trouble about Turbo', *BHAC* 1979/81 (1983) 303–19 = *Historia Augusta Papers* (1983) 168 ff.; *CP* no. 94; Dobson, *Primipilares* (1978) no. 107 (still relying on Ritterling, *RE* 12.2 (1925) 1445 f., for the date when II Adiutrix came to Aquincum); Fitz, *Verwaltung* I (1993) 339 ff.

16 *HA Had.* 2.3; *ILS* 308 = Sm. 109. – Iul. Mar[ ]: *CIL* XVI 41; Eck, *Chiron* 12 (1982) 324; Strobel, in Knape and Strobel, *Deutung von Geschichte* (1985) 51 ff., prefers to identify the governor with (Ti.) Jul(ius Candidus) Mar(ius Celsus) (*PIR²* J 241); not impossible, if not entirely plausible.

17 B.W. Jones, *Domitian* (1992) 193 ff. The main sources: Suetonius, *Dom.* 17, 23; Dio 67.15–16; 68.1 f.; Philostratus *V. soph.* 1.2.

18 Syme, *Tacitus* (1958) 1 ff., 627 ff.

CHAPTER 4 *PRINCIPATUS ET LIBERTAS*

1 Sources for the reign of Nerva are excerpted in A.R. Birley, *Lives of the Later Caesars* (1976) 29–37. – Verginius: Pliny, *Ep.* 2.1.4 f. – Antoninus: *Epit. de Caes.* 12.2–3; *PIR²* A 1086. – Frontinus: J 322. – Corellius: C 1294. – Pliny, *Ep.* 9.13.2 ff.

2 Pliny, *Ep.* 9.13.6 ff. – army commander: identified as M. Cornelius Nigrinus by

Alföldy and Halfmann, *Chiron* 3 (1973) 331–73 = Alföldy, *Römische Heeresgeschichte* (1987) 153 ff.; generally accepted, cf. e.g. Caballos Rufino, *Senadores* (1990) 103 ff. – dismissals and replacements: Syme, *Tacitus* (1958) 631, is the classic analysis; lengthy discussion in Schwarte, *BJ* 179 (1979) 147 ff.; Strobel, in Knape and Strobel, *Deutung von Geschichte* (1985), especially 41 ff., both stressing the key role of the Guard Prefect Casperius Aelianus. – Capitol: Pliny, *Pan.* 5.2–4.

3 Verginius: Pliny, *Ep.* 2.1.1–6; 6.10. – Tacitus, *Agr.* 3.2, 3.1.

4 mutiny: Pliny, *Pan.* 6.1 ff., 8.1–3; Dio 68.3. 3 f.; *Epit. de Caes.* 12.6–8. Discussed at length by Strobel, in Knape and Strobel, *Deutung von Geschichte* (1985) 9 ff.

5 Dio 68.4.1 f.; *Epit. de Caes.* 13.6; Pliny, *Pan.* 7.6.-Frontinus and Ursus: Pliny, *Pan.* 60.6 (not named). Frontinus was *cos. III ord.*, Ursus *cos. III suff.*, in 100, *FO²* 93 f. – Agricola: Tacitus, *Agr.* 44.5.

6 *HA Had.* 2.5–6.

7 *HA Had.* 2.6; *ILS* 308 = Sm. 109. – one other case: L. Minicius Natalis jr. (*PIR²* M 620). – Trajan's move: Eck, *Statthalter* (1985) 45 ff. – fifteen years later: *HA Had.* 10.2 ff., cf. pp. 117 f. above. – horses and dogs: cf. Pliny's story about an extravagant young man: *Ep.* 9.12. – new system: Schönberger, *JRS* 59 (1969) 158 ff.; *Ber. der röm-germ. Komm.* 66 (1985) 368 ff. – Avitus: Pliny, *Ep.* 8.23.5.

8 Dio 68.4.2; *Epit. de Caes.* 13.3; *HA Had.* 2.6.

9 favour: *HA Had.* 2.7. – deification: Pliny, *Pan.* 11.1 ff. – Mausoleum: *Epit. de Caes.* 12.12. – letter: Dio 68.5.2. – Frontinus, Ursus: *FO²* 45. – Palma: *PIR²* C 1412. – Senecio: C.P. Jones, 'Sura and Senecio', *JRS* 60 (1970) 98–104. – An important new document, a military diploma of AD 98 for the army of Lower Germany, was to have been published by the late Jules Bogaers. It was issued when Trajan was already Emperor but – exceptionally – still named as the commanding general of the auxiliary units. It must be hoped that a text will soon become available.

10 Casperius: Dio 68.5.4, cf. Strobel, in Knape and Strobel, *Deutung von Geschichte* (1985) 27 ff., 37 ff., 44. – Suburanus: Pliny, *Pan.* 67.8; Dio 68.16.1–2; Victor, *Caes.* 13.9; *CP* no. 56; Syme, *Tacitus* (1958) 56. As Werner Eck points out to me, Suburanus may have been made Guard Prefect of Trajan as new Caesar the previous autumn. – Horse Guards: Speidel, *Riding for Caesar* (1994) 15 ff., 38 ff. – Capito: *PIR²* O 62.

11 Pliny, *Ep.* 10.1, 10.2.

12 Tacitus, *Agr.* 39.1. – his father: assumed to be the man in Pliny, *NH* 7.76. – Tacitus, *Germ.* 37.2–5.

13 move to Danube: Pliny, *Pan.* 12 f. – Servianus, Avitus: Pliny, *Ep.* 8.23.5; Eck, *Chiron* 12 (1982) 332. – Pliny, *Pan.* 12–13, 20–24. – Plotina: Dio 68.5.5.

14 *HA Had.* 2.7–9. – boys, wine: Dio 68.7.4. – oracle: discussed by Michelotto, *Rend. Ist. Lomb.* 113 (1979) 324 ff.

15 Sura: *HA Had.* 2.10; Dio 68.15.4–6; Julian, *Caes.* 327A. – Frontinus: *PIR²* J 322. – Sabina: *HA Had.* 2.10. – Matidia: *PIR²* M 367.

16 quaestor: A.R. Birley, *Fasti* (1981) 12 ff. – *VIIvir*: *ILS* 308 = Sm. 109. Schumacher, *Priesterkollegien* (1973) 116 f., assumes that Hadrian gained his priesthoods after the consulship. Syme, 'A dozen early priesthoods', *ZPE* 77 (1989) 241–59 = *RP* VI (1991) 421 ff., discusses cases when the distinction came much earlier in the senatorial career.

17 Pliny, *Ep.* 4.8.3. – Marius Priscus: ibid. 2.11.12. – Sabinus: *CIL* XI 8020; *CIL* XIV 3579. Cf. Schumacher, *Priesterkollegien* (1973) 111 f. – Pliny, *Ep.* 10.13.

18 Schumacher, *Priesterkollegien* (1973) 108 ff., nos. D 12, 14, 11, 20 (to be revised by *PIR²* N 60), 3.

19 attendance: Suetonius, *D. Aug.* 38.2. – instalments: Pliny, *Ep.* 3.18.4. – aim: ibid. 3.18.2 f., *Pan.* 4.1 – Dio of Prusa, *Or.* 1.

20 *HA Had.* 3.1. – Isaeus: *IG* II/III² 3632, 3709; Pliny, *Ep.* 2.3.

21 *HA Had.* 3.2. It seems difficult to date Hadrian's responsibility for the senatorial record any later; if he had this duty while quaestor, it was exceptional. – Tacitus' use of the *Acta*: Syme, *Tacitus* (1958) 186 f., 278 ff., 295 f.

22 25 March: the Arvals sacrificed for his victory and return on this day, Sm. 1. – *comes*: *ILS* 308 = Sm. 109. – On the Dacians and the war, Strobel, *Dakerkriege* (1984), especially 56 ff., 155 ff., is the fullest modern account.

23 *HA Had.* 3.2–3.

24 This is essentially the solution of Alföldy, *Legionslegaten* (1967) 23 f. The alternative, as argued against Alföldy by Barnes, *Sources of the* HA (1978) 33, 41 f., is unsatisfactory: to accept the date 105 for the tribunate and to amend *Subsurano bis et Serviano iterum* for his praetorship to *Sura ter et Senecione iterum*, giving the year 107. This would mean that Hadrian's career was retarded rather than accelerated – hardly plausible.

25 Servianus: Pliny, *Ep.* 3.17; *PIR*² J 631. – Livianus: C 913. – Lusius: L 439. – Laberius: L 9. – On the war, Dio 68.9.1–10.2; Strobel, *Dakerkriege* (1984) 162 ff., and its results, 202 ff.

26 Senecio (Caballos Rufino, *Senadores* (1990) 295 ff. – but his Spanish origin is only a guess) and Livianus (*PIR*² C 913) are explicitly called Hadrian's friends in *HA Had.* 4.2. – Falco: A.R. Birley, *Fasti* (1981) 95 ff.; for his origin (Sicilian), Salomies, *Adoptive Nomenclature* (1992) 121 ff. – Quadratus Bassus: *PIR*² J 508. – Atilius: G 181; Syme, *RP* VII (1991) 629 ff. – Cilnius: Schumacher, *Priesterkollegien* (1973) 112 f., cf. Eck, *Chiron* 12 (1982) 332, note 205. – Apollodorus: *PIR*² A 922; Ridley, *Athenaeum* 77 (1989) 551 ff.

27 *HA Had.* 3.5. F. Kolb, 'Die Paenula in der Historia Augusta', *BHAC 1971* (1974) 81–101, at 95–9, demonstrates that the story cannot be genuine as it stands.

28 Classicus: Pliny, *Ep.* 3.4, 3.9, 6.29. – Bassus, ibid. 4.9, 5.20, 6.29, 10.56–7. – voting tablets: ibid. 4.25.

29 *HA Had.* 3.8. – Licinius Nepos: Pliny, *Ep.* 4.29, 5.4.2, 5.13.1, 6.5. – Nigrinus: 5.13.6. – Celsus: *PIR*² J 882.

30 infringing: Dio 68.10.3. – new legions: Syme, *Danubian Papers* (1971) 91; Strobel, *Dakerkriege* 97 ff. – 4 June: *FO*² 18 = 5m. 19. – *HA Had.* 3.6; *ILS* 308 = Sm. 109.

CHAPTER 5   THE YOUNG GENERAL

1 I Minervia: *RE* 12.2 (1925) 1420 ff.; Strobel, *Dakerkriege* (1984) 86 f., 203 note 8 (perhaps stationed in occupied south-west Dacia from 102 to 105). – deity: J.-L. Giraud, 'Domitien et Minerve: une prédilection impériale', *ANRW* 2.17.1 (1981) 203–22.

2 On the second war, Strobel, *Dakerkriegen* 205 ff. – bridge and opening of war: Dio 68.13.1–14.1. – deserters: 68.11.3. – Longinus: 68.12.1–5. – Pliny's prayer: *Pan.* 94.5. – Neratius: *HA Had.* 4.8; *PIR*² N 60; Eck, *Chiron* 12 (1982) 330 note 195, 338 note 332.

3 On Priscus: R.A. Bauman, *Lawyers and Politics . . . Augustus to Hadrian* (Munich 1989) 194 ff.; but his attempt to identify him with the Neratius who governed Lycia-Pamphylia is totally misplaced: *dikaiodotes* in *IGR* III 1511 does not mean 'jurist'; it is simply a standard label for the governor in Lycia, cf. the cases in Thomasson, *Laterculi* I (1984) 276 ff., nos. 5, 10, 14, 15; no. 6 is clearly Neratius Pansa. – Marcellus: *PIR*² N 55. – Servianus: Dio 69.17.3, where Xiphilinus has 'Traianos', emended by Zonaras unjustifiably to 'Adrianos', cf. Michelotto, in *Studi Gatti* (1987) 174.

4 In general, Strobel, *Dakerkriege* 211 ff. – Cl. Maximus: *AE* 1969/70. 583; Speidel, 'The captor of Decebalus', *JRS* 60 (1970) 142–53 = id., *Roman Army Studies* I

(Amsterdam 1984) 173 ff., with *add.*, 408 f. – Gemonian steps: Sm. 21. – Nabataean kingdom: Bowersock, *Roman Arabia* (1983) 76 ff. – mopping up, etc.: Strobel, *Dakerkriege* 219 f.; Piso, *Fasti* (1993) 4 ff.

5 Sabinus: Roxan III 148; Piso, *Fasti* (1993) 10 ff.; Pliny, *Ep.* 9.2, cf. 6.18. – *col. Ulpia Sarmizegethusa*: *CIL* III 1443 = Sm. 479; Strobel, *Dakerkriege* 226 f. – settlers: Eutropius 8.6.2. – spectacles: Dio 68.15.1; Sm. 21.

6 *HA Had.* 3.6–7; *ILS* 308 = Sm. 109. – Sura: *PIR²* L 253. – Senecio: Syme, *Danubian Papers* (1971) 248 ff. = *RP* VI (1991) 145 ff. (originally published as 'Pliny and the Dacian wars', *Latomus* 23 (1964) 750–9).

7 Division of Pannonia: Alföldy, in Hajnóczi (ed.), *Pannonia* (1994) 30. – decisive phase: Strobel, *Dakerkriege* 214 ff.

8 Jazyges: Mócsy, *Pannonia* (1974) 19 ff., 94 f.; Strobel, *Dakerkriege* 57 f., 205 notes 3–4. – *HA Had.* 3.9; Dio 68.10.3.

9 palace: Zsidi, in Hajnóczi (ed.), *Pannonia* (1994) 213; Póczy, ibid. 224–7.

10 *HA Had.* 3.9; cf. Tacitus, *Agr.* 9.4, *HA Had.* 13.10.

11 patronage: E. Birley, *Roman Britain and the Roman Army* (1953) especially 141 ff., repr. in id., *Roman Army Papers* (1988) 153 ff. – Falco: Pliny, *Ep.* 7.22. – Marcellus: ibid. 3.8. – Clodius Sura: *ILS* 6725; *PME C* 206. – Latro: *CP* no. 104 and *add.* – Note also a former tribune of II Adiutrix (name unknown) who rose high under Hadrian, *AE* 1976. 676; *CP Supp.* no. 109A.

12 Turbo: *HA Had.* 4.2; *PIR²* M 249 (fuller bibliography, p. 318, note 15, above).

13 Gallus: *PIR²* A 654. – Bradua: A 1298; A.R. Birley, *Fasti* (1981) 92 ff. – on the consulship, ibid. 24 f. – *HA Had.* 3.10; *CIL* VI 2016.

14 *in absentia*: suggested by Barnes, *Sources of the HA* (1978) 42 note 43 (but in my view for the wrong reasons). – Julius Maximus: *CIL* XVI 164; *PIR²* J 426. – 'adopted': *HA Had.* 3.11. – Sura's death: *PIR²* L 253; Syme, *RP* V (1988) 410, 486, 569. – Minicius: Syme, 'Hadrian and the senate', *Athenaeum* 62 (1984) 31–60 = *RP* IV (1988) 295 ff., at 37 = 302. – speeches: Julian, *Caes.* 327B; *HA Had.* 3.11. – Trajan's history: known only from a few words cited by the grammarian Priscian 6.13 (p. 205 Keil).

15 Pliny, *Ep.* 8.18.

16 Via Appia: *CIL* VI 10229; new fragment, *AE* 1976. 77 = 1978. 286. – Julia Paulina: line 15 now gives her full name. – On the identification of the testator and other details, I follow Syme, 'The Testamentum Dasumii: some novelties', *Chiron* 15 (1985) 41–63 = *RP* V (1988) 521 ff.

17 one of us: Pliny, *Pan.* 2.4. – Optimus: ibid. 2.7, 88.4. – wife, sister: Sm. 106. – Marsyas: *RE* 14.2 (1930) 1993 f., cf. 1554 and *Supp.* 4 (1924) 504. The seal is a further confirmation, not, it seems, previously exploited, that his mother was a Marcia (assumed from his sister's name Marciana); cf. R.-C. no. 521. – looked stupid: Syme, *Tacitus* (1958) 39. – Dio of Prusa: Philostratus, *V. soph.* 1.2. – *alimenta*: Pliny, *Pan.* 27; Sm. 435–8; *Epit. de Caes.* 12.4. – land: Pliny, *Ep.* 6.19.4.

18 riches: Johannes Lydus, *De mag.* 2.28, as corrected by Carcopino, cf. Strobel, *Dakerkriege* (1984) 221 f. – building: Pliny, *Pan.* 29.2; Dio 68.16.3; Sm. 374 ff.; in general, L. Richardson, *A New Topographical Dictionary of Ancient Rome* (Baltimore–London 1992), e.g. 18 f. (Aqua Traiana), 175 ff. (Forum), 251 f. (Mercati), 397 f. (Thermae). – Apollodorus: Dio 69.4.2.

19 Genitor: Pliny, *Ep.* 9.17. Tacitus: ibid. 7.20, 8.7, cf. 9.14. – unnamed author: ibid. 9.27. – Caninius: ibid. 8.4. – Capito: ibid. 8.12.

20 Senecio: *RE* 3A.2 (1927) 1188–92 (Groag); C.P. Jones, *Plutarch and Rome* (1971) especially 54 ff. – Fundanus: Syme, *RP* VII (1971) 603 ff. – *corrector*: Pliny, *Ep.* 8.24.

21 Maximus: Halfmann, *Senatoren* (1979) 136 no. 40. – presence at Athens: *ILS* 308 = Sm. 109; *HA Had.* 19.1; Phlegon, *FGrH* 257, fr. 36.xxv (cf. p. 322, note 12,

below). – Philopappus: Halfmann 131 ff. no. 36; *PIR²* J 151; Baslez, *DHA* 18 (1992) 89 ff. – Parthian empire: e.g. Schippmann, *Grundzüge* (1980) 59 f. – Pliny: his mission is dated by Sherwin-White, *Commentary* (1966) 80 ff., to 109–111; Eck, *Chiron* 12 (1982) 349 f. note 275, prefers 110–12 (more convincingly).

CHAPTER 6   ARCHON AT ATHENS

1 Falco: A.R. Birley, *Fasti* (1981) 95 ff. – friends: *HA Had.* 4.2 (in the context of AD 113) lists Sosius Senecio, Aemilius Papus, Platorius Nepos, Claudius Livianus and Marcius Turbo.

2 Epictetus: *PIR²* E 74; Millar, *JRS* 55 (1965) 141 ff. – close terms: *HA Had.* 16.10.

3 Arrian: Wheeler, *Flavius Arrianus* (1977) 1 ff.; Syme, 'The career of Arrian', *Harvard Studies in Classical Philology* 86 (1982) 181–211 = *RP* IV (1988) 21 ff. – house of Quadratus: Epictetus, 3.23.23. – twice consul: 4.1.53.

4 *annona*: Epictetus, 1.10.2–8. – Maximus: 3.7. – procurator-governor of Epirus: 3.4; identified with Cn. Cornelius Pulcher (*PIR²* C 1424) e.g. by Syme, *RP* IV 26. – worthlessness of preferment: e.g. Epictetus, 1.19.17 ff., 4.1.45 ff., 4.7.21 ff.; cf. *HA Had.* 20.1. – kinship, adoption: Epictetus, 1.9.7, 1.3.1, cf. Millar, *JRS* 55 (1965) 143.

5 Epictetus, 1.25.15; 2.22.22; 3.13.9–13.

6 Epictetus, 1.16.9–14. – Dio, *Or.* 36.17; cf. Apollonius, *Ep.* 63, 76. – Hadrian's beard: *HA Had.* 26.1. Walker, *J.Hist.Coll.* 3 (1991) 265 ff., is illuminating on the topic. Cf. also P. Zanker, *Die Maske des Sokrates* (Munich 1995), but his ch. 5, pp. 109–251, although called 'Hadrians Bart', does not have much on Hadrian; he does not cite Walker (or quote Dio and Apollonius).

7 Ambracia . . . Leucas: Arrian, *Anab.* 2.16.5 f.; *Indica* 41.2–3. – his hunting: clear from his *Cyneg.* – inscription: *SIG³* 827, emended by A. Plassart, *Fouilles de Delphes* III 4 (Paris 1970) no. 290 – Nigrinus' mission: Syme, *RP* IV 24 f.; Eck, *Chiron* 13 (1983) 187 note 479; Thomasson, *Laterculi* I (1984) 193 no. 24. – father, uncle: Plutarch, *Mor.* 478B, 487E, 548B, 632A; C.P. Jones, *Plutarch and Rome* (1971) 51 ff.

8 Senecio: Plutarch, *Mor.* 75B, 612C–E, 613C–D, 666D–E, etc.; *Theseus* 1.1; *Demosthenes* 1.1, 31.4; C.P. Jones, *Plutarch and Rome* 54 ff. – Fundanus: Syme, *RP* VII (1991) 603 ff. – Plutarch and Delphi: Jones 26, 43, etc.; Swain, *Historia* 40 (1991) 318 ff. – Hadrian may also have visited Coronea in Boeotia at this time, since he was honoured by a statue there before becoming Emperor: *IG* VII 2879.

9 Philopappus: Plutarch, *Mor.* 48E, 628A–B; *PIR²* J 151. – Balbilla: J 650.

10 Herculanus: Plutarch, *Mor.* 539A ('Herclanus' – not cited in *PIR²* J 302); 546D–E. The view taken here of the date of birth of Herculanus needs justifying (Antony Spawforth, who takes a different view, *ABSA* 73 (1978) 249 ff., kindly drew my attention to a number of difficulties, which I seek to resolve in 'Hadrian and Greek senators', *ZPE* 116 (1997) 209 ff.).

11 Dioscuri: *IG* V 1, 489, 971; *PIR²* J 151; cf. Spawforth, *ABSA* 73 (1978) 249 ff. (on his relations; but I differ on the chronology of his career, cf. previous note). – rise of Greeks: Halfmann, *Senatoren* (1979) 71 ff.; Syme, *RP* IV (1988) 1 ff. – house of Tullus Ruso: Fronto, *Ad M. Caes.* 3.2.1, p. 36 van den Hout.

12 Olympian Zeus: Strabo 9.1.6, p. 396; Vitruvius 7, *praef.* 17; *IG* II/III² 4099; Suetonius, *D. Aug.* 60; cf. Kienast, *Festschr. Lippold* (1993) 202 = id., *Kleine Schriften* (1994) 363. – deme Besa: Graindor, *Athènes* (1934) 14 note 1. – Trebellius: *IG* II/III² 4193; *AE* 1947. 69. – Crispus: *AE* 1971. 436. – Domitian: *IG* II/III² 1996 = MW 121. Cf. also p.321 note 21, above.

13 Tacitus: his proconsulate: Eck, *Chiron* 12 (1982) 353 note 289; Syme, *Tacitus*

(1958) 513, discussing Tacitus, *Ann.* 2.53, 55. – deified, Augusta: Sm. 22. Sabina's great-grandfather, the elder Trajan, had also been deified: M. Durry, 'Sur Trajan père', in *Les empereurs romains d'Espagne* (Paris 1965) 45–54 (deification shortly before Trajan's departure for the east).

14 Sm. 22. – *ex manubiis*: A. Gellius, *N. Att.* 13.25.1. – column: Claridge, *JRA* 6 (1993) 5 ff., makes a good case for the decoration of the Column being of Hadrianic date.

15 Parthia split: cf. e.g. Schippmann, *Grundzüge* (1980) 59 f. – Callidromus: Pliny, *Ep.* 10.74. – Axidares, etc.: Dio 68.17.1 ff. – young man: Pliny, *Pan.* 14.1. – *profectio*: Arrian, *Parthica* fr. 35 (anniversary of adoption, which was three months before Nerva's death, 27 January, *Epit. de Caes.* 12.9); Malalas 270 has 'October'; cf. Lepper, *Parthian War* (1948) 28 ff. – Augustae: R.-C. nos. 631, 681. – Misenum fleet, Turbo: *CIL* XVI 60; *AE* 1955. 225.

CHAPTER 7   THE PARTHIAN WAR

1 Dio 68.17.2 f.

2 Details in Eck, *Chiron* 12 (1982) 353 ff. – Homullus: Pliny, *Ep.* 5.20.6, cf. 4.9.215; also mentioned 6.19.3. – told Trajan: *HA Sev. Alex.* 65.5 (perhaps apocryphal, cf. p. 318 note 6, above).

3 Senatorial governors: Eck, *Chiron* 12 (1982) 353 ff. – Nepos: A.R. Birley, *Fasti* (1981) 103. He had command of the legion I Adiutrix in the Parthian expedition, it may be assumed. – Falco: ibid. 99. – Prefects: Syme, 'Guard Prefects of Trajan and Hadrian', *JRS* 70 (1980) 64–80 = *RP* III (1984) 1276 ff., at 66 f. = 1280 f. – Egypt: Thomasson, *Laterculi* I (1984) 347 f. – friends: *HA Had.* 4.2.

4 Palma, Celsus, Senecio: Dio 68.17.2. – enemies: *HA Had.* 4.3. There is virtually no evidence for Trajan's *comites* and it is purely my own speculation that Palma and Celsus were among them. – Laberius: *HA Had.* 5.5. – Bruttius: Pliny, *Ep.* 7.3; *AE* 1950. 66; *IRT* 545; Syme, 'Praesens the friend of Hadrian', *Studies I. Kajanto* (Helsinki 1985) 273–91 = *RP* V (1988) 563 ff., at 281 = 570. – Crassus: Dio 68.3.2; 68.16.2; *HA Had.* 5.5 f.; *PIR²* C 259.

5 Maximus: *PIR²* J 426. – Catilius: Halfmann, *Senatoren* (1978) 133 ff., no. 38. – Quietus: *PIR²* L 439. – Hadrian: *HA Had.* 4.1 – not yet, however, in spite of claims to the contrary, legate of Syria.

6 route: Dio 68.17.3; Malalas 11.3–4, p. 270. Longden, *JRS* 21 (1931) 1 ff., declined to accept Malalas' authority for dates, a particularly crucial matter as concerns the earthquake (below and note 13). Although some new evidence has come to light, in general Longden's chronology seems to me more acceptable than the alternative, based on Malalas, which has now become canonical (cf. note 13, below).

7 Zeus Casius: *Anth. Pal.* 6.332; Arrian, *Parth.* fr. 36. – Heliopolis: Macrobius, *Sat.* 1.23.14.

8 not promising: Lightfoot, *JRS* 80 (1990) 115 f. – Abgar: Dio 68.18.1; Arrian, *Parth.* fr. 45.

9 Satala, Arsamosata: Dio 68.19.2. – durbar: Dio 68.18.2. – kings: Eutropius 8.3.1; Festus, *Brev.* 20; Arrian, *Peripl.* 11.2; Dio 68.19.2. – Amazaspus: *IGR* I 192. – coinage: *BMC* III 115, 120, 222.

10 Dio 68.19.1–20.4. – *rex*: *BMC* III 103, 106. – killed: Fronto, *Princ. hist.* 18, p. 212 van den Hout; Eutropius 8.3.1.

11 Bruttius: Arrian, *Parth.* fr. 85; *AE* 1950. 66; *IRT* 545. – Arrian: Johannes Lydus, *De mag.* 3.53 = Arrian, *Parth.* fr. 6, cf. Wheeler, *Flavius Arrianus* (1977) 27 ff.; Syme, 'The career of Arrian', *Harvard Studies in Classical Philology* 86 (1982) 181–211 = *RP* IV (1988) 21 ff., at 187 f. = 27 f. – Quietus: Themistius, *Or.* 16.250. – submitting:

Dio 68.18.3ᵇ – 23.1. – Catilius: *ILS* 1338 and *add.* = Sm. 197. – Haterius: *ILS* 1338 = Sm. 262a. – false reports, Optimus : Dio 68.23.1–2.

12 Dio 68.21.1–3; 22.1–2; Arrian, *Parth.* fr. 46.

13 earthquake: Dio 68.24.1–25.6. – Hadrian: Malalas 11.15, p. 278. – Ignatius: Malalas 11.10, p. 276. – Sunday 13 December: Malalas 174, defended at length by Lepper, *Parthian War* (1948) 54 ff., 99 ff. Note the doubts of I. Henderson in her review of Lepper, *JRS* 39 (1949) 121–4. – Pedo replaced: *AE* 1911. 95; 1949. 23; *FO²* 48; O. Salomies, 'Zu Konsuln der Jahre 115, 135, 195 n. Chr.', *Arctos* 23 (1989) 165–78. – Ignatius commemorated in the east on 20 December: *ODCC²* 688 f. In fact, 20 December was the anniversary of the translation of his remains to Antioch: T. Camelot, *Ignace d'Antioche, Polycarpe de Smyrne, Lettres* (*Sources chrétiennes* 10, 1969) 13. This is unlikely to have bothered Malalas. – In support of a date for the earthquake early in 115 one may add the coins, *BMC* III 100, celebrating Jupiter's protection of Trajan, assigned to spring 115 by Mattingly, ibid. lxxxii. In favour of Lepper's (or Malalas') dating one might at first sight adduce the entry in the *Fasti Ostienses* – not available to Lepper: *[Id. Dec. terrae m]otus fuit*, thus restored and assigned to AD 115 by Vidman, *FO²* 48. But on inspection it is clear that neither the exact positioning of the fragment nor its restoration are at all certain.

14 Dio 68.26.1–4. – acclamations (VIII–XI): Lepper, *Parthian War* (1948) 44 f. – Quietus: Dio 68.22.2.

15 lead army: Dio 68.26.42. – Dura: Sm. 312. – Ozogardana: Ammianus Marcellinus, 24.2.3. – rioting: *CPJ* 435; cf. Barnes, *JJS* 36 (1985) 153 ff., for an important revision of the standard chronology of the Jewish diaspora revolt, showing that it began only in spring 116.

16 planned . . . Ctesiphon: Dio 68.1–2. – daughters, throne: *HA Had.* 13.1.

17 Parthicus: Dio 68.28.2. – despatches: Sm. 23. – anniversary: Guey, *REA* 50 (1948) 60 ff. – coinage: *BMC* III 118 f., 221 f. – Assyria: Eutropius 8.3.2, 8.6.2; Festus, *Brev.* 14, 20. Maricq, *Syria* 36 (1959) 257 ff., argued for the acceptance of these statements and this localisation of the new province; against, Lightfoot, *JRS* 80 (1990) 121 ff., followed by Millar, *Near East* (1993) 101; but cf. Potter, *ZPE* 88 (1991) 282 f., defending Maricq's view. – barge: Arrian, *Parth.* fr. 67.

18 Persian Gulf: Dio 68.28.3–29.3. – despatches: Sm. 23. – Babylon: Dio 68.30.1.

19 rebellion: Dio 68.29.4. – Jewish uprising: Applebaum, *Jews and Greeks* (1979); Barnes, *JJS* 36 (1985) 153 ff. – Armenia: Dio 75.9.6 (misplaced). – Maximus, Quietus, Seleucia: Dio 68.30.1–3. – Parthamaspates: Dio 68.30.3.; *BMC* III 223 = Sm. 51.

20 revolt: Dio 68.32.1–3; Eusebius, *HE* 4.2.3; Orosius 7.12.6; Sm. 59–60. – timing: *CPJ* 160–408d. – legion defeated: *CPJ* 438. – Memphis: *CPJ* 439, cf. 520 and the unpublished Oxyrhyncus papyrus discussed by Frankfurter, *JJS* 43 (1992) 208 ff. At Oxyrhyncus a defeat of the Jews was still celebrated in the late second century: *CPJ* 450. – Turbo: Eusebius, *HE* 4.2.3–4. – Cyprus: *ILS* 9491 = Sm. 284.

21 Quietus: Eusebius, *Chron.* 219 Karst; *HE* 4.2.5; Jerome, *Chron.* 196e Helm. Cf. Barnes, *JJS* 36 (1985) 156 ff.

22 Dio 68.31.1–4.

23 determined: Dio 68.33.1. – Bassus: Habicht, *Pergamon* VIII 3 (1969) no. 21; *PIR²* J 508; Strobel, in *Festschr. Lauffer* (1986) 942 ff.; Piso, *Fasti* (1993) 23 ff. – Syria: Dio 69.1.1, 2.1; *HA Had.* 4.6. – Phlegon: *FGrH* 257, fr. 36 IX. – Daphne: Ammianus Marcellinus, 22.12.8. – Zeus: *HA Had.* 2.9, cf. Michelotto, *RIL* 113 (1979) 324 ff. – enemies, second consulship: *HA Had.* 4.3–4. – Quietus: Dio 68.32.5; Eusebius, *HE* 4.2.5.

24 rumours: *HA Had.* 4.5. – no further step: ibid. 4.8–9. – illness: Dio 68.33.1–3. – On Trajan, J. Bennet, *Trajan. The Perfect Prince* (London 1997) (which I have not yet been able to consult) will doubtless be found valuable on many aspects.

CHAPTER 8   THE NEW RULER

1 letter, despatch: *HA Had.* 4.6–7. – dream: Dio 69.2.1. – donative: *HA Had.* 5.7.

2 97: cf. pp. 35 f. above. – stage-managed: Dio 69.1.1–2; *HA Had.* 4.10. Cf. Merten, *Festgabe Straub* (1977) 247 ff.; Temporini, *Frauen* (1978) 142 ff.

3 Attianus: *HA Had.* 5.5–6. – Neratius: *HA Had.* 4.8, cf. pp. 50 f. above. – Servianus: Dio 69.17.3 (Trajan in the version of Xiphilinus; Zonaras changed this to Hadrian, misunderstanding the context, cf. Michelotto, in *Studi C. Gatti* (1987) 174.)

4 Bruttius: *AE* 1950. 66; *IRT* 545; Syme, 'Praesens the friend of Hadrian', *Studies I. Kajanto* (Helsinki 1985) 273–91 = *RP* V (1988) 563 ff., at 278 f. = 568 f., 282 f. = 571 f. – Macer: Pliny, *Ep.* 3.5. – historian: Servius, ad *Aen.* 5.556; *PIR²* B 20–1. – Tacitus: Syme, *Tacitus* (1958) 465 ff.

5 evacuation: Fronto, *Princ. hist.* 11, p. 209 van den Hout; Eutropius 8.6.2; *HA Had.* 5.3, 9.1. – Parthamaspates: *HA Had.* 5.4 (wrong name). – Osrhoene: Drijvers, *ANRW* 2.8 (1977) 874 f. – Cato: *HA Had.* 5.3, cf. 16.6; Priscian, *Gramm.* 2.88.9.

6 *HA Had.* 5.8; *PIR²* L 439.

7 Clementianus: *CP* 150*bis* (61) and *add.*, *Supp.* p. 43; Alföldy, *Noricum* (1974) 244, dates his next but one post to *c.* 120. – Mauretania: *HA Had.* 5.2, 5.8, 6.6; Gutsfeld, *Nordafrika* (1989) 88 ff. – deliverer: cf. *Or. Sib.* 5.46 ff., 8.50 ff., 12.164 ff., cf. M. Hengel, 'Hadrians Politik gegenüber Juden und Christen', *Journal of the Ancient Near Eastern Society* 16/17 (1984/5) 153–82, at 155 ff. – rebuild Temple: Schürer, *Jewish People* I (1973) 535 ff.; Schäfer, *Aufstand* (1981) 29 ff.

8 Haterius, Hosidius: Scheid, *Collège* (1990) 384 ff. – Eudaemon: M. Aurelius, *Med.* 8.25; *HA Had.* 15.1; *CP* 110. – new Prefect: *POxy* 3781 (in post on 25 August 117). – edict: *Digest* 27.1.6.8, cf. Bowersock, *Sophists* (1969) 30 ff. – Another possible *comes* of Hadrian in 117–118 is C. Cilnius Proculus, cf. Halfmann, *Itinera* (1986) 249. He was a fellow-member of the *VIIviri epulonum*, Schumacher, *Priesterkollegien* (1973) 112 f.

9 remains: *HA Had.* 5.9–10. – letter to senate: ibid. 6.1–2.

10 Traianopolis: Dio 68.33.2; *Digest* 50.15.1.11, discussed by Zahrnt, *ZPE* 71 (1988) 245 ff.

11 Phaedimus: *ILS* 1792 = Sm. 176. The publication of this inscription by H. Dessau, 'Die Vorgänge bei der Thronbesteigung Hadrians', in *Festschrift H. Kiepert* (Berlin 1898) 85–91, spawned an extensive literature: cf. e.g. Weber, *Hadrianus* (1907) 40, 54; Henderson, *Hadrian* (1923) 35 f., for opposing views. Temporini, *Frauen* (1978) 152 ff., has a useful summary of the debate. – propensities: Dio 68.7.4.

12 *HA Had.* 5.2, cf. Weber, *Hadrianus* (1907) 50. – Turbo: *HA Had.* 5.8.

13 Bassus: C. Habicht, *Pergamon* VIII 3 (1969) no. 21; *PIR²* J 508; Piso, *Fasti* (1993) 28; Strobel, *Festschr. Lauffer* (1986) 942 ff., 947 ff. – armies sent ahead: *HA Had.* 6.6.

14 honours: *HA Had.* 6.3–4. – coins: *BMC* III 124, 237. Kienast, *Kaisertabelle* (2nd edn 1996) 128–34, gives a helpful summary of Hadrian's reign; ibid. 32 f., he supports the view (which I share), against e.g. Follet, *Athènes* (1976) 48 ff., that Hadrian renewed his *trib. pot.* on 10 December, i.e. that he was *trib. pot. II* from that day in 117.

15 beard: *HA Had.* 26.1, discussed above, p. 61.

16 *PGiessen* 3 = Sm. 519; den Boer, *Ancient Society* 6 (1975) 203 ff. – Orion: *Suda*, s.v.; further, Phlegon, *FGrH* 257, fr. 23 (an Orion evidently wrote about Adria, Hadrian's *ultima origo*).

17 coins: *BMC* III 245; cf. Syme, *Tacitus* (1958) 471 f., 771 ff.; Castritius, *JNG* 14 (1964) 89 ff.; Martin, *Mél. Seston* (1974) 327 ff.; Van den Broek, *Myth* (1972).

18 Catilius: *HA Had.* 5.10. – Daphne: Ammianus Marcellinus 22.12.8. – inscription: *CIL* VI 5076, cf. Weber, *Hadrianus* (1907) 57 ff., followed e.g. by Halfmann, *Itinera* (1986) 190, 194.

19 *IGR* III 208 = Sm. 498.

20 Dionysus: *IGR* III 209 = *SEG* VI 58–9; dated to 117 by Halfmann, *Itinera* (1986) 195.

21 *IGR* IV 349 = Sm. 61 = Ol. 58B. – Bassus: Habicht, *Pergamon* VIII 3 (1969) no. 21; Wesch-Klein, *Funus Publicum* (1993) 32 f.

22 Falco: A.R. Birley, *Fasti* (1981) 95 ff. – Nepos: ibid. 103, improved by Eck, *Chiron* 12 (1982) 360 note 315; *HA Had.* 4.2, 15.2, 23.4.

23 conquests abandoned: Fronto, *Princ. hist.* 11, p. 209 van den Hout; Eutropius 8.6.2. – bridge: Dio 68.13.6. – Strobel, *Festschr. Lauffer* (1986) 943, 952.

24 Fronto: see previous note.

25 wintered: Syme, *Tacitus* (1958) 243; 'Journeys of Hadrian', *ZPE* 73 (1988) 159–70 = *RP* VI (1991) 346 ff., at 160 = 347, and elsewhere. Syme suggests, plausibly, that Arrian may have been Hadrian's host. – honorary office: Robert, *Bulletin de Correspondence héllenique.* 102 (1978) 522 ff. – Delphi: Ol. 62. – Astypalaea: *IGR* IV 1013 c = Sm. 449a = Ol. 64.

26 Florus: *HA Had.* 16.3; cf. Nadel, *RSA* 12 (1982) 183. – V Macedonica: ibid. 2.2; *ILS* 308 = Sm. 109; *RE* 12.2 (1925) 1575 f. – Piroboridava: R.O. Fink, 'Hunt's *Pridianum*: British Museum Papyrus 2851', *JRS* 48 (1958) 102–16, cf. Syme, 'The Lower Danube under Trajan', ibid. 49 (1959) 26–33; id., *Danubian Papers* (1971) 108, 133 f.; Strobel, *Dakerkriege* (1984) 54 f., 134; id., *Festschr. Lauffer* (1986) 923 f. – *HA Had.* 6.8.

27 *ILS* 852–3, Pola: he had probably been deposed and was living in exile at this pleasant Adriatic city. – Borysthenes 'Alanus': *CIL* XII 112 = Sm. 520; Nadel, *RSA* 12 (1982) 181 ff.

28 Turbo: *HA Had.* 6.7, 7.3; Roxan I 21; *PIR²* M 249. – Nigrinus: *ILS* 2417 = Sm. 192. See further below.

29 *HA Had.* 7.1; Dio 69.2.5.

30 *HA Had.* 7.1. For this interpretation, Premerstein, *Attentat* (1908) 9 ff., especially 15 f., here somewhat modified in the light of new evidence. It is conceivable that Nigrinus was legate of Moesia Superior at the time of Bassus' death and had taken over Dacia as well temporarily, cf. M. Claudius Fronto during the Marcomannic wars, *ILS* 1097–8. The existence of Quadratus Bassus was then not known to Premerstein, whose later attempt to interpret the Pergamum inscription, 'C. Iulius Quadratus Bassus Klient des jüngeren Plinius und General Trajans' (*Sitzungsberichte der Bayerischen Akademie der Wissenschaften*, phil.-hist. Abt. 1934, Heft 3), was not a complete success, cf. Habicht, *Pergamon* VIII 3 (1969) 53 ff. Further, Premerstein's use of Polemo's *De physiognomia* to cast light on the affair must also be rejected (cf. below, p. 336, note 22). – Nigrinus' stepson: *HA Had.* 23.10, cf. p. 289 above.

31 Faventia . . . a journey: *HA Had.* 7.2, cf. *Ael.* 2.8. – fall from power: *HA Had.* 4.3.

32 *HA Had.* 7.1–4; 9.3. The existence of a conspiracy is doubted by most modern scholars, e.g. Syme, *Tacitus* (1958) 485, 599 ff., and frequently elsewhere.

33 Nigrinus: Pliny, *Ep.* 5.13.6, 5.20.6, cf. 7.6.2. – father and uncle: Plutarch, *Mor.* 478B, cf. 487E; 548B. – 'most admired': Plutarch, Loeb edn VII, p. 170. – Thrasea: Pliny, *Ep.* 6.29.1.

34 attendance: Talbert, *Senate* (1984) 152 ff. – allusions: Cizek, *Bull. Ass. G. Budé* 3 (1980) 279 ff., compares Tacitus, *Ann.* 16.16. Strack 42 note 40 and 52 f. note 58 found a variety of echoes in Tacitus, *Ann.* and Syme, *Tacitus* (1958) 482 ff., compared the events of 117–18 with Tacitus, *Ann.* 1, on the 'first crime of the new principate' (1.6.1), the adoption of Tiberius (1.7.7), and the four *capaces imperii*, rivals of Tiberius who all came to a bad end (1.13.2–3). Temporini, *Frauen* (1978) 157 ff., has a useful résumé of these and other contributions.

35 *ILS* 2417 = Sm. 192: his subsequent promotion is taken by Speidel, *Guards* (1978)

29 f., 88; id., *Riding for Caesar* (1994) 47 f., as corroborating the plot by Nigrinus. Worth considering, if not wholly convincing. – younger Quietus: *PIR²* A 1409; Eck, *Chiron* 13 (1983) 162.

36 Dio 69.9.6; *ILS* 2558 = Sm. 336, as interpreted by Speidel, *Ancient Society* 22 (1991) 277 ff.

37 Philostratus, *V. soph.* 2.14.

38 *ILS* 1029 = Sm. 224; Roxan II 86; *PIR²* M 619. As Werner Eck kindly informs me, yet another new diploma shows that Natalis was already in Upper Pannonia in 112.

39 barbarians: Dio 69.9.6. – Mursa: Steph. Byz. 458 M; Mócsy, *Pannonia* (1974) 119; Zahrnt, in Olshausen and Sonnabend, *Hist. Geographie* (1991) 469 ff., regarding it as the last 'genuine' (as opposed to titular) *colonia* founded in the Danubian provinces.

40 Mócsy, *Pannonia* (1974) 139 ff., 143 ff. has details on all these, except for Halicanum (S. Soproni, *'Municipium Halicanum'*, *Folia Archaeologica* 30 (1979) 91–8).

41 *HA Had.* 5.2. Falco: *AE* 1957. 336; A.R. Birley, *Fasti* (1981) 99 f.

42 new settlement: Piso, *Fasti* (1993) 30 ff., has the latest information. – Napoca: *CIL* III 6254, 14465. – Drobeta: *CIL* III 6309 = 8129, etc. – Malva: *colonia* in *CIL* XVI 144 of AD 230; but identified with Romula by Piso, *Fasti* (1993) 85 note 18; that place was still a *municipium* under M. Aurelius, *CIL* III 753, etc.

43 *HA Had.* 6.7, 7.3; 9.4; *PIR²* M 249.

44 *HA Had.* 9.4.

45 Eck, *Festschr. Lippold* (1993) 247 ff., convincingly reinterprets *AE* 1958. 189 = 1960. 152, as evidence for Turbo as Guard Prefect – probably in 118–19, although he does not rule out a date later in the reign. – diploma: Roxan I 21.

46 Moesia Inferior: Eck, *Chiron* 13 (1983) 150 and note 338. – Pliny, *Ep.* 7.24, cf. 6.11, 6.29, 9.13. – son-in-law: Syme, 'Ummidius Quadratus *capax imperii*', *Harvard Studies in Classical Philology* 83 (1979) 287–310 = *RP* III (1984) 1158 ff., at 309 = 1177.

47 Mastor: Dio 69.22.2–3. – Borysthenes: *CIL* XII 1122 = Sm. 520.

CHAPTER 9   RETURN TO ROME

1 *Fort. Red.*: *BMC* III 238, 248 f., 400, 403, 405. – Arvals: Sm. 6 (p. 22); for the date, Weber, *Hadrianus* (1907) 81 ff.

2 *BMC* III 401 f., 404 f.

3 new consuls: Arval Acts, Sm. 6 (p. 21). – Barbarus: Thomasson, *Laterculi* I (1984) 396. – Bassus: Syme, 'Spanish Pomponii: a study in nomenclature', *Gerión* 1 (1983) 249–66 = *RP* IV (1988) 140 ff., at 259 ff. = 152 ff. (discussing *AE* 1973. 200). – Matidia cherished: *CIL* XIV 3579 = Sm. 114. – Servianus . . . deference: *HA Had.* 8.11.

4 Pliny, *Pan.* 22–3. – *HA Had.* 9.8, 20.1.

5 gold pieces: *HA Had.* 7.3. – Postumus: Tacitus, *Ann.* 1.6.1. – *congiarium*: *HA Had.* 7.3; *BMC* III 404.

6 Sm. 6 (p. 22), cf. Scheid, *Collège* (1990) 384 ff.

7 Tacitus, *Agr.* 45.1.

8 Dio 69.2.6. – *HA Had.* 7.4, cf. Dio 69.2.4. – Nerva: Dio 68.2.3.

9 Attianus: *HA Had.* 8.7, 9.3–4. – old man: born 5 April AD 40, if, as seems plausible, Caballos Rufino, *Senadores* (1990) 35 f., is right in attributing to him the horoscope in Hephaestio Thebanus 2.18.54–61; *Epit.* 4.26.44–51. – estates: *ILS* 8999; *CIL* XI 2607 (Elba); *CIL* XIV 3039 (Praeneste); Baetica: Caballos Rufino, *Senadores* 35 and note 63. – Similis: Dio 69.19.2; *HA Had.* 9.5; Dobson, *Primipilares* (1978) no. 105.

10 Septicius: Pliny, *Ep.* 1.1. – Suetonius' career: known principally from *AE* 1953. 73 and *HA Had.* 11.3; cf. *CP* 96. – *Famous Men*: cf. Wallace-Hadrill, *Suetonius* (1983) 30 ff. – dedicate: Johannes Lydus, *De mag.* 2.6. – Thurinus: Suetonius, *D. Aug.* 7.1.

11 *signum*: Sm. 6 (p. 20). – expansion: Suetonius, *D. Aug.* 21.2.

12 not well received: *HA Had.* 9.1–2. Note also Eutropius 8.6.1 (*Traiani gloriae invidens*). – Cato: ibid. 5.3. – Suetonius, *Nero* 18 (*etiam ex Britannia deducere exercitum cogitavit, nec nisi verecundia, ne obtrectare parentis gloriae videretur, destitit*), looks like a sly hit at Hadrian's treatment of Trajan's Dacia, cf. Syme, 'The travels of Suetonius Tranquillus', *Hermes* 109 (1981) 105–17 = *RP* III (1984) 1337 ff., at 112 = 1343 f.

13 theatre: *HA Had.* 9.1–2. – plans: cf. above pp. 111 ff. – corn: Strack 63; *BMC* III 402, 405, 406.

14 *HA Had.* 6.5.

15 *HA Had.* 7.5.

16 arrears: *HA Had.* 7.6; Dio 69.8.1²; monument: *ILS* 309 = Sm. 64a. – coins: *BMC* III 417 = Sm. 64b. – relief: Plate 8 – economic activity: thus R.P. Duncan-Jones, *Structure and Scale in the Roman Economy* (Cambridge 1990) 59 ff.; 66 f.

17 *HA Had.* 7.7, 7.9, 3.8, 7.11.

18 *HA Had.* 7.8; Strack 59 f.; *BMC* III 409; cf. Pliny, *Pan.* 27.1.

19 Strack 61 f.; *BMC* III 409 f.; 415; 418, 421.

20 ashes: Dio 69.2.3; cf. Wesch-Klein, *Funus Publicum* (1993) 111 ff. – Nerva: *Epit. de Caes.* 12.12, cf. Dio 69.23.1. – triumph: *HA Had.* 6.3. – games: Dio 69.2.3. – balsam: *HA Had.* 19.5. – Temple: Boatwright, *City* (1987) 74 ff. – Column: Claridge, *JRA* 6 (1993) 5 ff., argues convincingly that the reliefs are of Hadrianic date. – Cf. on Trajan's posthumous honours Kienast, *Chiron* 10 (1980) 391 ff. = id., *Kleine Schriften* (1994) 503 ff. I am not persuaded by Kierdorf, *Tyche* 1 (1980) 147 ff., that the posthumous triumph had taken place in 117, before Hadrian's return. *HA Had.* 6.3 (*triumphum . . . recusavit ipse atque imaginem Traiani curru triumphali vexit*) surely implies Hadrian's personal participation.

21 games: *HA Had.* 7.12, 8.2; Dio 69.8.1²–2. – bread and games: Juvenal 10.81. – indifferent: id. 11.201–4.

22 *HA Had.* 19.8; Dio 69.6.1–2.

23 *CP* 95; *PIR²* H 29–30.

24 army commands: Eck, *Chiron* 13 (1983) 150 f. – Latinianus: known from a new diploma as legate of Pannonia Superior in 125: Eck and Roxan, in Frei-Stolba and Speidel (eds) *Festschr. Lieb* (1995) 74 ff., hence possibly in Inferior by 119/120. – Severus: *ILS* 1056 = Sm. 217; *CIL* XVI 68; Roxan I 47; A.R. Birley, *Fasti* (1981) 106 ff. – foremost: Dio 69.13.2.

25 Britain: cf. below and note 31. – *strategus*: *CPJ* 443 = Sm. 58. – damage: ibid. 447, 449. – confiscation: ibid. 445, 448. – tax-alleviation (known from nine papyri): Bonneau, *Le fisc* (1971) 176 ff. – accusations: *CPJ* 158a = Sm. 517.

26 consul: *HA Had.* 8.5. – Rusticus: Syme, 'The Testamentum Dasumii: some novelties', *Chiron* 15 (1985) 41–63 = *RP* V (1988) 521 ff., at 62 = 544 (stemma), and elsewhere. Dasumii are now attested at Italica: *AE* 1991. 1028 f.; hence the family may derive from there rather than Corduba. – Nepos: Eck, *Chiron* 13 (1983) 150 ff.

27 *HA Had.* 8.5–6, 9.7, Dio 69.7.1, *HA Had.* 8.8–10, 8.1, Dio 69.7.2–3.

28 *HA Had.* 20.1; Dio 69.7.1–2; *HA Had.* 8.3.

29 *HA Had.* 8.4. Cf. Sm. 1 for the list of consuls.

30 Catilius: Halfmann, *Senatoren* (1979) no. 30, cf. no. 18, established his origin. – dinner: Pliny, *Ep.* 3.12. – marriage: Syme, *Chiron* 15 (1985) = *RP* V (1988) 521 ff., at 54 f. = 535 f. – Servianus: *HA Had.* 8.11.

31 *Fort. red.*: Strack 82 ff., 85 ff.; *BMC* III 410, 412, 420, 273 (Hercules). – Britannia:

Toynbee 53 f.; *BMC* III 412. – Victory, etc.: *BMC* III 266 f., 418; 255 (Mars); 264 (Peace); 254 f. (Jupiter); 259 (Rome). Note also the galley, 269 f. – Alexandria: Vogt, *Alex. Münzen* (1924) I 97 f., II 42 f. – *virtus*: *BMC* III 421.

32 Campania: *HA Had.* 9.6, cf. Tacitus, *Ann.* 3.47.3, 4.57.1, 58.2, discussed by Syme, *Tacitus* (1958) 487 f., 524. – Tiberius' astrology: Tacitus, *Ann.* 6.20.2, cf. Syme, *Tacitus* 524 f. – Hadrian's: *HA Had.* 16.7, *Ael.* 3.9.

33 Hellenic identity: cf. M. Leiwo, *Neapolitana. A Study of Population and Language in Graeco-Roman Naples* (Helsinki 1994). – benefactions: *HA Had.* 9.6; cf. Boatwright, *Chiron* 19 (1989) 252 ff., citing *CIL* X 4574 (Caiatia), 6652 (Antium), *ILS* 843 (Nemi). – demarch: *HA Had.* 19.1.

34 Ol. 62–3; 69.

35 *HA Had.* 20.7, 20.9–11.

36 Sm. 333 = Ol. 70 (with alternative translation for 'gain credit'); discussed by Williams, *JRS* 66 (1976) 72 f.

37 *Digest* 47.21.2; cf. Syme, 'Hadrian the intellectual', in *Les Empereurs romains d'Espagne* (1965) 243–53 = *RP* VI (1991) 103 ff., at 245 = 105, reading a little more into it than Williams, *JRS* 66 (1976) 71 f. – Gentianus: *ILS* 1046 = Sm. 237a.

38 Euphrates: Dio 69.8.3; Pliny, *Ep.* 1.10; Philostratus, *V. Apoll.* 8.7.11. – Epictetus: *HA Had.* 16.10, cf. Chapter 6, above. – Favorinus: cf. above, pp. 193 ff.

39 Sm. 7 (p. 23); *CIL* XIV 3579 = Sm. 114.

40 Matidia: *PIR²* M 367; R.-C. no. 681. – Sabina: Eck, in *Festschr. Straub* (1982) 227 ff.; R.-C. no. 802. – coins: *BMC* III 281. – honours: *HA Had.* 9.9, 19.5. – Arvals: Sm. 7 (p. 23).

41 Sm. 7. – Suetonius, *D. Aug.* 21.2.

42 Sm. 452 = Ol. 71.

43 Ol. 72.

44 Ol. 73 (the comment on Plotina's Greek style is by Oliver, p. 179). – Heliodorus: *HA Had.* 16.10, cf. above, p. 182.

45 *Sent. Hadr.* 12.

46 Boatwright, *City* (1987) 58 ff., 74 ff.

47 *RE* Supp. 15 (1978) 1494 ff. (M. Steinby).

48 *HA Had.* 19.9; Boatwright, *City* (1987) 43 ff.

49 Augustan: Boatwright, *City* (1987) 33 ff. – coins: Strack 102 ff.; *BMC* III 282, 422, 423. – Numa: Zoepffel, *Chiron* 8 (1978) 391 ff. – *pomerium*: Boatwright 64 ff.; Bellen, *Forschungsmag. Mainz* 2 (1986) 5 ff.

50 Temple: Kienast, *Chiron* 10 (1980) 400 ff. = id., *Kleine Schriften* (1994) 513 ff.; Boatwright, *City* (1987) 99 ff. – Decrianus, Apollodorus: *HA Had.* 19.12–13.

51 Dio 69.4.1 ff., *HA Had.* 15.9–11.

52 Strack 105 ff.; *BMC* III 278; cf. Beaujeu, *Religion* (1955) 128 ff.; Martin, *Providentia* (1982) 278 ff.

CHAPTER 10   TO THE GERMAN FRONTIER

1 *proconsul* in 121: Weber, *Hadrianus* (1907) 99, gives a list. – *HA Had.* 10.1.

2 Matidia: *HA Had.* 9.1 f. – coins: Toynbee 84 f.; *BMC* III 491, 521–2, 531. 'Gallia' stands, of course, for all four Gallic provinces.

3 Lugdunum: Halfmann, *Itinera* (1986) 197, regards this as probable, citing R. Chevallier, *ANRW* 2.3 (1975) 921 f., 926, for building work there under Hadrian. Weber, *Hadrianus* (1907) 106, 108, assumes that he wintered in Germany. – snows: Dio 69.9.4. – Turbo: *PIR²* M 249 – assumed to have remained behind, as the other prefect was with Hadrian. – Verus: *PIR²* A 695. – M. Aurelius' birth: *HA M. Aur.* 1.5.

4 Empress, officials: *HA Had.* 11.3. – Bradua: *ILS* 8820; A.R. Birley, *Fasti* (1981) 92 ff. – Neratii: *PIR²* N 55, 60. – Natalis: *ILS* 1061 = Sm. 225; *PIR²* M 620. Tacitus' comment, *Ann.* 4.57 f., about Tiberius' retinue when he set off 'at last' (for Campania in AD 26) deserves mention here: it was restricted, only one senator, the Guard Prefect (Sejanus) and one other knight, otherwise men of letters, not least Greeks, whose conversation would provide relief (*ceteri liberalibus studiis praediti, ferme Graeci, quorum sermonibus levaretur*). Whether or not Tacitus had Hadrian in mind when writing about Tiberius (why not?), the last category indeed had a place in the *comitatus* of AD 122 – Septicius and Suetonius, for sure, *ex officio*, but also representing Latin *studia*; perhaps Arrian was of the company as well.

5 Tacitus: *Germ.* 29.4. – Schönberger, *JRS* 59 (1969) 160 ff.; *Ber. der R-G-K* 66 (1985) 369 ff.

6 *HA Had.* 12.6.

7 symbolic: Baatz, in *Roman Frontier Studies 1969* (1974) 117 f., insists that there was nothing fundamentally new about Hadrian's measure, merely a technical improvement. But the symbolic value was surely immensely important, a *finis* after all, despite Virgil, *Aen.* 1.279 f. – Tacitus: *Ann.* 4.32.1–2; 11.20.1–2.

8 converting: cf. note 5, above. – *HA Had.* 10.2.

9 *HA Had.* 10.2; 5.3 (Cato). – Scipio: Appian, *Iberica* 85–6. – Metellus: Sallust, *Jug.* 44–5.

10 *HA Had.* 10.2–5.

11 *HA Had.* 10.6–8. – Gracchus: Plutarch, *Gracch.* 5.1. – later sections: *HA Had.* 17.2, 20.10. Note also 21.9, on his generosity to the troops.

12 forts: *HA Had.* 10.6, also Dio 69.9.1; cf. Tacitus, *Agr.* 20.2. – stores: *HA Had.* 11.1.

13 Dio 69.9.1–4; *Epit. de Caes.* 14.10–11; Vegetius 1.8, 1.27; Arrian, *Tact.* 44.1. – ranking of officers, viz. the creation of the *militia quarta* for the commanders of *alae milliariae*. E. Birley, 'Promotions and transfers in the Roman army: senatorial and equestrian officers', orig. in *Carnuntum-Jb.* 1957, 3–20 (in German), repr. in id., *Roman Army Papers* (1988) 93 ff., at 106.

14 Toynbee 126; *BMC* III 501 f., 496, 533 (mines), 502 (army).

15 Ovilava, Cetium: Alföldy, *Noricum* (1974) 82. – *met(alla)*: *BMC* III 533. – statue: Wegner, *Hadrian* (1956) 33 and Taf. 12a. – Augsburg: Zahrnt, *ZPE* 72 (1988) 179 f. – Raetian army: *BMC* III 502. – Clementianus: *CP* 150*bis* (60) and add., Supp. p. 43; Alföldy, *Noricum* (1974) 244, dates his service *c.* 120. – Censorius: *CP* 97*bis*.

16 Arrian, *Indike* 4.15–16, often discussed. Cf. Grassl, *Chiron* 12 (1982) 250 ff., for a plausible hypothesis about when Arrian might have been at the Inn (viz. in 122 with Hadrian).

17 Auderienses: *CIL* XIII 7063, 7353. – Taunenses: *ILS* 7077, 7080, 7090, 7096. – Mattiaci: *CIL* XIII 7061 ff., 7266, 7271, 7281, 7587. – Forum Hadriani: *Tab. Peut.*; *CIL* III 4279. – Batavi: Tacitus, *Germ.* 29; Speidel, *Riding for Caesar* (1994). – Tungri: M.-T. Raepsaet-Charlier, '*Municipium Tungrorum*', *Latomus* 54 (1995) 361–9 (now conceding that the Tungri were in Germania Inferior, not Belgica).

18 Suetonius, *Cal.* 8; *D. Claud.* 1.2, cf. Tacitus, *Ann.* 2.8.1; Suetonius *D. Tit.* 4.1, discussed by Syme, 'The travels of Suetonius Tranquillus', *Hermes* 109 (1981) 105–17 = *RP* III (1984) 1337 ff., at 112 = 1343. – Nepos: *CIL* XVI 69 = Sm. 347; A.R. Birley, *Fasti* (1981) 100 ff.

19 Toynbee 86 ff.; *BMC* III 345–6; Tacitus, *Germ.* 17.3; *BMC* III 500.

CHAPTER 11   HADRIAN'S WALL

1 *HA Had.* 11.2. Halfmann, *Itinera* (1986) 190, 195 f., is confident about the date.

2 *HA Had.* 11.2–12.1; 15.3 (Florus). – coins: Toynbee 53 ff.; *BMC* III 490 (*adventus*), 498 (*exercitus*), 508 (Britannia), 425, 433 (*exped. Aug.*). The connection of the latter with Britain is denied by Mattingly, ibid. pp. clxvi f., without good reason; cf. Strack 70 f. – Sabinus: *ILS* 2726 = Sm. 276; *CP* no. 118 and *add.*; A.R. Birley, *Fasti* (1981) 292 f. – Agrippa: *ILS* 2735 = Sm. 265; *CP* no. 120; Birley, *Fasti* 292 ff. – appeal: Bowman-Thomas, Tabulae Vindolandenses II no. 344, cf. p. 135 and note 21 below.

3 *HA Had.* 5.2; – Falco: A.R. Birley, *Fasti* (1981) 95 ff. – coins . . . 119: *BMC* III 412; Strack 70 f.; Toynbee 54. – Fronto, *De bello Parthico* 2, p. 221 van den Hout.

4 A.R. Birley, *Fasti* (1981) 220 ff.

5 *CIL* XVI 69 = Sm. 347. – Nepos: A.R. Birley, *Fasti* (1981) 100 ff. – Varro: ibid. 239 f. (and *ILS* 1047). – Laelianus: ibid. 273 f. (and *ILS* 1094+1100).

6 Sabina, Septicius, Suetonius: p. 139 and note 26 below. – Marcellus: *PIR²* N55; A.R. Birley, *Fasti* (1981) 87 ff. Pliny, *Ep.* 3.8. – Bradua: Birley, *Fasti* 92 ff. (on *ILS* 8824a).

7 *HA Had.* 11.2, 12.1. – Voorburg: above p. 121 and note 7.

8 Suetonius, *D. Titus* 4.1. ; cf. Syme, *Tacitus* (1958) 779; 'The travels of Suetonius Tranquillus', *Hermes* 109 (1981) 112 = *RP* III (1984) 1343. – Christians: Eusebius, *HE* 4.8.6–9.3, on which the sceptical view of Nesselhauf, *Hermes* 104 (1976) 348 ff., seems to me the most convincing. For Granianus and Fundanus as proconsuls: and for Fundanus' successor in Asia, Pompeius Falco, Eck, *Chiron* 13 (1983) 155 ff. – Suetonius with Pliny – inferred by Syme from Pliny, *Ep.* 10. 94.1. (Whether or not one reads *nunc* instead of *hunc*, Pliny here indicates that he has got to know Suetonius better.)

9 *CIL* XVI 69 = Sm. 347. – Agrippa: *CP* no. 120; *PME* M 5; A.R. Birley, *Fasti* (1981) 292 ff. – Baienus: *CP* no. 126, *PME* B 14; Birley, *Fasti* 307 f.

10 Stevens, *Building of Hadrian's Wall* (1966), 39, 62, argued that work on the Wall began in 120; against, Breeze and Dobson, *Hadrian's Wall* (3rd edn 1987) 64. For details of the Wall and all its associated works: E. Birley, *Research on Hadrian's Wall* (1961); Daniels (ed.), Bruce, *Handbook* (13th edn 1978); Breeze and Dobson; Daniels (ed.), *Eleventh Pilgrimage* (1989); Breeze, in Maxfield and Dobson (eds), *Roman Frontier Studies 1989* (1991), 35 ff.; Crow, ibid. 44 ff., both with full bibliography. Of other recent studies one may note: Dobson, *Arch. Ael.* 14 (1986) 1 ff.; Wooliscroft, ibid. 17 (1989) 5 ff.; Mann, ibid. 18 (1990) 51 ff.; Maxfield, ibid. 18 (1990) 247 ff.; Hill, ibid. 19 (1991) 33 ff.; Hill and Dobson, ibid. 20 (1992) 27 ff. Some further items are cited below.

11 II Adiutrix: Németh, in Hajnóczi (ed.), *La Pannonia* (1994) 141; and cf. p. 32 above. – surrender: Tacitus, *Historia* 2.1 (*perdomita Britannia et statim missa*). – withdrawal: e.g. Salway, *Roman Britain* (1981) 165 f.

12 Haterius: *ILS* 1338 = Sm. 262a; *CP* no. 95; *PME* H 1. – Anavionenses: A.L.F. Rivet and C. Smith, *The Place-Names of Roman Britain* (London 1975) 249 f. Haterius' presence in Britain *c.* AD 100 is now dated by an unpublished Vindolanda writing-tablet, Inv. 93/1379, a letter from him to Flavius Genialis, referring inter al. to *Coria* (Corbridge, cf. note 19). – 'enforced enrolment': Schönberger, *JRS* 59 (1969) 167; D. Baatz, *Kastell Hesselbach und andere Forschungen am Odenwald Limes* (Berlin 1973) 54 ff., 71 ff., argues that the *numerus*-Kastelle later known to have been occupied by *Brittones* had already received these units as garrison by *c.* 100.

13 Bowman and Thomas, Tabulae Vindolandenses II (1994) nos. 164, 344.

14 *RIB* 1319–20. – Arrian, *Indica* 18.11; Diodorus 17. 104. – Oceanus and Tina coins: thus Toynbee 139 f.; *BMC* III 257 f.; 390. – Roman Newcastle: E. Birley, *Research on Hadrian's Wall* (1961) 161 ff. – bridge: Daniels (ed.), Bruce, *Handbook* (1978) 62.

15 Breeze and Dobson, *Hadrian's Wall* 27 ff., 73.

16 *RIB* 1051. For this interpretation (as the text of a speech by Hadrian), Cantarelli,

Studi e doc. di storia e diritto 19 (1898) 132 f. (subsequently rather neglected). Other views: E. Birley, *Research on Hadrian's Wall* (1961) 159.

17 Frontinus, *De aquis* 2.123. – plaster . . . Dionysius (Diodorus 14.18): Crow, *Britannia* 22 (1991) 58 f. – Hadria: Phlegon, *Olympiads*, *FGrH* 257, fr. 23. (He also mentions an alternative founder, Adrius the Messapian, son of Pauso.) Hadria (Atri), 6 miles inland from the Adriatic, (re)founded as a Latin *colonia* between 290 and 286 BC (Livy, *Perioch.* 11), was a city of the *Praetuttiana regio* (the southern part of Augustus' *regio V*), in which Illyrian elements are not surprisingly detectable. No reference to Phlegon in the lengthy but slightly strange article on the *Praetuttiana regio* by M. Hofmann, *RE* 22.2 (1954) 1639–73 (but information e.g. about the manufacture of *Knackebrot* in the 'Großdeutsches Reich').

18 Falco's Sicilian origin: Salomies, *Adoptive . . . Nomenclature* (1992) 123 f. – China: thus Stevens, *Latomus* 14 (1955) 384 ff.; against, Campbell, *Historia* 28 (1989) 371 ff. – Greek barriers: Hodgson, *Hist. of Northumberland* II 3 (1840) 149 ff.; Crow, in *Studien zu den Militärgrenzen Roms* III (1986) 724 ff. – Jupiter: Virgil, *Aen.* 1.279 f.; cf. also remarks by A.R. Birley, *Trans. Durham & North'd* 3 (1974) 13 ff. O. Lattimore, 'Geography and the ancient empires', in M.T. Larsen (ed.), *Power and Propaganda. A Symposium on Ancient Empires* (Copenhagen 1979) 35–40, at 37 ff., has a view similar to my own: 'both the great Wall of China and the fortified frontiers of the Roman empire, though they have always been regarded as necessary "to keep out the barbarians", were in fact constructed by the Chinese and the Romans to limit their own expansion.' All the same, Hadrian was influenced by Greek notions of 'walling out the barbarians'. Whittaker, *Frontiers* (1994) and in Kennedy, *Roman Army* (1996) 27 (citing Crow and others), does not do justice to these aspects.

19 The name *Coria*: Bowman and Thomas, Tabulae Vindolandenses II p. 96 f. – Florus: *HA Had.* 16.3 (*ambulare per Britannos*). – outposts: Daniels (ed.), Bruce, *Handbook* (1978) 209 ff., 295 ff.; E. Birley, *Research on Hadrian's Wall* (1961) 235 ff., 242 ff. – altar: *Britannia* 10 (1979) 346 no. 7 = *AE* 1979. 388.

20 coins: *BMC* III pp. 318, 466, 480. – commercial dealings: e.g. Bowman and Thomas, Tabulae Vindolandenses II nos. 180, 343; R. and A. Birley, 'Four new writing-tablets from Vindolanda', *ZPE* 100 (1994) 431–46, at 440 ff.; A.R. Birley, 'Supplying the Batavians at Vindolanda', *Proc. 16th Int. Congress of Roman Frontier Studies, Rolduc 1995* (forthcoming). Cf. now A.K. Bowman and J.D. Thomas, 'New writing-tablets from Vindolanda', *Brittania* 27 (1996) 229–328 (with, at 326 ff., improved readings of one text from *ZPE* 100, 440 ff.). – dedications: e.g. *RIB* 990, 1723. – Laelianus: Fronto, *Ad Verum imp.* 2.19, p. 128 van den Hout.

21 R. Birley, *Vindolanda. The Early Wooden Forts* I (1994), esp. 125 f. – petition: Bowman and Thomas, Tabulae Vindolandenses II nos. 180, 344 (not interpreting 'Your Majesty' as the Emperor). Cf. A.R. Birley, art. cited in note 20. (Part of no. 344 is illustrated here as Plate 17.)

22 'another visitor': Camden, cited by E. Birley, *Research* (1961) 6. – Cerialis to Brocchus: Bowman and Thomas, Tabulae Vindolandenses II no. 233; other, still unpublished, writing-tablets further document Cerialis' hunting. – *vertragi*: Arrian, *Cyneg.* 2–3; *tetrafarmacum*: *HA Had.* 21.4 (cf. p. 25 above). – Pennines: *RIB* 1041. – Silvanus Cocidius: *RIB* 1207, 1578; cf. further E. Birley, 'The deities of Roman Britain', in *ANRW* 2.18.1 (1986) 3–112, at 59 f.

23 coastal system: E. Birley, *Research on Hadrian's Wall* (1961) 126 ff.; Daniels (ed.), Bruce, *Handbook* (1978) 260 ff.; Breeze and Dobson, *Hadrian's Wall* (1987) 43 ff.; G.D.B. Jones, *Britannia* 7 (1976) 236 ff., 13 (1982) 283 ff., reporting on recent research and arguing that some kind of palisade connected the coastal installations. Cf. the summaries by Jones and R.L. Bellhouse in Daniels, *Eleventh Pilgrimage* (1989) 92 ff., 89 ff. – Agrippa at Maryport: *RIB* 823–6 (dedications to Jupiter Best and Greatest, at least two of them also to the Emperor's *numen*).

24 Octavius: Bowman and Thomas, Tabulae Vindolandenses II no. 343 (especially lines 20–1). – milestones: *RIB* 2244; 2265; 2272, on which cf. Zahrnt, *ZPE* 73 (1988) 195 ff.

25 Wroxeter: *RIB* 288, cf. comments by Salway, *Roman Britain* (1981) 185 ff. on Wroxeter and other British towns, and 189 f., 547 f., on the Fens.

26 *HA Had.* 11.3. The reading *in eius usu*, with *eius* referring to Sabina, is preferred in the edition by Callu et al., ad loc. Schulz, *Hadrian* (1904) 62 f., seems to have been the first to infer that Sabina and the dismissed officials were in Britain with Hadrian and that this 'Skandal' took place there. This was also the view of Syme, *Tacitus* (1958) 501, 778 ff.; id., 'The travels of Suetonius Tranquillus', *Hermes* 109 (1981) 105–17, at 112 ff. = *RP* III (1984) 1344 ff.; and elsewhere. The *ab epistulis* was normally in attendance, wherever the Emperor went, Millar, *Emperor* (1977) 90 f., cf. ibid. 6, 127 f. – *Famous Whores*: known only from Johannes Lydus, *De mag.* 3.64. – Tiberius: Suetonius, *Tib.* 43–5. – *Epit. de Caes.* 14.8.

27 *HA Had.* 11.4–6.

28 The existence of the *castra peregrina* under Trajan is guaranteed by *ILTun* 778, the career of the former *princeps peregrinorum* Q. Geminius Sabinus: Dobson, *Primipilares* (1978) 222 f., no. 103. – Dedication to Septicius: Johannes Lydus, *De mag.* 2.6.

29 Above, p. 142.

30 *BMC* III 412, 490, 498, 508; Toynbee 53 ff. [Cf. Add., p. 359 below.]

CHAPTER 12   A NEW AUGUSTUS

1 *HA Had.* 12.1, 3–4.

2 *HA Had.* 12.1; Dio 68.8[1]; Vogt, *Alex. Münzen* (1924) I 99, II 45. – Haterius: Thomasson, *Laterculi* I (1984) 348. – Strobel, *ZPE* 71 (1988) 268 ff., argues that there was a serious uprising in Egypt at this time: not convincing. – Vestinus: *IGR* I 136 = Sm. 264; *CP* 105; *PIR*[2] J 623 (both assuming a date late in the reign, for which there seems to be no evidence. The date proposed here is of course equally conjectural).

3 Rammius a possible Guard Prefect: Syme, 'Guard Prefects of Trajan and Hadrian', *JRS* 70 (1980) 64–80 = *RP* III (1984) 1276 ff., at 72 = 1290. For Narbo, cf. *CIL* XII 4416, Q. Rammius Q. l. Fronto. There are other Rammii (not a common name) in Narbonensis.

4 *HA Had.* 16.3–4. The missing line has been much discussed; cf. Callu et al., *Hist. Aug.* (1992) 117 note 158. W.D. Lebek kindly tells me he would prefer a different verb to *latitare* in Florus' third line.

5 Florus, *Vergilius orator an poeta* 1 ff. On Florus cf. *RE* 6.2 (1909) 2761 ff.; Garzetti, *Athenaeum* 42 (1964) 136 ff.; Bessone, *ANRW* 2.34.1 (1993) 80 ff.

6 Florus, poems 1, 2, 4, 6, 8.

7 Florus, *Epit., praef.* 8; 2.30.29; 2.33.51, 2.34.66. The date at which this work was written is not clear. I incline to a Hadrianic date, although it cannot be proved. The indication in the preface – 'not much less than two hundred years from Caesar Augustus to our age' – is too vague to allow precision. Cf. the works cited in note 5 above.

8 wintered: *HA Had.* 12.3. – Nemausus: ibid. 12.2; Dio 69.10.2–3a. – epitaph: *CIL* XII 1122 = Sm. 520. – horses and dogs: *HA Had.* 20.12.

9 Rivet, *Narbonensis* (1988) 256 ff.

10 *CIL* XII 1122 = Sm. 520. I prefer to understand the end of line 4 as *et ruscos*, 'and thickets', rather than *Etruscos*, which is out of place with Pannonian boars. (Henderson, *Hadrian* (1923) 17 note 2, has a characteristically sarcastic comment on this.) Thus Nadel, *RSA* 12 (1982) 182. – Bucephalus: Plutarch, *Alex.* 61. – new city in Asia: *HA Had.* 20.13, cf. above, p. 164.

11 tiles: *CIL* XV 691 ff.; cf. Temporini, *Frauen* (1978) 11 ff.; R.-C. no. 631. Since Hadrian could well still have been in Gaul at the beginning of AD 123, there is no obstacle (*pace* Temporini) to the Nemausus basilica being inaugurated on Plotina's death. – *exactor*: *ILS* 4844 = Sm. 142. – Dio 69.10.3¹–3a.

12 Syme, 'More Narbonensian senators', *ZPE* 65 (1988) 1–24 = *RP* VI (1991) 209 ff., especially 12 ff. = 220 ff., surveys these people. Cf. *PIR*² A 715, 1513, D 126, 152, 167, 182–3. – Macedo: *ILS* 6998.

13 bulwark: Cicero, *Pro Fonteio* 13. – Arcanus: *ILS* 1064; *PIR*² A 333; Martial 8.72.3.

14 Licinianus: Martial 1.49.19 ff., 40. – Sura: *CIL* II 4282; *ILS* 6956, etc. Cf. Syme, 'Rival cities, notably Tarraco and Barcino', *Ktèma* 6 (1981) 271–85 = *RP* IV (1988) 74 ff., at 276 = 81 f. – arch: erected not at the wish of Sura, but of a homonymous ancestor under Augustus, see G. Alföldy, 'Der römische Bogen über der Via Augusta bei Tarraco (Arc de Berà) und seine Inschrift', *Klio* 78 (1996) 158–70, summarising and slightly emending X. Dupré i Raventós, *L'arc romà de Berà (Hispania Citerior)* (Rome 1994) – Pedanii: *RE* 19.1 (1937) 23 f. (Groag).

15 Alföldy, *RE* Supp. 15 (1978) 599 ff., 617 ff.; *Tarraco* (1991) 24 ff. – summoned: Livy 26.19.12, 51.16. – Augustus: Florus, *Epit.* 2.33.51. – rebuilt: *HA Had.* 12.3.

16 Temple: Tacitus, *Ann.* 1.78; Alföldy, *Tarraco* (1991) 43 ff.

17 On Hadrian exploiting this anniversary, Strack 12 ff.; *BMC* III cxv, clxvii; M. Grant, *Roman Anniversary Issues* (Cambridge 1950) 101 f.; Syme, *Tacitus* (1958) 248, 496. Suetonius, *D. Aug.* 21.2 (contrast 31.5). – On Tacitus' insinuation, Syme, *Tacitus* 517 and elsewhere.

18 levy: *HA Had.* 12.4. – 1,000 men: *ILS* 2726 = Sm. 276.

19 *HA Had.* 12.4 has been much discussed: cf. Syme, 'Hadrian and Italica', *JRS* 54 (1964) 142–9 = *RP* II (1979) 617 ff., at 145 f. = 622 ff.; Nierhaus, in *Corolla Swoboda* (1966) 151 ff.; Gagé, *REA* 71 (1969) 65 ff.

20 *HA Had.* 12.5. – Calpurnius Flaccus: *ILS* 6946; Pliny, *Ep.* 5.2; A.R. Birley, *Fasti* (1981) 237. – gild statues: *ILS* 6930.

21 coinage: *BMC* III 501. – Segisama: Florus, *Epit.* 2.33.48; Orosius 6.21.3. – Quartinus: *CIL* XIV 4473, XIII 1802, improved by Alföldy, *Fasti* (1969) 79 ff.

22 coinage: Toynbee 102 ff.; *BMC* III 340, 346, 511–12. – Dio 69.10.1. – request: A. Gellius, *NA* 16.13.4. – lavish scale: cf. e.g. García y Bellido, in *Les empereurs romains* (1965) 7 ff.; Caballos Rufino, *Itálica* (1994) 109 ff. – *ILS* 5973, Villanueva de Cordoba, registers a Julius Proculus adjudicating boundaries between three Baetican communities, his verdict *confirmatum ab imp. Caesar[e] Hadriano Aug.* Alföldy, *Fasti Hisp.* (1969) 166 f., identifies Proculus as the *cos. suff.* 109 (*ILS* 1040), suggesting that he was with Hadrian as *comes* in Spain and appointed *iudex* for the purpose. (Date and identification rejected by A.U. Stylow in the new edition of the inscription, *CIL* II² 7 (1995), 776.) More is now known, and even more can now be conjectured, about the Proculus *cos.* 109: he was apparently *cos. II*, presumably under Hadrian, perhaps *suff. II* in 134 or 137, more likely perhaps the intended colleague, as *cos. ord.*, of Servianus *cos. III ord.* in 134, below note 4 to Chapter 21. The information comes from a new fragmentary inscription at Larinum: G. De Benedettis and A. Di Niro, *L'anfiteatro di Larinum. Iscrizioni, monete, sepolture* (Molise 1995) 21 ff., whose restorations need improving. Werner Eck kindly showed me a copy of this publication. Cf. further remarks in A.R. Birley, 'Hadrian and Greek senators' *ZPE* 116 (1997) 231 ff.

23 frontiers: *HA Had.* 12.6–7.

24 Gutsfeld, *Nordafrika* (1989) 88 ff., especially 98 ff., argues that the *motus* was invented, a confusion with the trouble of 117; this seems too extreme. – Antoninus: *HA Ant. Pius* 5.4.

25 *HA Had.* 12.8. – Quartinus: Alföldy, *Fasti* (1969) 79 ff.

CHAPTER 13   RETURN TO THE EAST

1 'most poorly documented': Halfmann, *Itinera* (1986), 197. – *HA: Had.* 12.8. – coinage: Vogt, *Alex. Münzen* (1924) I 100, II 46.

2 road-building: *CIL* VIII 10114 = 22173; seventeen further milestones from AD 124, Labrousse, *Mél. soc. toul.* 2 (1948) 143 note 111, who firmly argues for a visit to Africa by Hadrian on his way to the east, although he dates it a year too early, following Strack 73 ff.; Halfmann, *Itinera* (1986) 197, rejects a visit. – Metilius: Thomasson, *Laterculi* I (1984) 396; *PIR²* M 549.

3 On Phlegon as a source for the imperial itinerary, Weber, *Hadrianus* (1907) 94 ff. – 'Furnita': *FGrH* 257 fr. 22. Weber 120 failed to identify this as Furnos. – Furnos Minus: Gascou, *ANRW* 2.10.2 (1982) 281 f. – Furnos Maius: N. Ferchiou, 'Quelques inédites de Furnos Maius', in *L'Africa Romana* 2 (Sassari 1985) 179–88.

4 Bradua: *ILS* 8824; A.R. Birley, *Fasti* (1981) 92 ff.

5 ravaged: Orosius 7.12; Applebaum, *Jews and Greeks* (1979) 269 ff. – baths: Sm 60. – address: thus the editor on Ol. 122. – benevolence: Ol. 120–1. – coins: Toynbee 121; *BMC* III 524. – new city: Orosius 7.12; Syncellus 659, 19, etc., cf. Weber, *Hadrianus* (1907) 119 f. – Hadrianopolis: located by G.D.B. Jones and J.H. Little, *JRS* 61 (1971) 67 ff.

6 Crete: a visit is assumed by Strack 77; dismissed by Halfmann, *Itinera* (1986) 197. Cyprus: on Flaccus, A.R. Birley, *Fasti* (1981) 237. – explorer: Tertullian, *Apol.* 5.7. – Quartinus: Alföldy, *Fasti* (1969) 79 ff.

7 Malalas 278 f., cf. Weber, *Hadrianus* (1907) 231 f. – 'Baths': *Comptes-rendus de l'Académie des Inscriptions* (1989) 535 no. 1. – temple: Suda, s.v. Iovianus. – coinage: Vogt, *Alex. Münzen* (1924) I 100, II 46.

8 The commemorative coinage later celebrates both the *exercitus Syriacus* and *exercitus Cappadocicus*, *BMC* III 503, 498. Both armies saw Hadrian several times. – Parthian rival kings: Schippmann, *Grundzüge* (1980) 64; Karras-Klapproth, *Pros. Studien* (1988) 114 ff., 201 f. – Parthamaspates and Ialud: *HA Had.* 5.4; Weber, *Hadrianus* (1907) 119; Drijvers, *ANRW* 2.8 (1977) 874 f. – daughter, throne: *HA Had.* 13.8.

9 coinage: *BMC* III 425, 433, 434 (*expeditio*); 254, 437 (Janus). – Orosius 7.19.4.

10 Praesens: Eck, *Chiron* 13 (1983) 160 note 379. – Armenians: *HA Had.* 21.11.

11 Neocaesarea, Nicopolis, Amasia: Weber, *Hadrianus* (1907) 265; D. Magie, *Roman Rule in Asia Minor* (Princeton 1950) 1460. Dated by Halfmann, *Itinera* (1986) 198, to 123 rather than 131 (as Weber). – Phlegon: *FGrH* 257 fr. 18. – Strabo: R. Syme, *Anatolica. Studies in Strabo* (Oxford 1995) 357.

12 Arrian, *Periplus* 1.1. – Xenophon, *Anab.* 4.7.21 ff.

13 Arrian, *Periplus* 1.2 ff. – harbour: ibid. 16.6.

14 Hyssus: Arrian, *Periplus* 3.1. – native rulers: ibid. 11.2–3, 18.3. – Cotys: ibid. 17.3; *FGrH* 257 fr. 17; *PIR²* J 276 (with stemma); Nadel, *RSA* 12 (1982) 186 ff.

15 Arrian, *Periplus* 12.2. – Septicius: Pliny, *Ep.* 1.1. – Suetonius on Pliny's staff: argued from Pliny, *Ep.* 10.94.1, by Syme, *Tacitus* (1958) 779, and 'Biographers of the Caesars', *Museum Helveticum* 37 (1980) 104–28 = *RP* III (1984) 1251 ff., at 123 = 1269.

16 Sinope: Pliny, *Ep.* 10.90. – Amisus: 10.92. – Amastris: 10.97. – Suetonius: 10.94. – Christians: 10.96–7. – Sinope, bishop: the father of the heretic Marcion, Epiphanius, *Panarion* 42; cf. *ODCC²* 870 f.

17 Heraclea: *Bulletin de correspondence héllenique* 9 (1885) 68 f.; Weber, *Hadrianus* (1907) 125. – Nicomedia coinage: Toynbee 126; *BMC* III 524. – earthquake: Syncellus 659, 7; *Chron. Pasch.* 475, etc.; Weber, *Hadrianus* 127 f. – Nicaea gates: *IGR* III 37. – coins of Bithynia: Toynbee 51 f.; *BMC* III 490, 520–1.

18 aqueduct: Pliny, *Ep.* 10.37. – Nicaea theatre: 10.39. – *Graeculi*: 10.40.2, cf. *HA Had.* 1.5. – Lake: 10.41. Cf. on this theme Mitchell, *Harvard Studies in Classical Philology* 91 (1987) 333.

19 Bithynium: Pliny, *Ep.* 10.39.5–6. – Hadriane: Weber, *Hadrianus* (1907) 126; Le Glay, *BCH* 100 (1976) 357 ff., has a convenient list of towns in Asia which received Hadrian's name. – home-town: Dio 69.11.2. – Mantinium: Robert, *A travers l'Asie Mineure* (1980) 132 ff. – portraits: Kähler, *Villa* (1950) 177 ff., followed by Grenier and Coarelli, *MEFR* 98 (1986) 252, regards at least one of the figures in the *tondi* from the Arch of Constantine as depicting Antinous in autumn 130, aged about 20. On this question, p. 284, above – team of builders etc.: *Epit. de Caes.* 14.5. – Trajan's reluctance: Pliny, *Ep.* 10.18.3, 40.3, cf. 62.

20 Catilius: Halfmann, *Senatoren* (1979) 133 ff., no. 38. – Cassii: ibid. 194 no. 123; on Cassius Agrippa, A.R. Birley, *Fasti* (1981) 241 f.

21 Hadrian's friend: *HA Had.* 15.4. – prosecution: Pliny, *Ep.* 7.6, 7.10.1. – ruin: ibid. 10.70–1.

22 Polemo, *De Physiognomia*, ed. G. Hoffmann, in R. Foerster, *Scriptores Physiognomici Graeci et Latini* I (Leipzig 1893) 138 ff. Exploited by Premerstein, *Attentat* (1908) 46 ff., but his attempt to identify Lusius Quietus in this text and date the journey to 118 has not convinced. Text improved by Bowersock, *Sophists* (1969) 120 ff., dating the journey to 124; and cf. now Weiss, *Chiron* 25 (1995) 218 ff.

23 Polemo: details in *PIR²* A 862. – his ancestors and connections: Sullivan, *ANRW* 2.7.2 (1980) 913 ff. – kinsman pupil: Philostratus, *V. soph.* 1.25.4 (not named).

24 Philostratus, *V. soph.* 1.25.2.

25 Philostratus, *V. soph.* 1.25.3. – Bassus and Trajan: Syme, *Tacitus* (1958) 510 f.; 'Hadrian as philhellene: neglected aspects', *BHAC 1982/83* (1985) 341–62 = *RP* V (1988) 546 ff., at 356 f. = 558 f. – long train: Philostratus, *V. soph.* 1.25.2.

26 coins: Toynbee 130; *BMC* III 496. The *exercitus* coins are omitted in *BMC*; cf. Strack 143 and no. 815. – Oresta: Weber, *Hadrianus* (1907) 15 ff. – statue: *CIG* 2020. – legate: Eck, *Chiron* 13 (1983) 158, cf. 169. – Coela: F. Grelle, *L'autonomia cittadina fra Traiano e Adriano* (Naples 1972) 180, 212 ff. P. Gavius Balbus, procurator of the Thracian Chersonese, was honoured by the *municipium* of Coela, *IKEph* VII 1, 3048: Eck, in Eck (ed.), *Pros. und Sozialgeschichte* (1993) 370 ff. – road-building: *CIL* III S 14207³⁵, cf. 7615. – victory over Scythians: *IGR* I 884; Nadel, *RSA* 12 (1982) 187. – further north: thus Weber, *Hadrianus* 151. – Praesens: Eck, *Chiron* 13 (1983) 160. – Polemo: *De Phys.* 139.

CHAPTER 14 A SUMMER IN ASIA

1 Florus: 1.40.15. – Propertius: 3.22.1 ff. – Tryphaena: *PIR²* A 900. – Mucianus: Syme, 'Pliny the procurator', *Harvard Studies in Classical Philology* 73 (1969) 210–36 = *RP* II (1979) 742 ff., at 203 ff. = 744 f. – earthquake: Malalas 279.

2 Falco: Eck, *Chiron* 13 (1983) 158. His son died in 180, aged 62: *ILS* 1106. – Polla: J. and L. Robert, *Bulletin épigraphique* 90 (1977) 418 f., no. 489, on *IGR* IV 779–80. – 300 years earlier: an inference from the *Scholiast* on Lucian, *Icarom.* 24, quoted by Schulz and Winter, *Asia Minor Studien* 1 (1990) 36 note 30, where this temple is said to have taken as long to finish as that of Olympian Zeus at Athens. – Apollonis: Polybius 22.20. – Pliny, *Ep.* 10.41.5.

3 gold thread: Pliny, *NH* 36.98. – whole province: *IGR* IV 140, cf. Schulz and Winter, *Asia Minor Studien* 1 (1990) 37 ff. – *neocorus*: ibid. 49 ff. – temple construction: ibid. 56 ff.

4 Hadriane, etc.: Weber, *Hadrianus* (1907) 132 f.; cf. Le Glay, *BCH* 100 (1976) 358 f. – Apollonia, Miletopolis: *IGR* IV 128 f.; 121–3; Weber 132 and notes 418–19. – 500 cities: e.g. Philostratus, *V. soph.* 2.1.3. – Parium: *CIL* III 374; Weber 133 note 476. – Ajax: Philostratus, *Her.* 288. – Alexandria Troas: *CIL* III 7282; Weber 133.

5 *HA Had.* 20.13; Dio 69.10.2; Weber, *Hadrianus* (1907) 131; Robert, *Documents d'Asie Mineure* (1987) 133 ff.; on Hadriania and Hadriani, p. 262, above.

6 Polemo, *De phys.* 138 ff.

7 alleged attempt: Premerstein, *Attentat* (1908) 46 ff.; better interpreted by Bowersock, *Sophists* (1969) 120 ff. – Nigrinus: Dio 69.2.5. – Tarraco: *HA Had.* 12.5. – Athens: ibid. 13.2.

8 Polemo, *De phys.* 160 ff. (Favorinus); 148 (Hadrian); cf. *Scriptores Physiognomici* II 51 f.

9 Zeus the Hunter: Robert, *Documents d'Asie Mineure* (1987) 133 ff. – letter: Ol. 79. The interpretation by Weber, *Hadrianus* (1907) 136 ff., is doubted by D. Magie, *Roman Rule in Asia Minor* (Princeton 1950) 1478, and Ol., ad loc.

10 population of Pergamum: Galen 5.49 K. – On the city, W. Radt, *Pergamon* (Cologne 1988), especially 239 ff. on the Trajaneum. – Quadratus and Bassus: *PIR²* J 507–8.

11 Satan's throne: *Revelation* 2.13. – temple-wardenship: Price, *Rituals* (1984) 252 f. – Asclepieum: Le Glay, *BCH* 100 (1970) 347 ff. – New Asclepius: *IGR* IV 351; Weber, *Hadrianus* (1907) 135.

12 Library: *RE* 3.1 (1897) 414 f. – Bassus' monument: Habicht, *Pergamon* VIII 3 (1969) 43 ff. – Camerinus: Eck and Roxan, in Frei-Stolba and Speidel (eds), *Festschrift Lieb* (1995) 77 f. – Rufinus: *PIR²* C 1637.

13 Nico: *PIR²* A 226. – Galen: ibid. G 24. – attendant's eye: Galen 5.17 f. K. Galen has only two other mentions of Hadrian: that he had a work dedicated to him by Favorinus, 1.40 f. K., and that he approved of the edition of Hippocrates by the doctor Artemidorus Capito, 15.21 K.

14 Mytilene: *IGR* IV 84–7, 89; Weber, *Hadrianus* (1907) 135 f. – Sardes: Polemo, *De Phys.* 138, as amended by Bowersock, *Sophists* (1969) 120 ff. – Thyatira, Nacrasa: *IGR* IV 1196–9; 1160; Weber 138. – Saittae: Weiss, *Chiron* 25 (1995) 213 ff.

15 Polemaeanus: *PIR²* J 260; Halfmann, *Senatoren* (1979) 111 f., no. 16. – Julius Pardalas: *PIR²* J 448. – Menemachus: Plutarch, *Mor.* 798 A ff., 805 A ff. – ridiculous: ibid. 811 B f. – further quotations: ibid. 813 D ff.; 813 E f.; 825 D; 814 C f.; 814 F f.

16 Plutarch dead: C.P. Jones, *Plutarch* (1971) 34. – statue: *SIG³* 829A = Sm. 487. – Bassus: Halfmann, *Senatoren* (1979) 119 f., no. 26. – Major: ibid. 153 ff., no. 54. – Arrian: ibid. 146 f., no. 56. The much debated identification of the historian with the proconsul Arrianus who composed a Greek epigram for an altar to Artemis at Corduba, *AE* 1974. 370, remains conjectural, of course: but Bosworth, *ANRW* 2.34.1 (1993) 238 ff., seems to me to make it even more plausible (from the content of the poem). Meanwhile, J. Beltrán Fortes, 'Arriano de Nicomedia y la Bética, de nuevo', *Habis* 23 (1992) 171–96, has argued that the style of carving demands a third-century date for the stone; I am not convinced. (Werner Eck, who himself finds Beltrán's case more persuasive than I do, kindly drew my attention to this article.) – Charax: Halfmann 161 f., no. 73.

17 *Anth. Pal.* 12, especially 17, here quoted. For Strato's date, Bowie, in Russell (ed.), *Antonine Literature* (1990) 56 f.

18 Trocetta: *AE* 1957. 17. – Peducaeus: Eck, *Chiron* 13 (1983) 160. – Tmolus: Weber, *Hadrianus* (1907) 139 and note 504.

19 Polemo, colossal sum, etc.: Philostratus, *V. soph.* 1.25.2; *IGR* IV 1398, 1431. – second Wardenship: Price, *Rituals* (1984) 258.

20 Augustus and Ephesus: cf. e.g. *RE* Supp. 12 (1970) 263 f. – Erythrae Landing Festival: *IGR* IV 1542. – Ionian League: *RE* 18.3 (1949) 601–5. – Panionios: *IKEph* 1501; Weber, *Hadrianus* (1907) 217. – Antimachus: Dio 69.4.6; *HA Had.* 16.2. – Plato: Plutarch, *Lysander* 18.5. – Quintilian: *Inst. or.* 10.1.53. – Plutarch, *Timoleon* 36.2. – Artemis: *Antimachi Colophonii Reliquiae*, ed. B. Wyss (Berlin 1936), fr. 75.

21 A gigantic inscription, mentioning Hadrian in the nominative case, hence no doubt as restorer of the temple, was on view at Claros in March 1990 (evidently not

published: referred to indirectly by J. and L. Robert, *Bulletin épigraphique* 1962, 199). – Tacitus: Eck, *Chiron* 12 (1982) 353. – Germanicus: Tacitus, *Ann.* 2.54.

22 Oenoanda letter: Wörrle, *Stadt und Fest* (1988).

23 Gavii: Eck, in Eck (ed.), *Pros. und Sozialgeschichte* (1993) 368 ff. – Bassus: Pliny, *Ep.* 10.21, 86a.

24 Petronius Priscus: *AE* 1993. 447 (presumably before 128 from Hadrian's titulature). – petitions: Dio 69.6.3. Cf. Millar, *Emperor* (1977) 3, who cites similar stories.

25 hymn: Sm. 726 = *IKEph* 1145. – Paul: *Acts* 19.23 ff.

26 to Rhodes: *HA Had.* 13.1; Polemo, *De phys.* 138, as amended by Bowersock, *Sophists* (1969) 120 ff. – Erastus and Philocyrius: *IKEph* 1487–8. Sm. 72a and Ol. 82A unfortunately knew only the Erastus letter. Cf. on these and the implications Drew-Bear and Richard, in *Mél. Le Glay* (1994) 742 ff. – galley: Vogt, *Alex. Münzen* (1924) I 100, II 46.

27 Colossus: Malalas 279, discussed by Weber, *Hadrianus* (1907) 243 f. – Tiberius: Suetonius, *Tib.* 11–13. 'future Zeus', Apollonides, *Anthologia Palatina* 9.287, cited by Bowersock, in Millar and Segal (eds), *Caesar Augustus* (1984) 169 ff. (a valuable discussion of Tiberius on Rhodes and much else), at p. 181. – Tiberius and Hadrian, Syme, *Tacitus* (1958) 488, 517, and elsewhere. – Romaea, Caesarea: Price, *Rituals* (1984) 88. – Dio, *Or.* 31.121 f., praises the Rhodians for their Hellenism.

28 Praesens: Eck, *Chiron* 13 (1983) 160. – Nepos: still in Britain on 15 September 124, *CIL* XVI 70. – modifications: Breeze and Dobson, *Hadrian's Wall* (1987) 74 ff., on 'dislocation' in this year. – Egypt: Thomasson, *Laterculi* I (1984) 348. – City prefecture: Verus' successor, Lollius Paulinus, once colleague of Julius Quadratus as consul for the first time (*suff.* 94), was evidently in office before becoming *cos. II* (*ord.*), the Prefect's by now usual honour, at the beginning of 125, *PIR²* L 320.

29 *HA Had.* 13.1.

CHAPTER 15   A YEAR IN GREECE

1 'a few other cities': e.g. Boeotian Coronea, to judge from *IG* VII 2879, honouring him there before he was Emperor. – On the Mysteries: Mylonas, *Eleusis* (1961). – knives: *HA Had.* 13.2.

2 undertook rites: *HA Had.* 13.1; Dio 69.11.1. – priestess: *IG* II/III² 3575 = Sm. 71a. – precedents: Weber, *Hadrianus* (1907) 109 ff. – Augustus: Dio 54.9.7 ff. – Philopappus: proposed by Oliver, *AJP* 71 (1950) 295 ff.

3 Herodes in Pannonia: above, p. 89. – quaestor: *SIG³* 863 note 1 = Sm. 199b. New evidence on the career of his father (Roxan III 159: not consul until *c.* 132, rather than *c.* 108 or earlier) makes necessary some revision on Herodes' career, e.g. as in Ameling, *Herodes* (1983), II 1 ff. – father Atticus: *AE* 1919. 8 = Sm. 198 shows that he acquired *ornamenta praetoria*, honorary senatorial rank, perhaps from Trajan, even if it is now clear that Trajan did not make him a senator, let alone consul, as formerly assumed. Hadrian may initially have 'topped up' the *ornamenta* by making them *consularia*; and then have adlected him into the Senate later on. For further discussion, A.R. Birley, 'Hadrian and Greek senators' (*ZPE* 116 (1997) 209 ff.). – reform laws: Jerome, *Chron.* 198 Helm, etc.; Weber, *Hadrianus* (1907) 165 f.; Follet, *Athènes* (1976) 116 ff. – Pythodorus: Graindor, *Athènes* (1934) 32. – Council: Weber 163; Graindor 83 ff.; Follet 113 ff. – oil law: Sm. 443 = Ol. 92 . – fish: Sm. 444 = Ol. 77. – bridge: Jerome, *Chron.* 198 Helm; Weber 167. – favours: *HA Had.* 13.1.

4 Megara: Philostratus, *V. soph.* 1.24.3. – inscriptions: *IG* VII 70–2, 3491; Weber, *Hadrianus* (1907) 182. – Sabina: *IG* VII 73, 74. – Apollo: Pausanias 1.44.9. – road: ibid. 1.44.10. – milestone: *IG* VII 69. – edict: Ol. 56. – failure: Pausanias 1.36.3.

5 Epidaurus: *SIG³* 842 note 3; *IG* IV 1406; Weber, *Hadrianus* (1907) 182 f. – Pulcher: *PIR²* C 1424; *CP* 81. – Council: discussed by U. Kahrstedt, 'Zwei Probleme im kaiserzeitlichen Griechenland, II. Das Koinon der Achaier', *Symbolae Osloenses* 28 (1950) 70–5 (requiring revision in some details). – Plutarch: *Mor.* 86 B-D.

6 Troezen: *IG* IV 758; Weber, *Hadrianus* (1907) 183 f. – Hermione: *IG* IV 702. – Hera: Pausanias 2.17.6. – Nero: Suetonius, *Nero* 22 f.; Dio 63.21. – boys' race: Pausanias 6.16.4. – 30 December: *IGLS* IV 1265. – Council: *IG* VII 2711 f. – aqueduct, theatre: Spawforth and Walker, *JRS* 76 (1986) 102 f.; Piérart, in Frei-Stolba and Speidel (eds), *Festschr. Lieb* (1995) 7 ff.

7 revival of name: Pausanias 8.8.12. – Epaminondas: ibid. 8.11.8. On him cf. e.g. Cicero, *Tusc.* 1.2; Justin 6.8. – Caphisodorus: Plutarch, *Mor.* 761 D. – Poseidon: Pausanias 8.10.2.

8 Mantinium: cf. p. 158, above. – honour Antinous: Pausanias 8.9.7, etc.; Weber, *Hadrianus* (1907) 186 ff. – Antinoe: Pausanias 8.8.4; 8.9.5.

9 Tegea: *IG* V 2, 50; Weber, *Hadrianus* (1907) 188. – Sparta: *IG* V 1, 486 and 32 A, *SEG* XI 492, attest his presence. On Roman Sparta, Spawforth, in Cartledge and Spawforth, *Hellenistic and Roman Sparta* (1989) 93 ff., especially 105 ff., 127 ff. As he shows more clearly than had previously been done, the 'Greek renaissance', with its obsessive attention to ancient Hellenic glories, greatly restored the fortunes of Sparta, an essential and major component in the living museum which 'Old Greece' was becoming. – host: Spawforth, *ABSA* 73 (1978) 249 ff.; Halfmann, *Senatoren* (1979) 125 ff., no. 29. However, their early (Trajanic) dating of Herculanus' career is less convincing; cf. also *PIR²* J 302. I return to this question in more detail elsewhere, 'Hadrian and Greek senators' (*ZPE* 116 (1997) 237 ff.). – first Eurycles: *PIR²* J 301 (other members of family, 372, 587); G.W. Bowersock, 'Eurycles of Sparta', *JRS* 51 (1961) 111–18; id., in Millar and Segal (eds), *Caesar Augustus* (1984) 176 ff.; Spawforth in Cartledge and Spawforth (above) 93 ff. – 36th from Dioscuri: *IG* V 1, 971, 1172 = Sm. 210. – Arrian: *AE* 1974. 370; Eck, *Chiron* 13 (1983) 190. Cf. further note 16 to Chapter 14, above. – Plutarch: *Mor.* 539 A, cf. p. 63, above. – Falco: of his inscriptions only *ILS* 1035 includes the names of Herculanus, which he presumably inherited after the latter's death.

10 Caudus, Corone: *SEG* XI 494–5; Spawforth and Walker, *JRS* 76 (1986) 96 note 72. – aqueduct: Spawforth in Cartledge and Spawforth, *Hellenistic and Roman Sparta* (1989) 130, 216, citing 'pers. comm. from S. Walker'. – altars: *IG* V 1, 381–405. – Artemis Orthia: e.g. Plutarch, *Lyc.* 18.1; Philostratus, *V. Apoll.* 6.20, 7.42; Pausanias 3.16.10 f. – Atticus at Sparta: Spawforth, *ABSA* 75 (1980) 203 ff. – Laconian practices: Ol. 122.

11 Lycosura: Weber, *Hadrianus* (1907) 189 note 675. – Abea: *IG* V 1, 1352; Weber 189. – statues: Pausanias 5.12.6. – Zeus Apobaterios, coins: Weber 190 and note 679.

12 Pausanias 5.6.4–6.

13 Mummius: p. 24, above. – colonists: Pausanias 2.1.2. – Favorinus: in his speech attributed to Dio of Prusa, *Or.* 37.26. – statue: ibid. 1, 8. – benefactions: Pausanias 2.3.5.

14 Dionysia: *HA Had.* 13.1; Dio 69.16.1; *IG* II² 3287; Weber, *Hadrianus* (1907) 162 ff. – Epicureans: Ol. 73–4. – philosopher friend: *HA Had.* 16.10. In favour of the identification of friend, Epicurean and Avidius Heliodorus (as in *PIR²* A 1405): Birley, *Laverna* 5 (1994) 197 note 80; the letter of 125 has been re-edited by Follet, *REG* 107 (1994) 158 ff.; the addressee is now read as 'our Heliodorus', removing one difficulty over the identification with Avidius (which Follet herself, however, still rejects).

15 Bowersock, *Sophists* (1969) 118 f., discussing Secundus' Arabic text, para. 9. Cf. Perry, *Secundus* (1964) 127. – tribune: ibid. 72–3.

16 Eusebius, *HE* 4.3. Cf. *ODCC²* 84 f.; 1149.

17 temple: Vitruvius 7, pr. 15; Strabo 9.1.16, 396; Suetonius, *D. Aug.* 60. – went sour: Kienast, in *Festschr. Lippold* (1993) 203 f. – enclosure: thus Willers, *Panhell. Programm* (1990), especially 99 f., whose interpretation I largely follow.

18 aqueduct: *ILS* 337 = Sm. 396; Spawforth and Walker, *JRS* 75 (1985) 98 f. – Library: thus Willer, *Panhell. Programm* (1990) 14 ff. But cf. p. 219, above and note 11. – Roman Agora: Kienast, in *Festschr. Lippold* (1993) 192, 201.

19 Eros: Pausanias 9.27.1. – verses: *IG* VII 1828. – Socrates: Xenophon, *Symp.* 8.3–15. Lambert, *Beloved* (1984) 61, doubts whether Hadrian's poem implies that his relationship with Antinous had already begun. Who can tell?

20 Plutarch: *Mor.* 748 E–771 E. The quotations are from 748 F; 749 C ff.; 750 A ff.; 751 A; 752 C ff. – Roman attitudes: MacMullen, *Historia* 31 (1982) 484 ff.

21 *Epit. de Caes.* 14.5. – Vitalis: *ILS* 7741.

22 Lebadea: cf. Plutarch, *Mor.* 411 F. Pausanias 9.39 describes the consultation. On Trophonius' significance for Hadrian, p. 255, above. Guarducci, *Bull. Mus. Imp.* 12 (1941) 156, and in *Les empereurs* (1965) 217, believes in a visit; Weber, *Hadrianus* (1907) 177, has a different (unconvincing) explanation. Hadrian was honoured by Lebadea as benefactor and saviour: *IG* VII 1675.

23 Ol. 108, 109. Later letters, ibid. 110–18.

24 Pausanias 10.35.4, 6.

25 letter: Ol. 75, with useful discussion. Augustus' measures are mentioned by Pausanias 10.8.3–5.

26 Plutarch dead, honoured: C.P. Jones, *Plutarch* (1971) 34. – statue: *SIG*³ 829A = Sm. 487. – settled conditions: Plutarch, *Mor.* 408 B. Cf. on Plutarch and Delphi Swain, *Historia* 40 (1991) 318 ff. – Homer question: *Anth. Pal.* XIV 102.

27 *frumentarius*, office: *ILS* 9473 = Sm. 334a. – letter from Tibur: Ol. 74*bis*. – honoured by Hellenes: *SIG*³ 835A. Instructive remarks on this 'league' by C.P. Jones, *Chiron* 26 (1996) 45 f. – religious days: A. Plassart, *Fouilles de Delphes* III 4 (Paris 1970), 307, col. III.

28 Tempe: *HA Had.* 26.5. – Macedonia: from the coins (*BMC* III 494, 524). – Nicopolis: *SEG* XI 493; Halfmann, *Itinera* (1986) 203. – Herodes: *SIG*³ 863 note 1 = Sm. 199a. Further, A.R. Birley, *ZPE* 116 (1997), 209 ff.

CHAPTER 16 *PATER PATRIAE*

1 Dyrrachium: Ol. 56. – Megara road: Pausanias 1.44.10; *IG* IV 69. – northern Greece: Halfmann, *Itinera* (1986) 203.

2 Etna: *HA Had.* 13.3. – coins: Toynbee 128 ff.; *BMC* III 496, 516 f. – Falco: Salomies, *Adoptive Nomenclature* (1992) 121 ff. – Latro: *CP* 104.

3 preferred Cato: *HA Had.* 16.6. – consul Verres: *CIL* VI 2081 + 32378 = Sm. 10; *AE* 1962. 391 = Roxan I 26.

4 Hadrian's construction of an artificial harbour for Lupiae in the heel of Italy, mentioned in passing by Pausanias 6.19.9 (who somehow got the idea that that town, modern Lecce, had replaced Sybaris, which is a long way away, in the instep) may go back to this journey. The family of the future M. Aurelius (so much favoured by Hadrian) claimed descent from the legendary founder of the place, *HA M. Aur.* 1.6 (from Marius Maximus): this may have helped to set Hadrian's benefaction in train. – Via Traiana, Falco: above, p. 58. – Venusia: *ILS* 6485. – Aeclanum: *CIL* IX 1111. – Eggius: *PIR*² E 5; cf. Boatwright, *Chiron* 19 (1989) 238 ff. – improve Via Appia: *CIL* IX 6072, 6074 f.; *AE* 1930. 122. – Beneventum: the Arch has often been studied, cf. e.g. F.J. Hassell, *Der Trajansbogen in Benevent* (Mainz 1966), who, however, argues that the whole work was complete in 114 and not altered; against, e.g. F.A. Lepper, *JRS* 59 (1969), reviewing Hassell, especially 259 ff. – Neratii: *PIR*² N 56 ff. – Tervetia: Phlegon, *FGrH* 257 fr. 21. – Terventum: *CIL* IX 2565.

5 Coins: Strack 83 (not in *BMC* III). – Pantheon: Boatwright, *City* (1987) 43 ff. – Deified Trajan: *HA Had.* 19.9; *ILS* 306 = Sm. 141a.; Boatwright, *City* 74 ff. – Janus: *BMC* III 254, 437.

6 Delphi letter: Ol. 74*bis.* – Tibur: Syme, 'Spaniards at Tivoli', *Ancient Society* 13/14 (1982/3) 341–63 = *RP* V (1988) 94 ff. – Vopiscus: Statius, *Silv.* 1.3, cf. 1 *praef.* – Minicii: Syme, *RP* V 99 f.; *ILS* 1061 = Sm. 225; 1029 = Sm. 224. – Papus: *HA Had.* 4.2; Syme, *RP* V 100 f.

7 The literature on the villa is very copious. Cf. e.g. Kähler, *Villa* (1950); Boatwright, *City* (1987) 138 ff. – names: *HA Had.* 26.5.

8 Juvenal's farm: 11.65. – arts . . . Caesar: 7.1 ff. – writers of history: 7.98 ff. – Florus: *HA Had.* 16.3–4. – Voconius: Apuleius, *Apol.* 11. – Voconius Victor: Martial 7.29; 11.78.

9 famous exchange: *HA Had.* 15.12 f. – Philostratus: *V. soph.* 1.8. 1 ff.

10 Dio 69.3.4, 6. – *On Exile*: A. Barigazzi (ed.), *Favorino di Arelate: Opere* (Florence 1966) 347 ff. Swain, *ZPE* 79 (1989) 150 ff., doubts whether Favorinus was really exiled, perhaps rightly.

11 *HA Had.* 15.10–13. 'Thirty Legions': perhaps marginally relevant as an argument for the continued existence of IX Hispana at this time. If it had already been destroyed, the total would have gone down to twenty-nine. But the exchange between Emperor and intellectual is of course not dated.

12 *HA Had.* 16.8–10.

13 late Roman work: Charisius, *Gramm. Lat.* 1, 209. – Scaurus: A. Gellius, *NA* 11.15.3; *HA Ver.* 2.5. – *obiter.* Charisius 219. – *praeter propter.* Gellius, *NA* 19.10.5 ff. – obsolete words: ibid. 1.10. – colour: ibid. 2.20.

14 glass ball game: *ILS* 5173; Champlin, *ZPE* 60 (1985) 159 ff. – Lollius: *PIR*² L 320. – young Marcus: *HA M. Aur.* 4.1, 1.2, 1.10.

15 *FO*² 49, discussed by Vidman 115 f. – office: cf. *HA Had.* 19.1. – Ostia restored: Boatwright, *Chiron* 19 (1989) 254 f. – other towns: ibid. 242 f., 257 f., 261. – Gabii: Juvenal 3.192, 7.4, 10.100. – Veii: Boatwright 243 f. – Etruria: *HA Had.* 19.1. – Formiae: *CIL* X 6079. – Tarracina: *ILS* 1066.

16 G. Alföldy, 'Hadrian als Magister der fratres Arvales', *ZPE* 100 (1994) 464–8.

17 Achaians: Ol. 78 A–B. – Stratonicea: Ol. 79–81. – Eudaemon: *ILS* 1449 = Sm. 283; *CP* 110.

18 palace, Horti: Boatwright, *City* (1987) 150 ff.

19 *FO*² 49, as restored by Syme, 'Transpadana Italia', *Athenaeum* 63 (1985) 28–36 = *RP* V (1988) 431 ff., at 28 = 432. – Trebula: *AE* 1972. 153. – Laberia: *PIR*² L 15. – Aequicoli: *CIL* IX 4116. – Lacus Fucinus: *ILS* 302 = Sm. 388; *HA Had.* 22.12. – Hadria: *HA Had.* 1.1; 19.1; and cf. note 17 to Chapter 11, above. – Cupra: *ILS* 313.

20 Cingulum: *CIL* IX 5681. – Maenius: *ILS* 2735 = Sm. 265; *CP* 120. – Firmum: *CIL* IX 5353. Ancona: *ILS* 1068; ibid. 298 records a new mole for the harbour.

21 Faventia: *HA Ael.* 2.8, *Ver.* 1.9. – Quietus' letter: *CIL* III 355 = Sm. 454b. – favour: above, pp. 289 ff. – Vicetia: R.-C. no. 681. – Comum: *ILS* 6725. – Caesernii: *AE* 1957. 135 = Sm. 195; *ILS* 1068. – kinsman: *CP* 109. – Marcellus: *AE* 1934. 231. – Concordia: cf. *CIL* V 1822, Pedania L. f. Secunda, and 8699, Ser. Julius Pardalas.

22 *FO*² 49; *HA Had.* 19.8. – *salus Aug.:* Strack 93 f.; *BMC* III 476 f., 486. *Epit. de Caes.:* 14.9. – fractured: *HA Had.* 26.3.

23 *HA Ant. Pius* 2.1–3.1; *Had.* 22.13; *M. Aur.* 11.6; discussed by Eck, *HA Coll.* n.s. 1 (1991) 183 ff.

24 Appian, *BC* 1.38; Tacitus, *Ann.* 13.4.2. – Coins: Toynbee 166 ff.; *BMC* III 347, 352, 361.

25 Proculus: *ILS* 1080 = Sm. 212; A.R. Birley, *ZPE* 116 (1997) 234 f. – Albucius: Suetonius, *De rhet.* 6. – Augustus: Suetonius, *D. Aug.* 58.1–2.

26 Augustus: *Res Gestae* 35; Dio 55.10.10, etc. – Tiberius: Suetonius, *Tib.* 26.2, 67.2. – Hadrian's speech: Charisius, *Gramm. Lat.* 1. 222. – Antium: Philostratus, *V. Apoll.* 8.20. – Tacitus: Pliny, *Ep.* 2.1.6. – *pater patriae*: Jerome, *Chron.* 199 Helm (AD 128); Eck, in *Festschr. Straub* (1982) 217 ff.

27 *HA M. Aur.* 4.2–3; Dio 69.21.2; 71.35.2; *HA M. Aur.* 1.4; A.R. Birley, *Marcus Aurelius* (1987) 232 ff.

28 Salan: above, p. 183. – Dio 69.17.1; Hephaestio of Thebes, ed. D. Pingree (Leipzig 1973) 2.18.62 ff. – parents' marriage: Pliny, *Ep.* 6.26.

29 Nepos: *HA Had.* 23.4. – modifications: Breeze and Dobson, *Hadrian's Wall* (1987) 74 f. – Severus: *ILS* 1056 and *add.* = Sm. 217; *RIB* 739, 1550; Dio 69.13.2. Two newly discovered diplomas, issued on 16th and on 20th August AD 127, both to be published in *ZPE*, supply the names of hitherto unknown governors of Lower Germany and Britain, respectively L. Coelius Rufus and L. Trebius Germanus. The former (*cos.* 119) had been governor of Upper Moesia in 120, the latter had been consul *c.* 124 (A.R. Birley, *Fasti* (1981) 237) and was presumably related to C. Trebius Maximus (*cos.* 122) and C. Trebius Sergianus (*cos. ord.* 132). I am grateful to Werner Eck for information about the new documents, which I hope to discuss further at a later date.

CHAPTER 17   AFRICA

1 Augustus: Suetonius, *D. Aug.* 47. – élite: cf. Champlin, *Fronto* (1980) 5 ff. – Pactumeius: *Inscr. lat. de l'Algérie* II 644 = MW 298. – Suetonius: *AE* 1953.73 = Sm. 281; *CP* 76. – Fronto: *Pan. Lat. Vet.* 8 (5). 14.2.

2 Caesernius: *AE* 1957. 135 = Sm. 195. – his father: *CIL* XVI 56; CP 67. – Horse Guards: above, p. 212. – Arrian: *Cyneg.* 24.1–5, cf. Bosworth, *ANRW* 2.34.1 (1993) 230, 261.

3 governors: Thomasson, *Laterculi* I (1984) 396 f. – Major: Halfmann, *Senatoren* (1979) 143 ff., no. 54. – Catullinus: perhaps Spanish, Syme, 'The career of Valerius Propinquus', *RP* V (1988) 579–607, at 603. – Latro: *CP* 104. – Gavius: Thomasson 419 f.; *CP* 105*bis*; *Supp.* p. 33 (defective); Eck, in Eck (ed.), *Pros. und Sozialgeschichte* (1993) 368 ff.

4 *HA Had.* 13.4; 20.4, 22.14. – aqueduct: A. Audollent, *Carthage romaine* (Paris 1901) 56 f., 183 ff.

5 Utica: Gascou, *ANRW* 2.10.2 (1982) 183. – Fabius Hadrianus: Cicero, II *Verr.* 1.70; Livy, *Per.* 86.

6 A. Gellius, *NA* 16.13. – Lepcis: A.R. Birley, *The African Emperor Septimius Severus* (London 1988) 16 ff. – *quinquennalis*: *HA Had.* 19.1.

7 Gaius, *Inst.* 1.96; *ILS* 6780 (Gigthis); Gascou, *ANRW* 2.10.2 (1982) 192 f.; Sherwin-White, *Citizenship* (1973) 255 f.; M. Zahrnt, '*Latium maius* und Munizipalstatus in Gigthis und Thisiduo in der Africa proconsularis', *ZPE* 79 (1989) 177–80.

8 Gascou, *ANRW* 2.10.2 (1982) 182 (Bulla), 188 (Lares), 190 (Thaenae). – Marius: Sallust, *Jug.* 90.2. – Caesar: *Bell. Afr.* 77.1. – Gascou 186 f. (Uthina, Col. Canopitana), 191 (territory of Carthage).

9 native communities: Gascou, *ANRW* 2.10.2 (1982) 183 ff. He does not include Mactar, which he argues, 197 f., only later (under Commodus) went straight from native community to *colonia*, because it is still called a *civitas* in the 160s, *CIL* VIII 11799 + *ILAfr.* 200 + *AE* 1960. 114. This does not necessarily mean it was not a *municipium*, especially as a dedication made there in 145 was by *[mu]nicip[es]*, *CIL* VIII 11811 (which otherwise has to be explained away). As a *colonia* Mactar had the title *Aelia* Aurelia, *ILS* 458, *AE* 1949. 47, etc. – Lollius Urbicus: A.R. Birley, *Fasti* (1981) 112 ff. – Antistius Adventus: for his career, A.R. Birley, *Fasti* (1981) 129 ff.

The name 'Adventus': I. Kajanto, *The Latin Cognomina* (Helsinki 1965) 349. To press this extreme conjecture further, the *praenomen* Quintus indicated birth in July (Quinctilis): H. Peterson, 'The numeral *praenomina* of the Romans', *Transactions of the American Philological Association* 93 (1952) 347–54; perhaps, then, a pointer to Hadrian's presence at Thibilis in July 128. – Salvius Julianus: *HA Did. Jul.* 1.2, cf. *ILS* 8973; Schumacher, *Priesterkollegien* (1973) 313.

10 laws: conveniently accessible as Sm. 463–4; see now D. Kehoe, *The Economics of Agriculture of Roman Imperial Estates in North Africa* (Göttingen 1988).

11 altars: *CIL* VIII 2609 f.; Le Bohec, *Troisième légion* (1989) 373. – *limes*: ibid. 369 ff. The system was first detected by J. Baradez, *Fossatum Africae* (Paris 1949), whose interpretation of it (naturally outdated in various respects) it is now fashionable to criticise.

12 Gemellae: *AE* 1950. 58; Le Bohec, *Troisième légion* (1989) 370 f. – for a concise account of the frontier works, Daniels, in Wacher (ed.), *Roman World* (1987) 242 ff.- Ad Majores: *CIL* VIII 2478–9 = 17969, 17971.

13 Cf. E. Birley, in *Carnuntina* (1956) 25 ff. = id., *Roman Army Papers* (1988) 15 ff.

14 column: Cassend and Janon, *Bull. arch. alg.* 7.1 (1977–9) 239 ff. – address: Sm. 328.

15 *HA Had.* 10.2; Fronto, *Princ. hist.* 11, p. 209 van den Hout, on which see Davies, *Latomus* 27 (1968) 75 ff., reading *salicibus* for *salibus*, and with an excellent discussion of Hadrian's training programme.

16 Sm. 328.

17 Le Glay, in *Mél. Seston* (1974) 277 ff., developed by Speidel, *Guards* (1978) 29 f.; cf. id., *Riding for Caesar* (1994) 49. – Arrian on cavalry, *Tact.* 32–44; Wheeler, *Flavius Arrianus* (1977) 361 f., is sceptical; Bosworth, *ANRW* 2.34.1 (1993) 259 ff., believes Arrian may have been at Lambaesis with Hadrian in 128, plausibly enough.

18 Sm. 328. – Catullinus: *PIR²* F 25.

19 Gascou, *ANRW* 2.10.2 (1982) 180 f. – Quiza: *CIL* VIII 9697 = 21514.

20 Africa: Toynbee 33 ff.; *BMC* III 506 f.; 487 f., 518 f. – Mauretania: Toynbee 123 ff.; *BMC* III 512 ff.; 494 f., 501.

21 *AE* 1940. 99 = Sm. 200; cf. *Res Gestae* 12; Dio 54.10.2.

CHAPTER 18   *HADRIANUS OLYMPIUS*

1 September 128: inferred from *IG* II/III² 2040, combined with the literary sources, Graindor, *Athènes* (1934) 38; Follet, *Athènes* (1976) 108, 110 ff.; Halfmann, *Itinera* (1986) 203. – secret rituals: Clement of Alexandria, *Protrepticus* 21.2. – *cistophori*: Kienast, *JNG* 10 (1959–60) 61 ff. = id., *Kl. Schriften* (1994) 489 ff. with addenda, 500 ff., defending his view against Metcalf, *Cistophori* (1980) 89 f., who prefers *ren(ovavit)*.

2 Fuscus: cf. p. 201 above. – Antinous: cf. Lambert, *Beloved* (1984) 100 ff.; Barnes, *JRA* 2 (1989) 259.

3 Statianus: *ILS* 1068. – Natalis: *SIG³* 840, Olympia: of course, Natalis did not himself drive, but merely paid for, the chariot that won in 129. – L. Macedo: *IGR* IV 869, Colossae, cf. below and note 24. – Viator: Speidel, *Guards* (1978) 29 f. – Eudaemon: *CP* 110. – Heliodorus: cf. p. 182 and note 14, above.

4 sarcastic: Dio 69.3.5; Philostratus, *V. soph.* 1.22; cf. *IKEph* 426, 3047.

5 Dacia: suggested by Piso, *Fasti* (1993) 48 f. – Severus: ibid. 42 ff.; Dio 69.12.2. – Herodes: p. 000, above. – Philopappus: *PIR²* J 151; Baslez, *DHA* 18 (1992) 89 ff. Pausanias 1.25.8 refers to his Mausoleum, without mentioning his name. – Balbilla: *PIR²* J 650; cf. above, pp. 250 ff.

6 second stay: *IG* V 1, 486; *SEG* XI 492. – *patronomos*: AD 127/8, A.S. Bradford, 'The

date Hadrian was eponymous *patronomos* of Sparta', *Horos* 4 (1986) 71–4 (could he still have been in office at the time of his visit?) – grain commissioner: *SEG* XI 491, on which Halfmann, *Itinera* (1986) 139; Spawforth, in Cartledge and Spawforth, *Hellenistic and Roman Sparta* (1989) 152 f.

7 Atticus: he was not consul until *c.* 132, as is now known from Roxan III 159, rendering previous discussions obsolete. As he had previously received honorary praetorian rank (Sm. 198) and his son was already a senator, he must be assumed to have been adlected *inter praetorios* at latest *c.* 130. – Herculanus: the early dating of his career by Spawforth, *ABSA* 73 (1978) 249 ff., also adopted by Halfmann, *Senatoren* (1979) 125 ff., no. 29, is surely to be rejected; cf. e.g. *PIR²* J 302 for the (previously favoured) view that he only became a senator under Hadrian (but the date of birth is still implausibly early). That an inscription of his from late in Trajan's reign gives no senatorial office (*IG* V 1, 380 = Sm. 137) may not be decisive, it is true. But if he only became eponymous magistrate (*patronomos*) at Sparta not long before 125 (so Halfmann, citing *IG* V 1, 32, 34, 44, 103, 1315; the dating of *patronomi* is still not entirely certain), he would by then have been around 50 if he had been born in the 70s. Surely too old (even if nothing is known of minimum age for this office). His senatorial career is given by *IG* V 1, 1172 = Sm. 210. For further discussion, A.R. Birley, 'Hadrian and Greek senators' *ZPE* 116 (1997) 209 ff.

8 descendant of Miltiades and Cimon: Philostratus, *V. soph.* 2.1.1. – victory commemorated: e.g. *Syll³* 835A, 854. – Pericles: Plutarch, *Per.* 17.

9 Amphictyons: above, pp. 186 f. – embassy . . . Nicopolis: *SEG* XI 493.

10 Willers, *Panhell. Programm* (1990) 26 ff., identifies the *temenos* of the Olympieion as the meeting-place of the Panhellenion, plausibly, in my view. But the matter is still controversial (another view e.g. in Spawforth and Walker, *JRS* 75 (1985) 78 ff.). C.P. Jones, *Chiron* 26 (1996) 29 ff., offers a new interpretation of Dio 69.16.1–2, 'the one certain [literary] reference to the Panhellenion', which he takes to be a building (not compelling, although he can cite parallels), and concludes from Dio's phrasing that the initiative came from the 'overseas' Greeks and not from Hadrian, who merely 'permitted' them (as Dio says) to go ahead, comparing the institution of the imperial cult in Asia and Bithynia in 30/29 BC, Dio 51–20.7. I am not convinced: even if this single sentence – in Xiphilinus' epitome, as he concedes; Dio's original account is lost – means what Jones believes, it is perfectly feasible that Hadrian should have 'permitted' the Greeks to carry out what he had himself inspired. Further, if one accepts Willers' identification of the Olympieion as the meeting-place for the Panhellenion, Polemo's statement in his speech at the opening ceremony (below, Chapter 20), that Hadrian's initiative (*horme*) to complete the building had been divinely inspired, Philostratus, *V. soph.* 125.3 (mistranslated in the Loeb edn), is enough to guarantee Hadrian's role as the creator of the new institution. This fundamental question aside, Jones's new study offers valuable insights on many related matters.

11 Pausanias 1.18.9. – new deme: Zahrnt, *Chiron* 9 (1979) 393 ff., thus emends and explains the fragment of Phlegon, *FGrH* 257, fr. 19. – on the various building projects I largely follow the interpretation of Willers, *Panhell. Programm* (1990). He discusses the 'Library', 14 ff., and, while accepting resemblances to the Forum Pacis at Rome, insists on 'der ausgeprägte Charakter als Hochschule'. See now also A. Karivieri, 'The so-called Library of Hadrian and the Tetraconch church in Athens', in P. Castrén (ed.), *Post-Herulian Athens – Aspects of Life and Culture in Athens AD 276–529* (Helsinki 1994) 89–113, who plays down the idea of a 'university' building; further Castrén, ibid. 2–4, stressing the resemblance to a Forum. (I am grateful to Professor Castrén for putting this valuable volume at my disposal.)

12 *ILS* 1067 = Sm. 228.

13 Pericles: Plutarch, *Per.* 8.2, 39.2. – Hadrian Olympios: Weber, *Hadrianus* (1907) 209 ff.

14 Perseus: e.g. Tarsus and Iconium, *RE* 4A.2 (1932) 2415; further, Strubbe, *Ancient Society* 15/17 (1984/6) 253 ff., especially 280 ff. – Spawforth and Walker, *JRS* 75 (1985) 78 ff., 76 (1986) 88 ff., offer the fullest recent discussion of the attested membership. It remains, of course, an argument *ex silentio* that great cities such as Ephesus, Smyrna, etc., did not join. I prefer to assume that they, and a great many other Greek cities as yet not attested, did become members.

15 *HA Had.* 13.8. – Parthian kings: cf. Karras-Klapproth, *Pros. Stud.* (1988) 114 ff.; 201 f.

16 *SC Juventianum*: *Digest* 5.3.20.6. – three jurists: *HA Had.* 18.1. – Juventius: *PIR²* J 882. – Neratius Priscus: N 60. – Marcellus: N 55. – Salvius: *ILS* 8973 = Sm. 236. Perhaps in Hadrian's suite: above, p. 257. – travelling *consilium*: cf. Crook, *Consilium* (1955) 56 ff., 135 ff., who does not, however, dwell on the practicalities involved, given Hadrian's travels.

17 Celsus proconsul: Eck, *Chiron* 13 (1983) 167. His predecessor, Lollianus Avitus, and his wife Terentia, may now have joined the imperial party, cf. above, p. 246. – Severus of Ancyra: *IGR* III 174 = Sm. 216, cf. 173 = 215.

18 Erastus and Philocyrius: *IKEph* 1487–8.

19 Ephesians honoured Hadrian: *SIG³* 839 = *IKEph* 274. – letter: Wörrle, *Chiron* 1 (1971) 325 ff., discussing *IKEph* 3016 = Ol. 187 in the light of *IKEph* 274. – Titianus: *IKEph* 677A.

20 Oxyrhyncus: Van Groningen, in *Studi Calderini-Paribeni* II (1956) 253 ff. – Tralles: *CIG* 2927; Wörrle, *Chiron* 1 (1971) 335 f.

21 Metcalf, *Mnemos.* 27 (1974) 59 ff.; id., *Cistophori* (1980) 16 f.

22 Miletus: A. Rehm (ed.), *Didyma* II. *Die Inschriften* (Berlin 1958), nos. 254, 356 – Dionysius, cf. above, pp. 216 f.

23 Laodicea: *IGR* IV 1033 = Sm. 73 = Ol. 68. The date is incomplete, but must be June rather than July in the light of the evidence for Apamea (note 25, below), cf. Halfmann, *Itinera* (1986) 204. – On the chamberlain Alcibiades and his family, Robert, *Etudes* (1938) 45 ff. – Major: Halfmann, *Senatoren* (1979) 153 ff., no. 54. – Patara, Modestus: *IGR* III 668, cf. Bowersock, *BHAC 1982/3* (1985) 82 ff.; Wörrle, *Stadt und Fest* (1988) 40 ff. – Paion of Side: Robert, *Stèle Kontoleon* (1980) 1 ff.; and cf. above, p. 251.

24 Laodicea: see previous note. – Macedo: *IGR* IV 869, as interpreted by Pflaum, *CP* 109. – Epictetus from Hierapolis: *Suda*, s.v. – Plutonium: Strabo 13.4.14, 629 f.

25 Apamea: according to an inscription, which he was due to publish, cited by C.P. Jones (in a review), *Phoenix* 37 (1983) 74; unfortunately, permission for his publication was then withheld, cf. Bowersock et al., *AJP* 108 (1987) 699 ff., for an account of the regrettable circumstances. The text still remains inaccessible to students, a curious state of affairs. – hunting-park: Xenophon, *Anab.* 1.2.7 ff. – tomb of Alcibiades: Athenaeus 13.574 f. – Melissa: located by Robert, *A travers l'Asie Mineure* (1980) 257 ff. By mishap, Halfmann, *Itinera* (1986) 206, puts Melissa in south Phrygia, near the wrong Metropolis, cf. Barnes, *JRA* 2 (1989) 249. – 'because of the name': Robert 259 note 11 approves this suggestion by J. Hatzfeld, *Alcibiade* (Paris 1949) 345 note 6. – marble quarries: Robert 221 ff. – 100 columns: Pausanias 1.18.9. – Julius Severus: *AE* 1938. 144, Dorylaeum. – coins: Toynbee 127 ff.; *BMC* III 496, 525.

26 Hadrianopolis: *RE* 7.2 (1912) 2174, no. 5. – imperial estates: Mitchell, *ANRW* 2.7.2 (1980) 1076 ff. – Archelais: *AE* 1976. 675. – Rosianus: cf. Pliny, *Ep.* 10.26.1 – Clemens: *ILS* 1067 = Sm. 228.

27 *HA Had.* 13.7. – *castra*: interpreted by Hirschfeld, *Kais. Verw.* (1905) 314 note 1, as meaning the imperial household. Likewise Teja, *ANRW* 2.7.2 (1980) 1116 f. (not

referring to Hirschfeld). Cf. id. 1093 f., on Cappadocian bakers. – Comana: Strabo 12.2.3, 535. – Horace: *Ep.* 1.6.39. – horses: Oppian, *Cyneg.* 1.171.

28 coins: *BMC* III 498 (*exercitus*); 508 f.; Toynbee 66 ff. – Arca: *ILS* 1403 (time of M. Aurelius), cf. Teja, *ANRW* 2.7.2 (1980) 1107.

29 *HA Had.* 13.8–9. – petty rulers: Arrian, *Periplus* 11.2–3, 18.3. – Bactrians: *HA Had.* 21.14. – Kanishka: cf. E. Yarshater (ed.), *Cambridge History of Iran* 3.1 (Cambridge 1983) 198 ff.

30 *HA Had.* 21.13; 13.9; 17.10–12; Dio 69.15.2; *HA Ant. Pius* 9.6. For different views, Syme, 'Hadrian and the vassal princes', *Athenaeum* 59 (1981) 273–83 = *RP* III (1984) 1436 ff., at 276 ff. = 1439 ff.; D. Braund, 'Hadrian and Pharasmanes', *Klio* 73 (1991) 208–19.

31 *HA Had.* 17.10; *Epit. de Caes.* 14.10; Tacitus, *Ann.* 2.26.3.

32 *HA Had.* 13.10. – On the governors: Eck, *Chiron* 13 (1983) 169 ff. – legionary legates: above, pp. 218, 221.

33 coins: G. Macdonald, 'The pseudo-autonomous coinage of Antioch', *Numismatic Chronicle*, 4th ser., 4 (1904) 105–35, at 126–9. – *HA* claims: *HA Had.* 14.1. – Severus: Dio 55.23.2. – *metropolis*: explained by Bowersock, *BHAC 1982/3* (1985) 75 ff. – there are no coins of Syria in the province series; but for coins which seem to show the *Tyche* of Antioch, *BMC* III 440. – benefactions: Malalas 277 f.

34 Antioch's 'rivals', Tyre already '*metropolis*': Bowersock, *BHAC 1982/3* (1985) 76, 77 f., 81. – Philo: *Suda*, s.v. For the fragments, *FGrH* no. 290, cf. A.I. Baumgarten, *The Phoenician History of Philo of Byblos* (Leyden 1981) 31 note 2.

35 Herennius: Pliny, *Ep.* 4.28.1; *Suda*, s.v. Hermippos; *PIR*² H 130.

36 Paulus of Tyre as advocate: *CPJ* 157, 158a. – hostility to Jews: argued by L. Troiani, *L'opera storiografica di Filone da Byblos* (Pisa 1974) 23 f., 34 ff.

37 Balbilla: *PIR*² J 650. – Balbillus: C 812–13; *CP* 15. Both distinguish delegate and Prefect, but cf. R. Merkelbach, 'Ephesische Parerga 21. Ein Zeugnis für Ti. Claudius Balbillus aus Smyrna', *ZPE* 31 (1978) 186–7. – betrothal to Drusilla: Josephus, *AJ* 19.355, 20.139. – Balbilla's family: *PIR*² J 149–51; and on the dynasty of Commagene, R.D. Sullivan, *ANRW* 2.8 (1978) 732 ff.

38 Cf. remarks on Antiochus IV and Hadrian by Willers, *Panhell. Programm* (1990) 101 f. – Antiochus' behaviour: Polybius 26.10; 28.18; 31.4. – Hadrian and the plebs: *HA Had.* 17.8. – Epicureanism: E.R. Bevan, *The House of Seleucus* (London 1902) 276 f., 304; O. Mørkholm, *Antiochus IV of Syria* (Copenhagen 1966) 113.

39 On the policy of the king one may still benefit from consulting the classic work of E. Bickermann, *Der Gott der Makkabäer* (Berlin 1937). K. Bringmann, *Hellenistische Reform und Religionsverfolgung in Judäa* (Göttingen 1983), has refined the chronology. (It may or may not be coincidence that the rebellion led by Bar-Kokhba was to break out more or less exactly three hundred years after that of the Maccabees.) Whatever the king really intended, the essential point in this context is: what did Hadrian think Antiochus was up to? – desecration: e.g. *I Macc.* 1.54: 'And on the fifteenth day of Chislev in the hundred and forty-fifth year, they builded an abomination of desolation upon the altar.' – Josephus, *AJ* 12.241.

40 Tacitus: *Historia* 5.8.2. – *epispasmos*: Schäfer, *Bar-Kokhba* (1981) 45 ff.; id., *Trib. to Vermes* (1990) 293 ff. – rebuild Jerusalem: cf. above, pp. 232 f. – forbade circumcision: *HA Had.* 14.2.

41 Paul and 'mutilation': *Ep. ad Phil.* 3.2; castration: *Ep. ad Gal.* 5.12. – extension of *lex Cornelia: Digest* 48.8.4.2, cf. Dio 67.2.3, Suetonius, *Dom.* 7.1. – Sepphoris: Millar, *Near East* (1993) 369 f.

42 Tacitus, *Historia* 5.8.2. – no danger: the new Parthian king, Vologaeses III, already had a rival, Mithridates IV, Karras-Klapproth, *Pros. Studien* (1988) 85. He began striking coins *c.* 130 – and, as it turns out, it was this Mithridates' son who was eventually to topple Vologaeses III and reign as Vologaeses IV, cf. Potter, *ZPE* 88 (1991)

277 ff., for a convenient text with illuminating discussion of the new inscription from Mesene. Potter, however, assumes, 281 f., that Vologaeses III had succeeded Chosroes soon after Hadrian's accession. I prefer to suppose that the two remained rivals until the disappearance of Chosroes c. 127/8; thus Karras-Klapproth 114 ff., 201 f. – abandoned ancestral religion: cf. Josephus, *AJ* 18.141 (offspring of Herod's son Alexander). – Berenicianus, Julianus: Halfmann, *Senatoren* (1979) 140 f., no. 47; 143, no. 53; note also C. Julius Agrippa, 140 f., no. 46. – H. perceived favourably by Jews at first: *Or. Sib.* 5.46 ff., cf. Schäfer, *Trib. to Vermes* (1990) 291 f., and id., *Bar-Kokhba* (1981) 237 ff., on positive treatment of Hadrian in some passages of the rabbinic literature.

43 Mt Casius: *HA Had.* 14.3. – dream: Dio 69.2.1.

44 Ulpian: *Digest* 50.15.1.1 – Berytus and Heliopolis: Millar, *Near East* (1993) 279 ff. – local dignitary: *IGLS* VI 2791.

45 Palmyra: the Greek text conveniently available as *IGR* III 1054 = Sm. 77. Palmyrene text in *Corpus Inscriptionum Semiticarum* II 3959. – status of Palmyra: generally taken to be part of the empire from the first century AD, thus Millar, *Near East* (1993) 34 f. For another view, J.C. Mann, in Roxan I, 217 ff. – tokens portraying Sabina: Salzmann, in *Festschr. Himmelmann* (1989) 361 ff. – Mesene: temple: Potter, *ZPE* 88 (1991) 283.

46 Cf. Bowersock, *Arabia* (1983); Millar, *Near East* (1993), especially 414 ff. – 'new province': Lewis, *Greek Papyri* (1989) nos. 16–22. – Nepos: ibid. nos. 23, 25–6. – Florentinus: *CIL* III 87 + 14148[10], Petra; Lewis no. 16. – Horse Guards: *AE* 1915. 42 = Sm. 332; cf. Speidel, *Riding for Caesar* (1978) 49, 62. – arch, statues: C.B. Welles, in C.H. Kraeling, *Gerasa. City of the Decapolis* (New Haven 1938) nos. 58, 143–5.

47 Petra 'Hadriane': Lewis, *Greek Papyri* (1989) no. 25. – coins: Toynbee 47 ff.; *BMC* III 489, 519.

48 coins: Toynbee 117 ff.; *BMC* III 493 f. – Sepphoris: note 41 above.

49 Dio 69.12.1–2. – coinage: Mildenberg, *Bar Kokhba War* (1984) 100 f. – promise: Schürer, *Jewish People* I (1973) 535 f.; Smallwood, *The Jews* (1976) 434 ff.

50 Cf. on the foundation of Aelia Capitolina e.g. Isaac, *Talanta* 12–13 (1980–1) 31 ff.; Zahrnt, in Olshausen and Sonnabend (eds), *Stuttgarter Kolloquium* (1991) 463 ff. – for the inferred principle that provinces with legionary garrison should have one *colonia* per legion, Mócsy, *Pannonia* (1974) 94. – Bostra: D. Kennedy and D. Riley, *Rome's Desert Frontier from the Air* (London 1990) 125 and figs. 71–2.

51 road-building: Applebaum, *Prolegomena* (1976) 19 f.; Smallwood, *The Jews* (1976) 431 f., 436 f.; Isaac and Oppenheimer, *JJS* 36 (1985) 40 f. – coinage: Mildenberg, *Bar Kokhba War* (1984) 99. – Tineius: Eck, *Chiron* 13 (1983) 169.

52 Dio 69.11.1; *HA Had.* 14.4. – Gaza: see next note – Caesarea: Schürer, *Jewish People* I (1973) 542 note 122; Smallwood, *Jews* (1976) 432 note 13. – Tiberias: Epiphanius, *Panarion* 30.12. – talmudic stories: discussed by Schäfer, *Bar Kokhba* (1981) 236 ff., except for the conversations with R. Joshua, which he regards as 'of no value for the historical Hadrian'.

53 Gaza's new era: Weber, *Hadrianus* (1907) 244 f.; M. Rosenberger, *City-Coins of Palestine* II (Jerusalem 1975) 54 ff. – festival: *Chron. Pasch.* I 474. – that Gaza belonged to Judaea is clear from Pliny, *NH* 12.64. – for the date of arrival in Egypt, see Chapter 19, note 4.

CHAPTER 19   DEATH IN THE NILE

1 Juvenal 15.1 f.; 27 ff., 44 ff.; Epiphanius, *De mens. et pond.* 14.

2 Titianus: *CP* 99; Thomasson, *Laterculi* I (1984) 348 f. – Viceroy: *RE* 22.2 (1954) 2356 f.

3 Dio 69.11.1. *HA Had.* 14.4; Appian, *BC* 2.86; *Anth. Pal.* 9.402; Appian, *Syriaca* 50; cf. Pekáry, *BHAC 1970* (1972) 195 ff.

4 fourteenth year: Vogt, *Alex. Münzen* (1924) I 102 f., II 53. – later version, ibid. 54. – plans for new *polis*: Zahrnt, *ANRW* 2.10.1 (1989) 676 f. – taboo: Pliny, *NH* 5.57.

5 sixteenth year issue: Vogt, *Alex. Münzen* (1924) I 104 f. – Sarapis talisman: *CPJ* 157 = Sm. 516. – other gods: Vogt II 53 ff.

6 personified province: Toynbee 28 ff.; *BMC* III 342, 379, 504 ff., 531. – Nilus: *BMC* III 347 f., 514 ff. – floods low in 130–1: Bonneau, *Crue* (1964) 346 f., 351.

7 Alexandria: Toynbee 39 ff.; *BMC* III 339, 344, 487 f., 507 f.

8 Eusebius-Jerome, *Chron.* 197 Helm; vers. Arm. 164 Schoene. – new quarter: Calderini, *Dizionario* I i (1935) 89 f., has some of the papyri references, completed, with new evidence, by P.M. Fraser, 'A Syriac *Notitia Urbis Alexandrinae*', *Journal of Egyptian Archaeology* 37 (1951) 103–8, at 104 ff. A 'Hadrianic Library' (a kind of archive) had already been created, in existence in AD 127: Calderini 104. – Sema: Strabo 17.1.8, 794. – body: Suetonius, *D. Aug.* 18.1; Dio 51.16.5.

9 On the Mouseion: *RE* 16.1 (1933) 801 ff. – library: *RE* 3.1 (1897) 409 ff. – Strabo's description: 17.1.8, 793 f. – Polemo: Philostratus, *V. soph.* 1.25.3. – Dionysius: ibid. 1.22.3. – Chaeremon: *PIR*² C 706. – Dionysius: *CP* 46. – Balbillus: *CP* 15. – Vestinus: *CP* 105.

10 Hadrian at the Mouseion: *HA Had.* 20.2. – For the following, cf. above: Pancrates (p. 241), Numenius (p. 252), Dionysius (p. 252 f.), Mesomedes (p. 252), Paion (p. 251), Balbilla (pp. 250 f.). – Heliodorus: his presence inferred from the birth of his son at Alexandria, as revealed by the papyrus published by A.K. Bowman, 'A letter of Avidius Cassius?', *JRS* 60 (1970) 20–6 = Ol. 185, the birth being dated to 130–131 by Syme, 'Avidius Cassius. His age, rank and quality', *BHAC 1984/5* (1987) 207–22 = *RP* V (1988) 689 ff., at 215 f. = 695 f.

11 On the *tondi*, I follow Kähler, *Villa* (1950) 177 ff.; Lambert, *Beloved* (1984) 118 f.; Grenier and Coarelli, *MEFRA* 98 (1986) 252. – royal beast: Aymard, *Chasses* (1951) 416 ff. – Hadrian's lion-kill: *HA Had.* 26.3. – medallion: Strack 129. – Athenaeus 15.677 d–f.

12 *POxy* 1085.

13 Cf. note 11 above on the *tondi*.

14 Canopus: Juvenal 15.44 ff. ; Strabo 17.1. 6 f., 800 f. – Villa: *HA Had.* 26.5; cf. now Grenier, *MEFRA* 101 (1989) 925 ff. – Germanicus: Tacitus, *Ann.* 2.60 f.

15 L. Macedo: *CP* 109. On II Traiana and related problems, Isaac and Roll, *ZPE* 33 (1979) 149 ff.; Keppie, in Kasher et al. (eds), *Greece and Rome* (1990) 54 ff.

16 Proculus: *CP* 113. – Naucratis: *RE* 16.2 (1935) 1954 ff.

17 Strabo on Heliopolis: 17.1.29, 806, cf. Herodotus 2.3, 7–9. – Papyrus: *ZPE* 33 (1979) 262.

18 magical papyrus: K. Preisendanz, *Papyri Graeci Magici* IV (2nd edn, Stuttgart 1973) 2441 ff.; H.D. Betz, *The Greek Magical Papyri in Translation* (Chicago 1985) 82 f. – Lucian: *Philopseudes* 34 ff.

19 *kondy*: Athenaeus 11, 478a.

20 phoenix: Van den Broek, *Myth* (1972), especially 70 ff., 105 ff. Tacitus, *Ann.* 6.28 believed the phoenix returned after 1461 years. – Censorinus: *De die natali* 21.

21 On Memphis: *RE* 15.1 (1931) 660 ff., especially 675 ff. (Ptah), 680 f. (Apis), 684 (Imhotep), 65 ff. (Serapis). – temple of Hadrian there: Weber, *Hadrianus* (1907) 258.

22 *ILS* 1046, 1046b = Sm. 237a–b. – hated: *HA Had.* 23.5–6.

23 cleruchs: Montevecchi, in *Neronia* IV (1990) 188 f.; Zahrnt, *ANRW* 2.10.1 (1989) 686. – Berenice, Arsinoe: Weber, *Hadrianus* (1907) 258.

24 December: Van Groningen, *Studi Calderini-Paribeni* II (1956) 253 ff. – May: Sijpestein, *Historia* 18 (1969) 109 ff. – Hellenised: cf. in general J. Krüger,

Oxyrhynchos. Studien zur Topographie und Literaturrezeption (Frankfurt 1990). – victory celebration: *CPJ* 450.

25 Hermopolis: Sijpestein, *ZPE* 88 (1991) 89 f.; Lewis, *BASP* 30 (1993) 29. – 22, 24 October: Weber, *Drei Unters.* (1911) 22; Graindor, *Athènes* (1934) 159 f., on Plutarch, *De Iside et Osiride* 356C; Lambert, *Beloved* (1984) 127.

26 Dio 69.11.2–4. – Paulina: cf. Grimm, in *Festschr. Parlasca* (1990) 33 ff.

27 *HA Had.* 14.5–7; Victor, *Caes.* 14.5–7.

28 Lanuvium: *ILS* 7212 = Sm. 165; cf. Voisin, *MEFRA* 99 (1987), especially 262 ff. – various gods: cf. now Voisin, *Mél. Le Glay* (1994) 730 ff. – drowned . . . divine: Herodotus 2.90; Tertullian, *De baptismo* 5; cf. F.L. Griffith, 'Herodotus II.90. Apotheosis by drowning', *Zeitschrift für Agyptische Sprache* 46 (1910) 132–4; S. Eitrem, 'Tertullian *de baptismo* 5, sanctified by drowning', *Classical Review* 38 (1924) 69; S. Morenz, 'Zur Vergöttlichung in Ägypten', *Zeitschrift für Agyptische Sprache* 84 (1959) 132–43 ; Lambert, *Beloved* (1984) 125. – *devotio*: *RE* 5.1 (1903) 277 ff.

29 Dio 69.11.2. – Balbillus: Suetonius, *Nero* 36.1; Tacitus, *Ann.* 15.47.

30 Cf. U. v. Wilamowitz-Moellendorff, *Der Glaube der Hellenen* II (Berlin 1932) 483 note 2; Yourcenar, *Mémoires* (1951) 187; Lambert, *Beloved* (1984) 128 ff. – note e.g. Lucian, *Vera hist.* 28: 'never have commerce with a boy of more than eighteen'; and similar sentiments in *Anth. Pal.* 12.4, 12, 25–7.

31 30 October: thus in the *Chron. Pasch.* I 223 (albeit under the year 122). – Bes: Weber, *Drei Unters.* (1911) 20, 21; Graindor, *Athènes* (1934) 14; Follet, *Athènes* (1976) 62; but cf. Lambert, *Beloved* (1984) 127, for caution.

32 Thebes: below and notes 33–4. – Germanicus: Tacitus, *Ann.* 2.61. – Hadrian's Gate: Weber, *Hadrianus* (1907) 257, and *RE* 19.2 (1938) 2113, can only cite Baedeker for this. Cf. also E. Bernand, *Les inscriptions grecques de Philae* II (Paris 1969), Plates 79, 83–5, 107.

33 Bernand, *Colosse* (1960), nos. 28–31. No. 32 is a fragmentary dedication by Sabina herself. – Titianus: ibid. 24.

34 Bernand, *Colosse* (1960) nos. 28 ff. No. 29, line 12, is amended by M.L. West, 'Balbilla did not save Memnon's soul', *ZPE* 25 (1977) 120. – Strabo on the Colossus: 17.1.46, 816. – lesbian: Bowie, in Russell (ed.), *Antonine Literature* (1990) 62.

35 Bernand, *Colosse* (1960) nos. 11–12, cf. Robert, in *Stèle Kontoleon* (1980) 1 ff. – Faustus: Bernand no. 60; dated to Hadrian's time by Piso, *Fasti* (1993) 214 ff. The expansion of CETACO[S] is my own.

36 Choiak: Weber, *Hadrianus* (1907) 257. – birthday: *ILS* 7212 = Sm. 165. – further itinerary: Sijpestein, *Historia* 18 (1969) 112 ff. (who goes astray in making the hunt later, p. 115).

37 Mesomedes: *Suda*, s.v.; *HA Ant. Pius* 7.8; *PIR²* M 503. – Numenius: *Suda*, s.v. – Curium: Lebek, *ZPE* 12 (1973) 101 ff. – Pancrates: Athenaeus 15.677 d–f. – Tebtunis papyrus: *Papiri della R. Università di Milano* I (Milan 1937), 174 ff.

38 Dionysius' poem is now available with Greek text and German translation by K. Brodersen, *Dionysius von Alexandria. Das Lied von der Welt* (Hildesheim 1994). His dating (p. 11) to early in the reign is, however, unconvincing; cf. below on the River Rhebas. – acrostichs: lines 112–34, 513–32. – Gades: lines 11, 65, 176, 451, 456. – Adria: lines 92, 100, 102, 380, 481. – Carthage: lines 145–7. – Tiber: lines 352–4. – Ilium: lines 815–18. – Rhebas: lines 794–6, explained by Bowie, in Russell (ed.), *Antonine Literature* (1990) 71, as a compliment to Antinous.

39 *AE* 1991. 1461, Heraclea Pontica, shows that the name 'Antinoean' had already been assumed by the actors' association before the end of AD 130. Lambert, *Beloved* (1984), 177 ff., gives full coverage of the Antinous cult. – Eunostus: *RE* 6.1 (1907) 1136 f.

40 Zahrnt, *ANRW* 2.10.1 (1989) 677 ff.; Montevecchi, in *Neronia* IV (1990) 183 ff.

41 road: Sm. 423. – Antinoeia: *Bulletin épigraphique* 1952, no. 180.

42 Weber, *Hadrianus* (1907) 249 ff., led the way in interpreting these names. A fuller list than that available to Weber is provided by Calderini, *Dizionario* I 2 (Madrid 1966) 106 ff. 'Meleitorios' (given here, p. 108, under Pauleinios as well as Osirantinoeios) must surely be a misreading of Kleitorios. – Paulina: cf. note 26, above.

43 The original location of the obelisk at Antinoopolis, not at Rome (or Tivoli), is now established by A. Grimm and D. Kessler, in Meyer (ed.), *Obelisk* (1994) 84 ff., whose translation is here followed.

44 most learned: the Egyptologist P. Derchain, *Le dernier Obélisque* (Brussels 1987), has contributed an engaging fiction about one of these persons. – coins: Vogt, *Alex. Münzen* (1924) II 53. – games: *Bulletin épigraphique* 1952, no. 180. – Philadelphian contest: L. Moretti, *Iscrizioni agonistiche greche* (Rome 1953) 244 ff., no. 84, discussed by Grimm, in *Festschr. Parlasca* (1990) 39 f. – sacrifice: Seneca, *Quaest. nat.* 4.2.7.

45 new appointments: Eck, *Chiron* 13 (1983) 172. – Salvius Julianus: *ILS* 8973 = Sm. 236; *Digest* 46.3.36 indicates that he was in Egypt. – Heliodorus: cf. note 10, above. – Caesernii: *AE* 1957. 135 = Sm. 195; *ILS* 1068.

46 *BMC* III 1552 f., 1617; Strack 138; A.C. Levi, *NC* 8 (1948) 30 ff.; cf. for a different interpretation Ritner, in Simpson (ed.), *Religion and Philosophy* (1989) 103 ff.

CHAPTER 20 ATHENS AND JERUSALEM

1 weapons: Dio 69.12.2, cf. *HA Had.* 11.1. – hideaways: Dio 69.12.3. – Antinous statue at Caesarea: R. Savignac, *Revue biblique* 13 (1904) 84, no. 2.

2 Syria 'again': Dio 69.12.2. – Cilicia coins: Toynbee 69; *BMC* III 490. – credentials: cf. C.P. Jones, *Dio Chrysostom* (1978) 75; ample detail in Strubbe, *Ancient Society* 15–17 (1984/6) 253 ff., for these aspirations to be Hellenic in origin.

3 ceased to exist: Syme, 'Observations on the province of Cilicia', in *Anatolian Studies Buckler* (Manchester 1939) 299–332 = *RP* I (1979) 120 ff., especially 325 ff. = 141 ff. – own *koinon*: Ziegler, *Studien zum antiken Kleinasien* III (1995) 183 ff.

4 'no mean city': *Act. apost.* 21.39. – enthusiasm for philosophy: Strabo 14.5.13, 673 f. – Athenodorus: Strabo 14.5.14, 674 f.; *PIR²* A 1288. – Dio Chrysostom: *Or.* 34. 7–14; 45–53; 9; 34; 38–42; 21–33. Cf. C.P Jones, *Dio Chrysostom* (1978) 76 ff.

5 rivalries: – Tarsus Argive: Strabo 14.5.12, 673. – Olba, Mallus: id. 14.5.16, 675 f.; cf. Ziegler, in Hödl and Grabmayer (eds), *Leben in der Stadt* (1995) 86 ff., 95. – 'three *eparchiae*': *AE* 1961. 320; *ILS* 8827; cf. *AE* 1938. 4 (Severan).

6 *Digest* 22.5.3.1; 3 (Rufinus); 4 (Maximus); cf. Thomasson, *Laterculi* I (1984) 419 f.; 2 (Verus). Williams, *JRS* 66 (1976) 71, infers that Hadrian composed the letters himself.

7 Paion: above, p. 240. – Attalia: *IGR* III 771; ibid. 773, a tower flanking the Arch, was donated by Domitia Sancta, who also set up a statue to Hadrian's sister Paulina; cf. Halfmann, *Itinera* (1986) 131. – Perge and the Plancii: *JRS* 55 (1965) 56 ff.; Halfmann, *Senatoren* (1979) 128 f., no. 31; cf. Syme, 'Legates of Cilicia under Trajan', *Historia* 18 (1969) 352–66 = *RP* II (1979) 774 ff., at 365 f. = 787 f.

8 evil reputation: Strabo 14.5.7, 671, cf. Cicero, II *Verr.* 4.21. – its origin and early history: *RE* 19.2 (1938) 1876 ff. – new gateway: *TAM* II 3, 1187 = *SEG* XXXI 1299. – statues: *Tituli Asiae Minoris* II 3, 1191, 1194, 1193, 1192. – Sufenas and Atticus consuls: Roxan III 159; cf. Wörrle, *Stadt und Fest* (1988) 39 ff., for Sufenas' governorship. Atticus was also, it seems, made a member of the prestigious *XVviri sacris faciundis*, Ameling, *Herodes* (1983) II 132 f.

9 second Temple Wardenship: the date when this was approved remains uncertain: *IKEph* 428, honouring Ti. Claudius Piso Diophantus, may identify the man who

successfully petitioned Hadrian; cf. further C.P. Jones, *JHS* 113 (1993) 149 ff. – statue-base: *AE* 1977. 797 = *IKEph* 734; Champlin, *ZPE* 21 (1976) 78 ff., makes a good case for identifying the polyonymous honorand with young Fuscus. I cannot follow him in all details. – sculpture: thus Hahland, *JÖAI* 41 (1954) 54 ff.

10 coins: Toynbee 49 ff.; *BMC* III 344 f., 490, 519 f. – two further new cities: Schwertheim, *Epigr. Anat.* 6 (1985) 37 ff.; id., *IKHadrianoi* (1987) 156 ff., on nos. 56, 129. – back to Cyzicus, local office: Merkelbach and Schwertheim, *Epigr. Anat.* 2 (1983) 149.

11 coins: Toynbee 122 f.; *BMC* III 352, 494.

12 winter for the third time: clear from *SIG*³ 842, Epidaurus, cf. Halfmann, *Itinera* (1986) 208. – Mysteries, fragmentary letter: A. Plassart, *Fouilles de Delphes* III 4 (Paris 1970), 308; but Follet, *Athènes* (1976) 109, prefers to refer the Mysteries there mentioned to new ones for Antinous. – letter of 132: Sm. 445 = Ol. 85.

13 priestess: *IG* II/III² 3575 = Sm. 71a. – Pausanias: 1.3.2. – Dio: 69.16.1–2.

14 *HA Had.* 19.2 (by mishap this sentence is omitted in A.R. Birley, *Lives of the Later Caesars* (1976) 78). For comparison, cf. Robert, *Gladiateurs* (1940) 313.

15 Arrian, *Periplus* 6.2, 10.1 (Latin report); Trapezus (1.1–2.2), Dioscurias (10.3–4); Athens (3.4–4.1); Apsarus (6.1); manoeuvres (3.1, 6.2, 10.3); Phasis fort (9.3–5); Amisus (15.3, cf. Pausanias 1.18.6); Rhea (9.1); 11.2–3, 18.3 (client kings).

16 Cotys: Arrian, *Periplus* 17.3, cf. Phlegon, *FGrH* 257, fr. 17; *PIR²* J 276. – island of Achilles: *Periplus* 21.1–23.4.

17 *Digest* 49.14.2.1.

18 seven years before: Dio 69.16.1 – if this dating can be pressed; Jones, *Chiron* 26 (1996) 33 f., believes 'holding the highest office' in this passage ought refer to his archonship, which would put it back in 112, and wonders if he might have been archon again, viz. for 131/2. I prefer to believe that Dio's text, as we have it, is garbled. – Pausanias: 1.18.6. – Dio: 69.16.1. – *HA*: *Had.* 13.6. – Erichthonius: Pausanias 1.24.7.

19 Pausanias 1.5.5; 1.18.9.

20 Philostratus, *V. soph.* 1.25.3.

21 *temenos*: thus Willers, *Panhell. Programm* (1990) 36 ff., 54 ff. – chairman: Sm. 257; *CP* 81; cf. below, note 28 to Chapter 21. – members: Spawforth and Walker, *JRS* 75 (1985) 79 ff.; cf. above, note 14 to Chapter 18, on the question of membership. Cf. also Strubbe, *Ancient Society* 15–17 (1984/6) 280 ff., on eagerness to prove Hellenic credentials. – Amisus: Arrian, *Periplus* 15.3.

22 *Panhellenia*: Wörrle, *Chiron* 22 (1992) 337 ff., is able to show conclusively that they were first held in 137. – games at Athens: Geagan, *ANRW* 2.7.1 (1979) 397 f., has a useful summary. – portrait in Parthenon: Pausanias 1.24.7. – Benjamin, *Hesperia* 32 (1963) 57 ff., has a valuable discussion of the numerous altars (almost 100) honouring Hadrian at Athens.

23 Achaia coins: Toynbee 25 ff.; *BMC* III 349, 517 f. – Hadrian's Gate: *IG* II² 5185. On the Gate and its significance, Willers, *Panhell. Programm* (1990) 68 ff. – new deme: Zahrnt, *Chiron* 9 (1979) 393 ff., convincingly interprets Phlegon, *FGrH* 257, fr. 19.

24 no account: Dio 69.13.1. – Solomon's tomb: id. 69.14.2. – insurgents: id. 69.12.3. There is a vast literature on the Jewish war under Hadrian: I note here Schürer, *Jewish People* I (1973) 534 ff.; Smallwood, *The Jews* (1976) 428 ff.; Applebaum, *Prolegomena* (1976); Schäfer, *Aufstand* (1981); id., in Davies and White (eds), *Tribute to Vermes* (1990) 281 ff.; Mildenberg, *Coinage* (1984); Isaac and Oppenheimer, *JJS* 36 (1985) 33 ff. The fact that the documents discovered over thirty years ago have still not been published in full hardly needs re-emphasising (cf. Millar, *Near East* (1993) 545 f.). Some were published in *DJD* II; others by Y. Yadin in the *Israel Exploration Journal* 11 (1961), 12 (1962); and those in Greek are now

available in Lewis, *Greek Papyri* (1989). For a new checklist see now Cotton et al., *JRS* 85 (1995) 229–31, nos. 293–331, giving *DJD* II numbering or for the unpublished ones *PYadin**.

25 sally-ports: Gichon, *JQR* 77 (1986) 15 ff. – Marcellus and C. Julius Severus: *IGR* III 174 = *ILS* 8826 = Sm. 216. – XXII Deiotariana: Keppie, in Kasher et al. (eds), *Greece and Rome* (1990) 54 ff., is the latest discussion.

26 Fronto, *De bello Parthico* 2, p. 221 van den Hout: *quid? avo vestro Hadriano imperium optinente quantum militum a Iudaeis, quantum a Britannis caesum?* – Dio 69.14.3, 13.1–2.

27 'Other races': cf. Applebaum, *Prolegomena* (1976) 57 f.; Mor, *JJS* 36 (1985) 200 ff.

28 different category: cf. Isaac, *SCI* 7 (1983/4) 68 ff. – Christian writers: Justin, I *Apol.* 31.6; Eusebius, *HE* 4.6.2; 4.8.6; Jerome, *Chron.* 201 Helm; *Vers. arm.* 168 ff. Schoene; *Adv. Rufinum* 3.31; Orosius 7.13.4. – On Bar Kokhba: Schäfer, *Aufstand* (1981) 51 ff., discusses the sources systematically; cf. Mildenberg, *Coinage* (1984) 55 ff., 73 ff.

29 earliest document: Cotton et al., *JRS* 85 (1995) no. 293 = *PYadin* *42 (April 132). – latest: ibid. no. 310 = *DJD* II no. 22 (new reading).

30 *Numbers*: 24.17. – R. Akiba: Schürer, *Jewish People* I (1973) 543 f.; Schäfer, *Aufstand* (1981) 55 f. – star sign: Mildenberg, *Coinage* (1984) 44 f. – *Ezekiel* 37.24–5.

31 Akiba: cf. especially Herr, *Scr. Hier.* 23 (1972) 113 ff. – coinage: Mildenberg, *Coinage* (1984) 69 ff. – symbols: I have tried to summarise Mildenberg 123 ff. – letter from Sh'imon: Cotton et al., *JRS* 85 (1995) no. 317 = *PYadin* *52.

32 Eleazar the Priest: Schürer, *Jewish People* I (1973) 544; Mildenberg, *Coinage* (1984) 29, 61 ff. – Jerusalem: recapture by the rebels doubted e.g. by Schäfer, *Aufstand* (1981) 78 ff. and Mildenberg, *Coinage* (1984) 17, 31, 49. Cf. further note 37, below. – re-circumcision: Smallwood, *The Jews* (1976) 445; Schäfer 45 ff. – Rabbi: Schürer 544 note 139; Mildenberg 30, on *PYadin* *56.

33 *PYadin* *56, *54, *55 (En Geddi). – *DJD* II no. 43 (Galileans). – *PYadin* *56 (Romans). – brothers: e.g. *PYadin* *49, *59.

34 Schäfer, *Aufstand* (1981) 173 (missiles), 144, 170 (finger), 171 f. (blasphemy; cf. *Psalms* 60.12); 148 (brothers).

35 Justin: *Dial.* 1.3, 9.3.; I *Apol.* 31.6. – Eusebius-Jerome, *Chron.* 201 Helm; Eusebius, *HE:* 4.6.2 – Jerome: *Adv. Rufinum* 3.31.

36 documents: listed by Cotton et al., *JRS* 85 (1995) 229 ff. – Babatha: N. Lewis, *Greek Papyri* (1989). – Salome: Cotton, *ZPE* 105 (1995) 171 ff. – possible reprisals: thus Smallwood, *The Jews* (1976) 442.

37 caves in Lower Galilee: Gichon, *JQR* 77 (1986) 26 ff.; id., *Rev. int. hist. mil.* 42 (1979) 88, 95. – cave near Jericho: J. Geiger, reviewing Millar, *Near East* (1993), in *Scripta Classica Israelica* 13 (1994) 200, referring to *Eretz-Israel* 23 (1992) 276 ff. (in Hebrew). – coins as basis: Mildenberg, *Coinage* (1984) 22 ff., 85 ff. – supplies by ship: *PYadin* *49 refers to a ship. – Jerusalem: it is clearly an *argumentum ex silentio* that the rebels did not re-take Jerusalem: lack of rebel coins found there and no reference to it in the documents. Yet the coin-legends show the immense importance attached to the Holy City. It should be reflected that the legionary fortress of X Fretensis has still not been located, cf. Geva, *IEJ* 34 (1984) 239 ff., for a discussion. This would have been a necessary target for rebel attack and a likely base. Further evidence may one day be forthcoming.

38 Dio: 69.14.3. – Talmudic sources: Schäfer, *Aufstand* (1981) 138 ff. – Clemens: *ILS* 2081 = Sm. 300. – *expeditio: ILS* 1065, 1071, 1092, *CIL* VI 3505; cf. V. Rosenberger, *Bella et expeditiones* (Stuttgart 1992) 97 ff., against Halfmann, *Itinera* (1986) 209 f., already criticised by Syme, 'Journeys of Hadrian', *ZPE* 73 (188) 159–70 = *RP* VI (1991) 346 ff., at 166 f. = 354 f., and Barnes, *JRA* 2 (1989) 254.

39 Plew, *Unters.* (1890) 89 ff., was the first, it seems, to exploit Apollodorus. Blyth, *GRBS* 33 (1992) 127 ff., has shed doubt on the authenticity of the attribution to Apollodorus of the *Poliorcetica.*

40 'whole world': Dio 69.13.3. – Severus: A.R. Birley, *Fasti* (1981) 106 ff. – Sisenna: ibid. 109 f.

41 Quinctianus: *AE* 1957. 135 = Sm. 195. – Priscus: *ILS* 1092. – Cornelianus: *RIB* 814. – Urbicus: *ILS* 1065 = Sm. 220. tribune: *CIL* VI 3505 = Sm. 331. – man from Cilicia: *CIL* X 1769, cf. E. Birley, *The Roman Army* (1988) 316 ff.

42 X Fretensis: *CIL* XVI, App. no. 13. – Voconius: *ILS* 8828. – Statianus: *ILS* 1068. – Proculus: *ILS* 1341; *CP* 113. – Dio: 69.13.3.

43 Eusebius: *HE* 4.6.2. – Severus: Dio 69.13.3.

44 Eusebius: *HE* 4.6.3. – rabbinic story: Schäfer, *Aufstand* (1984) 138. Cf. p. 359, below.

45 fragmentary letter: *DJD* II no. 45. – *imp. II*: *CIL* II 478; VI 974 – Severus: *ILS* 1056 = Sm. 217 – Marcellus: *AE* 1934. 231. – less generous: E. Birley, *Roman Britain* (1953) 24.

46 name changed: thus in *CIL* XVI 87 of November 139. – Dio's figure: 69.14.1. – captives sold: *Chron. Pasch.* I 474; cf. Jerome, *In Jerem.* 21.15, *In Zach.* 11. 4–5. – Christian writers: Eusebius, *HE* 4.6.3; Jerome, *In Sophon.* 1. 15 f. – statue of Hadrian: Jerome, *In Esaiam* 1.2.9. – temple of Jupiter: id., *Comm. in Matt.* 24.15. – Aphrodite: Eusebius, *V. Constantini* 3.26. – coins: Schürer, *Jewish People* I (1973) 554 f. – pig: Jerome, *Chron.* 201 Helm.

47 statue: Foerster, *'Atiqot* 17 (1985) 139 ff.; Gergel, *AJA* 95 (1994) 231 ff. – pieces from Egypt, etc.: Hoffmann, in *Festschr. Helck* (1984) 585 ff. (but that Hadrian fought a local war in Egypt is unconvincing). – coins: *BMC* III 475, 485; A.C. Levi, *NC* 8 (1948) 30 ff.

48 Pausanias: 1.5.5. – Tertullian: *De praescript.* 7.9.

CHAPTER 21   THE BITTER END

1 curt response: *IGR* I 149 = Ol. 86. – Quinctianus: *AE* 1957. 135 = Sm. 195.

2 Moesia coins: Toynbee 125; *BMC* III 495, 501. – Major: *CIL* XVI 78; Eck, *Chiron* 13 (1983) 172, assumes he was there some time before 134. – Dacia: Toynbee 78 f.; *BMC* III 498 f., 510 f. – younger Bassus: first attested in Dacia 13 December 135, *ILS* 2301; Piso, *Fasti* (1993) 53 f.

3 *exercitus Delmaticus*: Strack 143, no. 796 (not in *BMC* III). – Vitrasius: Eck, *Hist. Aug. Coll. Parisinum* (1991) 189 ff. – temple to Antinous: *AE* 1972. 500, Municipium D(ar)danorum. – coins: *BMC* III 534 f.

4 *CIL* III 10281 had Servianus and another consul, whose name (in the ablative) ending in O and between 6 and 9 letters long, was erased. In several other inscriptions Servianus is named as consul without a colleague, A. Stein, *RE* 10.1 (1917) 887 f. C. Julius Proculus (*cos. suff.* 109) may have been the original colleague. For evidence that he was labelled '*cos. II*', note 22 to Chapter 12, above. (Perhaps he just happened to die at the turn of the year and was replaced by Varus.) – Paulina, Fuscus: above, pp. 247, 262.

5 Strack 126 f., 133 f.; *BMC* III 315 ff., 323 f., 393 note, 450 ff., 457, 464 f., 474, 478.

6 Nepos: *CIL* XVI 78 (April 134) – III Cyrenaica in fighting: *ILS* 1071 = Sm. 234. – Dio: 69.16.3.

7 Dio 69.8, cf. 66.17.2 (Vespasian).

8 Nepos: *HA Had.* 23.4, cf. 23.6; 4.2; 15.2. – Attianus, Septicius: 15.2. – Gentianus: 23.4, cf. 23.6. – Polyaenus (cf. Pliny, *Ep.* 10.70–1), Marcellus (*PIR²* N 55): 15.3. – Eudaemon, Heliodorus: 15.3, 15.15.5, both later Prefect of Egypt, Eudaemon in 142/3 as successor of Heliodorus, appointed in 137: Thomasson, *Laterculi* I (1984) 349. – Favorinus: 16.10. – exile: the inference from the discovery of his 'On Exile':

A. Barigazzi, *Favorino di Arelate: Opere* (Florence 1966) 347 ff.; the work is not regarded as evidence for a real exile by Swain, *ZPE* 79 (1989) 150 ff., but merely as an oratorical exercise.

9 Celer: the post is known from Philostratus, *V. soph.* 1.22.3; cf. *HA M. Aur.* 2.4, *Verus* 2.5; M. Aurelius, *Med.* 8.25. – Boeotia: Ol. 112, cf. 108–11. – Cyrene: Ol. 120. – Didyma: Ol. 87.

10 Polemo: Philostratus, *V. soph.* 1.25.3. – Herodes: ibid. 2.1.8.

11 Dio: 69.4.1–5. For the view that the story of his death cannot be right, Ridley, *Athenaeum* 77 (1989) 551 ff. E.L. Bowie suggests to me that the supposed criticism about the goddesses being unable to get up may even have been a subtle compliment, since the same had been said about Phidias' celebrated statue of Zeus at Olympia, Strabo 8.3.30, 353.

12 Victor, *Caes.* 14.1–4. On the Athenaeum, Braunert, *BHAC* 1963 (1964) 9 ff.; Boatwright, *City* (1987) 207 f. – Salvius: Jerome, *Chron.* 198 Helm, assigns his redaction of the edict to 131, which in any case looks the most likely year for his quaestorship, the office he held when carrying out the task (*ILS* 8973): Syme, 'The jurists approved by Antoninus Pius', *BHAC 1986/89* (1991) 201–17, at 206 f.

13 Boatwright, *City* (1987) 161 ff.

14 Boatwright, *City* (1987) 190 ff. There is copious literature on the *tondi*: cf. for recent contributions Oppermann, *Nikephoros* 4 (1991) 211 ff.; Turcan, *CRAI* 1991, 53 ff. My own view is close to that of Kähler, *Villa* (1950) 177 ff., and Coarelli, in Grenier and Coarelli, *MEFRA* 98 (1986) 252 f. (although their attempt to locate the original position of the Antinous obelisk on the Palatine must be rejected, above, p. 256, note 43). Oppermann 216 f. takes a basically similar position. He and Turcan both give good reasons for amending the traditional order of the eight scenes. Meyer, *Antinoos* (1991) 218 ff., cf. id., *Obelisk* (1994) 153 ff., allows at most a depiction of Antinous in one *tondo* out of eight. He also argues that three separate artists were at work (perhaps because the monument had to be erected quickly, one might suggest).

15 *ILS* 7212 = Sm. 165; cf. Voisin, *MEFRA* 99 (1987) 257 ff.

16 Grenier, *MEFRA* 101 (1989) 925 ff.

17 *CIL* VI 974; Strack 137; *BMC* III 335 ff. – crocodile: *BMC* III 475, 485; A.C. Levi, *NC* 8 (1948) 30 ff. – 'Typhonians': cf. Frankfurter, *JJS* 43 (1992) 203 ff. [Cf. p. 359, below.]

18 Ol. 88, A–C.

19 Dio: 69.15.1. – Alani and Iberia: Wheeler, *Flavius Arrianus* (1977) 101 ff., 223 ff., 227 ff. – Mithridates: Karras-Klapproth, *Pros. Studien* (1988) 85. – envoys: Dio 69.18.2.

20 Arrian's 'deterrence': Wheeler, *Flavius Arrianus* (1977) 272 ff. – Themistius: *Or.* 34.8. – IX Hispana: A.R. Birley, *Fasti* (1981) 220 f.

21 *HA*: *Had.* 21.8. – coins: Strack 184 ff.; *BMC* III 474 f. (*Roma Aeterna*); 334 (*Veneris felicis*); 337 f. (*vota publica*); 471, 483 (*liberalitas Aug. VI*); 472 (*liberalitas Aug. VII*).

22 Arrian, *Tactica* 32.3; 44.2–3. Cf. Wheeler, *GRBS* 19 (1978) 351 ff.

23 began to be ill: Dio 69.17.1. – health in Egypt: id. 69.11.3; Victor, *Caes.* 14.8. – obelisk: Meyer, *Obelisk* (1994) 84 ff. – *BMC* III 318 (no. 603); interpreted by Hannestad, *Anal. Rom. Inst. Dan.* 11 (1982) 97 ff. – adoption . . . fraudulent: *HA Had.* 4.10; Dio 69.1.1–4.

24 beauty: *HA Had.* 23.10, cf. *Ael.* 5.1. – secret oath: *Ael.* 3.8. – belated amends: thus Syme, *Tacitus* (1958) 601, and elsewhere. – bastard: Carcopino, *REA* 51 (1949) 262 ff. = id., *Passion et politique* (1958) 143 ff.; *REA* 67 (1965) 67 ff.; refuted e.g. by Syme, 'Ummidius Quadratus, *capax imperii*', *Harvard Studies in Classical Philology* 83 (1979) 287–310 = *RP* III (1984) 1158 ff., at 300 ff. = 1179 f. – tubercular: Dio 69.17.1. – daughter betrothed: *HA M. Aur.* 4.5; Prefect at Alban festival: ibid. 4.7, cf. *RE* 6.2 (1909) 2213–16. – Marcus as ultimate successor: Pflaum, *BHAC 1963*

(1964) 95 ff., plausibly in my view, explains the choice of L. Commodus in this way; cf. A.R. Birley, *Marcus Aurelius* (1987) 40 ff., 232 ff.

25 shows . . . Danube: *HA Had.* 23.12–13. – Jazyges: Dio 69.15.2. – Quadi: *BMC* IV *Antoninus Pius to Commodus* (1940) 204 f., 367 (*rex Quadis datus*). – adopted son of Turbo: *PIR²* F 305; Fitz, *Verwaltung* II (1993) 475 ff. – Nicomedes: *Chron. Pasch.* 163 – Rogatus: *ILS* 1450; *CP* 140. – Maximus: Fitz 483 ff. – coins: Toynbee 133 ff.; *BMC* III 363 ff., 543 ff. – everyone against: *HA Had.* 23.11: *invitis omnibus.*

26 Horoscopes: Hephaestio Thebanus, *Apotelesmatica*, ed. D. Pingree, 2 vols (Leipzig 1973–4), 2.18.21 ff., quotes three horoscopes supplied by an earlier astrologer, Antigonus of Nicaea: the first, that of Hadrian, 22–52; the second, 54–61, most plausibly identified with Acilius Attianus, Caballos, *Senadores* (1990) 35 f.; the third, clearly the young Pedanius Fuscus, 62–6. (However, I do not accept that the passage in Hephaestio 2.18.65, where his parents are said to have met a violent death, is evidence for them being killed as late as 137.) Almost identical versions are also given in id. *Epit.* 4.26.12–56. One passage is omitted in Pingree's edition from the beginning of Hadrian's horoscope, found only in the Vienna Codex, *C. Gr. Vindob.* 108, fol. 301 ff. It is printed in the *Catalogus codicum astrologorum Graecorum* VI, ed. W. Kroll (Brussels 1902) 68, lines 7–9, and is translated by Cramer, *Astrology* (1954) 165; this may allow the dating of Fuscus' attempted coup to November 137, as suggested by Martin, *Providentia* (1982) 302.   Dio: 69.17.1. – *HA*: see next note.

27 *HA: Had.* 15.8; 23.2; 23.8, 25.8. – last moments: Dio 69.17.2. On Servianus, cf. now the lengthy study by Michelotto, in *Studi Gatti* (1987) 143 ff. I cannot follow him in all particulars. – 'many others': *HA Had.* 23.8. – Polyaenus, Marcellus: ibid. 15.4.

28 Cyrene, Barca: Ol. 120, re-edited and reinterpreted by C.P. Jones, *Chiron* 26 (1996) 47 ff. – *Panhellenia* first held in 137: Wörrle, *Chiron* 22 (1992) 337 ff. – Herodes first archon: so Ameling, *Herodes* (1983) I 61. A likelier year for his presidency, Philostratus, *V. soph.* 2.1.5, is perhaps 141. J.H. Oliver, *Marcus Aurelius. Aspects of Civic and Cultural Policy in the East* (Princeton 1970) 92 ff., has a helpful collection of inscriptions registering office-holders in the Panhellenion. For Pulcher, ibid. 118; also *PIR²* C 1424; *CP* no. 81. – Celer (who may have been *ab epistulis tout court* and not just *Graecis*) is named as Secretary by Philostratus, *V. soph.* 1.22.3; assumed identical with the man who taught M. Aurelius and his adoptive brother Lucius, *HA M. Ant.* 2.4; *Verus* 2.5; cf. M. Aur., *Med.* 8.25. Origin at Corinth suggested by A.R. Birley, *Locus virtutibus patefactus?* (Opladen 1992) 48 (with a discussion of known *ab epistulis*, 41–54). On known Caninii at Corinth, see now A.J.S. Spawforth, 'Roman Corinth: the formation of a colonial elite', in A.D. Rizakis (ed.), *Roman Onomastics in the Greek East. Social and Political Aspects* (Athens 1996) 167–82, at 176 f.

29 death of the Caesar: *HA Had.* 23.15–16; *Ael.* 6.6–7; Dio 69.20.1. – Sabina: *HA Had.* 23.9; *Epit. de Caes.* 14.8; R.-C. no. 802.

30 wailing: *HA Had.* 26.8–9. – dreams: 26.10.

31 birthday, adoption: *HA Had.* 26.6 (with another omen); Dio 69.20.1–5; *HA Ant. Pius* 4.4–7.

32 *HA Ant. Pius* 1.9, 2.8, 2.11, 2.1; Dio 69.21.1–2. – condition: *HA Ant. Pius* 4.5; *M. Aur.* 5.1; *Verus* 2.13 (the last two confused).

33 For the view that Marcus was Hadrian's real choice as heir (but still too young in 138), A.R. Birley, *Marcus Aurelius* (1987) 232 ff. In particular, the relief from Ephesus which puts Lucius, the son of Aelius Caesar, in a more prominent position than Marcus, can hardly support the case that Lucius rather than Marcus was intended as principal heir, as argued by Barnes, *JRS* 57 (1967) 65 ff., especially 78 – as Barnes concedes (78 note 84), with one exception art historians date the relief to

the 160s, when Lucius, by then Emperor, was at Ephesus in person, and needed to be flattered. – Quadratus, Catilius: *HA Had.* 15.7; 24.6–7 (Catilius had particularly lamented the adoption of Antoninus.) – Titianus: *HA Had.* 15.6; *Ant. Pius* 7.3–4.

34 Turbo: *PIR²* M 249; Syme, 'Guard Prefects of Trajan and Hadrian', *JRS* 70 (1980) 64–80 = *RP* III (1984) 1276 ff., at 72 ff. = 1290 ff. – successors: *HA Had.* 24.9, referring to 138, has *praefectis*, plural. – Gavius and Petronius: Syme, op. cit. 75 = 1293. – strictness: *HA Ant. Pius* 8.7. – Severus, Major, Praesens: Thomasson, *Laterculi* I (1984) 311. – Nepos: Fitz, *Verwaltung* I (1993) 478 f. – Urbicus: A.R. Birley, *Fasti* (1981) 112 ff.

35 Augustus' letter: A. Gellius, *NA* 15.7.3. – astrologer: *HA Had.* 16.7; *Ael.* 3.9.

36 Tibur: *HA Had.* 23.8. – magic rites, etc.: Dio 69.20.1; 22.1–4.

37 Mastor, Antoninus: *HA Had.* 24.8–11. – doctor's tombstone: H. Solin, *Arctos* 21 (1987) 128 ff. – episodes: *HA Had.* 25.1–5.

38 autobiography: Dio 69.11.2 (Antinous); *HA Had.* 7.2 (consulars); 1.1 (Aelii); 3.3 (drinking); 3.5 (tribune); Vespasian (Dio 66.17.1); *HA Had.* 16.1 (Phlegon). It is worth asking whether Phlegon's work on long-lived persons (*Makrobioi*) and on marvels (*thaumasia*), including sex-changes, may not have reflected Hadrian's particular interests. Note also that the *Olympiads*, *FGrH* 257, fr. 23, had an entry on Adria, the *ultima origo* of the Aelii, making it a Greek colony, founded by Dionysius I of Syracuse.

39 papyrus: *PFayum* 19 = Sm. 123, as interpreted by Bollansée, *Ancient Society* 25 (1994) 279 ff.

40 dream: *HA Had.* 26.10. – poem: ibid. 25.9, discussed fully in the Epilogue that follows. – calm shattered: Dio 69.22.4.

41 *HA Had.* 25.6–7; Dio 69.23.2. Baldwin, *Gymnasium* 90 (1983) 546, argues persuasively for the meaning 'hated'.

EPILOGUE *ANIMULA VAGULA BLANDULA*

1 The poem is given in *HA Had.* 25.9. Its authenticity was authoritatively defended by Cameron, *Harvard Studies in Classical Philology* 84 (1980) 167 ff. (here quoted). I have elaborated my interpretation in *Laverna* 5 (1994) 176 ff., giving particular weight to Sajdak, *Eos* 20 (1914–15) 147 ff. (in Polish), summarised in *Berl. Ph. Woch.* 36 (1916) 765 ff. Sajdak first spotted the echoes of Ennius, from a fragment attributed to his *Andromache*, O. Ribbeck, *Tragoediarum Romanorum Fragmenta* (Berlin 1907) I 27, and thus took the adjectives in the fourth line with *loca*, not *animula*. This had already been done by another Polish scholar, K. Morawski, *Dwaj cesarze rzymscy: Tyberyusz i Hadryan* (Cracow 1883), 96, whom he cites (I am grateful to E. Dabrowa for procuring a copy of the relevant part of this work). This interpretation was first given general currency, independently (it seems), by T. Birt, *Römische Charakterköpfe* (Leipzig 1913) 329. Birt's translation provoked a debate which still goes on. – For Hadrian's love of Ennius: *HA Had.* 16.6. – The text and punctuation of lines 3–4 was, convincingly in my view (except that he retained *nudula* in line 4), established by Mariotti, *Studia Florentina* (1970) 233 ff. (cf. also id., *Scritti in Memoria di A. Ronconi* II (Florence 1988) 11 ff.). I have given an almost complete bibliography in the *Laverna* article and therefore refrain from further references here. I there overlooked V. Bejarano, 'El emperador Adriano ante la tradición romana', *Pyrenae* 11 (1975) 81–98, at 94 with note 71, the only author apart from myself to accept Sajdak's hesitant conjecture *nubila* for *nudula*.

2 *HA Had.* 14.11 (retaining Hohl's emendation; cf. Callu et al., in their edition, n. 143, and Baldwin, *Gymnasium* 101 (1994) 445 f. for alternatives); *Epit. de Caes.* 14.6.

3 Wegner, *Hadrian* (1956) 72 f.

4 Den Boer, *Mnemosyne* 8 (1955) 123.

5 Cf. further A.R. Birley, *Laverna* 5 (1994) 202 ff., citing among others André, *ANRW* 2.34.1 (1993) 607.

6 Thus the medical man Petrakis, *W. Journ. Medicine* 132 (1980) 87 ff., who draws attention to the diagonal earlobe creases visible in Hadrian's portraits, evidently a symptom of heart disease; further to what is known as 'Type A behavior' , of which the characteristics are being 'competitive, achievement-oriented, involved in multiple activities with deadlines, impatient with slowness in others, [liking] to set a rapid work pace, and [tending] to be hostile and aggressive.' (I owe this reference to the late Dr D.A. Dixon.)

7 Wegner, *Hadrian* (1956) 72, cf. 25 f., on the latest portrait-type.

8 In other words, Hadrian does not feature in Book 1 of the *Meditations*. There are not many references elsewhere in the work. 8.25, mentioning that Celer survived Hadrian, may refer to the *ab epistulis* Caninius Celer; 8.37 names two men called Chabrias and Diotimus, probably freedmen, who mourned Hadrian. Other mentions are very impersonal.

9 Fronto, *Ad M. Caesarem* 2.4.1, p. 25 van den Hout; *Princ. Historiae* 11, pp. 208 f. van den Hout (I accept the emendation *salicibus* by Davies, *Latomus* 27 (1968) 75 ff.).

10 Ael. Aristides, *Or.* 26 K: the passages cited are Chapters 31–3 and 18 (the Persian king). On the speech, Swain, *Hellenism and Empire* (1996) 274 ff., sees less genuine enthusiasm for Rome on the author's part than commonly held. Cf. also id. 256 n. 10 on the birthplace (Hadriani rather than Hadrianutherae). – Another speech preserved in the works of Aristides, *Or.* 35 K, addressed to the Emperor himself, has generally been supposed to be the work of an unknown orator from the next century. A case has been argued for it being by Aristides himself, and in praise of Antoninus, making repeated hostile comparisons, scarcely veiled, with his predecessor. Thus C.P. Jones, 'Aelius Aristides EIS BASILEA', *JRS* 62 (1972) 134–52; id., 'The EIS BASILEA again', *Classical Quarterly* 31 (1981) 224–5. For example, the ruler who is addressed had refrained unlike 'previous emperors' from 'accusing people of plotting and punishing them with death or exile' (Chapter 9); and he 'checked . . . the irrational and violent lunges' in the body of empire (Chapter 13). Still, although Hadrian's behaviour towards the Greeks was erratic, Jones exaggerates Hadrian's harsh treatment of some of them, *JRS* 62 (1972) 145: the philosopher Euphrates was not 'ordered', but permitted, to commit suicide; that Apollodorus was 'put death' and Favorinus 'relegated to an island' is far from certain (cf. pp. 112, note 51; 281, note 11; 341, note 10, above). The attribution has been supported, e.g. by Champlin, *Fronto* (1980) 83 ff., 165 and A.R. Birley, *Marcus Aurelius* (1987) 87 f., 227 – but the weight of scholarly opinion against now seems decisive: Swain, *Hellenism and Empire* (1996) 266 note 50, cites relevant contributions.

11 Dio 69.23.2; 69.9.4; *Epit. de Caes.* 14.11. – training and discipline: cf. Chapters 10 and 11, above. – concessions: J.B. Campbell, *The Emperor and the Roman Army 31 BC–AD 235* (Oxford 1984) 214, 231 ff., 277 f., 285 f., 310 – diplomas: G. Alföldy, 'Die Truppenkommandeure in den Militärdiplomen', in W. Eck and H. Wolff (eds), *Heer und Integrationspolitik* (Cologne–Vienna 1986) 385–436 = id., *Römische Heeresgeschichte* (1987) 89 ff., at 400 ff. = 104 ff., discusses naming of officers' *origo*. J. Morris and M. Roxan, 'The witnesses to Roman military diplomata', *Arheoloski Vestnik* 28 (1977) 299–333, find that from AD 133 onwards the order of witnesses went by seniority. – *militia quarta*: E. Birley, *Roman Britain and the Roman Army* (1953) 149 = *Roman Army Papers* (1988) 158 f. – G. Wesch-Klein, 'Hadrian, der exercitus Romanus und die pax Romana' (forthcoming), offers more on army matters. I am grateful to the author for letting me see her paper in typescript.

12 few further transfers of legions: cf. E. Ritterling, *RE* 12.1 (1924) 1293. – *HA* on frontier-works: *Had.* 11.2; 12.6. – Aristides: *Or.* 26 K. 80 ff. – Antonine Wall: W.S. Hanson and G.S. Maxwell, *Rome's North-West Frontier. The Antonine Wall* (Edinburgh 1986). – studied insult: cf. A.R. Birley, *Trans. Durham and Northumberland* 3 (1974) 15 ff. – On Hadrian's frontier policy as a whole, I still find much to be said for the view of E. Birley, in *Carnuntina* (1956) 25 ff., repr. in id., *Roman Army Papers* (1988) 12 ff. That the artificial running barriers owed something to Greek traditions of 'walling out the barbarians' is convincingly stressed by Crow, in *Stud. Militärgrenzen Roms* III (1986) 724 ff. Three ambitious works, two very recent, have a lot to say about Roman frontier policy: E.N. Luttwak, *The Grand Strategy of the Roman Empire* (Baltimore–London 1976); B. Isaac, *The Limits of Empire. The Roman Army in the East* (Oxford 1990); Whittaker, *Frontiers* (1994). Only the last offers much on Hadrian and I am not particularly convinced. Cf. further E.L. Wheeler, 'Methodological limits and the mirage of Roman strategy', *Journal of Military History* 57 (1993) 7–41, 215–40, a detailed review of Isaac and Whittaker (in the first, French, edition), and comparison with Luttwak. Whittaker offers a partial reply in Kennedy (ed.), *Roman Army* (1996) 25 ff. Cf. also above, notes 10 and 18 to Chapter 11.

13 On the consular 'governors' in Italy, Eck, *Historiae Aug. Coll.* n.s. I (1991) 183 ff. – *cursus honorum*: thus Syme, 'Hadrian and the Senate', *Athenaeum* 62 (1984) 31–60 = *RP* IV (1988) 295 ff., at 51 ff. = 316 ff. Two other men seem to have been intended as *cos. II ord.*, P. Metilius Nepos for 128 (*PIR²* M 545) and C. Julius Proculus, perhaps for 134, above, note 22 to Chapter 12, note 4 to Chapter 21. And on the question of 'eastern' consuls, A.R. Birley, 'Hadrian and Greek senators' *ZPE* 116 (1997) 225 f. – equestrian *ab epist.* etc.: *HA Had.* 22.8, cf. Callu et al., ad loc. – *advocatus fisci*: *HA Had.* 20.6; *AE* 1975. 408. – Hadrian as 'reformer': e.g. Hirschfeld, *Kais. Verw.* (1905) 476 ff.

14 Cf. the judicious restraint of Crook, *Consilium* (1955), Chapter 5 and App. 3. – Edict: *ILS* 8973; Victor, *Caes.* 19.2; Eutropius 8.17, etc. – *HA*: especially *Had.* 8.8–9; 18.1–11; 22.1–8. – rescripts: F. Pringsheim, 'The legal policy and reforms of Hadrian', *JRS* 24 (1934) 139–53, at 146. Pringsheim's paper is one of a good many which attribute far-reaching legal initiatives to Hadrian. Cf. especially d'Orgeval, *Hadrien* (1950) and (more restrained) A. d'Ors, 'La signification de l'oeuvre d'Hadrien dans l'histoire du droit romain', in *Les empereurs romains d'Espagne* (Paris 1965) 147–68. Note the critical review of d'Orgeval by W. Kunkel, *Gnomon* 24 (1952) 486–91 (repr. in id., *Kleine Schriften* (Weimar 1974) 602–7). Kunkel likewise, in his *Herkunft und soziale Stellung der römischen Juristen* (Weimar 1952) 291 ff., denies the great significance attached to a 'reform' of the *consilium principis*, to the Edict and to rescripts. – *Latium maius*: Gaius, *Inst.* 1.96; attested by *ILS* 6780 (Gigthis) and by implication 6781 (Thisiduo), from the reigns of Pius and Hadrian respectively; cf. Sherwin-White, *Citizenship* (1973) 255 f. Cf. also pp. 207, 342 (note 7), above.

15 Dio: 69.5.2–3; 10.1. – *HA*: 19.2 cf. 20.4–5. – *Epit. de Caes.*: 14.4–5. – Fronto: *Princ. Historiae* 11, p. 209 van den Hout. – Athens: Dio 69.16.1–2; *HA Had.* 13.6; 19.3; 20.4; Pausanias 1.3.2. – Rome: *HA Had.* 19.9–13. Dr Susan Walker informs me that M.T. Boatwright is planning a monograph on Hadrian's building in the provinces, a colossal undertaking. Such a work would nicely complement Boatwright's *Hadrian and the City of Rome* (1987). On one aspect of Hadrian's activity as restorer or 'founder' of Greek cities, cf. Follet, in Létoublon (ed.), *Colloque Chantraine* (1992) 241 ff.

16 Cf. above all the various contributions by Zahrnt, especially *ANRW* 2.10.1 (1989) 669 ff. and in Olshausen and Sonnabend (eds), *Kolloquium* (1991) 463 ff.

17 Tertullian: *Apol.* 5.7, *omnium curiositatum explorator*. *curiositas* has a pejorative

sense, cf. Tertullian, *Idol.* 9; 10.9. – Julian: *Caes.* 311 C–D. – *HA: Had.* 17.8; 26.5. – *Epit. de Caes.* 14.6, of which *HA Had.* 14.11 is surely another version. – Dio: 69.2.5 (mildness); 3.2–3 (ambition, jealousy); 5.1 (strictness . . . skill).

18 Synesius, *Ep.* 148; *De Regno*, especially 13 f. – A travelling emperor with a large entourage of course imposed heavy expenses on all the places he visited. But in effect this no doubt meant that the rich spent on public works, to the general benefit. In any case, Hadrian certainly disbursed from imperial funds in many cases. Whether this – and for example his tax remission of AD 118, cf. above pp. 97 f. and note 16, or his measures on use of imperial domain, cf. above p. 208 – can be called 'Hadrianic economic policy' is another matter. A good many aspects which could be discussed under this rubric have had to be omitted from the present study – e.g., not a word on the *lex metallis dicta* of Vipasca (Sm. 439 f.). There are, after all, limits to what can be covered in a biography.

ADDENDUM

1 Part of a tombstone found at Vindolanda in May 1997 may throw more light on the troubles in Britain under Hadrian. It commemorates a centurion called *T. Ann[ius? . . .]*, probably acting commander of the Vindolanda garrison at that time, *[coh. I] Tungr[orum]*, who was 'killed in the war', *in bell[o . . . inter/fectus.* The dating is not quite certain, however. What appears to be the date by consuls could refer to the year 134. If so, this officer could have been killed in the Jewish war, rather than in renewed fighting in northern Britain, as Paul Holder points out to me, having taken reinforcements from Britain to Judaea.

2 Werner Eck kindly informs me that the supposed evidence for Hadrian becoming *imperator II*, which marked the end of the Jewish war, before the end of AD 135 is highly doubtful, and that the war may have gone on into 136. Further, in his view the Roman casualties were even higher than has been assumed hitherto (e.g. much of the original auxiliary garrison of Judaea may have been wiped out). It is to be hoped that he will soon publish a new study of this question.

BIBLIOGRAPHY

The following list is mainly, but not exclusively, of items cited more than once in the notes. Titles of books and journals abbreviated in the notes are here given in full.

Alföldy, G. *Die Legionslegaten der römischen Rheinarmeen (Epigraphische Studien 3,* Graz–Cologne 1967)
—— *Fasti Hispanienses. Senatorische Reichsbeamte und Offiziere in den spanischen Provinzen* (Wiesbaden 1969)
—— *Noricum* (London 1974)
—— *Konsulat und Senatorenstand unter den Antoninen* (Bonn 1977)
—— *Römische Heeresgeschichte. Beiträge 1962–1985* (Amsterdam 1987)
—— *Tarraco* (Tarragona 1991)
—— 'La Pannonia e l'Impero Romano', in: G. Hajnóczi (ed.), *La Pannonia e l'Impero Romano* (Rome 1994) 25–40
Ameling, W. *Herodes Atticus,* 2 vols (Hildesheim 1983)
André, J.-M. 'Hadrien littérateur et protecteur des lettres', *ANRW* 2.34.1 (1993) 583–611
Applebaum, S. *Prolegomena to the Study of the Second Jewish Revolt (AD132–135) (British Archaeological Reports* supp. ser. 7, Oxford 1976)
—— *Jews and Greeks in Ancient Cyrene* (Leiden 1979)
Aymard, J. *Essai sur les chasses romaines des origines à la fin du siècle des Antonins* (Paris 1951)
Baatz, D. 'Zur Grenzpolitik Hadrians in Obergermanien', in: E. Birley, B. Dobson and M.G. Jarrett (eds), *Roman Frontier Studies 1969* (Cardiff 1974) 112–24
Baldwin, B. 'Hadrian's death in the *Historia Augusta*', *Gymnasium* 90 (1983) 546
—— 'Hadrian's character traits', *Gymnasium* 101 (1994) 455–6
Barnes, T.D. 'Hadrian and Lucius Verus', *Journal of Roman Studies* 57 (1967) 65–79
—— *The Sources of the* Historia Augusta (Brussels 1978)
—— 'Trajan and the Jews', *Journal of Jewish Studies* 36 (1985) 145–62
—— 'Emperors on the move', *Journal of Roman Archaeology* 2 (1989) 247–61
Baslez, M.F. 'La famille de Philopappos de Commagène, un prince entre deux mondes', *Dialogues d'histoire ancienne* 18 (1992) 89–101
Beaujeu, J. *La religion romaine à l'apogée de l'empire* I. *La politique religieuse des Antonins (96–192)* (Paris 1955)
Bellen, H. 'Die Weltreichsidee des Kaisers Hadrian', *Forschungsmagazin der Johannes Gutenberg-Universität Mainz* 2 (1986) 5–16
Benario, H.W. *A Commentary on the* Vita Hadriani *in the* Historia Augusta (Chico, Cal. 1980)
Benjamin, A.S. 'The altars of Hadrian in Athens and Hadrian's Panhellenic Program', *Hesperia* 32 (1963) 57–86

Bernand, A. and Bernand, E. *Les inscriptions du Colosse de Memnon* (Paris 1960)

Bernier, Y. 'Génèse et fortune littéraire des *Mémoires d'Hadrien*', *Cahiers d'études anciennes* 21 (1988) 7–25

Bessone, L. 'Floro: un retore storico e poeta', *ANRW* 2.34.1 (1993) 80–117

Birley, A.R. 'Roman frontiers and Roman frontier policy: some reflections on Roman imperialism', *Transactions of the Architectural and Archaeological Society of Durham and Northumberland* 3 (1974) 13–25

—— *Lives of the Later Caesars. The First Part of the Augustan History, with Newly Compiled Lives of Nerva and Trajan* (Harmondsworth 1976)

—— *The* Fasti *of Roman Britain* (Oxford 1981)

—— *Marcus Aurelius. A Biography* (2nd edn, London 1987)

—— 'Hadrian's farewell to life', *Laverna* 5 (1994) 176–205

—— 'Indirect means of detecting Marius Maximus', *Historiae Augustae Colloquia*, n.s. III, *Colloquium Maceeratense 1992* (Bari 1995) 57–74

—— 'Marius Maximus the consular biographer', *ANRW* II.34.3 (1997) 2678–757

—— 'Hadrian and Greek senators', *Zeitschrift für Papyrologie und Epigraphik* 116 (1997) 209–45

Birley, E. *Roman Britain and the Roman Army* (Kendal 1953)

—— 'Hadrianic frontier policy', in: E. Swoboda (ed.), *Carnuntina* (Graz–Cologne 1956) 25–33

—— *Research on Hadrian's Wall* (Kendal 1961)

—— *The Roman Army. Papers 1929–1986* (Amsterdam 1988)

Birley, R. *Vindolanda. The Early Wooden Forts* I (Bardon Mill 1994)

Blyth, P.H. 'Apollodorus of Damascus and the *Poliorcetica*', *Greek, Roman and Byzantine Studies* 33 (1992) 127–58

Boatwright, M.T. *Hadrian and the City of Rome* (Princeton 1987)

—— 'Hadrian and the Italian cities', *Chiron* 19 (1989) 235–71

Boer, W. den 'Religion and literature in Hadrian's policy', *Mnemosyne* 8 (1955) 123–44

—— 'Trajan's deification and Hadrian's succession', *Ancient Society* 6 (1975) 203–12

Bollansée, J. '*P. Fay.* 19, Hadrian's Memoirs, and imperial epistolary autobiography', *Ancient Society* 25 (1994) 279–302

Bonneau, D. *La crue du Nil* (Paris 1964)

—— *Le fisc et le Nil* (Paris 1971)

Bosworth, A.B. 'Arrian and Rome: the minor works', *ANRW* 2.34.1 (1993) 226–75

Bowersock, G.W. *Greek Sophists in the Roman Empire* (Oxford 1969)

—— *Roman Arabia* (Cambridge, Mass.–London 1983)

—— 'Augustus and the east: the problem of the succession', in: F. Millar and E. Segal (eds), *Caesar Augustus: Seven Aspects* (Oxford 1984) 169–88

—— 'Hadrian and *metropolis*', *BHAC 1982/3* (1985) 75–88

Bowerstock, G.W., Habicht, C. and Jones, C.P. 'Epigraphica Asiae Minoris rapta aut obruta', *American Journal of Philology* 108 (1987) 699–706

Bowie, E.L. 'Greek poetry in the Antonine age', in: D.A. Russell (ed.), *Antonine Literature* (Oxford 1990) 53–90

Bowman, A.K. and Thomas, J.D. *The Vindolanda Writing Tablets.* Tabulae Vindolandenses II (London 1994)

Braunert, H. 'Das Athenaeum zu Rom bei den *SHA*', *BHAC 1963* (1964) 9–40

Breeze, D.J. 'The frontier in Britain, 1984–1989', in: V.A. Maxfield and M.J. Dobson (eds), *Roman Frontier Studies 1989* (Exeter 1991) 35–43

Breeze, D.J. and Dobson, B. *Hadrian's Wall* (London, 3rd edn 1987)

Bruggisser, P. '"Patience" d'un impatient. Hadrien à l'approche de la mort, de l'Histoire Auguste à Marguérite Yourcenar', in: *Historiae Augustae Colloquia*. n.s. 5 (Macerata, forthcoming)

Bruce, J.C. *see* Daniels, C.M.

Caballos Rufino, A. *Los senadores hispanorromanos y la romanización de Hispania (siglos I–III)* (Ecija 1990)
—— *Itálica y los Italicenses. Aproximación a su historia* (Seville 1994)
Calderini, A. *Dizionario dei nomi geografici e topografici dell' Egitto greco-romano* I 1 (Milan 1935); I 2 (Madrid 1966)
Callu, J.P., Gaden, A. and Desbordes, O. *Histoire Auguste* I 1. *Introduction générale, Vies d'Hadrien, Aelius, Antonin* (Paris 1992)
Cameron, Alan *"'Poetae novelli'"*, *Harvard Studies in Classical Philology* 84 (1980) 127–75
Campbell, D.B. 'A Chinese puzzle for the Romans', *Historia* 28 (1989) 371–6
Cantarelli, L. 'Gli scritti latini di Adriano imperatore', *Studi e documenti di storia e diritto* 19 (1898) 113–70
Carandini, A. *Vibia Sabina. Funzione politica, iconografia e il problema del classicismo adrianeo* (Rome 1969)
Carcopino, J. 'L'hérédité dynastique chez les Antonins', *Revue des études anciennes* 51 (1949) 262–321 (repr. in: id., *Passion et politique chez les Césars*, Paris 1958, 143–222)
Carney, T.F. 'The political legends on Hadrian's coinage. Policies and problems', *Turtle* 6 (1967) 291–303
—— 'How Suetonius' *Lives* reflect on Hadrian', *Proceedings of the African Classical Association* 11 (1968) 7–24
Cartledge, P.A. and Spawforth, A.J.S. *Hellenistic and Roman Sparta. A Tale of Two Cities* (London 1989)
Cassend, J.-M. and Janon, M. 'La colonne d'Hadrien à Lambèse', *Bulletin d'archéologie algérienne* 7.1 (1977–9) 239–58
Castritius, H. 'Der Phoinix auf den *Aurei* Hadrians und Tacitus *Annalen* VI 28', *Jahrbuch für Numismatik und Geldgeschichte* 14 (1964) 89–95
Cazzaniga, I. 'Il *tetrapharmacum* cibo adrianeo (*HA Spart., Vit. Hadr.* 21,4, *Vit. Ael.* 5,4 e Philod. *P. Herc.* 1005, IV 10). Esegesi e critica testuale', in: *Poesia latina in frammenti* (Genoa 1974) 359–66
Champlin, E. 'Hadrian's heir', *Zeitschrift für Papyrologie und Epigraphik* 21 (1976) 78–89
—— *Fronto and Antonine Rome* (Cambridge, Mass. 1980)
—— 'Figlinae Marcianae', *Athenaeum* 71 (1983) 257–64
—— 'The glass ball game', *Zeitschrift für Papyrologie und Epigraphik* 60 (1985) 151–63
Cizek, E. 'L'éloge de C. Avidius Nigrinus chez Tacite et le "complot" des consulaires', *Bulletin del l'Association G. Budé* 3 (1980) 279–94
Claridge, A. 'Hadrian's Column of Trajan', *Journal of Roman Archaeology* 6 (1993) 5–22
Cotton, H.M. 'The archive of Salome Komaise daughter of Levi: another archive from the "Cave of Letters"', *Zeitschrift für Papyrologie und Epigraphik* 105 (1995) 171–207
Cotton, H.M., Cockle, W.H. and Millar, F.G.B. 'The papyrology of the Roman Near East: a survey', *Journal of Roman Studies* 85 (1995) 214–35
Cramer, F.H. *Astrology in Roman Law and Politics* (Philadelphia 1954)
Crook, J.A. *Consilium principis* (Cambridge 1955)
Crow, J.G. 'The function of Hadrian's Wall and the comparative evidence of Late Roman Long Walls', in: *Studien zur Militärgrenzen Roms* III *(13. Internationaler Limeskongress Aalen 1983)* (Stuttgart 1986) 724–9
—— 'Construction and reconstruction in the central sector of Hadrian's Wall', in: V.A. Maxfield and M.J. Dobson (eds), *Roman Frontier Studies* 1989 (Exeter 1991) 44–7
—— 'A review of current research on the turrets and curtain of Hadrian's Wall', *Britannia* 22 (1991) 51–63
Daniels, C.M. (ed.) J.C. Bruce, *Handbook to the Roman Wall*, 13th edn (Newcastle upon Tyne 1978)
—— 'Africa', in: J.S. Wacher (ed.), *The Roman World* (London 1987) 223–65

—— *The Eleventh Pilgrimage of Hadrian's Wall* (Newcastle upon Tyne 1989)

Davies R.W. 'Fronto, Hadrian and the Roman army', *Latomus* 27 (1968) 75–95

Devijver, H. *Prosopographia militarium equestrium*, 5 vols (Louvain 1976–93)

Dobson, B. *Die* Primipilares. *Entwicklung und Bedeutung, Laufbahnen und Persönlichkeiten eines römischen Offizierranges* (Bonn 1978)

—— 'The function of Hadrian's Wall', *Archaeologia Aeliana*, 5th ser., 14 (1986) 1–30

Dobson, B. and Hill, P.R. 'The design of Hadrian's Wall and its implications', *Archaeologia Aeliana*, 5th. ser., 20 (1992) 27–52

Drew-Bear, T. and Richard, F. 'Hadrien et Erastos, nauclère d'Ephèse', in: Y. Le Bohec (ed.), *L'Afrique, la Gaule, la religion à l'époque romaine. Mélanges à la mémoire de M. Le Glay* (Brussels 1994) 742–51

Drijvers, H.J.W. 'Hatra, Palmyra and Edessa', *ANRW* 2.8 (1977) 799–906

Dürr, J. *Die Reisen des Kaisers Hadrian* (Vienna 1881)

Eck, W. 'Hadrian als *pater patriae* und die Verleihung des Augustatitels an Sabina', in: G. Wirth (ed.), *Romanitas-Christianitas. Festschrift J. Straub* (Berlin 1982) 217–29

—— 'Jahres-und Provinzialfasten der senatorischen Statthalter von 69/70 bis 138/9', *Chiron* 12 (1982) 281–362 ; 13 (1983) 147–237

—— *Die Statthalter der germanischen Provinzen* (Bonn 1985)

—— 'Die italischen *legati Augusti pro praetore* unter Hadrian und Antoninus Pius', *Historiae Augustae Colloquia*, n.s. I *Coll. Parisinum 1990* (Macerata 1991) 183–95

—— 'Q. Marcius Turbo in Niedermösien', in: *Klassisches Altertum, Spätantike und frühes Christentum. Festschrift A. Lippold* (Würzburg 1993) 247–55

—— (ed.) *Prosopographie und Sozialgeschichte. Studien zur Methodik und Erkenntnismöglichkeit der kaiserzeitlichen Prosopographie. Kolloquium Köln 24.–26. November 1991* (Cologne 1993)

—— 'Überlieferung und historische Realität: ein Grundproblem prosopographischer Forschung', in: Eck (ed.), *Prosopographie und Sozialgeschichte* (1993) 365–96

Eck, W. and Roxan, M.M. 'Two new military diplomas', in: R. Frei-Stolba and M.A. Speidel (eds), *Römische Inschriften – Neufunde, Neulesungen und Neuinterpretationen. Festschrift H. Lieb* (Basel 1995) 55–99

Fitz, J. *Die Verwaltung Pannoniens in der Römerzeit* I–III (Budapest 1993–4)

Foerster, G. 'A cuirassed bronze statue of Hadrian', *'Atiqot* (English series) 17 (1985) 139–57

Follet, S. *Athènes au IIe et au IIIe siècle. Etudes chronologiques et prosopographiques* (Paris 1976)

—— 'Hadrien *ktistès kai oikistès*: lexicographie et realia', in: F. Létoublon (ed.), *La langue et les textes en grec ancien: actes du colloque Pierre Chantraine* (Amsterdam 1992) 241–54

—— 'Lettres d'Hadrien aux épicuriens d'Athènes (14.2.–14.3.125): *SEG* III 226 + *IG* II² 1097', *Revue des études grecques* 107 (1994) 158–71

Franke, T. *Die Legionslegaten der römischen Armee in der Zeit von Augustus bis Traian*, 2 vols (Bochum 1991)

Frankfurter, D. 'Lest Egypt's city be deserted: religion and ideology in the Egyptian response to the Jewish revolt (116–117 C.E.)', *Journal of Jewish Studies* 43 (1992) 203–20

Gagé, J. '"Italica adlectio": à propos de certaines formes du "ius Italicum" en Espagne au temps de Trajan', *Revue des études anciennes* 71 (1969) 65–84

García y Bellido, A. 'La Italica de Hadriano', in: *Les empereurs romains d'Espagne* (Paris 1965) 7–26

Garzetti, A. 'Floro e l'età adrianea', *Athenaeum* 42 (1964) 136–56

Gascou, J. 'La politique municipale de Rome en Afrique du Nord I. De la mort d'Auguste au début du IIIe siècle', *ANRW* 2.10.2 (1982) 136–229

Geagan, D.J. 'Roman Athens: Some aspects of life and culture', *ANRW* 2.7.1 (1979) 375–437

Gergel, R.A. 'The Tel Shalem Hadrian reconsidered', *American Journal of Archaeology* 95 (1994) 231–51

Geva, H. 'The camp of the Tenth legion in Jerusalem', *Israel Exploration Journal* 34 (1984) 239–48

Gichon, M. 'The Bar Kochba war – a colonial uprising against imperial Rome', *Revue internationale d'histoire militaire* 42 (1979) 82–97

—— 'New insight into the Bar Kokhba war and a reappraisal of Dio Cassius 69.12–13', *Jewish Quarterly Review* 77 (1986) 15–43

Graindor, P. *Athènes sous Hadrien* (Cairo 1934)

Grassl, H. 'Arrian im Donauraum', *Chiron* 12 (1982) 245–52

Gray, W.D. 'A study of the life of Hadrian prior to his accession', *Smith College Studies in History* 4.3 (Northampton, Mass. 1919) 139–209

Gregorovius, F. *Der Kaiser Hadrian. Gemälde der römisch-hellenischen Welt zu seiner Zeit* (Stuttgart, 2nd edn 1884); Eng. tr. by M.E. Robinson (London 1898)

Grenier, J.-C. 'La décoration statuaire du "Sérapeum" du "Canope" de la Villa Adriana. Essai de reconstitution et d'interprétation', *Mélanges de l'Ecole française de Rome – Antiquité* 101 (1989) 925–1019

Grenier, J.-C. and Coarelli, F. 'Le tombe d'Antinous à Rome', ibid. 98 (1986) 217–53

Greppo, J.-G.-H. *Mémoire sur les voyages de l'Empereur Hadrien et sur les médailles qui s'y rapportent* (Paris 1842)

Griffin, M.T. 'The Elder Seneca and Spain', *Journal of Roman Studies* 62 (1972) 1–19

Grimm, G. 'Paulina und Antinous. Zur Vergöttlichung der Hadriansschwester in Ägypten', in: *Das antike Rom und der Osten. Festschrift K. Parlasca* (Erlangen 1990) 33–44

Guarducci, M. 'Adriano e i culti misterici della Grecia', *Bulletino del Museo dell' Impero Romano* 12 (1941) 149–58

—— 'La religione di Adriano', in: *Les empereurs romains d'Espagne* (Paris 1965) 209–19

Guey, J. '28 janvier 98–28 janvier 198, ou le siècle des Antonins', *Revue des études anciennes* 50 (1948) 60–70

Gutsfeld, A. *Römische Herrschaft und einheimischer Widerstand in Nordafrika* (Stuttgart 1989)

Habicht, C. *Die Inschriften des Asklepieion. Pergamon* VIII 3 (Berlin 1969)

Hahland, W. 'Ebertöter Antinous–Androclus', *Jahreshefte des Österreichischen Archäologischen Instituts* 41 (1954) 54–77

Halfmann, H. *Die Senatoren aus dem östlichen Teil des Imperium Romanum bis zum Ende des 2. Jh. n. Chr.* (Göttingen 1979)

—— *Itinera Principum. Geschichte und Typologie der Kaiserreisen im römischen Reich* (Stuttgart 1986)

Hannestad, N. 'Über das Denkmal des Antinous. Topographische und thematische Studien im Canopus-Gebiet der Villa Adriana', *Analecta Romana Instituti Danici* 11 (1983) 69–108

Henderson, B.W. *The Life and Principate of the Emperor Hadrian AD 76–138* (London 1923)

Herr, M.D. 'Persecutions and martyrdoms in Hadrian's days', *Scripta Hierosolymitana* 23 (1972) 85–125

Hill, P.R. 'Hadrian's Wall: some aspects of its execution', *Archaeologia Aeliana*, 5th ser., 19 (1991) 33–9

Hirschfeld, O. *Die kaiserlichen Verwaltungsbeamten bis auf Diokletian* (2nd edn, Berlin 1905)

Hodgson, J. *History of Northumberland* II 3 (Newcastle upon Tyne 1840)

Hoffmann, I. 'Der bärtige Triumphator', in: *Festschrift W. Helck* (Hamburg 1984) 585–91

Isaac, B. 'Roman colonies in Judaea: the foundation of Aelia Capitolina', *Talanta* 12–13 (1980–1) 31–54

—— 'Cassius Dio on the revolt of Bar Kokhba', *Scripta Classica Israelica* 7 (1983/4) 68–76

Isaac, B. and Oppenheimer, A. 'The revolt of Bar Kokhba. Scholarship and ideology', *Journal of Jewish Studies* 36 (1985) 33–60

Isaac, B. and Roll, I. 'Judaea in the early years of Hadrian's reign', *Latomus* 38 (1979) 54–66

—— 'Legio II Traiana in Judaea', *Zeitschrift für Papyrologie und Epigraphik* 33 (1979) 149–56

Jones, B.W. *The Emperor Domitian* (London 1992)

Jones, C.P. *Plutarch and Rome* (Oxford 1971)

—— *The Roman World of Dio Chrysostom* (Cambridge, Mass. 1978)

—— 'The Olympieion and the Hadrianeion at Ephesos', *Journal of Hellenic Studies* 113 (1993) 149–52

—— 'The Panhellenion', *Chiron* 26 (1996) 29–56

Jones, G.D.B. 'The western extension of Hadrian's Wall: Bowness to Cardurnock', *Britannia* 7 (1976) 236–43

—— 'The Solway frontier: interim report 1976–81', *Britannia* 13 (1982) 283–97

Jones, G.D.B. and Little, J.H. 'Coastal settlement in Cyrenaica', *Journal of Roman Studies* 61 (1971) 64–79

Kähler, H. *Hadrian und seine Villa bei Tivoli* (Berlin 1950)

Karras-Klapproth, M. *Prosopographische Studien zur Geschichte des Partherreiches auf der Grundlage antiker literarischer Überlieferung* (Bonn 1988)

Kennedy, D.L. (ed.) *The Roman Army in the East* (Ann Arbor 1996)

Keppie, L.J.F. 'The legionary garrison of Judaea under Hadrian', *Latomus* 32 (1973) 859–64

—— 'The history and disappearance of the legion XXII Deiotariana', in: A. Kasher, U. Rappaport and G. Fuks (eds), *Greece and Rome in Eretz Israel* (Jerusalem 1990) 54–61

Kienast, D. 'Hadrian, Augustus und die eleusinischen Mysterien', *Jahrbuch für Numismatik und Geldgeschichte* 10 (1959–60) 61–9

—— 'Zur Baupolitik Hadrians in Rom', *Chiron* 10 (1980) 391–412

—— *Römische Kaisertabelle. Grundzüge einer römischen Kaiserchronologie* (Darmstadt 1990; 2nd edn 1996)

—— 'Antonius, Augustus, die Kaiser und Athen', in: *Klassisches Altertum, Spätantike und frühes Christentum. Festschrift A. Lippold* (Würzburg 1993) 191–222

—— *Kleine Schriften* (Aalen 1994)

Kierdorf, W. 'Apotheose und postumer Triumph Trajans', *Tyche* 1 (1986) 147–55

Knibbe, D. and Alzinger, W. 'Ephesos vom Beginn der römischen Herrschaft in Kleinasien bis zum Ende der Principatszeit', *ANRW* 2.7.2 (1980) 748–830

Kornemann, E. *Kaiser Hadrian und der letzte grosse Historiker von Rom* (Leipzig 1905)

Labrousse, M. 'Note sur la chronologie du premier voyage d'Hadrien', *Mélanges de la société toulousaine d'études classiques* 2 (1948) 125–47

Lambert, R. *Beloved and God. The Story of Hadrian and Antinous* (London 1984)

Lebek, W.D. 'Ein Hymnus auf Antinous', *Zeitschrift für Papyrologie und Epigraphik* 12 (1973) 101–37

Le Bohec, Y. *La troisième légion Auguste* (Paris 1989)

Le Glay, M. 'Hadrien et Viator sur les champs de manoeuvre de Numidie', in: *Mélanges d'histoire ancienne offerts à William Seston* (Paris 1974) 277–83

—— 'Hadrien et l'Asklépieion de Pergamon', *Bulletin de correspondance hellénique* 100 (1976) 347–72

Lepper, F.A. *Trajan's Parthian War* (Oxford 1948)

Levi, A.C. 'Hadrian as King of Egypt', *Numismatic Chronicle* 8 (1948) 30–40

Levi, M.A. *Adriano Augusto. Studi e ricerche* (Rome 1993)

—— *Adriano. Un ventennio di cambiamento* (Milan 1994)

Lewis, N. *The Documents from the Bar Kokhba Period in the Cave of Letters. Greek Papyri* (Jerusalem 1989)

—— 'Hadriani sententiae', *Greek, Roman and Byzantine Studies* 32 (1991) 267–80

—— 'Local provisioning of official visits', *Bulletin of the American Society of Papyrologists* 30 (1993) 29

Lightfoot, C.S. 'Trajan's Parthian War and the fourth-century perspective', *Journal of Roman Studies* 80 (1990) 115–26

Longden, R.P. 'Notes on the Parthian campaigns of Trajan', *Journal of Roman Studies* 21 (1931) 1–35

MacMullen, R. 'Roman attitudes to Greek love', *Historia* 31 (1982) 484–502

—— 'Hellenizing the Roman world (2nd century BC)', *Historia* 40 (1991) 419–38

Mann, J.C. 'The function of Hadrian's Wall', *Archaeologia Aeliana*, 5th ser., 18 (1990) 51–4

Maricq, A. '*Classica et orientalia* 6. La province d' "Assyrie" créée par Trajan. A propos de la guerre parthique de Trajan', *Syria* 36 (1959) 257–60

Mariotti, I. '*Animula vagula blandula*', in: *Studia Florentina . . . A. Ronconi* (Rome 1970) 233–49

—— 'Nota in margine ai poeti novelli', in: *Munus amicitiae. Scritti in memoria di A. Ronconi* II (Florence 1988) 11–21

Martin, J.-P. 'Hadrien et le phénix', in: *Mélanges d'histoire ancienne offerts à William Seston* (Paris 1974) 327–37

—— *Providentia deorum. Recherches sur certains aspects religieux du pouvoir impérial romain* (Rome 1982)

Maxfield, V.A. 'Hadrian's Wall in its imperial setting', *Archaeologia Aeliana*, 5th ser., 10 (1990) 1–28

Merkelbach, R. and Schwertheim, E. 'Die Inschriften der Sammlung Necmi Tolunay in Banduma. II. Das Orakel des Ammon für Kyzikos', *Epigraphica Anatolica* 2 (1983) 147–54

Merten, E. 'Die Adoption Hadrians', in: *Bonner Festgabe J. Straub* (Bonn 1977) 247–59

Metcalf, W.E. 'Hadrian, Jovis Olympius', *Mnemosyne* 27 (1974) 59–66

—— *The Cistophori of Hadrian* (New York 1980)

Meyer, H. *Antinoos. Die archäologischen Denkmäler unter Einbeziehung des numismatischen und epigraphischen Materials sowie der literarischen Nachrichten. Ein Beitrag zur Kunst- und Kulturgeschichte der hadrianisch-frühantoninischen Zeit* (Munich 1991)

—— *Der Obelisk des Antinoos. Eine kommentierte Edition* (Munich 1994)

Michelotto, P.G. 'Sul responso oraculare in *SHA vita Hadriani* 2,9', *Rendiconti dell'Istituto Lombardo* 113 (1979) 324–38

—— 'Intorno a Serviano cognato e vittima dell' imperatore Hadriano', in: *Studi C. Gatti* (Turin 1987) 143–92

Mildenberg, L. *The Coinage of the Bar Kokhba War* (Frankfurt am Main 1984)

Millar, F. 'Epictetus and the imperial court', *Journal of Roman Studies* 55 (1965) 141–8

—— *The Emperor in the Roman World (31 BC–AD 337)* (London 1977)

—— *The Roman Near East 31 BC–AD 337* (London 1993)

Mitchell, S. 'Population and the land in Roman Galatia', *ANRW* 2.7.2 (1980) 1053–81

—— 'Imperial Roman building in the eastern Roman provinces', *Harvard Studies in Classical Philology* 91 (1987) 333–65

Mócsy, A. *Pannonia and Upper Moesia* (London 1974)

366

Montevecchi, O. 'Adriano e la fondazione di Antinoopolis', in: *Neronia* IV. *Alejandro Magno, modelo de los emperadores romanos* (Brussels 1990) 183–95

Mor, M. 'The Bar-Kokhba revolt and non-Jewish participants', *Journal of Jewish Studies* 36 (1985) 200–29

Mylonas, G. *Eleusis and the Eleusinian Mysteries* (Princeton 1961)

Nadel, B. 'Aspects of Emperor Hadrian's policy in the northern Black Sea area', *Rivista Storica dell'Antichità* 12 (1982) 175–215

Németh, M. 'Roman military camps in Aquincum', in: G. Hajnóczi (ed.), *La Pannonia e l'Impero Romano* (Rome 1994) 139–52

Nesselhauf, H. 'Hadrians Reskript an Minucius Fundanus', *Hermes* 104 (1976) 348–61

Nierhaus, R. 'Hadrians Verhältnis zu Italica', in: *Corolla memoriae E. Swoboda dedicata* (Graz–Cologne 1966) 151–68

Oliver, J.H. 'Hadrian's precedent, the initiation of Philip II', *American Journal of Philology* 71 (1950) 295–9

—— *Greek Constitutions of Early Roman Emperors from Inscriptions and Papyri* (Philadelphia 1989)

Oppermann, M. 'Bemerkungen zu einem Jagddenkmal des Kaisers Hadrian', *Nikephoros* 4 (1991) 211–17

d'Orgeval, B. *L'empereur Hadrien. Oeuvre législative et administrative* (Paris 1950)

Pekáry, T. 'Das Grab des Pompeius', *BHAC 19/0* (1972) 195–8

Perowne, S. *Hadrian* (London 1960)

Perret, L. *La titulature impériale d'Hadrien* (Paris 1929)

—— *Essai sur la carrière d'Hadrien jusqu'à son avènement à l'Empire* (Paris 1935)

Perry, B.E. *Secundus the Silent Philosopher* (Ithaca 1964)

Petrakis, N.L. 'Diagonal earlobe creases, Type A behavior, and the death of Emperor Hadrian', *Western Journal of Medicine* 132 (January 1980) 87–91

Pflaum, H.-G. *Les carrières procuratoriennes équestres sous le Haut-Empire romain* (Paris 1961); *Supplément* (Paris 1982)

—— 'Le réglement successoral d'Hadrien', *BHAC 1963* (1964) 95–122

—— 'La valeur de la source inspiratrice de la *vita Hadriani* et de la *vita Marci* à la lumière des personnalités contemporains nommément citées', *BHAC 1968/69* (1970) 173–99

Piérart, M. 'L'empereur Hadrien et Argos. Une dédicace partiellement inédite d'un temple d'Héra. (SEG XI, 340+)', in: R. Frei-Stolba and M.A. Speidel (eds), *Römische Inschriften – Neufunde, Neulesungen und Neuinterpretationen. Festschrift H. Lieb* (Basel 1995) 7–16

Piso, I. *Fasti Provinciae Daciae* I. *Die senatorischen Amtsträger* (Bonn 1993)

Plew, J. *Quellenuntersuchungen zur Geschichte des Kaisers Hadrian* (Strasbourg 1890)

Póczy, K. 'La città di Aquincum sede del luogotenente della Pannonia Inferiore', in: G. Hajnóczi (ed.), *La Pannonia e l'Impero Romano* (Rome 1994) 221–31

Potter, D.S. 'The inscriptions on the bronze Herakles from Mesene: Volageses IV's war with Rome and the date of Tacitus' *Annales*', *Zeitschrift für Papyrologie und Epigraphik* 88 (1991) 277–90

Premerstein, A. v. *Das Attentat der Konsulare auf Hadrian im J. 118 n. Chr.* (*Klio* Beih. 8, Leipzig 1908)

Price, S.R.F. *Rituals and Power. The Roman Imperial Cult in Asia Minor* (Cambridge 1984)

Raepsaet-Charlier, M.-T. *Prosopographie des femmes de l'ordre sénatorial (Ier–IIe siècles)* (Louvain 1987)

Ridley, R.T. 'The fate of an architect: Apollodorus of Damascus', *Athenaeum* 77 (1989) 551–65

Ritner, R.K. 'Horus on the crocodiles: a juncture of religion and magic in late dynastic

Egypt', in: W.K. Simpson (ed.), *Religion and Philosophy in Ancient Egypt* (New Haven 1989) 103–16

Rivet, A.L.F. *Gallia Narbonensis. Southern Gaul in Roman Times* (London 1988)

Robert, L. *Etudes épigraphiques et philologiques* (Paris 1938)

—— *Les gladiateurs dans l'Orient grec* (Paris 1940)

—— 'Documents d'Asie Mineure V–XVII', *Bulletin de correspondance hellénique* 102 (1978) 395–543 (repr. in: id., *Documents d'Asie Mineure*, Paris 1987, 91–239)

—— 'Deux poètes grecs à l'époque impériale', in: *Stèle: Mélanges Kontoleon* (Athens 1980) 1–20

—— *A travers l'Asie Mineure* (Paris 1980)

—— *Documents d'Asie Mineure* (Paris 1987)

Roxan, M.M. *Roman Military Diplomas 1954–1977* (London 1978) (I); *1978–1984* (London 1985) (II); *1985–1993* (London 1994) (III)

Sajdak, J. 'Spór o Hadryanowe zegnanie ze swiatem', *Eos* 20 (1914–15) 147–58

—— 'Hadrians Abschied vom Leben', *Berliner Philologische Wochenschrift* 36 (1916) 765–7

Salomies, O. *Adoptive and Polyonymous Nomenclature in the Roman Empire* (Helsinki 1992)

Salway, P. *Roman Britain* (Oxford 1981)

Salzmann, D. 'Sabina in Palmyra', in: *Festschrift N. Himmelmann* (Mainz 1989) 361–8

Schäfer, P. *Der Bar Kokhba Aufstand. Studien zum zweiten Jüdischen Krieg gegen Rom* (Tübingen 1981)

—— 'Hadrian's policy in Judaea and the Bar Kokhba revolt: a reassessment', in: P.R. Davies and R.T. White (eds), *A Tribute to G. Vermes* (*Journal for the Study of the Old Testament* Supp. ser. 100, 1990) 281–303

Scheid, J. *Le collège des frères Arvales. Etude prosopographique du recrutement (69–304)* (Rome 1990)

Schiller, A.A. 'Sententiae Hadriani de re militari', in: *Festgabe U. v. Lübtow* (Berlin 1970) 295–306

—— '"Alimenta" in the *Sententiae Hadriani*', in: *Studi G. Grosso* IV (Turin 1971) 402–15

—— 'Sententiae et Epistulae Hadriani: vindication of a text' in: *La critica del testo. Atti del II. Congresso Int. della Soc. ital. di stor. di diritto* (Florence 1971) 717–27

Schippmann, K. *Grundzüge der Parthischen Geschichte* (Darmstadt 1980)

Schlumberger, J. *Die Epitome de Caesaribus* (Munich 1974)

Schönberger, H. 'The Roman frontier in Germany: an archaeological survey', *Journal of Roman Studies* 59 (1969) 144–97

—— 'Die römischen Truppenlager der frühen und mittleren Kaiserzeit zwischen Nordsee und Inn', *Bericht der römisch-germanischen Kommission* 66 (1985) 321–498

Schürer, E. *The History of the Jewish People in the Age of Jesus Christ (175 BC–AD 135)*, I, rev. edn by G. Vermes and F. Millar (Edinburgh 1973)

Schulz, A. and Winter, E. 'Zum Hadrianstempel von Kyzikos', *Asia Minor Studien* 1 (Bonn 1990) 33–81

Schulz, O.T. *Leben des Kaisers Hadrian* (Leipzig 1904)

Schumacher, L. *Prosopographische Untersuchungen zur Besetzung der vier hohen römischen Priesterkollegien im Zeitalter der Antonine und der Severer (96–235 n. Chr.)* (Mainz 1973)

Schwarte, K.H. 'Trajans Regierungsbeginn und der Agricola des Tacitus', *Bonner Jahrbücher* 179 (1979) 139–75

Schwertheim, E. 'Zu Hadrians Reisen und Stadtgründungen in Kleinasien', *Epigraphica Anatolica* 6 (1985) 37–42

—— *Inschriften griechischer Städte aus Kleinasien. Hadrianoi und Hadrianeia* (Cologne 1987)

Sherwin-White, A.N. *The Letters of Pliny. A Historical and Social Commentary* (Oxford 1966)
—— *The Roman Citizenship* (2nd edn, Oxford 1973)
Sijpestein, P.J. 'A new document conerning Hadrian's visit to Egypt', *Historia* 18 (1969) 109–18
—— 'Another document concerning Hadrian's visit to Egypt', *Zeitschrift für Papyrologie und Epigraphik* 88 (1991) 89–90
Smallwood, E.M. *Documents Illustrating the Principates of Nerva, Trajan and Hadrian* (Cambridge 1966)
—— *The Jews under Roman Rule* (Leyden 1976)
Spawforth, A.J.S. 'Balbilla, the Euryclids and memorials for a Greek magnate', *Annual of the British School at Athens* 73 (1978) 249–62
—— 'Sparta and the family of Herodes Atticus', ibid. 75 (1980) 203–20
Spawforth, A.J.S. and Walker, S. 'The world of the Panhellenion. I. Athens and Eleusis', *Journal of Roman Studies* 75 (1985) 78–104
—— 'The world of the Panhellenion. II. Three Dorian cities', ibid. 76 (1986) 88–105
Speidel, M.P. *Guards of the Roman Armies. An Essay on the Singulares of the Provinces* (Bonn 1978)
—— 'Swimming the Danube under Hadrian's eyes. A feat of the emperors' Batavi horse guard', *Ancient Society* 22 (1991) 277–82
—— *Riding for Caesar. The Roman Emperors' Horse Guard* (London 1994)
Stevens, C.E. 'Hadrian and Hadrian's Wall', *Latomus* 14 (1955) 384–403
—— *The Building of Hadrian's Wall* (Kendal 1966)
Strack, P.L. *Untersuchungen zur römischen Reichsprägung des zweiten Jahrhunderts* II. *Die Reichsprägung zur Zeit des Hadrian* (Stuttgart 1933)
Strobel, K. *Untersuchungen zu den Dakerkriege Trajans. Studien zur Geschichte des mittleren und unteren Donauraumes in der Hohen Kaiserzeit* (Bonn 1984)
—— 'Zu zeitgeschichtlichen Aspekten im "Panegyricus" des jüngeren Plinius: Trajan – "Imperator invictus" und "novum ad principatum iter"', in: J. Knape and K. Strobel, *Zur Deutung von Geschichte in Antike und Mittelalter* (Bamberger Hochschulschriften 11, Bamberg 1985) 9–112
—— 'Die Jahre 117 bis 119 n. Chr., eine Krisenphase der römischen Herrschaft an der mittleren und unteren Donau', in: *Studien zur Alten Geschichte. Festschrift S. Lauffer* (Rome 1986) 905–67
—— 'Zu Fragen der frühen Geschichte der römischen Provinz Arabien und zu einigen Problemen der Legionsdislokation im Osten des Imperium Romanum zu Beginn des 2. Jh. n. Chr.', *Zeitschrift für Papyrologie und Epigraphik* 71 (1988) 251–80
Strubbe, J.H.M. 'Gründer kleinasiatischer Städte. Fiktion und Realität', *Ancient Society* 15/17 (1984/6) 253–304
Sullivan, R.D. 'The dynasty of Commagene', *ANRW* 2.8 (1977) 732–98
—— 'Dynasts in Pontus', ibid. 2.7.2 (1980) 913–30
Swain, S. 'Favorinus and Hadrian', *Zeitschrift für Papyrologie und Epigraphik* 79 (1989) 150–8
—— 'Plutarch, Hadrian and Delphi', *Historia* 40 (1991) 318–30
—— *Hellenism and Empire. Language, Classicism, and Power in the Greek World* AD *50–250* (Oxford 1996)
Syme, R. *Tacitus* (Oxford 1958)
—— *Danubian Papers* (Bucharest 1971)
—— *Roman Papers* I–II (Oxford 1979); III (1984); IV–V (1988); VI–VII (1991)
—— *Historia Augusta Papers* (Oxford 1983)
Talbert, R.J.A. *The Senate of Imperial Rome* (Princeton 1984)
Teja, R. 'Die römische Provinz Kappadokien in der Prinzipatszeit', *ANRW* 2.7.2 (1980) 1083–124

Temporini, H. *Die Frauen am Hofe Trajans. Ein Beitrag zur Stellung der Augustae im Prinzipat* (Berlin–New York 1978)

Thomasson, B.E. *Laterculi praesidum* I (Gothenburg 1984)

Toynbee, J.M.C. *The Hadrianic School. A Chapter in the History of Greek Art* (Cambridge 1934)

Turcan, R. 'Les *tondi* sur l'arc de Constantin', *Comptes-Rendus de l'Académie des Inscriptions* (1991), 53–82

Van den Broek, R. *The Myth of the Phoenix* (Leyden 1972)

Van den Hout, M.P.J. (ed.) *M. Cornelii Frontonis Epistulae* (Leipzig 1988)

Van Groningen, B.A. 'Preparatives to Hadrian's visit to Egypt', in: *Studi A. Calderini & R. Paribeni* II (Milan 1956) 253–6

Vidman, L. *Fasti Ostienses* (2nd edn, Prague 1982)

Vogt, J. *Die alexandrinischen Münzen* (Stuttgart 1924)

Voisin, J.-L. 'Apicata, Antinous et quelques autres. Notes d'épigraphie sur la mort volontaire à Rome', *Mélanges de l'Ecole française de Rome – Antiquité* 99 (1987) 257–80

——— 'Antinous *varius, multiplex, multiformis*', in: Y. Le Bohec (ed.), *L'Afrique, la Gaule, la religion à l'époque romaine. Mélanges à la mémoire de M. Le Glay* (Brussels 1994) 730–41

Walker, S. 'Bearded men', *Journal of the History of Collections* 3 (1991) 265–77

Wallace-Hadrill, A. *Suetonius. The Scholar and his Caesars* (London 1983)

Weber, W. *Untersuchungen zur Geschichte des Kaisers Hadrianus* (Leipzig 1907)

——— *Drei Untersuchungen zur ägyptischen-griechischen Religion* (Heidelberg 1911)

Wegner, W. *Das römische Herrscherbild* II 3. *Hadrian Plotina Marciana Matidia Sabina* (Berlin 1956)

Weiss, P. 'Hadrian in Lydien', *Chiron* 25 (1995) 213–24

Wesch-Klein, G. *Funus Publicum. Eine Studie zur öffentlichen Beisetzung und Gewährung von Ehrengräbern in Rom und den Westprovinzen* (Stuttgart 1993)

Wheeler, E.L. *Flavius Arrianus. A Political and Military Biography* (University Microfilms, Ann Arbor 1977)

——— 'The occasion of Arrian's *Tactica*', *Greek, Roman and Byzantine Studies* 19 (1978) 351–66

Whittaker, C.R. *Frontiers of the Roman Empire. A Social and Economic Study* (Baltimore 1994)

——— 'Where are the frontiers now?', in: D. Kennedy (ed.), *The Roman Army in the East* (Ann Arbor 1996) 25–42

Willers, D. *Hadrians panhellenisches Programm. Archäologische Beiträge zur Neugestaltung Athens durch Hadrian* (Basel 1990)

Williams, W. 'Individuality in the imperial constitutions: Hadrian and the Antonines', *Journal of Roman Studies* 66 (1976) 67–83

Wörrle, M. 'Ägyptisches Getreide für Ephesos', *Chiron* 1 (1971) 325–40

——— *Stadt und Fest im kaiserzeitlichen Kleinasien* (Munich 1988)

——— 'Neue Inschriftenfunde aus Aizanoi I', *Chiron* 22 (1992) 337–76

Wooliscroft, D.J. 'Signalling and the design of Hadrian's Wall', *Archaeologia Aeliana*, 5th ser., 17 (1989) 5–19

Yourcenar, M. *Les mémoires d'Hadrien* (Paris 1951); Eng. tr. by G. Frick (London 1954)

Zahrnt, M. 'Die Hadriansstadt in Athen', *Chiron* 9 (1979) 393–8

——— 'Antinoopolis in Ägypten', *ANRW* 2.10.1 (1988) 669–706

——— 'Vermeintliche Kolonien des Kaisers Hadrian', *Zeitschrift für Papyrologie und Epigraphik* 71 (1988) 229–49

——— 'Zum römischen Namen Augsburgs', *Zeitschrift für Papyrologie und Epigraphik* 72 (1988) 179–80

——— 'Die frühesten Meilensteine Britanniens und ihre Deutung', *Zeitschrift für Papyrologie und Epigraphik* 73 (1988) 195–9

—— 'Zahl, Verteilung und Charakter der hadrianischen Kolonien (unter besonderer Berücksichtigung von *Aelia Capitolina*)', in: E. Olshausen and H. Sonnabend (eds), *Stuttgarter Kolloquium zur historischen Geographie des Altertums* 2–3 (1984–7) (Bonn 1991) 463–86

Ziegler, R. 'Zur Einrichtung des kilikischen *Koinon.* Ein Datierungsversuch', *Studien zum antiken Kleinasien* III (Bonn 1995) 183–6

—— 'Die Polis in der römischen Kaiserzeit: Selbstdarstellung und Rangstreitigkeiten', in: G. Hödl and J. Grabmayer (eds), *Leben in der Stadt. Gestern-heute-morgen* (Vienna 1995) 83–105

Zoepffel, R. 'Hadrian und Numa', *Chiron* 8 (1978) 391–427

Zsidi, P. 'Aquincum – the capital of Pannonia Inferior. Topography of the civil town', in: G. Hajnóczi (ed.), *La Pannonia e l'Impero Romano* (Rome 1994) 213–20

INDEX

Only limited reference is made to items in the Notes.

PERSONS

Most Romans are listed under their family name; and where applicable consular dates have been supplied. It was not feasible to construct a detailed entry for Hadrian himself: references to him in other entries are abbreviated 'H.'

Abgarus VII, ruler of Osrhoene, 68 f., 70 f.

Acilius Attianus, P., of Italica, H.'s guardian, 16, 58; date of birth, 327; Guard Prefect, 58, 67, 76, 77 f., 84; urged H. to suppress dissent, 77 f.; had 'conspirators' killed, 88, 91, 95; dismissed, 91, 96, 281

Acilius Glabrio, M'. (*cos.* 191 BC), 62

Acilius Glabrio, M'. (*cos. ord.* 91), 26, 31

Adamantius, writer on physiognomy, 166

Adrius, founder of Hadria, 332

Aelian, on tactics, 288

Aelii, of Italica, 12, 13, 198, 201, 299

Aelius Aristides, orator, 5, 303, 304, 357

Aelius Caesar, L., see Ceionius Commodus

Aelius Hadrianus, H.'s great-uncle, 308, 309; expert astrologer, 23; predicted H.'s accession, 37

Aelius Hadrianus Afer, P., H.'s father, 10, 19, 308, 309; cousin of Trajan's father, 12, 309; his career, 14; death, 16

Aelius Nico, father of Galen, 167

Aelius Rasparaganus, P., king of Roxolani, 86, 326

Aemilius Arcanus, L., of Narbo, made senator, 146

Aemilius Juncus, L. (*cos.* 127), 235 ; in Achaia, 282

Aemilius Papus, M., Spanish friend of H., 24, 58, 67, 192; at Tibur, 192

Aemilius Paullus, L. (*cos. II* 168 BC), 25

Afranius Burrus, Sex., of Vasio, Guard Prefect, 13

Agrippa, M. Vipsanius, built original Pantheon, 111

Agrippa Postumus, 95

Agrippina, the Elder, 121

Ajax, Achaean hero, his tomb restored by H., 164, 237

Akiba, Rabbi, 270,

Albucius Silo, C., of Milan, 200

Alcibiades, Athenian general, his tomb restored by H., 223, 237

Alcibiades, H.'s freedman chamberlain, 151, 222, 223, 240, 251

Alexander the Great, emulated by Trajan, 65, 72, 73, 75, 78, 131; perhaps by H., 131; at the Granicus, 163; his horse, 145; sacrificed to Ocean, 130 f.; made shaving fashionable, 61; his body inspected, 239

Amasis, Pharaoh, 243

Amazaspus, Iberian, 69

Amenhotep III, Pharaoh, 250

Ammianus Marcellinus, on Hadrian, 75

GEOGRAPHICAL

Single mentions in lists and references to places of origin (e.g. 'Dio of Prusa') have mostly been omitted; also references to Rome, except for individual buildings. Ancient rather than modern names have been used in most cases.

RELIGION

MISCELLANEOUS